WINE
APPRECIATION

WINE APPRECIATION

SECOND EDITION

RICHARD P. VINE, PH.D.

Professor, Enology, Department of Food Science
Purdue University

Wine Consultant
American Airlines

JOHN WILEY & SONS, INC.

New York ❖ Chichester ❖ Brisbane ❖ Toronto ❖ Singapore ❖ Weinheim

This publication is designed to provide accurate and
authoritative information in regard to the subect
matter covered. It is sold with the understanding that
the publisher is not engaged in rendering legal, accounting,
or other professional services. If legal advice or other
expert assistance is required, the services of a competent
professional person should be sought.

Library of Congress Cataloging in Publication Data:
Vine, Richard P.
    Wine appreciation / Richard P. Vine. —2nd ed.
      p.   cm.
    Includes bibliographical references and index.
    ISBN 0-471-15396-6 (alk. paper)
    1. Wine and wine making.   I. Title
TP548.V484 1997   96-8971
                               CIP

Printed in the United States of America

10 9 8 7 6 5 4 3

CONTENTS

FOREWORD

ROBERT MONDAVI

Richard Vine has done a masterful job in the new edition of *Wine Appreciation*. Its breadth and depth are unmatched in the field. We at Robert Mondavi Winery have known Richard for many years, and his commitment to wine matches our own. I always knew we had the grape varieties, climate and soils, and the people here in Napa Valley to grow wines that belong in the company of the great wines of the world. These are wines with their own style and character. We had the tenacity and desire to excel and today our wines are among the world's finest.

Richard has done the same thing with wine education, and with his colleagues at Purdue I believe he will bring the art and science of wine—and food—together in a new and exciting way.

Our shared feeling is that if more young people understand the role of wine in American society, the many positives as well as the detriments of abuse, we will have better people and a better society. Richard provides the academic rationale for embracing all of the good things about wine; taste, health, and general good sense and quality of life.

Here in Napa Valley we have much of the good life, in which wine plays an important role. Enjoy and learn from Richard's book, and come to see us!

PREFACE

America's love affair with wine has been a 300-year on-again-off-again thing since Colonial times. At this writing we are engaged in a serious courtship again—perhaps finally headed toward marriage. Medical research in the 1990s has produced evidence that a glass of wine every day may actually be good for us. Beyond the traditionally fickle attraction of the American palate to wine, we may now be able to see a bond between wine and health.

This book is not another comprehensive guide to the world's vineyards, vintners, or vintages. It is, rather, a compendium of these essential elements, and its primary emphasis is on wine and its relationship to humanity.

Modern anthropological discoveries indicate that human beings have appreciated wine for at least 8,000 years, probably much longer. This seems entirely plausible when one considers that wine is essentially a natural beverage that requires no brewing or processing; modern materials, machines, and methods serve only to perfect commercial wines.

No one can be sure how many millions of years microscopic yeast cells have existed on the surface of grape skins. Once the skins are broken, the yeasts convert the sugars inside the berries into alcohol and carbon dioxide gas—hence, the bubbling of fermentation.

Thus, wine will, literally, make itself. The first vintners may have been cave people who discovered the "magic" of fermentation when they left some crushed grapes in a crude container for a few days, the resulting beverage providing immeasurable relief for the pains of their daily lives.

In modern times wine remains one of our most natural and simple foods, yet it is a subject of study that has spawned a vast and complex body of knowledge. During the 80 centuries or more during which wine has developed as an integral part of Western civilization, nearly every major academic discipline has been applied to advance the state of its art. These disciplines are the focus of the first chapter of this book—the definition of wine, its horticulture, its microbiology, its biochemistry, and its classification.

Chapter 2 explains the significance of wine along the pathway of human history, its importance as a healthy substitute for polluted water, as a medicine, and as an anaesthetic. Also discussed is the elemental role of wine in advancing agriculture, economics, sociology, and theology. In this regard, Plato wrote, "Nothing more excellent or valuable than wine was ever granted by the gods to man."

Because wine has been closely associated with religion and human existence throughout its Old World history, it is ironic that the fundamentalist church in the New World has become the adversary of wine in the marketplace. It was this influence that led to National Prohibition throughout the 1920s and early

1930s. Unfortunately, ignorance about wines continues across much of America yet today.

By far the most important premise of this book is that knowledge can empower each reader to fully understand the pros and cons of wine consumption. To this end, moderate and appropriate consumption of wine, by people whose individual physiology and psychology qualify them to do so, is a principal learning experience.

British wine expert Hugh Johnson indicates that 1 of every 100 persons throughout the world is either a winegrower, a winemaker, or a wine marketer, and 1 of every 130 acres of cultivated land is a vineyard. There are more than 25 million acres of vineyards spread over the Earth, and the annual world wine harvest is sufficient to supply every adult in the world with about 12 bottles of wine per year. Although Americans now consume more wine than distilled spirits, our average annual per capita consumption of 2 gallons pales in comparison to the 18 to 19 gallons required by each Frenchman and Italian every year. One out of every 10 Americans is every bit as accomplished a wine consumer as the Europeans. This book is addressed to the other nine.

From simple beginnings have come thousands of different wines and the range expands with each new vintage and each new vintner. The scientific findings and romantic fancies about wine have produced an overwhelming body of literature, addressed to every conceivable aspect of the subject. Indeed, a collection of all the published wine dictionaries, wine encyclopedias, wine geographies, wine buying guides, wine textbooks, wine cookbooks, wine service manuals, and other related works would make a good-sized library in itself. The sheer magnitude of this information may discourage less motivated neophytes from acquiring a true appreciation of wine, perceiving it as an impossible feat in one lifetime.

There are many millions of wines produced every year, all of which will be, even from the same vineyard, different next year, and different again in the vintage after that. No other form of agriculture has such infinite variability, an essential element in every art form.

Wine as art is illustrated by some simple notions. How many consumer magazines are dedicated to orange juice? Has anyone ever heard of the Brotherhood of the Knights of Milk or the Society of Medical Friends for Coffee? Where might we find cellars harboring prized collections of colas? Do we ever find a grape juice shop?

True works of art must also stand the test of time and appreciate in value—music, paintings, sculpture, literature, drama, films, and wine, among others. Indeed, the word vintage is borrowed for many other things, such as "vintage cars," in order to portray their timelessness.

But is it realistic to assume that Americans can achieve the expertise in wine that is inherent in most European cultures? There is danger in expressing degrees of wine expertise. Some accomplished European enophiles may well be able to recognize select vintages and/or vineyard sources from taste alone. A native Burgundian, for instance, may approach wine appreciation with blind passion (and even blinder prejudice), inasmuch as wine is the very lifeblood of Burgundy. Although such expertise may be deep, it may also be narrow. That Burgundian would, in all likelihood, have great difficulty in making equally profound judgments about wines from Bordeaux, and even more trouble in judging wines from other countries.

This book will not afford the reader instant expertise. Despite what legends and myths may lead us to believe, there are no superhumans who can blindly pick up glass after glass of wine and identify the precise source and vintage of each through evaluation alone. Such performances must rely on what label statements disclose.

Thus, the ultimate purpose herein is to prepare the reader to identify wines by their labels, to appreciate the types of wines that are apt to provide pleasure. The true appreciator of wine will progress to have many favorites, each known by grape variety, vineyard locale, classification pedigree, and vintner source, all of which are disclosed on labels. The latter chapters of this book are addressed to precisely these issues.

A deep appreciation for wine then becomes a matter of experience. The level of expertise in any art is a measure of practice. Wine experts taste wine almost every chance they get. Judges on the national wine competition circuit may evaluate several thousands of wines every year. Buyers for large retail and restaurant chains, for airlines and steamship lines, may taste even more.

There are no shortcuts in this process. Fragments of knowledge, myths, and the lore of wine have turned many a hopeful novice into an arrogant wine snob. Some of the most common symptoms of this condition are name-dropping, citing the great vineyards and vintners while turning up the nose at more common wines, praising only dry (not sweet) wines while faulting those with any detectable degree of sweetness, and a predilection for European wines over their American counterparts. In point of fact, the quality of wine from the highly classified growths can often be disappointingly similar to that of less noble vineyards. Many of the truly great white wines of the world are sweet, and American wines often outdo European counterparts, even in European competitions.

Wine snobs can intimidate wine students, but not for long. A formal education about wine and the ability to make choices based on facts rather than fantasy, impart confidence. Although both the quantity and quality of wine education in America have increased greatly during the past several decades, wine still retains a certain mystique. Some perceive wine as a beverage reserved for the aristocracy or fear to use wine lest they commit a blunder in etiquette. Others cling to some of the many myths about wine that seem to survive in our country even today. This book is intended to be straightforward in debunking the snobbery, mystery, and obscurity surrounding the enjoyment of wines.

Of course, some dedicated students of wine will achieve the status of wine *connoisseur*. It is hoped that *Wine Appreciation* may serve these learners, as well as neophytes.

ACKNOWLEDGMENTS

Having discussed the seeds of rationale and reasoning for this book, I would like to recognize those who have been instrumental in its creation.

Dan Archibald, Dan Berger, Jerry Boyd, Russ Bridenbaugh, Julia Child, Sara Jane English, Craig Goldwyn, John Hailman, Mort Hochstein, Hugh Johnson, Linda Jones McKee, Jerry Mead, Bill Moffett, Tom Stockley, Bill Rice, Mike Rubin, Mike Stepanovich, and Bob Thompson are friendly media enophiles, as was the late Leon Adams. All have helped.

Chapter 3 exists because of the extraordinary knowledge provided by Dr. Douglas Stringer, noted Florida neurosurgeon and expert enophile, along with Gene Ford, who has devoted his life to the societal benefits of responsible drinking, and Elisabeth Holmgren, whose news releases from the Wine Institute have kept America informed on wine and health issues.

Chapter 4 owes much to Sue and Phil Nelson, Purdue University faculty members who are very well read, traveled, and accomplished in fine wine and good food; Sherry and Tom Storey; Susan and Marion Winkler, from Ole Miss, two splendid couples who epitomize Southern hospitality; to Nonnie Cameron, an authority on wine service, American Airlines International First Flight Attendant extraordinaire and housemother to more than 100 at Purdue's Sigma Phi Epsilon fraternity.

Among the many American vintners and wine marketers who were inspirational for Chapter 5 are Bob Bellus, Joe Bollinger, Don Carano, Jack Daniels, Ed Farver, Tom Fogarty, Fred Franzia, Darryl Groom, Peter Huwiler, Ron Johnson, Peter Kasper, Donn Kelly, Bernard La Borie, Mike Lambert, Marty Lee, David Lett, Ann Littlefield, Zelma Long, Orville Magoon, Francis Mahoney, Larry McGuire, Steve Meisner, Brian Moffatt, Robert Mondavi, Tim Murphy, Gil Nickel, Robert Palmer, Jim Pedroncelli, Janos Radvanyi, Jr., David Ready, Jack Schlatter, Jan Shrem, Bill Shill, Jack Stuart, Bill Stuht, Marimar Torres, Eric Wente, Hermann Wiemer, Hack Wilson, and Phil Woodward.

In Europe, Anthony Barton, Andreas Bauer, Albert Bichot, Guy Bizot, Jean-Claude Boisset, Luc Bouchard, Bartholomew Broadbent, Thierry Budin, Julie Campos, Daniel Cathiard, Jean-Michel Cazes, Armand Cottin, Hanns Christophe Wegeler-Deinhard, Valerie Delannoy, Robert Denby, Eugene DeRose, Philp DiBelardino, Georges DuBoeuf, Bill Deutsch, Robert Drouhin, Tim Enos, Hank Evans, Richard Herberger, Rob Janelli, Christopher Marshall, Philippe Menguy, Marcus Moller-Racke, Christian Moreau, Richard Mueller, Montse Painous, Robert Pulley, Brian St. Pierre, Dennis Robinson, Christophe Salin, Warren Strauss, Henry Stuart, Mickey Stuart, and James Symington have contributed considerably to making this book a reality.

There are also those with whom I have the pleasure of working on a daily basis: at Purdue University, my secretary, Michele Javens, is quite frankly, the very best. Essential team members include Sheri Fell, Steve Gauger, Linda Haar, Ellen Harkness, and Linda Milakis, who took calls, sent faxes, delivered illustrations, passed along messages, taught me how to work the new computerese, and in countless ways gave of their time and energies.

Also contributing are the members of my American Airlines "crew," Emily Bacic, Hortencia Barton, Mary Anne Brooks, Linda Daniel, Marc Evans, Mike Gunn, Bob Hayen, Diane Heard, John Jaynes, Henry Joyner, Koolsum Klavon, Deidre Meyer, Shirley Stacy, Randy Thomas, Jim Verges, and Chairman Bob Crandall, who, in demanding the best wines from the world's finest vintners, gave me the world's greatest job.

Valued most of all is the irreplaceable support from my wife, Gaye. She has sacrificed many evenings and weekends, bringing me countless cups of hot coffee—and, yes, a few glasses of good wine—while I simply thanked her and continued pounding away at the keyboard.

I am very grateful to one and all.

In vino veritas!

RICHARD P. VINE, PH.D.

WINE
APPRECIATION

1

INTRODUCTION

WINE: ORIGINS AND DEFINITIONS

Although experts disagree as to the exact origin of the term, many scholars now identify the Hittite script *wee-an* as the first "wine" word recorded, as early as 1500 B.C. The Georgians of ancient Armenia are also credited with a similar vocal reference to wine.

The *Oxford English Dictionary* traces the modern English word *wine* back to the Old English *win*, associated with the Latin *vinum*, which, in turn, is related to the Greek *oinos* and the archaic Greek *woinos*. The Greek *oinos logos* ("wine logic") is the origin of our term *enology* (or the British *oenology*), which is the science of winemaking. Thus, a modern-day winemaker is an *enologist*.

The common dictionary definition of wine is "an alcoholic beverage obtained by the fermentation of the juice of the fruit of the vine." The U.S. Bureau of Alcohol, Tobacco and Firearms (BATF or, more commonly, ATF) defines wine as "the product of the juice of sound, ripe grapes." A technical criticism of the latter statement is directed toward the phrase "sound, ripe grapes." There are several famous wines made from green grapes—and even more made from overripe grapes. More important, the ATF definition overlooks any stipulation for the all-important fermentation process necessary to generate "the product." *Wine*, as the word is used in this book, *is the product of fermenting and processing grape juice or must*. Crushed grapes, generally with all or some portion of the stems removed, are known as *must*.

Wine made from any fruit other than grapes is qualified, both by tradition and by ATF commercial regulation, by identifying that particular fruit. By itself the term *wine* implies the beverage is made from grapes. Otherwise it is labeled as "blackberry wine," "peach wine," "dandelion wine," and so forth.

❖ FERMENTATION

Fermentation is a natural process in which the grape sugars (mostly glucose and fructose) are transformed into ethyl alcohol and carbon dioxide gas. In 1810 the French chemist and physicist Joseph-Louis Gay-Lussac described this process in the following chemical equation:

$$C_6H_{12}O_6 \longrightarrow 2C_2H_5OH + 2CO_2$$
(grape sugars) $\longrightarrow$ (ethyl alcohol + carbon dioxide gas)

Today we know that wine fermentation is carried out by yeasts producing protein compounds called *enzymes,* catalysts that are directly involved with the sugar —> alcohol/CO_2 conversion. Students of the fermentation process learn that it very closely parallels the glycolysis cycle that is elementary to modern biochemistry, and that heat energy is also a product of the transformation:

$$C_6H_{12}O_6 \xrightarrow{\text{yeast enzymes}} 2C_2H_5OH + 2CO_2 + 56 \text{ kilocalories of energy}$$

Consequently, we are dependent on two very different plant forms for the making of wine: the grapevine and the yeast cell.

❖ THE VINE

The leaves, stems, and roots of the grapevine classify it biologically as a higher-form plant. Such plants are able to use sunlight to make sugars from carbon dioxide and water through the process of photosynthesis. Some of these sugars are used in the metabolic processes of the plant's life system. Another portion of these precious sugar compounds is stored in the grapevine's roots until *veraison,* a French term referring to that time when grapes commence to ripen and sugars are transported from roots to berries.

Taxonomically, the grapevine is classified as follows:

Group	Spermtophyta
Division	Tracheophyta
Subdivision	Pteropsida
Class	Angiosperm
Subclass	Dicotyledonae
Order	Ramnales
Family	Vitaceae (Ampelidaceae)
Genus	*Vitis*
Subgenera	Euvitis and Muscadinia

There are more than 50 known species of *Vitis,* and many of these are indistinguishable to all but highly skilled viticulturists. Origins of the vine are largely limited to the Northern Hemisphere, and the North American continent is particularly abundant in native species.

Vitis is a deciduous plant that climbs by grasping supporting objects with out-growths of very special leaf-type organs called *tendrils.* In the wild, vines may reach the tops of tall trees, but in culturing the vine, aptly called *viticulture,* the natural growth is generally controlled by annual pruning. Typically, vines in vineyards are trained on post-and-wire trellis supports designed to optimize both the quality and the quantity of the plant's yield. Exposure of grape leaves to sunlight increases the production of grape sugars by allowing photosynthesis to transform carbon dioxide, which will eventually result in grapes of varying levels of sweetness.

Note how the earlier chemical equation for fermentation compares with that of photosynthesis:

$$6\,CO_2 + 6\,H_2O \xrightarrow{\text{ultraviolet light}} C_6H_{12}O_6 + 6\,O_2$$

This process is diametric to fermentation. Carbon dioxide is now the substrate from which the reaction is fueled, catalyzed by the ultraviolet rays in sunshine, with sugar as the product and oxygen as a by-product.

Traditionally, grape quality is closely linked to sweetness levels attained in ripening. Severe pruning is often practiced to obtain smaller crops of higher quality, and more moderate pruning is generally associated with a larger quantity of lower-quality fruit.

As a rule, two buds emerge from the *abcission point* of each leaf on the vine. These buds are covered by a single cap, or *caliptra,* and in many varieties a third, or *tertiary,* bud is also found but rarely sprouts. Unless damaged by spring frost or some other malady, the primary buds sprout to produce new shoots, which will develop leaves and fruit. The flowers of the vine emerge on developing shoots. At the perimeter of the flower several male *stamens* produce pollen, which, by wind, insect activity, or other mechanical means, finds its way to the central female *pistil,* where fertilization takes place and formation of grape berries commences.

Shoots mature from a supple, green vegetative state to a hard woody cane, which is pruned according to any number of viticultural motives and designs. When primary buds or shoots are damaged, secondary buds then grow to produce a grape crop—almost always of lesser quality and quantity than would have been achieved by the primaries.

In any event, all fruit results from the current season's growth. Bunches of grapes may be composed of fewer than 10 berries each—in some of the more obscure varieties—to more than 300 berries in the most prolific types. Cluster shapes range from long, cylindrical forms (with or without lateral forms, called *shoulders*) to shorter conical structures. The grape is morphologically a true berry because it is a simple fruit with a pulpy *pericarp* consisting of four skin layers: epidermis, hypodermis, outer wall, and inner wall.

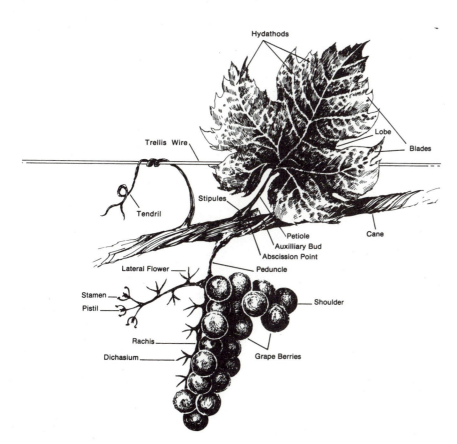

FIGURE 1.1 Morphology of grape cluster, tendril, leaf, and cane. (*Artwork by Larry Bost.*)

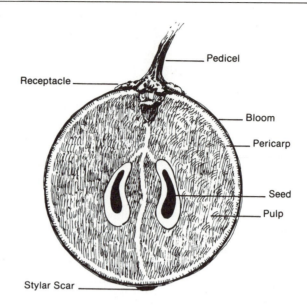

Pedicel

Receptacle

Bloom

Pericarp

Seed

Pulp

Stylar Scar

FIGURE 1.2 Morphology of a grape berry. The pericarp consists of epidermis, hypodermis, outer wall, and inner wall. *(Artwork by Larry Bost.)*

Generally, grapes are native to temperate zones, primarily between 40 to 50 degrees south latitude. The grapevine can, however, adapt to some rather difficult climate and soil conditions. In reproduction vines often form *clones,* offspring with slight variations in character responding to the natural selection process. As compared with the classic type, some clones may be more resistant to cold winter temperatures, others may require a shorter growing season, and still others may produce heavier crops, and so on. Some varieties have been cataloged with hundreds of different clones, from which selections are made to best meet vintner constraints and designs.

Young vines are propagated asexually, usually from cuttings or graftings grown in a nursery for a year or so. A newly planted vineyard may be allowed to produce a token number of grape clusters during its third year of growth, with other clusters pinched off shortly after bloom. It may be the fifth or sixth year before a full vintage of grape production is taken. All things considered, it is common to find these years of vineyard establishment costs totaling more than $6,000 per acre, not including the cost of land.

✪ EUVITIS

The subgenus Euvitis includes all the world's grapevines that produce grapes in clusters. The most important species of Euvitis is *Vitis vinifera,* the "Old World" grape that originated in Asia Minor.

VITIS VINIFERA

Vitis vinifera is cultivated around the world today as the true noble wine grape. Among literally hundreds of *vinifera* varieties are the famous Chardonnay, Sauvignon Blanc, Sémillon, Cabernet Sauvignon, Merlot, Pinot Noir, and Gamay—all native to France. In Italy the Trebbiano, Nebbiolo, and Sangiovese, are classic *vinifera* varieties, as is Johannisberg Riesling in Germany.

VITIS VINIFERA WHITE VARIETIES

Chardonnay (shar-doe-NAY). This classic variety is native to the Burgundy region of France but is grown around the world. It ripens in late midseason to

FIGURE 1.3 Springtime spraying in a Napa Valley *Vitis vinifera* vineyard. (*Courtesy of Napa Valley Vintners Association Association.*)

small, compact cone-shaped clusters of light green berries. (See Figure 1.4; color insert.) Chardonnay produces sparse crops—the very best quality from struggling vines in marginal soils and climates. It is famous for complex apple-citrus, honey-olive flavors from the noble vineyards in the Chablis, Meursault, and Montrachet districts in Burgundy. Chardonnay is also the principal variety grown in the Côte de Blancs district of Champagne.

Sauvignon Blanc (so-veen-YOHN-BLAWNK). The white Sauvignon is another classic variety native to France and also very popular in many other countries. The name is derived from the French *sauvage* ("wild"). It is a vigorous vine with long, loosely clustered yellowish-green berries maturing in early midseason. From the Pouilly-Fumé vineyards in the upper reaches of the Loire, Sauvignon Blanc wines are typically melonlike and perfumey in aroma and taste, or *fumé* in character—a style sometimes labeled "Fumé Blanc" in the New World. In Bordeaux and in much of northern California the wine has very little color, but a bold grassy-blossom flavor.

Johannisberg Riesling (yo-HANNES-berg REEZ-ling). Native to Germany, the Johannisberg Riesling is the principal variety grown there for that country's very best wines. The fruit takes the form of short cylindrical clusters of yellowish-gray berries dotted with russet spots. The prized Riesling, sometimes labeled as "White Riesling" in America and other countries, can result in a golden wine of intense floral-apricot flavor. It is a variety increasingly planted in the Great Lakes region and northeastern America, as well as in Oregon and, to a lesser degree, in California.

Sémillon (SEM-mee-yohn). This variety is most closely identified with the famed sweet wines made from purposely overripened grapes in the Sauternes district of Bordeaux. Clusters of Sémillon are comparatively small, with tightly compact yellowish-golden berries. Whereas Sauternes has a rich golden-amber hue and a profound honey-peach flavor, dry (not sweet) wine made from Sémillon has a shy yellow color with a delicate pear-melon character. It is growing in popularity in the warmer climes of California and Washington State.

Gewürztraminer (gah-VOORTS-trah-meener). Native to northern Italy, Gewürztraminer is generally considered the major variety of the Alsace wine growing region of northeastern France. It yields moderately heavy crops of small cylindrical bunches, tightly packed with small berries curiously yellowish-pink in color. The German *gewürz* ("spicy") refers to its ginger-cinnamon aroma. The acreage planted to Gewürztraminer has been slowly on the rise in the cooler climate locales of Oregon, the Great Lakes region, and the northeastern United States.

Pinot Grigio (PEEN-oh GREEZ-zyo). This is one of the most widely cultivated vines across the northern sectors of Italy and, as "Pinot Gris," can be found in many other European countries. It is known as "Rulander" in Germany, as "Szurkebarat" in the Tokay region of Hungary, and, aptly enough, as "Tokay d'Alsace" in the Alsace region of France. Its rich golden color and bold fig-almond flavor have prompted the establishment of many new vineyards of Pinot Gris in Oregon.

Chenin Blanc (SHEN-in BLAWNK). Native to the Loire Valley region in west central France, the Chenin Blanc variety is a vigorous and productive vine, yielding long, conical, compact clusters. Chenin Blanc typically has a delicate fruity flavor—a bit figlike in the best wines made from the variety. It has lost much of its once great popularity in America.

Cortese (coar-TAY-suh). An old classic vine, Cortese is again in the limelight because of the remarkable popularity building for wines from this variety grown in the now-famous Gavi district in the Piedmont region of northern Italy. New winemaking techniques have succeeded in extracting more of its delicate stony-almond flavor and taming its biting acidity. No major commercial interest has yet surfaced for planting Cortese in the United States.

Muscat de Frontignan (MOOS-kat dah frawn-teen-YAWN). One of many Muscat grape varieties that are prized for their bold, powerful fig-guava flavor, Muscat de Frontignan is widely cultivated in southern France. A close relative, Moscato, is grown in northern Italy for the famed Asti Spumante sparkling wines. Muscat de Frontignan produces elliptically shaped berries in compact medium-size clusters. Comparatively small acreages of this variety are cultivated in America.

Palomino (pal-oh-MEEN-oh). This variety is often erroneously referred to as Golden Chasselas in some winegrowing regions. Palomino is the principal grape grown in Spain for the production of the finest Sherry dessert and cocktail wines. It is a vigorous, productive vine, maturing its fruit in late midseason to large, frequently shouldered, clusters of greenish-yellow oblong berries. There are some commercial vineyards of Palomino in California, but new plantings are rare.

Pinot Blanc (PEE-noh BLAWNK). A variety closely identified with the lower districts in the Burgundy region of France, Pinot Blanc is named for its "pine cone" cluster shape—packed tightly with small green berries. Its wine is shy in flavor, recalling very light nuances of fig, melon, and raisins. Despite this delicacy, it is gaining some popularity among vintners in California.

Silvaner (sill-VAHN-ner). Silvaner (sometimes spelled "Sylvaner") is native to Germany and can generally be found in the warmer, less rigorous climates of this country's southern winegrowing districts. It matures to small, cylindrical, compact clusters of spherical yellow-green berries. Silvaner generally yields heavier crops, but less flavor intensity, than its sibling, the noble Johannisberg Riesling. The Alsace region in France cultivates many Silvaner vineyards. Interest in the variety has never been widespread in the United States.

Aligote (al-ah-GO-tay). This variety of Central France yields a rather ordinary white table wine. It is found mostly in the Challonais district of the Burgundy region.

Burger. A variety found in central California, the Burger is a heavy producer once widely cultivated in the Central Valley region for blending and for distilling into brandy.

Chasellas (SHA-sel-lahs). This variety of Switzerland and central France, also known as Fendant, yields a clean, but rather neutral white table wine.

Columbard. Found in central California, the Colombard variety is also called *French Colombard;* it yields a very fruity table wine.

Folle Blanche (FAHL BLANSH). Folle Blanche, also known as Picpoul, is cultivated for fresh, light wines in the southern Rhone Valley of central France. It is also a principal variety for the making of Cognac brandy.

Müller-Thurgau (MULE-luhr TOOR-gow). Cultivated in Germany, Müller-Thurgau is the hybrid offspring of a Johannisberg Riesling/Sylvaner cross; it makes very fruity white table wines.

Pedro Ximenez (PAY-droh HIM-en-eth). Pedro Ximenez is a variety cultivated for Sherry dessert wines in the Jerez de la Frontera region of Spain.

Prosseco. Grown in the Veneto region of northern Italy, Prosseco is best known for its quality sparkling wines.

Scheurebe (sha-RAY-buh). Scheurebe is a very fruity variety, cultivated principally in the Rheinpfalz, Rheinhessen and Franken regions of Germany.

Sercial. Cultivated in Madeira for table wines, Sercial is more widely known as the principal grape used for Madeira dessert wines.

Trebbiano. Known as Ugni Blanc in France, the Trebbiano variety takes its name from the Trebbia Valley in central Italy, across which it is planted to many thousands of acres.

Veltliner. Cultivated in Austria and Northern Italy, Veltliner is sometimes referred to as "Gruener Veltliner." Its fruity character is similar to that of Silvaner.

VITIS VINIFERA RED VARIETIES

Cabernet Sauvignon (cab-bare-NAY so-veen-YOHN). The quintessential red Sauvignon, Cabernet Sauvignon is perhaps the most famous grape in the world. There are diverse opinions as to its origin, but it remains the principal variety grown for the renowned châteaux estates across the Bordeaux region of France. The vine is vigorous and makes long, loose, conical clusters of small spherical blue/black berries. The deeply lobed leaves of Cabernet Sauvignon are often used as the models for viniculturally inspired artwork. (See Figure 1.5; color insert.) The wine is very dark ruby red with an aroma of green bell pepper and cedar and a flavor of black currants. Cabernet Sauvignon is widely grown in California and Washington State, with several other states adding to this acreage.

Merlot (MARE-loh). Next to Cabernet Sauvignon, Merlot is the most important grape variety grown in Bordeaux. Merlot clusters are long and conical, with compact medium-size, spherical, blue-violet berries. Wine from Merlot is typically a bit lighter in color density and texture than Cabernet Sauvignon; it has similar flavor components but is markedly more fruitlike in overall character. In recent years the demand for Merlot has achieved remarkable growth, and, commensurately, new vineyards have been established in California, Washington State, and other milder-climate states.

Pinot Noir (PEEN-oh nwah). Pinot Noir is the regal variety of the magnificent Côte d'Or ("Slope of Gold") of northern Burgundy in east central France. In Germany it is called "Spätburgunder." Pinot Noir makes its best fruit in cooler climates and poorer soils, conditions epitomized in Burgundy. It yields small blue berries, tightly packed in cone-shaped clusters. Red wine from Pinot is very light in color hue and density, with a distinctive coffeelike aroma and bramble-berry flavor. Some districts in California and Oregon are building fine reputations for the great Pinot, as are certain locales in upper New York and other eastern states.

Zinfandel (ZIN-**fun**-**dell**). Zinfandel is a variety closely identified with California vineyards. Controversy continues as to its origin; the most widely accepted notion is that it is perhaps the very same vine as the Primitivo di Gioia in southern Italy. Zinfandel is a productive vine, yielding large cylindrical clusters, tightly packed and often heavily shouldered. Its berries are spherical, with a small brown apical scar. Young wine has rich plum-berry flavors.

Sangiovese (**san-gee-oh**-VAYZ-**ah**). This is the revered vine of the Tuscany region in north-central Italy. A clone called Sangioveto is grown for the famous Chianti wines of Tuscany. Sangiovese requires a long, warm growing season in order to produce its best fruit. Clusters contain moderately large, oval black berries filled with an abundance of large seeds. Young Sangiovese wine has a dark scarlet-ruby hue and flavors recalling truffles and blackberries. Although the acreage of this variety planted in America is still very small, interest seems to be increasing among northern California vintners.

Nebbiolo (**neb**-BYO-**loh**). Along with Sangiovese, Nebbiolo is an aristocrat among red wine grapes in Italy. The grand vineyards of Barolo and Barbaresco in the Piedmont region are testimony to the famous Nebbiolo. It ripens late in the season to long conical clusters, which are often shouldered. Its medium-size berries are spherical and a foggy (*nebbioso* means "foggy" in Italian) gray-blue in color. Young Nebbiolo wine has a dark purplish-garnet color and is typified by an aroma of violets and a prunelike flavor. There are only a few commercial Nebbiolo vineyards in the United States, although interest is growing slowly.

Gamay (**gam**-AY). Gamay is the premier grape variety cultivated in the famous Beaujolais district of the Burgundy wine region in France. It should not be confused with Gamay Beaujolais, a variety that is neither Gamay nor Beaujolais, but rather a clone of Pinot Noir cultivated in California. Gamay is a vigorous vine, producing abundant medium-size conical, compact clusters of large, slightly elliptical blue berries. Young Gamay wine has a medium color density with a regal purplish hue, a black-cherry aroma, and a plum flavor. There are comparatively few U.S. vineyards planted to Gamay.

Barbera (**bahr**-BARE-**rah**). The Barbera variety is widely grown in northern Italy and in a few vineyards in California. This is a vigorous vine, yielding abundant conical clusters of dark blue elliptical berries. Its wine has a dark crimson hue and is often rather acidic and harsh until tamed by wood aging.

Grenache (**gren**-AHSH). Grenache is native to Spain, where it is called Garnacha, but is widely grown in the Rhone Valley of France for red wines and in California for the production of pink "blush" wines. Clusters of Grenache are short, conical, and often shouldered. Berries are of medium size, slightly elliptical, and loosely arranged, typified by a reddish-blue color. Renewed interest in the Rhone varieties has resulted in some recent plantings of Grenache in the United States.

Syrah (**sear**-RAH). Syrah was brought to the Rhone Valley by returning Crusaders. At that time it was called Shiraz, the name still used in Australia and other countries. Syrah ripens rather early, with moderate production of compact clusters of slightly oval-shaped berries. It is often confused with Petite Sirah, a totally different variety. Syrah has a dense blue-black hue and a truffle/tar-like aroma.

Cabernet Franc (cab-bare-NAY FRAHNK). Another of the grand Bordeaux varieties, Cabernet Franc is still used primarily for blending but is now enjoying increasing popularity as an individual variety, particularly in California and Australia. Cabernet Franc berries are a bit larger, with less density in color, acidity, and tannin, as compared with its Sauvignon cousin. The aroma of Cabernet Franc is distinctively like tobacco leaf with herbal and grassy nuances, and the young wine is characterized by a fresh but complex earthy-berry flavor.

Mourvedre (moor-VEHD-rah). Mourvedre is perhaps the same as, but surely a relative of, the Spanish Mataro vine. Cultivated in the Rhone Valley of France primarily for blending, Mourvedre is increasingly popular as a varietal red table wine in the United States. Clusters of Mourvedre are rather large, often double-shouldered, with spherical dark blue berries.

Aleatico (al-ee-AH-tah-ko). This variety of Southern Italy has a very fruity flavor and is grown mostly for dessert wines.

Alicante Bouchet (AL-ah-KAHN-tay boo-SHAY). Grown in southern France, Alicante Bouchet is a *teinturier,* meaning that its berries have pigmentation in the pulp as well as in the skins. This variety is often used in blending to augment color intensity.

Carignan **(CARE-in-yahn).** A variety cultivated in Spain and southern France, Carignan is very productive, and is widely grown in the Central Valley region of California.

Charbono **(shar-BO-noh).** Charbono (Charbonneau in France) a variety of northern Italy, produces a heavy-bodied, often rather tannic red table wine.

Corvino **(core-VEE-noh).** A northern Italian variety of distinctive character, Corvino is widely cultivated in the Bardolino and Valpolicella districts of the Veneto region.

Friesa **(free-AY-suh).** Friesa, a variety of Northern Italy, produces a rather ordinary red table wine.

Grignolino **(green-yo-LEE-noh).** The northern Italian Grignolino has a very fruity flavor and produces a distinctive red table wine.

Malbec. Malbec, a variety of central and southern France, is the same as the Pressac and Cot varieties and a close relative of the Cabernet family.

Mission. The southern California Mission variety was widely grown for ordinary red table wines until Prohibition.

Petite Sirah. This northern California variety is the same as the *Duriff* variety in the Rhone Valley of France. Its berries produce dense, dark, full-bodied, often tannic red table wine.

Refosco. This variety of central and northern Italy (Mondeuse in France) produces heavy crops for ordinary red table wine.

Souzao **(SOO-zoh).** A variety of northern Portugal, Souzao is a productive vine cultivated for red Port dessert wines.

Tempranillo **(tem-prah-NEE-yoh).** This variety of central Spain is the distinguished grape of the Rioja region.

Touriga. A variety of northern Portugal, Touriga is a productive vine culti-vated for red Port dessert wines.

VITIS LABRUSCA

The genus and species *Vitis labrusca* constitute the so-called fox grape. Some people contend that the character of *labrusca* varieties is related to an odor asso-ciated with foxes. This association takes a bit of imaginative stretch for anyone who has ever been close to these little animals. More plausible legends tell of foxes being attracted by the intense fruit flavor often associated with "grape" soft drinks, candies, and so forth.

VITIS LABRUSCA WHITE VARIETIES

Catawba (kah-TAW-bah). Catawba, a vine found growing in the wild near the Catawba River in North Carolina circa 1802, was discovered to be disease resistant, as well as productive and hardy. It was planted in Ohio in the middle 1800s and produced America's first commercial sparkling wine. It ripens late, with medium-size, conical bunches of large, pink-skinned spherical berries. The Catawba remains heavily planted in eastern U.S. vineyards, but interest in this variety is diminishing.

Delaware. Delaware County, Ohio, is the origin of the Delaware, a native American variety discovered during the early 1800s. It is widely cultivated in eastern U.S. vineyards, remaining primarily because of a once huge demand for "New York State Champagne," which has long since been replaced by California sparklers. Delaware ripens rather early to small cylindrical clusters of tiny spherical, pink-skinned berries. In the hands of a talented winemaker this variety can exhibit a pleasant, fruity aroma that is often compared to that of wine types found in Germany, Austria, and Switzerland.

Niagara. The Niagara is a vine developed by researchers in Niagara County, New York, during the 1860s. It is a *Vitis labrusca* hybrid with the parentage of Concord crossed with Cassady. In preferred locales Niagara is a vigorous and productive vine, its heavily scented flavor being the standard for rich, fruity native American white wines. Most vineyards of Niagara today are harvested for fresh table grapes and for white grape juice production.

VITIS LABRUSCA RED VARIETIES

Concord. The quintessential "foxy" grape, the Concord is a cultivar devel-oped in Concord, Massachusetts, during the 1840s and is better known for its juice, jelly, and table grape production than for wine. With inclusion of all its various uses, it is one of the most widely cultivated vines in the United States. Concord yields large crops of large, spherical blue-black berries, loosely arranged in moderate-size clusters.

Isabella. Introduced to the national scene in 1816, the Isabella is thought to have originated from the garden of Isabella Gibbs in South Carolina. Successfully grown for Episcopal communion wine in Hammondsport, New York, during the 1840s, it became widely planted in the Finger Lakes district. Isabella was also planted to some extent along the Swiss-Italian border region during the later 1800s. Few commercial vineyards of Isabella remain anywhere today.

Ives. There are several accounts as to the origin of Ives, but there can be no question about its dense color and rich grapey flavor. It was introduced by H. Ives in Ohio in 1844 and planted along the banks of the Ohio River during the

FIGURE 3.7   White wine color range.

FIGURE 3.8   Red wine color range.

FIGURE 1.4   Chardonnay cluster. *(Photo by author.)*

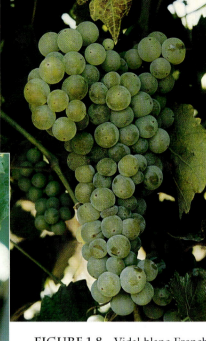

FIGURE 1.8   Vidal blanc French-American hybrid grapes. *(Photo by author.)*

FIGURE 1.5   Cabernet Sauvignon cluster. *(Photo by author.)*

FIGURE 5.33   Muscadine grapes. *(Photo by author.)*

FIGURE 7.16   Catarrato grapes, which produce Marsala wines. *(Courtesy of Italian Wine Promotion Center.)*

FIGURE 6.27   Noble mold grapes at Château Rieussec. *(Courtesy of Domaines Baron de Rothschild; photo by Michel Guillard.)*

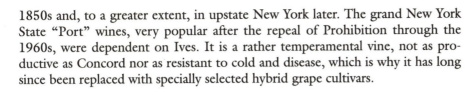

1850s and, to a greater extent, in upstate New York later. The grand New York State "Port" wines, very popular after the repeal of Prohibition through the 1960s, were dependent on Ives. It is a rather temperamental vine, not as productive as Concord nor as resistant to cold and disease, which is why it has long since been replaced with specially selected hybrid grape cultivars.

VITIS RIPARIA

The *Vitis riparia* species is referred to as the "post-oak" or "frost" grape by some viticulturists. It is widely adapted to almost all of temperate North America, but is most often found east of the Rocky Mountains from Canada to the Gulf Coast. Because of its hardiness in cold climates, it is often used for grafting as a rootstock or in grape breeding by researchers.

Other North American Euvitis grape species of note are *Vitis aestivalis, Vitis berlandieri, Vitis cinerea, and Vitis rupestris.*

MUSCADINIA

The subgenus Muscadinia is more commonly known in America's Deep South as "muscadine"—generally small, loose clusters of berries typified by a thick skin and dense pulp consistency and fairly bursting with jammy-fruit flavors. The bronze-skinned varieties are collectively referred to as "scuppernongs," and the reds are known as "muscadines." Most are actually hybrid cultivars in the *Vitis rotundifolia* species, the most commercially important of these being Carlos, Magnolia, Noble, and Tarheel.

HYBRIDS AND GRAFTING

Natural variations in grapevine and/or fruit morphology result in grapes identified by the term *varieties*. Some varieties, which have certain mutations apart from a morphological change, are differentiated by the term *clone*. Varieties and clones are both the result of natural selection.

Hybrids are, however, altogether another matter; in this case, man instead of nature is involved in the breeding of grapevines. The process is one whereby pollen is gathered from the male stamens of selected grape flowers and used to fertilize female pistils on other specific grape flowers. From the resulting meiosis a genealogical combination takes place in the developing grape seeds, which then reflect the attributes of each parent. Each new vine resulting from hybridization is called a *cultivar*, a term derived from *culti*vated *vari*ety.

The rationale for hybridization is to improve resistance to disease and adverse climate/soil conditions so as to increase yields and advance fruit quality. Unfortunately, it is common to find negative characteristics associated with dominant genes. History indicates that it may take hundreds of crosses to find just one cultivar worthy of commercial cultivation. University breeding programs continue, but state-of-the-art research looks to the advent of gene

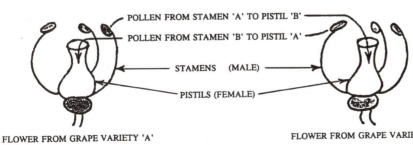

FIGURE 1.6 Diagram of cross-fertilization.

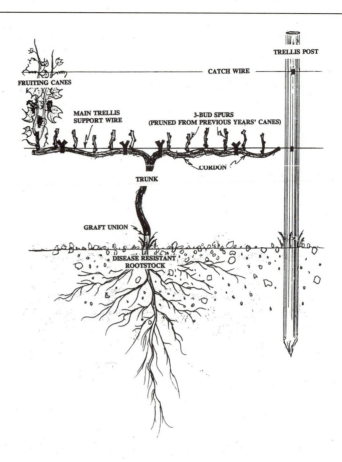

FIGURE 1.7 Grafted vine root-stock to fruiting vine scion wood.

splicing, which promises to make classic varieties increasingly resistant, thus offering greater productivity of better quality fruit.

Hybridizing should not be confused with *grafting*. In avoiding negative soil conditions, viticulturists often graft one variety onto another. Great care must be taken to ensure that the *xylem* and *phloem* sap-flow tissue matches perfectly between the *scion* (upper fruit-bearing variety) and the *rootstock* (root-support variety). Vines can be "bench-grafted" and propagated asexually in a nursery or "top-grafted" to change a mature vine from one variety to another in a vineyard.

FRENCH-AMERICAN HYBRIDS

The term *French-American hybrid* evolved from efforts to find vines resistant to the great *Phylloxera* root louse blight that ravaged most of the world's wine-growing community during the latter part of the nineteenth century. French *vinifera* vines, well known for fine wine quality, were bred with disease-resistant *labrusca* and *riparia* American vines.

Grafting classic *vinifera* scions atop the resistant American species allowed for replanting the classic French vineyards to their original varieties, but purists scorned the French-American hybrids as the bastard children of insensitive viti-culture.

Nevertheless, some French-American hybrids remain important cultivars, particularly in the eastern United States, where market acceptance of native wines has severely diminished during the past decade or so.

FRENCH-AMERICAN HYBRID WHITE CULTIVARS

Seyval Blanc (SAY-vahl BLAWNK). This cultivar is considered by many to be one of the finest of the French-American hybrids. It ripens midseason to large, compact, conical bunches of slightly elliptical greenish-yellow berries.

TABLE 1.1
COMPOSITION OF GRAPES AND NATURAL TABLE WINE

Component Compound	Approx. % in Grapes	Approx. % in Wine
Water	75.0	86.0
Sugars (fructose, glucose, with minor levels of sucrose)	22.0	0.3
Alcohols (ethanol, with trace levels of higher alcohols)	.1	11.2
Organic Acids (tartaric, malic, with minor levels of lactic, succinic, oxalic, etc.)	.9	.6
Minerals (potassium, calcium, with minor levels of sodium, magnesium, iron, etc.)	.5	.5
Phenols (flavonoids and nonflavonoids)	.3	.3
Nitrogenous compounds (protein, amino acids, humin, amides, ammonia, etc.)	.2	.1
TOTAL	99.0	99.0

ADAPTED FROM M.A. Amerine, et al., *The Technology of Wine Making*, 4th ed. (Westport, Conn.: AVI, 1967), pp. 111–112.

Well-made Seyval Blanc can compete favorably with some dry white wines made from Chardonnay and Pinot Blanc. This French hybrid was released in 1919 by Bertille Seyve and Victor Villard, who assigned it the Seyve-Villard number 5-276.

Vidal Blanc (VEE-**doll** BLAWNK). J.L. Vidal crossed Trebbiano with another hybrid to create Vidal 256 in Bordeaux. Despite its French origin, the hybrid matures fruit with a rather distinctive German character. Vidal Blanc has very long cylindrical clusters (almost always shouldered), tightly packed with small greenish-white berries with Riesling-like russet spots. (See figure 1.8; color insert.) It ripens late, often left on the vine for "late-harvest," a natural dehydration process that concentrates sugars and flavors. Late-harvest Vidal Blanc can compare to similar wines made from Sylvaner.

Vignoles (VEEN-**yoal**). A Missouri-grown Vignoles shocked the world in 1992 when it was selected as the Best-of-Show white table wine in a prestigious international wine competition held in California. Vignoles is a shy producer with tiny yellowish-white berries tightly packed in rather small clusters. Vignoles is often referred to in the literature as Ravat 51, the number given to it by French viticulturist J.F. Ravat in the 1930s.

FRENCH-AMERICAN HYBRID RED CULTIVARS

Chambourcin (SHAM-**burr-sahn**). A cultivar that has garnered considerable attention among eastern U.S. winegrowers during the past decade or so, Chambourcin may now be the most widely planted red cultivar. Chambourcin usually yields good crops of small blue berries, loosely clustered in long bunches, which ripen rather late during the vintage season. The young wine has a moderate garnet hue with abundant berry-cherry flavors. It was developed in France by Joannes Seyve, who gave it the hybrid number J.S. 26-205.

Chancellor. Chancellor is known for its rich plum-cedar aroma. If frequent mildew attacks can be controlled in the vineyard, Chancellor can be a bountiful producer. Clusters are long and loose, with medium-size berries that ripen in midseason. Chancellor wine is dense in ruby-violet color, heavy bodied, and can be quite astringent unless tannins are tamed in oak. This cultivar, originally known as Seibel 7053, is one of the most successful remaining from the many thousands of crosses made by Albert Seibel in the Landes region of France (south of Bordeaux) during the late 1800s.

Marechal Foch (MARR-shawl FOHSH). This is a cultivar that ripens early, with tiny berries tightly compacted in small clusters. Made from early-harvest fruit, young Foch wine can exhibit a moderate crimson hue and delicious cranberry-currant flavors. First identified as Kuhlmann 188-2, this hybrid cultivar was developed by Eugene Kuhlmann in the Alsace region of France.

❖ STRUGGLING VINE THEORY

It is universally accepted by fine wine growers that the best wines are made from grapes which are harvested from vines which struggle for existence. This is aptly known as the "struggling vine theory." There may be a scientific basis for this theory, in that the size of grape berries ripened on vines cultivated in rigorous soils and climates is smaller, as would be expected. Smaller berries have a greater ratio of skin surface area to total volume than do larger berries. In that most of the color and flavor of wines is extracted from the skins of grapes, it stands to reason that there would also be more colorful and flavorful wines made from smaller berries. Consequently, many of the world's greatest vineyards are found on steep stony hillsides and other environs that would be considered unacceptable for most any other form of agriculture.

❖ WINE COMPOSITION

Given that water, sugars, and most alcohols have no flavor, note that Table 1.1 indicates that only about 2 to 3 percent of the total grape composition accounts for the flavor difference between the very finest of wines and the poorest.
Note also that water content increases during fermentation. This is due primarily to the Embden-Meyerhof reaction, which diverts some of the sugars to the production of lactic acid, creating water as a by-product. In addition, yeasts produce enzymes that convert pyruvic acid to carbon dioxide gas and water.

ORGANIC ACIDS

Organic acids, principally tartaric and malic acids, combine to form the tartness of a wine (not sourness, which implies spoilage). Normally, about one third of the total acidity is lost because of fermentation, much as a result of tartrate crystal formation, as explained in the following paragraph. Sour wine, in wine terms called "acetic," is spoiled to vinegar by acetic acid bacteria. Sometimes this is referred to as "volatile acidity," in that such acidity can be distilled.

MINERALS AND METALS

Although most wine minerals have a small nutritive value in the human diet, they often pose a stability problem in winemaking. Potassium combines with tartaric acid to form crystals that can precipitate, often mistaken for broken glass particles by neophytes. Over longer periods of time calcium tartrates can form in similar fashion, but with much finer crystallization. Iron and copper can form hazelike suspensions called "casse" formations. Today, mineral analysis is generally performed by flame photometry, in which a wine sample is burned and precise wavelengths of light are passed through the flame and quantified by a receptor device. For each mineral, there is a specific wavelength of light to which it is sensitive.

PHENOLS, PHENOLICS, AND POLYPHENOLS

As shown in Table 1.1, table wines are composed of about 86 percent water and 11 percent ethyl alcohol, leaving only 3 percent of the remaining components to account for color, flavor, and body. A major group of compounds found in this small but essential portion of wine are called *phenols,* sometimes referred to as *phenolic* substances and/or *tannins.* Technically, each term refers to a different substance. The chemistry of these structures is very complex and diverse, each having important relationships in winemaking.

Phenols refer to the fundamental form of phenic acid, phenylic acid, and oxybenzene. A phenol very common to wine is hydroxybenzene. Phenolics are more complex structures formed from primary phenols, such as in ripening grapes and maturing wines. Tannins are condensed giant phenolic polymers, which can be precipitated by proteins such as the mucoproteins on the human palate, accounting for the "puckery" astringent effect when high-tannin wines are tasted.

Yet another family of phenolics are extracted by aging wines in barrels. These are varied, owing to the species of oak selected, the intensity of "toasting" given during construction, and the ratio of time/temperature employed in the cellar.

The entire family of phenols, phenolics, and tannins can be referred to as *polyphenols.* On average, about 65 percent of grape polyphenols are found in the seeds, 22 percent in the stems, and 12 percent in the skins, whereas only 1 percent is in the pulp. The quality and quantity of polyphenols in grapes is determined by species and variety, vineyard locale, and cellar management.

Polyphenols are categorized into two major groups, *flavonoids* and *nonflavonoids.* Flavonoids are large polymer molecules that include wine color, tannins, and *resveratrol* and *quercetin* compounds, among many others. Nonflavonoids are generally smaller molecules, primarily associated with oak flavor extracts such as cinnamic acid and vanillic acid.

COLOR

The pigmentation in grape skins, which eventually determines wine color, are phenolic flavonoids called *anthocyanins.* These are a group of five closely related anthocyanidin compounds constructed in combination with sugar residues called *glucosides.* There are monoglucosides having a single sugar residue and diglucosides with two. Anthocyanidins decompose rather rapidly without a glucoside component. Consequently, the stability of wine color is largely dependent on the anthocyanin glucoside structure.

It is principally the monoglucoside form that is associated with wines made from *Vitis vinifera* grapes; this is generally more stable than the diglucoside form identified with the red "muscadine" varieties belonging to the *Vitis rotundifolia* species. A varying density of purple hues is typical of the predominance of the monoglucoside anthocyanin *malvidin* in Cabernet Sauvignon, Merlot, and other *viniferas.* Some *Vitis labrusca* types, such as Concord, also possess a significant level of monoglucoside malvidin, but in concert with the other four monoglucoside anthocyanins, *cyanidin, delphinidin, peonidin,* and *petunidin.* Hybrid grapes, such as the French-American cultivars, each have a specific phenolic color profile, inherited from their breeding lines.

Color can be enhanced, however, by employing the *saignée* system of must concentration practiced in some European winegrowing regions. Some portion of the free-run juice is separated from the freshly pressed must and processed as blush wine, or as sparkling wine "blanc de noirs" components, or for blending. The remaining pomace is then either fermented by itself or added to other crushed grapes of the same types to increase the potential for increased pigment extraction. Exacting control over the extent of extraction is necessary to avoid generating distorted flavor profiles and saturated concentrations of phenolics, as well as excessive astringency, bitterness, and eventual color precipitates.

A simpler method to achieve red wine color enhancement is the simple blending of a "teinturier," a dense, inky wine made from Salvador, Colobel, and other heavily pigmented grape varieties. Sometimes color-rich press wine *fractions* (red wine extracted from fermented red grape must under heavy pressure) are employed in a similar manner. Vintners differ in their approach to this matter, as some feel that the blend strays from the ideals of varietal purity and others point out that many classic reds, such as Bordeaux, are themselves blends of different varieties.

New products made possible by membrane separation processing techniques have resulted in the isolation of concentrated pigments in retentate form. Although this may raise similar issues regarding varietal purity, there is far less concern, as comparatively little pigment is required to achieve favorable results.

FLAVORS

The literature often refers to chemical structures of flavor and an increasing amount of casual discussion centers on flavor chemistry. One of the most advanced wine flavor sources is Jean Lenoir, who manufactures the *Le Nez Du Vin* ("The Nose of Wine") aroma identification kits, which are highly recommended for the neophyte and even for more advanced enophiles.

Wine flavors are categorized into four major groups. *Primary floral and fruit aromas* are generally composed of terpene alcohol and/or ester compounds. *Primary vegetal aromas* are typically identified biochemically as one or another carbonyl groups and *primary wood aromas* are usually phenolic structures.

There are, of course, bad flavors in bad wines. Among these are burnt match, rotten eggs, and skunky tastes associated with sulfur residues. Others are vinegar and paint-thinner pungency resulting from bacterial spoilage. Still others are prune-like flavors associated from some portion of the grapes having decayed.

The entire spectrum of wine aromas and flavors are discussed in Chapter 3.

NITROGENOUS COMPOUNDS

Note in Table 1.1 that about half of the nitrogen compounds in grapes remain in the resulting wine—owing to the heavy demand made by yeasts during fermentation. Winemakers are concerned with the amount of protein remaining, as it can form a haze that is difficult to remove. Samples of wine are exposed to higher temperatures for several days in order to determine the likelihood of this haze forming. If more definitive quantitative analyses are required, testing is usually done by laboratories having greater technical capacity.

WINE MICROBIOLOGY

YEASTS

There are plenty of natural, or "wild," microscopic yeasts in the *cutin* of grape skins. The cutin, often called the "bloom," is a waxy coating on grape skins.

Given the patience, we can remove the bloom from grapes in much the same way we can shine an apple.

It was Theodor Schwann who first discovered that the transformation of sugar to alcohol in fermentation was caused by a "sugar fungus," the *Saccharomyces* organism. Louis Pasteur published a paper in 1857, reporting his observation of a similar microscopic organism that was responsible for wine fermentation. Prior to this time fermentation was thought to have been due to a phenomenon known as "spontaneous generation," loosely related to various forms of magic. The Hellenic Greeks called fermentation *zestos* ("boiling"), from which the term *yeast* was derived. Thus, the discipline of microbiology was born in France, largely in response to Pasteur's curiosity about wine fermentation.

Yeasts are egg-shaped cells about 1/300,000 of an inch in length. Because they lack stems, leaves, roots, and chlorophyll, yeasts are referred to as lower-form plants. In the tumult of fermentation they can reproduce once every half hour or so—a rate that can generate a huge population in a relatively short period of time.

Wild yeasts may, or may not, perform the fermentation function adequately. *Saccharomyces apiculata* are, as the name suggests, apiculated, with irregular shapes pointed at one or both ends. These and other natural yeasts can lose viability at some point well before fermentation is completed; the resulting wine is residually sweet and unbalanced. There is an additional hazard, in that some strains are also spoilage yeasts that can foul a wine with a "vinegar" (acetic acid) or "paint-thinner" (ethyl acetate) flavor. Even so, many classic wines are still fermented with natural yeasts.

Yeasts are taxonomically classified as follows:

Phylum	Thallophyta
Subphylum	Fungi
Class	Eumycetes
Subclass	Ascomycetes
Order	Endomycetales
Family	Saccharomycetaceae
Subfamily	Saccharomycoideae
Genera	Saccharomyces

Saccharomyces cerevisiae is the species within which the most important cultured wine fermentation yeasts are found. The variety *ellipsoideus* has many strains available for commercial vintners. Among these are *Champagne, Epernay, Montrachet,* and *Steinberg* offered in dehydrated pellets, which are stirred in warm water by winemakers just prior to inoculation into new grape juice or must for fermentation. Another common choice today are "killer yeasts," such as *Prisse de Mousse,* which have the ablility to overpower wild spoilage yeasts.

Alcohol is, as mentioned earlier, a by-product of fermentation, and most cultured yeasts have difficulty remaining viable in concentrations of alcohol exceeding 14 percent.

Most wine yeasts grow in suspension throughout the entire volume of fermenting juice. There are, however, also surface-growing yeasts defined as *Saccharomyces beticus,* more often referred to as *flor* yeasts. These microorganisms serve to transform alcohol into aldehyde and furfural compounds that are somewhat caramel and nutlike in flavor. This process occurs in "madeirized" wines, typical in Madeira and Sherry wines. Other surface-growing yeasts, such as the general *candida, kloeckera,* and *pichia,* are spoilage types that can cause rather dirty, or musty, "off" flavors.

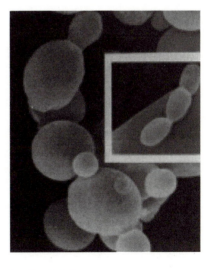

FIGURE 1.9 Electron microscope photo of Saccharomyces cerevisiae yeast cells and *Acetobacter aceti* bacteria (inset). *(Courtesy of Mississippi State University.)*

BACTERIA

The microbes most feared by wine masters are the vinegar bacteria, more properly known as *Acetobacter,* or acetic acid bacteria. Fortunately, we know that these one-celled organisms require oxygen to grow, a condition that can be controlled in well-equipped wineries. The most common strain of vinegar bacteria is *Acetobacter aceti,* although *Acetobacter pasteurianus* and *Acetobacter peroxydans* are also identified.

Another type of wine bacteria can be beneficial to some wines and detrimental to others. These are the well-known "malo-lactic" bacteria which, as their name suggests, transform malic acid to lactic acid, along with carbon dioxide gas as a by-product. Malic acid is an organic acid that has a rather apple-like flavor, wheras lactic acid has somewhat of a cheesy character. *Leuconostoc oenos* is the most widely cultured strain of malo-lactic bacteria and is often employed to add complexity to red wines and the heavier white wines.

Lactobacillus brevis is one of several malo-lactic bacteria species that may infect wine with a malady known as *tourne.* This can devastate acidity, leaving a wine insipid and lifeless. Another of the spoilage bacteria is *Lactobacillus buchneri,* which produces both lactic and acetic acid, resulting in a harsh, pungent wine, a condition sometimes referred to by the French as *piqure lactique.*

Pediococcus cerevisiae bacteria produce histamine in some wines, predominantly red table wines. Histamine is an organic compound that stimulates blood circulation and may play a role in nasal stuffiness, headache, and some allergic reactions.

A wine spoilage that the French call *vins filant* or *graisse* is also known as *amertume* in America. This disorder results from the action of *Leuconostoc mesenteroides,* which produces acrolein, a very bitter compound that is highly irritating to human nasal passages.

MOLDS

Although viticulturists may have to contend with such molds as black rot, downy mildew, powdery mildew, and others in the vineyard from year to year, there are few molds that directly affect the finished wine in the well-managed winery. Powdery mildew is also known as the dread oidium mold, which devas-

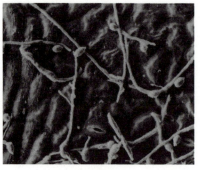

FULLY
RIPENED
BERRY

Botrytis cinerea
MOLD PERMEATES
BERRY SKINS—WATER
EVAPORATES INTO
ATMOSPHERE

BERRIES BECOME
CONCENTRATED WITH
SWEETNESS, COLOR,
AND FLAVOR

FIGURE 1.10   Electron microscope photo of *Botrytis cinerea.* *(Photo by Constance Rowinski and Bruce Bordelon.)*

tated vineyards in both Europe and America during much of the nineteenth century. In general, such molds unchecked can damage the fruit, which, in turn, may seriously deteriorate the resulting wine quality.

The famous "noble mold," or more properly, *Botrytis cinerea*, is an exception. When desired, and when grown in optimal conditions, this fuzzy gray mold permeates grape skins and allows internal water to evaporate. The resulting berries are shriveled, with concentrated tannins and sugars. Such grapes make the renowned *pourriture noble* (noble mold) wines of Sauternes in Bordeaux, France, and Edelfaule wines in Germany. Many similar late-harvest wines of both types are also grown in America. The loss of natural grape water and the delicate techniques required in making such wines successfully renders them expensive delicacies.

With unexpected rains or improper handling in the vineyard botrytized berries may also become infected with *Penicillium expansum*—not to be confused with the *Penicillium notatum* of medicinal fame. At first it can be observed as a white powderlike dust on grape berries, eventually maturing to an ominous bluish-green mold. Wines can be ruined with the compound trichoroanisole (TCA), which is formed in corks infected with this microorganism.

Various species of *Rhizopus* molds can be found in many winegrowing regions and are generally associated with summer bunch rot in vineyards. These molds can act in fermentation much like spoilage yeasts, converting sugars to ethanol and carbon dioxide gas. Under the microscope, these are seen as spherical sacs at the end of threadlike sporangiophores and are sometimes referred to as "pin molds."

❖ WINE CLASSIFICATION AND PRODUCTION METHODS

REGULATION

In America, wine is regulated nationally by the Bureau of Alcohol, Tobacco, and Firearms (ATF). However, production is far less regulated in the United States than in some European countries. In France, for example, the varieties of vine planted, the manner in which they are cultivated, maximum yields, and the type of wine made from those yields are all strictly controlled. In the United States, ATF wine regulations are directed more toward marketing control, with limits on how wines may be labeled, advertised, promoted, sold, and consumed.

Wine is classified in five categories:

Table
Sparkling
Dessert
Aperitif
Pop

The distinctions between the classes are based primarily on differences in their manner of vinification.

TABLE WINES

The overwhelming majority of the wine produced in the world falls into the table wine category. These wines range from the obscure and ordinary to the most expensive and celebrated classics. As the name suggests, table wines are designed for use at the table as a complement to good food. For the same reason, table wines are sometimes referred to as "dinner wines."

There are white, blush (pink), and red wines, which are the base wines needed to make every other wine type. Although neophytes may prefer wines with a little sweetness, the overwhelming preference among veteran wine consumers is for dry wines. Sugar blunts crisp acidity and has a tendency to mask delicate wine flavors.

Table wines may be *generic, proprietary,* or *varietal.* Generic wines are labeled for the geographic area in which they are grown, such as Burgundy, Bordeaux, Champagne, California, or New York State. ATF regulations permit the commercial use of a select list of European generic names by U.S. vintners, such as "New York State Champagne." Such use is controversial and considered by many to be consumer deception.

Proprietary wines are given unique names by their vintner, such as "Jamestown White," "Martha's Blush," "Hamburger Red," and so forth.

Varietal wines are labeled for the variety of grape predominantly used in their production, such as Chardonnay, Pinot Noir, or Cabernet Sauvignon. European wines are typically generic, their identity being geographic. Here are a few examples of generic wines, along with the varietals that are cultivated in the designated regions:

GENERIC	VARIETAL
White Table Wines	
Alsace (France)	Gewürztraminer
Chablis (Burgundy in France)	Chardonnay
Sancerre (Loire in France)	Sauvignon Blanc
Graves (Bordeaux in France)	Sémillon
Rheingau (Germany)	Johannisberg Riesling
Orvieto (Umbria in Italy)	Trebbiano
Red Table Wines	
Barolo (Piedmont in Italy)	Nebbiolo
Beaujolais (Burgundy in France)	Gamay
Medoc (Bordeaux in France)	Cabernet Sauvignon
Pomerol (Bordeaux in France)	Merlot
Chianti (Tuscany in Italy)	Sangiovese
Côte d'Or (Burgundy in France)	Pinot Noir

Among the most widely enjoyed American table wines are the "jug" wines that can be found in most markets. Unfortunately, these often have less than complimentary reputations, owing to the myth that "only expensive wines can be good." There are, in fact, some great bargains awaiting those who seek them out.

Jug wines are defined as any wines commercially marketed in a container of 1.5 liters capacity or larger. Wines offered in the bag-in-a-box package can also loosely be considered jug wines. Most jug offerings are California generic and varietal table wines; a few are from eastern American and European vintners.

To some extent, jug wines epitomize the many advances in wine production technology. Research has met consumer demands for freshness, flavor, and overall appeal with new techniques that allow wines to be made more quickly at less cost. To these specific ends, jug wines are primarily designed for immediate consumption and usually do not improve with bottle aging. One frequently hears that jug wines are "America's answer to the *ordinary* wines of Europe."

ATF rules require table wines to have an alcohol content not exceeding 14 percent by volume. Commercial table wines must remain "in bond" (federal excise tax—FET—unpaid) at the winery until $1.07 per gallon FET is paid to the ATF. Vintners producing less than 100,000 gallons per calendar year pay a rate of \$.17 per gallon FET. Vintners producing annually more than 100,000 gallons, up to 250,000 gallons, are subjected to a sliding scale.

The basic principles of table wine production are rather straightforward. Nevertheless, capturing the precious natural flavors from high-quality grapes can be a mystifying and frustrating task.

Across the global range of white table wines one can find examples varying in color from very pale, almost colorless, green, to rather dense golden hues. Sweetness can vary from bone dry to very sweet, and acidity from insipid to puckery tart. There is every imaginable shade of blush, or pink, or rose, with similar sweetness and acidity balances as in the whites. There are many hues of red wine pigmentation—crimson, ruby, and scarlet—each toned with shades of purple in youth and tawny-amber at maturity. The reds are almost always dry, or nearly so, and the classics often have firm acid structure and tannic astringency, which ensure long-term aging potential.

Vintners in America, Australia, Chile, and other countries in the New World are free to produce table wines in almost any combination of these qualities they choose, providing, of course, that cellar treatments and label graphics meet the standards enforced by regulations, which are often updated. European wine-growers, depending on the country and region, have far less freedom, owing to long-term tradition, which governments maintain as comparatively rigid interpretations of the desired wine qualities.

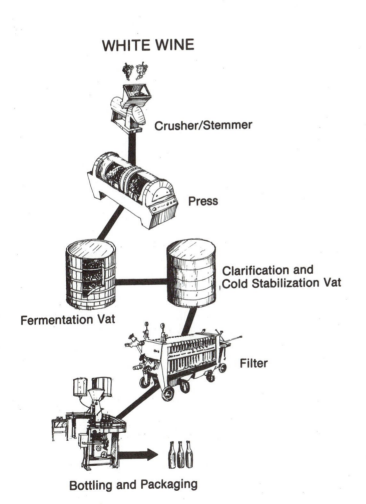

FIGURE 1.11   White table wine processing pathway.

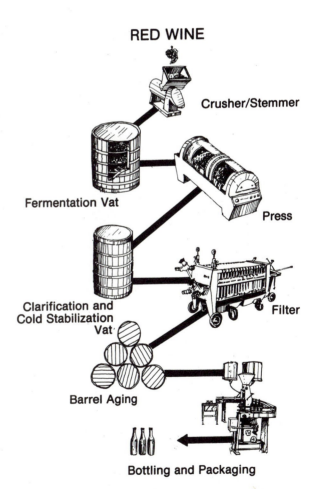

FIGURE 1.12   Red table wine processing pathway
(Artwork by Larry Bost.)

FIGURE 1.13 Crushing and destemming hand-harvested wine grapes. *(Photo by author.)*

White table wines are generally made from the juice pressed from white grapes and fermented at cooler temperatures, 50° to 60° F or so, for several weeks. Red grapes are also used, but not nearly to the extent of whites. Most grapes yield white or pink juice from the press, as pigmentation is contained almost entirely in the berry skins. Fermentation in contact with skins allows the red pigments to be extracted into the wine. Consequently, the chief difference between white and red fermentations is the time the grapes are pressed—before fermentation for whites and after fermentation for reds. Blush wines are typically pressed after only brief contact with the skins during fermentation.

VINTAGE SEASON. Winemakers carefully scrutinize grapes arriving at the winery and then supervise the weighing, crushing, and destemming that take place immediately. Stems, which contain tannins (complex phenolic compounds), can cause excessive astringency in white wines; therefore, stem removal is essential.

A small amount of sulfur dioxide, perhaps 40 to 60 mg/l, may be added to grapes as they enter the crusher hopper. This treatment inhibits the action of natural yeasts and bacteria but is insufficient to restrict the growth of cultured yeasts added later. Sulfur dioxide can also aggravate the extraction of astringent phenols. For this reason, many vintners have found ways to bring grapes from the vineyard in less time and at lower temperatures so as to forego the need for this sulfur treatment.

PRESSING. A large amount of *free-run* white juice (or red wine) runs through the press before any pressure is applied. This portion is often kept in a separate processing lot from the lesser quality press fraction.

For most of the best-known white wine varieties, a yield of more than 175 gallons per ton would be considered excessive. A bit greater gallonage is realized from reds, as some solid constituents are liquefied during fermentation. Higher pressures can extract bitter seed oils and increase the amounts of berry skin and pulp solids, which can mask delicate fruit flavors.

COOLING. Immediately after pressing, white wine juice is cooled in settling tanks maintained at about 55° F. After several days, the juice is *racked,* or decanted to a fermenting tank. The wine master then carefully measures the volume of the racked juice to be fermented. Red *must,* crushed and destemmed grapes, is not generally cooled unless ambient temperatures exceed 85° F or so.

ANALYSIS. Juice or must entering tanks is analyzed for sugar content, which is expressed in degrees *Brix,* roughly a percentage of sugar solids in solution. Each degree Brix is fermented by yeasts to yield about 0.535 percent ethyl alcohol by volume. In order to achieve 12 percent alcohol, 22.5° Brix is needed. Obviously, more sugar is necessary to have a sweet wine remaining after fermentation. Higher sugar levels are achieved by allowing grapes to overripen in the vineyard or by the addition of grape juice concentrates. Refined sugar may also be added, although this practice is strictly regulated and in some regions forbidden.

Acidity analyses and adjustments are made in much the same manner. Typically, the grapes of California are high in sugar and low in acidity, whereas the reverse is true in eastern America and northern Europe.

FERMENTATION. White wines of superior quality are dependent on simple but precise fermentation procedures. A healthy yeast culture inoculum generally serves to activate fermentation within several days, with complete fermentation taking place in several weeks. The fermentation reaction is *exothermic* (releases energy in the form of heat).

Consequently, fermentation in large tanks can build excessive temperatures, which can permit evaporation of precious fruit flavor compounds. The deep color, heavy body, and rich flavor components desired in most red table wines are extracted by fermentations in the 80° to 90° F range.

RACKING. During and after fermentation, *autolyzed*, or expired, yeast cells, along with grape pulp solids, precipitate to the bottom of fermenters in the form of a sediment called *lees*. To eliminate the risk of these sediments being decomposed by other microorganisms, which can create an unpleasant musty-mousy flavor character, several *rackings* (decantings) are performed during the first two or three months following fermentation. The wine is slowly drawn off its lees, by draining, pumping, or siphoning, and transferred to a clean vessel. To assimilate richness and flavor complexity in some white wine types, wine masters often choose to accept the risk and purposely allow the wine to remain *sur lies* ("on the lees") for several months or more.

BLENDING. Recorded history indicates that the blending of wines has gone on since ancient times. At first the process may have been more wine "mixing" than blending, as in wine mixed with seawater, honey, tree resins, and other additions to dilute spoiled wine so that it didn't taste so bad and to aid in preservation.

Blending is an element of wine production that has been described as a rather mystical operation by wine promoters. In the hands of an accomplished winemaker, blending is a tool to achieve an end product that exceeds the simple sum of its components—a classic synergy. Blending, an operation that may take place several months, or several years, after the vintage, is usually determined collectively by a group of people in authoritative association with the winery.

In one way or another, most of the great wines in the world are the product of blending. Even small vineyards in Burgundy blend wines from barrique (barrel) to barrique at each vintage. Large Bordeaux estates blend vineyard plot by vineyard plot, and free-run with press-wine, in order to achieve the perfect château style each year. In Champagne, blending is done on a large scale, the grand *assemblage*, with wines from various vineyards from different villages and, sometimes, across several vintages.

MERITAGE BLENDING. One of the fastest-growing changes in American winegrowing is *meritage* blending. An association of California vintners, following a 1980s nationwide contest in search of an appropriate term for rather Bordeaux-like whites and reds, established *Meritage* as an ATF-approved label designation in 1989.

The adoption of this category came with a set of rules which, loosely summarized, are as follows:

1. Membership in the Meritage Association is required in order to use the word *Meritage* on wine labels.
2. Meritage wines must be either white or red (no blush wines) and only grape varieties approved for classified Bordeaux commercial winegrowing may be used.
3. Wines labeled as *Meritage* must be the vintner's finest in its type—often identified as the most expensive in the line.
4. Meritage wines cannot also be varietal-labeled, although appropriate variety percentages can be listed subordinately.
5. A limit of 25,000 cases of production is permitted for each type from each vintage.

After a rather slow initial acceptance rate in the marketplace, meritage wines are becoming some of the more popular premium whites and reds to be found in fine wine shops. Much of this success has doubtlessly risen from the temptation to replace genuine Bordeaux with the Bordeaux-like meritage wines—at a much lower price. Recently, however, the meritage popularity has driven its prices to equal those of Bordeaux château wines, and some are bold enough to say that many of the New World meritage editions are even better than those older classics!

Large commercial wine houses often blend wines of different varieties in order to create "proprietary" types that have proven market demand. This is where barrels of wines that didn't make the grade in smaller wineries end up—"bulked-out" at sacrifice prices to become lost in huge batches of popular-priced blends. It is for this reason that some jug wines, carefully selected, can be truly superb values.

There is no magic to the process of blending. Successful blending, in its purest form, is synergistic—the result greater than the sum of its individual components. It is the creative ability of each individual winemaker that ultimately determines blending success. The form and character of each wine expresses the manner by which that product has been conceived to parallel market demand. There are, of course, blends that are "monuments" to various vintner egoist expressions. Often these motives are not shared by consumers and, consequently, such wines go begging in the marketplace.

CLARIFICATION. New wines are generally hazy or cloudy in appearance because of suspended particles of grape pulp, yeasts, and certain colloids that remain. In proper storage environments most of these will precipitate, except in white wines, in which protein and other colloids may remain. In reds an abundance of phenolic compounds are extracted from the skins during fermentation, which neutralizes such protein suspensions.

Winemakers use "fining" agents, such as gelatin and bentonite clay, which bond to suspended particles in white wines and ultimately provide the mass needed for precipitation. At the other extreme, reds must be clarified with proteins such as milk casein or by the time-honored Old World egg-white treatment, to soften astringent and bitter tannins. Care must be exercised, however, as such tannins are antioxidants, which slow the aging process. Wines designed for long life must contain sufficient tannins for the long haul. Consequently, this treatment, typical in the great Grand Cru reds of Burgundy and the château reds of Bordeaux, renders younger wines harsh and unpleasant until they begin to mature.

In every case, the most clever winemakers determine the lowest adequate levels of fining treatments to minimize color and flavor loss resulting from the action of most clarification agents.

STABILIZATION. New wines contain mineral and acid ions that eventually crystallize to form salts, which precipitate. The most common of these, as mentioned previously, is potassium bitartrate, or cream of tartar, which may look like small particles of broken glass but is harmless.

Small wineries keep wines in refrigerated storage, generally in the range of 26° to 27° F (wine at 12 percent alcohol freezes at about 25° F), for a month or so to accelerate the crystallization and precipitation of tartrate crystals. This time can be reduced by the addition of crushed crystals (taken from previous wine detartration precipitates) which aid in fostering development of crystal nuclei formation.

The cost of energy for refrigeration and special stainless steel storage tanks makes this operation expensive. The vast majority of fine red wines are not stabilized, because it is believed that they will eventually "throw" a sediment—which is expected in older red wines anyway—and are separated by decanting.

Large wineries may stabilize wines by using an ion-exchange column, which operates in the manner of a water softener. In a bed of resin beads, unstable potassium ions are exchanged for stable sodium ions. People on low-sodium diets should check with their physicians about consuming wines treated in this manner.

AGING. Wines will age in stainless steel, glass, and other rather nonporous storage tanks, but aging occurs much faster in wooden vessels, often referred to as "cooperage," a term taken from old sailing jargon. White and blush wines are increasingly aged in stainless steel because it allows pinpoint storage temperature control and interior aseptic control, both of which are essential to preserving the delicate color and elusive "terpene" flavor constituents found in Johannisberg Riesling, Gewürztraminer, and Muscat varietals.

Chardonnay, Sauvignon Blanc, Sémillon, and other whites may require limited oak aging, for perhaps just a few weeks to several months, to develop the desired character and complexity. French and American species of oak are widely used, often "toasted" to varying degrees on the interior walls for even broader effects in the final product.

Virtually all fine red wines are oak aged, often for one or two years or more. It is typical to find each succeeding vintage of a red wine aged in a similar regimen: for example, one third in new oak, another third in one-year-old barrels, and the balance in two-year-old cooperage—all for a period of two years; or an entire vintage stored in new barrels for one year and then racked to older barrels for another year. Comprehensive aging programs include the use of various species of French oak, such as *Limousin*, *Nevers*, and *Allier*, along with American oak from the preferred forests of Minnesota and Pennsylvania. Slavic oak, Hungarian oak, and other white oak species may also be used.

Prior to the 1970s, the toasting of oak barrels, a charring treatment, was employed throughout the bourbon whiskey industry but virtually unknown in wine production. Barrel aging, for wines, was produced by treating bare oak

FIGURE 1.14 Stainless steel fermentation tanks and oak barrel aging. *(Courtesy of Cap Rock Winery, Lubbock, Texas.)*

surfaces with only mild chemical soakings and rinsings. Robert Mondavi pioneered the notion of barrel toasting for wines made in California. Today, with toasting regimes ranging from very light to very dark, there is a growing school of thought that the level of toast given an oak barrel has a greater influence on flavor than the species of oak itself. This idea, as might be expected, has prompted even more research and debate on the topic. The following are some typical wine-aging regimens employed for oak barrel selection and toasting treatments.

Barrel Wood Species	Degree of Toast	Generally Accepted Utility
Allier	light-medium	dry whites
	medium-heavy	dry reds
American	medium-heavy	dry heavy-bodied reds
Limousin	medium-heavy	dry heavy-bodied reds
Nevers	light-medium	dry whites
	medium-heavy	dry reds
Tronçais	light-medium	dry whites
	medium-heavy	light-bodied reds
Vosges	light-medium	dry delicate whites

FILTRATION. Filtering is designed to remove any remaining suspended particles. Unfortunately, filtering also removes some portion of color and flavor, justifying some red wine labels that prominently state "Unfiltered" as a proud indicator of higher quality. This proclamation is sometimes used in combination with a disclaimer to excuse any haziness or precipitates present in the bottle.

Advances in food science and technology have provided many new processes and techniques readily applicable to producing higher-quality wines with greater efficiency. Small wineries may employ a disposable cartridge-type filter for up to a few hundred gallons at a time. Larger vintners have more complex units designed for both coarse and fine filtrations. One of the most significant developments in recent years is the ability to filter liquids through submicron porosity media to remove yeast and bacteria cells. In fine wine production, however, the application of this process must focus on adequate or optimal filtration in order to conserve precious color and flavor components.

BOTTLING. In large wineries bottling often depends on such factors as inventory depletion and sales projection. Estate vintners are faced with the same concerns, in addition to the need to determine the optimal time for a wine to leave the barrel or tank and commence its life in bottle.

Modern winemaking—from the first sampling of grapes prior to harvest, all the way through aging—depends a great deal on the results obtained by laboratory analysis. Bottling is no different. Important as these analytical indicators are, however, most well-run wineries depend on a collective association of people to determine bottling time. The greatest laboratory of all is the master's nose and palate.

Bottling involves great care in selection of the appropriately shaped bottle for each particular wine. The basis of such selection is tradition and consumer acceptability.

BOTTLES. There is considerable history involved with the shape of wine bottles. The original Roman shape was rather cylindrical, with an abrupt shoulder reduced down to a narrow neck. This was the principal influence on bottles as

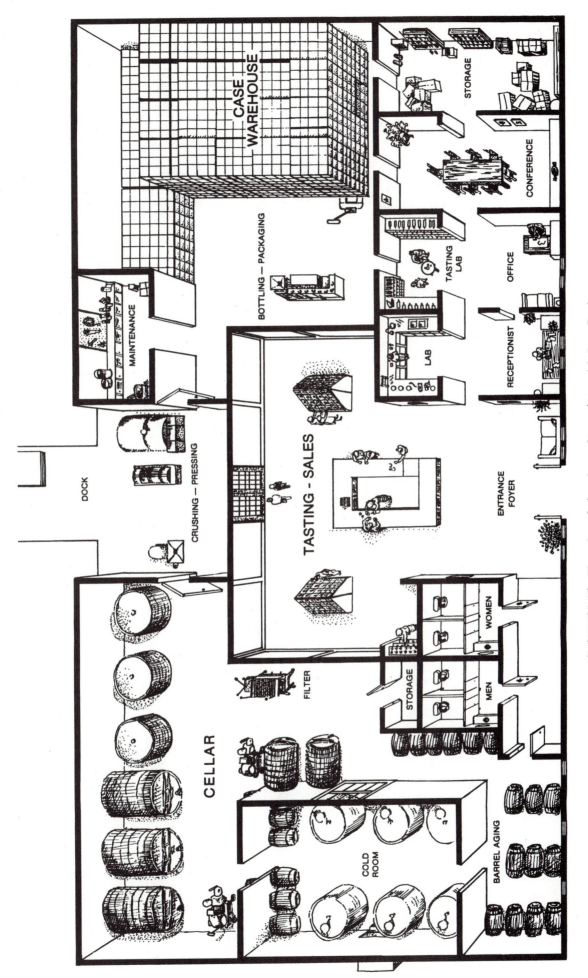

FIGURE 1.15 Floorplan of a boutique winery. (*Artwork by Larry Bost.*)

27

FIGURE 1.16
Traditional bottle shapes.

ROMAN RHONE | BURGUNDY | CHAMPAGNE | RHEIN | BORDEAUX | PORTUGAL SPAIN | LOIRE | FRANKEN

we know them today. As the Roman Empire progressed to the west, into Spain, Portugal, and Bordeaux in southern France, the bottle remained in this traditional shape. But the occupation of northern Europe over several hundred years was to evolve a new tradition—a more gradual slope in the shoulders as now expressed in the bottles from Burgundy, Champagne, and the Rhineland.

It is important that the "right" bottle be used for each table wine type. Tradition can, of course, be broken, but consumers who are well versed in wine will typically reject Burgundy-type wines bottled in Bordeaux-type bottles, and vice versa.

A "punt," or indented pushed-up bottom, is another tradition that is preserved by some vintners, usually for more expensive wines. The punt was first designed to provide added rigidity and strength to the bottle bottom. Later the punt was adopted to help secure bottles into machines for corking and labeling.

The following is a table of bottle shapes designed for popular varietal table wines:

BORDEAUX SHAPE

Sauvignon Blanc

Sémillon

Cabernet Sauvignon

Merlot

Nebbiolo

Sangiovese

BURGUNDY SHAPE

Chardonnay

Seyval Blanc

Chambourcin

Gamay

Grenache

Pinot Noir

HOCK (GERMAN RHINELAND) SHAPE

Gewürztraminer

Johannisberg Riesling

Vidal Blanc

The most common wine bottle size is 750 milliliters, or ¾ liter, which replaced the ⅕ gallon, or "fifth" (757 ml), bottle when the ATF changed to standardized metric measurements. The generally recognized range of wine bottle sizes is as follows:

COMMON WINE BOTTLE SIZES

Bottle Name	Volume
Split (or quarter bottles)	187 ml
Half bottle	375 ml
Bottle	750 ml
Magnum	1.5 l
Jeroboam	3.0 l
Imperial	6.0 l

Splits are used extensively in the transportation and hotel industries. Half bottles are designed chiefly for restaurant use at tables where only one or two people are dining. Magnums, or double bottles, are used primarily for festive occasions when eight or more guests participate. Some vintners fill a few half bottles and magnums along with the regular bottles at each vintage. Jeroboams and imperials are very expensive and difficult to handle.

Soft drink bottles, spirits bottles, and the like are rarely used by vintners as they create an impression of carelessness and questionable ethics.

CORKS. Corks are made from the bark of the cork oak tree, *Quercus suber,* and can cost more than 15 cents apiece, especially those in the higher-quality grades. Under ideal storage conditions, a cork may last two or three decades. Owners of old wine bottles sealed with the original corks should consider recorkage.

The bottle shapes discussed earlier are molded to a number of varying neck diameters, for which matching cork diameters are needed. Typical cork dimensions are 9 mm in diameter by 1.75 in long. Shorter corks are generally used for wines that are expected to be in bottle only several months; longer corks for reds are designed for years of bottle aging.

The best corks have designations such as "Extra Fine Quality" or "Grade AAA," indicating those that have minimal natural imperfections. They are chamfered (edges rounded off), dusted, coated with a thin coat of paraffin and/or silicone, and sterilized. These specifications add a few more pennies to cost but increase sealing integrity.

Some vintners choose to direct newly filled bottles to aging cellars in order

FIGURE 1.17 Corks cut from the bark of the cork oak tree. *(Photo by David Ferguson.)*

to transcend "bottle shock," a condition caused by the rigors of adding preservatives, mixing, pumping, final filtration, and handling throughout the bottling operation, which serves to disturb the integrity of bouquet and flavor. With several months of rest the wine returns to, or near to, its original state. The bottles may then be labeled or held for further aging.

LABELING. In small wineries labeling is often performed one bottle at a time; keen-eyed workers can place labels at exactly the right height so that bottles standing side by side have a uniformity of military precision. Larger vintners, as would be expected, economize with labor-saving machines that can turn out more than 40 bottles per minute, and giant wineries can produce several times that amount.

LABELS. Labels disclose the name of the winemaker, the wine grape variety or type, the vintage year, and other important information. The ATF has exacting rules relating to label statements and decor, which are strictly enforced in the wine industry.

The best labels are professionally designed to attract consumer attention. Others express lighter concepts—even tongue-in-cheek titles and artwork. Label design is actually a matter of taste, identification, and market demand.

CAPSULES. Capsules do not add any type of pilfer-proof seal to wine bottles. Their value is totally aesthetic, which is, nevertheless, important. They provide a "finished" look to the final product and express the degree of pride and craftsmanship of the vintner.

Up until the late 1980s lead and lead alloy capsules were the epitome of fine wine capsules—durable, efficient, rich in appearance, and expensive. When several controversial studies indicated the possibility of trace amounts of lead migrating from capsule into poured wine, lead was banned by the ATF.

Inexpensive capsules generally portray the contents as cheap wine. Great advances have been made in the appearance of heat-shrink PVC film capsules, and these offer substantial resistance to removal by indicating evidence of tampering. Even greater improvement has been achieved in replacing lead with tin-aluminum and aluminum polylaminate roll-on capsules. As in the use of corks, the diameter of a capsule must be precisely fitted to the bottle neck in order to avoid folding, wrinkling, or tearing when applied.

The notion that it is better to have no capsule at all than a bad one is gaining momentum in the United States. The revolutionary "B-Cap" closure system features a custom-designed, drip-resistant, flange-lip bottle mouth. Corks are driven as usual, but instead of a capsule, a small decorative paper circle is applied to cover the top of the cork. The full length of the cork is perfectly visible (although some vintners prefer to partially mask the cork with a narrow garnish strip applied around the bottle neck). The B-Cap marketers advertise it as "functional, economical, attractive, user-friendly, and environmentally correct."

Once bottles are labeled, they are immediately placed in cases. Some vintners choose to wrap bottles in tissue prior to casing in order to prevent scuffing of the label. Most cases are made of paperboard and hold 12 bottles; some are made of wood to hold fine wines from classic winegrowing regions around the world.

SPARKLING WINES

Sparkling wines are wines that "effervesce," or bubble. The first sparkling wines may have been made in the mid-1600s by a monk named Dom Perignon, thought to have been blind, and perhaps also the first to use plugs made from cork tree bark for bottle stoppers. Apparently the seal was so good that wine bottled in the autumn, before it was completely finished fermenting, built up some carbon dioxide gas pressure inside the bottle during storage, later released as "sparkling" bubbles when the cork was removed.

Nowadays many people use the terms "Champagne" and "sparkling wine" interchangeably. However, Champagne is a sparkling-wine-producing region in France, and the term is thus generic.

Ordinarily, fermentation pressure in a table wine bottle produces a very dangerous situation. Modern methodology for the traditional Champagne process, or *methode champenoise,* however, includes a highly controlled secondary fermentation of a low-alcohol table wine. Pressure may build to 100 lbs per square inch in specially designed bottles.

In the Champagne Region, the French are permitted to use only Chardonnay, Pinot Noir, and Pinot Meunier grapes, the latter two having blue-black skins but white juice inside the berry. *Blanc de Blancs* on the label indicates that the white sparkling wine is made exclusively from white grapes, and *Blanc de Noirs* is a white made exclusively from black grapes.

Other countries also produce sparkling wines by the bottle fermentation method. Sparkling wine fermentation in tanks is a process called *Charmat,* or the bulk process. According to European Economic Community (EEC) regulation, sparkling wine made in Germany must be labeled as *Sekt,* whereas in Italy it is referred to as *Spumante,* and in Spain as *Cava.* Much to the understandable dismay of the French Champagne vintners, ATF regulations permit the use of *Champagne* in labels on sparkling wines produced in the United States. The word *Champagne* must, however, be preceded with an approved U.S. appellation, such as "California Champagne," or "Napa Valley Champagne."

The driest of sparkling wines is generally referred to as *naturel;* also very dry are *brut* and *sec,* which are the most popular. *Demi-sec* is noticeably sweet, and *doux* very sweet. One also finds *dry* and *extra dry* on sparkling wine labels, which often indicate dryness somewhere between *sec* and *demi-sec.*

The federal excise tax (FET) rate on naturally fermented sparkling wines is $3.40 per gallon for all producers, regardless of annual output. Artificially carbonated, or "crackling," wines are taxed at a rate of $2.40 per gallon.

DESSERT WINES

As the term implies, dessert wines are those generally consumed with, or instead of, dessert courses. The British, dismayed by the poor quality of Portuguese table wines in the seventeenth and eighteenth centuries, perfected dessert wine-making in Portugal. These wines are now exemplified by sweet, rich Ports, most of which are still marketed under British brand names.

Dessert wines are usually made by the addition of grape brandy to a fermenting juice or must, less often to a completely fermented table wine. The brandy addition usually increases alcohol content to 19 to 20 percent by volume, not to exceed 24 percent by ATF regulations. FET is $1.57 per gallon for all commmercial vintners.

Credit is given to the medieval Moors, despite their Islamic prohibition, for inventing the distillation process from which "wine spirits," or brandy, is made. Wines having undergone a brandy addition are sometimes referred to as "fortified." Sherry from Spain, Madeira from the isle of Madeira, and Marsala from Sicily are also good examples of fine dessert wines.

The brandy used in wineries is "high-proof" wine spirits refined to more than 95 percent ethanol and, following approval by the ATF, is added in bond so as to avoid paying the comparatively very expensive brandy FET. Some states prohibit commercial vintners from storing high-proof brandy and the making of brandy additions for dessert wines.

APERITIF WINES

Aperitif wines are those designed to serve as appetizers to prime the palate before a special meal. Dubonnet®, Lillet®, and Pernod® are well-known brand names of light and dark aperitifs in Europe. Aperitif wines are consumed in the United States largely as cocktail mixers, such as dry vermouth in Martinis and sweet vermouth in Manhattans.

Aperitif wines are fortified with brandy, generally up to a level of 17 or 18 percent alcohol by volume, carrying the same $1.57 FET as exacted for dessert wines. ATF approval is required prior to producing each of these "special-natural" wines, as they are sometimes referred to. Essences from various barks, herbs, peels, roots, and/or spices, combined in a special, closely guarded, sometimes patented recipe, are added to create a consistently distinctive wine.

The history of this category may date to the ancient Greeks who added, among other things, honey, seawater, and wood resins to their wines. Coniferous resins are still added to Greek wines, such as the renowned *Retsina*.

POP WINES

Pop wine is a type thought by some to be named after its *pop*ularity among young adults and ethnic groups. Others testify that pop wines have a similarity to soda *pop*. Perhaps both sources apply. In any event, this is a category that has emerged and become popular just during the past several decades.

Commercially produced pop wines may be made at alcohol levels under 14 percent by volume, in which case they are subject to the table wine FET rate. In states permitting brandy additions, pop wines containing 14 to 24 percent alcohol by volume can also be made, in which case they are subject to the dessert wine FET rate.

In short, pop wines closely resemble aperitif wines, except that the added essences are more exotic, typically boldly pronounced fruit and/or berry flavors.

◈ THE AMERICAN WINE PRODUCER

There are more than 1,300 commercial vintners operating in 43 of the United States, supplied by another 8,000 growers of fruit from which their wine is made. Together they account for 10 out of every 12 bottles of wine consumed in America.

The late Louis Gomberg, a noted wine economist, observed that six different classes of wine-producing firms make up the U.S. wine industry. These classes are discussed in the following paragraphs.

THE GIANT VINTNERS

For a vintner to qualify as a "giant," its wine production facilities must have storage capacity in excess of 100 million gallons. Such vintners have comprehensive product lines, many different brand names, and global markets.

There are only two winemakers at this level in America. The E. & J. Gallo Winery headquartered in Modesto, California, is the largest wine producer in the world, with well over 400 million total gallons of capacity maintained by its four major production facilities. Principal Gallo wine brands are as follows:

E. & J. Gallo	Boone's Farm
Bartles and James	Thunderbird
Carlo Rossi	Andre
Livingston Cellars	Ballatore
Cooperidge & Sheffield	Totts
William Wycliffe	Turning Leaf

FIGURE 1.18 A giant winery in California. *(Photo by author.)*

The other giant is Canandaigua Industries, based in Canandaigua, New York, at the western edge of the famous upstate Finger Lakes wine region. Canandaigua has 12 principal winery locations across the United States, totaling more than 200 million gallons of capacity. Principal Canandaigua wine brands are as follows:

Richard's Wild Irish Rose	Widmer
Cook's	Deer Valley
Paul Masson	Dunnewood
Inglenook	Chase-Limogère
Taylor	St. Regis
Great Western	Manischewitz
Gold Seal	Cribari
Henri Marchant	J. Roget

THE CORPORATE VINTNERS

Gomberg's original categorization for vintners in the corporate category were publicly held producers having more than 50 million gallons of capacity. Activity in public offerings, buy-outs, sell-outs, consolidations, and mergers can be expected with public ownership, but activity has been so great that the principal member of the category, Canandaigua, has grown to become a giant. Several corporate vintners have recently dropped out of the wine business.

Others have grown to achieve more than 50 million gallons of capacity, but are not publicly held companies. Still others, such as Chalone and Robert Mondavi, have gone public but hold less than 50 million gallons of tankage. Consequently, this category may well need another name.

The Robert Mondavi Winery is a famous landmark in the Napa Valley, where its corporate headquarters are located. Other Mondavi wine estates include the huge Robert Mondavi Woodbridge winery in the Central Valley, Vichon Winery in the Napa Valley, and Byron Vineyard and Winery in Santa Maria, California.

Corporate vintners typically offer a number of brands, some in selected markets, some nationally, and some internationally.

The Heublein Corporation, based in Connecticut, is the largest of the corporate vintners, itself owned by Grand Metropolitan, PLC Ltd., in England. Heublein operates a large imported wine distribution business across the United States and owns Almaden Vineyards and Beaulieu Vineyards in California. Its total gallonage nearly qualifies Heublein as a giant.

FIGURE 1.19   Robert Mondavi Winery.   *(Photo by author.)*

The JFJ Bronco Wine Company, in Ceres, California, near Gallo, is another important member of this category, with the following brands found in the markeplace:

Forest Glen	Domaine Laurier
Foxhollow	Dreyer Sonoma
Hacienda	Estrella River
Silver Ridge	Forest Ville
Napa Creek	Grand Cru
Rutherford	Montpellier

The Wine Group, with corporate offices in San Francisco, has more than 50 million gallons of total capacity in producing the following brands:

Colony	Mogen David
Corbett Canyon	Summit
Franzia	Tribuno
Lejon	

Stimson Lane Vineyards & Estates is based at Château Ste. Michelle in Woodinville, Washington, just northwest of Seattle. Stimson Lane is owned by the U.S. Tobacco Company. The corporate wine group comprises Château Ste. Michelle, Snoqualmie Winery, M. W. Whitbey's, and Columbia Crest in Washington State, along with Conn Creek Winery and Villa Mt. Eden Winery in the Napa Valley.

Wine World Estates, based in the Napa Valley of California, was owned by the famous Nestlé food products company in Switzerland until it was sold in 1995 to a Texas investment consortium. The estates of Wine World are the historic Beringer winery in Napa Valley, Château Souverain in Sonoma County, and Meridian Winery in Paso Robles, California. Wine World also produces the well-known Napa Ridge wines.

Chalone Wine Group, which is publicly traded on the NASDAQ, has as its principal stockholder the Baron Eric de Rothschild, owner of Château Lafite-Rothschild and other famous winegrowing estates around the world. Chalone estates include Chalone Vineyard in Monterey County, Acacia Winery in the Carneros, and Carmenet Vineyard in Sonoma County.

The Brown-Forman distilling company in Louisville, Kentucky, owns Fetzer Vineyards and Bel Arbors in Mendocino County, along with Jekel Vineyards in Monterey County.

The Wine Alliance, based in Healdsburg, California, is owned by the huge Hiram Walker-Allied Vintners group headquartered in England. Principal estates operated by this corporate vintner are Clos du Bois in Sonoma County, Atlas Peak Vineyards and William Hill Winery in the Napa Valley, and Callaway Vineyards and Winery in Temecula, California.

The Seagram's Classic Wine Company owns both Sterling Vineyards and Mumm in the Napa Valley, along with the Montery Vineyard.

COOPERATIVES

There are only a few wine cooperatives in America remaining of the more than 40 that were established between 1934 and 1975. These firms primarily supply bulk wines to other vintners for blending, a market that has obviously eroded as a result of vastly increased vintner ownership of vineyards in more recent years. Principal cooperative vintners remaining in operation are Delano Growers Grape Products, Gibson Wine Company, and Sun-Maid Growers—all in the Central Valley region of California.

FAMILY VINTNERS

Family winemaking firms are typically closely held corporations with regional or national market distribution networks. There are more than 100 family-type vintners in the United States, most having entered the wine business after World War II. They range in size from less than 250,000 gallons capacity to the 40 million-gallon capacity of Delicato.

MOM-AND-POP WINERIES

Vintners in the mom-and-pop category are similar to family vintners, but much smaller. Most of the 500 or so mom-and-pop wine producers that entered commercial winegrowing since repeal of Prohibition have grown to become family vintners, have sold out, or have closed down. The greatest number of remaining American mom-and-pop wineries exist outside of California. These, primarily growers of native *Vitis labrusca* and French-American hybrid vines, have not been as attractive to corporate ownership as the California growers of *Vitis vinifera*.

THE BOUTIQUE WINERIES

The newest concept and most dynamic segment of premium wine production in America is the boutique winery. Since 1970 hundreds of such wineries have sprung up across the United States.

The typical boutique winery is a new, or newly remodeled, facility with state-of-the-art equipment directed by modern technology to produce small quantities of highest quality wines. Some of these wineries are owned by physicians, attorneys, and other professionals. Others are owned by corporations or by corporate executives. There is considerable foreign ownership in the boutique category, and many famous entertainers are also boutique vintners.

Collectively, the boutiques have grown to capture a large market share that was once the domain of prestigious European wine estates. Boutique wines are usually varietal table wines priced from a low of $8 to more than $60 per bottle retail.

FIGURE 1.20 Château St. Jean in Sonoma County, California. *(Photo by author.)*

✶ THE AMERICAN WINE MARKET

As mentioned earlier, wine marketed in the United States is under strict control of both federal and state authorities and often subject to local statutes as well. Much of this regulation has a history dating back more than 60 years, when Prohibition was repealed.

The 1933 repeal of National Liquor Prohibition was not a national mandate across America. To change from "dry" was a state's right; Mississippi was the last state to vote "wet," doing so in 1966, more than three decades after federal repeal. Even so, some states were and remain divided on the issue.

The social losers from the failed prohibition experiment were the fundamentalist churches rooted in the Protestant Reformation. That loss, however, remains in appeal as there are still many dry counties, dry townships, and other prohibitive political locales in the United States, collectively accounting for a massive neoprohibitionist force.

The financial losers with repeal were the underworld gangsters who had reaped heavy profits from bootlegging during National Prohibition. However, many of these individuals had the financial, production, and marketing resources to move quickly into the legal mode of wine production.

The winner in repeal was, of course, government. Legalized alcoholic beverages were an immediate source of tax revenue in an America trying to recover after the collapse of the stock market, dirt poor because of the Dust Bowl, the Depression, and the burdens of another World War on the horizon.

Consequently, the foundations for post-repeal regulation were born out of voter demand for strict limitations on when, where, and by whom alcoholic beverages could be marketed. These new statutes were also heavily concerned with strict qualifications to be met by individuals who were issued marketing licenses. Most important of all was the design of laws and enforcement procedures that would ensure collection of the excise taxes. From these circumstances arose the flavor and tenor of the ATF Code of Federal Regulations that exists today.

Along with ATF regulations are many state and local statutes that restrict the sale and consumption of wine in America. According to Frederic Butcher in his spring 1995 "Government Affairs" column in the *American Wine Society News,* of 254 counties in Texas, 79 are dry; and in the wet counties, options exist whereby communities may be divided so that one side of a street is dry and the other wet.

The sale of wine in some states is restricted to location, such as exclusively in liquor stores or in establishments properly licensed in accordance with state and local regulations. Retail wine licenses are often awarded on a quota basis, such as one retail permit granted for every 3,000 persons residing in the community. Such state and local regulations are not only extensive and complex, but also confusing, and certainly far beyond the scope of this text.

✶ THE THREE-TIER MARKETING SYSTEM

A classic three-tier system, including manufacturer, wholesaler, and retailer, applies to the wine business as it is conducted throughout most of America.

THE MANUFACTURER

The manufacturing element of the system is, of course, the vintner or the winery. The different types of wine manufacturer are discussed in detail earlier in this chapter. Included in manufacturing are marketing specialists such as the *négociants* and *eleveurs,* typically French-style wholesaler-like firms that buy wines in bulk from small producers and then "elevate" them through blending, aging, filtration, bottling, and packaging prior to sale. Vintners also sell bulk wines "in bond" (excise taxes unpaid) to other processors, but this commerce is not generally considered part of wine consumer product marketing. In all other cases, excise taxes are paid by the vintner upon shipping from the winery.

THE WHOLESALE CHANNEL

Wholesalers are typically governed by various forms of licensing, with accompanying fees and/or taxes, and limits on the solicitation of sales to retailers and restaurateurs.

THE RETAIL CHANNEL

The retailing of the three-tier marketing system is far more complex than the wholesale channel across the United States. There are hundreds of specific regulations governing how wine may be offered for sale to consumers. Sales may be restricted on certain days of the week (election days, holidays, Sundays, etc.) and at certain times of day, such as after midnight or before noon. There are age restrictions that qualify buyers. There are also limitations on the places where wines may be offered for sale, such as prohibition on campuses, at certain distances from churches, at polling places, and so on.

Some of these statutes reflect social attitudes and mores generated by the uncertainty that has existed since the days of National Prohibition. The great changes in American life-styles during the subsequent 50 years have rendered many of the old rulings unrealistic and, in even more cases, difficult to enforce.

In most locales across America a prospective wine retailer must secure and maintain a valid license in order to market wines legally. Usually, either an "off-premise" or an "on-premise" license is issued. An off-premise license permits the sale of wines in bottles or "packages" (from whence the term *package store* arises) for consumption off the retail premises. An on-premise license generally provides consent to the sale and service of wine to legal-age consumers on the premises, such as in restaurants, taverns, and hotels.

FIGURE 1.21   Wine tasting and retail sales in a boutique winery.   *(Photo by author.)*

Most states permit various departures from the three-tier system. There are, for example, considerable retail sales made directly to consumers who visit and tour American wineries. Some vintners also operate as wholesalers in market areas adjacent to their winery premises. Still others operate restaurants at their wineries, having both off- and on-premise retail licenses.

⬧ MONOPOLIES

There are 12 states in which the wholesale marketing of wines is controlled, in whole or in part, by state monopolies:

Alabama	Montana
Idaho	New Hampshire
Iowa	Oregon
Maine	Pennsylvania
Michigan	Utah
Mississippi	Wyoming

State and county monopolies purchase wine directly from vintners and negotiants, usually from a listing that is approved and periodically updated by authorized ABC (Alcohol Beverage Control) board members. In some cases the governing authority warehouses and distributes wines to "State Stores" for retail sale. In other cases only certain classes of wines are sold through state-owned outlets, the remaining classes offered to properly licensed retail entrepreneurs. Some states allow certain licensees to share the retail market with the state. In still other instances, the state monopoly comprises only the wholesale channel, with all retail wine sales being made in privately owned outlets.

Table wine sales in food stores are prohibited in 12 states. Wine consumers are permitted to have wine shipped to them, at this writing, in only 13 states, where "reciprocal shipment" laws have been enacted.

⬧ ADVERTISING

The federal Alcoholic Beverage Labeling Act requires that all alcoholic beverages bottled after November 18, 1989, must include the following message on every label:

Government Warning: (1) According to the Surgeon General, women should not drink alcoholic beverages during pregnancy because of the risk of birth defects. (2) Consumption of alcoholic beverages impairs your ability to drive a car or operate machinery, and may cause health problems.

Unfortunately, this message fails to distinguish between alcohol use and abuse. More important, this statement also fails to indicate that many physicians prescribe wine in moderate amounts to reduce the risk of heart disease, improve the digestion of food, enhance absorption of key minerals and vitamins in the human body, and to achieve other therapeutic effects.

The 1993 version of the Sensible Advertising and Family Education Act (SAFE), as originally presented by Al Gore (D., Tenn.), Joseph Kennedy (D., Mass.), and Strom Thurmond (R., S.C.), proposed that wine labels be made with a rotating series of seven different warning topics relating to wine consumption. The objection raised by this legislative proposal was that each label would give a wine consumer only one of seven important warning messages. This unrealistic idea involved so many logistical problems that it had little chance of passage.

A bill introduced by Patricia Schroeder (D., Colo.) proposed that jurisdiction over alcoholic beverage labeling requirements be taken from the ATF and given to the Food and Drug Administration. Further, Ms. Schroeder suggested that labels provide a list of calories and ingredients, much like food labels, and toll-free telephone numbers that consumers could call. Again, that the ATF and FDA could share regulatory authority is unrealistic.

A Code of Advertising Standards was adopted by the California wine industry in 1978. Among its provisions are agreement on depicting no sports figures in wine advertising, using no ads in which wine would appeal to people below the legal drinking age; designing no advertising that associates wine with driving; and the encouragement of wine consumption with food.

✦ THE CONSUMER

Wine consumption is primarily an urban practice. The largest U.S. wine markets are in greater Los Angeles, New York City, Chicago, Boston, and Washington, D.C., which accounted for an aggregate 22.4 percent of total U.S. wine sales in 1992. San Diego, Philadelphia, Oakland, Detroit, Seattle, San Francisco, Houston, Baltimore, and Miami totaled another 11.5 percent. Note that all the cities making up these statistics are Atlantic, Pacific, or Great Lakes port cities. More than half of all wine consumed in America is consumed within a few miles of coastline periphery. Wine consumption is thus also cosmopolitan.

According to *Jobson's Wine Handbook 1993*, females made 53.8 percent of all U.S. wine purchases in 1992. In this same year it was the 25 to 34 age group that bought 25.9 percent of total wines, along with 23.6 percent in the 35 to 44 age segment.

FIGURE 1.22 The annual charity wine auction in the Napa Valley. (*Courtesy of Napa Valley Vintners Association.*)

TABLE 1.2

PREFERENCE OF WINE AS AN ALCOHOLIC BEVERAGE

| | *Percentage of Preference* | | |
	Spirits	*Wine*	*Beer*
Females	27	42	8
Males	16	14	64
College Graduates	17	41	38
High School Graduates	24	23	48
Whites	21	28	47
Blacks	28	21	50
Republicans	19	31	45
Democrats	23	27	45
$50K+ income	18	40	36
$20–30K income	24	25	49
Total United States	21	27	47

Adapted from *Jobson's Wine Handbook 1993* (New York: Jobson Publishing, 1993), p. 126.

TABLE 1.3

DEMOGRAPHICS OF AMERICAN WINE CONSUMERS

	Percentage Consuming Wine
Did not graduate from high school	26
Attended college	47
College graduates	55
Rural residents	32
Suburban residents	45
Urban residents	42
Craft employed	39
Administrative employed	48
Professional/managerial employed	54

Adapted from *Jobson's Wine Handbook 1993* (New York: Jobson Publishing, 1993), p. 126.

A study conducted by the University of California at Davis Graduate School of Management, published in *Wine Business Monthly* magazine, indicates that the U.S. wine market entered another boom during 1994. This research polled grape growers, vintners, and wine marketers, who collectively agreed that there are six major forces driving this sharp upswing in wine sales:

- Perceived health benefits
- Affordable wine prices
- Economic well-being
- More sophisticated palates
- An increase in the number of wine drinkers
- Better marketing

The United States has the strictest laws relating to minimum age of wine drinkers. A family dining in an American restaurant may not offer a teenager a taste of wine. This is, however, perfectly legal across the border in Canada. Minimum ages for the consumption or purchase of wine in other countries are as follows:

COUNTRY	MINIMUM AGE
Portugal	no limit
Switzerland	14–16 depending on region
Austria	16–18 depending on region
France	16
Germany	16
Italy	16
Spain	16
Netherlands	16
Australia	18
Finland	18
Norway	18
Sweden	18
United Kingdom	18
New Zealand	20
Japan	20
United States	21

Total U.S. wine consumption reached a peak of 589.5 million gallons in 1986. Current trends indicate that this mark will be surpassed during the mid to late 1990s.

2
WINE HISTORY

Fossils found in France and Germany reveal that a vigorous plant bearing some resemblance to the rambling European *Ampelopsis* existed some 500 million years ago. This was probably the prolific ancestor of the vine that now bears wine grapes.

North American fossilized rocks indicate that grape seeds were borne by vines during the Tertiary period. *Vitis,* the genus of the grapevine, first appeared during the same geologic era, perhaps 50 million years ago.

One of the first distinct species to emerge was *Vitis sezannensis,* apparently named after Sézanne, the locale in the Champagne region of France where some of the earliest vine fossils were found. *Sezannensis* is strikingly similar to *Vitis rotundifolia,* the muscadine grape that is native to the southeastern United States. Later, between 10 and 15 million years ago, several more species of *Vitis* evolved, among which were *Vitis vinifera,* the historically renowned vine from which hundreds of classic European wine varieties have been cultivated.

Paleontologists date the phenomenon of fermentation back more than 100 million years, to the Mesozoic era. Most authorities agree that crude fermented beverages made from grapes and other fruits were familiar to early humans more than 100,000 years ago. There can be little doubt that Cro-Magnons enjoyed some form of wine.

Fossilized seed packs from mounds in the south central European lakes region have given archaeologists definite evidence that humans have consumed the grape in one form or another since at least the Stone Age. In Neolithic times, about 8,000 years ago, the lake-city dwellers in what is now northern Italy made wine and enjoyed it with a rather varied menu of bread, fish, meats, shellfish, and soups.

The exact time when humans introduced wine into their diet may never be determined, but we can be sure that it long predates the recorded history.

FIGURE 2.1 Fossilized leaf of *Vitis balbiani.* *(Courtesy of Sorbonne Geological Laboratory; photo by Roger Viollet.)*

❖ THE CRADLE OF WINEGROWING

Vine culture may have commenced in the Far East, in Mesopotamia, or in Egypt—we cannot be sure. All were important centers of early civilization and primitive winegrowing. The Greek god of wine and fertility, Dionysus, was thought to have arrived from the Orient; hence the notion of ancient Chinese dynasties having first planted the vine. There can be no doubt, however, that the Mesopotamian Persians made wine some 6,000 years ago in the Tigris-Euprates river region, in what is now Iraq.

Some authorities contend that the first commercial vineyards were located northwest of Mesopotamia, across modern-day Turkey and over the Caucasus mountains into Georgia. According to the Bible, Noah landed his ark in these mountains, on Mount Ararat, subsequently planting vines and making wine. In Genesis 9:20–21, it is written:

And Noah began to be an husbandman, and he planted a vineyard: And he drank of the wine, and was drunken.

This account indicates that Noah brought vines with him from Transcaucasian lands, which, prior to the great flood, had been crudely cultivated since Neolithic times.

Some of the first written references to grapes are dated at about 2400 B.C. Wine had perhaps its first religious symbolism during the rites of Mithra, the Persian god of light, when violent ceremonies included mixing blood with wine.

There are Sumero-Akkadian documents that affirm that the pre-Islamic Arabs drank wine in early Mesopotamia, and one archaic Persian poem rhapsodizes:

The wineskin is a kingdom to him who possesses it, and kingdom therein though small, how great it is!

The Tigris-Euprates river basins formed a "fertile crescent" in which agriculture provided an abundance of food and wine. People could buy or barter for their daily fare. As a result, energies were increasingly spent in honing skills for other arts and crafts. The number of artisans and craftsmen grew to meet an increasing demand; an economy emerged, and so did Babylon (Baghdad) as the first urban center in the west.

The very delicate glassware and intricately designed pottery of the Mesopotamians that remain indicate that their culture developed with remarkable creativity and craftsmanship, and we may think that they cultivated a sense for fine wine as well. By 2250 B.C. wine had become a common article of commerce.

To the west of Mount Ararat, in what is now Turkey, the Hittites made wine, perhaps as early as 1900 B.C. Although this is not nearly as early as Georgian or Mesopotamian winegrowing, the Hittites are recognized for the word *wee-an,* one of several terms that could have evolved to the word "wine" as we know it in modern times.

The laws of the Babylonian king, Hammurabi, drafted in the eighteenth century B.C., threatened stern punishment for any who tried to pass off bad wines as good. There were, no doubt, many poor wines during those times, as the natural alcohol content would have been insufficient to serve as a reliable preservative against spoilage to vinegar by bacteria.

Yet despite the great fertility of the Mesopotamian crescent, succeeding generations increasingly preferred wines from the mountain slopes. The Assyrian king, Assurnasirpal, ordered vine varieties from all around the Middle East to be planted upriver in the high country—back toward Mount Ararat. The best of these wines are said to have come from the region centered around Nineveh, more than 250 miles up the Tigris. This had long since become sacred land, home to the wine goddess, Siris. Wines were brought downriver in small boats, which are described in detail by the Greek historian Herodotus:

> *The boats which come down the river to Babylon are circular and made of skins. The frames which are of willow are cut in the country of the Armenians above Assyria, and on these which serve for hulls, a covering of skins is stretched outside, and thus the boats are made, without either stem or stern, quite round like a shield. They are then entirely filled with straw, and their cargo is put on board, after which they are suffered to float down the stream. Their chief freight is wine stored in casks made of the wood of the palm tree. When they reach Babylon, the cargo is landed and offered for sale; after which the men break up their boats, sell the straw and the frames, and loading their asses with the skins, set off on their way back to Armenia.*

This early form of boat recycling made wine transport very expensive, and only the privileged could afford such wines. The common drink was a beerlike brew doubtlessly made from part of the huge barley and wheat crops cultivated in the rich topsoils along the two rivers. It was the food and drink from this agriculture, traded and taxed in kind, which supported an economy and allowed Babylon to emerge as the center of Persian culture.

Sennacherib (705–681 B.C.) and Nebuchadnezzar (circa 605–562 B.C.), famous in the Old Testament as kings of Babylonia, both planted extensive vineyards in Persia. Cambyses II, son of Cyrus the Great, conquered the Egyptians in 525 B.C. and took the great empire southwestward into the Nile Valley. Surely Cambyses and his successors, Darius and Xerxes, drank wine from Egyptian vines, which have a history equal to that of Persia's.

A thousand years later Muhammed conquered the Persians and converted them to the religion of Islam, which demanded total abstinence from fermented beverages in this life. The Koran allows for wine drinking only in the afterlife when, without a worldly body, there is no influence from the alcohol. This first prohibition, however, had little initial effect, because the Persians continued to drink wine heavily and maintained ample supplies.

❖ PALESTINE

The link between Persia and Egypt was Palestine, the Hebrew holy land. Damascus and Jerusalem are some 500 miles west of Baghdad, and Memphis on the Nile was yet another 300 miles to the southwest.

For both Syria and Egypt the source of cedar lumber was from the upper reaches of Palestine, in Phoenicia, which we now know as Lebanon. The threads of history suggest that lumber, honey, and wine, among other commodities, could have transgressed the three cultures. Phoenicians were to become traders on a grand scale, shipping goods the entire length and width of the Mediterranean.

The art and craft of Hebrew winegrowing doubtlessly grew from the time of Babylonian aggression and occupation. Hebrew wines were typically sweetened with honey, sometimes spiced, and often diluted with water. King Solomon, who preferred the wines grown on the slopes of Mount Engedi, wrote, "My beloved is to me a cluster of henna blossoms in the vineyards of Engedi."

Drinking to excess had been tolerated for centuries and, by way of pagan celebration, even encouraged. The Old Testament scriptures contain many references to wine celebrations, as in this eloquent passage from Joel (2:23–24):

> *Be glad then, ye children of Zion, and rejoice in the Lord your God: for he hath given you the former rain moderately. . . . and the latter rain in the first month. And the floors shall be full of wheat, and the vats shall overflow with wine and oil.*

FIGURE 2.2 Joshua and Caleb returning from the Promised Land. Woodcut by Hans Sebald Beham (Germany, 1500–1550). *(Courtesy of the British Museum.)*

But it is also in the Bible that we find the first warnings about excessive wine consumption. The Book of Proverbs is replete with stern admonitions, as exemplified by Proverbs 23:19–21:

Hear thou, my son, and be wise, and guide thine heart in the way. Be not among winebibbers; among riotous eaters of flesh: For the drunkard and the glutton shall come to poverty; and drowsiness shall clothe a man with rags.

The celebrated Canaan grape was a legend even in biblical times when Moses dispatched Joshua and Caleb to Palestine on a mission to learn more about the "land of milk and honey." To portray the grandeur they found in the Promised Land, the two envoys returned with a single cluster of grapes so large that they carried it on a pole between them. Although the size of this cluster may have stretched a bit as the event was continually recalled, there is living evidence of extraordinary grape clusters grown in Palestine. The variety, Aramon, still cultivated in Palestine, yields clusters exceeding five pounds in weight.

Related to the Canaanites were the Semites, called "Sidonians" in the Old Testament, whom we recall as the Phoenicians in ancient history and as Lebanese in our time. Lebanon, or Phoenicia, grew from settlements heavily influenced by Persian culture, which was, of course, deeply steeped in wine.

✦ EGYPT

The ancient Egyptians considered wine a gift from their most divine god, Osiris, the son of Heaven and Earth. The spirit of Osiris came from Palestine, where his body was thought to have emerged from the sea. Hieroglyphic inscriptions portray Osiris as the "Lord of the vine in flower."

Tombs of the pharaohs contain art treasures that clearly portray scenes of gathering grapes and winemaking amidst the festivity of dance and song. One such relic at the burial site of Phtah-Hotep is estimated to be 5,000 years old, ranking in age with the early accounts of wine in Babylon.

The importance of wine to the Egyptian monarchs is apparent by the numerous grape seeds that have been discovered in the crypts of the great pyra-

FIGURE 2.3 Ancient Egyptian viticulture and winemaking. Tomb of Nakht, fifteenth century B.C. *(Courtesy of The British Museum.)*

mids at Giza, suggesting a desire for bountiful wine crops in the hereafter. The hieroglyphic account of offerings made at the funeral of Pharaoh Peppi II mentions the wines of Letopolis and Pelusium. Other archaic writings admire the wines from the vineyards of Buto, Kakenie, Kenemen, Suanit, and Tjetje.

The Roman scholar Pliny the Elder described two Egyptian wines, *ecbolada,* which according to this account was an aphrodisiac, and *sebennytic,* one of the choicest selections. Perhaps most famous of all the old Egyptian wines was *arp hup,* from Anthylla, which Cleopatra poured for Antony. The vineyards of Anthylla flourished on the banks of Lake Mareotis and yielded grapes that made an impressive wine, charmingly described by the Greek geographer Strabo: "Its color is white, its quality is excellent, and it is sweet and light, with a fragrant smell."

The Egyptians probably made mostly sweet wines, both red and white. They began the process by crushing the grapes with their feet, a romantic rite that lives on today as a joyful symbol of winemaking. The crushed grapes were pressed in sacks, the juice then collected and fermented in earthenware jars called *amphorae.* When the sediment settled, the new wine was racked (decanted) and kept in other amphorae sealed with tree resins. On the wall of an ancient winery in Esna it is written:

> *This is the wine cellar, the place for the produce of the vine is in it. One is merry in it. And the heart of him who goes forth from it rejoices.*

Egyptian wine taxes were collected in currency, not in kind, suggesting a complex economy associated with the wine industry. Fine wines were often identified by inscriptions on the amphorae that held them. These hieroglyphic "labels" usually related to a certain hierarchy of quality, such as a "Wine fit for the pharaoh," or "Wine for the praise of souls in heaven."

FIGURE 2.4 Wine service to an Egyptian pharaoh. *(Courtesy of the National Geographic Society; Artwork by Lloyd K. Townsend.)*

Although a few of these wines enjoyed grand reputations, history implies that some were barely acceptable and, most likely, many others were not even that. The best wines were consumed by the pharaohs and the members of their households, along with their priests and soldiers. Elaborately decorated alabaster bowls and shallow silver cups were typical in service to the privileged. Egyptian wine service ware was also fashioned from gold, bronze, ivory, bone porcelain, and glass.

The common people of Egypt received grape wine only on special occasions. Everyday peasant fare was either a drink made from palms or *shebdou,* a pomegranate wine mixed with water and served in simple clay cups.

The Egyptians reserved some wines for special purposes, such as for the alluring wine-based perfume used by Queen Nefertiti. Egyptian physicians often prescribed a compound of wine, stramony, and opium for treating colic and depression. A powder made from pulverized Memphis stone was mixed with wine or vinegar as a styptic to stop the bleeding of wounds. Wine was even used as a cleansing fluid in part of the embalming procedure before mummification.

Most of the great Egyptian vineyards were located along the banks of the Nile River, from Thebes to Memphis—just to the south of what is now Cairo. Inscriptions in the pyramids of Saqqâra tell of the "Water of Rebirth," the "holy water" that enriched the soil in the vineyards as the river flooded. During the dry season, however, the vineyards required irrigation—a tedious task that involved carrying water in animal skins up from the river. Trees were used as a trellis support on which vines were trained, a system that is still maintained in many Middle Eastern vineyards.

As the Egyptian empire grew, so did its demand for wine, in quantities much greater than the Nile vineyards could supply. During the seventeenth and sixteenth centuries B.C., Egypt came to depend on wines from occupied Phoenician vines and additional imports from Ethiopia, Greece, and Syria.

By 1400 B.C. Egypt had lost Phoenicia to the many Hittite raids from the north. In the prevailing state of chaos the Phoenicians grasped their opportunity for independence. They were fearless sailors and clever traders, expressing their freedom by venturing out into the sea to profit from commerce with countries all around the Mediterranean perimeter.

During the next several hundred years the Phoenicians became enormously successful and rich. The cities of Carthage and Utica on the north coast of Africa were born from Phoenician trade, which included wine.

❖ GREECE

The Phoenicians brought an alphabet system of writing and a numerical system of counting to Greece. Phoenician trade is also credited with bringing both vines and wines across the eastern Mediterranean Sea from Egypt to Greece. There could, however, also have been a knowledge of Persian wine in Greece through the Grecian wars led by the successsors to Cyrus the Great, and an influence by the Hittites centuries before that.

In any event, it seems probable that the first Greek plantings of the vine were upon land that was already being used for pasture, grain crops, and olive groves. In the *Odyssey*, Homer wrote of the vineyard of Alcinous:

> *There flourishes a fertile and luxuriant vine,*
> *Whose clusters in part are dried by the sun*
> *In the more open and airy places, and elsewhere*
> *They are gathered by hand from the leafy stalk,*
> *Or pressed out by the feet in the great vats:*
> *Sour are the grapes here, there fragrant are the blossoms,*
> *And the grapes are purple and gold.*

Homer relates that the crude wine made from the wild vines growing near the Cyclops was so bad that the monster preferred to wash down his meal of two men with sheep's milk. The legend continues that Odysseus then gave Cyclops a Thracian wine from Ismarus, made from cultivated vines. The beast found such enormous pleasure in this wine that he quaffed until he became drunk, which gave Odysseus the opportunity to blind Cyclops's single eye.

Homer's works praised the wines from Arne in Boeotia, promising that the wines from Heraea caused men to decrease their sense of reason and increase the fertility of women; further, that the wines from Cyrene and Troezen induced abortions. Most Grecian women were allowed to drink wine, but the Spartans forbade it and were most stern in enforcing this rule.

Wine fermentation in classical Greece lasted for about nine days, the new wine being decanted into amphorae and sealed by lids coated with pine pitch. The Greeks added various types of flavor compounds, such as gums, herbs, honey, pepper, seawater, and pine pitch resin. All of these additions served to delay the transformation of wine into vinegar and to make the result more appetizing. Drinking unmixed wine was thought to be barbaric. The Greek *retsina* wine still made in our time is a good example of the flavor of their time. Such mixtures were made in earthenware pots called *kraters*.

Among the most fascinating of Greek relics are their wine *amphorae*, the two-handled jugs that were also used for the storage of honey and oil. Jugs with only one handle were called *oinochoe*, from the prefix, *oinos*, meaning "wine" in classical Greek.

Grecians drank their wines out of a large, two-handled cup known as a *skyphos*. All Greek wine vessels were made from a rich black clay and magnificently decorated with tributes to Zeus, Aphrodite, Dionysus, and all their gods and goddesses, each attended by equally mythical dryads, nymphs, and satyrs.

Early Greek wine masters buried their amphorae, a technique employed to protect their wine from the destructive effects of exposure to air and high tem-

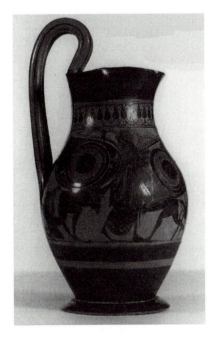

FIGURE 2.5 Greek oinochoe depicting Dionysus between two satyrs, fifth century B.C. (*Courtesy of the Lowie Museum of Anthropology, University of California, Berkeley.*)

FIGURE 2.6 The Parthenon on the Acropolis—center of the Golden Age of Greece. *(Photo by author.)*

peratures. This practice may also indicate that wine cellars did not exist prior to Homeric Greece. Excavations in the ancient Athenian *agora* ("marketplace") to the west of the great Acropolis, indicates that Greek wine may have been made and/or stored in special rooms.

As in Mesopotamia and Egypt earlier, wine became the principal beverage in Greece. In all periods of Greek literature, wine was called upon by the great chroniclers to express the color and feeling of their experiences. As Theognis explained: "Wine is wont to show the mind of man."

Primitive forms of Grecian culture ripened in the Golden Age of Greece—often referred to as Hellenic Greece. Wine was used with, and then replaced, blood as a sacrifice to the gods. Homer pointed to this practice when he described the meeting of King Agamemnon and Odysseus in the *Iliad:*

> *They drew wine from the bowl in cups, and as they poured it on the ground they made their petition to the gods that have existed since time began.*

Dionysus, the wine god and son of the Greek paternal deity, Zeus, was an extremely important expression of Hellenic culture. First seen as a beardless youth, Dionysus evolved into a strong young man with a full beard—at times portrayed erotically as a bull, a ram, and a stag—and, finally, an old man. He was also depicted holding a vine-pruning knife, a clear indication of the importance the Greeks placed on cultivating their vines. The image of Dionysus as a fat, drunken delinquent appeared much later in pagan Rome, where he was renamed Bacchus.

Greek mythology relates some celebrations of Dionysus as drunken orgies that became extremely violent and bloody. At one such gathering the mythic poet Orpheus was said to be dismembered for failing to honor Dionysus. Although these revels continued for centuries at Delphi and Thebes, eventually the savagery softened into more humane festivities. The cult of Dionysus evolved into seasonal reunions held four times a year.

The first festival, known as the "lesser Dionysia," was probably an assemblage for the first tasting of the new vintage.

FIGURE 2.7 Ancient Greek theater at the base of the Acropolis.
(Photo by author.)

The second gathering was named the "Lenaea,"
after the place where it was first located. This cele-
braton honored the vintage at a "feast of winepress-
es" and was often the occasion for new plays to be
acted out by rival groups and judged by the thesp-
ian hierarchy. The genius of Euripides at age 25 is
expressed in his first play, *The Daughters of Pelias,*
but he was not to win favor with the judges until he
was 40, a comparatively old man at that time.
Euripides harbored a morbid temperament that
became a source of amusement for young Athenian
playwrights. Aristophanes made grand satire of
Euripides in several stage productions. This was the
foundation for classic Greek tragedy and comedy.
Thus, it was Dionysus, and wine, which gave us the
very beginnings of theater as we know it today.

The third Dionysiac festival lasted three days
and was designated the "Anthesteria." This was
considered perhaps the most joyous feast of all. It
began when the wine amphorae were opened, and
everyone, family and servants alike, joined in the
celebration.

The "greater Dionysia," the fourth festival, last-
ed for about a week and was held in March. Wealthy Greeks would lavish food
and *ambrosia,* the fabled "wine of the gods," upon the citizenry while games
and sideshows went on in much the same manner as at modern-day carnivals.

Greek art portrays Dionysus with leaves and clusters of grapes in his hair, as
though he was a living "vine god," giving people wine that made them feel
merry and productive.

Although wine had become the staple beverage of Greece by the time of
Homer, it was several hundred years later, perhaps not until 700 B.C., that
Greek land was cleared exclusively for vineyards. By the fifth century before
Christ the Greeks had developed an evening event called a "symposium," a

FIGURE 2.8 Grecian grape
pressing. Artwork on a sixth-century
B.C. amphora. *(Courtesy of the Museum of
Thessalonia; photo by Greek Exports
Promotion Organization.)*

gathering of artisans, scholars, and local squires for the appreciation of wine. Aristophanes, circa 448 B.C., wrote:

And dare you rail at wine's inventiveness:
I tell you nothing has such go as wine.
Why, look you now; 'tis when men drink they thrive,
Grow wealthy, speed their business, win their suits,
Make themselves happy, benefit their friends.
Go fetch me out a stoup of wine, and let me
Moisten my wits, and utter something bright.

Socrates took the symposium a step further, using the gatherings to teach, establishing perhaps the earliest root of public education. His great wisdom is eloquently portrayed in the following passage:

So far as drinking is concerned, gentlemen, you have my approval. Wine moistens the soul and lulls our grief to sleep while it also wakens kindly feelings. Yet I suspect that men's bodies react like those of growing plants. When a god gives plants too much water to drink they can't stand up straight and the winds flatten them, but when they drink exactly what they require they grow straight and tall and bear abundant fruit, and so it is with us.

The symposium followed the evening meal's heavily salted or spiced desserts, such as cheese, figs, nuts, and dried olives. Although the Greeks were not known for gourmet cooking, they did know how to leave the palate dry and ready for more wine, which they genuinely enjoyed. A century after Socrates, Plato wrote: "Nothing more excellent nor more valuable than wine was ever granted mankind by God."

Aristotle, a renowned philosopher and Plato's most famous student, remarked: "The chief object of the dessert, besides the pleasure to the palate which its dainties afforded, was to keep up the desire of drinking."

Hippocrates, the father of medicine (to whom all modern physicians take the famous Hippocratic oath) and a contemporary of Socrates, used wine extensively in treating ailments. Among many of the Hippocratic prescriptions was wine from Crete for tetanus and highly aromatic wines for the mentally infirm. Wine was used for snake bites, bee stings, and fungal poisonings, as a hemlock antidote, and, when steeped with herbs, as an ointment for wounds.

Much of what we know about early eastern Mediterranean winegrowing and wine appreciation was recorded by Herodotus. He was a tireless traveler and researcher, having made extensive journeys during the fifth century B.C. throughout Persia, Egypt, and his native Greece. Cicero, the Roman orator and statesman, referred to Herodotus as the father of history.

About 50 years before the birth of Christ, the Roman poet Virgil wrote of contemporary Greek viticulture:

Plant your vines neatly, and let the neat rows crossed by regular alleyways form a perfectly symmetrical plot. They should be like a legion before a great battle where the cohorts are deployed and drawn up in the open countryside.

One heavy red wine from the island of Cos was noted for precipitating a crystal sediment called *faecula coa,* which was gathered and used in cooking as a crude form of cream of tartar. The most famous wines probably came from the vineyards of Arvisian and Phanaean, which Virgil acclaimed as the finest growths in Greece.

The Greeks used manure to fertilize their vineyards, and Pliny the Elder, the first-century (A.D.) Roman naturalist, described six methods for pruning the vines, each suited to different grape varieties and soil types. Pliny claimed that there were too many separate varieties of the vine to distinguish them all. Greeks did, however, recognize *Alopecis, Argitis, Basilica, Dracontios, Graecule,*

Mareotica, and *Psitia* for white wines. Reds were made from *Amephystos* and *Helvennaca.* Because where a wine was grown became much more important than the grape variety that produced it, a geographical nobility evolved among the winegrowers.

Pliny preferred the wines from Cyprus, Oenoe, and Samos. The wines from Phyrigia, mixed with honey, were favored Greek wines in Rome, as were the wines of Chios, Lesbos, Miletus, and Smyrna. Many Greek islands produced wine, and still do: Euoea, Icaria, Mykonos, Naxos, Tenos, Thera, and others, in addition to those previously mentioned.

The Greeks were probably the first to publicly advertise wine, using images of Dionysus on their coins as the medium. The price of wine in Hellenic Greece varied widely with the quality of the product. Five gallons of wine from Chios were valued equivalent to one ox!

The Greeks were also great innovators and teachers of the winegrowing art. Grecian colonies were established along the northern rim of the Mediterranean, from Italy to Gaul (France) and Iberia (Spain). Along with their knowledge of wine, they took their entire culture westward. The influence of the Golden Age of Greece—literature, mathematics, theater, education, philosophy, medicine, history, and economy—remains at the foundation of our Western civilization.

⊠ ROME

The gift of wine was enjoyed in Italy long before the existence of the Roman Empire. Recall from the beginning of this chapter that the lake-city dwellers in what is now northern Italy enjoyed wine with their food some 8,000 years ago.

In the ninth century B.C., and probably earlier, Etruscans made wine in what are now the superb winegrowing regions of Lazio and Tuscany in central Italy. The Etruscans were most likely refugee Hittites driven from their Turkish homeland.

The Greeks ventured westward to Italy taking Dionysus and all their gods with them. The names of most of the Greek gods changed to names identified with the pagan culture in the new land. Athena, goddess of wisdom, became Minerva; Poseidon, god of the sea, became Neptune; Dionysus became Bacchus; and *oinos* became *vinum.* Noble vines from Greece were planted throughout their colonies—*Greco di Gerace* and *Greco di Tufo* are white wines that are made in southern Italy yet today.

Italy was the jewel of the Mediterranean, its extensive coastline dominating the sea in every direction. The austere, rocky shores were fine for winegrowing, but soils suitable for grain were inland and there were plenty of mouths to feed. The Italian peninsula had become parceled into Greek and Phoenician colonies to the south and Etruscan settlements to the north. For common people—fishermen, shepherds, and agrarians—life was a struggle. Bacchus continued as the vine god, his bounty a relief from the pains of the times.

Observing that the grapes gathered from the vineyards of higher elevations made better wines, the poet Horace remarked: "Bacchus loves the hills."

It was wine from the higher slopes that was preferred by the Mesopotamians too, continuing the notion that "struggling vines" growing on poor hillside soils yield fruit that has smaller berries with more concentrated color and flavor. Richer land is thought to allow vines to grow lush with heavy bunches of grapes, which dilutes the essences needed for wines of fine quality.

There are plenty of poor hillside soils in Italy, and so much wine was made there that the countryside was first called Enotria, or "Vineland." It was amidst a loose confederation of Latium villages, at about 750 B.C., that the legend of Romulus emerged and his name taken to unify the locale as Rome.

Farther south, Greek colonists at Cumae, near Mount Vesuvius and Naples, made *Falernian,* a wine that had become famous by the fourth century B.C. The poet Martial wrote of it as "immortale Falernum!" Falernian did seem to be immortal—a very heavy-bodied dark red wine with a remarkable capacity for aging, often reported to exceed 50 years.

In general, the wines of Rome were more robust than the delicate wines of Greece, although the Greek selections were usually more aromatic. The common Romans probably preferred their wines to be sweetened with honey, regardless of where they were made.

Julius Caesar served wine from the Greek islands of Chios and Lesbos, as well as the grand domestic Falernian. Caesar also enjoyed the honored *Mamertine* wine grown near Messina on the island of Sicily.

The winegrowing arts advanced during the Roman Empire to a high level of sophistication. Cato the Elder, born in 234 B.C., wrote a book on farming that described grape growing and winemaking methods in considerable detail. He also told of a potion made of myrtle berries and wine. Mrytle was the sacred tree of Venus, the goddess of love and beauty, known as Aphrodite in Greece. Cato's special wine was considered an aphrodisiac, which perhaps accounts for its popularity among Rome's elderly senators.

Columella was a second-century B.C. Roman naturalist dedicated to the improvement of grape and wine culture. He took great care in the handling of his plant materials. Despising the Greek practice of adding flavorings and seawater to wine, he wrote:

We judge to be best every kind of wine which can grow old without any treatment, nor should anything at all be mixed with it, which might dull its natural flavor. For that wine is immeasurably the best, which needs only its own nature to give pleasure.

The Bacchanalia, held in the sacred woods near Rome, reverted to the violence and brawling of the first Dionysiac rites. A special senate committee investigated following some particularly violent revelry in 186 B.C., and the Senatus Consultum de Bacchanalibus was passed, which made such celebrations illegal.

The favorite wine of Caesar Augustus was *Setine.* This must have delighted Virgil, because the Setine wines were grown on the hillsides above Verona, not far from his birthplace in Mantua. Also made in this area was a white wine called *Rhaetic,* a distant forerunner of today's popular *Soave* from the same locale. Rhaetic was particularly good with oysters, another of the fabled aphrodisiac foods held dear by the ancient Romans.

The second *Georgic* by Virgil indicates that Romans distinguished and selected wines according to how they best complemented different courses served during their meals. Like the wines of Hellenic Greece, Roman wine types were defined by their geographical origin. White wines, such as Rhaetic, were drunk young, whereas Falernian wines were often older than those who were fortunate enough to drink them. Roman wines were purchased, stored, and served with great care, similar to the meticulous attention given to fine wines today.

Both Columella and Pliny were dedicated wine scholars and authors. Both knew of intricate methods of vine propagation, grafting, vineyard site selection, and trellis training. They were accomplished wine judges and passionate about proper wine service. Some 70 years after the birth of Christ, Pliny declared Rome the "wine capital of the world" and provided detailed descriptions of more than 90 grape varieties, along with precise data on how they should be cultvated. Pliny advised that the wine of Alba was good for coughs, diarrhea, and fever. These were his views on the medical properties of wine:

FIGURE 2.9 Statue of Bacchus at Château Mouton-Rothschild. *(Photo by author.)*

Wine on its own is a remedy. It will improve the strength and the blood of a man! It settles the stomach, it allays unhappiness and worries.

Other well-known wines of Roman times were *Babia, Galea, Status, Trebellicum,* and *Veliternus,* among others—all from the Calabria region, which is located in the "foot" of the lower Italian peninsula. *Surrentinum,* another Calabrian wine from Sorrento, was especially rich and hearty, requiring at least 25 years of aging, according to the Roman experts. Nevertheless, it was still considered to be too thin by the emperors Caligula and Tiberius. Caligula rejected it as *nobilis vappa,* or "wine that is good for nothing."

To the east of Rome, in the province of Abruzzi, ordinary wines called *Consentia, Rhegium,* and *Tempsa* were grown by peasants who paid their taxes in kind.

Despite Columella's disapproval, many Roman wines were ameliorated, mostly with honey, but also with herbs, resins, spices, and seawater—all in the Greek tradition. Pliny stated that even Romans of nobility were served debased wine.

Petronius, a notorious rake at the court of Nero and the author of the *Satyricon,* directed that guests be served the most expensive wine in Rome—a 100-year-old Falernian. Martial wrote that he "wanted not merely to drink the kisses left in the loved one's cup but to kiss lips moist with old Falernian."

Falernian became highly esteemed and placed in a class with the epicurean wines imported from the Greek islands of Chios, Lesbos, and Cos. Greek wines were very expensive in Rome, and Lucullus, a military and political leader, recalled that his father never offered more than one glass of Greek wine, even at the most lavish of dinners.

The Romans made and stored their wines in amphorae, carrying on the Greek and Egyptian traditions. Many of the Roman wine vessels were, however, much larger than those of their eastern Mediterranean predecessors; the very largest of these amphorae, called *doria,* were more akin to small tanks or vats.

Roman wine masters heat-treated their wines in a type of kiln called a *fumaria,* hence the many references to "smoky" wines in the works of Latin writers. Amphorae were filled with wine and then protected with a thin floating layer of olive oil before being sealed with a plaster closure. The containers were then placed in the fumaria and heated. Although they did not know about vinegar spoilage being the result of aerobic bacteria, the Romans did sense a relationship between air exposure and spoilage. The fumaria served to drive out the air—the vinegar bacteria could not survive—and the wine lived. Ovid wrote: "He draws the wine which he had racked in his early years when stored in a smoky cask."

Many of the common Greek and Roman amphorae were fashioned with ungainly looking pointed bottoms, a feature that allowed them to be stood upright in dirt floors. The points also slipped easily into leather or raffia slings for easy pouring, or hung in storage harnesses from the mainstays inside wine shops. This system must surely have been the forerunner of the raffia-covered fiasco bottles commonly used in more modern times for wines from Chianti and Orvieto in Italy. Glassmaking was a well-known art form in classical Roman times, but glass was used mostly for wine service, not for bottles.

Vintage years were inscribed on Roman amphorae, but age was much more important than the particular year of grape harvest. Columella felt that nearly all wines improved in quality with aging. Wines were often dated by being named in honor of the then-reigning emperor.

In bringing civilization to the barbarians of the western Mediterranean, the Greeks and Romans realized that wine was one of their most effective allies. Wherever a colony was founded they would plant a vineyard. These were the seeds that grew to become today's vast European wine industry.

FIGURE 2.10 Eastern Mediterranean amphora, first century B.C. *(Courtesy of the Corning Museum of Glass.)*

✪ CHRISTIANITY

Throughout history, there were many influences on wine and its meaning to humankind, but none more powerful and enduring than that of Jesus Christ. The Bible contains 165 direct references to wine, 155 of which are found in the Old Testament. These scriptures chronicle the history of humankind before Christ, dating from the time recorded in Genesis, when Noah landed his ark on Mount Ararat. Christ knew that to his people, wine was essential, that it had been spiritually symbolic in many earlier cultures. He knew that the Greeks and Romans had drunk of their "vine god"; thus his message to his followers: "I am the true vine."

There are vivid descriptions of wine drinking as well as wine imagery in the Bible, along with much advice about the best uses for wine. There can be no question that the Bible portrays wine as God's gift to humankind, as illustrated in Genesis 27:28:

Therefore God give thee of the dew of heaven, and the fatness of the earth, and plenty of corn and wine.

Another example appears in Psalms 104:14–15:

He causeth the grass to grow for the cattle, and herb for the service of man: that he may bring forth food out of the earth; and wine that maketh glad the heart of man.

And yet another in Proverbs 3:10:

So shall thy barns be filled with plenty, and thy presses shall burst out with new wine.

There are several Old Testament passages concerning winemaking, such as in Judges 9:27:

And they went out into the fields, and gathered their vineyards, and trode the grapes, and made merry.

But it is in Ecclesiastes, a 12-chapter book in the Old Testament thought by some to have been written by King Solomon, that we find numerous references to the virtues of wine drinking:

Go thy way, eat thy bread with joy, and drink thy wine with a merry heart; for God now accepteth thy works.

—*Ecclesiastes 9:7*

A feast is made for laughter, and wine maketh merry.

—*Ecclesiastes 10:19*

As mentioned previously, the Old Testament also provides plenty of warnings about drinking wine to excess, as in Proverbs 23:29–30:

Who hath woe? who hath sorrow? who hath contentions? who hath babbling? who hath wounds without cause? who hath redness of eyes? They that tarry long at the wine; they that go to seek mixed wine.

But what of wine in the time of Christ, in the New Testament? There is the first miracle, when Christ turned water into wine at the marriage feast at Cana in Palestine. We find in the Gospel according to John 2:6–11:

And there were set there six waterpots of stone, after the manner of the purifying of the Jews, containing two or three firkins apiece. Jesus saith unto them, Fill the waterpots with water. And they filled them up to the brim. And he saith unto them, Draw out now, and bear unto the governor of the feast. And they bare it. When the ruler of the feast had tasted the water that was made wine, and knew not whence it was: (but the servants which drew the water knew;) the governor of the feast called the bridegroom, And saith unto him, Every man at the beginning doth set forth good wine; and when men have well drunk, then that which is worse: but thou has kept the good wine until now. This beginning of miracles did Jesus in Cana of Galilee, and manifested forth his glory; and his disciples believed on him.

Again, we read in Matthew 9:17:

Neither do men put new wine into old bottles: else the bottles break, and the wine is runneth out, and the bottles will perish: but they put new wine into new bottles.

We read in 1 Timothy 5:23 the very famous quotation of St. Paul, who surely must have known the value of wine as an aid to digestion:

Drink no longer water, but use a little wine for thy stomach's sake and thine often infirmities.

Perhaps it was the fact that wine is perptually renewed each vintage that explains why Jesus Christ consecrated wine to his blood. Every Christian Communion yet today, since the very first at the Last Supper nearly 2,000 years ago, includes the passage found in 1 Corinthians 11:25:

This cup is the new testament in my blood: this do ye, as oft as ye drink it, in remembrance of me.

Wine thus became an element of the Christian ritual—and of the church. Wherever Christianity flourished, wine would become necessary.

⊠ GAUL (FRANCE)

Greek expeditions landed in Southern Gaul at about the same time they arrived in Italy, between 800 and 600 B.C.

Looking for new sources of food, the Greeks colonized the port of Massilla, the city now known as Marseilles, France. Grecian colonies were also established at Monoikos (Monaco) and Kikae (Nice).

The first vines cultivated in Gaul were planted by the Greeks on the hillsides near their seaports. Trading stations were established, where bartering was done with the native Gallic tribesmen. But widespread development of wine in Gaul was impeded lest the colonial wines offer too much competition to those grown in mother Greece. According to the historian Diodorus Siculus, the currency was slaves, and the price of one amphora of wine was one young boy.

The Gauls had emigrated from several northern cultures, but were mostly Celts and Teutons—certainly beer drinkers, but their taste for Greek wines soon emerged. The Gauls lacked the materials and skill to duplicate the Greek wine amphorae, however, and used instead wooden barrels for the storage of their wine, much the same as those made 1,000 years earlier in Persia. The wood was porous, which allowed wines both to mature and to spoil rather quickly, a dilemma also encountered centuries before.

When the Roman Empire supplanted Greece as the major Mediterranean power, the Greek colonists along the coast of Gaul petitioned Rome for support against the Gallic barbarians. Rome responded and occupied the province. To this day the southeastern coastal region of France is called Provence.

Roman occupiers taught the native Gallic tribes the ways of wine and how to establish vineyards along the banks of the rivers, in the forests, and on the valley slopes. These original vineyards were centered in what is now the Hermitage on the eastern banks of the central Rhone Valley. Although those vines have long since been replanted many times, that land remains today as prime vineyard sites along the Rhone River.

By 125 B.C. there were two centers of commmerce established by the Romans, one at Norbo Martius (Narbonne) and the other at Portus Veneris (Port-Vendres). Both were situated on a highway that had been constructed to link Italy with Spain. In a short time Narbonne evolved as the primary trading center of Gaul, and the surrounding region became known as Narbonensis, known today as the Languedoc.

The Romans exported wine into the Narbonensis by large merchant ships that carried amphorae and doria. One of the twentieth-century *Calypso* expeditions led by Jacques Cousteau was successful in locating one of these ships buried about 130 feet deep in the mud-bottomed sea just a few miles to the southwest of Marseilles. This ship had been commissioned by the wealthy Roman merchant Marcus Sestius in the third century B.C.; it had carried Cycladic wines loaded at the Greek port of Delos and some Latium wines from Italy. A total of some 1,000 amphorae and 800 vases were found, many of which were sealed and intact. The wine was sampled but proved to be a disappointment, as it had become a pale, lifeless liquid and certainly quite different from the flavorful drink the ancients had tasted more than 22 centuries earlier.

Trade was expanded northward and westward from the Narbonensis, with depots for wine amphorae along several main routes. Some of the wines were carried overland by burro train, and other trade was carried up and down the Rhone and Saone by flat-bottomed boats. Wine commerce also extended on into the Teutonic Rhineland, which required both land and water transportation. This activity flourished, and the Narbonensis became very affluent. Pliny described the colony as "not really a province but a part of Italy itself."

The Romans needed grain, not wine, inasmuch as most Italian soils were too poor to grow abundant crops. Consequently, as the Roman Empire grew, an economy was planned that proposed Provence and other territories become regions of grain farms rather than vineyards. This was formally decreed by a Roman edict prohibiting new vineyard plantings. However, clever provincial winegrowers circumvented the law by arranging for deceptive sales of land to Roman civil servants and soldiers who were exempt from the planting restric-

FIGURE 2.11 Diver observing amphorae in Roman ship wreckage. *(Courtesy of the National Geographic Society.)*

tion. The vineyards would be planted and tended by the native provençals until the vines matured. Then the Romans would "sell" the tract back. Vineyards that already existed were not affected by the prohibition. Apart from this fraud, there was out-and-out disregard for the Roman decree as well.

The large numbers of soldiers involved in Caesar's conquest of Gaul required great volumes of wines, most of which were produced in the Narbonensis and were probably of rather poor quality. Mixing wine with herbs, honey, and spices was continued in Gaul.

The Pax Romana was delivered to Bordeaux by Crassus in 56 B.C., who found vineyards already flourishing there. *Vitis biturica,* the Spanish grape called *Biturigia,* may have been brought from northern Spain to Burdigala, or Bordeaux, in southern Gaul. Some think the Biturigia to be the ancestor of Cabernet Sauvignon, one of the most celebrated vines now cultivated around the world.

To the northeast, near what is now Burgundy, the *Allobrogian* vine was discovered, a vine producing small black pine-cone-shaped clusters of grapes that ripened before the first autumn frost. This variety is almost certainly the progenitor of today's suberb Pinot Noir, which yields precious red Burgundies. Other grape varieties that survive from early Gallic winegrowers are Carignan, Chasseslas, and Muscat, but such vines as *Amethyston, Aminea, Bailic, Maronea,* and *Nomentum,* carried from Greece and Italy, seem to have disappeared.

During the rise of the Roman Empire, wine quality in the Narbonensis and Provence improved. With centuries of winegrowing experience the Romans were prepared to recognize better varieties of the vine growing in the wild and were equipped to try new methods to advance the state of the art.

The Narbonensian expansion into Gaul resulted in a huge production of contraband wines, so immense that the imported Roman wines were almost totally replaced by domestic products. The Italian winegrowers appealed to the Emperor Domitian for relief from this loss of market for their exports. In A.D. 92, the Narbonensian consul was ordered by Rome to uproot half of the Gallic vineyards. This decree proved to be as much a blessing for the Narbonensians as it was for the Italian wine exporters. Winegrowing had spread so profusely that it threatened other critically needed agricultural produce. Succeeding provincial governors, however, found the Domitian edict difficult to enforce, and in A.D. 276 Emperor Probus repealed the statute.

As a result of the original Narbonensian trade routes, winegrowing reached the Rhone Valley in the first century A.D. Burgundy was established as an important viticultural area in the second century. Farther north, third-century Roman soldiers were employed to clear woodlands covering the hillsides around Reims so that land there could be worked and planted with vines. This was to become the famous Champagne district northeast of Paris. Many of the original vineyard plots are still cultivated, having been many times planted anew. The spread of Roman winegrowing ended a century later in the Rhineland of Germania.

FIGURE 2.12   Roman caves in the Champagne Region of France. *(Courtesy of C.I.V.C.)*

⬧ GERMANIA

Grapevines grew wild in the Rhineland long before the arrival of the Roman legions. The first wine drunk there, however, was probably that brought from Italian vineyards by Caesar's armies. Some historians believe that Emperor

FIGURE 2.13   Roman wine boat statue in Trier, Germany. *(Courtesy of the German Wine Information Bureau.)*

Probus may have brought the first cultivated vines to Germany in the third century. A Roman glass bottle, containing traces of its original wine, was relatively recently discovered near Speyer along the Rhine River.

The desperate need for grain in Italy continued, but the steep banks of the rivers Mosel and Rhine were not adaptable to any serious agricultural use other than the cultivation of the grapevine. Consequently, the Romans set the Germanic natives to work on the establishment of vineyards.

In Roman times Trier was known as the *Augusta Trevisorum,* or the "capital beyond the Alps." Roman emperors and other dignitaries often visited there, and some even lived there, which contributed greatly to social activities and festivities that resulted in large amounts of wine consumption.

According to Ausonius, the Roman proconsul from Bordeaux, there were many vineyards flourishing along the hillsides of the winding Mosel by the fourth century. As he said in one of his many poems: "Oh Mosel, you have so much wine."

Despite this great wine bounty, there is evidence that the best wines of ancient Roman Germany were imported from Gaul or Italy for the aristocracy who could afford such fare. It was not for another several centuries, however, that truly fine wines would be grown in the Mosel or the Rhineland.

◈ IBERIA

Whether the grapevine is native to the Iberian peninsula remains open to question. There is evidence that the Phoenicians were the first to bring wine to Spain, perhaps as early as the seventh century B.C. Some of the earthenware wine vats used by the Phoenicians in Cyprus are quite similar to those used in Aragon by contemporary Spaniards.

Roman forces first occupied Spain during the Second Punic War, two centuries before the birth of Christ. For 17 years Hannibal, the great Carthaginian general, won monumental battles against the Romans, but the victory finally went to Rome. Yet another several hundred years would pass before Hispania was totally secured by the Roman Empire.

Much as they did in Gaul, the Romans made great advances in winegrowing technology in Spain. Wine made there was fermented and stored in large jars called *orcae*. These earthenware vessels are still used in the winegrowing regions of La Mancha and Montilla.

Wines from the newly settled Spanish provinces were exported to Italy in large volumes. This market was relatively short-lived, however, as the edict of Emperor Domitian in the first century A.D., which limited vine plantings in Gaul, also curtailed the establishment of new vineyards in Spain.

As the Roman legions penetrated the interior of the Iberian peninsula, the need for wine outweighed Domitian's decree as it had in Gaul. Important winegrowing centers were developed, with the sweet wines of Malaga being a favorite of the times. Columella, a Roman born in Spain, wrote of Malaga wines in both his *Agricultura* and *De Re Rustica*. Democritus, Pliny, and Virgil also praised the wines of Malaga.

❖ FALL OF THE ROMAN EMPIRE

Perhaps the vineyards on the slopes of Mount Vesuvius best symbolize the beginnings of the fall of the Roman Empire. Here is how Martial described the scene following the massive volcanic eruption in A.D. 79, when Pompeii and Herculaneum were deluged:

> *Here is Vesuvius, once covered with green pastures, whose prolific fruit used to fill our wine presses. Here were vineyards which Bacchus preferred to those of Nysa. In ancient times satyrs would have danced on these hills, the home of Venus and Hercules. The flames have destroyed it all, and everything is covered up by that mountain of cinder. Surely even the gods did not intend this.*

Gaius Caesar, perhaps better known as Caligula, initially ruled Rome with compassion and generosity, but severe illnesses drove him to become a vicious tyrant, and he was assasinated in A.D. 41. The Praetorian Guard proclaimed Claudius to succeed as Roman emperor. This ruler became cruel and greedy under the influence of his wife, Messalina, whom he executed in A.D. 48. Claudius then married his niece, Agrippina, who is thought to have poisoned him six years later via mushroom soup laced with toadstools. Agrippina's son, Nero, became the last of the Caesar emperors in Rome and married Claudius's daughter, Octavia. Andromachus, a physician, was made responsible for the health of Nero. Among his charges was to taste the emperor's wine first; this was nothing new, but perhaps the first time the act was boldly publicized.

Galen, unquestionably the most renowned physician since Hippocrates, looked after the health of Emperor Marcus Aurelius. The genius of Galen still lives in his remarkable antidotes and treatments made from exotic plants and animals, some of which are, in one form or another, still prescribed today. But the single medication at the center of all Galen's apothecary was fine wine in moderate daily rations. He eloquently expresses the quality of wines in the emperor's cellar:

> *So in execution of my duty, I deciphered the vintage marks on the amphorae of every Falernian wine and submitted to my palate every wine over twenty years old. I kept on until I found a wine without a trace of bitterness. An ancient wine which has not lost its sweetness is the best of all.*

Emeror Marcus Aurelius wrote *Meditations*, a synopsis of morality and philosohical strength, yet he lived during the period following the Caesar emperors, when Rome was in its most depraved state. The military downfall of the Roman Empire was caused, in large part, by Gothic forces from the Baltic Sea region in Lithuania, Poland, and Sweden. Savage Gothic armies and navies

FIGURE 2.14 Gilded Roman oinochoe, second century A.D. *(Courtesy of the Corning Museum of Glass.)*

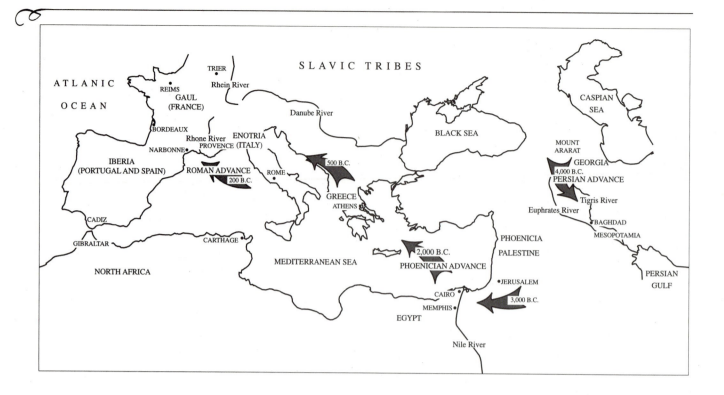

FIGURE 2.15 The course of winegrowing in the early history of Western civilization.

had been a constant menace to the Roman provinces in eastern Europe since the time of Christ. The fierce Teutons, in what is now Austria and Germany, had eroded Roman occupation, as had the Franks to the west. For 19 years, until his death at age 59, Emperor Marcus Aurelius was able to put down the uprisings of barbarians and the traitorous plots conceived by some of his own provincial generals.

The end of the great Roman Empire can be dated in many ways, but it is probably best marked by the death of Emperor Marcus Aurelius in A.D. 180. With Frankish victories, Gaul became France.

✦ THE MIDDLE AGES

Western civilization is greatly indebted to the Christian monks for the continuance of winemaking during the period of history following the end of the Roman Empire until the beginning of the great Renaissance—a 1,000-year epoch called the Middle Ages.

Monks, of course, did more in preserving and restoring civilization than just make wine. They maintained hospitals, schools, and libraries, provided leadership for the church, distributed charity, and looked after cultural and social services. But their expertise in winegrowing was unique. Their monasteries were the only communities that had the resources for research and improvement of winemaking skills. Monks used methods and devices in their wine cellars that were unknown to lay vintners. There can be no question that winegrowing would have taken far longer to develop in Europe without the essential contributions made by the church.

During the latter part of the sixth century bloodshed and turmoil engulfed much of Europe. Wars among the Franks, Teutons, and Goths wreaked havoc in France and Spain, bringing death and destruction. Many vineyards were laid waste. International trade had become well established and was not significantly affected by the European wars until the seventh century, when the Muslims from northern Africa gained control of the Mediterranean. With Islamic abstinence from wine drinking, the maritime wine trade, which had commenced with the Phoenicians more than 2,000 years before, came to an end.

Despite the devastation left by centuries of war, the monks survived, as did their monasteries. Under the direction of Pope Gregory the Great, new abbeys were developed during the early seventh century; virgin land was cleared and new vineyards established. Monks began to grow grapes and make wine in every conceivable locale, testing even the harsh environments of Ireland and Poland.

The monks, guardians of the purity of God's grapes, eventually fell to making potions instead of wines, adding flavors and spices in the manner of pagan Greece and Rome. Wines that had gained poor reputations, such as those grown at the St. Wandrille Abbey in Normandy, were often called *pigments,* as they were concocted by a *pigmentarius,* or pharmacist.

Medieval white wines were clarified with fish-bladder isinglass, and red wines of the times were cleared with egg whites, as many classic European wines are still treated today. Lesser-quality grapes were eaten as fresh fruit or used in pickling brines for cheese and ham. Inadequate wines were allowed to turn into vinegar. *Pomace,* skins and seeds remaining in the wine presses, was used to feed livestock. Prunings from the vines made very aromatic fireplace fuel.

The alliance between the monks and the peasants was an essential factor in the medieval economic structure. While learning the science and art of winegrowing, the serfs became Christians. All grapes were required to be pressed in the abbey cellars, the abbey taking one-tenth of the resulting wine production as a feudal tithe called a *dime,* or *zehnt.* In addition, the peasants were not allowed to sell any of their wine until the inventory in the monastery was fully marketed. The monasteries were usually exempt from wine taxes as well.

These marketing advantages for the monasteries resulted in the church's becoming wealthy. The system encouraged the monks to lavish resources on improving their wines. Most important was the resource of time, centuries of collected evidence relating to which variety of vine in which vineyard locale consistently made the best wine. Peasant vineyards were forced into producing quantity rather than quality. Most of the wines made from the common grapes were quaffed shortly after they were made, certainly within a year. Wine had

FIGURE 2.16 St. Goar monastery on the Rhine River in Germany. *(Courtesy of the German Wine Information Bureau.)*

FIGURE 2.17 Tapestry depicting feudal winegrowing. *(Courtesy of the Musée de Cluny, Paris.)*

long since become a staple of the diet and an important ingredient in making bad food more palatable.

Small villages began to form around the monasteries, and vineyards were planted by farmers who had mastered the monks' technology. As viticulture became a major form of agriculture, the great European vineyard system began to develop toward the grand and noble structure we know today.

Charlemagne, son of Pepin and grandson of Charles Martel, ascended as king of the Franks in 771. He defeated the Lombards and Saxons of Germany, drove the Saracens out of Bordeaux, and forced the Moors out of Spain. In A.D. 800, after putting down an insurrection in Italy, Charlemagne was crowned by Pope Leo III, on Christmas Day, as the first Holy Roman Emperor. He reunited western Europe by zealously promoting agriculture, the arts, commerce, and education.

During the reign of Charlemagne (742–814), the Catholic Church was protected and viticulture encouraged. Charlemagne gave many gifts of land to the church across Europe, with the proviso that new vine plantings be made. Under the protection of this great king, monastic winegrowing commenced to achieve a level of consistent quality previously unknown, and the church became even richer.

Charlemagne was a scholar, spoke Greek and Latin, and devised a system of grammar for his own French language. Under his creative influence, the Holy Roman Empire endured for 1,000 years. During and following Charlemagne's reign, Europe enjoyed some measure of peace and tranquility. The monasteries flourished and some even grew to become cities. The citizenry of the great abbey of St. Martin at Tours, for example, exceeded 20,000 peeople.

Unfortunately, this period of quiescence was short-lived, as Saracen invaders, among others, laid siege to monasteries all across Europe. Although much of the wealth held by the church was pillaged by the raiders, resources remained to organize and finance the Crusades of the tenth, eleventh, and twelfth centuries—wars designed to regain the Holy Land for Christendom from the Islamic Saracens.

Crusaders returned from the Holy Wars carrying Middle Eastern vines for wine. They introduced Muscat de Frontignan into the vineyards of southern France. The classic Syrah, which now typifies the heavy dark red wines of the Rhone, is the same vine as *Shiraz*, which is native to the Tigris-Euphrates river valleys in Iraq.

During the latter part of this era new orders of monks appeared — Carthusians, Cistercians, Hospitallers, and Templars—who brought down the monopoly over monasticism held by the Benedictines. Much of this development can be credited to noblemen who, following Charlemagne's example, endowed the church with money, abbeys, land, and vineyards—and the church became wealthy again.

The finest remaining example of a winegrowing monastery is the perfectly preserved Clos de Vougeot in northern Burgundy. In 1110 some rather poor, undeveloped land, as well as some fine vineyard property situated near the river Vouge, was given to the Abbey of Citeaux by Guerric of Chambolle. The Cistercian monks cultivated the Vouge land and expanded their vineyards, adding even more to their estate as they could afford it. About 40 years later they built their first wine cellars. By 1336 the Citeaux monks had developed a vineyard estate of about 125 acres, around which they constructed a stone wall, which thus became the Clos de Vougeot. Wine connoisseurs for centuries have considered the wines produced by this abbey to be among the finest of all Burgundies. Abbot Jean de Bussiere was made a cardinal after shipping 30 hogsheads of Clos de Vougeot to Gregory XI in honor of his papal election.

The Cistercian monks of Eberbach in the Rhineland cleared a portion of the dense Steinberg Forest, which was given to them by the archbishop of Mainz at about the same time the Vouge land was bequeathed to the Cistercians in Burgundy. More than 60 acres of vines were planted within a stone wall, making the Kloster Eberbach the largest and most highly esteemed monastery vineyard in all of Germany.

The most important bestowal of vineyard property of all time was made during the twelfth century: the dowry of Eleanor of Aquitaine, which included all of the present winemaking region of Bordeaux in southwestern France. Eleanor married Henri Plantagenet, Comte d'Anjou, in 1152, and they lived at the castle of Chinon on the Loire. Henri became King Henry II of England two

FIGURE 2.18 The Chinon castle.
(*Courtesy of* Food and Wines from France.)

years later, and the combined Aquitaine-Plantagenet wine lands became the possession of England, remaining so for about 300 years. The union of Eleanor and Henri resulted in the birth of Richard, who became legendary as the Crusader king, Richard the Lion-Hearted.

During the reigns of Henry II and Richard, huge amounts of wine were shipped from Bordeaux to England. The demand for Bordeaux wines grew even further. A thousand casks were ordered just for the coronation of Edward II in 1307. The fine red wines of the Aquitaine became so popular in England that King Edward III issued regulations that forced shipping bases to be established in Bordeaux to serve only English ships. The large number of ships built as a result of this law became the first great English navy.

Geoffrey Chaucer, author of the *Canterbury Tales*, relates his impressions of wine in England during the fourteenth century:

> *Now keep ye from the white and from the red*
> *And namely from the white wine of Lepe*
> *That is to sell in Fish Street as in Chepe.*
> *This wine of Spain creepith subtilly*
> *In other wines, growing fast by,*
> *Of which there rises such fumositee*
> *That when a man has drunken draughtes three,*
> *And wenith that he be at home in Chepe*
> *He is at home right in the town of Lepe*
> *Not at the Rochelle, or at Bordeaux town.*

("The Pardoner's Tale," ll. 100–109)

According to Chaucer there were then three distinct categories of wine: beverage (table) wines, dessert wines, and medicinal wines. Red beverage wines were mostly the very dark types grown in the Languedoc, the same region as the Narbonensis settled by the Romans more than 1,000 years previously. Whites from Nantes on the Loire and Rochelle in Bordeaux were less popular. Comparatively expensive were the Portuguese and Spanish dessert wines, reserved for special occasions and as expressions of hospitality. One favorite medieval drink in England was *Hippocras,* a Greek-styled medicinal wine, as the name would suggest, made of a mixture of wine and spices. The aristocracy often added a bit of very expensive sugar to demonstrate their wealth.

The shipping center in the Loire Valley was Orleans, but only a few wines were exported from there. England had a thirst for *claret,* a British colloquialism for red Bordeaux wine. English rule led to the clearing of great expanses for new vineyards in the Aquitaine. By the mid-fifteenth century, however, all of the British interests in French wine had been lost. French forces led by Joan of Arc drove the English out of the Loire Valley in 1429. In 1453, with the defeat of Marshal Talbot, the British surrendered Bordeaux and ended the Hundred Years' War, which had, once again, devastated many vineyards. With the demand for claret being much more difficult to supply, the English turned to the wines of Germany, Italy, Portugal, and Spain.

As the Middle Ages came to an end during the late 1300s, war had again left the monks heirs to European winegrowing. With well-organized and centralized labor forces, the monks brought a highly professional approach to growing grapes and making wine. Hundreds of monasteries had developed extensive vineyards, with many more operating modest plots of vines. Most were planted with a range of grape varieties. For their time, monastic wine cellars were efficiently designed, constructed, and operated in order to optimize wine quality. The monks used calendars for planning and kept records of their data. These efforts mark the beginning of vineyard and wine classifications in Europe as they are known today.

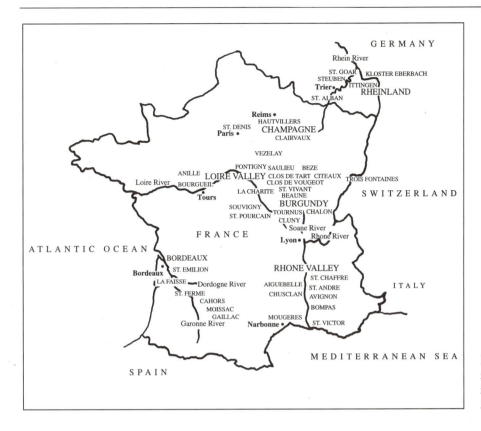

FIGURE 2.19 Sites of abbeys, monasteries, and nunneries important in developing winegrowing during the Middle Ages.

❖ THE RENAISSANCE AND THE EIGHTEENTH CENTURY

For a period of almost 70 years during the fourteenth century, the popes refused to live in the Vatican of Rome, making their home, instead, at Avignon on the Rhone River in the south of France. The wines of *Châteauneuf-du-Pape* (the "new home of the Pope") gained considerable distinction and notoriety. When the popes eventually returned to Rome, following the pleas of Francesco Petrarca, more well known as Petrarch, they became essential leaders in the Renaissance movement, in which not only European culture but also the art of wine was reborn.

FIGURE 2.20 The Roman Colosseum. *(Photo by author.)*

Wine is a recurrent motif in the great artworks of the Renaissance, as seen, for instance, in Michelangelo's famous *Bacchus* (1496) and, in a Christian context, Leonardo's *Last Supper*. The scientific revolutionary Galileo had a deep appreciation for fine wine; he is quoted as having said: "Wine is light, held together by water." What a remarkably foresighted observation—hundreds of years in advance of the discovery of photosynthesis and the chemical analysis of wine. Francis Bacon (1561–1626) was another father of modern science. His *Novum Organum* outlined the process of identifying and testing hypotheses. Bacon loved wine and is credited with this quotation:

> *Old wood to burn! Old wine to drink!*
> *Old friends to trust! Old authors to read!*

Shakespeare, like Galileo born in 1564, lived in a land and a time when water was considered (and perhaps often was) unfit to drink. At breakfast and midday ale and beer were drunk, and wine in the evening. Sherry, the fortified wine from Spain, was a favorite beverage of Elizabethan England, and the poet himself was partial to *sack*, as the wine is called in his plays. References to wines of all types abound in Shakespeare's plays. In *Much Ado About Nothing*, Leonato bids farewell: "Drink some wine ere you go; fare you well."

Talbot makes clear his wishes in Henry IV:

> *No other satisfaction do I crave*
> *But only—with your patience—that we may*
> *Taste of your wine, and see what cares you have;*
> *For soldiers' stomachs always serve them well.*

Iago, in the tragedy *Othello*, praises wine:

> *Come, come, good wine is a good familiar creature if it be well-used: exclaim no more against it.*

There is the famous line of Brutus in *Julius Caesar*:

> *Speak no more of her.—Give me a bowl of wine.—In this I bury all unkindness.*

And, finally, from the drinking party in Act 2 Scene 7, of *Antony and Cleopatra*, we read:

> *Come, thou monarch of the vine,*
> *Plumpy Bacchus with pink eyne!*
> *In thy fats [vats] our cares be drown'd,*
> *With thy grapes our hairs be crown'd:*
> *Cup us till the world go round,*
> *Cup us, till the world go round!*

The church peerage, vintners, and licensed tavern operators were the only people allowed to maintain wine cellars during Elizabethan England. Nearly all wines were imported from the European Continent, and most of these were rather young and inexpensive, being drawn from barrels, butts, casks, hogsheads, pipes, and other wooden shipping containers. In 1542, Dr. Andrew Borde published a dietary, which includes the following:

> *Moderately dronken, it doth actuate and doth quycken a man's wyttes, it doth comfort the hert, it doth scoure the lyuer; specyally yf it be whyte wyn, it doth reioyce all the powers of man and doth nowrysshe them; it doth engender good blode, it doth comforte and doth nourysshe the brayne and all the body, and it resolueth fleume; it ingendereth heate, and it is good agaynst heuyes and pencyfulness; it is full of a agylyte; wherefore it is modsonable; specyally whyte wyne, for it doth mundyfye and clense wounds & sores. Furthermore, the better the wyne is, the better humours it doth ingender.*

Dr. Borde relates his personal wine preferences:

I do take good Gascon [Bordeaux] wyne, but I wyl not drynke stronge [fortified] wynes, as Malmsey, Romney, Romaniske wyne, wyne Qoorse, wyne Greke and Secke [rather] a draught or two of Muscadell or Basterde, Osey, Caprycke, Aligant, Tyre, Raspyte, I wyl not refuse; but whyte wyne of Angeou or wyne of Orleance [Loire], or Renyshe [German] wyne, whyte or red, is good for al men.

Borde also advised that the Portuguese Osey wine was best taken as a dessert wine: "not good to drynke with meate, but after meate."

In 1568, one of Queen Elizabeth's personal physicians, Dr. William Turner, wrote the first English-language book addressing the topic of wine. The lengthy title given to the work was *A new Boke on the natures and properties of all wines that are commonly used here in England, with a confutation of an error of some men, that holds that Rhenish and other small white wines ought not to be drunken of them that either have, or are in danger of the Stone, the reume, and divers other diseases, made by William Turner, Doctor of Phisicke.*

The Renaissance was a grand rebirth of creative thought expressed in every art form, including wine. As the influence of the Renaissance began to spread from Italy, commercial winegrowing made renewed advances across Europe.

Monasticism was one of the primary targets of the great religious Reformation that spread, along with the Renaissance, throughout western Europe in the sixteenth century. It was inevitable that winegrowing would also suffer heavily. Most reformers argued that monastic life was a waste of time and showed contempt for God. Martin Luther, himself an ex-friar, wrote that "monks are the fleas on God Almighty's fur coat."

There is no question that the monasteries had grown too numerous, perhaps too wealthy, and, in some cases, corrupt. Some had become no more than comfortable retreats for the spiritual-minded aristocracy. By the 1520s about half of the abbeys in western Europe had failed.

Peasants raided the cellars of Kloster Eberbach along the Rhine River in 1525, and a ransom of 18,000 gallons of wine was demanded. Protestants purged the caves of Schloss Johannisberg numerous times during the 1560s. In France the abbeys came under severe attacks during the Wars of Religion, which were fought from 1562 to 1598. In one instance the Huguenots orgiastically sacked the abbey at Pontigny in Chablis while wearing monks' robes.

FIGURE 2.21 Kloster Eberbach.
(Courtesy of the German Wine Information Bureau.)

The monasteries remained easy prey to pillage and plunder throughout the Thirty Years' War, which raged in central Europe from 1618 to 1648. Some of the abbeys were to eventually recover, but never again would monastic wine-growing approach the intensity and breadth it had attained at its zenith during the Renaissance.

In the mid-seventeenth century war again broke out between England and France. The House of Stuart fell, and the reign of Louis XIV, the "Sun King," commenced. Once more the claret wines from Bordeaux were denied the English, who had to console themselves with poor-quality dry red "Ports" from Portugal. One Scottish verse describes their discontent:

> *Firm and erect the Highland chieftain stood*
> *Old was his mutton and his claret good.*
> *"Thou shalt drink Port," the English statesman cried.*
> *He drank the poison—and his spirit died.*

Determined to improve the quality of these wines, British merchants went to Portugal and literally "invented" the sweet red Port dessert wines that are widely known today. British vintners knew that the deep, dark red grapes of the Douro River valley matured to a high sugar content. When all of this sugar was fermented, the result was the strong, harsh traditional Port wine that had been drunk and disparaged in England. The wine masters developed a process whereby brandy was added at a precise time during fermentation, arresting further yeast activity and preserving some of the natural sweetness in the wine. Some purists quickly challenged this practice, however, insisting that such wines were not natural—a notion that persists in some circles to this day.

Wine lodges, or cellars, in the cities of Vila Nova de Gaia and Oporto, situated where the Douro empties into the Atlantic, still bear the names of these original Port inventors and shippers: Croft, Dow, Graham, McKenzie, Offley, Sandeman, Warre, and others. Oliver Cromwell is credited with introducing this new Port to the British Isles. Port became the wine of England, just as Madeira was adopted as the wine of colonial America.

In France there was keen competition between the winegrowers of Burgundy and Champagne for lower taxes and other conveniences from Louis XIV. Both provinces produced fine red wines from the celebrated Pinot Noir

FIGURE 2.22 The city of Vila Nova de Gaia, center of the British Port Trade. *(Photo by author.)*

vine. Louis XIV also prized Bordeaux wines, calling them "the Nectar of the Gods."

The change of Champagne from red wine to sparkling white wine is credited to a blind monk, Dom Perignon, cellarer at the Benedictine Abbey of Hautvillers from 1668 until 1715. Dom Perignon stoppered his bottles of new wine with cork plugs. Wine bottles filled and corked before fermentation kept the carbon dioxide gas generated from dissipating. Upon pulling the cork and feeling the bubbles on his palate, Dom Perignon is said to have exclaimed, "My God, I am drinking stars!"

Fagon, personal physician to Louis XIV, was admonished for endorsing the new sparkling wine, which the Burgundians insisted was a "fast-living wine." In 1700 people from Champagne gathered at the medical school at Reims, the capital city of the province, and proclaimed that Champagne was the most pleasant and wholesome wine one could drink.

Champagne was made fashionable at court by King Louis XV, whose reign brought prosperity to all the major vineyard districts in France. Exports were increased to Russia and the Scandinavian countries, as well as to the French colonies and settlements in Africa, India, and America.

Credit for using the cork plug even before Perignon was claimed in England, Italy, Portugal, and Spain. Across several decades of time, these instances may well have been rather coincidental. In any event, the cork, as a vastly improved seal for wine bottles, brought an entirely new dimension to winemaking expertise in the eighteenth century. It became possible to age wines in the bottle for long periods of time, dispensing with the need to drink wines young. Wine evolved from a healthy and hearty diet staple into an infinitely variable beverage, which became certainly the first, and arguably the only, truly fine art form in agriculture.

✛ THE GREAT REVOLUTIONS

Winegrowing suffered yet again during the French Revolution and the Napoleonic wars. Vineyards and wine cellars were damaged or destroyed, some even seized outright. The Clos de Vougeot vineyards were sold at public auction in more than 60 individual parcels.

In the Rhineland, Napoleon secularized all of the religious orders with the 1801 Treaty of Luneville. As a result, many of the principal German vineyards were similarly divided among numerous small holders, who gave their family names to the new estates.

Despite the ravages of war and revolution, the first half of the nineteenth century was a "Golden Age of Wine." Gay-Lussac's chemistry introduced important new applications of the scientific method to winemaking. Superb quality vintages seemed to occur rather regularly, and new generations of connoisseurs emerged to appreciate them. The nobility, bankers, land barons, and the nouveau riche merchant-princes spared no expense in the development of great vineyards and wine cellars. The division and classification of districts, subdistricts, villages, and specific vineyards was accompanied by a growing acceptance for scientific precepts. Even so, political oppression in Europe and the promise of gold in California lured many winegrowers to the New World.

Louis Pasteur started a revolution of a very different kind. His first experiments were with wine yeasts, giving birth to the discipline of microbiology. In 1866, Pasteur wrote:

When one sees beer and wine go through profound alterations because these liquids have been the host to microscopic organisms, one is obsessed by the thought that the same kind of thing can and must happen sometimes with men and with animals.

FIGURE 2.23 *The Good Wine Tasters.* Lithograph by Claude Thielley (France, 1811–1891). *(Courtesy of the Seagram Museum Collection.)*

Because of Pasteur's discoveries people were faced with the realization that fermentation was not magical or mystical after all, but a natural product unveiled by science.

Wine masters commenced to hand down scientifically based expertise to apprentices, and succeeding generations began to leave much less to chance. Research yielded new materials and techniques by which wines could be made and preserved with consistently higher quality. The age of packaging arrived, along with the widespread use of labels adorning previously naked bottles.

The wine art was married with wine science in the 1800s, with a greater bounty of offspring in winegrowing and wine appreciation than ever before. But disaster loomed just ahead.

✤ THE *PHYLLOXERA* BLIGHT

The *oidium fungus,* a powdery mildew that can devastate a grape crop, invaded France in 1847 and spread to the rest of western Europe several years later. Some native American vines seemed to be resistant to the disease, an attribute which interested European winegrowers to the extent that they imported some vine plant materials from the United States for experimentation. Little did anyone know that these plants carried a tiny root louse, *Phylloxera vastatrix,* which would prove to be far more destructive than the mildew.

The *Phylloxera* was discovered in 1868 by Planchon in southern France. Spreading quickly underground, it was undetected by the *vignerons* (growers) until it had become a full-fledged epidemic. Most French vineyards were destroyed in less than 20 years.

The root louse spread considerably more slowly across the cooler mesoclimates of Germany than in other European countries, the first report of the scourge there arriving from the Rhinepfalz in 1874.

One suggestion for getting rid of the killer louse was to flood vineyard floors long enough to drown the pest but not rot the vines. Unfortunately, most European vineyards were on hillsides. Grafting, which had been studied since the time of the Roman naturalist Columella, proved to be the most effective technique in combating the *Phylloxera* invasion. Classic European *Vitis vinifera* varietal scions were grafted onto native American *Vitis labrusca* rootstocks, which were resistant to the louse. Hundreds of thousands of these rootstock materials were imported from the United States, mostly from Missouri and Texas, each season until the massive project was completed. Never before, or since, have such massive resources been employed in the salvation of an agricultural industry. The great vineyards of Europe were reestablished, thriving yet today on American roots.

Appellation (geographical origin) control by the French government required that only certain designated varieties could be replanted in specific vineyard districts. This proved to be at least some compensation for the blight, in that many of the vague regional and subregional boundaries that had existed previously could become more clearly defined. Moreover, many of the original patchwork "succotash" vineyards were planted anew with singular varietal selections.

The destruction caused by Napoleon at the beginning of the nineteenth century, and by the *Phylloxera* epidemic toward its end, forever altered the wine map of Europe. The Old World wine masters had to pick up the pieces of crumbled monastic cellars and afflicted vineyards. The task of rebuilding was formidable.

As a result, the great château estates of Bordeaux, the precious tiny vineyard plats of Burgundy, and the grand houses of Champagne were reborn. European winegrowing entered the twentieth century with vineyards strictly defined as to vine variety and an advancing winemaking technology. Wines were created such as the world had never known before.

Nevertheless, by 1880 many winegrowers on the Continent were left financially ruined, and they emigrated to South Africa, Australia, New Zealand, and the Americas. Those who came to the United States brought new philosophies and skills to the fledgling American wine industry. This European seed found a fertile opportunity.

FIGURE 2.24 Vine grafts being planted in nursery. *(Courtesy of C.I.V.C.; photo by the French Ministère de l'Agriculture.)*

❖ THE NEW WORLD

In comparison with the 6,000 years of winegrowing history in the Old World, the 400-year span of New World vines and wines seems minuscule. But it should be remembered that most of the major development in Europe has taken place during these same four centuries. Few modern-day European wine producers can boast of continuous ownership since before the seventeenth century.

Grapevines grow abundantly in the United States. In nearly every state at least one type of vine or another can be grown. Of the 50-odd species and thousands of varieties known, a greater selection of vine types can be grown in America than in any other nation.

This profusion of vines is doubtlessly what Leif Erikson found when he first visited the North American continent. The following passage is from *The Discovery of America in the Tenth Century*, written several centuries ago by Charles C. Prasta:

> *Leif, son of Eric the Red, bought Byarnes' vessel, and manned it with thirty-five men, among whom was also a German, Tyrker by name. . . . And they left port at Iceland, in the year of our Lord 1000.*
>
> *But when they had been at sea several days, a tremendous storm arose, whose wild fury made the waves swell mountain high, and threatened to destroy the frail vessel. And the storm continued for several days, and increased in fury, so that the stoutest heart quaked with fear; they believed that their hour had come. . . . Only Leif, who had lately been converted to Christ our Lord, stood calmly at the helm*

and did not fear; . . . And behold! While he spoke to them of the wonederful deeds of the Lord, the clouds cleared away, the storm lulled; and after a few hours the sea calmed down, and rocked the tired and exhausted men into a deep and calm sleep. And when they awoke, the next morning, they could hardly trust their eyes. A beautiful country lay before them . . . and they cast anchor, and thanked the Lord, who had delivered them from death.

A delightful country it seemed, full of game, and birds of beautiful plumage; and when they went ashore, they could not resist the temptation to explore it. When they returned, after several hours, Tyrker alone was missing. After waiting some time for his return, Leif, with twelve of his men, went in search of him. But they had not gone far, when they met him, laden down with grapes. Upon their enquiry, where he had stayed so long, he answered: "I did not go far, when I found the trees all covered with grapes; and as I was born in the country, whose hills are covered with vineyards, it seemed so much like home to me, that I stayed a while and gathered them." . . . And Leif gave name to the country, and called it Vinland, or Wineland.

An enchanting story, and convincing too, as wild grapevines are still prolific along the coastline of eastern America.

◈ EASTERN AMERICA

A ship's log kept by navigator Giovanni da Verrazano dated in 1524 made note of vines in what is now North Carolina, and the possibility of making wine from them. During the mid-1500s, French Huguenots settled in Florida and made America's first wines from some of the native grapes found there. This fruit was from the subgenus Muscadinia and species *Vitis rotundifolia*, known today as the Muscadine varieties. These New World grapes must have seemed strange to the Huguenot wine masters, because Muscadines ripen their fruit by individual berries in small clumps, rather than in large clusters. Further, the flavor of Muscadines is very exotic as compared with the more subtle nuances found in the Old World *Vitis vinifera* grapes.

In 1565, Sir John Hawkins, a British admiral, reported on making wine from the native Florida grapes during his visits there. It seems likely that the Florida wines met with little favor among the early settlers.

Farther north, Captain John Smith wrote of his observations in Virginia during the early seventeenth century:

Of vines great abundance in many parts that climbe the toppes of highest trees in some places, but these beare but few grapes.

There is another sort of grape neere as great as a Cherry, they [probably Indian natives] call Messamins, *they be fatte, and juyce thicke. Neither doth the taste so well please when they are made in wine.*

As the seventeenth century progressed, hope continued that the European vines could be successfully grown in the New World. Viticulture was encouraged through economic incentives and even required by law in some places. In New York wine could be made and sold without taxation. Virginia promulgated a law whereby "all workers upon corne and tobacco shall plant five vynes . . . upon penaltie to forfeit one barrell of corne."

The major inspiration for the soon-to-be-frustrated hopes of early colonial *Vitis vinifera* pioneers was, of course, the profusion of wild vines; if the native vines grew so luxuriantly, they reasoned, the cultivated European varieties should do all the better. The failures were, of course, not the fault of any person

FIGURE 2.25 Williamsburg cooper craftsman in Virginia. *(Photo by author.)*

but, rather, the result of the then unknown *Phylloxera* root louse, plus a lack of hardiness against the colder winter temperatures. These adverse conditions thwarted eastern American winegrowing for more than two centuries.

Thomas Jefferson maintained a very keen interest in American vineyards, but continued to import wine from Europe, where, as ambassador to France, his appreciation for wine was well known by his peers. As secretary of state, Jefferson chose the wines for President Washington. When Jefferson became president, he paid for his wines personally, keeping careful inventory records. He also assisted in stocking the presidential cellars of John Adams, James Madison, and James Monroe.

The first cultivation of native American *Vitis labrusca* vines is credited to John Alexander, a Pennsylvanian whose viticultural research in the late 1700s brought forth the aptly named "Alexander" grape. The Alexander became famous for its heavy production of fruit and stalwart resistance to disease and cold winters. The wine from Alexander, however, still fell short of the wines from the prized vines from mother Europe.

Jean Jacques Dufour left his native Vevey, in Switzerland, during the late 1700s, eventually settling in southeastern Indiana along the Ohio River. By 1804, Dufour's first vines were planted near the new little village of Vevay, near Madison, in what is now Switzerland County. Others followed his lead, and the region soon became known as the "Little Rhineland," owing to the ascending riverbank terraces on which hundreds of acres of the Alexander vine were planted.

The Alexander grape variety interested Thomas Jefferson and Henry Clay, who provided encouragement for Dufour to write *The American Vine Dresser's Guide*, first published in 1826. In 1809, following some of his own unsuccessful *Vitis vinifera* experiments at Monticello, Thomas Jefferson stated, "It will be well to push the culture of this grape [Alexander] without losing time and effort in the search of foreign vines which it will take centuries to adapt of our soil and climate." But Jefferson was not the only early hopeful winegrower with good foresight. William Penn also suspected that the proper course was to move toward cultivating native *labrusca* vines.

John Adlum, of Georgetown, D.C., introduced the *Vitis labrusca* variety Catawaba, named for the Catawba River in North Carolina, where the vine was discovered in the wild. The comparatively delicate fruit flavor of Catawba brought it quickly to the attention of winegrowers. Without modesty, Adlum informed the world that giving the world the Catawba grape had provided a greater service to America than if he "had paid the national debt."

Thomas Jefferson never lost his optimism that American winegrowing would eventually be achieved on a commercial scale, despite his fondness for the fine wines from Europe. His foresight is evident in a statement made in 1808: "We could in the United States make as great a variety of wines as are made in Europe, not exactly of the same kinds, but doubtless as good."

And later he said:

Wine being among the earliest luxuries in which we indulge ourselves, it is desirable it should be made here and we have every soil, aspect & climate of the best of wine countries . . . these South West mountains, having a S.E. aspect, and abundance of lean & meager spots of stony & red soil, without sand, resembling extremely the Côte of Burgundy from Chambertin to Montrachet, where the famous wines of Burgundy are made.

Jefferson kept a "Garden Book" at Monticello from 1766 to 1826, in which he kept data on his vine plantings and experiments. Among his notes is recorded the planting of "30 plants of vines from Burgundy and Champagne with roots, 30 plants of vines of Bordeaux with roots."

FIGURE 2.26 Wine elevator from the wine cellar to the dining room at Thomas Jefferson's Monticello. *(Courtesy of the Vinifera Wine Growers Association; photo by Ed Roseberry.)*

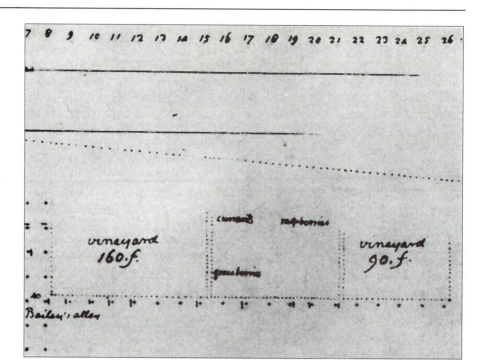

FIGURE 2.27
Notes from Thomas Jefferson's
Garden Book.
*(Courtesy of the the Vinifera Wine Growers
Association; photo by Alderman Library,
University of Virginia.)*

An entry of several years later reports the planting of several famous Italian vines, which included *Trebbiano* and *Aleatico,* among others. The Garden Book does not, however, show any significant success at the Monticello vineyard in testing any of the European selections.

◈ BIRTH OF THE AMERICAN WINE INDUSTRY

The first commercial American winery may have been the Pennsylavania Vine Company, situated near Philadelphia and founded by Pierre Legaux in 1793. Legaux was a Frenchman determined to succeed in cultivating French grapes, but like all previous attempts to grow the vaunted *vinifera,* this was yet another failure. In 1818, Thomas Eichelberger constructed a winery near York, Pennsylvania.

FIGURE 2.28 The Brotherhood
Winery. *(Courtesy of the Brotherhood Wine
Company.)*

Located in Washingtonville, New York, about 50 miles northwest of New York City, the Brotherhood Winery has a vast expanse of caves that challenge the magnificence of many in Europe. Founded in 1816 by a French immigrant shoemaker, Jean Jacques, Brotherhood remains the oldest operating winery in the United States.

Nicholas Longworth amassed a huge ownership of land in middle America during the early 1800s. He was reputed to be the largest single payer of land taxes in the nation. Longworth built a majestic winery on Adam's Hill in Cincinnati, extending the "Little Rhineland" approximately 50 miles northeastward along the Ohio River from Vevay, Indiana. Longworth was so highly impressed by Adlum's Catawba grape that he planted a large acreage of the variety near his winery in the early 1820s. Longworth made the first American "Champagne," labeling his product as "Sparkling Catawba." Longworth had great pride in his wine, declaring that it was even superior to the sparkling wine from Champagne in France.

Henry Wadsworth Longfellow, a noted wine critic and connoisseur, was intrigued by the lofty claims of Nicholas Longworth and paid a visit to the Ohio winery in the mid-1850s to taste Longworth's sparkling wine. Impressed and convinced, Longfellow wrote a poem in 1854, entitled "Catawba Wine," which proclaims:

FIGURE 2.29 Nicholas Longworth. *(Courtesy of* Wine East *magazine; photo by Linda Jones McKee.)*

> *Very good in its way*
> *Is the Verzenay,*
> *Or the Sillery soft and creamy;*
> *But Catawba wine*
> *Has a taste more divine,*
> *More dulcet, delicious, and dreamy.*

Longworth's wine must have been truly remarkable, as Longfellow's testimonial ranking it superior to the French Champagne from Verzenay is very high praise.

The church, this time the Protestant denominations, also had a profound influence on the development of the wine industry in New York. Elijah Fay, a Baptist deacon, planted the first vineyard in western New York State in 1818.

More notable, however, are the vineyards of central New York State nestled along the Finger Lakes. Local legend has it that when God finished making the heavens and earth, he laid his hand on that particular site to bless his creation; hence, the great handlike impression that distinguishes the Finger Lakes map. Geologists point out, however, that the glens and hills of the Finger Lakes region resulted from the clawing effects of the Ice Age.

In either event, St. James Episcopal Church still stands today as the landmark in Hammondsport, at the southern tip of the "thumb" of the Finger Lakes, Lake Keuka, where the New York State wine industry began. Father William Bostwick propagated cuttings of Catawba and Isabella, another native *labrusca* variety, into roots and planted them behind the church in 1829 in order to make wine for his Anglican Eucharist.

The success of Bostwick's work became well known and attracted the interest of several prospective commercial vintners. In 1860, Charles Champlin, along with several other investors, founded the Pleasant Valley Wine Company just south of Hammondsport in Rheims, New York. The original cave was lined with stone walls more than six feet thick, a remarkable cellar that remains a monument to the first federally licensed winery in America.

Champlin's obsession was to make the finest Champagne in the New World, certainly to improve on the lauded wines of Longworth in Ohio. He hired Jules Masson, a French wine master, to ensure that the very best New York State "Champagne" was made. In 1871 a tasting of some of the first wine from Pleasant Valley was held at the Parker House hotel in Boston. Among the

prestigious critics was Marshall Wilder, then president of the American Horticultural Society, who proclaimed that Champlin's sparkling wine was "great" wine from the new "western" world. Thus, the famous "Great Western" name was born and became the trademark for the Pleasant Valley Wine Company.

The early 1860s marked the beginning of a promising era for American winegrowing. In no less than 20 states and territories significant vineyard planting and winery investments were taking place. Mary Todd Lincoln was the first to serve American-grown wines in the White House.

The success of Champlin and Longworth, among others, awakened new commercial winegrowing interests in the east and prompted considerable vineyard expansion, in turn, bringing about fierce competition in the marketplace for scarce consumer dollars.

On the west side of Lake Keuka, north of Hammondsport, the Urbana Wine Company was founded in 1865 by Clark Bell and associates. Urbana was later renamed the Gold Seal Winery. John Widmer, from Switzerland, built his Widmer Winery in Naples, New York, west of Hammondsport.

The new market potential for barrels, casks, and vats enticed cooper Walter Taylor, descendant of a sailing ship captain, to set up a cask-making shop on Bully Hill, at the foot of which the village of Hammondsport is situated. Taylor's farm was in an area known for large stands of white oak timber and, high on Bully Hill, overlooked miles and miles of the young but dynamic New York State wine industry. Taylor also dabbled in winemaking, but his expertise lay in the crafting of fine cooperage, much of which went into service at the local wineries under credit agreements.

The wine production capacity of the Finger Lakes district grew faster than the market's propensity to consume, and the competition proved to be too much for many of the financially weaker vintners. As this situation worsened, Walter Taylor was ultimately forced to act on his delinquent accounts receivable, often taking bulk wine inventories for payment. Taylor and his three sons, Fred,

FIGURE 2.30 Finishing New York State "Champagne" at Gold Seal in Hammondsport, New York, circa 1900. *(Courtesy of Joseph E. Seagram & Sons, Inc.)*

Clarence, and Greyton, promptly found themselves deeply involved in the wine business. During the ensuing 50 years the Taylor family parlayed this somewhat impromptu start into one of the largest wineries of its time.

During the mid-1800s the Catawba and Isabella grape varieties found their way to Missouri and were adapted to yield large bounties of fruit. This success attracted widespread plantings there, much as in New York.

Many of the Missouri growers were inexperienced with grapes, however, and did not recognize infestations of the dreaded black rot fungus. The attack of this disease throughout the heartland of America discouraged even dedicated believers. A large number of the old Swiss growers in the Little Rhineland of Indiana moved to northern Ohio, where they joined German immigrants in establishing vineyards near Sandusky and on the Bass Islands in Lake Erie.

Ephraim Bull, of Concord, Massachusetts, introduced eastern vine growers to the Concord variety. It was the flagship product of Bull's research with vine hybrids and was released in 1854 after seven years of testing. The Concord was bred from disease-resistant native *Vitis labrusca* varieties, and despite the then astronomical cost of $5 per vine, it was of interest to the sparse wine industry remaining in Missouri.

Along with another new disease-resistant and highly productive variety called "Norton's Virginia," Concord rekindled commercial winegrowing enthusiasm in Missouri. By the mid-1860s Missouri's vineyards had expanded to the largest acreage ever, making it the leading grape-producing state in the Union. It was during this time that the first rootstock materials were taken from American vineyards to combat the *Phylloxera* root louse in Europe. Nurserymen Bush and Meissner of St. Louis published their initial catalog in 1869, and by 1876 a French translation was being used by European winegrowers to order the rootstocks necessary for the great grafting project in the Old World.

The finest years for Missouri viticulture proved to be the 1860s, as production later grew to far oversupply demand. New York City newspaper editor Horace Greeley advised: "Go west, young man, go west," and people were doing exactly that. The Gold Rush, the land grants, and the transcontinental railroad were among the many fascinations of the time, offering opportunity in the west. Viticulture Professor Husmann moved from Missouri to California, where he proclaimed that California was "the true home of the grape." In 1870, California took the lead as the largest winegrowing state in America, a position the Golden State has never since relinquished.

❖ WESTERN AMERICA

Winegrowing in the western states was pioneered, as in Europe and in eastern America, by the church. The "island" of California was first recognized by Pope Alexander VI in 1493. Spain made expeditions to explore the California coastline in 1542 and 1602. The conquistadores found new frontiers to explore along the western shores of the Americas, and vineyards were established in their wake.

The European *Vitis vinifera* vines, which had not done well in the eastern states, flourished in the western New World. In fact, vines grew so well that in 1595 the king of Spain decreed that new vineyard plantings were to be terminated in the provinces. The edict was intended, of course, to maintain sales of Spanish wine to the west, and it remained in effect for nearly 150 years. This Spanish decree offers an interesting historical parallel to a similar abatement made by Rome some 1,500 years earlier to curtail vineyard plantings in its colonial European provinces.

FIGURE 2.31 Mission San Diego.
(Photo by author.)

Despite the order from Madrid, Franciscan missions continued planting vines in the Americas. The first vineyard in the *Baja*, or lower California, was established at Mission Xavier by Father Juan Ugarte in the late 1690s.

Gaspar de Portola, explorer-captain of the Eighth Company of Dragoons, arrived in Mexico from Spain in 1767. The following year he was ordered by General José de Galvez to establish missionary settlements in *Alta* (upper) California to prohibit Russian fur trappers and British explorers from taking over the Spanish territorial claims.

De Portola embarked upon his project in March 1769 with a small force of soldiers and a devout missionary priest, Padre Junipero Serra. It was Serra's responsibility to teach the native American Indians the ways of Christianity in order to subdue any pagan violence which might be encountered. The procession arrived in California in July of the same year, and Serra raised the cross that marked the first mission, San Diego. Because Padre Serra knew he would need wine, he brought vines and planted the very first vineyard in California.

More missions were established northward, each a hard day's ride in the saddle apart, along a route that became known as El Camino Real. By 1771 the vineyard at the San Gabriel Mission had become a large plot, called the *vina madre* (mother vineyard) because of its superior soil and weather conditions. By the end of the eighteenth century Serra had carried his vines to five outposts in southern California: San Diego, San Juan Capistrano, San Buenaventure, San Gabriel, and Santa Barbara. His mission vines flourished in the California sun, and the wines they produced, though perhaps not of the finest quality, were abundant. In all, there were 12 missions constructed as El Camino Real progressed to San Luis Obispo, Santa Cruz, San Jose, and yet further north, the last begun in 1823 by Father José Altimira at Sonoma.

As merchant ships began to stop more frequently at ports along the Alta California coast, the missions of El Camino Real increasingly came into contact with the outside world, which, in turn, brought about more demand for wine production during the early 1800s.

This growth was short-lived, however, as the Mexican revolt against Spain resulted in the curtailment of all agricultural endeavors by the missions. The situation worsened; some of the early church vineyards in California were abandoned, and others were destroyed by the enraged monks themselves. Consequently, although the birth of California wine must be credited to the church, the remarkable development of the California wine industry was achieved by the commercial laity.

Joseph Chapman planted the first commercial vineyard in California on the Los Angeles pueblo land in 1824. Chapman was originally an easterner who had gained experience in viticulture by working at Junipero Serra's Santa Ynez and San Gabriel missions.

Jean-Louis Vignes, a native of Bordeaux, planted about 100 acres of vines in southern California prior to 1833. The vineyard became the property of two Sansevaine brothers, nephews of Vignes, in the 1850s. The Sansevaines reportedly brought cuttings of several *Vitis vinifera* varieties from their French vineyard, but no record has yet been found to indicate what the selections were or how they performed.

Vineyards continued to prosper in California under Mexican rule until after the War of 1846. Junipero Serra's mission vines proved to be hardy, vigorous, and exceptionally well adapted to California. Some specimens eventually grew to become truly magnificent plants. The U.S. Department of Agriculture reported that a single vine, the *Carpinteria* vine, had a trunk nearly three feet in diameter and once yielded a crop of eight tons of grapes! According to Ruth Teiser in her book, *Winemaking in California,* the Carpinteria vine was dug up and sent off to the 1876 Exposition in St. Louis.

With the concentrated efforts of the monks, winegrowing had developed faster in southern than in northern California. With Mexico's loss of California to the United States in 1846, and the Gold Rush of 1849, that situation was quickly reversed. Many European winegrowers emigrated to the San Francisco area seeking refuge from political oppression in Europe and a mother lode of gold in the Sierra foothills. California welcomed this new populace and encouraged land investments for vineyards. The State Agricultural Society promised that "capital put into vineyards would bring greater returns than when outlayed in fluming rivers for golden treasures."

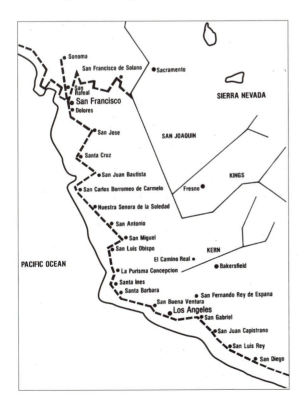

FIGURE 2.32 El Camino Real, the mission trail.

FIGURE 2.33 Count Agoston Haraszthy. *(Courtesy of Buena Vista Vineyards and Winery.)*

California wine in the mid-1800s was made primarily from Serra's mission vines—good, but far from the grand wines made from the *Vitis vinifera* in Europe. Count Agoston Haraszthy, an exiled Hungarian, changed all that. Haraszthy initially emigrated to Wisconsin in the early 1800s, planting vines and building a beautiful stone winery near what is now the village of Prairie du Sac. His vines probably died, from either *Phylloxera* or the Wisconsin winters, or both. In any event, about one year prior to the Gold Rush, Haraszthy moved to the Sonoma Valley, near the last mission of El Camino Real.

Count Haraszthy's optimism over the possibilities of quality winegrowing became infectious in northern California. He developed the Buena Vista Vinicultural Society and was determined that the wine industry there should be built on a sound foundation. His speeches and articles prescribed that only the finest varieties of *Vitis vinifera* should be planted on only the choicest land, and that only the latest viticultural methods be used.

In 1861, Governor Downey delegated Haraszthy to make a trip to Europe to select the finest vine stocks there and to bring cuttings from them back to California. About 300 different varieties were shipped, but difficulties in handling and labeling the plant materials resulted in some of the varieties becoming either mislabeled or lost altogether. It took years to untangle the puzzle of identifying varieties, some of which, such as the now famous Zinfandel, have yet to be positively traced.

The estate and winery at Buena Vista were lavish, their cost eventually leading to Haraszthy's bankruptcy. With further financial support denied, Haraszthy left California for Brazil quite mysteriously. The many classic vines of the Old World remained, however, and have since become a perpetual monument to his dedication.

Ten miles to the east of Sonoma is the Napa Valley, thought by many to be the single finest winegrowing district in America. A number of choice European varieties were planted there in the 1860s, some via Haraszthy's Sonoma project and others by Samuel Branna, who had made a selection of classic vines during his own personal tour through Europe.

The reputation of the wines being grown in the Napa Valley spread rapidly. Robert Louis Stevenson commented in the 1880s that the Napa locale was "where the soil sublimated under sun and stars to something finer, and the wine

FIGURE 2.34 The first Haraszthy vineyard in Sonoma. *(Photo by author.)*

is bottled poetry." Stevenson went on with his lauds, comparing Napa wines with those from the great growths of Bordeaux and Burgundy, namely, Château Lafite-Rothschild and the Clos de Vougeot.

The future seemed very bright indeed, but Sonoma and Napa vines were soon attacked by the *Phylloxera* root louse in much the same manner as vines in Europe had been. Having studied winegrowing in Michigan and Mississippi, Eugene Waldemar Hilgard, later of *Hilgardia* magazine fame, was named the first professor at the grape and wine laboratory at the University of California at Berkeley. Through the work of Hilgard and the ex-Missourian Hussmann, the *Phylloxera* was finally held in check.

With the root louse out of the way, a general opinion emerged that the potential of the California wine industry was limitless. As in New York and Missouri earlier in the century, wine production in California was developed far in excess of demand. This situation was aggravated further by get-rich-quick schemers who marketed cheap, poor-quality wines. These efforts crashed in the late 1860s, bringing about a depressed market for California wines. Industry leaders learned that more technical and economic knowledge was required before California wines could become the American standard. Professor Hilgard wrote in 1879:

> *As the depression was, beyond doubt, attributable chiefly to the hasty putting upon the market of immature and indifferently made wines, so the return of prosperity has been, in great measure, the result of steady improvement in the quality of the wines marketed—such improvement being partly due to the introduction of grape varieties better adapted than the Mission grape to the production of wines suited to the taste of wine-drinking nations.*

Two colossal personalities led the recovery of California winegrowing in the 1880s—George Hearst and Leland Stanford. Hearst made a fortune in mining, became a U.S. senator, and helped launch the monumental publishing career of his son, William Randolph Hearst. George Hearst also purchased a 400-acre tract in Sonoma County, but *Phylloxera* promptly killed his vines. Undaunted, Hearst ordered new grafted vines, replanted, and ultimately attained production capacity of nearly 250,000 gallons of wine each year.

Stanford, railroad magnate and patron of Stanford University, built a winery amid the 350 acres of vineyard he owned near San Jose. By 1888 his output exceeded one million gallons.

Because of such projects as these, California vineyards once again expanded to the point of overproduction. A subsequent recession was even worse than that which took place in the previous decade. Grapes were sold for less than $10 per ton and wines for less than 8¢ a gallon.

To make matters worse, another mysterious disease was found in southern California vineyards. Some vines there rather suddenly became defoliated and died. This condition, which bewildered plant pathologists for decades, was finally identified as a bacterium introduced to vines by a leafhopper insect. It was called "Pierce's Disease," and, to date, no cure has been found. Pierce's Disease, generally found in subtropical climates, was doubtlessly involved in many of the *vinifera* failures experienced in the warm, humid climates in the southeastern sector of the United States.

Some pioneers were not deterred by the economic and biological threats. In the Napa Valley a Finnish sea captain, Gustave Niebaum, bought the Inglenook vineyard in 1879 and built an impressive stone winery in the Gothic style. Niebaum had an intense desire to grow the finest wine possible, an obsession that led to a strict "white-glove" inspection policy in his cellars. Today the Niebaum estate vineyards and winery are owned by the famous film producer-director, Francis Ford Coppola.

Georges de Latour, a Frenchman from Perigord, bought a Napa Valley grainfield and orchard property on which he planted vines personally selected from France. Fernande de Latour, his wife, named the small estate "Beaulieu," or "Beautiful Place." Fine wines were also made at Beaulieu Vineyard, long since having come to be known as simply "BV."

French winegrowers were reluctant to admit that California could grow Old World grapes well enough to be capable of entering into serious competition with the wines of Europe. The gauntlet was dropped. American vintners were invited by the French to enter their wines in competition at the Paris World Exposition of 1889. The results stunned the international wine scene—U.S. vintners won 42 medals awarded by French wine judges! Among the California winners were Beringer, Cresta Blanca, Inglenook, Krug, and Schramsberg. Stone Hill of Missouri was a medalist, as was Great Western from New York State.

⬧ PROHIBITION

For some 80 years it had been building—a disaster worse than any disease or depression yet known to American vintners. It was a reflection of the profound and perhaps excessively rapid change in the fabric of American life. As wine had been a symbol of the church throughout the entire history of Western civilization, the church had become, ironically, the primary influence used to destroy it.

The end of the Civil War had not ended America's differences. Dynamic advances in industrial technology, a huge influx of immigrants coupled with a population explosion, increased urbanization, lingering influences from the Victorian era, and Protestant sectarianism—all contributed to the idea that alcohol, in any form or measure, was sinful and a detriment to the welfare of mankind.

The movement formally began with the 1846 passage of Prohibition in Maine, with Massachusetts, Rhode Island, and Vermont following suit in 1852. More notable, however, was the 1880 enactment of Prohibition in Kansas. The moving force behind this action was the infamous Carrie Nation, who assumed, at one time or another, the roles of judge, jury, and executioner in taking action against any facility that might have had anything to do with an alcoholic beverage. Her disregard for private property and human rights spread quickly. As a result, much of our early American wine history was lost when books, diaries, and journals were burned by the Prohibitionists.

The first signal of National Prohibition came with the so-called Dry Movement. Proponents demanded that any mention of wine be struck from textbooks and from the *U.S. Pharmacopoeia*. The "Drys" published books claiming that the word *wine* in the Bible was really grape juice, at the same time advocating the ban of classical Greek and Roman literature that mentioned wine. By the time World War I broke out in Europe, a total of 33 states had voted to go dry. By 1919 the Drys had succeeded in gaining wartime prohibition. The Eighteenth Amendment to the U.S. Constitution, in conjunction with the Volstead Act, brought National Prohibition to all of America in 1920.

Vintners who had seen this ban taking shape geared up their production and marketing forces for medicinal, sacramental, and salted cooking wines, which remained legal under the Volstead Act. Some wine masters went into the grape juice business, but many were forced to close their doors altogether.

Consumers who were determined to keep drinking wine found ways around Prohibition. Fake churches and synagogues were founded for the purpose of dispensing legal sacramental wines. Wine was often prescribed as "medication" for all sorts of human conditions.

FIGURE 2.35 Carrie Nation ready for battle. (*Courtesy of Kansas State Historical Society.*)

Of all the schemes, perhaps the most blatant was the sale of an array of grape juice products with a pill of dehydrated dormant yeast attached for home winemakers. The complete package was usually labeled with a printed warning not to add the pill: "Because if you do, this will commence fermenting and will turn into wine, which would be illegal."

Millions of European-born Americans blatantly made wine, forcing governmental legalization of home winemaking. The law was, and remains, that the head of each American household is allowed to make up to 200 gallons per year for personal and family consumption. Some growers converted their vineyards from wine grapes to juice grapes. Concord growers knew that their grapes made high-quality grape juice. In fact, the founder of Welch's grape juice company was a devout Prohibitionist.

The owners of Stone Hill Wine Cellars at Hermann, Missouri, had the novel idea of remodeling their cellars into caves for mushroom farming. The Glen Winery in Hammondsport, New York, was transformed into a storehouse for pioneer aviator Glenn Curtiss's airplane parts.

A number of vintners desperately tried to continue their operations in secret, illegally, becoming bootleggers—those who sold beverage alcohol without license and without paying excise taxes. Alva Dart, from Hammondsport, was one of many clever bootleggers in that locale during Prohibition. His bootleg produce was transported in the fuel tank of his Model T Ford and, when he and others stopped for gasoline at a very special filling station, the attendant actually pumped the wine or brandy from the car into an underground storage tank. "Gasoline" delivery trucks served to take the resulting products to outlying distribution points.

For the most part, though, such efforts were ultimately discovered and destroyed by U.S. Treasury officers, or T-Men, who, standing amid the rubble of a winery just destroyed, would strike triumphant poses for news photographers.

Ironically, most of the bootleggers who prospered were criminals who had access to the gangster network of underground labor and resources that could circumvent or corrupt the enforcement efforts of the T-Men. It was a conflict with which the names Al Capone and Eliot Ness will be connected forever.

California vineyard land actually grew during National Prohibition, totaling more than 640,000 acres. Most of the grapes grown were of the variety *Alicante Bouschet,* which resisted spoilage in storage and transport. More important was that this variety was so dark and dense that one gallon of crushed grapes could be ameliorated with another gallon or more of water and sugar. The resulting wine, often referred to as "Dago Red," gave the bootleggers a beverage they could market cheaply to lower-income people.

Despite the tenacity of the T-Men, the nation was well supplied with alcoholic beverages in countless ways, the memorable "speakeasy" private clubs being perhaps the most colorful. Bootlegger greed eventually made Prohibition wine expensive—and made the gangsters rich. Desperate alcoholics who couldn't afford the contraband prices resorted to drinking rubbing alcohol, aftershave lotions, colognes, and the like, which were made from butanol, methanol, and other toxic alcohols.

It didn't take long for America to realize that the "great experiment" of National Prohibition was a huge mistake. There were many attempts at reversing the Volstead Act, as well as some proposals for modification of the Prohibitionist regulations, but such efforts were fragmented with egoistic disunity. Thomas Jefferson's statement, a century earlier, rang vividly appropriate: "No nation is drunken where wine is cheap."

Finally, recognizing that National Prohibition was destroying America, politicians commenced to rally around the demand for repeal. The impetus, of course, came not from the underworld, for they had built an empire with Dago Red and bathtub gin.

Nor did the repeal movement originate with the legal vintners. They were, except for the remaining medicinal and sacramental wine producers, long since out of business. The support for repeal came from a force perhaps best described as a national conscience. Early in December 1933 repeal took effect, bringing to an end 14 years of devastation to the entire country—and particularly the American wine industry.

◆ AMERICAN WINE IN THE TWENTIETH CENTURY

Repeal came during the midst of the Great Depression, which was a major hurdle for commercial winegrowing recovery. Consequently, few winegrowers in 1933 believed that American vines and wines could ever be resurrected to become a viable industry again, much less ever offer serious competition to the wines of Europe, which had made great advances in both production and marketing during the American Prohibition.

Apart from the Italian-Americans who continued to drink Dago Red, the new generation of young Americans who had matured without any knowledge of wine during Prohibition found dry table wines to be an unfamiliar, "sour," foreign type of drink. In addition, many states voted to remain Prohibitionist, especially in the Deep South. Mississippi remained so until 1966. Other states voted in rigorous tax laws and government control, and still others heavily restricted marketing activities.

Perhaps the only positive thing born out of National Prohibition was the need to start over again from scratch. The Prohibition years had effectively buried many of the traditional vines, wines, and practices that had been detrimental to the advancement of the winemaking art. With the slate wiped clean, there was an opportunity to formulate a truly American wine industry, rather than a poor imitation of that in Europe. In any event, American winegrowers, presented with the ruins of abandoned vineyards, decayed cellars, and broken lives, began their work anew.

One of the first positive steps was the formation of the Wine Institute in California by a group of experienced winegrowers led by Leon Adams, a young newspaperman and wine enthusiast. The establishment of quality standards for California wines, and the belief that good-quality, inexpensive table wine should be made and marketed to a wine-educated American public, were among the principal ideas expressed by the founders.

Despite their scarcity of funds, vintners were persuaded by the California State Department of Agriculture to tax themselves as a way of funding a trade association, now known as the Wine Institute. This body created educational materials necessary in the ongoing struggle to win Americans from "hard drink" to wine. Subsequently, Adams wrote *The Wine Study Course,* which proved to be one of the most significant educational tools for promoting intelligent wine consumerism across all of America.

Unfortunately, along with the Wine Institute literature, there also surfaced a plethora of articles and books written by self-proclaimed experts who disseminated wine fallacy and snobbery. The notion that only certain wines should accompany specific entrées—and then at precise serving temperatures and in specific types of stemware—and other nonsense confused and intimidated the potential American wine consumer.

Nevertheless, the U.S. wine industry slowly reemerged. Franklin Delano Roosevelt saw to it that American wines were once again served in the White House.

It was during the late 1930s that several foresighted pioneers were to make a permanent mark on the American wine industry, each with a very different philosophy of winegrowing.

Philip Wagner was a Baltimore newspaper editor and an amateur winemaker. After visiting Europe, Wagner had become deeply interested in some of the little-known French-American hybrid vines. These had been developed as an alternative attempt to save Europe from the *Phylloxera* root louse. The idea had been to breed new cultivars of grapes from parentages of *vinifera, labrusca, riparia, rupestris,* and other species, endeavoring to combine the disease resistance and high productivity of the native American selections with the high wine quality of the European lines. From thousands of crosses, several hundred promising new hybrids were developed, each identified by a number code instead of a name. Those that captured Wagner's attention were imported and propagated in his Maryland nursery.

Wagner befriended many winegrowing people in the east, particularly in New York State. Greyton Taylor, youngest son of the Taylor Wine Company founder, planted experimental plots of Wagner's imported hybrids. Success required that the number codes be changed to marketable names, the best whites now known as *Seyval Blanc, Vidal Blanc,* and *Vignoles,* along with reds, *Chambourcin, Chancellor,* and *Marechal Foch.*

The French-American hybrids were instantly rejected by *vinifera* purists and *labrusca* traditionalists. It took more than 20 years to perfect the viticultural and vinification techniques necessary to result in competitive wines. Today, they compete very well indeed. In 1992 a Missouri Vignoles was determined by more than 30 premier wine judges at the New World Wine Competition in California to be the "Champion White Table Wine," besting more than 700 competing entries. Nevertheless, a lack in national market acceptance still plagues wines made from the French-American hybrid cultivars.

Another prominent post-Prohibition figure was Charles Fournier, who emigrated in 1934 from the Champagne Region in France to the Gold Seal Vineyards in Hammondsport. Fournier was warned that *Vitis vinifera* would not survive the disease and harsh winters encountered in upstate New York, but he experimented anyway. A decade or so later, Fournier was introduced to Dr. Konstantin Frank, a winegrower refugee born in Russia. Fournier was convinced by Frank that it was possible to grow Old World vines in colder climates by carefully selecting hardy rootstocks for grafting and employing cultivating practices learned in mother Russia. Dr. Frank was hired by Fournier to work in the Gold Seal vineyards, and they experimented together with the tender *vinifera.* During the late 1950s they succeeded in harvesting the first commercial quantities of Old World grapes grown in eastern America. While devastating winters still elicit caution and fear among eastern winegrowers, the development of Old World wines continues to advance, building on the breakthroughs by Frank and Fournier.

Brothers Ernest and Julio Gallo had their roots in Asti, in the Piedmont Region of Italy. The Gallos first grew grapes at Antioch, California, where their parents had immigrated from Italy via South America. During Prohibition the Gallo family shipped grapes for home winemaking to Chicago and New York. Instead of the Alicante Bouschet variety, however, they marketed the higher-quality Zinfandel.

Following the repeal of Prohibition, the Gallos became interested in the commercial wine business and leased a warehouse in Modesto from the Santa Fe railroad in which to commence their initial operations. Demand for their bulk wines grew rapidly, and by World War II Gallo wines were also competing for consumers in the retail marketplace. The marketing genius of Ernest and the production expertise of Julio combined in a mangagement team of unequaled

FIGURE 2.36   Philip Wagner. *(Courtesy of* Wine East *magazine; photo by Linda Jones McKee.)*

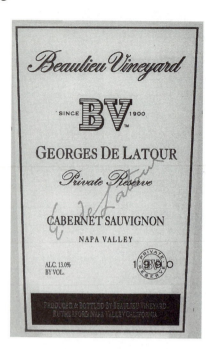

drive and success. In less than 40 years Gallo became the largest single winery in the world. Its success heralded the greatest growth in the U.S. wine industry to date.

Perhaps the most significant contributions to the development of American wine, certainly to the American industry becoming recognized as a world-class producer, were made by Andre Tchelistcheff. Born to Russian aristocracy in 1901, his plans were to become a physician, but he was trained in military school. When the Bolsheviks took over, Lieutenant Tchelistcheff left the Russian Army for Czechoslovakia, where he studied agronomy. Following postgraduate work in viticulture and enology at the Institut National Agronomique in Paris, he worked at a number of classic European vineyard estates. At the age of 37 he emigrated to California, where English would be the eighth language in which he would become fluent.

Andre Tchelistcheff found an opportunity with Georges de Latour, owner of Beaulieu Vineyard, a rather ordinary property in the Napa Valley. The vast Old World knowledge and skill of Tchelistcheff soon gave BV wines a distinction that became an American standard. He reserved the very best Cabernet Sauvignon from each vintage for bottling as Beaulieu Vineyard *Georges de Latour,* the first of what we now see as "reserve" wines from many other vintners. At 72 he retired from BV and embarked upon yet another career as consultant for 20 vintners in California, Oregon, and Washington. Each of these firms, among them Buena Vista, Château Ste. Michelle, Clos Pegase, Firestone, Jordan, Niebaum-Coppola, Simi, and Stag's Leap Wine Cellars, has also achieved grand stature. There can be no question that the late Andre Tchelistcheff was truly the "Dean of American Winemakers."

✣ THE AMERICAN WINE BOOM

The interest in table wines grew quickly during the late 1940s, heavily influenced by returning American servicemen who brought home from Europe a newly acquired appreciation for wine. Subsequently, a burgeoning commercial airline industry brought European wine to even more Americans.

The quest for wine technology was again rekindled. The American Society of Enologists was founded in 1950 at the University of California at Davis, where wine researchers followed up the early work of Hilgard at Berkeley.

Funding was made available in other states for commencing or renewing viticulture and enology programs of study. As both European and American wine masters conducted intensive research programs, the traditions of Old World methodology gave way to innovations based on New World technology.

The forward steps were by no means confined only to production. There were many new ideas for wine marketing too. New and more efficient distribution channels gave better access to retail-shelf space and restaurant wine lists. People began to tour the wineries, learning the jargon and sampling wines. Vintners printed sales promotion pamphlets replete with wine cookery recipes and down-to-earth wine serving tips. Slowly the shrouds of wine snobbery and intimidation commenced to fall.

One public relations program that gained attention was that of George Lonz, whose winery was on Middle Bass Island, in Lake Erie, several miles off the shore of Port Clinton, Ohio. Lonz devised tongue-in-cheek publicity releases showing his wines surrounded by young ladies in cheesecake photographs. Popular music concerts, more than 20 years before Woodstock, are still recalled in northern Ohio.

In Michigan there was innovation in wine types, including particularly wines flavored with synthetic essences in somewhat the same style as the ancient

Greek and Roman wines. A mixture of "Michigan Champagne" and "Sparkling Burgundy" made a bubbly called "Cold Duck," which became an overnight national sensation and died a few years later as quickly.

By far the most important contribution of the 1950s was a simple, commonsense idea expanded on by Frank Schoonmaker, a devoted and highly respected American wine authority. Schoonmaker's concept was that the labels of American-made wines should carry the name of the grape variety rather than continuing to borrow the traditional European geographic names. A wine made from Pinot Noir grapes in a style similar to that of French Burgundy would no longer be labeled "California Burgundy" but, rather, "California Pinot Noir." The names of the great German varieties, Johannisberg Riesling and Sylvaner were much more honest and descriptive terms on labels than, for instance, "California Rhine Wine."

The conversion proved to be rather easy in California, especially in the Napa, Sonoma, and other north coastal districts where many of the classic Old World varieties had been grown since the Haraszthy influence a century earlier.

In the east, however, conversion to varietal labeling proved to be more difficult. The native American grape varieties, such as Catawba and Concord, were not internationally known, and the French-American hybrid cultivars were not yet widely planted. Consequently, many eastern vintners retained the practice of using European geographic names, such as "New York State Burgundy," "Ohio Rhine Wine," and "Michigan Chablis," among many others. Although many of these wines were good, the practice was nonetheless false labeling, as native and hybrid grapes cannot be vinified to *vinifera* character. Consequently, commercial eastern winegrowing in the east became suspect to consumers during the 1950s and 1960s.

As the 1980s began, several American wine fads had come and gone: the previously mentioned Cold Duck, a Spanish-inspired mixture of fruit and light red wine called Sangria, and a plethora of flavored wines led by Gallo's "Boone's Farm" brand.

The 1990s wine boom in America gathered momentum via a totally different operational philosophy—the establishment of more than 1,000 small boutique wineries. The typical estate was a few acres of prime Napa or Sonoma land planted to several select *vinifera* varieties, centered by a state-of-the-art production facility housed in an architectural masterpiece. Although most of this development occurred in the North Coast counties of California, boutique wineries emerged in most every state. These new vintners prided themselves on individual wine character and style, yet they were unified by the common goal of producing wines of ultimate quality, wines that could challenge the classical Old World vineyards.

Small wine contests became comprehensively structured competitions. Wine consumption surpassed that of all distilled spirits combined. New consumer wine periodicals kept Americans abreast of news from the vineyards, chapters of national and international wine societies and brotherhoods grew quickly, and there emerged a national interest in fine wine such as America has never before experienced. It is now common to find large metropolitan wholesale distributors carrying portfolios of several thousand selections for retail wine shops and restaurant wine lists.

Much of this success is credited to the technological advances in winegrowing across

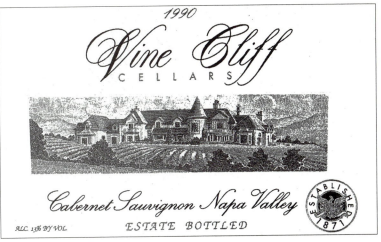

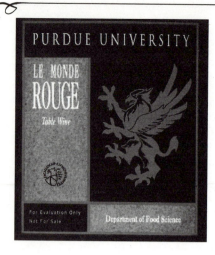

the United States. Credit must be given to the University of California at Davis for pioneering viticulture and enology research. Other institutions have contributed significantly in this effort too, among which are the Universities of Arkansas, Florida, Missouri, and Pennsylvania, along with the California State University at Fresno, Cornell University, Michigan State, New Mexico State, North Carolina State, Ohio State, Oregon State, Purdue, Texas A&M, Virginia Tech, and Washington State.

This new technology, which ultimately led to the production and marketing of quality wines at lower cost, continues to provide the science necessary to further affirm the virtues of moderate wine consumption.

3

WINE AND HUMAN PHYSIOLOGY*

Each of us carries around a laboratory for sensory evaluation in the form of primary sense organs—visual, olfactory, and gustatory. These allow the perception of seeing, tasting, and feeling wine. Certainly these senses are more finely tuned in some people than others, but most anyone can develop superior abilities to evaluate and judge wine.

The drinking of wine has different effects upon different people. There is exciting new research that indicates that sensible wine consumption may have profound therapeutic effects. Those who can drink wine should do so with carefully monitored moderation—though some should not drink wine at all.

◆ SENSORY EVALUATION OF WINE

The interaction of human sensory organs with the environment supplies the basic information by which the world is perceived. Nerves transmit this information to the brain, where it is evaluated and interpreted. For any given sensation, there are specialized nerve endings and cells that can be trained to higher levels of acuity.

The sensory pathways involved in the evaluation of wine include the *visual,* *olfactory,* and *gustatory.* Each transmits messages to a different part of the brain. Thus, because information for vision is gathered in the eye, information for smell gathered in the nose, and information for taste gathered by the tongue and mouth, people actually see, smell, and taste in specialized areas of the brain called, respectively, the visual cortex, olfactory cortex, and gustatory cortex.

VISUAL—THE SENSE OF SIGHT

Sight is the dominant human sense. The sensory receivers (the rods and cones of the retinas) in the eyes comprise more than 70 percent of the total sensory

*Updated from material in the first edition written by Dr. Douglas L. Stringer.

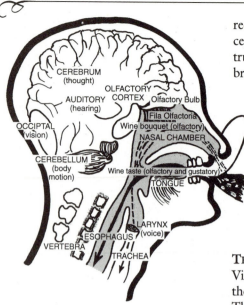

FIGURE 3.1 Functioning of the human sensory system.

receptors of the human body. The two physical factors affecting our visual perception are light, which is interpreted as brightness, and the colors of the spectrum, which are interpreted from varying wavelengths. In vision, our eyes and brain are actually performing at least eight functions simultaneously:

1. Discrimination between light and dark
2. Perception of color
3. Image reproduction, or form vision
4. Visual acuity
5. Spatial perception, or sense of depth
6. Perception of motion, or resolution of images in time
7. Appreciation of brightness or intensities of light
8. Recognition and comparisons of new images with old images

THE VISUAL PATHWAY

Visual impressions are transported through the lens of the eye to a membrane at the back of the eye, called the retina, where the rods and cones are located. That information is then projected through the optic nerve and optic tracts, which go to both of the brain's occipital lobes, where the images are portrayed.

Visual interpretation of an object seen at any given moment is a result of the comparison of that image to previous experiences of that object or something similar. An analysis of an image takes place in the occipital lobes, situated in the back of the head just above the neck. Interpretation, comparison, and image storage, however, take place in the frontal and temporal lobes of the brain. The identification of wine color, for example, can occur only if there have been previous visions of wines that can be compared to make a judgment.

OLFACTORY—THE SENSE OF SMELL

The sense of smell is not as highly developed in humans as it is in other animal species, but we can refine and train our ability to detect odors. Tea tasters and perfume sniffers may have such discriminating nose that they can identify thousands of odors. People often remark how a certain smell brings with it images, associations, or memories of past experiences. The smell of freshly baked bread or cookies, for example, may instantly conjure up one's entire childhood.

The olfactory system is very complex. In addition to perceiving odors and calling upon memory to make associations with great immediacy, it stimulates other nerve systems that are involved with emotional behavior patterns. The aromas of many foods trigger salivation and lip smacking. The identification of smell, like vision, is based on comparisons of what is currently being smelled with what has been previously smelled. The sense of smell is also difficult to quantify. Even though the human sense of smell lags behind that of other animals, it can still detect minute traces of odors much more quickly than sophisticated chemical analysis.

Olfactory receptors quickly become accustomed to changing odors. This adaptation process is apparent, for example, when a person enters a room that has a distinctly unpleasant odor. After several minutes the odor is less noticeable. However, if the person goes outside for a few minutes and then returns, once again the unpleasant odor is perceived. The sense of smell is, therefore, easily exhausted in human beings. For this reason wine judges must be very careful in pacing and limiting their activity.

THE OLFACTORY PATHWAY

The olfactory nerve cells are located high up in each nostril. As one sniffs, odor-bearing air is directed to these cells in the nasal cavity. To perceive odors most

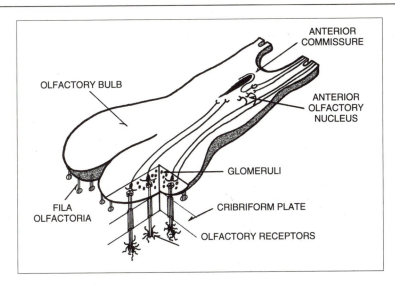

FIGURE 3.2 Diagram of the human olfactory system.

intensely, it is best to take quick, deep sniffs so that the odors can reach high up in the nose. Subtle smells, such as wine bouquet, may not reach the olfactory nerve cells if sniffing is weak. Although it is not fully known how the entire olfactory system works, it is thought that a crude indication of smell takes place in the olfactory bulb and subtle smell discriminations occur in the olfactory cortex—each of these located in different parts of the olfactory lobe in the brain.

Some researchers belive that certain olfactory nerve cells respond only to certain odors and that different odors are projected to different parts of the brain. A unique phenomenon known as "cross-talk" occurs when a person smells an odor. As the odor stimulates the nerve cells, this stimulation may also be transmitted from one nerve cell to another. With such sharing of information by various cells, the person is able to interpret intensities of smell, probably from the number of nerve cells that are stimulated.

The brain's response to odor is very rapid, and its recovery from odors can also be rapid, depending on the character and intensity of the odor. Recovery can vary from a few seconds to several minutes. In most cases, a person can identify more than 70 odors in one hour if proper concentration is maintained. People can detect an intense odor diffused to one millionth the concentration of a weak odor.

GUSTATORY—THE SENSE OF TASTE AND MOUTH FEEL

The human capability to taste is less sensitive than the ability to smell. It takes a much more intense stimulus to activate our taste buds than to stimulate olfactory nerve cells. By some estimates it takes approximately 20,000 times more molecules to induce a taste sensation than a smell sensation. It stands to reason, then, that a stimulus strong enough to induce taste should make an impression on the olfactory system. But this is not always the case. Open a salt shaker and smell deeply. Only a faint smell is perceived, if any. Do the same with the sugar bowl. It is difficult to perceive salt or sugar in the olfactory sense.

Human beings have four basic gustatory sensations:

1. Acid—sensed most intensely on the back of the tongue
2. Sweet—perceived primarily on the front of the tongue
3. Bitter—tasted primarily on the back of the tongue
4. Salt—perceived primarily on the sides of the tongue

The center of the tongue has comparatively fewer taste buds and is usually considered "taste blind." This part of the palate is, however, important in contributing to overall tactile sensitivity in the mouth—the "mouth feel," which is generally called *body* in wine evaluation.

The sense of taste, like the sense of smell, can be easily fatigued. Taste may be further inhibited by *adaptation,* which is also a response to overstimulation. Usually there is rapid recovery from both adaptation and fatigue, but one must allow sufficient time before tasting results will be accurate again. Wine judges should allow at least two minutes for recovery between wine evaluations. Adaptation and fatigue of the four major tastes vary considerably. Consider the following:

1. The adaptation to salt does not affect sensitivity to salty tastes.
2. Adaptation to acidic (sour) taste reduces the taster's sensitivity to all other tastes. However, recovery of sensitivity to sourness is rapid because most common acids are easily rinsed away by saliva or water.
3. Adaptation to one particular type of sugar may or may not reduce sensitivity to other sugars. Sugar and other sweeteners do not fatigue sensitivities to each other. Recovery of sensitivity to most sugars occurs more rapidly than recovery for other sweeteners.
4. Bitterness may last longer than the other three basic gustatory tastes. A bitter taste may persist for more than a minute, even after rinsing the tongue with saliva or water. This is probably because bitter compounds have an affinity for the skin and remain longer.

The smallest amount of a compound needed to actively stimulate taste bud nerve cells is called *threshold concentration.* The threshold concentration for sweetness is greater than for saltiness, for saltiness greater than for acidity, and for acidity greater than for bitterness.

The perception of taste is, however, relative. Well-practiced tasters with keen sensitivity may taste a substance at less than 5 percent the concentration needed to make an impression on a novice taster. Temperature can also significantly change sensitivity of taste for various substances. Cold sweet wine tastes less sweet than the same wine at room temperature.

There is a decrease in human sensitivity to taste with age, because the total number of taste buds declines markedly after a person reaches the late thirties or early forties. Babies have more than 10,000 taste buds, which explains why they usually dislike spicy foods. Mature individuals, who have fewer and less sensitive

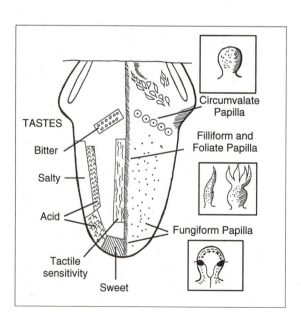

FIGURE 3.3 Diagram of gustatory sites on the human tongue.

taste buds, may prefer more salt and spiciness in their food. Elderly people may prefer even greater levels of seasonings.

THE GUSTATORY PATHWAY.

Human taste buds are bulb shaped and allow dissolved substances to enter through a pore in order to interact with taste cells. Taste buds are grouped into *papillae,* which are distributed in different parts of the tongue. These papillae are what give the tongue a rough surface. Each papilla has about 250 taste buds and may contain various types of buds that respond to different tastes. Many nuances of taste are the result of the different patterns of taste buds in the papillae. The intensity of taste is believed to be caused by the frequency with which each taste cell is stimulated. The ends of taste bud cells are in contact with "taste nerves," which transmit taste messages to the brain. Gustatory messages enter the brain stem via the chorda tympani nerve at the junction of the pons and the medulla.

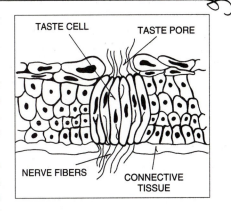

FIGURE 3.4 Diagram of a human taste bud.

✤ FLAVOR AND TASTE

As discussed earlier, the human palate discriminates in reaction to taste for saltiness, acidity, sweetness, and bitterness. It is equally discriminating in distinguishing taste for flavors. Thus "taste" often becomes a confusing concept, as obviously it is simultaneously involved with both olfactory and gustatory sensations. Consider these examples:

1. The saltiness and flavor of soy sauce
2. The tart acidity and flavor of a green apple
3. The sweetness and flavor of milk chocolate
4. The bitterness and flavor of almonds
5. The tart acidity, moderate sweetness, citrus flavor, and thin body of grapefruit juice
6. The bland acidity, cloying sweetness, maple flavor, and heavy body of syrup

It becomes necessary to make common sense of the concept of taste for application to wine evaluation, description, and communication. Much of what is discussed and written about wine refers to perceptions "in the nose" and "on the palate." This concept, of course, is much more complex to a wine taster than to an ear, nose, and throat physician or a flavor chemist. Students learning about wine can perhaps rest a bit easier knowing that it may take years to develop a keen palate.

✤ MAKING IT WORK

Each person has a given set of abilities and talents. A good training regimen can improve levels of proficiency for most any human function. One should not be discouraged if the first few attempts at grasping subtle flavors achieve faint results or are futile.

One of the best approaches is to develop a "flavor memory," to concentrate on certain odors and flavors easily identified in everyday life so that they can be retrieved from memory. For example, few people think much about the common essences of roses, melons, figs, green bell peppers, tobacco, cedar, and vanilla. These and hundreds of other such flavors are important elements in evaluating and appreciating wine.

FIGURE 3.5 Le Nez du Vin. *(Photo by David Ferguson.)*

The development of a sharp flavor memory takes determination, time, and practice. Start with concentrating on simple, elemental flavors. One of the best references is the *Le Nez Du Vin* ("The Nose of Wine") aroma identification kit. Invented by French flavor expert Jean Lenoir, this is highly recommended for the neophyte and even for more advanced enophiles. As one adds more and more flavors that can be identified and instantly retrieved from memory, a vocabulary will develop, serving to provide increasing expertise whereby one can better appreciate the many complexities in fine wines and effectively communicate with other wine enthusiasts.

❖ WINE JUDGING

It would be unfortunate if a reader of this book has begun with this section, especially if the intention is to scan the next few pages rapidly in the hope of becoming an instant expert. It just doesn't work that way. Becoming a proficient wine judge, as in attaining mastery of any discipline, requires fundamental knowledge, dedication, patience, and practice.

Even with all the recent advances made in analyzing the chemistry of wine, no researcher has yet devised a method of accurately quantifying a wine's "goodness" or "badness." There are, of course, wine critics who continue to publish exacting numerical ratings for dozens of wines, assigning this wine a "68" and that one a "94" and so forth. These people are less willing to try repeating such precise ratings for the same wines tasted blind in a public forum.

Wine judgments will always remain an individual matter. Yet wine evaluation has advanced considerably from the realm of snap judgments based on highly subjective hedonic scales with such categories as "dislike," "like," "like a lot," and so on. During the past two decades there have been several endeavors by wine researchers and magazine publishers to standardize the judging scale.

DESCRIPTIVE TERMINOLOGY

Despite the fact that science can quantify virtually all wine components through chemical analysis, there still exists only a rudimentary language for communicating what wine actually tastes like. Flavor and taste values are exceedingly difficult to describe unless one is a food technologist, and even then the language is valid only with other food technologists.

Consequently, it is necessary to use other common and familiar sensory values as points of reference, such as "ruby red," "hazy," "peach," "tart," and "thin," to name only a few among hundreds. The aspiring wine appreciator must learn the basic sensitivities that wine produces in the eyes, in the nose, and on the palate.

AMBIGUOUS TERMINOLOGY

It is unfortunate that many people get started in wine appreciation speaking a nondescript and confusing language. Words such as *racy* and *supple* may make the discussions of wine critics more interesting, but they have no definitive meaning in accurately communicating wine character. Has anyone ever really experienced a "dumb" wine, or a "fat" wine, or a "takes no prisoners" wine? Wine judging remains subjective enough without the use of such jargon.

JUDGMENT OF THE VISUAL MODE

The visual character of a wine is divided into two major categories, clarity and color, as well as effervescence in the case of sparkling wines.

CLARITY

The common procedure in evaluating clarity is to hold the wineglass by the stem or base so that a constant light source behind the glass can filter through the wine. Wine with perfect clarity has no trace of suspended particles or lint. The four generally accepted echelons of wine clarity are:

> Brilliant
>
> Clear
>
> Hazy
>
> Cloudy

To replicate a hazy condition, fill an 8-ounce wineglass half full with water and add one drop of whole milk—two or three more drops will render a cloudy mixture.

COLOR.

The first concern for color is its *hue*, or an identity of specific color value such as "straw-gold," or "ruby-red." This is followed by a judgment on color *intensity*, the quantity of hue present in the wine. Color evaluations are best made against a stark white background, such as plain white paper or a white table napkin. By looking downward through the glass, one can perceive variances in both hue and intensity as stationary light passes through different depths of the wine. Obviously, the wine will have the same color hue throughout, but intensity will seem denser in the center of the glass where the wine is deeper. Conversely, intensity will be lighter around the edge of the glass where the wine is more shallow. Some judges prefer to make this examination by holding the glass at

FIGURE 3.6 The visual mode.
(Photo by David Ferguson.)

various angles and looking from side to side through the bowl or the glass. Whichever approach is adopted, a judge should use it consistently.

The following are examples of typical color judgments (See also Figures 3.7 and 3.8; color insert):

WINE TYPE	COLOR HUE	COLOR INTENSITY
Dry Vermouth	pale celery	extremely light
Sauvignon Blanc	pale straw	very light
Chardonnay	straw	light
Sauternes	golden	moderate
Blush	pink	light
Anjou Rosé	rose	moderate
Pinot Noir	crimson red	light
Merlot	scarlet red	moderate
Cabernet Sauvignon	garnet red	dark
Port	ruby red	dense
Tawny Port	amber red	moderate
Oloroso Sherry	amber	dark

JUDGMENT OF THE OLFACTORY MODE

Flavor is the single most important element in wine judging. It involves the most sensitive human organ, the nose, and is generally the primary factor in deciding wine quality. For all these reasons the entire scope of the olfactory mode comprises the greatest number of points on every good cardinal (numerical) scale of wine judging.

The first concern is that of *bouquet,* often referred to as the "nose" by wine judges. Wine bouquet, or nose, is perhaps best compared to a bouquet of flowers. Each flower in the bouquet expresses its own characteristic odor, which contributes to a complex array of smells. In the case of wine, the part of the bouquet that is grape flavor is called the *aroma.* The combination of the aroma with odors resulting from the winemaking process results in a complex array of smells collectively referred to as bouquet. A Chardonnay wine, for example, may have a slight ripe olive and herbal aroma, which is typical of Chardonnay grapes. The nose may also detect a "buttery" flavor resulting from a special malo-lactic bacterial fermentation and a "vanilla" flavor owing to oak-barrel aging. The combined olive-herbal aroma and butter-vanilla flavors constitute the entire bouquet of this Chardonnay. A properly trained human olfactory and temporal system can identify, classify, store, and recall hundreds of different flavors. Some of these are delicious experiences, whereas others are unpleasant, resulting from winemaking problems. An experienced wine judge is familiar with both.

Dr. Ann Noble, enology researcher at the University of California at Davis, has succeeded in formulating a standardized system of wine flavor terminology, generally referred to as the "aroma wheel." It employs a three-tier system of primary, secondary, and tertiary levels of flavor definition. Although not yet perfect, the system does establish a basis on which people can now communicate effectively in discussing the many varied olfactory impressions experienced in the vast world of wine.

In many white grape varieties we find *primary floral aromas.* Among these are acacia, honeysuckle, linden, jasmine, rose, peony, and violet. These flavor values are most often found in grapes that have been harvested slightly before maturity, prior to the formation of *primary fruit aromas* in full maturation.

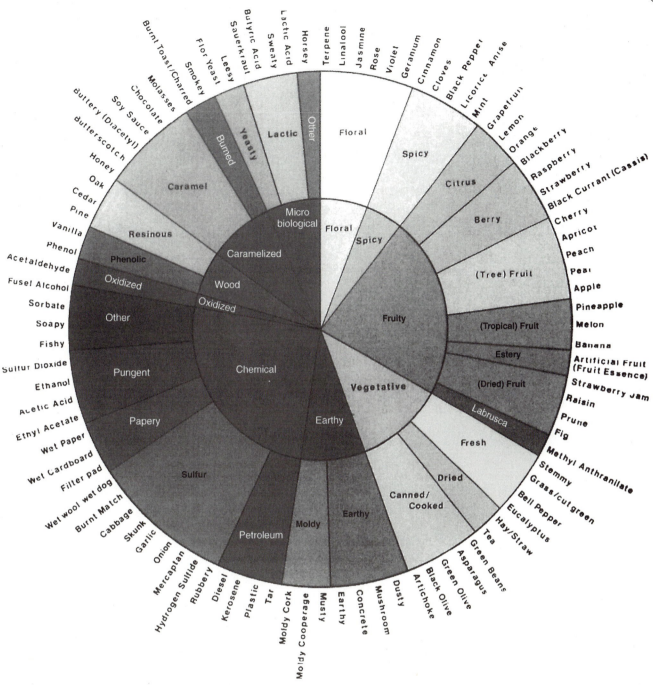

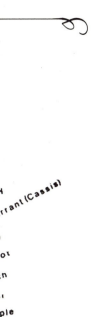

FIGURE 3.9 The Aroma Wheel.
(Adapted from A.C. Noble et al, "Progress Towards a Standardized System of Wine Aroma Terminology," American Journal of Enology and Viticulture 35, no.2 [1984]: 107–109).

Many of the primary floral and fruit aromas exist in the form of higher terpene alcohols such as citronellol, linalol, and geraniol. These are commonly found in Johannisberg Riesling, Gewürztraminer, Vidal Blanc, Vignoles, and most of the Muscat varieties.

Other aromas are identified in the form of esters. Among these are the isoamyl acetate, associated with bananas; ethyl propionate, associated with apples; and methyl anthranilate, found in the native American *Vitis labrusca* cultivars such as Niagara and Concord.

Primary fruit aromas in red grapes, frequently identified as cherry, black currant or cassis, strawberry, raspberry, and plum, are often used as flavor descriptives in evaluation of wines made from Chambourcin, Gamay, and Pinot Noir. Many of

FIGURE 3.10 The olfactory mode.
(Photo by David Ferguson.)

these aromas are found in ester forms. Strawberry flavor is attributed principally to several butyrate compounds. Raspberry is identified with ethyl caprote.

Heavy floral and fruit aromas extracted from mature or slightly overripe grapes require particularly close attention in order to avoid oxidation and microbiological infection. This involves culling out bad clusters (called *triage*), cool 50° to 55° F fermentation in sanitized stainless steel tanks, rackings (decanting) sparged with nitrogen, absolutely full tankage for storage, minimal finings, cold storage stabilization, and prompt bottling.

Another flavor group comprises the *primary vegetal aromas*. Good examples of these are anise, green pepper, tobacco leaf, and tea. Aromas in this group are often structured in the form of carbonyl compounds, such as the methoxy-isobutyl-pyrazine that is the principal aroma component associated with bell peppers. These compounds can be very complex, such as the aroma associated with Cabernet Sauvignon, 2-methoxy-3-isobutylpyrazine. Vegetal aromas can also exist as phenols, such as cinnamic acid that is found in grass and tobacco. This character is most often desired in very heavy red wines, for instance, those traditionally made from Cabernet Sauvignon, Chancellor, and Merlot.

Yet another group, *primary wood aromas,* is exemplified by briar, cedar, hazelnut, resin, and oak. These aromas generally exist in the form of phenolic compounds, such as vanillin, which is the aroma component associated with oak. Wood aromas can also be carbonyl compounds such benzaldehyde, the aroma associated with bitter almond.

Chemical flavors in wine are generally associated with the decomposition of ethyl alcohol to acetic acid by various species of spoilage bacteria. Ethyl acetate, described as a "paint-thinner" aroma, is often associated with acetic acid formation. Ethyl acetate can, however, metabolize independently from action by certain species of yeast.

An earthy character, sometimes described as "barnyard," is attributed to fermentation products resulting from the action of *Brettanomyces* yeast. Some wine judges call this condition simply "Brett." The occurrence of Brett in white wines is almost always considered a flaw, although judges often differ in opinion as to a little of this flavor contributing positively to the complexity of some reds.

Another set of spoilage flavors found in wine is due to one or another form of sulfur degradation. These conditions usually arise from elemental sulfur dusted on vines, essential in controlling various types of mildew and molds in vineyards. Sulfur is also an important natural constituent in the synthesis of essential proteins in grapevines. Whether dusted or natural, elemental sulfur on or in grapes can be transformed by both cultured and wild yeasts into hydrogen sulfide, or a "rotten eggs" character, in wine.

Sulfide compounds can be further degraded by bacterial action into one or another mercaptan compounds which emerge in various types of complex compounds. At best, this is manifested in an "asparagus," "cabbage," or "green bean" flavor. As may be expected, this can sometimes be confused with primary vegetal flavors. At worst, mercaptan spoilage is expressed in a "rubbery" aroma, or a foul "wet dog" smell, or, worst of all, a "skunky" character.

Moldy-musty flavors arise from either moldy grapes, moldy barrels, or some other exposure of the wine to a source of mold. Molds will not grow directly in wine due to its alcohol content.

Flavors that seem "cooked" or "brown apple" in character are often due to oxidation of wine resulting from extended exposure to air and/or higher temperatures (over 65°F) in processing and storage. These flavors can also be categorized with "prune" flavors that come from grapes that are overripened and/or have decayed. Some wines, such as Madeira, are purposely heavily oxidized to produce high levels of aldehyde compounds that result in a pronounced "nutty-caramel" flavor.

The first phase of olfactory judgment commences with the examination of bouquet and should be made while the wine is in a glass on a countertop or tabletop. The judge will be smelling only the vapors that the wine gives off at rest. The nose is inserted into the glass, and several deep sniffs are taken, the judge making a mental note of each reaction. Sometimes closing the eyes may help concentration. These primary judgment notes are then recorded.

After a few seconds rest another examination of bouquet should be made immediately after the wine has been fully swirled around the inside walls of the glass. The glass stem is grasped and the bowl gently rotated. This significantly increases the surface area of the wine, from which volatile flavor can evaporate into the chamber for the nose to receive. Again the nose is inserted into the glass, several deep sniffs are taken, and a mental note is made of each reaction. These secondary judgment notes are also recorded.

The second phase of olfactory judgment takes place in the mouth with the taste buds employed as evaluators of wine flavor constituents. The mouth should be freshly rinsed clean with water, then a small sip of wine is taken from the glass and rolled around the mouth. The flavors may, or may not, be the same as those identified in the nose. The palate may identify new flavors altogether or the same flavors with different intensity. These primary judgments are recorded, and the wine is spit out into a bucket.

After a few seconds' rest, a small nibble of cheese and unsalted cracker is taken, and the mouth is rinsed clean again for making the second flavor judgment. This time a sip of wine is drawn in the mouth along with a little air—an action almost like whistling in reverse. The wine is rolled around in the mouth, with air drawn in to stimulate taste buds and accentuate shy flavors. The secondary judgment impressions are recorded, and the wine is spit into the bucket as before.

JUDGMENT OF THE GUSTATORY MODE

There is comparatively little gustatory sensation in the nose. High alcohol content, carbon dioxide bubbles, and some measures of acidity and phenolic compounds are detectable in the nose and may contribute to wine flavor. Consequently, experienced judges usually make olfactory and gustatory evaluations simultaneously while the wine is on the palate. For beginners it helps to make gustatory judgments more deliberately until expertise is developed.

As mentioned previously, the upper surface of the tongue is constructed of several thousand various types of *papillae,* which are expanded skin protuberances, each papilla containing about 250 taste buds. Each bud delivers taste information directly to the brain via special transmitter nerves.

Conventional wisdom often identifies four human gustatory senses, *acidity, sweetness, bitterness,* and *saltiness.* These senses are supplemented by *tactile,* or mouth-feel, sensations of touch on the palate.

ACIDITY

Total acidity in wine is the sum total of the acids present. These consist primarily of *tartaric, malic, lactic,* and *acetic* acids. Typically, total acidity in wine is measured between .5 and 1.0 percent of total wine composition. Tartaric acid has very little perceptible flavor. Malic acid is a bit like green apple in character, while lactic acid has a buttery-cheesy flavor, and acetic acid is vinegary.

Acidity is perceived mostly on the back of the tongue by *foliate papilla* cells in various degrees of tartness, from which the term *tartaric acid* is derived.

FIGURE 3.11 The gustatory mode. *(Photo by David Ferguson.)*

The following is a typical range of acidity expressed in wine judging:

Insipid

Bland

Balanced

Tart

Harsh

SWEETNESS

Sweetness can mask total acidity on the palate. A beginning wine enthusiast should devote some time to studying the interaction of these two gustatory influences. A suggestion is to pour three glasses of the same wine. In one dissolve a pinch of ascorbic acid, and in another dissolve a pinch of sugar. Compare all three to ascertain whether or not differences can be detected. If not, dissolve another pinch and try again. Continue until the additions are readily obvious on the palate. In a fourth glass blend together equal parts of the acid- and sugar-treated wines. Compare the resulting blend with both the high-acid wine and the high-sugar wine. This exercise shows how acidity and sweetness serve to neutralize each other on the palate and illustrates the term *sugar-acid balance*. The following is a typical range of sweetness expressed in wine judging:

Bone dry

Dry

Semidry

Sweet

Cloying

Glucose, or corn sugar, is the least sweet of the common sugars. Sucrose, which is cane sugar, is a bit sweeter on the palate, but fructose, or natural fruit sugar, produces the greatest gustatory sensation of sweetness.

Glucuronic acid is a sweetening compound found in wines that have been made from overripened grapes infected with the "noble mold," *Botrytis cinerea*. The background and description of this phenomenon are given in the discussion of Sauternes in Chapter 6.

BITTERNESS

Bitterness in wines is usually attributed to phenolic compounds extracted mostly from grape seeds. A good example of this gustatory sensation can be experienced by biting into a few grape seeds and chewing them for a minute or so before spitting them out.

A related gustatory characteristic is astringency, also resulting from phenolic compounds, but extracted principally from grape skins and stems. Wine judges often use the term *tannin* in relating to puckery astringency—a rather leathery, aspirinlike sensation on the palate.

Tannins are a special group of phenols that serve to slow the wine-aging process by inhibiting oxidation potential. Wine aging is, thus, wine oxidation. Vintners desiring long-lived red wines purposely conduct fermentations with extended periods of contact with grape skins in order to extract greater amounts of tannin. As would be expected, these young red wines have very astringent, unpleasant tannins. Over years of aging, however, the tannins eventually give way to the inevitable oxidation-aging process and develop a soft tealike flavor. During that time, all of the other flavor constituents in the wine also mature into what has, it is hoped, made the wait worthwhile.

The following is a typical range of bitterness expressed in wine judging:

Smooth

Astringent

Coarse

Tannic

Harsh

SALTINESS

Other than in some cooking wines, there is no salt in wine. Recall from earlier discussion that unsalted crackers are recommended for palate neutralizers during wine judging. The reason is that salt is a flavor intensifier. Whereas sweetness can mask flavor, saltiness can enhance it. Salt is often overused in ordinary restaurants to make deficient food flavors more expressive.

TACTILE SENSATIONS

The tactile phase of gustatory examination has to do with the manner in which a wine embraces the palate, more often referred to as "mouth-feel" by food scientists. A wine judge considers wine *body* in regard to whether it feels light and thin or full and heavy. Heavy-bodiedness results from dissolved solids in the wine, such as sugars, color pigments, and glycerol. Intrinsically, sweet wines have more body than drys, but it is the relative degree of body for each individual wine type that is the judgment criterion. A little glycerine mixed into a light, dry white wine can create the effect of heavier body.

Higher concentrations of ethyl alcohol in wine can contribute to a slight burning sensation in the nose and on the palate. Mix enough unflavored vodka with water to make a solution of about 13 percent alcohol, a common level in table wines. If the vodka is 80 proof, it is about 40 percent alcohol by volume. Mixing two parts of water with one part of vodka results in a little more than 13 percent alcohol by volume.

Smell and taste a glass of plain water and then the ethyl alcohol solution, both at room temperature. The ethanol mixture should have no flavor, but there should be a gustatory sensation—perhaps a slight burning in the nostrils and on the tongue. Then chill both the water and the ethanol solution to refrigerator temperature and repeat the evaluation. The refrigeration should significantly mute the gustatory effect of the alcohol—a term called "closed", or decreased volatility. Then heat both solutions to a lukewarm temperature and try the experiment again. The heated alcohol solution should produce a profound burning effect because of the irritation in nasal passages due to increased volatility—a term called "hot" or "strong" by wine judges.

AFTERTASTE

Aftertaste relates to how long both the olfactory and gustatory effects remain on the palate after the wine has been spit out. The common judgment terminology for aftertaste is simply "short," "lingering," and "long." As a rule of thumb, lengthy aftertaste is a virtue. Some very high-quality wines are, however, also delicate and shy, precluding any measure of lengthy aftertaste.

Proceed with judging the gustatory mode in precisely the same manner as used in tasting in the olfactory mode. After a few seconds' rest take a small bite of cheese and unsalted cracker. Rinse out the mouth with water and take a sip of wine. Roll it around the mouth to obtain the full effects of acidity, sweetness, and bitterness. Spit out the wine and record all impressions. While recording, make a judgment as to the length of the aftertaste.

Remember that this entire discussion has to do with wine judging, and not with wine drinking. When wine is swallowed there is an additional set of olfactory and gustatory impressions made in the back of the mouth and in the pharyngeal passage of the throat. For obvious reasons, wine judges cannot swallow every wine presented to them in a whole day of wine competition.

JUDGMENT OF OVERALL IMPRESSION

As the term indicates, judges use overall impression to rate the combined visual, olfactory, and gustatory impressions of each wine.

More often than not, judgment of overall impression is relegated to a rather "fudge-factor" role. A given wine might possibly score only moderately when scrutinized mode by mode, whereas all the modes may fit together very nicely. In this case a judge would be generous in scoring overall impression; the opposite holds true, as well.

❖ SCORING

CARDINAL SCALES

There are many cardinal (numerical) scales used in evaluating wines, several of which are particularly popular among professional wine people.

The simplest of cardinal scales includes various symbols, such as stars, which are awarded to wines in some consumer wine guides and magazines. This, of course, provides such a narrow sense of value that it may not mean much. For example, a two-star wine may be construed as only half as good as a four-star wine. On most scales of this type a two-star wine is very good, and a four-star wine is particularly outstanding. Even more confusing is that the two-star wine may be a far better price value. Another common problem with such scales lies in interpreting absolute values, such as the difference between no star and one star. Does no star mean the wine is worthless, or is not recommended, or is just OK?

Probably the most widely used cardinal scale is the 20-point scale devised by the University of California at Davis. Here is how it was originally structured:

DAVIS 20-POINT CARDINAL SCALE

CRITERIA	MAXIMUM POINTS
Clarity	2
Color	2
Aroma	4
Bouquet	2
General Flavor	2
Total Acidity	2
Tannin	2
Body	1
Sugar	1
Overall Impression	2
TOTAL	20

Note how the visual, olfactory, gustatory, and overall impression modes are structured. Listed between the olfactory and gustatory modes is "General Flavor," often a source of confusion for beginners, and particularly so in that it is valued at a meager two points maximum. If one can accept the notion that flavor can be smelled in the nose and tasted in the mouth, the concept can be grasped. If we can further accept the notion that the nose is much more sensitive to flavor than the mouth, then the four points for aroma and two points for general flavor make good sense. The rest of the components in the scale are easily understood.

Wines scoring less than 10 total points have serious faults and are not considered worthy of any distinction whatsoever.

Scores of 13 to 14 points signal obvious but not serious faults; wines in this range may be considered bronze medal winners.

Judges agreeing across the board in the 15 to 16 points range are generally responding to wines that reveal no specific flaws, but rather some deficiency in expression of color and/or flavor intensity. These are silver medal winners.

Gold medals go to wines expressing distinctive character and virtually faultless composition, those scoring 17 points or more.

The 20-point scale, although widely accepted, is not always used consistently. Some judges rearrange point values to suit their personal preferences. For example, they will reduce the "clarity" category to one point and upgrade "color" to three points—obviously placing much more importance on the hue and intensity of color than whether the wine has brilliant clarity.

A very common arrangement is as follows:

MODIFIED 20-POINT CARDINAL SCALE

CRITERIA	MAXIMUM POINTS
Visual	3
Nose	6
Taste	6
Aftertaste	3
Overall Impression	2

This modification allows for a more realistic integration of olfactory and gustatory sensory perception taking place simultaneously.

Every version of the 20-point scale is simple to use and adequate but, like all scales, has its shortcomings. One major fault is the failure to provide a "trueness-to-type" criterion. For example, a wine may be judged nearly faultless as a Chardonnay, but the label discloses it is really a Sauvignon Blanc. Thus, it is not true to its type or variety. Another flaw concerns the lack of a price/value measurement. Consider a $10 California Pinot Noir which scores 17 points and a $90 Burgundy (also a Pinot Noir) that also scores 17 points. The 20-point scale offers little indication of the far greater value of the $10 wine.

Consequently, there are also an increasing number of 100-point scales, typically used by wine writers. The 100-point scale is, of course, familiar to everyone. As mentioned earlier, this results in finite scores such as "Chardonnay of 88 points," or "Château Mysterie 1993 awarded 91 points." Thus one may perceive wines as *A* s, *B* s, *C* s, *D* s, and *F* s, graded like assignments in school. Or others may consider such wine scores on a percentile—"this wine is 91 percent

WINE EVALUATION CHART

NAME: _____

PLACE: _____

DATE: _____

WINE	PRICE	APPEARANCE 3 MAX	AROMA/ BOUQUET 6 MAX	TASTE 6 MAX	AFTERTASTE 3 MAX	OVERALL 2 MAX	TOTAL 20 MAX
1							
2							
3							
4							
5							
6							
7							
8							
9							

COMMENTS:

FIGURE 3.12   Modified 20-point cardinal scale format.

APPEARANCE (the visual mode—what one is seeing in a wine)

The color and clarity of a wine can be an indication of it's character—of potential qualities and flaws. Darker colors (both reds and whites) generally indicate heavier, more full-bodied wines. Rosé wines should be pink, perhaps just a bit of orange tint to older selections. All wines should be transparent—younger whites brilliant, while older selections may exhibit a very slight haziness, and very old reds often "throw" a noticeable sediment.

3 - Excellent	- brilliant with outstanding characteristic color
2 - Good	- clear with characteristic color
1 - Poor	- excessive haziness andlor uncharacteristic color
0 - Objectionable	- cloudiness and/or very poor color

AROMA AND BOUQUET (the olfactory mode—what one is smelling in a wine)

This second step in wine evaluation is directed towards aroma (fruit flavor) and bouquet (fruit flavor plus added odors from vinification). Swirl the wine inside the glass to expand the surface area from which flavor esters can evaporate. Take several large whiffs. Some wines may be herbaceous, while others are fruity—experience serving to distinguish which should be which. In every case the result should be balanced (not either neutral or overpowering) and, most importantly, pleasant. This mode is often called the "nose" in organoleptic testing.

6 - Extraordinary	- outstanding in character with exceptional balance in bouquet constituency
5 - Excellent	- characteristic and well-balanced
4 - Good	- distinguishable and adequately balanced
3 - Fair	- somewhat neutral and/or slightly unbalanced
2 - Poor	- undistinguishable and detectable "off" odors
1 - Unacceptable	- obvious "off" odors and unbalanced
0 - Objectionable	- offensive odors and very unbalanced

TASTE (the gustation mode—what one is tasting in a wine)

The human tongue can detect variances in acidity, bitterness, and sweetness, levels in wine—typical values for each wine type are learned with experience. Other portions of the mouth are anatomically connected to the olfactory lobe and are, therefore, sensitive to specific flavors and essences associated with the "nose" of each wine—again judged authoritatively through continued practice. Take a small sip and "wash" it around the mouth so that all surfaces are given a chance to experience the wine—"whistling" in some air to activate taste bud activity. Generally, after ten to fifteen seconds of examination, the wine is spit out.

6 - Extraordinary	- outstanding in character with exceptional balance of acidity and sweetness
5 - Excellent	- characteristic and well-balanced
4 - Good	- distinguishable and adequately balanced
3 - Fair	- somewhat neutral and/or slightly unbalanced
2 - Poor	- undistinguishable and detectable "off" flavors and/or unbalanced
1 - Unacceptable	- obvious "off" flavors and unbalanced
0 - Objectionable	- offensive flavors and very unbalanced

AFTERTASTE (the taste and flavor values that linger following completion of the gustatory mode)

Take a second, perhaps smaller, sip of the wine and swallow—endeavoring to judge how long the taste and flavor constituents remain detectable in the mouth. Lighter wines may linger only momentarily, while heavier wines can last for perhaps a dozen seconds or more.

3 - Excellent	- outstandingly pleasant aftertaste, lasting beyond normal duration of time
2 - Good	- pleasant aftertaste, lasting a normal duration of time
1 - Poor	- little or no distinguishable aftertaste
0 - Objectionable	- unpleasant aftertaste

OVERALL IMPRESSION (the trueness of type and price/value judgement one determines in a wine)

The total quality level achieved by a wine in comparison to other wines of the same variety or type, and in regard to the monetary price, is addressed in this mode. This not a "fudge factor" used indiscriminately to give or take points in response to subjective notions.

2 - Excellent	- outstanding example of the variety or type and/or and exceptional value for the money
1 - Good	- representative of the variety or type and/or an acceptable value for the money
0 - Poor	- uncharacteristic of the variety or type and/or an unacceptable value for the money

SCORES

18 - 20	- truly great wines, unusually superior attributes orchestrated in a faultless character
15 - 17	- excellent wines, perhaps faulted only by a shyness of one or another attributes
12 - 14	- good wines, with perhaps only one or two detectable faults
9 - 11	- poor wines, with obvious faults
0 - 8	- objectionable wines, having many faults

FIGURE 3.13   Modified 20-point scale rationale (reverse side).

good"—or hold some similar notion. Although this rating makes for good prose, and very good marketing ploys for the fortunate vintners who receive high marks, it nevertheless approaches the mystical. No judge has a palate so finely tuned as to repeat such definitive scoring consistently. Following is an example of a common 100-point scale:

100-POINT CARDINAL SCALE

CRITERIA		MAXIMUM POINTS
Color		
	Hue	5
	Intensity	5
Clarity		
	Suspension	5
	Precipitate	5
Nose		
	Aroma	10
	Bouquet	10
Palate		
	Flavor	10
	Acidity	5
	Sweetness	5
	Body	5
	Length (aftertaste)	5
Overall Impression		
	Balance	10
	Trueness to Type	10
	Price-Value Relationship	10
TOTAL		100

Note that a new consideration, "precipitate," enters the scale. In this case, the entire bottle would need to be available for evaluation, as sediments could easily escape detection in individual glasses. As compared with the 20-point scales, the 100-point scale increases the value placed on overall impression to the same as that given to the olfactory mode.

HEDONIC SCALES

In circles where wine evaluation includes people who are unfamiliar with wine, it is common to find simple scales relating only to the relative level of pleasure participants may experience during the tasting. Hedonic scales can be custom designed to fit any wine tasting occasion.

❖ THE WINE-JUDGING SCENARIO

Realistically, one can never expect to find absolutely perfect conditions in which to judge wine. Even so, such concerns are subjective, as judges view the ideals of wine judgings differently. Further, conditions are dynamic, changing from morning to afternoon, impressions fading with fatigue and differing before and

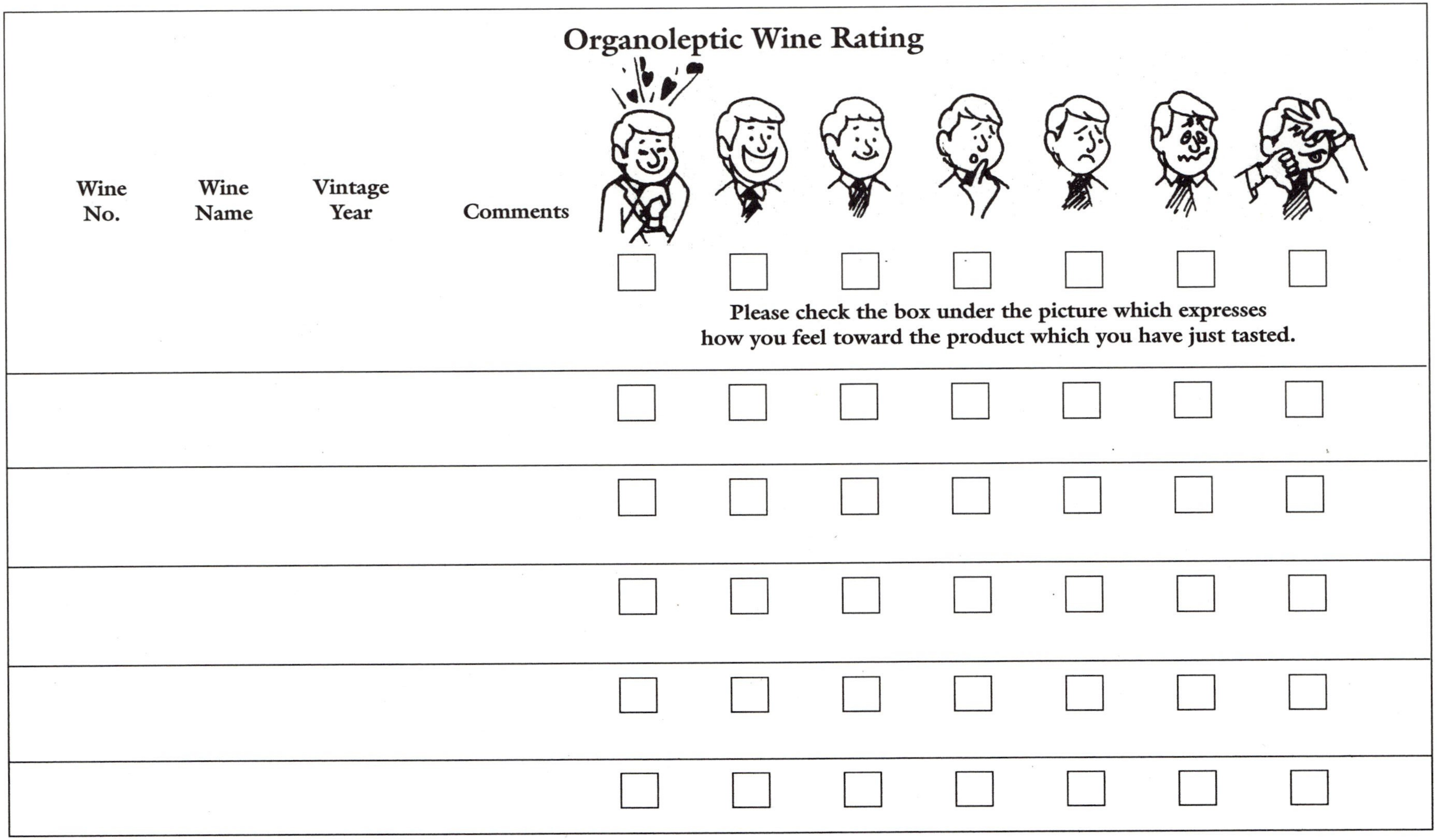

Organoleptic Wine Rating

Wine No.	Wine Name	Vintage Year	Comments							
			☐	☐	☐	☐	☐	☐	☐	
			☐	☐	☐	☐	☐	☐	☐	
			☐	☐	☐	☐	☐	☐	☐	
			☐	☐	☐	☐	☐	☐	☐	
			☐	☐	☐	☐	☐	☐	☐	

Please check the box under the picture which expresses how you feel toward the product which you have just tasted.

FIGURE 3.14 An hedonic scale.

after meals, and so on. Nevertheless, there is a checklist from which a good wine-judging architect designs a competition; its components are presented in the following paragraphs.

ENVIRONMENT

The judging room should be located where there is minimal noise—away from street traffic and busy hallways. People setting up and removing flights (groups) of wineglasses should strive to maintain soft communication only as necessary. Wine judging should take place in an odor-free environment well away from kitchens, laboratories, lavatories, and the like. The temperature should be on the cool side—66° to 70° F, which compensates for the added layer of the traditional stark-white lab jacket worn by a judge. Light should be a constant incandescent source. Fluorescent illumination and other types of light can interfere with the evaluation of wine color.

JUDGING AREA

The judging area should be sufficiently large that judges have several feet of free space between each other. A solid white Formica-type countertop or plain white tablecloth is preferred so that wine colors are not distorted.

JUDGING AMENITIES

Each judge should be outfitted with a lab jacket or apron, bottled water, unsalted crackers, fresh sourdough bread, small chunks of Monterey Jack or Muenster cheese, a spit bucket, large cloth napkins, and, of course, plenty of score sheets and pencils.

WINEGLASSES

All wineglasses should be identical in size and shape so that wines in the same class can be closely scrutinized for color and clarity. Wineglasses should be free of logos and other adornments and without any tint or color. Ideal is the 8-ounce tulip shape, hot-water cleaned (without detergent) just before using.

WINE SAMPLES

There should be at least four bottles of each wine entered into the judging, all brought to cool room temperature and organized according to type, origin, color, sweetness, and so on, as may be desired.

GROUND RULES

A thorough understanding of the guidelines *before* judging is much better than trying to change the rules midway into the contest. Prior to the judging, work out seating arrangements, caution against gestures and utterances that may bias fellow judges' opinions before scores are disclosed, set time limits for evaluations, and answer any questions about the guidelines.

PROCEDURE

Wines to be judged together should be opened and poured at the same time. If there are a large number of samples, they should be divided into flights of six to eight at a time. Each glass should be clearly marked on its stem or base with a code number/letter so that no confusion arises about the identity of that entry when scores are posted. Glasses should be consistently filled to about one-third capacity so that there is minimal visual variance between entries.

FIGURE 3.15 Setting up behind the scenes at a large wine competition. *(Courtesy of Indiana State Fair Wine Competition; photo by Dave King, Purdue University.)*

❖ WINE COMPETITIONS

A person new to the world of wine will soon hear about wines winning all sorts of accolades—a gold medal here, a silver there, a sweepstakes somewhere else, and so on. The major point to be made about wine competitions, and particularly the most prestigious ones, is that they are refereed evaluations made by panels of judges—not the single opinion of a wine expert. Wine experts always have their individual favorite varietals and their preferred styles, which translates, to one degree or another, to personal bias. A well-organized wine competition with panels consisting of noted wine writers, wine educators, wine retailers, restaurateurs, and those in other disciplines with wine expertise, results in a forum where personal bias is minimized.

Wine competitions are usually organized by wine categories, such as Chardonnay, Sauvignon Blanc, Gewürztraminer, Pinot Noir, Merlot, Cabernet Sauvignon, and every other popular varietal. The larger and more comprehensive competitions may have more than 2,000 wines entered in 50 or more different categories.

These categories may be further segmented as follows:

Chardonnay 1993 and younger	$15 and higher per bottle retail
Chardonnay 1992 and older	$15 and higher per bottle retail
Chardonnay 1993 and younger	$14 and lower per bottle retail
Chardonnay 1992 and older	$14 and lower per bottle retail

Conversely, some obscure varietals may be categorized together as "Miscellaneous White Vinifera," and "Miscellaneous Red Vinifera," and so forth.

Competitions may be structured with any number of panels, each comprising three to five judges. The various panels are assigned different categories and segments. The four segments of Chardonnay, listed in the preceding example, would probably be assigned to four different panels. This arrangement permits

FIGURE 3.16 Judging at a major national wine competition. *(Courtesy of Indiana State Fair Wine Competition; photo by Dave King, Purdue University.)*

each panel to judge an array of different categories, thus reducing the propensity for palate fatigue and monotony.

Each panel is served flights of six to ten glasses coded with a number/letter system known only to the "back room" or "pit crew" staff. Each flight contains wine of the same category, and judges take 15 to 30 minutes to make their evaluation. A panel coordinator, or a senior "anchor judge," then takes a poll of the judges to ascertain whether each of the wines will be eliminated because of obvious flaws or retained for a second evaluation in the "medal round." The judges are then given a few minutes to rinse the palate with water, plus perhaps a bite of bland cheese and unsalted cracker. With the judges' palates revived, another flight of wine is presented. The better competitions do not allow judges to taste more than 25 samples per hour or for more than six hours a day.

As a rule, retained wines are marshalled together for the following day, when the fresh palates can determine which win the gold, silver, and bronze. Each of these flights takes a bit longer, as one or another of the panelists may encourage fellow judges to see their points of view. Generally, the majority rules, but deadlocks often occur so that an "acclaim" must be made. Say that one judge votes gold, another two silver, and another two bronze. The acclaim by the panel coordinator in this instance would probably be an award of a silver medal.

Most wine competitions require panels to acclaim one single wine a "Best of Class." The entire throng of judges may then be assembled at the end of the competition to vote on an overall "Sweepstakes Winner." Sometimes there is a sweepstakes vote for whites and another for reds.

The entire competition may take several days. The judges, often from various states and countries, are treated like visiting royalty with gourmet dinners, receptions, media interviews, and other activities. The validity of the judges' findings is important, as consumers can be far more confident of a refereed medal symbolizing wine value than any individual critique.

Wine competitions are not without controversy. There are all manner of complaints, some straightforward and others contrived, from both vintners and judges, about how various and sundry details of each competition is administered. There are also varying opinions as to the merit of wine competitions. One school of thought holds that although gold medals bring great glory to winning entries, silver and bronze medals may be deleterious, implying flaws of one sort or another. Another point of view is that it is better to win a silver or a bronze than to receive no recognition at all. Like wine judging itself, wine competitions are totally subjective.

❖ WINE NUTRITION

As discussed in Chapter 2, it is likely that the human race linked wine with food long before recorded history. But what about wine as a food in itself?

The most important food value in wine is carbohydrates from ethyl alcohol and sugars. Wine is a better therapeutic agent than a food source. A large body of research is building, relating to the growing number of benefits provided by wine consumption by people who are physically and psychologically able to enjoy it.

ALCOHOL

Ethyl alcohol is a substance found in every human body. The enzymatic breakdown of starches and sugars results in the production of about one ounce of ethanol in the body every day. Although individuals may be total abstainers from drinking alcohol, there is no one who is without at least some ethanol in his or her body.

There is plenty of evidence that wine alcohol complements other carbohydrates in providing the energy required for every vital metabolic process in the human body. Excessive wine consumption, particularly with insufficient levels of other carbohydrate types, creates adverse nutritive effects. Most studies indicate that about 10 percent of a person's daily carbohydrate allowance could safely be consumed in the form of wine alcohol.

The alcohol in dry white table wine contains approximately 100 calories per 4-ounce serving—about 110 calories for dry reds. Although this low level can easily fit into most diets, it is argued that wine alcohol contains "empty calories," calories provided by constituents devoid of nutritious components such as minerals and vitamins. On the other hand, research shows that wine alcohol enhances the absorption of other nutrients from food, particularly calcium, iron, magnesium, phosphorus, and zinc.

TABLE 3.1	
SUGGESTED LIMITS OF ALLOWABLE DAILY WINE CONSUMPTION	
Weight of Individual (lbs.)	Ounces of 12% Alcohol Table Wine
110	13
132	15
154	18
176	20
198	23
220	25

Adapted from *Johns Hopkins Medical Journal* (February 1981), p.62.

In small quantities wine can be a relaxant or a tranquilizer. In large quantities wine alcohol becomes a depressant. Wine alcohol dilates capillaries, helping oxygen in the bloodstream to reach body extremities. Alcohol is known to increase gastric secretions such as to stimulate appetite and aid in the digestion process.

The first digestive action of alcohol is in the stomach, where the enzyme alcohol dehydrogenase decomposes a significant portion of ingested foods and beverages. The remainder of the alcohol enters the bloodstream through the small intestine and travels to the liver, where further breakdown occurs. Women produce only about half the alcohol dehydrogenase in the stomach as compared with men, and, thus, pound-for-pound in weight, should expect to digest only about half as much alcohol in the same period of time. The consumption of food with wine is particularly important in retaining the blood alcohol levels permitted by drivers returning home from a lunch or dinner out.

More than 90 percent of alcohol in the bloodstream is metabolized by the liver, the remainder eliminated by exhaling and through kidney function. The human body uses the energy generated from this metabolism; the excess ethanol circulates in the bloodstream and, when circulated through the brain, causes an intoxication effect until the liver can catch up. Wine alcohol cannot lodge in organs and other human tissues as do harmful drugs. The overall physiological effects of wine alcohol depend more on the amount absorbed from the gastrointestinal tract into the bloodstream than the total volume of wine consumed.

Thus, the effect of alcohol on the body varies with the weight and sex of the individual, the amount of food in the stomach, the degree to which one is accustomed to ingesting alcohol, and the type of beverage in which the alcohol is consumed. The rise in blood alcohol per ounce consumed is much smaller with wine than with spirits. Wine is more apt to be diluted by the simultaneous consumption of food. Wine alcohol taken on an empty stomach reaches the bloodstream in 15 to 20 minutes, but on a full stomach it may take more than 60 minutes.

To calculate a BAC beyond one hour, a factor of .015 can be employed in relation to body weight, number of four-ounce glasses of wine, and time. For example, a 160-pound person having five glasses of wine over a two-hour period would calculate an initial BAC of .117 and then subtract (.015 × 2), or .03, to arrive at an adjusted BAC of .087. One is cautioned, however, that this chart is composed of averages calculated from studied data. The only factor that can reduce BAC is time. The liver metabolizes alcohol at a rate of approximately

TABLE 3.2

TABLE OF APPROXIMATE BLOOD ALCOHOL CONCENTRATIONS (BAC)

| Body Weight (lbs.) | *Number of Four-Ounce Glasses of Wine in One Hour* | | | | | |
	1	2	3	4	5	6
100	.040	.075	.115	.150	.190	.225
120	.035	.065	.100	.125	.155	.190
140	.030	.055	.080	.105	.135	.160
160	.025	.050	.070	.095	.115	.140
180	.020	.040	.065	.085	.105	.125
200	.020	.040	.055	.075	.095	.115
220	.015	.035	.050	.070	.085	.100
240	.015	.030	.050	.065	.080	.095

Adapted from the Rutgers Blood Alcohol Content Table.

one 4-ounce glass of wine per hour. Coffee, cold showers, or exercise will not accelerate the process.

Consider these BAC levels:

BAC Level	Human Physiology
.050	Impaired reaction time
.100	Marked loss of motor control
.200	Mental and physical instability
.400	Subject may become comatose
.500	Risk of death

Most states use a BAC limit of .100 to establish legal intoxication. There are BAC limits of .080 in some locales. In the early 1990s a "zero tolerance" BAC was proposed in California. Violation would, of course, be extremely difficult to prosecute as the human body produces minute quantities of natural alcohol without having consumed any whatsoever. In addition, small amounts of alcohol are consumed with some fruit juices and medicines.

A food balance is prescribed by virtually all registered dieticians. Excessive consumption of any carbohydrate, fat, or protein can create metabolic problems. Diets out of balance with high fat content are well documented as resulting in heart and vascular problems. Diets heavy in protein can cause ammonia toxicity and difficulties in the metabolism of other foods. Obviously, a diet high in whole milk and cream, containing substantial amounts of fat and protein, imposes a double risk—a problem addressed by the dairy industry years ago when low-fat milk, half-and-half, and light cheese products were introduced.

One of the greatest dangers of high-dose wine alcohol consumption is the risk for alcoholic fatty liver, cirrhosis, and other liver diseases. Many of the neurological disorders and deficiencies attributed to the abuse of alcohol can also be seen in patients with nutritional imbalances. Except for acute intoxication and alcoholic seizures, most cases are actually due to nutritional deficiencies rather than any direct toxic effect of wine or its alcohol. Alcohol abusers usually have diets low in calories other than those provided by alcohol and deficient in vitamins and minerals.

VITAMINS AND MINERALS

Studies indicate that the vitamins and minerals in wine reflect both the soil in which the grapes were grown and the winemaking techniques used.

B Vitamins
A 4-ounce glass of red table wine provides about 50 percent of the minimum daily requiement of pyridoxine and about 10 percent of riboflavin. Only a trace of thiamine is found in wines.

P Vitamins
Current literature does not precisely quantify the minimum daily requirement of P vitamins in the human diet or the amount that wine may contribute. Wine, to the extent it contains P vitamins, is thought to involve strengthening of blood capillaries. Other medical references characterize this group of vitamins as having a "tonic effect."

Iron
Wine is known to be an effective iron supplement. Dry white table wines contain about 5 milligrams per liter and reds contain 6 milligrams per liter. A 4-

ounce glass of dry red wine provides about 5 percent of the recommended daily iron requirement. Approximately 80 percent of the iron in wine is present in the ferrous form, which is readily available for metabolism in the human body.

POTASSIUM

Most wines contain 600 to 1,000 milligrams of potassium per liter. No recommended daily allowance for this mineral has been established, but a 4-ounce glass of wine provides a significant share of what many registered dieticians recognize as sufficient daily potassium intake.

SODIUM

The sodium content of wine may be a concern to people on low-salt diets. The average concentrations of sodium in wine types are as follows:

WINE TYPE	MILLIGRAMS PER LITER
Table wines	.8
Sparkling wines	.7
Dessert wines	1.0

Some wines, particularly those made by larger vintners, are treated with ion-exchange processing, whereby unstable potassium ions are replaced with soluble sodium ions. The resulting wines are much higher in sodium content. If at risk, one should inquire of vintners before consuming their wines.

CALCIUM

Most wines have about 60 to 70 milligrams of calcium per liter. A 4-ounce glass of dry table wine provides less than 1 percent of the recommended daily calcium requirement.

SULFITES

Sulfur, in the yellow rhombic form, was first used as a preservative in wines several centuries ago. Early in this century it was found that the sulfur dioxide form, in a smaller dosage, was more effective. The use of sulfites is to inhibit oxidation and to discourage bacteria and yeast growth in order to maintain precious colors and flavors. Although ATF regulations permit total sulfur dioxide usage up to 350 milligrams per liter, modern alternatives such as sterile filtration permit most vintners to use less than one third that amount, and many even far less than that. Wine yeasts may naturally produce up to 20 milligrams per liter of sulfites during fermentation.

The well-known antialcohol group, Center for Science in the Public Interest (CSPI), in 1990 published an article entitled "Wine Preservatives Causing Unpleasant Allergic Reactions." The implications of this release were that sulfites are toxic and that vintners are using increasing amounts of sulfites in winemaking.

The truth of this issue is that some people, several percent of the population, mostly asthmatics, are allergic to sulfites—which *are* found in wines, but decreasingly. What CSPI failed to mention is that dairy products, dried fruits and fruit concentrates, seafoods, bakery products, processed potatoes, vegetables, and many other foods, as well as wines, contain a few milligrams of sulfites per liter. Obviously, the advice of a physician is recommended for anyone suspecting an allergy or any other reaction to sulfites, whether from wine or any other food. The ATF now requires that all wines containing more than 10 milligrams of sulfites per liter must include the statement "CONTAINS SULFITES" on the label.

LEAD

In 1991 the U.S. Food and Drug Administration (FDA) suddenly became concerned with the levels of lead in wine. A large-scale analysis of California wines discovered lead levels averaging 21 parts per billion (ppb). Similar analyses indicated that typical spaghetti with meat sauce contained an average of 60 ppb of lead, and spinach 39 ppb. Even oranges, whole wheat bread, and dill pickles, among hundreds of others foods, have higher lead contents than wine does.

However, research conducted by the California Department of Health Services does indicate that long-term storage of wines, particularly higher-alcohol dessert wines such as Ports and Sherries, can leach lead out of crystal decanters. Calculations showed that lead content in dessert wines stored 24 hours in crystal decanters would increase up to 60 ppb, and the same wines stored 10 days would increase up to 106 ppb.

Fine wines have traditionally been sealed with decorative tin-lead alloy capsules covering the top of the bottle over the cork. In addition to the issues addressed by the FDA investigation, there was also considerable concern about the amount of lead in wines poured over a freshly cut capsule. Ironically, less-expensive wines sealed with aluminum and plastic capsules were not at risk. Although results of the studies of lead from capsules were varied and thus inconclusive, the ATF decreed that lead and lead alloy capsules were to be discontinued by January 1, 1992.

THE MEDITERRANEAN DIET

In January 1993 more than 300 health and nutrition experts from around the world gathered in Boston for the 1993 International Conference on the Diets of the Mediterranean. This assembly was jointly sponsored by the Harvard University School of Public Health and the Oldways Preservation & Exchange Trust, a nutritional education group based in Boston. The World Health Organization (WHO) joined with Harvard and Oldways at the 1994 meeting of the conference held in San Francisco.

Out of these gatherings came the first, and now revised, "Mediterranean Diet" concept. This concept is based on the dietary traditions of Crete, Greece, Italy, Lebanon, Morocco, Portugal, Spain, Tunisia, Turkey, southern France, and other areas and is closely associated with the traditional areas of olive cultivation.

The Mediterranean Diet is conceptualized as a pyramid starting with essential daily foods, including whole-grain breads and pasta, along with fruits, vegetables, beans, legumes and nuts, certain dairy products, and olive oil. Fish, poultry, eggs, and sweets are prescribed "a few times per week," and lean red meat "a few times per month (or somewhat more often in very small amounts)."

There are three keys to the Mediterranean Diet. First is its dependence on regular physical activity; second is its proposal for consuming food with wine in moderation; and third is its geographical association with olive growing. The rationale is as follows:

Olive oil, high in monounsaturated fat and rich in antioxidants, is the region's principal fat. In the optimal, traditional Mediterranean diet, total fat can be as high as 35–40% of calories, if saturated fat is at or below 7–8% and polyunsaturated fat ranges from 3–8% with the balance coming from monounsaturated fat [in the form of olive oil]. Variations of this diet where total fat [again, principally olive oil] is at or below 30%—such as is found in the traditional diet of Southern Italy—may be equally optimal.

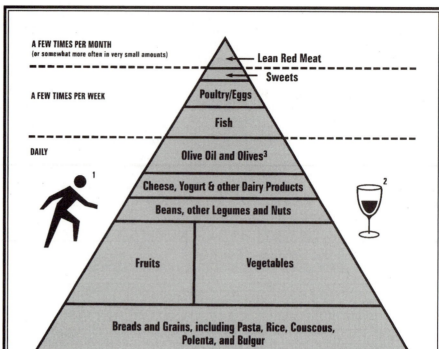

A FEW TIMES PER MONTH
(or somewhat more often in very small amounts)

← Lean Red Meat

← Sweets

A FEW TIMES PER WEEK

Poultry/Eggs

Fish

DAILY

Olive Oil and Olives[3]

Cheese, Yogurt & other Dairy Products

Beans, other Legumes and Nuts

Fruits   Vegetables

Breads and Grains, including Pasta, Rice, Couscous, Polenta, and Bulgur

Source: 1993 International Conference on the Diets of the Mediterranean

[1]Regular physical activity is vital to maintaining good health and optimal weight and was an important characteristic of the rural Mediterranean lifestyle in the 1960's.

[2]Following Mediterranean tradition, wine can be enjoyed in moderation primarily with meals (1–2 glasses/day, for women and men respectively). It should be considered optional and avoided whenever consumption would put the individuals or others at risk.

[3]Olive oil, high in monounsaturated fat and rich in antioxidants, is the region's principal fat. In the traditional diet of Crete (and much of Greece) in 1960, it appears that total fat was safely as high as 40% of calories, with saturated fat at 8%, polyunsaturated fat at 3% with the balance (29%) coming from monounsaturated fat (in the form of olive oil). Variations of this diet where total fat (again, principally olive oil) was at or below 30%—such as was found in the traditional diet of Southern Italy in the 1960's— appear to have been equally healthy. The question of whether a lower or higher fat Mediterranean-style diet is generally best suited for contemporary lifestyles—or what specific levels of total fat (principally monounsaturated) are optimal for which populations under which circumstances— deserves further investigation. If one adopts a Mediterranean-style diet, olive oil should replace—*and not be added to*—other fats and oils, especially saturated and hydrogenated fats.

FOR MORE INFORMATION

This pyramid was presented by Walter Willett, M.D., Dr. P.H., Professor and Chairman of the Department of Nutrition, Harvard School of Public Health, at the "1993 International Conference on the Diets of the Mediterranean," jointly organized by Harvard School of Public Health and Oldways Preservation & Exchange Trust. For more information and to receive a complete set of discussion notes for this Optimal Traditional Mediterranean Diet Pyramid, please contact Oldways Preservation & Exchange Trust at 45 Milk Street, Boston, MA 02109 Telephone: (617)426-7696. (revised February 16, 1993).

FIGURE 3.17 The Mediterranean Diet. *(Courtesy of Oldways Preservation & Exchange Trust, Harvard School of Public Health.)*

There are many sources of information relating to the pros and cons of wine in the human diet. The U.S. Department of Agriculture and the U.S. Department of Health and Human Services offer published dietary guidelines by which diets, including moderate amounts of alcohol, can be nutritiously well balanced. The American Dietetic Association and the American Heart Association have similar publications available relating to moderate wine consumption in a healthy diet.

◈ WINE THERAPEUTICS

Although all of the following material in this section is supported by scientific research, each person should consult with her or his physician before consuming wine for any therapeutic purpose.

WINE AND GERIATRICS

Galen, a second-century A.D. physician and writer in ancient Rome, has been credited with describing wine as "the nurse of old age."

Increasing age impairs human abilities to deal with day-to-day emotional stress and deterioration of physical well-being. A British study reported by the American Heart Association indicated that lifelong total abstainers from alcohol have double the risk for stroke as compared with moderate wine drinkers.

Frequent complaints of the elderly are lack of appetite, insomnia, and difficulties with the bowels and urinary tract. Wine alcohol improves the blood lipid profile, decreases thrombosis, and reduces the reaction to stress. Because ethanol cannot be synthesized to fat, it becomes a body energizer.

Wine cannot, of course, remedy all the changes that inevitably occur with aging. However, moderate wine consumption is increasingly prescribed by physicians as a simple "P vitamin" tonic to help make later years more pleasant. A small glass of wine taken at bedtime is considered preferable to barbituates and other sleeping medications. Wine is thought to have many more subtle benefits that have yet to be calculated through research and analysis.

Physicians and physiologists agree that moderate wine consumption frequently brings about a better outlook on life—a more robust, energetic feeling and a more congenial attitude among geriatric patients. Typically, wine encourages and enhances cooperation, conversation, and laughter. It is not uncommon to find nursing homes and hospital geriatric wards across America rationing out the daily small glass of wine before bedtime.

WINE AND CARDIOVASCULAR DISEASE

The alcohol in wine increases blood flow through the blood vessels, including arteries and veins, in organs such as the kidneys, liver, heart, and brain and in the skin. For this reason, wine has traditionally been prescribed in the treatment of certain disorders of blood circulation such as Raynaud's disease and Buerger's disease. Wine has also been used to reduce the anxiety component of hypertension, although care must be taken to prescribe wines that are low in sodium content.

THE FRENCH PARADOX

The blockbuster news concerning research on the beneficial effects of wine on the heart and circulatory system was made public on November 17, 1991, when the CBS *60 Minutes* television program presented a segment entitled "The French Paradox."

Reporter Morley Safer interviewed Dr. R. Curtis Ellison, a Boston University cardiologist who had closely studied the ability of the French, who have a low propensity for heart attack, to consume far greater quantities of fat and cholesterol than Americans, who have a high risk for heart disease.

Dr. Ellison theorizes that certain constituents in red wine, probably phenols such as resveratrol, break down LDL (low-density) "sticky" cholesterol attached to artery walls and blood platelets into HDL (high-density) cholesterol, which can then be carried by the blood to the liver for processing into waste. Reduced LDL cholesterol buildup diminishes the chance for arteriosclerosis, restriction of the blood circulatory system, and thus lessens the pressure needed for the heart to deliver the same amount of blood to body extremities.

Resveratrol is a compound produced by vines to ward off diseases in the vineyard. Ironically, grapes from vineyards of less prestige probably have more cholesterol content, because they typically have greater exposure to disease organisms.

Ellison explains: "Only in moderate wine amounts, on a regular basis, do you get these mechanisms, without getting an overshoot." An "overshoot" is an increased risk of heart disease, cancer, and other disease, from consuming too much wine.

In November 1995, CBS aired another *60 Minutes* program that updated "The French Paradox." A research project in Denmark was cited in which thousands of people who regularly drink beer, wine, and spirits, as well as abstainers from alcohol-containing beverages, were studied over many years to determine whether there was any correlation between mortality and levels of consumption. Significantly shorter life was observed among the abstainers and the heavy drinkers. Consumers of several glasses of wine daily were observed to achieve remarkably longer life. Dr. Ellison was interviewed again and disclosed a plethora of new evidence indicating that moderate, regular consumption of wine seems to be the most healthful choice.

The question arises as to whether the same amount of resveratrol consumed in wine can be ingested by eating red grapes or drinking red grape juice. Research findings completed thus far seem to indicate that most of the resveratrol is contained in the skins and seeds of grapes. Although grape skins are readily eaten, grape seeds are not. Apparently, red wine fermentation leaches out resveratrol, which juice processing cannot do.

ANTIOXIDANTS

The oxidation of LDL on blood platelets and arterial walls is thought to be the reaction that causes damage to arteries, leading to blood restriction, or blockage, which can result in a heart attack. Approximately 50 different antioxidants are known to exist in red wine. University of California at Davis research reported in the April 24, 1993, issue of *The Lancet* indicates that two of these antioxidants, quercetin and catechin, are more powerful than resveratrol and twice as effective in inhibiting oxidation of LDL cholesterol.

WINE AND DIABETES

Dry table wines with low sugar content can be an excellent and regular energy source for those on diabetic diets. Wine may also be substituted for fat in diabetic diets without producing ketosis, the accumulation of excessive ketones in the body.

According to an April 1995 bulletin published by the Wine Institute, research directed by Dr. Eric Rimm at Harvard University, in association with a similar study made in England, resulted in the conclusion that "moderate alcohol consumption among healthy people may be associated with increased insulin sensitivity and a reduced risk of diabetes."

The feeling of well-being that wine induces can help the diabetic person accept the need for a strict diet. Alcohol, with the possible exception of sugar, is the most easily digestible food substance. Unlike sugar, however, ethanol is readily metabolized without insulin. It should be noted that immediately following the intake of wine, blood sugar levels rise slightly. This brief hyperglycemic period is followed by a period of lower glucose level that may last in excess of four hours. Although marked ketosis has been noticed in some diabetic patients who drink alcoholic beverages, no such effect has occurred when the alcohol consumed is a dry table wine.

People on a diabetic diet who take oral medication for control of diabetes, such as Tolbutamide, sometimes experience flushing, profuse sweating, and a moderate drop in blood pressure after drinking wine on an empty stomach. If a person has or suspects diabetes, he or she should consult with a physician before making wine a regular part of the diet.

WINE AND EPILEPSY

In some epileptic patients alcohol has been shown to raise the potential for seizures and thus increase their susceptibility to them. There is no direct evidence that wine alcohol itself causes eptileptic seizures but, rather, that it may decrease the brain's seizure avoidance mechanism. An epileptic person may not be able to metabolize Dilantin, a drug commonly prescribed for seizure control, after drinking wine. It is important to note, however, that many more seizures occur after the abrupt withdrawal of high levels of wine alcohol than with mild-to-moderate consumption.

WINE AND GLAUCOMA

The metabolism of small amounts of alcohol can reduce the pressure of intraocular fluid so as to help relieve eye pain. It is essential, however, that wine taken to help relieve glaucoma be prescribed by a physician.

WINE AND LIVER DISEASE

Cirrhosis is a diffuse liver disease characterized by a significant loss of liver cells, the collapse of the supporting cellular network, and a distortion of the vascular system. Although cirrhosis is often considered a disease solely associated with heavy drinking, it also occurs among nondrinkers. In any case, liver disease sufferers should consume no wine whatsoever.

WINE AND DRUG INTERACTIONS

Most of the research undertaken regarding the interactions of wine and drugs has focused on the impact of alcohol on drug metabolism and its impact on the effects of those drugs. Comparatively little research, however, has been conducted specifically on wine. Three possible types of drug and wine interactions may occur:

1. The alcohol may have a direct impact on the drug, either increasing or inhibiting its action.
2. The metabolism of the alcohol may affect the metabolism of the drug.
3. Most important, the alcohol may alter the effects of the drug within the human body.

Alcohol is known to increase the effects of such drugs as sedatives, tranquilizers, and antihistamines. In many cases drug overdoses are due to the augmenting effects of alcohol on drugs.

Marijuana has been shown to delay the effects of alcohol for a short period of time; the effects of high blood alcohol may then occur suddenly.

Certain drugs, such as some of the oral drugs used for the treatment of diabetes, produce a reaction similar to that of Antabuse, a drug prescribed for recovering alcoholics to purposely make the effects of alcohol unpleasant. This reaction may include a flushing of the skin and face, an increased heart rate, nausea, and vomiting.

Research findings indicate that some of the components of wine may adversely affect certain blood pressure medications. Thus, if wine is consumed, the patient's blood pressure may become elevated in spite of continuation of the appropriate dose of medication.

WINE AND NEUROLOGICAL DISORDERS

The first effect of acute alcohol intoxication is the inhibition of higher brain functions, commencing with a feeling of relaxation, followed closely by loss of judgment and personality changes, varying from placidity to combativeness, and impaired coordination.

DELIRIUM TREMENS

Delerium tremens, a disease often referred to as the "D.T.s," is a serious complication of alcoholism seen most often with abrupt withdrawal from alcohol and the concurrently abrupt withdrawal of the sedative effects from alcohol. It produces marked neurological activity and irritability. The first symptoms of delir-ium tremens are usually restlessness, irritability, loss of appetite, elevated temperature, agitation, nightmares, hallucinations, and seizures. Respiration and heartbeat rates become rapid. Unless the patient is treated quickly and appropriately, death can occur.

KORSAKOFF'S PSYCHOSIS, OR WERNICKE'S ENCEPHALOPATHY

A syndrome often associated with chronic alcoholism, Korsakoff's psychosis, or Wernicke's encephalopathy, begins with difficulties of eye movement, difficulty in walking, and dementia. The onset can be sudden. The syndrome, once identified, is treated with thiamine (vitamin B_1). The visual and walking difficulties generally respond rather quickly, although the mental symptoms may not improve.

DEHYDRATION AND MALNUTRITION

Several changes within the structure of the brain have been described in people with nutritional deficiency and/or alcoholism. One is marked by symptons that include abnormalities of eye movement, facial weakness, difficulty with speech, and difficulty with swallowing. These are thought to be related to dehydration, which may accompany alcoholism and malnutrition.

MARCHIAFAVA-BIGNAMI'S DISEASE

Marchiafava-Bignami's disease was originally identified in Italian men who drank large quantities of red wine. However, there have been sporadic cases reported in other countries, in people who consumed other types of wines and other alcoholic beverages. More recent evidence indicates that this condition is a nutritional deficiency seen in alcoholics rather than a toxic effect of alcoholism. Symptoms include emotional disorders, intellectual deterioration, convulsive seizures, and varying degrees of tremor, rigidity, and paralysis, among other neurological disorders. Duration ranges from several weeks to months, and recovery is possible in varying degrees if abstinence from alcohol and adherence to good nutrition are established and maintained.

PERIPHERAL NEUROPATHY, OR NEURITIC BERIBERI

Most of the cases of peripheral neuropathy, or impaired peripheral nerve functioning (also called neuritic beriberi), seen in alcoholics are identical to those caused by nutritional deficiencies. This disease results from a deficiency of B-complex vitamins, particularly vitamin B_1.

CEREBELLAR DEGENERATION

Cerebellar degeneration, a form of brain degeneration generally caused by nutritional deficiencies, is seen in alcoholics as well as nonalcoholics who suffer from nutritional disorders. There is marked atrophy of certain brain centers, which may result in acute difficulty with walking and can be cured through early prognosis, prompt withdrawal of alcohol, and treatment with B-complex vitamins.

The chronic form of alcoholic cerebellar degeneration develops over a period of many weeks or months and may progress to a point at which the patient is confined to a wheelchair. There is less likelihood of recovery from severe cases.

MYOPATHY

Myopathy is a disease involving muscle changes during chronic alcoholism. It is still uncertain whether the chronic muscle deterioration and tenderness observed in alcoholics is due to the effects of malnutrition on the nerves, or whether there is a direct toxic effect of excessive alcohol on muscle tissue.

HEADACHE

Certain foods, principally those containing caffeine, seem to be correlated with headaches. Some cheeses, chocolates, and nuts are also reportedly linked to headache, as is red wine. One explanation of this may be that headache occurs in reaction to the phenolic compounds in red wine that are missing in whites. Another may be that headache is produced by the amino acid histidine, transformed into histamine, which can cause nasal and sinus irritation (the reason people treat themselves with antihistamines). Headache produced by wine is a very complex question that could involve many dietary, life-style, and environmental influences for each individual. Sufferers of headaches after drinking wine should consult their physicians before drinking again.

STROKE

A bulletin published by the Wine Institute cites a 1994 paper published in *Stroke,* the journal of the American Heart Association, which revealed that the risk of stroke for total abstainers of alcoholic beverages is more than twice that for moderate drinkers.

WINE AND CANCER

ETHYL CARBAMATE

The late 1980s scare publicity on the possibility of ethyl carbamate presence in wines and other alcoholic beverages was initiated by the Center for Science in the Public Interest (CSPI). This was yet another of several media vehicles used for its well-documented motives in support of neo-prohibitionist activities.

It is true that all wines, as well as all fermented foods, such as bread, cheese, sauerkraut, soy sauce, vinegar, and yogurt, to name only a few, contain some ethyl carbamate (urethane). The concentration is generally measured in parts per billion for table wines.

Canada, acting on information provided by the World Health Organization (WHO), set legal limits for ethyl carbamate in wines. Subsequently, the U.S. Food and Drug Administration and several major universities spent millions of dollars studying the extent to which ethyl carbamate may be responsible for causing cancer. Research was inconclusive as to the carcinogenicity of minute levels of ethyl carbamate. Although there is no ATF regulatory maximum set for ethyl carbamate in wines, the U.S. wine industry adopted new winemaking materials and methods to minimize this substance.

The American Council on Science and Health (ACSH) publicly criticized the CSPI for "needlessly frightening consumers about urethane." The ACSH related that a 4-ounce glass of wine has less ethyl carbamate toxicity potential than a strip of bacon. Further, an ACSH news bulletin stated that "there is no evidence of human—or any other illness—ever being caused by this substance."

BREAST CANCER

According to a 1995 study published in the *Journal of the National Cancer Institute,* there was no increased risk of breast cancer found among women who were moderate wine consumers. There was, however, a modest increase of risk correlated with similar consumption levels of other alcoholic beverages.

This report was preceded by a 1993 issue of *Cancer Causes and Controls,* a British publication, which concluded: "Even at moderate levels of alcohol intake, a 50 percent increase in risk of breast cancer was found."

A similar study sponsored in the same year by the U.S. National Institute of Health found no increased or decreased risk of breast cancer from moderate alcohol consumption. A 1989 study published by the National Cancer Institute in the *International Journal of Epidemiology* indicated no increased breast cancer risk with moderate drinking levels. A 1988 study conducted by the Permanente Medical Group in Oakland, California, found that the risk of breast cancer increased with more than three drinks of alcohol per day.

SKIN MELANOMA

The American Wine Alliance for Research and Education (AWARE) reports, "At this point, there is no evidence that wine drinking is associated with melanoma."

A study in China indicated that the consumption of allium vegetables, which contain quercetin and which include garlic and onions, may actually reduce the risk of stomach cancer. Quercetin is a phenolic compound also resulting from the fermentation of red grapes into wine. Although considerable research has been conducted relating to the properties of certain phenols in citrus juices, soy sauce, and tree barks as effective inhibitors of skin cancer, there has been no research conducted on wine phenols as such agents.

EXCESSIVE ALCOHOL CONSUMPTION

Excessive alcohol drinkers are subject to increased rates of oral, pharyngeal, esophageal, and stomach cancer, rates that soar among drinkers who are also smokers. One of the principal counterclaims to the French Paradox, discussed earlier, is that although the French may suffer less per-capita incidence of heart attack than Americans, it is compensated for by a higher incidence of gastrointestinal cancer among excessive wine drinkers.

WINE AND PREGNANCY

There is considerable controversy over the findings from several major research projects relating to the consumption of wine during pregnancy. However, there can be no question that alcohol in the blood of a pregnant woman is transmitted though the placenta to the fetus without biosynthesis.

At some level of exposure to alcohol each fetus is at risk of suffering fetal alcohol syndrome (FAS). This condition results in low birth weight, along with anomalies of physical and mental development. A fetus is particularly vulnerable early in the term when major body systems are being developed. Alcohol ingestion also increases the risk of miscarriage.

Although well-documented studies indicate low correlations of FAS with low wine consumption during pregnancy, and the genetic ability of pregnant women to be affected differently by the same amount of ingested alcohol, it is highly recommended that expectant mothers consume no alcohol during the entire term.

NURSING MOTHERS

Dr. Ruth Lawrence, author of the 1989 book *Breastfeeding: A Guide for the Medical Profession,* explains that

> *Therapeutically, alcohol has been recognized as an excellent adjunct to nursing, if used judiciously. A glass of wine, a mug of beer, or cocktail, especially in the early evening when some mothers may be under tension to feed the infant and family, will provide the relaxation necesssary to remit adequate letdown.*

La Leche League International, a breastfeeding educational association, recently published a guide entitled *The Womanly Art of Breastfeeding,* in which it is stated, "An anxious, overtired mother may find that an occasional glass of wine, beer, or other alcoholic drink helps her to relax."

Conversely, a 1989 study published in the *New England Journal of Medicine* revealed results showing that nursing babies whose mothers drank at least one drink of alcohol each day scored marginally lower on motor development tests than infants fed by mothers who had consumed lesser amounts of alcohol.

✛ WINE AND ALCOHOLISM

Wine in moderation continues to be an inexhaustible source of pleasure. The key word here is *moderation,* for wine or any form of alcohol in excess can be a serious danger to the drinker—and a terrible burden for the drinker's family and friends. Anyone who writes about the pleasures and benefits of alcoholic beverages has a responsibility to discuss the risks of alcohol dependency and alcoholism.

Modern medicine has advanced to recognize alcoholism as primarily a medical problem. Monumental funding has been given to research devoted to identifying the hereditary, cultural, and emotional factors associated with the disease. Out of this has come the knowledge that people who drink brandy, tequila, vodka, whiskey, and other beverages high in alcohol content are more prone to alcoholism than those who drink beer and wine. This accounts in part for the high level of alcoholism in countries such as Poland and Russia, where high-alcohol spirits dominate consumption statistics. In France, Greece, and Italy, the most popular alcoholic beverage is wine, and the risk of alcoholism is considerably lower.

Research has also demonstrated that the drinking patterns of low-risk and high-risk groups are marked by significant sociological and cultural influences. In the low-risk group there is an early, unemotional initiation to the drinking of alcoholic beverages, usually within a family group and with meals. Unfortunately, across most of America the initiation to alcoholic beverages usually occurs during adolescence, usually away from home, and the first experience often involves drinking to excess. There is a social stigma attached to excessive consumption of alcoholic beverages and drunkenness. In groups that are prone to alcoholism, high levels of alcohol are consumed, often before meals, for the purpose of becoming intoxicated—the resulting drunkenness being culturally accepted or even encouraged.

Alcoholism, or alcohol addition, is a complex problem, difficult to identify and even more difficult to cure. Genetic, biological, social, and psychological factors each contribute to the disease. It is known that alcoholism has some ties with heredity and that children of alcohol-addicted parents constitute a high-risk group that should be targeted for prevention efforts. It is also known that reinforcement of positive cultural and social drinking patterns can reduce the incidence of drinking problems.

Although annual per capita alcohol consumption across the U.S. is less than in Europe, Americans have more problems with alcohol abuse—a paradox that begs even more study. We should identify social and cultural norms in societies where alcoholism is rare and alcohol abuse is discouraged. Public programs designed to incorporate these elements should be given a chance to work.

There is a need to educate children to develop a positive attitude toward alcohol abuse as a disease—that it can be prevented with commonsense decision making. There is a further need to continue this education process as children become young adults, discouraging the use of alcoholic beverages for self-medication to alleviate stress, or physical distress, or to cure emotional problems.

Wine has traditionally been associated with pleasure. If consumed in moderation, as it should be, wine can be a joy to the human senses as well as a valuable therapeutic adjunct in the diet.

Unfortunately, there is still far more pressure on society and government to fund alcohol control than for research into an understanding of alcohol. In 1993 the National Institute of Alcohol Abuse and Alcoholism (NIAAA) reported funding approximately 700 alcohol research projects totaling more than $165 million. As may be expected, most of these projects involve alcohol abuse and control. Ironically, some of these studies have proven positive to moderate alcohol consumption.

❖ SUMMARY

The following indications and contraindications have been found to associate with wine consumed by normal, healthy, adult human beings. It is essential, however, that every individual consult with his or her physician regarding the effects of consuming wine.

MAJOR INDICATIONS

1. Wine can be used as a mild tranquilizing agent to counter emotional tension and anxiety, as long as low blood alcohol levels can be maintained over extended periods.
2. Wine may be a useful component of the normal diet, providing energy and aiding the digestive process.
3. Because alcohol is metabolized without insulin, dry wine may serve both as a useful source of energy and as a valuable psychological adjunct to the diabetic diet.
4. Dry wines have been used effectively to stimulate appetite in such eating disorders as anorexia nervosa.
5. Presumably because of its tranquilizing action, wine has helped obese patients maintain prescribed weight-reducing diets.
6. In cardiovascular diseases, wine has been found beneficial as a tranquilizing agent. It may also prove useful where there is a need to dilate blood vessels and improve dull or monotonous diets. Recent epidemiological studies, provocative even if not yet totally conclusive, suggest that wine in the diet may actually help protect against heart disease. Related evidence shows that certain phenols can break down low-density "sticky" cholesterol from arterial wall into high-density cholesterol delivered in the bloodstream to the liver for waste processing.

7. Naturally made wine is low in harmful sodium and high in beneficial potassium, which suits the dietary needs of many cardiac patients who are on low-sodium diets, taking diuretics and supplemental dietary potassium.

8. In the care of convalescent patients, and especially among geriatric populations, wine may be an ideal way to improve nutrition, relieve emotional tension, and supply mild sedation.

9. Wine used as a food with other foods at mealtimes may play a vital role in developing a cultural or sociological protective pattern against excessive drinking.

MAJOR CONTRAINDICATIONS

1. The most important contraindication to the use of wine is the inability of some patients to ingest alcohol in any form without contracting alcohol dependency.

2. Wine is usually not recommended in the presence of inflammation, irritation, or ulceration of the mouth, throat, esophagus, or stomach. Like all other alcoholic beverages, it is contraindicated in gastritis, any condition that causes excessive gastric secretions, gastric cancer, or bleeding in the upper digestive tract.

3. In healing duodenal ulcers, wine may be helpful for some patients but not for others.

4. All alcoholic beverages are clearly contraindicated in disease of the pancreas and should be used with caution in the presence of confirmed or suspected liver disease.

5. Use of alcoholic beverages is to be avoided in the presence of acute kidney infection.

6. Persons with severe heart muscle damage and chronic congestive heart failure should not drink alcoholic beverages. Other cardiac patients should limit their use of alcohol.

7. All alcoholic beverages should be used cautiously or not at all in people suffering from epilepsy.

8. Alcohol in any form may react to increase the effects of such drugs as barbituates, tranquilizers, narcotics, and similar medications. When these drugs are prescribed, the use of wine must be carefully supervised and controlled.

9. The link between maternal alcohol abuse and fetal damage has been recognized since ancient times. Growth retardation in the baby, congenital defects, and reduced intellectual formation can occur with excessive alcohol intake by expectant mothers.

10. Wine and other alcoholic beverages are usually contraindicated in diseases of the prostate or diseases of the genitourinary tract.

4
WINE SERVICE

The appreciation of wine has meant different things to different cultures throughout history. The ancients probably appreciated wine most as a relief from thirst and pain. To them, wine was a perfume and a medicine. The Greeks of the golden Hellenic age had a greater appreciation of their wines after they were mixed with seawater or herbs, spices, or resins. In Rome, mealtime conversations were often devoted to in-depth wine evaluations. It was Jesus at the Last Supper who made wine the symbol of his blood, a symbol now recognized the world over. Monks dispensed wine as a staple of the diet for locals and travelers during the Middle Ages. During the Renaissance, wine became an article of trade, taxation, and economic leverage. Artists and writers thoughout the ages have portrayed the appreciation of wine.

As the state of the winegrowing arts has improved with advances in science and technology, the quality of wine has improved as well. Consequently, there is greater opportunity to enjoy wine in America than ever before. Many cities in the United States offer wine selections that are unmatched even in Europe. The major wine distributors in America offer thousands of different selections in their portfolios.

Some Americans enjoy a glass or two of wine every day, whereas others prefer wine only during special events or occasions. To whatever degree it is incorporated into a life-style, one will be much better able to appreciate wine if one knows how to deal with it. Such knowledge includes the selection, buying, storing, and presentation of wine.

❖ WINE SELECTION

Knowing how to select an appropriate wine for any occasion, be it a meal at home, a celebration, or a formal dinner, ranks among the most valuable of social graces. Properly matching wine to food, personalities, and mood can turn a simple gathering into a memorable event and is a superb reflection on a host. Many people, unfortunately, find the prospect of wine selection so intimidating that they forgo the pleasures of wine altogether. This is totally needless. There are no absolutely perfect wine choices. Deciding on an appropriate wine is a matter of preparing one's mind for common sense.

There are, of course, guidelines and traditions associated with wine selection, but some have recently begun to modulate. Ordering red wine with fish was an unforgivable travesty just a decade ago. Today such a choice is rather commonplace and fun to try; there is even a book entitled *Red Wine with Fish*, written by wine experts Joshua Wesson and David Rosengarten.

In recent years, especially in America, there has been an active trend toward innovation in matching wine with food and occasion. Such experimentation can, of course, be taken to extremes. Some people refuse to acknowledge any guidelines and seem to revel in silly combinations which have no manner of relationship. Still others are so tightly bound to rules that they consider a dinner ruined if a given wine selection is not totally perfect. More and more people are trying new and different combinations of wine and food; they are fully acquainted with wine traditions, but feel comfortable in adding a personal touch as well.

Discoveries can be made that become personal favorites and even establish new conventions. Like an expert chef improving freely on a classic recipe, seasoned enophiles know exactly how unorthodox they can be. They also know that experimenting at home with close friends or relatives can be a very enjoyable way to create new wine and food combinations. Imposing on the boss and the boss's spouse to serve as guinea pigs for a brainstorming session should be avoided. Research has its time and place; as ever, common sense should prevail.

Most people want to be familiar with the fundamentals before attempting to improve on them. The suggestions in this chapter should be enough to get started. Try them first and, if they work out, make adjustments in the seasoning of the food or the intensity of the wine. Once a good match is made, there will be less worry and more fun in preparing for an occasion.

✖ WINE MATCHMAKING

The first consideration in matching wine and food should be the season of the year. Most people prefer cold or iced drinks in the hot summer months. Thus, chilled dry white and blush, or rosé, wines are sensible choices and go perfectly with such summer fare as crab and shrimp. Dry red table wines are frequent autumn and winter choices, as they most often complement hearty foods such as beef entrées and red-sauce Italian and Mexican dishes.

The following sections provide basic wine and food pairing suggestions. These lists are by no means comprehensive and are subject to differences of opinion.

LUNCHEON

Most people prefer their luncheon wines to be inexpensive and informal, often jug wines that are light, fresh, and fruity. Although luncheons of several courses are commonplace in Europe, most Americans do not have the inclination to linger over lengthy luncheons so as to savor the complexity and richness of fine wines. Luncheon fare for most people in the United States is simple and nicely complemented by good ordinary wine. There are, of course, very special luncheons for which the occasion may appropriately call for more formal wine service. In this case, the dinner guidelines for wine service apply. With the afternoon activities yet to come, common sense again dictates the appropriate quantity of luncheon wine to be consumed.

The simplicity of white, blush, or red jug wine allows for food pairing to be equally simple. A nice shrimp salad would seem perfect with a lightly chilled delicate white wine. A festive pink ham luncheon entrée matches well with a blush

FIGURE 4.1 Wine and foie gras (goose liver pâté). *(Courtesy of* Food and Wines from France.*)*

wine, and a richer Tex-Mex luncheon plate may call for a cool room-temperature red. If it is difficult to discern a commonsense match, ask the opinion of a favorite restaurateur or wine retailer.

APERITIFS

Serving wines as cocktails, a rather recent notion in American dining, is an ideal innovation for wine aficionados inasmuch as cocktail drinks made with distilled spirits can dull the taste buds for fine food and wine served later. The preference for higher-alcohol aperitif wines is giving way to the universal popularity of simple white and blush table wines prior to lunch or dinner. Sparkling wines are also excellent cocktail wines if they are dry and have good, crisp acidity.

A wine cocktail hour offers the host an opportunity for creativity in devising fresh ideas for food and wine pairings. Here are some suggestions for canapés and hors d'oeuvres:

❧

CHARDONNAY (WHITE BURGUNDY) OR SEYVAL BLANC

Capers
Herring
Olives
Shellfish

❧

SAUVIGNON BLANC (GRAVES BLANC)

Avocado
Eggs
Sardines
Smoked salmon

⤜⤏

GEWÜRZTRAMINER (ALSACE) OR DRY VIGNOLES

Calamari

Chicken

Sausage

⤜⤏

CHAMPAGNE OR DRY WHITE SPARKLING WINE

Caviar

Pâté

⤜⤏

FINO SHERRY OR DRY MARSALA

Mushrooms

⤜⤏

DRY BLUSH WINE

Ham

⤜⤏

GAMAY (BEAUJOLAIS) OR MERLOT

Cream cheese

Dried beef

Short ribs

SOUP

The soup course allows for a range of options in wine matchmaking. Thin broths such as chicken soup were once served with dry Fino Sherry, although this is a high-alcohol wine (technically, a dessert wine) and a bit heavy for contemporary fare. Chowders go well with dry white wines and soups with beef generally match up with light red wines. Some hosts omit wine for the soup course, feeling that two liquids don't work well together.

The following are some suggested wine selections with soups:

⤜⤏

CHARDONNAY (WHITE BURGUNDY) OR SEYVAL BLANC

Clam chowder

Oyster stew

Vichyssoise

⤜⤏

SAUVIGNON BLANC (GRAVES BLANC)

Bouillabaisse

⤜⤏

GAMAY (BEAUJOLAIS) OR MERLOT

Minestrone

Oxtail

Vegetable

FINO SHERRY OR DRY MARSALA

Consommé
Gazpacho
Mushroom
Onion

ENTRÉES

The entrée wine is, of course, the most important selection for any dining occasion, whether simple or formal. For many people, it entails the most difficult decision.

Gone are the days when one could apply the simple rule "white wines with white meats, red wines with red meats, and rosé wines with anything." The difficulty is not that the rule is wrong, but that it falls far short of creative sensitivity when the modern marketplace offers so many fine wines to choose from.

The more educated the palate, the more varied the choices. As one experiences more and more fine dining occasions, specific tastes and flavors can be filed away in memory to be used as the basis for future wine and food pairing possibilities.

Consider, for example, a light filet of sole enjoyed at a business dinner several months ago that matched up well with a Chardonnay. The Chardonnay had a delicate fig-olive-oak flavor—dry, with a crisp acidity on the plate and finished with a lingering aftertaste. It was the perfect combination. The Chardonnay may then be a good choice tomorrow night for a filet of fish dinner with friends. If these guests are not particularly experienced with wine, perhaps a spicier, fruitier Gewürztraminer, with a touch of sweetness, may be a better match.

Another instance: A simple cold salmon plate was ordered during a luncheon with co-workers last week. It was delicious and matched up well with the house white. That same plate with a little imagination could become a magnifi-

FIGURE 4.2 Wine and fish entrées.
(*Courtesy of* Food and Wines from France.*)*

cent first course for a special dinner party coming up. Because these guests know quite well the ways of wine, the choice would be a fine dry white, perhaps a Chardonnay from a popular vintner.

Yet another example: At a gourmet function attended with friends, some marvelous beef ribs with a rich cherry sauce were served. The wine was a velvet-textured Pinot Noir with a soft briar-coffee bouquet and long-lasting earthy flavors—delicious. Trying this recipe with those same friends might be an opportunity to switch to a fruitier, less-complex Gamay red.

Finally, suppose an interesting Tex-Mex recipe is featured in a magazine, the recommended wine being a Cabernet Sauvignon. Guests at a promotion celebration may enjoy this, although if most of these people are younger and perhaps sensitive to a heavy Cabernet, a softer Merlot may be a better selection. Guests at a retirement celebration may enjoy this same dish, and a rich, full, well-aged Cabernet Sauvignon will doubtlessly match up very well on more mature taste buds.

Experiences like these should build more definite ideas as to wine selection choices. For instance, suppose a delicately poached filet of halibut or orange roughy is decided on. Chardonnay is definitely the wine of choice, but which one? An inexpensive, good quality California Chardonnay may be chosen for a casual dinner with close friends or relatives. A California Chardonnay from the Carneros that has recently received a gold medal or a high recommendation may be a more appropriate choice for guests who appreciate fine wine.

Consider a dinner party featuring roast duckling or turkey. These birds have both light and dark meat, which, along with the variables of basting, stuffing, and other flavor influences, can make a roast fowl a rather complex entrée to match with a single wine. There is a good chance that a larger bird may be at the center of a table seating of eight people or more. A bottle of inexpensive Johannisberg Riesling, fruity and with just a touch of sweetness, may pair well with the lighter meats and please those who are unfamiliar with wine. For guests who know wine, an Oregon Pinot Noir of high repute may be delicious with the darker meat.

It is fun to match the ethnic character of entrées with wines from the same culture. For example, chicken cacciatore is a natural with Italian white wines,

FIGURE 4.3 Wine and fowl.
(*Courtesy of* Food and Wines from France.)

and one would expect a host to serve a French red with Coq au Vin. Much of California cuisine is, in fact, designed around California wine flavors.

Taken a step further, it is even more fun to design a dinner around wines made from the same grape variety but grown in different countries. To illustrate, Beef Bourguignonne could be served with, of course, red Burgundy. Because the Burgundy is grown from Pinot Noir, it is both interesting and educational to serve a Pinot Noir from California, and perhaps a third from Oregon, side by side to see how each compares and matches up with the beef entrée.

The idea, again, is to use common sense. A pairing may not always work out exactly right, but most guests will identify with the rationale of a host in pusuing ideal wine and food matchmaking.

The following are a few fundamental wine matchmaking ideas:

CHARDONNAY (WHITE BURGUNDY) OR SEYVAL BLANC

Boiled shellfish

Butter sauce fish and shellfish

Coquilles St. Jacques

Poached fish

SAUVIGNON BLANC (GRAVES BLANC)

Broiled fish

Broiled shellfish

Cream sauce fish and shellfish

GEWÜRZTRAMINER (ALSACE) OR DRY VIGNOLES

Barbecued chicken

Chicken stir fry

Fried fish

Fried shellfish

Szechuan dishes

JOHANNISBERG RIESLING (GERMANY) OR VIDAL BLANC

Bratwurst

Broiled pork chops

Roast fowl light meat

Hunan dishes

PINOT GRIS OR SOAVE (VENETO)

Alfredo sauce dishes

Canelloni

Carpaccio

Pesto dishes

ROSÉ (ANJOU OR TAVEL) OR BLUSH

Barbecued pork
Boiled or baked ham
Shish-kebab
Tripe

PINOT NOIR (RED BURGUNDY) OR CHAMBOURCIN

Beef Bourguignonne
Beef Wellington
Prime rib
Chateaubriand
Coq au Vin
Lamb
Roast beef
Roast fowl dark meat
Standing rib roast

GAMAY (BEAUJOLAIS) OR MERLOT

Barbecued beef
Beef pot roast
Beef stew
Beef stir fry
Brunswick Stew
Charcoal-broiled beefsteak
Coq au Vin
Mutton

CABERNET SAUVIGNON (RED BORDEAUX) OR ZINFANDEL

Beef Stroganoff
Cassoulet
Crown roast of beef
Steak Diane
Steak Tartare
Sweetbreads
Tournedos of beef

NEBBIOLO (PIEMONTE) OR SANGIOVESE (TUSCANY)

Carbonara
Fusilli
Lasagne
Ravioli
Spaghetti
Veal Parmigiana

FIGURE 4.4 Wine and dessert.
(Courtesy of Food and Wines from France.*)*

DESSERT

Nowadays many dinners across America end with coffee after the entrée. With the constraints of diets and food budgets, the popularity of dessert wine has receded considerably in recent years. Fine Ports and Madeira types have remained after-dinner favorites among wine connoisseurs, however. In any event, a special occasion can be festively celebrated with decanting a delicious old Vintage Port.

More often than not, dessert wines are offered instead of dessert rather than with dessert. A heavy Oloroso Sherry can be delicious, but often just too heavy with a rich dessert course. Sometimes a sweeter sparkling wine, such as Asti Spumante, can better serve as a refreshing light dessert wine.

The following are some classic dessert wine combinations:

SAUTERNES AND OTHER LATE-HARVEST WHITE WINES

Carrot cake

Cheesecake

Cream puffs

Peach or apricot pie or cobbler

ASTI SPUMANTE-LIGHT, SWEET, SPARKLING WHITE OR RED WINES

Angel food cake

Baked Alaska

Cherries Jubilee

Cherry pie

Dessert soufflé

PORT OR TAWNY PORT

Fruitcake

OLOROSO OR CREAM SHERRY

Crepes Suzette
Maple torte
Mincemeat pie
Nut cakes
Zabaglione

WINE ENEMIES

In any discussion of which foods go with which wines, it should be mentioned that some foods and seasonings simply don't lend themselves to wine matchmaking very well.

Vinegar, for example, kills the flavor of wine. Thus, any dressing that is vinegar-based should not be the first choice in the presence of fine wine. This can be a problem for the salad course unless one chooses to serve the salad course after the entrée, as is done in France. For a guest at dinner, it is often difficult to escape this conflict, in which case one can cleanse vinegar from the palate by slowly eating small bites of bread with a few sips of water in between.

Some of the worst enemies of wine are, unfortunately, also holiday favorites. Cranberries, molasses, onions, tomatoes, and pineapple top the list. Asparagus fights wine, as do candied and creamed vegetables. Foods that are heavily flavored with citrus are also difficult to match with wines gracefully.

Strong spices such as chili, curry, and garlic do not lend themselves well to pairing with light wines but can work well with hearty reds. Matching white wines and egg dishes is a challenge, and it is a particularly talented enophile who can find a good wine pairing for chocolate.

✠ WINE AND CHEESE

Someone once remarked that wine and cheese go together like love and marriage. Casanova believed that the silky, soft red Burgundy from Chambertin and Roquefort cheese combined to make an aphrodisiac. Truly, this is an extraordinary pairing of wine and cheese, but whether or not it will generate much desire must be, of course, left to each individual to judge. Not all wines and cheeses make such sensational partnerships; basic principles may help in making sensible selections.

A common myth holds that white wines should never be served with cheese. There can be no question that the bold flavors of some classic cheeses, such as Boursault, Camembert, and Swiss, seem to do best with rich red wines. On the other hand, there are some heavily flavored cheeses that do well with both red and white wines. A good example is Blarney with Sauvignon Blanc or Cabernet Sauvignon. Some of the lighter cheeses, such as Fontina, Gouda, and Havarti, are overwhelmed by heavy red wines and balance much better with fine white wine.

As a rule, young wines call for rather new cheeses and, conversely, aged wines marry well with aged cheeses. Matching wines and cheeses from the same country can be helpful in making good selections too. For instance, a fresh, light Brie pairs up very well with a delicate young red Burgundy. Both have youth and both are, of course, French. Bel Paese from Italy is perfect with Barolo or Chianti. New York State Cheddar and a Long Island Merlot are a delicious combination. Monterey Jack combines well with most any well-made California red from the Monterey Peninsula.

FIGURE 4.5 Wine and cheese.
(Courtesy of Food and Wines from France.*)*

Some people offer cheeses and fancy crackers as canapés with wine before dinner, but such hors d'oeuvres can be so filling that they actually blunt the appetite. Consequently, wine and cheese best follow the entrée course at dinner, as is done in Europe.

The following are some wine and cheese pairings that have proven successful:

CHARDONNAY (WHITE BURGUNDY)
OR SEYVAL BLANC

Gourmondise

Havarti

Jarlsberg

Tilsit

JOHANNISBERG RIESLING (GERMANY) OR
VIDAL BLANC

Liederkranz

Limburger

Muenster

SAUVIGNON BLANC (GRAVES BLANC)

Blarney

Bonbel

Brick

Gouda

St.-Paulin

SOAVE (VENETO) OR TREBBIANO

Fontina

❦

GAMAY (BEAUJOLAIS) OR MERLOT

Camembert

Cheddar

Edam

Gjetost

Swiss

❦

PINOT NOIR (RED BURGUNDY)
OR CHAMBOURCIN

Appenzeller

Brie

Cheshire

Monterey Jack

Port du Salut

Roquefort

❦

CABERNET SAUVIGNON (BORDEAUX)
OR ZINFANDEL

Blarney

Bleu

Boursault

Gruyére

Stilton

❦

NEBBIOLO (PIEMONTE)
OR SANGIOVESE (TUSCANY)

Bel Paese

Fontinella

Gorgonzola

Provolone

A well-chosen combination of light red wine, creamy cheese and fresh fruit with light crackers is a perfect end to a formal luncheon or casual dinner. For those who have a taste for dessert wines after a formal dinner, old Vintage Port served from a crystal decanter is a classic when served with aged cheese, fruits, nuts, and light sugar biscuits.

❖ WINE COOKERY

Although wine has been used in cooking for many centuries, even predating the ancient Greeks, French housewives probably should be credited with the first widespread use of wine in cooking. They learned that the cheaper, more ordinary cuts of fish and meat could be made much more palatable and interesting by using wine as an integral ingredient. Thus, wine became an essential part of French food preparation, considered by many today to be the world's finest cuisine. Both traditional and developing cultures of American cookery are increasingly turning to the special goodness of wine.

A common worry in wine cookery is the consumption of wine by children. This need not be a difficulty as it takes only a little heat for the alcohol to evaporate, in much the same manner as the alcohol in vanilla extract disappears when a simmering temperature is reached.

All types of wine may be used regularly for cooking. The easiest and cheapest access to cooking wine is the proper use of leftover aperitif and dinner wines. These can be recorked and stored in the refrigerator until needed for a recipe. It is best if the recorked bottles are full, which may require some blending. Some purists argue against this practice, but it is more important to store full bottles so that minimal air (oxygen) is left in the bottles. Thus, a good case can be made for saving whites together in one bottle and reds together in another. Some noted chefs subscribe to the adage, "Cook with the same wine that you drink." Although this may be all right in some cases, it remains idealistic, impractical, and very expensive. We can and should resist deglazing a fry pan with a Grand Cru Burgundy for making sauce. Another old truism is "Wines unfit for drinking are unfit for cooking." It is easier to subscribe to this dictum, inasmuch as harsh or overacidic wines can ruin the balance of a delicate recipe. Old oxidized wine flavors are amplified in cooking and can overpower other flavors.

Most experienced cooks tend to avoid the wines specifically labeled "cooking wine" that are offered in some supermarkets. Typically, these are not made from wines of high quality and frequently have been infused with various herbs and salts that preclude personal seasoning preferences.

Wine enhances the natural flavors of many foods. It can add subtle nuances of its own, and red wines can be the source for rich color enhancement in some recipes. French and Italian cuisines depend heavily on sauces to bring texture and flavor to many dishes. The moderate acidity of wine serves well as a marinade to tenderize meats, and wine is indispensable in taming the excessively powerful flavors of wild game.

There are no specific rules for cooking with wine. On the contrary, wine can bring endless variation to a single recipe. Some chefs poach eggs and fish in red wine, and others prepare red meat sauces with white wines. There are some guidelines, however.

Karen and Richard Keehn, California vintners, have spent years experimenting with wine cookery. They are experts in the matching of wine with herbs, spices, and other food flavoring components. They believe that it is the choice of seasonings that links food to wine. Based on a careful selection of one or two herbs and a spice in each recipe, there are certain predictable patterns that can be used to make the best choice of a wine to accompany a particular dish, and vice versa.

The first consideration in this approach is to identify a wine's elemental fruit flavor and then to select a seasoning compatible with that character. For example, dry Sémillon usually has flavors reminiscent of apples, melons, and pears. These fruits are often paired with spices and with herbs that have mint or licorice flavors. Thus, try matching Sémillon wines with foods seasoned by mint or basil, and anise or tarragon, and cinnamon or cloves.

Following are some adaptations of the Keehn's theories, as a guide to anticipating the effect of wine and seasoning matchmaking:

1. The more delicate the wine flavor, the more delicate the seasoning can be, such as a delicate Sauvignon Blanc with the subtle flavors of dill, chervil, or parsley.

FIGURE 4.6 Culinary Institute of America in the Napa Valley. *(Photo by author.)*

2. The more powerful the wine flavor, the more powerful the seasoning can be, such as a rich Chardonnay with sage or Cabernet Sauvignon with rosemary or caraway.

3. Some wines have an inherent spiciness and can be combined with seasonings having spicy properties, such as a dry Gewürztraminer with mustard or ginger or Zinfandel with black pepper or allspice.

4. Some wines are made in a fruitier and sweeter style, which usually complements seasonings that are tart or salty, such as a delicate blush wine with prosciutto.

5. The excessive use of strong seasonings, i.e., anise, cilantro, garlic, ginger, pepper, salt, and sugar, can overpower the flavor of wine.

6. Some vegetables have acids that compete with wine flavors, i.e., artichokes, asparagus, sorrel, and spinach. The judicious use of cheese, cream, and other dairy products in vegetable recipes can help to diminish these acids.

7. Wine flavors are at their best when added in cooking 10 minutes or so prior to serving. This helps to protect wine flavor components from becoming distorted.

8. Serve simpler foods with restrained seasoning when serving older wine vintages, because the subtle, complex flavors so valued in mature wines can easily be masked by powerful food flavors or seasonings.

◈ WINE BUYING

Beware of fine wine bargains in an unfamiliar store—these are not always what they appear to be. Sometimes wines offered at greatly reduced prices are suspect to having been stored improperly, or the stock is an unsaleable closeout, or something worse. It has been said many times: If it seems too good to be true, it probably is.

The best course is to cultivate a relationship with a reputable wine merchant. When a consumer shows an interest in learning more about wines, a good retailer will quickly return that attention. As the merchant gets to know individual tastes, sensible suggestions can be made. It doesn't take long to become a "privileged" customer who receives notices about special shipments coming in, upcoming sales, and free tastings. Most retailers have more time to talk and visit early in the week, after busy weekend activities are over.

Fine wines are not typically a bargain business. New vintage releases are usually bought up rather quickly by the same privileged customers. Most vintners allocate heavily to important urban markets, sending comparatively little to smaller markets. It may make sense for wine enthusiast friends to consider making store visits together. The cost of travel, even if just into the city from suburbia, can be divided among the number of participants. The economy of buying together can be very rewarding, not to mention the fun of making the event a social outing.

Good wine buys can also be found by visiting wineries. Many vintners offer "library" wines—older wines in quantities too small to sell in the general marketplace. A winery visit is particularly good, as it provides a chance to taste each wine before buying. Don't expect to pay less at the winery, because vintners must protect the integrity of their retailers' shelf prices. Before large quantities of wines are purchased at a winery, think through the exercise of transporting them home. Each case of table wine weighs about 35 pounds. For those traveling in the heat of summer, it will be necessary to carry each case into the cool motel at night, and back out again in the morning, and then figure out a way to keep the cases from overheating during the day.

WINE INVESTING

Yet another element of wine appreciation is the value of the various wines. For some of the pedigreed European wines the investment record has been favorable, as well as for a few selections of New World wines from well-established vintners of high repute. The vast majority of wines are, however, made for consumption and do not appreciate in value. Beyond any advice, pro or con, to a prospective wine investor is the question of how such investments might be sold later. Wine, as an alcohol beverage, requires a license for sale, a hurdle that in many cases is legally insurmountable.

WINE OPINIONS

Without personal sampling and evaluation, there is no foolproof source of opinion for determining the quality and value of wines. As mentioned earlier, the experience of friends and relatives in whom one has confidence, or advice provided by a reliable retailer, is usually the best bet. It should go without saying that heeding the idle banter of wanna-be wine experts can prove to be an expensive lesson.

The results of national and international wine competitions are typically good indicators of wine values. Although some wines entered are purposely designed by vintners to be "prizefighters" in these events, and are therefore limited in quantity, their value has still been decided by a refereed panel of judges, rather than determined by a single person's opinion. Because some of these competitions attract more than 2,000 entries, the list of medal winners is ponderous and difficult to publish. The best source of this information is a subscription to the following magazine:

Wine East
620 North Pine Street
Lancaster, PA 17603

A synopsis of California wines in competition is published in this booklet:

California Wine Vintners
Varietal Fair
4022 Harrison Grade Road
Sebastopol, CA 95472

WINE PERIODICALS

There are several dozen good magazines that include news and information helpful to sensible wine buying. The most popular of these are as follows:

Decanter
Priory House
8 Battersea Park Road
London SW8 4BG, England

Mead On Wine
P.O. Box 2798
Carson City, NV 89702-2796

The Wine Enthusiast
P.O. Box 39
Pleasantville, NY 10570-0039

The Wine News
353 Alcazar Avenue
Coral Gables, FL 33134

Wine Spectator
M. Shanken Communications, Inc.
387 Park Avenue, South
New York, NY 10016

A word of caution about wine guides and newsletters. There are many of these available; some are reliable and others are not. The recurring difficulty with these publications is that they typically express a singular opinion. Wine buying guides are much safer when they embody the collective advice of a panel of qualified judges.

EVERYDAY WINES

Fortunately, America is a nation where jug wines are plentiful, inexpensive, and often very good quality for the money. There are American jug wines available at less than $3 per liter, at about the same price as most French *vin ordinaire*, and often a much better value. Jug wines usually lose very little of their freshness if they are reclosed securely and stored in the refrigerator.

Even the wealthiest wine enthusiast wants to pay the lowest prices, but this may take some shopping around. The fact remains that the very same wine can be found at different retailers with significant variations in price. One reason for this may be the type of retailer. Wine shops cannot compete with supermarket chains, which have high-volume buying power to leverage lower unit prices and can then offer wines with less markup. Another reason for price variations can be that a given wine may be a loss leader, priced lower to attract customers to the store.

SPECIAL WINES

In deciding what wines to buy for special occasions, it helps to think about the nature of the occasion, the number of guests invited, and consumption control. These factors will help determine appropriate purchase quantities. Most important of all: be sure to have designated drivers available for those who choose to overconsume.

Most people calculate about two glasses of 3 ounces each per person. Each 750 milliliter (.75 liter) bottle contains about eight glasses. Thus, one bottle of wine should do nicely for four people. If the gathering calls for more than six bottles, it may make sense to negotiate a price for a full case with the retailer and to store the remaining bottles in the household wine cellar.

In typical American homes the most special events of the year occur during the holiday season. The traditional Thanksgiving turkey is often served with slightly sweet Gewürztraminer or Johannisberg Riesling. These wines match up well with the meal and are also good selections for those who are infrequent wine consumers. For similar reasons, a Christmas ham is well paired with a festive blush wine.

New Year's Eve celebrations are famous for Champagne toasts, but if the French bubbly is too expensive, there are plenty of good sparkling wines available that are just as festive for a lot less money.

A good bottle of deep, dark, heavy red wine is perfect for Valentine's Day—a fine Merlot is ideal. A lovely accompaniment to a very special steak dinner, this wine can suit both the day's romantic mood and the chilly winter season.

There is, of course, no wine poured for the children at weddings, baptisms, and christenings, but adults have celebrated these blessed events with Champagne and sparkling wines throughout the history of our country. Caterers and retailers are often able to assist in arranging for wine fountains and other appropriate accoutrements to make such receptions even more memorable.

For a sweltering Fourth of July, almost anything cold tastes good. Ribs slowly broiled on the charcoal grill can be matched well with a cool, crisp Gamay. When wine is purchased in the warmer months, make sure that it doesn't suffer in the heat.

Sooner or later, most wine enthusiasts are "tricked and treated" by Halloween friends in silly costumes bearing empty wineglasses. This is a great time to arrange an informal get-together before the holiday season when people begin to plan trips and family celebrations. Halloween brings the first taste of cooler weather across much of America, and a hearty pot roast brings good friends together, especially with a nice mature bottle of Pinot Noir or Burgundy decanted at the table.

The end of the football season, the beginning of the basketball season, and the anticipation of the holidays—all bring gatherings of good food, fine wine, and great people.

Throughout the entire year there are occasions when thoughtful wine selections can express the good taste and judgment of a host or hostess. Such selections reflect intellect, culture, and a charisma that is fun for people to be around.

GIFT WINES

Buying wine as a gift can be a happy experience when one is familiar with the preferences of the recipient. There are few holiday gifts other than wine that can be given again and again, thus reducing the anxiety of trying to find just the right gift every time. On the other hand, the giver may find new wines that will be fun for the recipient to try.

Wines come in a wide range of prices. Find a wine appropriate to the person and the occasion. An overexpensive wine may make the recipient uncomfortable. A cheap wine is never a good gift idea; it's an insult even among close friends. Retailers often have handsome gift boxes available for their best customers.

When invited to dinner at a friend's home, it shows good taste to bring a $10-$15 bottle of sparkling wine. A new home might be celebrated by friends going together to buy a case of mixed favorite wines to stock the new wine cellar.

✛ THE PERSONAL WINE CELLAR

Wines purchased for everyday drinking can be stored in the refrigerator. An extra jug or two can be kept on the pantry floor.

Buying wines for stocking private wine cellars requires first, of course, that one has a proper place to lay them down. The term *laying down* refers to the practice of placing wine bottles on their sides, so that the wine is kept in contact with the cork to keep it from drying out and breaching the seal. Dry corks shrink, allowing air to enter the bottle, which can oxidize rich color and flavors to ruin.

People buy wine for laying down for a number of reasons. Larger wine purchases are usually less expensive on a per-bottle basis. Promising vintages are usually priced lower when purchased at an early age and allowed to mature in the home wine cellar. Taking bottles of the same wine out of the cellar over a long period of time allows observation of the maturing taking place during aging. Wine collection is a superb hobby. Perhaps above all, wine is fun to have around, an endless topic of conversation, and a good stock in the home wine cellar is always conveniently at hand.

A good way to become familiar with different wines to lay down is by attending wine-tasting parties and programs. Progressive vintners, distributors, retailers, and restaurateurs sponsor such programs. There are also national and international wine appreciation organizations such as the American Wine Society and the Knights of the Vine, among others. Perhaps best of all are private gatherings with friends, to which each participant contributes a different wine to share. This keeps the cost down and provides a superb opportunity to learn.

The wine storage area should be kept at a cool temperature, ideally about 55° F, without much fluctuation. This is important for all wines, but particularly for sparkling wines, fine whites, and blush types. Because cooler temperatures are generally found nearer the floor, store sparkling wines nearest the floor, white and blush above them, then red, with dessert wines uppermost at chest height. It is not recommended that any wines be stored near the ceiling. Wine storage should be well clear of heating ducts, appliances, and drafts.

Sunlight can have a devastating effect on wine. Good wine storage should have minimal light, only whatever incandescent lighting is necessary to find one's way around and to read labels and the cellar inventory log book.

Vibration should be minimized in order to minimize sedimentation. Humidity should also be kept moderate if possible. Wine storage facilities that are consistently at less than 55 percent relative humidity can dry out corks. Conversely, humidity in excess of 85 percent can cause molding of labels and capsules.

Consider the representations of the "dream kitchen," so often fitted with a wine storage unit over the refrigerator. Although this may look good, it is the worst of all worlds for wine—complete with heat, vibration, humidity, and light.

Many people convert closets or cupboards into wine storage areas. Some just pile their wines on ordinary wooden planks, using bricks to create sufficient space for bottles in between. Others lay cylindrical drain tiles in tiers along a supporting wall, inserting one bottle inside each tile. Old refrigerators can serve well when their thermostats are properly adjusted up a few degrees. Wooden crates, still used by some fine wine shippers, can make very fine storage containers.

Paperboard wine cartons may be used temporarily but can mold because of high humidity and collapse on wet floors. The major criteria are that wine storage racks and shelves be stable and accessible.

Once the wine cellar is set up, one should establish an inventory log so that a record of incoming and outgoing bottles, dates, and other pertinent data can be kept. Some keepers of larger cellars develop locator codes for quick reference; for instance, a wine with a C2 code would be in row C in the second slot, and so forth. Tasting notes and scores can also be kept in the log.

Wine enthusiasts who don't have access to an environmentally controlled storage area, or an underground cellar, now have access to some ingenious wine storage units. These range in capacity from several dozen to several hundred bottles and are fully temperature and humidity controlled. They are usually priced a bit more than comparably sized refrigerators but offer fine furniture finishing and a special pride for the owner.

⬧ WINE PRESENTATION

One of the most pervasive myths in wine lore is that red wines should be opened an hour or more in advance of being served. There are several explanations given to support this practice. One is that stale gases collect during aging in the ullage (space below the cork and above the wine) of the bottle, and advance uncorking allows these to escape. Another is that exposure of the wine to air permits it to "breathe," amplifying bouquet and dissipating and mellowing tannins. A third rationale is that opening a bottle long before service gives sulfur dioxide, sometimes used in excess as a wine preservative, time to dissipate. There may be some truth in these notions but most are questionable.

Opening a bottle actually introduces very little oxygen and may, in fact, serve to deteriorate older reds. A renowned wine writer, Alexis Bespaloff, once conducted an experiment whereby he served prominent vintners their own wines, one set having been opened an hour before and another set just prior to serving. The vintners tasted from coded glasses, not knowing which wine was which. They consistently preferred the wines that had been uncorked just prior to pouring.

During the last several decades there have been some wine connoisseurs, wine writers, and would-be wine experts who have introduced a multitude of "right and wrong" wine service codes. Some of these rules are plain and others fancy. By and large, they have been contradictory and confusing to wine novices interested in learning the straight and narrow. Unfortunately, many Americans have gone away perplexed and intimidated by the hype, willing to do without wine rather than risk committing a social blunder. There is no need for such confusion. Wine can and should be as common at the table as bread or cheese —and it is just as easy to serve.

TEMPERATURE

The proper temperature for any wine is entirely a personal matter. There are those who argue that it is heresy to chill red wines, and others contend that a slightly chilled Gamay or Beaujolais makes for a better match with barbecued beef and other beef dishes. Much more important is, of course, for each person to establish his or her own preferences through experience, experimentation, and serendipity.

One may find that some wines taste better at different temperatures with different dishes. A favorite Chardonnay, for example, may be preferred at about 60° F with Trout Almandine. With a filet of flounder in a light cream sauce the same wine may do better at about 50° F. Similarly, most any wine may seem more refreshing served at cooler temperatures in summer, and more hearty served a bit warmer in winter.

The colder a wine is, the less it evaporates its bouquet vapors, a condition referred to as "closed." Conversely, the warmer a wine is, the more it evaporates its bouquet vapors and its alcohol, a condition referred to as "strong." Although cold wines may be refreshing in warmer weather, they may also be rather tasteless. Furthermore, heating delicate wines to force more bouquet vapors distorts their flavor.

The time necessary to reach the desired temperature varies, of course, with the beginning temperature of the wine. If the home wine cellar is maintained at 55° F, there may be no need to chill a white or blush wine at all, but perhaps just a few minutes in the refrigerator prior to dinner. If a wine has just been brought home from the store and is at 70° F or so, it will take about 30 minutes to chill down to 55° F in a refrigerator (about half that time in an ice-water bucket). Placing a bottle in the freezer for a quick chill is not a good idea. Sooner or later this practice will result in a forgotten bottle that has frozen and broken.

The idea of serving reds at room temperature is derived from Old World notions about what ambient room temperature is. In this case, it may be better stated as "cool room temperature." Red wine service in Europe is at 65° F or so. The same red wine at an American 72° F room temperature is much stronger and less expressive of its fruit.

Sparkling wines of all colors are chilled at the table in an ice-water bucket. If left there for too long the temperature of the wine will, of course, continue to fall, which may be too cold for some people. Anticipating this eventuality, a smart host will put less ice in the bucket to begin with. An ice bucket is a nice touch of hospitality and imparts a festive air. Buckets of silver and pewter are the best, but nicely fashioned chrome and stainless steel buckets can also do very well.

UNCORKING

A first attempt at opening a bottle of wine can be a traumatic experience, especially if other people are observing the event. Perhaps it's better to try it alone a few times in order to develop a smooth technique, perhaps even a bit of flair.

There are all manner of cork-removal devices with a wide range of prices. A simple $2 two-pronged "ah-so" unit is available, which straddles the cork and binds it during withdrawal. Heavy-duty, professional counter-mounted units offer one-stroke uncorking, at a cost of several hundred dollars for the fancy ones. Two of the most common and practical corkscrews are the wing type with metal side levers that, when pressed down, leverage the cork out. The "captain's knife" or "waiter's friend" is a bit like just one half of the wine type, with leverage gained by pulling up on one side of the device.

Most wine bottles have a ring molded into the glass at the top of the neck. It is just beneath this ring that the capsule covering the cork is to be cut all around, totally exposing the bottle top for wiping clean before cork removal is started. Some of the newer bottles do not have capsules, and the process of uncorking can thus commence straightaway. Start the corkscrew at an angle for about a full turn, then straighten it so as to go directly vertical down through the center of the cork. This binds the cork and allows for more effective removal of crumbly or otherwise unsound corks. Exert only enough pressure to ease the cork out. If possible, remove the cork while the bottle is standing upright on a counter or table. If it becomes necessary to use the knees as a vise, or to wrestle with the bottle in order to pull the cork, be excused from guests and perform the task in another room.

Sparkling wines require special attention. The carbon dioxide gas inside the bottle exerts pressure on the cork and makes the bottle potentially dangerous unless it is handled properly. The initial step is to chill the wine to reduce the gas pressure. Then cut the capsule just beneath the wire hood fitted over the

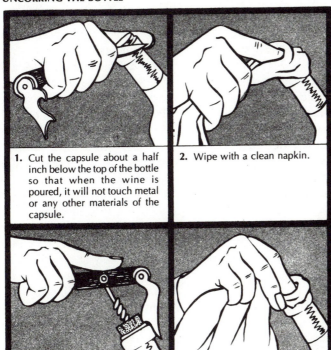

1. Cut the capsule about a half inch below the top of the bottle so that when the wine is poured, it will not touch metal or any other materials of the capsule.

2. Wipe with a clean napkin.

3. Insert the corkscrew into the center of the cork and work it in until it reaches the bottom of the cork or goes as far as it can. Draw out the cork as gently as possible. In this way, the wine is not shaken and the cork is less likely to break.

4. Wipe the bottle neck, inside as well as out.

FIGURE 4.7 Illustration of uncorking a table wine bottle using a "captain's knife." *(Courtesy of* Food and Wines from France.*)*

cork. With one hand grasp the bottom of the bottle firmly, making sure that the top of the bottle is pointed away from everyone. Then undo the wire hood and remove it gently so as not to disturb the cork. Take the cork firmly in the free hand and hold it stationary while the hand grasping the bottom slowly twists the bottle. The cork should commence to loosen and push out. It should be gripped tightly so that removal is slow and easy, which is a bit more difficult with plastic stoppers than with real corks. Allowing a sparkling wine cork to fly out freely with a great loud pop may be attention getting, but because of the danger it shows very poor judgment.

DECANTING

Some wines, especially aged reds and dessert wines, will precipitate, or "throw" a sediment. Sedimentation of this type is common, particularly in naturally made wines without extensive clarification and filtration treatments. Beware, however, of young white and blush wines that exhibit a noticeable sediment. This may indicate that the wine has decomposed because of air leakage past the cork, or that the wine has degenerated in some other way. This condition may be found in tandem with a hazy clarity and a color hue that has become excessively yellow or brown. Some older whites, such as German late-harvest types, Bordeaux Sauternes, and older white Burgundies, may mature in the bottle with a bit of sediment and an attractive golden hue.

Most U.S. vintners go to great lengths to ensure that their wines are free of any appreciable sedimentation. There are differing views on this condition. In

Europe, wine sediments are excused and even held up as evidence of Old World wine artistry. Americans are often quick to criticize any wines that have thrown a sediment and, consequently, many New World vintners explain on their labels or in their literature the nature of fine wine sediments.

Sediment is bitter and can reduce the full pleasure of a wine in much the same manner as grounds in coffee. The wine to be decanted should be disturbed as little as possible beforehand. Several hours before decanting the bottle should be taken from its horizontal cellar storage position and stood upright on a table or counter, preferably in a decanting cradle. This allows any disturbed sediment to resettle.

Unless one has a wine cellar service area with a special table for decanting, the operation is usually performed on a buffet or at a corner of the dining table. Bottles are uncorked a few minutes or so before serving, whether or not they are to be decanted. This permits any sediment disturbed during uncorking to resettle and head-space gases, if any, to dissipate.

A candle or soft light should be on hand before the decanting process is started. Take the opened bottle firmly and steadily and position it so that the light is angled for good visibility through the bottle neck. The bottle is then gently tipped for pouring into the decanter, held equally firmly by the other hand. The pouring continues steadily until the first signs of sediment appear; the bottle is then raised and set aside. If all goes well, no sediment should appear in the neck until 90 to 95 percent of the wine has been decanted. The decanter is closed with its stopper and readied for service at the table.

A fine silver funnel may also be employed for this purpose. Some delicate old wines develop aromatic nuances that are very fragile. Rough handling can evaporate these precious flavors away.

It is a good idea to develop a decanting technique by practicing before attempting it in front of guests. One may even want to enlist an accomplished enophile for a bit of tutoring. Decanting is not difficult, nor is it mystical. Carving a roast turkey properly is far more involved.

WINEGLASSES

The first element of pouring is what the wine will be poured into—wineglasses. Serving wine in water tumblers or cocktail glassware is not recommended. Such glasses work, of course, but getting the most out of a good bottle of wine requires the proper glass—the right tool for the right job.

Unless there is a desire and the means for different shapes and styles of crystal wineglasses, there is no real need for more than a single service of all-purpose tulip-shaped stemware. A set of 12 heavy-duty 8-ounce stems should not cost more than $40, and often significantly less. Avoid glasses that have a heavy bead around the lip, as these are uncomfortable in the mouth and appear cheap and coarse. Most service glassware is made of good, durable glass—striking the fingernail against the bowl should produce a nice ringing sound. Fine leaded-crystal wineglasses give a loud resonant ring. Such elegance is, of course, sometimes very expensive. Steuben and Waterford, for instance, have stems priced at several hundred dollars each.

The bowl of the glass allows for swirling, which increases the surface area of the wine from which bouquet vapors are amplified. Most wine authorities recommend bowls without color, engraving, or other adornments, because the wine is easier to examine, judge, and appreciate in plain, clear "flint" glass.

Care should be taken in the proper cleaning and storage of wineglasses. An extra rinse cycle in the dishwasher can ensure that all detergent residuals have been washed away. The preferred method is hand washing with scalding hot water and wiping dry with a fine linen cloth. Keep wineglasses in as neutral an

FIGURE 4.8 Traditional wineglass shapes.

environment as may be practical. Glasses housed in varnished cabinets or in a cupboard with kitchen spices can pick up odors that will be evident in the wine. Cardboard boxes are particularly notorious for imparting a "papery" smell to wineglasses. Try this interesting experiment: Take a wineglass out of the cupboard or its cardboard shipping carton, wash it thoroughly and roll it up in plastic wrap. A few days later, unroll the glass and immediately compare its smell to the odor of the glasses on the cupboard shelf or in the cardboard carton to ascertain whether there is a difference.

The all-purpose tulip-shaped glass is designed for aperitif wines, entrée wines, and dessert wines. It is not, however, satisfactory for sparkling wines. These require a special glass, preferably a tall, narrow "flute" that can display the expensive bubbles. Some of the best sparkling wine glasses have small, rough surfaces blown into the bottom of the bowls to serve as focal points from which the bubbles are released and effervesce to the surface of the wine like tiny strings of pearls.

Some people offer Port and other dessert wines in a smaller 4-ounce version of the tulip-shaped glass. Sherry should be served in a *copita*, taller and more slender, and perhaps a bit more elegant, than the small tulip.

There are many traditional wineglass shapes and styles that evolved from Old World winegrowing regions. One of the most interesting is the German *roemer*, which some people refer to as a Hock glass, from the English name for wines shipped from Hochheim. The bowl of the Alsatian wineglass is reminiscent of the German *roemer*, but has a slender green stem from its French influence. The *roemer* stem flares out like a bell.

A modern Loire wineglass exhibits a thin, graceful stem upon which is a straight-sided and flat-bottomed bowl, creating something of a "tumbler-on-a-stem" effect. A wineglass from the Mosel-Saar-Ruwer region in Germany is much like the Loire glass, except for a nearly spherical-shaped bowl.

Lovers of fine Bordeaux and Burgundies find the large "Paris goblets" appealing. These are reminiscent of brandy snifters, but with a wider opening in the bowl and a much taller stem. These are fun, but impractical to all but those who have the money and space for them.

A collection of wineglasses can add a great deal to the pleasures of wine and are a timeless gift. Nevertheless, it must be remembered that a single service of 12 all-purpose service stemware can suffice very nicely. If a wine tasting with friends is planned, an additional set or two may be needed. It is perfectly all right to borrow wineglasses from friends and neighbors too.

POURING

Wineglasses are placed at the upper right of the place setting, about two or three inches from the "two o'clock" position of the plate. If more than one

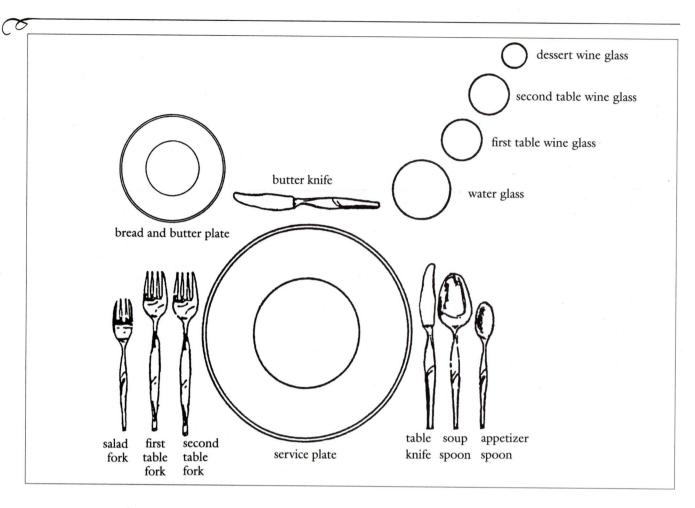

FIGURE 4.9 Typical formal dinner place setting.

glass is to be used during the course of the meal, these may be appropriately lined up in the order in which they will be used. The first will be nearest the plate, the second behind it, and then the third.

No more than three wine glasses should be set at each place. If more than three wines are being served, the used stems should be removed and a new service added between appropriate courses during the meal. The first pour of wine should properly be made in the host's wineglass. This allows any bits of cork that may have dropped into the wine to be separated from the guest's portions. The host evaluates the wine, rejecting it if it is not up to par. This custom also alludes to the ancient practice of the king's wine taster giving approval to the wine.

An all-purpose wineglass is usually filled about one-third full, certainly never more than one-half full. The decanter or bottle should not touch the lip of the glass while it is poured. When the pour is finished, the bottle may be twisted a quarter turn or so to help prevent dripping. Some prefer to wrap the bottle neck in a white service towel—a nice gesture in good taste. There are also drip rings that fit over the necks of bottles. Dessert wines should be poured in much the same way, but with smaller serving portions.

Sparkling wine glasses should be poured about three-fourths full. This may, however, take two pours, as the first touch of wine in the glass generally foams up quickly. After that pour settles, a second pour can be made up to the appropriate filling height. Great care should be taken in pouring sparkling wines, as it is easy for the foaming to cause overflowing and leave guests with dripping wet hands—an embarrassing situation.

An offer of an additional pour may be made when the level in a guest's glass falls below a remaining sip or two. When the level of wine in a person's glass does not recede, it is usually a sign that the person does not care for the wine.

The host should not badger that person to drink more, even when other guests may be accepting additional helpings. Neither should that person be embarrassed with an offer of some other wine. Merely make a mental note that she or he does not enjoy that particular selection and that it is not a good future choice in this company.

There are, of course, those whose glasses seem always to be empty. This is a delicate situation and should be handled with common sense and diplomacy. Take a firm stand on even rationing around the table with each pour. Overlook remarks by overimbibers and ignore their pleas for what is obviously too much wine.

✖ WINE IN RESTAURANTS

Pairing wine and food in a restaurant is governed by the same general principles as wine matchmaking at home. In some restaurants the wine list may be limited, and selecting the right wine may be something of a challenge. Some eateries may also provide little care for their wine inventories. In such cases it is often best not to order any wine at all. In some locales the law permits "brown bagging," whereby diners may bring their own wine selections and pay a "corkage fee" for the restaurant's service of chilling, uncorking, and pouring the wine.

If a restaurant has a wine list, chances are it also has one or more "house wines." These are usually good ordinary jug wines sold by the glass or carafe. As a rule, these can be good values and offer an economical alternative to buying a whole bottle.

It is perfectly acceptable to order house wines during luncheon at a favorite restaurant. Each member of the party can order the wine of her or his choice, white, blush, or red. This wine can be ordered first and served as a sort of mini-cocktail while the food is being prepared. One may properly limit oneself to just one glass and sip this throughout the entire luncheon. If the luncheon includes an appetizer course, the fare may call for two different house wines. Of course, at more formal luncheons common sense calls for a selection from the wine list.

THE WINE LIST

Among the many times when a person is happy about studying wine appreciation, it is when a sommelier brings the wine list to the table. Unless it is presented to a gathering of wine enthusiasts, the list is usually passed around the table until it finds the "resident expert." Dealing with the wine list can win a great deal of regard and respect from such a group.

The person who orders the wine will be dealing with the wine server who, in upscale restaurants, is called a *sommelier*. Generally, this person will offer specific suggestions for wine selection. This is not only fun, but often very enlightening as well. The final decision is, of course, not up to the sommelier—don't be bullied or intimidated—the customer is always right. If an unusual choice is decided upon, see it through; perhaps the sommelier will learn something too.

A wine list is nothing more than that—a list of the wines the restaurant has, or should have, available. The better restaurants regularly update their lists. It can be embarrassing to order one wine after another, only for the waiter to return apologizing for its not being in stock. If the restaurant employs a sommelier or has a headwaiter in charge of wine service, it is a good bet that the wine list is up to date.

A wine list can be made on a chalkboard on the restaurant wall, given on a single page included in the menu, communicated in hand-written entries in a modest folder, or presented in an impressive leather-bound volume embracing hundreds of wines. Approach each in the same way, searching for items that are familiar, or, if the occasion is appropriate, looking for something new to try. It is

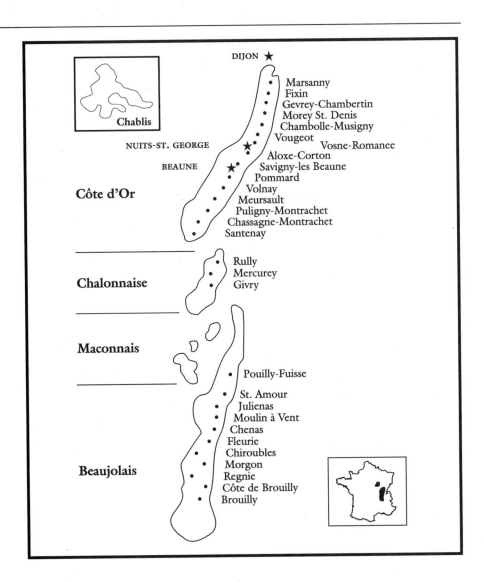

DIJON ★
• Marsanny
• Fixin
• Gevrey-Chambertin
• Morey St. Denis
• Chambolle-Musigny
• Vougeot
Vosne-Romanee
★•
Aloxe-Corton
Savigny-les Beaune
Pommard
• Volnay
• Meursault
• Puligny-Montrachet
• Chassagne-Montrachet
Santenay

Chablis

NUITS-ST. GEORGE

BEAUNE

Côte d'Or

Chalonnaise
• Rully
• Mercurey
• Givry

Maconnais

• Pouilly-Fuisse

• St. Amour
• Julienas
• Moulin à Vent
• Chenas
• Fleurie
• Chiroubles
• Morgon
• Regnie
• Côte de Brouilly
• Brouilly

Beaujolais

FIGURE 4.10—Page 52 from Anthony's wine list—Burgundy. *(Courtesy of Anthony's.)*

perfectly acceptable to ask the sommelier's opinion. A few exchanges of good conversation can start a rewarding relationship with a good sommelier.

There are, of course, thousands of exceptional wine lists in restaurants in America—and in Europe and other countries too, of course. One of the very best may be the wine list at Anthony's, an exquisite award-winning restaurant in Tuscon, Arizona. It certainly lends itself ideally to demonstrate the proper design for a user-friendly wine list.

Selecting a wine can sometimes be difficult because of guests' ordering different entrées. If one orders poached fish, another shrimp scampi, and yet another lamb, and the host would really prefer a steak, how can he or she deal with such variability? A possible solution is to inquire whether the restaurant offers half-bottles, each containing .375 liters, instead of the regular .750 liter size. If so, two or more selections may be ordered to match the guests' food choices. If the restaurant does not stock half-bottles, the key remains to choose those wines that best match the guests' entrée selections. The host might suggest a rich, full-bodied Chardonnay or white Burgundy to pair with the fish and shrimp and a young Pinot Noir or soft Merlot to pair with the lamb and steak. A rosé is not the answer unless the guests suggest it.

The host of a restaurant party has the final word on the wine to be selected. She or he should poll the group beforehand to see what entrées are being considered. Hosting a group of wine aficionados can be great fun, as they are usu-

France—White Burgundy

Bin	Winery	Cru	Vintage	½ Btl.	Bottle	Magnum

Chablis

Bin	Winery	Cru	Vintage	½ Btl.	Bottle	Magnum
6032	Albert Pic		1990		39.00	
6033	Jean Marc Brocard "Vaillons"	Premier Cru	1990		40.00	
6034	Dauvissat "Les Clos"	Grand Cru	1990		80.00	

Côte de Beaune
Corton-Charlemagne

Bin	Winery	Cru	Vintage	½ Btl.	Bottle	Magnum
6036	Domaine Chevalier	Grand Cru	1987		88.00	
6037	Louis Latour	Grand Cru	1990	45.00		

Meursault

Bin	Winery	Cru	Vintage	½ Btl.	Bottle	Magnum
6038	Louis Jadot		1991		35.00	
6039	Francois Jobard		1990		66.00	
6040	Louis Jadot "Les Perrières"	Premier Cru	1989		90.00	

Puligny-Montrachet

Bin	Winery	Cru	Vintage	½ Btl.	Bottle	Magnum
6041	Château de Puligny-Montrachet		1991		50.00	
6045	LeFlaive "Combettes"	Premier Cru	1992		116.00	
6046	LeFlaive "Bienvenues Batard Montrachet"	Grand Cru	1992		176.00	

St. Aubin

Bin	Winery	Cru	Vintage	½ Btl.	Bottle	Magnum
6049	Louis Latour		1991		26.00	

Chassagne Montrachet

Bin	Winery	Cru	Vintage	½ Btl.	Bottle	Magnum
6050	Louis Latour		1990		40.00	
6053	Duc de Magenta "Clos de la Chapelle"	Premier Cru	1991		55.00	
6055	Domaine Romanee Conti "Montrachet"	Grand Cru	1989		500.00	
6057	Marquis de Laguiche "Montrachet"	Grand Cru	1988		225.00	
6059	Louis Jadot "Le Montrachet"	Grand Cru	1984		260.00	
6060	Louis Jadot "Le Montrachet"	Grand Cru	1990		288.00	

FIGURE 4.11 Page 53 from Anthony's wine list—White Burgundy selections. *(Courtesy of Anthony's.)*

ally eager to experiment with wine and food pairings. Sometimes, particularly when the host is not very knowledgeable about wine, a guest may be asked to do the ordering. Similarly, a guest may privately ask the host's permission to select a wine. In the latter case, the guest is responsible for paying the wine check.

For obvious reasons, an uncorked bottle brought to a table is unacceptable. The server should present the bottle "label forward" in order to confirm it is the correct brand, wine type, and vintage. The capsule seal is then cut, and the mouth of the bottle is wiped clean with a service towel. The cork is then pulled and offered to the person who ordered the wine.

The cork must be inspected for three things:

1. The name and/or logo and the vintage years should be clearly printed on the cork to ensure authenticity of the wine.

2. Wine stains should not run the full length of the cork, which could indicate leakage and possible spoilage owing to oxygen exposure inside the bottle.

3. The cork should smell like wood and wine, not dirty or moldy. Decayed cork has a musty odor that may, or may not, have infected the wine—a condition often referred to, aptly enough, as "corky."

The server should pour a small portion of the wine into the glass of the person who ordered it. That person should check color, clarity, and bouquet. In the case of a suspect cork, the bouquet should be inspected *very* carefully to ensure that the wine does not smell like an old potato cellar. A small sip is then taken to ensure that the wine measures up to what it should be. This entire exercise should take place in less than 30 seconds.

If the wine is approved, a gentle nod indicating so is given to the server, who will then pour. She or he should fill glasses no more than one-third full, clockwise around the table, to ladies first, then gentlemen, and the host last.

If the wine is disapproved, the host quietly asks the server to accompany him or her with the bottle to discuss the situation with the maître'd.

Pouring should take place in the same manner as discussed previously for service in the home. During pouring, the neck of the bottle should not touch the lip of the glass. As each pour is made, the bottle should be turned a bit as it is withdrawn in order to prevent dripping. A plain white service towel may be held under the bottle as it is moved from guest to guest. When all are served, toasts and sentiments can be expressed.

Chilled wines, which include most whites and all sparkling wines, should be placed in an ice-water bucket near the table. As the bottle is removed for pouring, the service towel should be on hand to wrap around the bottle to prevent dripping. As in wine service at home, discussed earlier, glasses are filled one-third full, allowing for close inspection of the wine to better appreciate color and clarity. Portions of this size also allow for swirling, increasing the surface area of the wine from which the precious bouquet vapors rise, and provide plenty of space in the glass for the nose to gracefully receive this bouquet.

All wines should be brilliantly clear, perhaps only older reds excused for a bit of haze. Most reds beyond five years old or so should be decanted by the sommelier prior to service.

If the server offers more wine amid conversations, the host may gesture with an affirmative nod or, if no more wine is desired, simply place a hand slightly above the glass and tacitly gesture, "No, thank you." It is permissible for a guest to ask for more wine if the group is composed of close friends or relatives. Otherwise, it is appropriate to wait until it is offered.

Unfortunately, there are still restaurants in America that have marvelous food, superb coffee service, attentive wait staff, but pitiful wine offerings and inept service. Red wines may arrive ice cold, or white wines may be presented right off the shelf with no chill whatsoever. A waiter may bring a bottle to the table already uncorked and abruptly commence pouring without waiting for the host's evaluation or approval. Don't make a point of passionate disapproval in front of guests. Endure such an experience without an embarrassing confrontation; then return to the restaurant in a day or so for a word with the manager. A positive approach may help this restaurant to get started on a promising wine selection and acceptable service, in which case everybody wins.

◆ WINE TASTINGS

Wine tastings are becoming some of the most popular social events in America. They can be simple private gatherings or more formally organized as part of business occasions. There are wine tastings that serve as fund-raisers and others that are the focus for bringing special groups of people together. The list is endless.

The wine neophyte can learn a lot about how to organize and administer a private wine tasting by attending similar events held by friends and associates. Larger commercially sponsored events are also valuable in formulating ideas.

FIGURE 4.12 — Sharing bottles at a private wine-tasting party. *(Courtesy of Napa Valley Vintners Association.)*

An ideal group is 8 to 12 people, a number that most living rooms can accomodate comfortably. A regular 750 ml bottle of wine can be stretched to serve 12 if each taster is limited to 2 ounces, which is plenty when six or eight different wines are to be evaluated.

It is common for each couple or individual participant to bring a bottle of wine appropriate to the theme of the tasting. This, of course, helps considerably to reduce the expense for the party giver and may also be something of a "homework assignment" if each contributor presents a short discussion about the background of her or his particular wine. Some groups prefer taking turns as host, with the host being responsible for securing all the wines for the tasting. Experience generally proves the former plan works better than the latter. In either event, it is mandatory that all refrain from smoking and wearing heavy colognes and perfumes.

A wine tasting may be conducted casually in a living room or family room centered around a coffee table or game table. Some prefer to conduct the tasting a bit more formally around the dining room table. A kitchen does not usually serve well unless it has sufficient space apart from the cooking area, and fluorescent lighting distorts the color of blush and red wine pigments to orange and brown. Whatever room is selected should have minimal noise and a comfortable temperature. An out-of-doors setting may be fine as long as there are agreeable conditions—no insects or street noise, comfortable temperatures, calm breezes, and moderate sunlight with plenty of shade.

Wine tastings generally preceed dinner and can take the form of an extended cocktail hour—but without fancy canapés and hors d'oeuvres to confuse the taste buds. Ideally, each wine being judged should be followed with just a simple unsalted cracker or piece of white bread, then perhaps a small bite of bland cheese to neutralize the palate and, finally, a sip of bottled water to cleanse the palate in readiness for the next wine. There should, of course, be sufficient pencils and score sheets on hand. Some of the more serious enophiles may carry their own record book so they can refer back to their notes as needed.

The order of serving is usually dry wines first, progressing to the sweetest last. Whites are first, then blush, and reds last. Dryness takes priority over color in ranking. A sweet white, for example, would be served after the dry red wines were finished. Generally, between four and eight wines are sampled at a private tasting.

Wine tastings can be organized in many ways. The following paragraphs give examples of popular types.

VARIETAL WINE TASTINGS

Wine tastings are often conducted to evaluate various varietal wines produced by a single vintner:

Chardonnay

Sauvignon Blanc

Gewürztraminer

Pinot Noir

Merlot

Cabernet Sauvignon

HORIZONTAL WINE TASTINGS

A horizontal wine tasting is designed to evaluate the same varietal wine grown by various vintners during the same vintage year:

Clos Pegase Carneros Chardonnay	Carneros
Husch Anderson Valley Chardonnay	Mendocino
Flora Springs Napa Valley Chardonnay	Napa County
Chimney Rock Stag's Leap District Chardonnay	Napa County
Ferrari-Carano Dry Creek Valley Chardonnay	Sonoma County
Murphy-Goode Alexander Valley Chardonnay	Sonoma County

This selection is from well-known Chardonnay vintners across the North Coast Counties region of California.

Another version of the horizontal wine tasting is designed to evaluate the same vintage in a geographic area, such as in Bordeaux:

Château Duhart-Milon Rothschild	Pauillac in Médoc
Château Lascombes	Margaux in Médoc
Château Léoville-Barton	St. Julien in Médoc
Château Bouscaut	Cadaujac in Graves
Château Haut-Bailly	Leognan in Graves
Château Smith Haut-Lafitte	Martillac in Graves

These are wines grown in six different townships across two of the major red wine districts of Bordeaux. A more detailed explanation of the Bordeaux districts and their wines is provided in Chapter 6.

Yet another version of a horizontal wine tasting comprises wines taken from the same varietal and the same vintage, but from diverse regions around the world:

Chablis Premier Cru	Chablis in Burgundy
Puligny-Montrachet Premier Cru	Côte de Beaune in Burgundy
Chardonnay	Barossa Valley in Australia
Chardonnay	Maipo Valley in Chile
Chardonnay	Carneros in California
Chardonnay	Finger Lakes in New York

VERTICAL WINE TASTINGS

A collector often has a favorite vintner or vineyard from which vintage upon vintage has been laid down in the cellar. It is great fun to bring out various vintages to see how they compare:

FIGURE 4.13 Wine tasting after a winery tour. *(Courtesy of Napa Valley Vintners Association.)*

Robert Mondavi Reserve Cabernet Sauvignon 1978

Robert Mondavi Reserve Cabernet Sauvignon 1981

Robert Mondavi Reserve Cabernet Sauvignon 1985

Robert Mondavi Reserve Cabernet Sauvignon 1986

Robert Mondavi Reserve Cabernet Sauvignon 1988

Robert Mondavi Reserve Cabernet Sauvignon 1992

Note that the oldest vintage is served first. The notion supporting this is that the palate is more sensitive to subtle nuances of flavor, whereas the tannins of younger vintages can fatigue the palate quickly. There are many who prefer the opposite arrangement of vintages for their own reasons.

There are, of course, many other ways of organizing wine tastings. Although the examples given here are moderately expensive wines, that is not to say that more modest selections cannot be assembled in the same manner. On the contrary; for most people who live on a budget, a good share of the fun in wine tastings is discovering inexpensive wines that are also good.

TOASTS AND SENTIMENTS

The touching of glasses following profound, moving, or jolly words is a tradition that has greatly enriched the history of Western civilization. Here are some of the finer sentiments:

> *Eat, drink, and be merry,*
> *For tomorrow we shall die!*
>
> *Adapted from Isaiah 22:13*

> *The wine urges me on, bewitching wine, which sets even a wise man singing and laughing gently . . .*
>
> *—Homer*

> *Wine is wont to show the mind of man.*
>
> *—Theognis*

No thing more excellent nor more valuable than wine was ever granted mankind by God.

—Plato

In vino veritas. (In wine there is truth.)

—Plato (adapted from Alcaeus)

What is better adapted than the festive use of wine in the first place to test and in the second place to train the character of a man, if care be taken in the use of it? What is there cheaper or more innocent?

—Plato

Wine moistens the soul and lulls our grief to sleep, while it also awakens kindly feelings.

—Socrates

Quickly, bring me a beaker of wine so that I may whet my mind and say something clever.

—Aristophanes

Where there is no wine, there is no love.

—Euripides

Wine brings to light the hidden secrets of the soul, gives being to our hope, bids the coward fight, drives dull care away, and teaches new means for the accomplishments of our wishes.

—Horace

No poem was ever written by a drinker of water.

—Horace

It warms the blood, adds luster to the eyes,
And wine and love have ever been allies.

—Ovid

Nothing is more useful than wine for strengthening the body and also more detrimental to our pleasures if moderation be lacking.

—Pliny the Elder

Wine refreshes the stomach, sharpens the appetite, blunts care and sadness, and conduces to slumber.

—Pliny the Elder

Wine not only strengthens the natural heat but also clarifies the turbid blood and opens the passages of the whole body.

—Rufus of Ephesus

Wine is at the head of all medicines . . . where wine is lacking drugs are necessary.

—The Babylonian Talmud

Wine was given by God, not that we might be drunken, but that we might be sober. It is the best medicine when it has moderation to direct it.

—St. John Chrysostom

The benefits of wine are many if it is taken in the proper amount, as it keeps the body in a healthy condition and cures many illnesses.

—Maimonides

And that you may the less marvel at my words,
Look at the sun's heat that becomes wine
When combined with the juice that flows from the vine.

—*Dante*

If a man deliberately abstains from wine to such an extent that he does serious
harm to his nature, he will not be free from blame.

—*St. Thomas Aquinas*

He said: "I see well it is necessary,
Where that we go, good wine with us carry
For that will turn rancour and disease
To accord and love, and many wrong appease.

—*Geoffrey Chaucer*

I feast on wine and bread, and feasts they are.

—*Michelangelo*

Wine is light, held together by water.

—*Galileo*

If God forbade drinking would He have made wine so good?

—*Richelieu*

A meal without wine is like a day without sunshine.

—*Brillat-Savarin*

Old wood to burn! Old wine to drink!
Old friends to trust! Old authors to read!

—*Sir Francis Bacon*

Beer is made by men, wine by God!

—*Martin Luther*

Let's drink to our friend and host.
May his generous heart, like his good wine,
    only grow mellower with the years.

—*Unknown*

While there's life on the lip,
    while there's warmth in the wine,
One deep health I'll pledge,
    and that health shall be thine.

—*Unknown*

Drink to me only with thine eyes,
And I will pledge with mine;
Or leave a kiss but in the cup,
And I'll not look for wine.

—*Ben Jonson*

A Book of Verses underneath the Bough,
A Jug of Wine, a Loaf of Bread—and Thou
Beside me singing in the Wilderness—
Oh, Wilderness were Paradise enow!

—*Omar Khayyám*

I wonder often what the Vintners buy
One half so precious as the stuff they sell.

—*Omar Khayyám*

Come, love and health to all:
Then I'll sit down.
Give me some wine, fill full,
I drink to the general joy o' the whole table.

—Shakespeare

Good wine is a good familiar creature if it be well used, exclaim no more against it.

—Shakespeare

Tis mighty easy, o'er a glass of wine,
On vain refinements vainly to refine,
To laugh at poverty in plenty's reign,
To boast of apathy when out of pain.

—Charles Churchill

What though youth gave love and roses,
Age still leaves us friends and wine.

—Thomas Moore

Wine is the divine juice of September.

—Voltaire

A glass of good wine is a gracious creature,
And reconciles poor mortality to itself,
And that is what few things can do.

—Sir Walter Scott

A glass of wine is a great refreshment after a hard day's work.

—Beethoven

Drink in itself is a good creature of God and to be received with thankfulness, but the abuse of drink is from Satan.

—Increase Mather

Behold the rain, which descends from heaven upon our vineyards, and which enters into the vine roots to be changed into wine; a constant proof that God loves us and wants to see us happy.

—Benjamin Franklin

My manner of living is plain and I do not mean to be put out of it. A glass of wine and a bit of mutton are always ready.

—George Washington

Clearly, the pleasures wines afford are transitory—but so are those of the ballet, or of a musical performance. Wine is inspiring and adds greatly to the joy of living.

—Napoleon Bonaparte

Wine is the intellectual part of a meal, meats are merely the material part.
—Alexander Dumas

I think wealth has lost much of its value if it not have wine . . .
—Ralph Waldo Emerson

Then a smile and a glass and a toast and a cheer,
For all the good wine, and we've some of it here.

—Oliver Wendell Holmes

I give you health in the juice of the vine,
The blood of the vineyard shall mingle with mine;
Thus let us drain the last dew drop of gold,
And empty our hearts of the blessings they hold.

—*Oliver Wendell Holmes*

This song of mine
Is a Song of the Vine,
To be sung by the glowing embers
Of wayside inns,
When the rain begins
To darken the drear Novembers.

—*Henry Wadsworth Longfellow*

If you drink nothing but water
You'll never write anything wise;
For wine is the horse of Parnassus
That hurries the bard to the skies.

—*Lord Byron*

Wine cheers the sad, revives the old, inspires the young, makes weariness forget
his toil.

—*Lord Byron*

Oh, for a draught of vintage that hath been
Cool'd a long age in the deep delved earth,
Tasting of Flora and the country green,
Dance, and Provençal song, and sunburnt mirth!

—*John Keats*

I have lived temperately, eating little animal food. Vegetables constitute my
principal diet. I double, however, the doctor's glass and a half of wine, and even
treble it with a friend!

—*Thomas Jefferson*

I think it is a great error to consider a heavy tax on wines as a tax on luxury.
On the contrary, it is a tax on the health of our citizens.

—*Thomas Jefferson*

God in his goodness sent the grapes
To cheer both great and small;
Little fools will drink too much
And great fools none at all.

—*Unknown*

You Americans have the loveliest wines in the world, you know, but you don't
realize it.

—*H.G. Wells*

A waltz and a glass of wine invite an encore.

—*Johann Strauss*

The flavor of wine is like delicate poetry.

—*Louis Pasteur*

Back of this wine is the Vintner,
    and back through the years, his skill
And back of it all are the vines in the sun,
    and the rain, and the Master's will.

—*Unknown*

Wine of California . . . inimitable fragrance and soft fire . . . and the wine is bottled poetry.

—Robert Louis Stevenson

Thy sacred emblems to partake—
Thy consecrated bread to take
And thine immortal wine!

—Emily Dickinson

"Have some wine?" the March Hare said, in an encouraging tone.
   Alice looked all round the table, but there was nothing on it but tea. "I don't see any wine," she remarked.
   "There isn't any," said the March Hare.
   "Then it wasn't very civil of you to offer it," said Alice angrily.

—Lewis Carroll

One not only drinks wine, one smells it, observes it, tastes it, sips it and . . . one talks about it.

—King Edward VII

Wine is one of the most civilized things in the world . . . and it offers a greater range of enjoyment and appreciation than, possibly, any other purely sensory thing which may be purchased.

—Ernest Hemingway

Penicillin cures, but wine makes people happy.

—Sir Alexander Fleming

A bottle of wine begs to be shared; I have never met a miserly wine lover.

—Clifton Fadiman

To praise, revere, establish and depend;
To welcome home mankind's mysterious friend;
Wine, true begetter of all arts that be;
Wine, privilege of the completely free;
Wine, the foundation, wine the sagely strong;
Wine, bright avenger of sly-dealing wrong.

—Hilaire Belloc

Wine improves with age—I like it more the older I get.

—Unknown

Making good wine is a skill, fine wine an art.

—Robert Mondavi

Abstinence from wine may not help you live longer, but it will sure seem like it.
—Professor G.S. Howell

5
THE WINES OF AMERICA

There are more species of the vine native to America than to any other nation. Almost every state has at least several species of vine in cultivation and an even larger selection of interspecific hybrids. It is this genetic heritage that makes viticulture possible in the marginal winegrowing regions, particularly in the extremes of cold and warm climates. The U.S. encompasses an extremely broad geology and wide diversity of climatic conditions in which to cultivate the vine. Commercial winegrowing exists in 44 of the 50 states in our Union.

With production of 448 million gallons in 1993, the United States ranks fourth in worldwide production of wine, after Italy, France, and Spain. Italy produces about 1.8 billion gallons per year, France is close behind with approximately 1.7 billion gallons, and Spain with a distant 975 million gallons vinified each year. Prior to its breakup, the Soviet Union produced about 450 million gallons annually. Argentina is now the world's fifth largest winegrowing nation, with about 380 million gallons each vintage.

At about two gallons per person annual wine consumption, Americans rank far below the top nations. The French and Italians not only produce a lot of wine, they also drink a great deal of it, both nations consuming at rates of about 19 gallons per capita annually—nearly tenfold the U.S. rate.

About three quarters of the wine consumed by Americans is made in America. California alone produces about 90 percent of the wine made in the entire United States. California is unquestionably the vinous center of the country, but there is still a great deal of vitality in the wine industry across the rest of the nation despite a declining overall percentage of wine produced by other states. While the number of large bottling plants in the eastern states dwindles, the number of small boutique vintners continues to increase. State and local authorities are taking a more active role through supportive legislation in encouraging "farm wineries" to thrive.

Most European governments exercise far more control over vineyard boundaries, grape varietal selection, and winemaking technique than is found in

America. This does not mean that American vintners produce lesser quality wines. On the contrary, vastly improved technologies have been introduced into American winegrowing, and the results have often been exemplified by U.S. wines winning in competitions against classic European vintners.

Some, perhaps most, of these tehnologies are developed through U.S. research efforts, some by land-grant universities, and others generated within the wine industry itself. The lower levels of governmental control have served to broaden the experimental horizons of U.S. wine researchers and have made possible the expansion of commercial winegrowing to new regions in America.

⬥ CLASSIFICATION

The U.S. Congress has decreed authority for appellation (geographically restricted location) of wine origin petitions to be administered by the ATF. This bureau evaluates each application and requires that specific cause be shown as to why each area should be considered unique for such special recognition. Following approval by Congress, the appellation of origin may then be displayed on labels of wines whose grapes have been grown within the boundaries of that particular locale.

The system does not yet include the restrictions and classification standards found in Europe that result in wines of many different pedigrees or orders of classification. Nevertheless, the federal government has, with this first step, opened the door for the initiation of an American wine classification system. The current approval list of U.S. vineyard appellations are as follows:

ATF AUTHORIZED U.S. VINEYARD APPELLATIONS (AVA)

ARIZONA

Sonoita

ARKANSAS

Altus

Arkansas Mountain

Ozark Mountain

CALIFORNIA

Alexander Valley

Anderson Valley

Arroyo Grande Valley

Arroyo Seco

Atlas Peak

Ben Lomond Mountain

Benmore Valley

Carmel Valley

Carneros

Central Coast

Chalk Hill

Chalone

Cienega Valley

Clarksburg

Clear Ranch

Cole Ranch

Cucamonga Valley

Dry Creek Valley

Dunnigan Hills

Edna Valley

El Dorado

Fiddletown

Guenoc Valley

Hames Valley

Howell Mountain

Knights Valley

Limekiln Valley

Livermore Valley

Lodi

Madera

McDowell Valley

Mendocino

Merritt Island

Monterey

Mount Harlan

Mount Veeder

Napa Valley

North Coast

North Yuba

Northern Sonoma

Oakley

Oakville

Pacheco Pass
Paicines
Paso Robles
Potter Valley
Russian River Valley
Rutherford
St. Helena
San Benito
San Lucas
San Pasqual Valley
Santa Clara Valley
Santa Cruz Mountains
Santa Maria Valley
Santa Ynez Valley
Shenandoah Valley
Sierra Foothills
Solano County Green Valley
Sonoma Coast
Sonoma County Green Valley
Sonoma Mountain
Sonoma Valley
South Coast
Spring Mountain
Stag's Leap
Suisun Valley
Tephra Ridge
Temecula
Willow Creek
York Mountain

COLORADO
Green Valley

CONNECTICUT
Southeastern New England
Western Connecticut Highlands

INDIANA
Ohio River Valley

KENTUCKY
Ohio River Valley

LOUISIANA
Mississippi River Delta

MARYLAND
Catoctin
Cumberland Valley
Linganore

MASSACHUSETTS
Martha's Vineyard
Southeastern New England

MICHIGAN
Fennville
Lake Michigan Shore
Leelanau Peninsula
Old Mission Peninsula

MISSISSIPPI
Mississippi Delta

MISSOURI
Augusta
Hermann
Ozark Highlands
Ozark Mountain

NEW JERSEY
Central Delaware Valley
Warren Hills

NEW MEXICO
Messilla Valley
Middle Rio Grande Valley
Mimbres Valley

NEW YORK
Cayuga Lake
Finger Lakes
The Hamptons of Long Island
Hudson River
Lake Erie
North Fork of Long Island

OHIO
Grand River Valley
Isle St. George
Lake Erie
Loramie Creek
Ohio River Valley

OREGON
Columbia Valley
Rogue Valley
Umpqua Valley
Walla Walla Valley
Willamette Valley

PENNSYLVANIA
Central Delaware Valley
Cumberland Valley
Lake Erie
Lancaster Valley

RHODE ISLAND
Southeastern New England

TENNESSEE
Mississippi Delta

TEXAS
Bell Mountain
Escondido Valley
Fredericksburg
Messilla Valley
Texas High Plains
Texas Hill Country

VIRGINIA
Monticello
North Fork of Roanoke

Northern Neck—George Washington
  Birthplace
Rock Knob
Shenandoah Valley
Virginia Eastern Shore

WASHINGTON STATE
Columbia Valley
Nooksack Valley
Walla Walla Valley
Yakima Valley

WEST VIRGINIA
Kanawha River Valley
Ohio River Valley
Shenandoah Valley

WISCONSIN
Lake Wisconsin

Although geographical source and vine variety are relied upon to identify wines, particularly the classic wines from Europe, great wines are also a product of superior grape quality and vintner ability. Appellation of origin statements on labels do not, in themselves, guarantee superior wine products.

American winegrowing can do little about the nobility of European vineyards, and absolutely nothing about the 1,500-year head start that mother Europe has on U.S. commercial winegrowing. There can be no question that there is value in this grand history and tradition. It should be remembered, however, that this does not necessarily mean that the actual wine quality behind a classic label measures up to its price tag. It is fun to have someone pour similar wines from different origins in coded glasses—"blind" to all tasters willing to test their palates. Often the differences between the $15 American and the $115 European wines are difficult to measure. This is, of course, where the reality of U.S. wine value shines brightly.

❖ CALIFORNIA ❖

California is the premier winegrowing state in America, producing more than 400 million gallons annually during the 1990s. In 1994 there were 744 commercial vintners and 333,000 acres of wine grape vineyards cultivated in California.

Virtually all of the wine production in California is derived from Old World *Vitis vinifera* vine stocks brought to the state from Europe during the mid-1800s. As would be expected, this has created a rivalry between U.S. and European growers of the same grape varieties. Such contention is continually expressed in the wine media through vintage quality and price/value comparisons, such as California Chardonnay versus White Burgundy, or California Cabernet Sauvignon compared with Red Bordeaux. Sometimes there are formal competitions conducted to determine top honors. Although these activities result in a measure of objectivity for wine writers and marketers, evaluation should remain subjective for wine consumers. If wine is truly an art form, then its value remains a matter of personal taste and preference.

CLIMATE

The weather in California is dominated by two primary influences: the mountain ranges and the Pacific Ocean. Both the coastal mountains and the Sierra

FIGURE 5.1 California winegrowing regions.

Nevada range run north-south through the state. Between the two ranges is the broad, flat Central Valley, often referred to as the San Joaquin Valley.

Small valleys and bays along the coastline open channels for cool ocean air to penetrate inland, moderating temperatures and creating many localized weather patterns called *mesoclimates*. Fog is created where the ocean air meets the warmer inland air. The degree to which this fog penetrates inland often determines the varieties of grapes that can be grown in a given area. Regions such as the North Coast, Central Coast, and South Coast in California are locales where the penetration of ocean air moderates the climate. Travelers to San Francisco take cool-weather clothing even for the summer. The Central Valley, much farther inland, where this ocean influence is not a factor, remains rather uniformly warm and dry over its 400-mile length between Sacramento and Bakersfield.

Researchers at the University of California at Davis have devised a system for classifying viticultural areas according to "heat summation" to assist growers in determining the vine varieties that should grow best in a particular area. Heat summation is an indication of the relative length and warmth of the growing season and is expressed in terms of "degree days." These are calculated by including all the growing season days between the last day of frost in the spring and the first day of frost in autumn. Each day's daylight temperature, in degrees Fahrenheit, is then averaged and 50 degrees are subtracted from this figure (vine growth is insignificant at 50° F); the balance is that day's "degree days." For example, if the average temperature on a given day is 68° F, the result is 18 degree days. Adding up the season-long total of degree days in a particular area produces a total referred as the heat-summation figure.

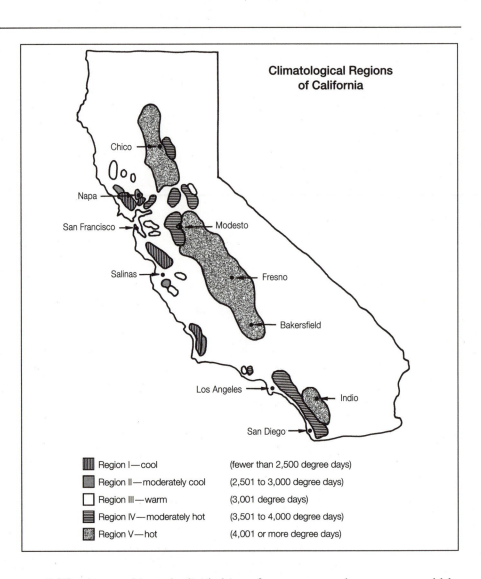

**Climatological Regions
of California**

Chico

Napa

San Francisco

Salinas

Modesto

Fresno

Bakersfield

Los Angeles

Indio

San Diego

	Region I—cool	(fewer than 2,500 degree days)
	Region II—moderately cool	(2,501 to 3,000 degree days)
	Region III—warm	(3,001 degree days)
	Region IV—moderately hot	(3,501 to 4,000 degree days)
	Region V—hot	(4,001 or more degree days)

FIGURE 5.2 Viticultural climatological regions of California.

California was ultimately divided into five segments where grapes could be grown, ranging from Region 1, the coolest, to Region 5, the warmest. Vines such as Chardonnay, Johannisberg Riesling, and Pinot Noir, which are native to cool European climates, yield better wine quality in the coastal regions of California. On the other hand, vines such as Sauvignon Blanc, Cabernet Sauvignon, and Merlot, are native to much warmer environs and generally do much better inland.

VITICULTURAL DISTRICTS

Appellations of origin are defined by regions, in which there are districts, in which there are subdistricts. The North Coast Region comprises five districts situated just north of San Francisco Bay: Napa County, Sonoma County, Carneros, Mendocino County, and Lake County. Several of these districts are further classified into several subdistrict appellations, such as the Alexander Valley, Dry Creek Valley, Russian River Valley, and Sonoma Valley in Sonoma County.

✖ NORTH COAST COUNTIES

NAPA COUNTY

The village of Yountville honors the memory of George Yount, originally from North Carolina, who first planted mission grapes in Napa County during the 1840s.

FIGURE 5.3 Sparkling wine caves at Schramsberg. *(Courtesy of Jack Davies.)*

Napa County is thought by many to be the single finest winegrowing district in America. A number of choice European varieties were planted here in the 1860s, some arriving via Count Agostin Haraszthy's Sonoma project and others with Samuel Branna, who had made a selection of classic vines during his own personal tour through Europe.

Robert Louis Stevenson spent considerable time in the Napa vicinity, even part of his honeymoon at the sparkling wine estate founded by Jacob Schram in 1862. During the 1970s the Davies family resurrected the Schram caves, which had closed during National Prohibition.

High regard for the initial wines grown in Napa County spread rapidly. Robert Louis Stevenson commented in the 1880s that the Napa locale was "where the soil sublimated under sun and stars to something finer, and the wine [was] bottled poetry." Stevenson went on with his lauds, comparing Napa wines to those from the great growths of Bordeaux and Burgundy—namely, Château Lafite and the Clos de Vougeot—high praise, indeed.

Napa County is situated north of San Francisco Bay and includes the famous Napa Valley, which runs in a 25-mile-long flank along the eastern slopes of the Mayacamas range.

Because of the of ocean influence, the coolest microclimates of Napa County are in its southernmost extreme, where fog rolls northward from the

FIGURE 5.4 Ocean fog rolling into the southern Napa Valley. *(Courtesy of Napa Valley Vintners Association.)*

bay. Here the soil is less fertile, and the area was previously used primarily for pastureland. This is the type of environment found in Burgundy and, as one might expect, the choice for cultivating Chardonnay and Pinot Noir vines.

Napa Valley

Proceeding north to the city of Napa, where the Napa Valley commences, the ocean influence subsides. Consequently, the Napa Valley is rather warm as compared with other locales in the North Coast. There is a deep gravel loam topsoil over much of the valley floor, perfect for the longer growing season required by such varieties as Sauvignon Blanc, Cabernet Sauvignon, and Merlot.

Many people regard the Napa Valley as the most sophisticated, and least agrarian, of the North Coast districts. This may be due to its citizens' subtle display of wealth and the building/zoning restrictions that exemplify modern-day aristocratic exclusivity. The Napa Valley has perhaps the most expensive agricultural land in all of America, with vineyard land, when it can be found, often selling for more than $50,000 per acre.

Perched high on the rim of the extinct Mount Veeder volcano in the Mayacamas Mountains is the tiny Mayacamas Vineyards. The vines, terraced into hillsides well more than 2,000 feet in elevation, are among the highest in Napa County. The old stone winery on the estate was built in 1889 by John Henry Fisher. In 1968, San Francisco stockbroker Robert Travers bought Mayacamas and has continued its high standards for Chardonnay and Cabernet Sauvignon. Mayacamas Cabernets are noted for an exceptional density, often requiring a decade before they can be enjoyed.

About nine miles north of Napa city, near the town of Yountville, is Domaine Chandon, which represents the first major entry of a European wine company into California. In 1973, Moët-Hennessy, the parent company of the French Champagne giant Moët & Chandon, bought 850 acres of prime land, situated mostly in the lower reaches of Napa County, where the traditional Champagne varieties, Chardonnay and Pinot Noir, flourished.

The company began producing an American sparkling wine, using the traditional French Champagne methodology. In 1977 an architectural masterpiece of a winery was constructed to embrace the three million bottles of capacity needed to meet consumer demand. The winery now includes first-class visitor facilities and a truly superb restaurant. Domaine Chandon makes several sparkling wine types and is one of the premier tourist attractions in the southern portion of the Napa Valley.

The magnificent Far Niente stone winery was old when Prohibition was declared and slowly decayed until 1979, when it was purchased by Gil Nickel,

FIGURE 5.5   Domaine Chandon winery.

who endured the expensive task of renovating the facility to a beauty and quality far beyond its original grandeur. He named the property after the Italian phrase *dolce far niente*, translated as "it is sweet to do nothing." The Far Niente caves are filled with some of the finest — and among the most expensive — Chardonnay and Cabernet Sauvignon.

The mission-style architecture of the Robert Mondavi Winery in Oakville is an easily recognized landmark with its bell tower facade, as featured on the famous label.

Born in Italy, Robert Mondavi emigrated with his family from Italy to California at the age of 10. Twenty years later, in 1942, his family purchased the Charles Krug winery. A man in intense innovation and creativity, Robert Mondavi was frustrated by family strife, an ongoing conflict thought to be the basis for the long-running *Falcon Crest* television series.

In the mid-1960s Mondavi struck out on his own and finalized a funding package that permitted him to build what has become one of the premier wineries in all of the United States. It was Mondavi who introduced the use of the term *Fumé Blanc* for dry Sauvignon Blanc produced in an aromatic wood-aged style. Constantly searching for ways to improve, Mondavi experimented with variable fermentation techniques and intricate barrel-aging methods, which are now legendary. His staff conducts many educational programs at the winery and across the country. The winery is open to the public and is an essential tourist stop in the Napa Valley.

In 1980, Mondavi announced a joint venture with the late Baron Philippe de Rothschild, master of the renowned Château Mouton-Rothschild estate in Bordeaux. The result was construction of the grand Opus One estate in the Napa Valley, which now produces perhaps the single finest red wine in America.

Gustave Niebaum, as discussed in Chapter 2, was captain of a trading ship running seal furs from Alaska. Having made a fortune, he bought the then highly prized Inglenook wine estate in 1879 and set about his cellars with a demand for "white-glove" sanitation. The Niebaum estate grew to rank with the best in the Napa Valley, the equal of Beaulieu and Beringer. Succeeding generations let things slip, and the Inglenook name, mansion, and cellars were eventually sold to the giant Heublein beverage conglomerate. The vineyard portion of the estate was sold to film producer-director Francis Ford Coppola. While Heublein relegated the grand old Inglenook brand to labels of jug wines, Coppola created the Niebaum-Coppola wine estate. In 1994 he was able to reunite the original mansion and cellars with his vineyards. While the Inglenook name is gone, Niebaum-Coppola has arrived with a verve that promises rebirth of this historic site.

FIGURE 5.6   The Niebaum-Coppola wine estate. *(Photo by author.)*

The Grgich Hills winery is named for its founders, Mike Grgich and Austin Hills, the latter a member of the well-known San Francisco coffee-importing family. A Croatian by birth, Grgich came to this country in 1958 with a background in wine production and worked for 20 years at some of the best wineries in the Napa Valley, among them the Beaulieu Vineyards, Robert Mondavi, and Château Montelena. He achieved international acclaim in 1976 when, as Château Montelena winemaker, his 1973 Chardonnay won a gold medal at the famous Bicentennial invitational blind tasting conducted in France against highly ranked White Burgundies. The Grgich and Hills partnership was subsequently founded in 1977 and, as would be expected, a major share of its production has been Chardonnay.

A short drive up Spring Mountain road west of St. Helena, in the middle of the Napa Valley, brings one to Spring Mountain Vineyards, best known today for the Victorian mansion featured in the popular 1980s television series *Falcon Crest*.

The estate was built in the late 1800s by the Parrott family, which had made a fortune in wine distribution, among other ventures. It is now the property of an investment consortium headed by Mike Farrell, one of the premier winemakers in the Napa Valley.

The ornate gothic Rhine House of Beringer Vineyards, with 1,000 feet of 1870s limestone tunnels and caves, is another of the most popular tourist attractions in the Napa Valley. The main road passing in front of the property is "tunneled" between two rows of magnificent trees.

Beringer was founded in 1876 by Frederick and Jacob Beringer, who had emigrated from the Rhineland winegrowing region in Germany. The winery has operated continuously since 1879, making alternative products during Prohibition, and remained in the Beringer family until 1970, when it was purchased by the Nestlé Company. Nestlé sold the estate in 1995 to a Texas firm. With more than 2,500 acres of vineyards, Beringer is one of largest vintners in the Napa Valley. More important, Beringer wins more gold medals and accolades for quality than most smaller boutique vintners.

Situated on a hilltop just south of Calistoga is Sterling Vineyards, unquestionably one of the most picturesque winery estates in the world. Visitors ascend the crest by a short tramway ride. From the balconies of the beautiful Moorish-inspired winery buildings there is a view of the entire northern portion of the Napa Valley. The winery itself is a showcase of tile mosaics, fountains, elegant wall hangings, stained glass windows, and even an operating carillon, not to

FIGURE 5.7 The Beringer Rhine House. (*Photo by author.*)

mention the state-of-the-art cellars that visitors may see in detail by virtue of self-guided tours. Sterling was founded in the early 1960s by English paper magnates Peter Newton and Michael Stone, who sought to produce the highest-quality table wines. Its reputation grew rapidly and found a ready market. In 1977, Sterling was sold to Coca-Cola and six years later resold to the Seagram Corporation.

Clos Pegase wines age in caves amidst priceless works of art collected by publisher Jan Schrem. Among the finest in the gallery is Redon's *Pegasus*. This magnificent painting of the famous winged horse of Greek mythology is faithfully reproduced on Clos Pegase labels in homage to the legend that Pegasus gave birth to wine and art when his hooves released the sacred Spring of the Muses. A competition sponsored by the San Francisco Museum of Modern Art resulted in renowned Princeton archictect Michael Graves' winning the commission to design the Clos Pegase winery—to build a "temple to wine."

Caymus Vineyards was founded in 1971 by the Charles Wagner family in the heart of Napa Valley. Early on it was readily apparent that Cabernet Sauvignon vines on this land matured fruit of an exceptional richness with a dense ruby color, immense cherry-cedar bouquet, and heavy-bodied consistency. Aged in an array of various types of oak, the result has truly advanced the state of Napa Valley winemaking. At the top of a long list of impressive awards Caymus has won is that for its 1990 Special Select Cabernet Sauvignon: the *Wine Spectator* magazine 1994 selection as the single finest wine in the world.

Although a relative newcomer to winegrowing, Silverado Vineyards has already become a California classic. It is owned by the Disney family, an estate left by the late entertainer Walt Disney. The majestic winery sits atop one of the

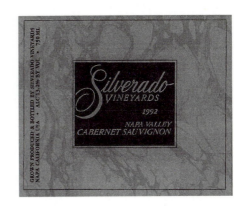

Stag's Leap foothills in the southeastern reaches of the Napa Valley. Expert winemaker Jack Stuart has earned the great respect that the Silverado brand commands in the marketplace.

Stag's Leap Wine Cellars takes its name from the rocky promontory that brings the Napa Valley to an abrupt end at its southeastern extreme. Stag's Leap is also an approved appellation given to the entire vineyard locale at the south end of the Silverado Trail.

Founder Warren Winiarski left an academic career at the University of Chicago to pursue an interest in commercial winemaking. After an apprenticeship with several area winemakers, he commenced producing his own wines in 1972. The Winiarski claim to fame came when his 1973 Stag's Leap Wine Cellars Cabernet Sauvignon was awarded first place, ahead of several classic Bordeaux châteaux, at the 1976 Bicentennial wine competition in Paris. The high regard for wines from this estate has ever since been building on that stunning achievement.

A World War II combat aviator, Sheldon "Hack" Wilson settled in postwar South Africa to found what was to become a large chain of soft drink bottling plants. Several decades later he sold out and brought his fortune home to California. Taken with the beauty of an obscure golf course beneath the magnificent Chimney Rock in the Stag's Leap end of the Napa Valley, Wilson bought the facility, plowed up half of the golf course, and established what has become one of the most remarkable smaller estate wineries in the area. The architecture of the winery is Cape Dutch, very unusual for anywhere in America, but expressed perfectly on this site. More important, Chimney Rock Cabernet Sauvignon is winning both the accolades of the press and the palates of the public. Visitors are welcome, both at the winery and at the remaining nine-hole golf course.

SONOMA COUNTY

To the west, a dozen miles or so across the Mayacamas mountains, is Sonoma County, a much larger winegrowing district than Napa County and with a vastly different character. The Sonoma winegrowing atmosphere seems to be generally less aristocratic and more agrarian.

The Sonoma County district is best known for wines grown in four major subdistricts: Alexander Valley, Dry Creek Valley, Russian River Valley, and the Sonoma Valley. Wines grown in these locales may be labeled with their appropriate appellation name, which may also be used in conjunction with "Sonoma County." Wines blended from two or more appellations in this district are generally labeled as simply "Sonoma County."

FIGURE 5.9 Sonoma County vineyards. *(Photo by author.)*

The climate of Sonoma County is diverse, ranging from a designation of less than Region 1 in some areas, where vines fail commercially, to well into Region 3 amid the inland valleys.

ALEXANDER VALLEY

Grapevines were first planted in the Alexander Valley in the 1840s by Cyrus Alexander, a pioneer farmer who possessed extraordinary judgment for fine vineyard environs. Alexander's decision to settle here was doubtlessly influenced by the beautiful landscape stretching in every direction. By the late nineteenth century there were several wineries operating nearby, but most of the Alexander Valley grapes went to wineries in other parts of Sonoma County.

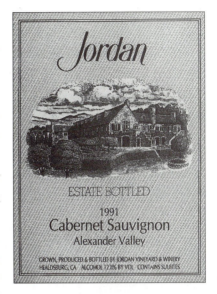

The Alexander Valley is the most inland of the four Sonoma County wine subdistricts and thus has a moderately warm climate ranging between Regions 2 and 3, depending on how each vineyard is situated in elevation and exposure to the sun. Since the ATF has approved the Alexander Valley as an appellation, investment has been vigorous. Today there are a broad selection of wines available with Alexander Valley labels.

At the western edge of the valley is its capital, the demure city of Healdsburg, which is a delightful place to visit. Its old town square is lined with quaint shops and eateries that can provide take-outs for an impromptu picnic.

Colorado oil magnate Tom Jordan first planned to buy a château in Bordeaux, but decided instead to build his own château, tucked back in the hills between the Alexander Valley and Healdsburg. The goal was to make a Bordeaux-style red that could fully compete with the high-ranking château growths. He proceeded to plant several hundred prime acres with pedigreed stocks of Cabernet Sauvignon and Merlot vines and, later, some Chardonnay as well.

The magnificent château winery was built and equipped with the latest in technology. Jordan's first vintage was 1976, the wine from which was released in 1980. It immediately won the attention of both the wine media and the marketplace. Although most Alexander Valley wines are modestly priced, Jordan commands premium prices. Added to the line more recently is a sparkling wine, "J," which has also won enviable accolades.

It was amid the festivity of their 1984 New Year's Eve party that neighbors Tim Murphy and Dale Goode were introduced to wine marketer David Ready. A mutual friendship developed, and the founding ideas for Murphy-Goode wine cellars emerged soon after. The partners own some of the most esteemed vineyards in the Alexander Valley.

DRY CREEK VALLEY

From the Warm Springs Dam northwest of Geyserville to the Dry Creek's confluence with the Russian River just south of Healdsburg, is found the warmest appellation in Sonoma County, primarily owing to its lower elevation and open exposure to the sun. Even so, there are some equally warm locales in the Alexander Valley.

A brilliant MIT engineering student, David Stare, was a 1950s wine buff whose drive and enthusiasm for wine was far greater than for academics. Beset and frustrated throughout the 1960s with the unrealistic ambition for commercial winegrowing he decided, nevertheless, to take the big step in 1972 and founded Dry Creek Vineyards. If Sonoma County Sauvignon Blanc is the best in the world, then Dry Creek Fumé Blanc is the "crème de la crème" and more than a match for the classified growths in the Graves district of Bordeaux.

Don Carano's enthusiasm for fine food and wine was inspired by his grandmother, Amelia Ferrari, and the fine cuisine traditional to her native Italy. The magnificent Ferrari-Carano villa and estate winery situated in the upper Dry Creek Valley is testimony to the remarkable success the Carano family has achieved in bringing together tradition and style in their creation of superb food and wine.

FIGURE 5.10 Aging cellars at the new Ferrari-Carano villa in the Dry Creek Valley. *(Courtesy of Ferrari-Carano Vineyards and Winery.)*

Founded in 1880, Geyser Peak Winery survived several ownerships after the repeal of National Prohibition. In the simplest terms, most of those ownerships did little to enhance the reputation of the estate. Bag-in-the-box wines were made there, along with vinegar. All that changed when the Trione family acquired the winery in 1982 and brought the Geyser Peak winery back to its prime. True glory, however, returned only when Daryl Groom was hired as winemaker in 1989. Groom was the vaunted artisan of Penfold's Grange Hermitage, Australia's most famous and expensive red wine. In just a few years under Groom's direction (twice voted California "Winemaker of the Year"), Geyser Peak has become one of the premier vintners in California.

Wines from the vineyards belonging to the late actor Raymond Burr, who lived in the small village of Geyersville, were made at the Pedroncelli Winery, situated in a small canyon just to the west of town. This is one of the older Sonoma County family wineries that was founded at the repeal of Prohibition, only to find itself in the midst of the Great Depression. A frugal and clever businessman, Pedroncelli produced bulk wines for other vintners, bypassing the high cost of labor, machines, and materials to produce inventories of bottled goods for an uncertain market demand. However, once the Depression had subsided, Pedroncelli supplemented bulk production with a few wines bottled under his own label.

In the 1950s, sons John and Jim embarked upon an extensive modernization of the facility and today produce a full range of table wines. With the burden of development cost long behind them, the Pedroncelli brothers continue to offer fine wines at comparatively low prices. Consequently, Pedroncelli wines are routinely listed in the "Best Buy" category of wine reviews.

Piper-Sonoma is a scion of the famous Champagne vintner, Piper-Heidsieck, in France. Despite this influence, the sparkling wines of Piper-Sonoma are made for the American palate, with lighter texture, a bit less tart acidity, a little more fruit character, but all with the same fine structure and tiny bubbles that result only from the fermented-in-the-bottle method of Champagne—and at much less the price.

RUSSIAN RIVER VALLEY

Russians came to this part of Sonoma County in the early 1800s seeking the rich furs of the otter and seal through their great skill as trappers. Little did they know—or, probably, care—that a century and a half later this locale would be one of the very few places in America that could cultivate the regal Pinot Noir vine to a quality matching Grand Cru Burgundy. Dehlinger, Gary Farrell, Iron

Horse, Laurier, Robert Stemmler, and Williams-Seylem are among the Russian River Valley vintners that consistently win highest honors for Pinot Noir wines grown in the United States.

SONOMA VALLEY

The Sonoma Valley, often referred to as "The Valley of the Moon," is arguably the most well known of the Sonoma County subdistricts. It is in Sonoma city that the last of the El Camino Real missions was built, with construction commencing in 1823. Ten years later, General Mariano Vallejo, a 26-year-old Mexican Army lieutenant, was dispatched to shut down the Sonoma Mission. Vallejo governed the Sonoma locale for three decades, during which he became interested in winegrowing and was fascinated by Count Agostin Haraszthy's Buena Vista project. It was through the combined influence of Vallejo and Haraszthy that the southern tip of the Sonoma Valley became the cradle of fine California winegrowing.

Rugged mountaintops protect valley and foothill vineyards, which are manicure perfect. A stop for lunch or a picnic in the town of Glen Ellen recalls a bit of the old-time California ambiance; a visit to the Smothers Brothers wine shop near Kenwood recalls more recent times.

Determined to bring excellence to Sonoma Valley table wines, the Lee and Sheela families purchased the rustic 1906 Pagani Winery in 1970. It has since emerged beyond excellence and is truly one of the premier wineries in America. Renamed Kenwood Vineyards, it embraces two magnificent legacies. The first of these is the Jack London vineyard estate, situated high above the valley, where Cabernet Sauvignon produces small crops of superb quality grapes. The second is the production of rather Rothschild-like editions of Kenwood "Artist's Series" Cabernet Sauvignon, with labels fashioned around original artwork selected for each vintage. Both of these red wines have dense body, brilliant garnet-scarlet hues, and rich cedar-plum flavors.

One of the newest Sonoma Valley wine estates is the Carmenet estate which is actually atop Moon Mountain, with some vineyards planted in holes blasted out of the rock with dynamite. One of the most popular Carmenet wines is the "Dynamite Red." This magnificent place offers a spectacular view of Sonoma Valley below. Carmenet enjoys a reputation for heavy-bodied, rich, dark red wines made in the château estate style of Bordeaux in France, whereby wines grown from Cabernet Sauvignon, Merlot, Cabernet Franc, Malbec, and Petit Verdot vines are blended together. The French refer to this collection of five varieties as the "Carmenet."

FIGURE 5.11 The Jack London vineyards. *(Photo by author.)*

Another venerable member of the Sonoma Valley wine community is Sebastiani Vineyards, founded in 1904. The history and philosophy of Sebastiani are similar to those of other Italian immigrant winemakers who settled in the North Coast region. Sebastiani specializes in well-made and modestly priced table wines, both under the traditional Sebastiani brand and the new Vendange label. The story of Sebastiani is a Mondavi-like saga; a family split occurred in the 1980s, when company president Sam Sebastiani, fired by his mother, left the company and started his own Viansa Winery at the south edge of Sonoma city.

The Fisher tradition of excellence began in 1886, when the first carriages from the family coach works heralded what was to become the Fisher Body Corporation, eventually the body supplier for all of General Motors automobiles. The first vineyards were planted in 1973 by Juelle and Fred Fisher on Mayacamas Mountain hillsides overlooking the lush, green Sonoma Valley. Their pride in heritage and craftsmanship is symbolized by the familiar coach insignia found on their wine labels.

As discussed in Chapter 2, the first of the Sonoma wineries was Buena Vista, the property made famous by Count Agoston Haraszthy. Records recently unearthed seem to indicate that wine was made there before Haraszthy ever arrived—perhaps by General Vallejo's brother, Salvador, as early as 1849.

It is certain, however, that Haraszthy founded his own Buena Vista at the northeastern edge of Sonoma city in 1857. The vineyards surrounding the winery were planted with the numerous vine varieties he brought back from Europe. The winery consisted of two stone buildings constructed across the front of a series of tunnels and caves—truly a showplace in its day. The barns were shaken and several of the tunnels collapsed during the great earthquake of 1906.

Frank Bartholomew, a UPI correspondent in World War II, bought Buena Vista at auction, sight unseen, in 1943 and operated the estate until 1968, when he sold the winery but kept the old Haraszthy homestead. Both properties have now been reunited under the ownership of the Racke family, prominent European wine marketers. They continue a marvelous restoration of the old stone buildings and welcome visitors at this magnificent place. Buena Vista wines, however, are now made at a modern facility situated a few miles farther south in the Los Carneros district.

FIGURE 5.12 Wine tasting and retail in the old Buena Vista winery. *(Courtesy of Buena Vista Vineyards and Winery.)*

LOS CARNEROS

The Los Carneros district comprises the combined lower reaches of both Napa and Sonoma Counties as they border the shore of San Pablo Bay. The county boundary line divides the area such that labels often indicate either "Carneros-Sonoma" or "Carneros-Napa" to further define their geography.

The rolling lowlands of the Carneros region, bringing together the southernmost reaches of the Napa and Sonoma valleys, was once considered a locale too harsh in climate and too poor in soil for quality winegrowing. However, the Carneros has proven to bear superb fruit in these Burgundian-like conditions. The Acacia Winery, part of the Chalone-Rothschild wine alliance, produces consistently superior wines from Chardonnay and Pinot Noir grapes.

The extensive pioneering achievements of Francis Mahoney during the 1970s convinced skeptics that Los Carneros could emerge from common pastureland to premier viticultural land. The poor soils and Region 1 climate here have since constituted one of the premier locales in all of California for exceptionally fine Chardonnay and Pinot Noir. These vine varieties are native to Burgundy, which epitomizes poor soil and harsh weather winegrowing. In Mahoney's Carneros Creek cellars young wines are aged in French oak barrels. His Chardonnay has a sumptuous boxwood-citrus flavor profile, and the Pinot Noir has a complex cherry-coffee-bramble-briar character. Both wines are perennial gold medal winners.

MENDOCINO COUNTY

Just north of Cloverdale, where Sonoma County ends, Mendocino County begins. This is another of the picturesque districts that make up the North Coast Region. A drive along Route 101 on a clear day can be enchanting, offering the blue-gray-green colorscape of creeks, mountain rock, and vineyard-laden foothills dividing small valleys in which superb winegrowing is rewarding some of California's newest vintners.

Viticulture here is less concentrated than in either Napa or Sonoma Counties. Vineyards are often interspersed with orchards and row crops. It is this splendid diversity of agriculture on display that creates the charming character of Mendocino County.

ANDERSON VALLEY

The newest and most remote of all the winegrowing locales in the Mendocino County district, the Anderson Valley is also the coolest, virtually all of it classified as Region 1. As expected, the cool-climate vine varieties gather most attention here, and justifiably so. Anderson Valley wines from Chardonnay, Gewürztraminer, and Pinot Noir vines now rival the Carneros for truly superb quality.

The tiny Husch Winery was founded in 1971. Despite its youth, as compared with many other northern California vintners, Husch is still the oldest wine firm in the Anderson Valley of Mendocino County. In 1979, Husch was sold to the Oswald family, who merged their La Ribera Ukiah Vineyards with the estate. Husch Chardonnay, Pinot Noir, and Gewürztraminer are among the most sought-after wines grown in Mendocino County.

REDWOOD VALLEY

One of the greatest success stories in all of California winegrowing is that of the Fetzer family. Originally from Nebraska, Bernard and Kathleen Fetzer moved to the Redwood Valley from Oregon in the early 1950s. Their expertise was in lumber, but they soon became intrigued with the lush vineyards that surrounded Ukiah, the capital city of the rich and famous Mendocino farmlands.

The Fetzers bought a former stagecoach inn, large enough to house their bounty of 11 children. They called it the "Home Ranch," and the 40 acres of

vines that came with it became an obsession. The first few crops wre sold to other vintners, and the cash received was literally plowed back into their vineyards. It was only natural that a family with an extraordinary work ethic such as theirs would soon recognize the value-added potential of their fine grapes and respond to the challenge of commercial winemaking. The result was success of titanic proportions. In 20 years Fetzer became one of the 10 largest wineries in America. Barney Fetzer passed away in 1981. Widow Kathleen and her 11 children continued to operate the facility for another 10 years and then sold it to the Brown-Forman Distilling Company.

LAKE COUNTY

Truly a special place, Lake County includes majestic mountains to the west, a large serene lake, and bountiful agriculture. Along with its attraction for wine enthusiasts, Lake County is also popular as a remote weekend and vacation paradise.

Founded in 1888 by the renowned British actress Lillie Langtry, Guenoc was her manifest commitment to "create the greatest claret in the country." Although there is little evidence to indicate she ever attained that lofty goal, there can be no question that this grand Guenoc Valley vineyard is now one of the premier producers of Cabernet Sauvignon, Cabernet Franc, and the other Bordeaux "Claret" grapes in America. Situated just outside the Napa County border, some 90 miles north of San Francisco, Guenoc is now part of a 23,000 acre estate operating under the ownership of the Magoon family who, despite being the most medal-winning vintner in the United States, never seem to reach perfection. There are few wine values to equal Guenoc.

Corporate attorney Jess Jackson shares the Old World belief that the finest wines are created through skillful blending, that no single vineyard is capable of contributing all the components necessary to orchestrate perfection. Jackson describes each vineyard as another "color for the canvas," reflecting an artistry and craftsmanship that have brought his California wines an astonishing level of success.

His accomplishment is unparalleled. The modest original winery has now expanded to become one of the largest premium vintners in the United States. Further, Jess Jackson has invested wisely, purchasing fine vineyards along the way to ensure a continuing supply of grapes meeting his demanding standards. The Jackson success has also grown to include ownership of other wineries, among which are Robert Pepi, Stonestreet, Cambria, and La Crema.

At this point it may be well to consider how the various geographic statements on a label indicate a "pecking order." Note the following example of how value increases as appellation becomes more closely defined and limited:

ORIGIN OR APPELLATION	TYPICAL PRICE	INTERPRETATION
American	$6.00	• Grapes could have been grown anyplace in the United States. • Has virtually no prestige. • Vintage dating not permitted.*
California	$8.00	• At least 75 percent of the grapes must have been grown in California. • Up to 25 percent of the grapes could have been grown in some other state. • Generally an appellation used for ordinary wine. **

North Coast Region	$10.00	• At least 85 percent of the grapes must have been grown anyplace in Napa County, Sonoma County, Carneros, Mendocino County, and/or Lake County.
		• Reputation of vintner is more important.
Sonoma County District	$12.00	• At least 85 percent of the grapes must have been grown in Sonoma Valley, Alexander Valley, Dry Creek Valley, Russian River Valley, and/or any part of Sonoma County.
		• Carries prestige, but reputation of vintner is also important.
Sonoma Valley Subdistrict	$14.00	• At least 85 percent of the grapes must have been grown within the bounds of Sonoma Valley.
		• Carries high prestige, but reputation of vintner is also important.
Jack London Ranch Vineyard	$18.00	• A "Vineyard Designated" wine.
		• At least 95 percent of the grapes must have been grown in the Jack London Ranch Vineyard in the Sonoma Valley.
		• Carries very high prestige.***
Estate Grown or Estate Bottled		• Grapes are grown from vineyards owned or leased by the vintner.
		• Prestige is totally dependent on reputation of vintner.
Reserve Statements		• Highest quality wine.
		• Prestige is totally dependent on reputation of vintner.

* ATF regulations permit grapes to be transported from one state to another, made into wine, and then vintage dated, providing the state in which the wine is made permits vintage dating and regulates retail sales exclusively in that state.

** There are some vintners that purposely blend together wines with specific, finite prestige appellations in order to achieve a more complex and superior final product, in which case the "California" appellation does not accurately reveal value. Success of these wines in the marketplace depends entirely on vintner reputation.

*** Most Vineyard Designated wines are the property of, or the exclusive production of, a single vintner and are therefore generally recognized as highly prestigious.

A close examination of the label at right reveals that this wine was grown in vineyards once owned by the famous author Jack London, now operated by the Kenwood Vineyards company. The vines on the Jack London Ranch are in Sonoma Valley, which is in Sonoma County, which is part of the North Coast Counties region of California.

It is essential that one learn how to judge the value of wines by interpreting their labels. Consider the statements found on the front and back labels of a Chardonnay produced by the Clos du Bois Winery in Geyserville, California:

- Brand or producer name.
- The vintage or year in which the grapes were grown.
- Vineyard designation. Grapes from the "Calcaire Vineyards" are grown exclusively for Clos du Bois.
- The appellation "Alexander Valley" is a specific locale within Sonoma County.
- The specified grape variety. At least 85 percent of the grapes used must be of the specified variety. When a grape variety is used for wine identity, the wine is thus a *varietal* wine.
- Production statement. "Produced and bottled by" requires that at least 75 percent of the wine be made from grapes processed by the bottler. "Made and bottled by," "cellared and bottled by," and other such statements have no real meaning in identifying production.
- Alcohol content (may be omitted if the words "Table Wine" appear on the label). Table wines must not exceed 14 percent alcohol by volume.
- ATF "warning" statement, required on all beverages containing alcohol that are marketed in the United States.
- ATF "sulfite" statement, required on all wines containing sulfites (which are used as preservatives).

❖ THE SIERRA FOOTHILLS

The Sierra Foothills region best exemplifies the early European influence on California winegrowing. Located to the southeast of Sacramento, the Sierra foothills are famous as 1849 Gold Rush territory.

The opportunity to stake a claim and strike it rich attracted hundreds of French, Germans, and Italians, to search for the "mother lode." Few found wealth. Sierra gold mining was short-lived, and the European miners who also knew how to grow wine grapes returned to that occupation. By 1860 there were more vineyards in the Sierra foothills than in either Napa or Sonoma.

Although the region boasts one of the most majestic landscapes in all of California winegrowing, it was also one of the most difficult to travel prior to the advent of paved highways. This difficulty, along with a cooler climate and a longer distance to the San Francisco market, allowed commercial winegrowing to progress much faster in Napa and Sonoma during the latter 1800s and early 1900s. During the wine boom of the 1960s, however, serious investments were made in Amador, Calaveras, El Dorado, Mariposa, and Nevada Counties, which make up the Sierra Foothills region.

This locale is best known for intense red Zinfandel with rich color and flavor, which compares favorably with the regal red Zinfandel wines grown by the Lytton Springs, Rafanelli, and Ravenswood wineries in the Dry Creek Valley of Sonoma County.

Robert Trinchero is the inventor of the popular "White Zinfandel," which is really pink or blush in color. Although his first wines were red Zinfandels under the Sutter Home Amador label, he was far more successful with white and blush wines. As a consequence, he built a huge production facility in the middle of the Napa Valley during the late 1980s. He recently acquired the Montevina Winery near Plymouth and continues high-quality production of red Zinfandels under both the Sutter Home and Montevina labels.

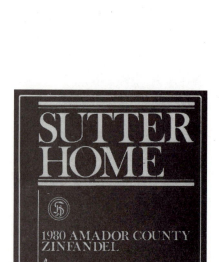

Baldinelli Vineyards and Shenandoah Vineyards in Plymouth are highly reputable vintners of the grand Sierra Zinfandel. The Boeger Winery in El Dorado County and the Stevenot Winery in Calaveras County are just two more of the vintners that have made the Sierra Foothills region one of the best "discovery" tours for enophiles visiting this part of California.

⊠ CENTRAL COAST COUNTIES

The major share of the Central Coast winegrowing region is situated to the south of San Francisco, extending down the California coastline nearly to Los Angeles. The Golden State's earliest history of cultivating vines and making wines is found here with the El Camino Real mission trail running its entire length. It is in this region that the infamous Hayward, San Andreas, and other earthquake faults pose a constant threat to California wine cellars.

The northern portion of the Central Coast Counties region comprises four counties joined around the periphery of San Francisco Bay: Alameda, Santa Clara, Santa Cruz, and San Mateo. The traditions of winemaking in these counties date from the first settlement of the San Francisco area. The pressures of urbanization, however, have driven winegrowers south. As the north has seen vineyards pushed out, the south has planted anew.

The southern sector of the Central Coast Counties region includes the counties of San Benito, Monterey, San Luis Obispo, and Santa Barbara. Although many labels on wines grown here simply give the appellation "California" as a geographical source, there is an ever-increasing proportion of premium-quality wine grapes being harvested in this area.

Cool coastal temperatures and fog penetrate some of the valleys in this area, resulting in Region 1 and Region 2 climates, which encourage the cultivation of Chardonnay and Pinot Noir. Further inland there are locales where Sauvignon Blanc and Cabernet Sauvignon, among other warm weather vine varieties, are grown.

ALAMEDA COUNTY

In the southwestern corner of Alameda County, in Mission San Jose, is the historical Warm Springs property once owned by railroad magnate Leland Stanford

FIGURE 5.13   Coastal mountain barrier of cool ocean fog. *(Photo by author.)*

in the nineteenth century. Stanford, patron founder of Stanford University, built a winery on his 350-acre estate and by the late 1880s was producing more than one million gallons per year—a monumental output for its time.

Modern-day Alameda County is far different. The bay coast is industrial and urban, influencing the Contra Costa hills and pushing eastward toward the Livermore Valley. The late Ernest Wente, of Wente Bros. Winery fame, recalled some 20 wineries operating in the Livermore Valley during the late 1890s and just several thousand people living there then. At the time of his death in 1983 only a few vintners remained and the population of Alameda County was well over one million.

LIVERMORE VALLEY

Situated about 50 miles southeast of San Francisco is the Livermore Valley. Coastal fogs do not cross over the Contra Costa hills, and, as a consequence, this is one of the warmest districts in the Central Coast region. Its landscape reminded the first French settlers of southern Bordeaux. As would be expected, they planted Sauvignon Blanc, Sémillon, and Cabernet Sauvignon vines. These varieties continue to be the principal selections cultivated and produce the best wines grown in the Livermore Valley.

Carl Wente, founder of Wente Bros. winery in 1883, sold all his wine in bulk. Discouraged by Prohibition, Wente sold the business to two of his sons, Herman and Ernest. The brothers struggled financially to keep the business alive and, at repeal, were among the first premium wine vintners to become nationally distributed. Herman's reputation as one of California's premier wine-makers grew quickly.

In 1981 the Wente firm, led by its fourth-generation president, Eric Wente, purchased another 955 acres of land to add to its already formidable estate. The new acreage included the original ranch purchased a century earlier by Carl Wente. It was here that Sémillon and Sauvignon Blanc vines, thought to have originated from Bordeaux's fabled Château d'Yquem vineyard, had been planted. The old winery buildings on the property have been fully restored for sparkling wine production. The Wente restaurant at the winery is one of the finest in the area.

Concannon Vineyards, Wente's neighbor in Livermore, is equal in age and tradition. James Concannon emigrated from Ireland to America in the 1860s— first to New England and then west to California's Barbary Coast. It was there that he learned of Catholic Archbishop Alemany's need for additional sacramen-

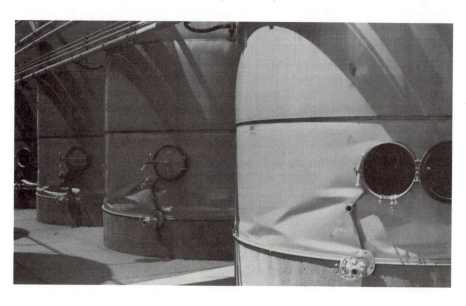

FIGURE 5.14 Wine tanks following an earthquake at Wente Bros. Winery. *(Photo by author.)*

tal wine in San Francisco. A small winery was constructed in 1883 to process the harvest of Concannon's young vineyards, and the wine quickly gained favor with both clergy and laity.

Founder Concannon passed away just after the turn of the century, and the winery was handed down to subsequent generations, dedicated to the production of premium wines. In the 1980s and 1990s the estate was sold and resold several times, during which time its grand reputation faded. Most recently the Wente family has formed a consortium of owners that has taken control of Concannon, and the restoration of this landmark estate indicates that it will soon return to prominence as one of the great Livermore wine producers.

SANTA CLARA COUNTY

West and across San Francisco Bay is Santa Clara County where a few vineyards remain, symbolic of what was once one of the largest winegrowing centers in California.

The Almaden Vineyard estate at Los Gatos came into prominence during the 1950s under the ownership of Louis Benoist. A marketing genuis, Benoist took the advice of wine writer Frank Schoonmaker, who suggested dropping generic wine names, such as "California Burgundy," and creating variety-named wines, exemplified by "California Chardonnay" and "California Cabernet Sauvignon." It took a monumental investment of time and money to convert both vineyards and production to this revolutionary idea. The first varietal wines were released in the 1960s, and this new wave of honesty in labeling took the American wine market by storm. Ironically, some of the new vineyards were almost immediately forced out of production by the roots of what would become the Silicon Valley. Eventually Almaden was sold, and now the name exists as a brand for huge wine production facilities in the Central Valley region.

A similar story involves the winery that Paul Masson built in the hills above Saratoga, near Los Gatos. Masson came to California from Burgundy in the late 1870s and took a job with Charles Lefranc, founder of Almaden. When Lefranc died, Paul Masson bought out part of the family estate and commenced to build a national reputation for fine "California Champagne." The Masson success grew with innovative products and packaging over several decades, but the estate was slowly displaced to Monterey County and the Central Valley region to become another of the corporate brands.

FIGURE 5.15 Paul Masson. *(Courtesy of Paul Masson Vineyards.)*

Although the Mirassou family has been making wine in Santa Clara County since 1854, wines bearing the Mirassou label did not attain any significant distribution until the late 1960s. With more than a century of experience in selling bulk wine to other vintners, and a loyal following of customers who drove some distances to obtain Mirassou wines directly at the winery, the fifth generation of Mirassous felt it was time to market consumer wines under their own label. With their own estate vineyard land falling to urbanization, new Mirassou vineyards were planted to the south, in Monterey County. The family still maintains "Home Ranch" vineyards in Santa Clara County, but only a fraction of those held several decades ago. Mirassou pioneering was an integral part of developing mechanical grape harvesting and crushing in the vineyard to reduce costs and improve wine quality.

SAN MATEO COUNTY AND SANTA CRUZ COUNTY

The industrial and urban sprawl south of San Francisco has driven almost all commercial winegrowing out of San Mateo and Santa Cruz Counties. Only a few small-scale vintners remain. Most of these are, however, professional people who pride themselves on making world-class quality wines, epitomizing the concept of the boutique winery.

Exemplifying these smaller winemakers is Cronin Vineyards, owned by computer expert Duane Cronin. At 8,000 gallons total capacity, Cronin would be dwarfed by the million-gallon Almaden and Paul Masson wineries that existed in this locale before development replaced them. Vintages of Cronin Chardonnay are among the very best, competing with the finest cru in Burgundy.

Dr. Thomas Fogarty, a cardiovascular surgeon, planted vines and built his modern winery overlooking the Silicon Valley during the early 1980s. His efforts are best known for a dry style of Gewürztraminer, a crisp white wine bursting with classic spicy fruit character that has reached lofty heights in competition across the United States. Vintage after vintage, Thomas Fogarty has won more prestigious medals for this varietal than any other vintner in America.

A completely different operational philosophy is found at the Grahm family's Bonny Doon Vineyard in Santa Cruz. Randall Grahm has brought humor to commericial winegrowing, spoofing, on his labels, some of the stuffy terms and identities used in the industry. One among several is a Bonny Doon "Grand Crew" wine, whereby Grahm associates the superior efforts of his employees with the prestigious Grand Cru classified vineyards in France.

SAN BENITO COUNTY

The historical center of San Benito County is Mission San Juan Bautista, built by the Franciscans in the late 1790s. The friars planted vines here, as at the other missions of the El Camino Real.

A few miles south of this mission, in the Cienega Valley, a small commercial winegrowing estate was founded by William Palmtag during the middle 1850s. Unfortunately, the winery building was constructed directly atop the San Andreas earthquake fault. The Cienega Valley Winery still operates, but with each tremor the cracks in the winery floor widen a little more—a keen tourist attraction.

Of the three recognized San Benito viticultural locales, Cienega Valley, Paicines, and the Limekiln Valley, it is the Limekiln Valley that has received the most recent attention. The small Calera Wine Company was founded by the Jensen family in 1976. Josh Jensen had previously studied winegrowing in Burgundy for several years and was convinced that the finest Pinot Noir could be produced only from vines cultivated in limestone subsoils. The Limekiln Valley locale was an obvious site selection for building "Calera"—Spanish for "Limekiln." The superb quality of the Jensen Pinots today indicate that his theory is precisely correct.

MONTEREY COUNTY

The thought of Monterey generally brings to mind the serenity of Monterey Bay, commercial fishing, a year-round resort, and the posh residential vicinity of Carmel and other nearby communities. On the 120-mile southwest trip from San Francisco to the Monterey Peninsula, much of the agriculture seen along the road is devoted to artichokes, not vineyards. Monterey winegrowing is found inland, amid vastly different environs. The ocean air is so cold near the bay shore that grapes will not ripen adequately, and these same breezes have a cooling effect on down the valley to Greenfield.

SALINAS VALLEY
The Salinas Valley is an 80-mile-long expanse of prime agricultural flatlands, continuing as far as Monterey Bay. This locale is often referred to as the "Salad Bowl of America," because of its huge amounts of iceberg lettuce in continu-

ous production. Vines are cultivated on the benchlands on either side of the valley. Soil drainage is excessive here, with the result that most vineyards require irrigation.

The principal winegrowing area of the Salinas Valley is situated between Soledad and King City. Here the dramatic effects of the ocean air can be measured; classification ranges from Region 1 (Soledad) to Region 3 (King City).

For the most part, the Salinas Valley has been developed over the past two decades by large Santa Clara "refugee" corporate wineries investing in large winegrowing projects. The vines planted here are the same classic varieties of *Vitis vinifera* cultivated in the vacated Silicon Valley locale, although the sheer magnitude of the Salinas acreage more closely resembles the gigantic San Joaquin Valley region.

To the east, in the Gavilan Mountain foothills, however, are some smaller vineyards that have earned lofty praise for quality. The Chalone vineyard, dating from 1920, exists in stark contrast to other winegrowers in the locale. Not only is it far older than most others in this district, it is the flagship vintner of a small NASDAQ corporation that includes several other estate wineries in California. A major share of the company is held by the Baron Eric de Rothschild, famous as the owner of the grand Château Lafite-Rothschild in Bordeaux.

Chalone is situated on a windy limestone hilltop east of Soledad, and the small quantities of superb Chardonnay and Pinot Noir grapes harvested there each vintage are convincing testimony for the "struggling vine theory" in producing highest-quality wines.

FIGURE 5.16 Chalone vineyards in the Gavilan foothills. *(Courtesy of Chalone, Inc.)*

SAN LUIS OBISPO COUNTY

If Monterey County is considered adolescent in the history of California viticulture, San Luis Obispo and its neighboring counties to the south are mere infants. Most vintners in this district have commenced operations just since 1980.

Yet despite their youth, several vintners have emerged with such consistent quality that they have already captured national attention. Among these are Arciero, Castoro, Creston, Edna Valley, and Meridian, all in the area centered by the city of Paso Robles.

SANTA BARBARA COUNTY

Vineyard development in Santa Barbara County has evolved in three areas— Santa Maria and Sisquoc Valleys to the north and Santa Ynez Valley to the south. This district is rapidly building a fine reputation for all the cool-climate varieties.

Established in 1974 by A. Brooks Firestone, of automobile tire fame, Firestone Vineyards is one of the oldest wine producers in Santa Barbara County. The 1978 Firestone Chardonnay won a double gold medal at the 1981 International Wine & Spirits Competition in Bristol, England. There were only five such awards given that year, and this was the only one presented to an American winery.

In 1984, Byron "Ken" Brown founded Byron Vineyards and Winery in the Santa Maria Valley. With a cool Region 1 climate, Santa Maria is a locale traditionally devoted to strawberry production. Only the Chardonnay vine can consistently ripen its fruit to full maturity. Each vintage develops slowly, yielding grapes exceptionally rich in flavor. As a consequence, there are few vintners in America, even in the world, that can match the heavy character of Byron Reserve Chardonnay. During the early 1990s, Brown sold the Byron estate to Robert Mondavi but stayed on as general manager and winemaker. Seeing great potential, Mondavi has invested heavily in expanding this promising venture.

Santa Barbara Pinot Noir is typified by bold essences of briar and bramble-berry fruit, perhaps the best quality to be found in all of southern California. One of the very best of these wines bears the Wild Horse label. Founded in 1982, this winery and its owner-winemaker, Ken Volk, have gained a national reputation.

❖ SOUTH COAST COUNTIES

During the 1960s a small Region 3 winegrowing area emerged southeast of Los Angeles near the town of Temecula. This may be considered a rediscovery, as Spanish missionaries had grown wine in nearby San Diego more than two centuries earlier.

Vines were planted in a planned agricultural/industrial development called Rancho California, which has since grown to enormous success. Though the region is 23 miles from the ocean at its nearest point, a gap in the coastal hills allows cool, moist breezes to penetrate the vineyards.

The first to plant commercial vineyards in the Temecula locale was Ely Callaway, a retired textile executive who founded the Callaway Vineyard & Winery in 1974. He later sold the firm and turned his remarkable entrepreneurial abilities to making high-grade golf clubs.

Under the ownership and direction of the Winery Alliance, which also operates Clos du Bois in Sonoma, Callaway has grown to become one of the premier vintners of distinctively delicate wines from warmer climate vine varieties.

❖ CENTRAL VALLEY

The Central Valley, a gigantic fertile plain often referred to as the San Joaquin Valley, lies between the coastal mountain range and the Sierra Nevadas in central California. It commences just south of Sacramento and stretches southward almost to Bakersfield, making it nearly 400 miles long. At some points it is nearly 100 miles wide. With few exceptions, the Central Valley is classified as a very warm Region 4 or 5 throughout its length. The world's largest single vineyard plots are found in this region, and this vast, flat expanse yields more than 75 percent of all the grapes grown in California.

In addition to producing nearly all of America's table grapes and raisins, the Central Valley has been known since Prohibition for most of the Port- and Sherry-type dessert wines grown in California. This great valley is the home of

FIGURE 5.17 A huge Central Valley vineyard. *(Photo by author.)*

the ubiquitous Thompson Seedless, the ultimate all-purpose grape harvested for the table, sun-dried for raisins, crushed for white table wines, and distilled for brandy.

During the 1980s the Central Valley made great strides in applying advanced viticultural techniques developed by the California State University at Fresno. This resulted in widespread planting of Sauvignon Blanc, Sémillon, Cabernet Sauvignon, and Merlot, among other classic vine varieties—all thought previously to be too delicate to withstand the higher temperatures in this region. The heavy tonnage of fruit produced from these vines lacks the intensity of flavor and color found in cool-climate locales, but success in developing low-cost "fighting varietal" table wines in the Central Valley has taken the world standard for *vin ordinaire* production a step higher.

The standard has been raised yet another step by the application of enological techniques to America's everyday wines grown in this huge valley. Machine harvesting at night, when temperatures are much lower, has reduced fruit oxidation. Gentle bladder-type pneumatic tank presses have reduced skin, pulp, and seed particle sediment, which can be a source of bacterial spoilage. Pinpoint control of fermentation temperature, stainless steel aseptic storage tanks, and membrane media sterile filtration, have each markedly contributed to San Joaquin wines being among the best there are for the money.

These technologies, along with the natural endowments of the "Big Valley" itself, and the determination of California's large producers to provide maximum quality and value, have combined to make this region a major center of the worldwide wine industry.

The Forest Glen label exemplifies the true state of the art in modern winemaking technology. High-yield grapes grown across the vast San Joaquin are masterfully vinified and barrel aged to produce wines that can often compete with those from vineyards in the North Coast region. The vintner behind this achievement is the giant JFJ Bronco firm, which also makes other similar hightech wines of excellent value under the Rutherford, Silver Ridge, Grand Cru, and Domaine Laurier labels.

The giant of San Joaquin, of California, and of the entire world, is the E. & J. Gallo winery. Gallo is the largest wine producer in the world, with a storage capacity of several hundred million gallons.

Ernest and Julio Gallo founded their Modesto, California, winery in 1933. It was originally housed in a rented warehouse and is still entirely owned and operated by the Gallo family. Their success is a story of truly remarkable foresight, fortitude, and savvy.

To convey the relative size and importance of Gallo in the American wine industry is a challenge. Its bottling capacity of more than three million bottles per day is greater than the entire annual production of most American or European wineries in a year. The bottling facility at Modesto makes its own bottles.

Gallo research and development have created standards for quality at affordable pricing, delivered through a comprehensive distribution network, and have contributed heavily to advancing the appeal of wine in an America that still hangs on to some vestiges of Prohibitionism. Dollar-for-dollar, there are perhaps no wines in the world that are better values than those with the Gallo label —some selections are better than wines costing several times as much.

❖ THE NORTHWEST ❖

The region known as the Northwest, or the Pacific Northwest, includes the winegrowing areas of Washington, Oregon, and Idaho. None of these states has a long history of *Vitis vinifera* wine production, although *Vitis labrusca* grapes

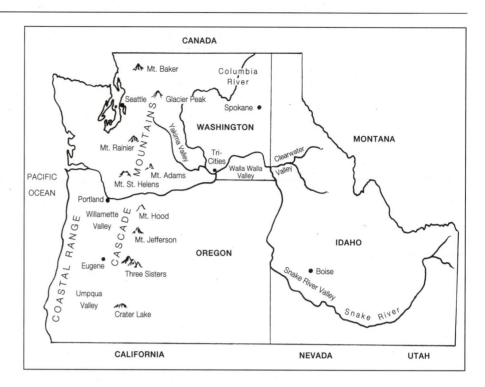

FIGURE 5.18 Northwest wine-growing regions.

have been grown in Washington and Oregon for many years. Despite their geographic proximity, the winegrowing locales of these three states have little in common.

In Washington, the majority of vineyards are cultivated on the east side of the Cascade mountains in what may be described as a temperate desert, which depends heavily on irrigation. As would be expected, Washington vines are princpally warm-climate varieties, Sauvignon Blanc, Sémillon, Cabernet Sauvignon, and Merlot being the leaders.

Oregon's winegrowing is clustered along the western perimeter of the state between the coastal mountains and the Cascades. Here one finds mostly Chardonnay, Gewürztraminer, Pinot Gris, Pinot Noir, and other cool-climate varieties planted widely.

Idaho is, of course, much farther inland, and vineyards there are generally situated in river valleys at elevations of 2,000 feet. The climate is characterized by moderate rainfall and fluctuating temperatures.

The growth of vineyard acreage in this tristate region has been explosive. In 1963 there was only one commercial winery in the region producing wines from the classic European varieties, and now there are nearly 200.

❖ WASHINGTON

With 85 vintners producing seven million gallons of wine per vintage, Washington is third after California and New York in quantity of wine production among the fifty states. A good share of Washington's vineyards produces grapes for jams, jellies, juice, and concentrate.

There were no wineries in Washington State before 1933, and from that time until the mid-1960s the only commercial wines made there were from native American *Vitis labrusca* varieties. Attempts were made to produce wines from French-American hybrids, but these did not succeed. It was the wine amateurs and hobbyists of the state, who thirsted for better wines and were willing to make their own, who triggered the *Vitis vinifera* wine-grape revolution in Washington viticulture. A group of amateur winemakers, mostly University of Washington professors frustrated with being unable to obtain reliable supplies of Old World grapes, decided to plant their own vineyards. To avoid regulatory complications from the ATF, the group founded their own winery in 1967, calling it, aptly enough, the Associated Vintners. When Andre Tchelistcheff, of Beaulieu Vineyard fame in the Napa Valley, came to Washington in 1967 to assess the possibilities for a premium wine industry there, he sampled a wine made by one of these amateurs and was duly impressed. His counsel and guidance to the region's vintners doubtless contributed heavily to the Northwest wine explosion.

COLUMBIA VALLEY

Most of the vineyards in Washington are cultivated in the Columbia Basin and Yakima Valley irrigation projects, which have converted a million acres of sagebrush to productive farmland. The average annual rainfall of the region is only about eight inches, because the Cascade mountains to the west block off most of the moisture-laden clouds arriving from the Pacific Ocean. The soils are predominantly sandy loam, requiring only sufficient water from irrigation to make them arable. Because there is little history of the *Phylloxera* root louse in the region, some of the vines are own-rooted, rather than grafted. The greatest threat to profitable viticulture in these southeastern Washington valleys seems to be the danger of early winter freezes.

Some of the very first Washington State wines were produced by American Wine Growers, Inc., a firm created by a merger of the Pommerelle and Nawico wineries in 1954. Pommerelle was a fruit and berry wine firm in Seattle, and Nawico made dessert wines in the Yakima Valley. They instituted a long-term project of phasing out sweet wine production, releasing their first premium dry table wines in 1967. These were specially labeled as the "Ste. Michelle" brand, a namesake of the famous French monastery in Normandy. Later a group of Seattle-area investors purchased American Wine Growers, Inc. and renamed the company "Ste. Michelle Vintners." In 1974 the firm was sold to the U.S. Tobacco Company.

With the financial backing of U.S. Tobacco, Ste. Michelle Vintners was able to purchase the historical Hollywood Farm, which had been established in the outskirts of Seattle in 1912 by wealthy lumberman Fred Stimson. U.S. Tobacco designed and built an Empire-style mansion on the estate during the mid-1970s

FIGURE 5.19   Château Ste. Michelle. *(Courtesy of Château Ste. Michelle.)*

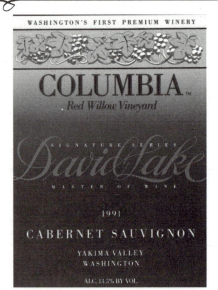

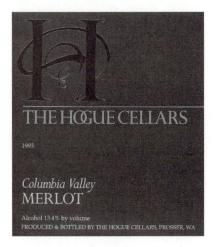

in order to house additional administrative and production facilities for their wine operations. This is a grand wine manor, adorned by arboretum landscaping, serene ponds, and lush greenery—all now known as "Château Ste. Michelle." Visitors are cordially welcomed to tour the charming château and taste award-winning wines in a setting more akin to the aristocratic countryside of Bordeaux, France, than the northeast Seattle suburb of Woodinville.

Château Ste. Michelle, along with its subsidiary Columbia Crest production facilities in the Yakima Valley and Columbia River Gorge, constitutes the largest winegrowing operation in all the Northwest Region.

Each of the University of Washington professors who founded the Associated Vintners brought expertise from a different discipline in creating this new winegrowing entity. Although it required several changes of location to keep up with the logistics of growth in processing and marketing, the firm flourished. As it grew, ownership evolved from a closed consortium to a corporation, and the name eventually changed to become the Columbia Winery. This highly regarded winery, now headquartered in Woodinville, Washington, is a neighbor of Château Ste. Michelle.

The Hogue family cultivates the noble Sémillon vine on the rich, sun-drenched eastern Washington soils. From the earliest wines made in Gary Hogue's daughter's playhouse and sold over a card table, to the impeccable vintages of today, the Hogue name on a bottle of Sémillon continues to be synonomous with delicate, but crisp, dry white wine expressing delicious pear-peach flavors. Without precedent anywhere, Hogue Sémillon won Best of Show honors for white table wine two consecutive years at the highly prestigious West Coast Wine Competition.

The Preston winery was founded in 1976 just to the northeast of Pasco in Washington's southern Columbia River basin. The Preston family first planted *Vitis vinifera* vines there during the early 1970s in fulfillment of a dream to produce top-quality table wines that could compete with those of California and Europe. Since that time Preston continues its impressive record of awards and accolades. The winery features an elevated tasting room situated so that visitors may enjoy wine tasting while viewing a panorama of vineyards embraced by breathtaking countryside.

The Leonetti Cellars may be the finest producer of Merlot in the United States. Founded in 1977 by Nancy and Gary Figgins, this Walla Walla winery may be considered the "Pétrus" of America. Like Pétrus, a small unclassified Pomerol château in Bordeaux that makes the world's most lauded and expensive Merlot, Leonetti quietly makes vintage after vintage of truly superb Merlot. This wine will demand a dear price, if one is fortunate enough to find a bottle, but will be well worth the cost.

FIGURE 5.20   Washington vineyards in the Yakima Valley. *(Photo by author.)*

◈ OREGON

WILLAMETTE VALLEY

Most of the winegrowing activity in Oregon has been in the Willamette Valley southwest of Portland. In close proximity to the Pacific Ocean, this area enjoys plenty of natural rainfall and is a haven for cool-climate varieties. The region has built a sterling reputation for Pinot Noir, but also produces exceptional Chardonnay, Johannisberg Riesling, and Gewürztraminer as well.

The excitement in Oregon wines has focused on David Lett's pioneering success with Pinot Noir, a wine that can be grown in a wide variety of places but performs distinctively in only a very few. California struggled to produce a first-class Pinot Noir for decades until Los Carneros, and, later, a few agreeable cool-climate sites in the higher elevations of Sonoma and Monterey counties, were planted. In the 1983 American Wine Competition conducted by the Beverage Testing Institute, which is open to all U.S. vintners, Oregon winegrowers clearly emerged as the leading producers of the regal Pinot Noir.

More recently the Yamhill County appellation in the Willamette Valley has made news as a "giant killer" in successful competition against some of the finest red Burgundies grown from the Pinot Noir in mother France.

Northern Oregon seems to be most suited to sparkling wine production. Frequent rains are likely during the harvest, but this is not a drawback inasmuch as sparkling wine production allows the wineries to harvest Chardonnay and Pinot Noir grapes early so as to obtain higher acidity levels.

The 95 commercial vintners in Oregon comply with state statutes that are even more restrictive than U.S. federal regulation. Oregon wines with varietal labels must contain 90 percent of the named variety, as opposed to the 75 percent required by the ATF. No European generic names may be used on their *Vitis vinifera* wine labels. Consequently, one will not find "Oregon Chablis" or "Oregon Burgundy" wines in the marketplace. An Oregon label must also show the locale in which the grapes were grown, and all grapes used must come from the region so specified. If, for example, a label states "Yamhill County," then 100 percent of the grapes must have been grown there. These restrictions were initiated and promoted by Oregon growers and vintners to protect and enhance the reputation of Oregon wines.

David Lett was the first to establish commercial Pinot Noir winegrowing operations in this region. He was in search of the best place to grow the elusive Pinot and, after deciding that the Umpqua Valley to the south was a bit too warm, in 1965 he settled in the Willamette Valley near the town of Dundee and founded his Eyrie Vineyards wine estate. He has been growing exceptional

FIGURE 5.21   The first Oregon Pinot Noir vineyard. *(Courtesy of Eyrie Vineyards.)*

wines from Pinot Noir and Pinot Gris ever since. Lett is best known for a well-publicized tasting by international experts, in which his 1975 Pinot Noir placed second against a number of highly classified French Burgundies personally selected for the competition by the renowned Burgundy shipper Robert Drouhin.

Drouhin was duly impressed with the quality of the Eyrie Vineyards' Oregon Pinot Noir, which outpaced nearly all of his classic Burgundies during the 1975 competition in New York. He decided to visit and investigate the virtues of the Willamette Valley. Ultimately, he invested in prime vineyard land there and constructed one of the most scenic and well-equipped wineries in the Dundee locale. The Domaine Drouhin Oregon Pinot Noir has been very impressive—with prices to match.

Another of the great pioneering forces in Oregon is David Adelsheim, who, along with his wife, Virginia, founded the innovative Adelsheim Vineyard winery near Newberg, Oregon, in 1971. Although the many prestigious awards for superb Adelsheim Pinot Noir portray their distinction as vintners, the Adelsheims' philosophy has been dedication to tireless experimentation. It has been Pinot Noir under the Adelsheim label that has won many of the grand awards accorded to Oregon wines since the late 1970s.

When Susan Sokol and William Blosser were first married, the idea of owning and operating their own winery was little more than a dream they shared from time to time. Having moved to Oregon from California, then to North Carolina, and back once more to Oregon, the Blossers planted their first 18 acres of Chardonnay, Johannisberg Riesling, and Pinot Noir in the early 1970s near David Lett and other enterprising new vintners on the outskirts of Dundee. The first few crops were sold to these vintners before the Sokol-Blosser winery was completed in time for the 1977 vintage. The Blossers moved cautiously and prudently in designing, constructing, equipping, and staffing their wine-production facilities. Their dream was realized, and today Sokol-Blosser is among Oregon's most respected vintners.

One of the largest wineries in Oregon is the highly regarded Knudsen-Erath facility, a winery founded by partners Cal Knudsen and Richard Erath. Their first plantings of Chardonnay, Johannisberg Riesling, and Pinot Noir were made in 1969.

The Knudsen-Erath philosophy is based on the "natural" approach to winemaking—using knowledge and experience to help "guide" wines, with minimal processing so that the resulting wines can be the best that they can be from each vintage of grapes. Erath explains that he does not employ ultrahigh technology and equipment to "steamroller" the wines. The winery, located west of Dundee, is a favorite stop for visitors traveling to and from the Pacific Coast.

The crown jewel of Oregon winegrowing is the magnificent King Estate, established in 1991. The King family, leaders in the communications industry,

FIGURE 5.22 King Estate.
(Courtesy of the King Estate.)

spared no expense in building what is one of the premier château wineries in the entire world. Cutting-edge science is seen at every turn in both vineyards and winery.

The King Estate philosophy takes wine production to another level. Each case of wine is imprinted with the signature of every employee at the facility, evidencing a pride and purpose that have won deserved praise from both wine critics and consumers. An enviable list of awards and medals has already commenced to build.

❖ IDAHO

The wine industry in Idaho is located almost exclusively in Sunny Slope, an area south of Boise along the Snake River. Vineyards are planted on southerly foothill exposures at an elevation just under 2,000 feet. The growing season has long hours of sunlight without excessive heat, and cool nights. Grapes ripen slowly throughout the long growing season and therefore retain good acid levels for well-balanced wines. Growers find extended periods of winter sunshine to be their greatest difficulty. Reflected light from the snow cover can sun-scald the vines, and higher temperatures can coax vines out of dormancy into a vulnerable vegetative state, leaving them vulnerable to damage with the next winter freeze.

Of the 13 vintners in Idaho, the largest is Ste. Chapelle, founded in 1976 as a joint venture of Richard Symms and William Broich. The estate comprises 180 acres of vines and twice that amount contracted from other growers. Chardonnay and Johannisberg Riesling have been consistently successful varietals for Ste. Chapelle, but the winery has also developed a promising line of sparkling wines.

❖ THE NORTHEAST ❖

Many native vines were discovered in the early seventeenth century by the Frenchman Samuel de Champlain, as he explored the islands in the St. Lawrence River. One of these islands was so overgrown with vines, doubtlessly *Vitis labrusca,* that Champlain named it "Bacchus Isle."

FIGURE 5.23 Northeast wine-growing regions.

The major hurdle for competitive commercial winegrowing in the northeast was the postulate that the region could grow only the native *Vitis labrusca* vines, which could withstand disease and the harsh climate, but which were overwhelmingly full of "foxy" fruit flavor. Beauchamp Plantaganet, in a London-published text describing the colonies, made these observations of the native grapes:

> Thoulouse Muscat, Sweet Scented, Great Fox *and* Thick Grape; *the first two, after five months, being boiled and salted and well fined [clarified], make a strong red Xeres [Sherry]; the third, a light claret; the fourth, a white grape which creeps on the land, makes a pure, gold colored wine.*

The "Great Fox" that Plantagenet identified was probably a variety of *Vitis labrusca*, a species delivering its heavily scented fruit in moderate-sized clusters. Even in modern times *foxy* is a rather loose sensory term used to describe the aroma and flavor typical of the *labrusca* species, of which the Niagara and the Concord are prime examples.

❖ NEW YORK

It seems incredible today, but the Dutch planted grapevines on Manhattan Island during the 1650s. The early vintners of New York State faced problems well beyond the simple maladies of climate and disease. The entire length of upstate New York, from Albany to Buffalo, was known in the nineteenth century as the "burned-over district" because of the number of revivalists, spiritualists, utopians, and other purveyors of religious and social causes who swept through the region in waves, rousing the populace to varied levels of frenzy and false promise. Twice before 1860, some 60 years before National Prohibition was declared, New York State passed prohibition laws that were either repealed or declared unconstitutional.

It is curious that the region could grow as a wine center during this period. That wineries such as Taylor, Pleasant Valley, and Widmer could survive the latter 1800s, then Prohibition and the Great Depression between two World Wars, is particularly remarkable.

FIGURE 5.24 Fred, Greyton, and Clarence Taylor, circa 1960. (*Courtesy of* Wine East *magazine; photo by Linda Jones McKee.*)

During the expansive "wine boom" years of the 1960s the American wine market thirsted for more wine than California could market. Management of some of the older, more well established vintners, such as the Taylor Wine Company, identified this desire as an unending demand for most any palatable wine product. Heavy investments were made in plantings of more native *Vitis labrusca* vines and in the buildings and equipment to process their fruit. California caught up in the 1970s, with stunning wines from both traditional vintners and the new high-tech boutique wineries in the North Coast region. Taylor, Gold Seal, and other vintners lacking prudent foresight fell quickly, their facilities remaining today as eerie, empty monuments to poor judgment.

In the 1960s and 1970s other enterprising eastern U.S. winegrowers turned their attention to the exciting new French-American hybrid grapes. Thousands of vine crosses had been made decades earlier in Europe as an alternative to losing the battle with the invading *Phylloxera* root louse. French vine parentage was indexed for high-grade fruit quality, and American vine parentage was indexed for disease resistance and winter hardiness.

The threat of vine-killing disease and harsh winters discouraged even the boldest of eastern U.S. winegrowers from cultivating the regal *Vitis vinifera* European wine varieties. Dr. Konstantin Frank's first successes with special clones, grafting, and trellis training techniques paved the way for an increasing number of trial plantings across the entire northeastern quadrant of the United States. This technology continues to advance, and plantings of Old World varieties have increased dramatically during the 1980s and 1990s.

Cornell University—in particular, its Geneva Experiment Station—has contributed heavily to advancing the state of wine art and craft across New York State. Indeed, Cornell has been a major contributor to technical wine literature for the entire cool-climate wine industry. In 1993 there were 108 vintners in New York State with a total production of 18 million gallons—a distant second to California.

FINGER LAKES

The Finger Lakes Region of west central New York State enjoys a unique and varied topography. Formed by glacial erosion at the end of the last Ice Age, the Finger Lakes area is a series of long, narrow parallel lakes with steep gravel-shale slopes that provide good soil drainage. Cold winter winds out of the north and west form a vortex over the warmer water in the lakes and bring a few degrees of increased temperature to the vineyards.

Keuka Lake, with its familiar Y-shape, is the cradle of both the aviation and wine industries in New York. Hammondsport, a sleepy village at the southern tip of the lake, was once the capital of the big New York state wineries—Taylor, Great Western, Golden Age, and others. In its heyday Hammondsport locals proudly displayed a picture of the world's first flying boat being launched. Its caption read,

The world's first flying boat (made in Hammondsport)
Christened by Glenn Curtiss (made in Hammondsport)
With Great Western Champagne (made in Hammondsport)

Today, Curtiss and the big wineries are memories, and, as far as commercial winegrowing is concerned, Hammondsport is much like a ghost town.

Founded in 1945 by the Sands family, the Canandaigua Wine Company took over the old Virginia Dare brand, which had been founded by Captain Garrett in North Carolina. Production was directed to eastern U.S. sweet table wines, exemplified by Richard's Wild Irish Rose and other popular types during the "wine booms" of the 1950s and 1960s. Marvin Sands masterfully kept costs low and profits high, building and buying estates until Canandaigua is now second only to Gallo in size among U.S. vintners.

In stark contrast to the mega-size of Canandaigua, the tiny Vinifera Wine Cellars remains a living and growing tribute to its founder, Dr. Konstantin Frank. Dr. Frank was a Russian-born iconoclast, a very outspoken champion of *Vitis vinifera* winegrowing in the eastern United States. Having escaped the Russian Revolution, Frank emigrated to America in 1951 and was hired by Cornell University as a common vineyard hand. His knowledge of growing Old World grapes in his native Russia was suspect by the professors, but it gained the attention of Charles Fournier, the French-born president of Gold Seal Vineyards near Hammondsport.

Fournier hired the Russian, and after several years of experiments Dr. Frank bought his own land, planted Chardonnay and Johannisberg Riesling vines, and by 1965 had wines on the market under the Vinifera Wine Cellars label. Frank passed away in 1985, but his family carries on his tradition.

Walter S. Taylor, son of Greyton Taylor and namesake grandson of the Taylor Wine Company founder, became the patron saint of French-American hybrid enthusiasts. Fired from the family business in the late 1960s for making denigrating remarks about the production philosophy of Taylor wines, Walter Taylor promptly started his own winery on Bully Hill at the original site of his grandfather's winery and cooperage firm.

FIGURE 5.25 The late Dr. Konstantin Frank (*center*) receiving the Vinifera Wine Growers Association Monteith Trophy from Elisabeth Furness and R. de Treville Lawrence. (*Courtesy of* Wine East *magazine; photo by Linda Jones McKee.*)

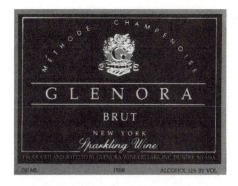

FIGURE 5.26 The Bully Wine Company "mask" label. *(Courtesy of Bully Hill Wine Company.)*

FIGURE 5.27 Finger Lakes vineyards. *(Photo by author.)*

Several years later the Taylor Wine Company was sold to Coca-Cola, which insisted that Walter Taylor discontinue the use of the Taylor name on his labels. In the midst of an ensuing lawsuit, young Taylor hired college students, using felt-tip pens, to draw lines through the word "Taylor" on each of his wine labels. Then banditlike masks were drawn on the portraits of his father and grandfather displayed in some of the Bully Hill labels and promotional materials. Walter Taylor lost the litigation, but his brilliant manipulation of publicity endeared the underdog Bully Hill brand to many wine imbibers.

Founded by a group of independent growers in 1977, Glenora Wine Cellars is one of the largest producers of *Vitis vinifera* wines in the eastern United States. Today, with a breathtaking view of Seneca Lake, the Glenora winery is a favorite tourist stop for sampling some of the best sparkling wine produced in America; it was the winner of the New York Governor's Cup in 1993 and is a perennial gold medalist in tough competitions.

Richard and Cynthia Peterson first planted vines at their Romulus, New York, estate in 1969, later expanding their French-American and *Vitis vinifera* plantings to 30 acres. Their Swedish Hill Vineyard estate winery opened in 1985. In 1994 it won the New York Governor's Cup and is a consistent gold-medal winner in every competition entered.

Hermann J. Wiemer, whose winery and vineyards are situated just north of Glenora in Dundee, New York, is a native of Bernkastel, Germany. After extensive training in all aspects of viticulture and enology at Geisenheim Institute in the Rhineland, Wiemer came to the United States, where he spent a number of years as grower and winemaker at Bully Hill vineyards. In 1973 he bought land on the west side of Seneca Lake and established his own vineyard and winery estate there. Johannisberg Riesling wines under the Hermann J. Wiemer label are consistent winners of awards and medals.

LAKE ERIE—CHAUTAUQUA AND NIAGARA

Despite an early history of winegrowing dating from 1818, when Baptist minister Elijah Fay and his son, Joseph, planted the area's first vineyards, the Lake Erie-Chautauqua Region in the western corner of New York State suffered most from the long "dry" tradition of the area. Esther McNeil organized America's first chapter of the Women's Christian Temperance Union in nearby Fredonia during the early 1870s. In 1873, Dr. Charles Welch, an ardent Prohibitionist, found the town of Westfield in Chautauqua County a welcome home to start his grape juice business in 1897.

This region may have the best climate in New York State, except, perhaps, Long Island, for growing top-quality wine grapes. The buffering effect of Lake Erie's warmer waters protects the strip of shoreline extending from Ohio through the northwest tip of Pennsylvania and across the western border of New York State. This effect extends the growing season by inhibiting frost formations, tempering cold winter winds, and contributing to heavier snow precipitation, which serves to insulate delicate vine trunks. A similar effect is found in Niagara County along the southwestern shores of Lake Ontario.

The favorable climate and soils of this area are, however, not devoted principally to fine wine vines, but to the historical Concord that is in great demand by the huge Welch's grape juice co-op operations in Westfield. Yet the real excitement in Lake Erie-Chautauqua and Niagara is generated by the new small farm and boutique wineries that have emerged during the past several decades. Most of these have entered the premium wine market with wines made from *Vitis vinifera* and French-American hybrid vines.

HUDSON VALLEY

The Hudson Valley region is one of the oldest winegrowing locales in the United States. Records indicate that small vineyards were planted near the city of New Paltz in the 1600s. This area is burdened with colder mesoclimates than experienced by other major winegrowing regions in New York State. Consequently, most of the commercial wines grown in the region are made from native *Vitis labrusca* and French-American hybrid vines.

The Benmarl Wine Company is well known as one of the great innovators in both grape growing and winemaking. In the 1970s owner Mark Miller financed the purchase of a historical 1700s estate by selling one-vine mini-estates. The "owners" could tend their vines or leave them to Miller; the important thing was that their ownership permitted them to buy Benmarl wines at a discount.

LONG ISLAND

The history of winegrowing on Long Island can be traced back to the sixteenth century, but it is only during the most recent decades that there has been significant interest in the region for commercial wine production. Most of Long Island's wine industry is located on the North Fork of the isle's eastern extremity. The waters of Long Island Sound and the Atlantic Ocean virtually surround the region, providing consistently moderate temperatures that average about 2,600 degree-days of growing season, as compared with approximately 2,400 in the best upstate winegrowing districts.

The vineyards on Long Island are nearly all planted to *Vitis vinifera*—Chardonnay, Johannisberg Riesling, Gewürztraminer, and Cabernet Sauvignon. But the crown jewel of the North Fork has become Merlot, for which it has earned grand accolades from both wine critics and consumers. *Wine Spectator* magazine sponsors an annual charity benefit "barrel tasting" of the new Merlot vintages, hosted by a different vintner each year.

Founded in 1983 by Robert J. Palmer, a New York City advertising executive, Palmer Vineyards has already earned an enviable list of top awards for quality. Palmer's 50 acres of estate vineyards include Chardonnay and Gewürztraminer, but it is the Palmer Cabernet Sauvignon and Merlot vines that produce truly world-class wines.

Dr. Herodotus Damianos established Pindar Vineyards in 1979. With more than 200 acres of *Vitis vinifera* vineyards, Pindar is now the largest winery on Long Island.

The Lenz Winery was established in 1983 near the town of Peconic, Long Island, by Peter Carroll and John Pancoast. The estate Merlot is its pride, but Lenz Chardonnay and Gewürztraminer have also been consistent medal winners.

Villa Banfi is famous throughout the world as a shipper of both popular and classic Italian wines. John and Harry Mariani, principals of Villa Banfi, developed this 60-acre estate winery near Old Brookville, New York, in 1983. A limited amount of exquisite Chardonnay has been released, and Pinot Noir is expected in the near future.

The Bedell Vineyards family winery was founded in 1985 near Cutchogue on the North Fork of Long Island. Only *Vitis vinifera* varieties are cultivated on the 28-acre estate. Bedell wines, in particular the Merlot, are considered among the best grown on Long Island.

❖ PENNSYLVANIA

In Colonial times there were many attempts to grow Old World vines commercially in Pennsylvania, including a failed endeavor by William Penn himself.

John Alexander, a Pennsylvania vine researcher during the late 1700s, was perhaps the first person to cultivate native American *Vitis labrusca* varieties. He named one of his more promising selections for himself—the Alexander—which became famous for its heavy production of grapes and remakable resistance to disease and cold winters. But the wine from Alexander paled in comparison to that from the regal *Vitis vinifera*.

America's first commercial American winery, the Pennsylvania Vine Company, was founded by Pierre Legaux near Philadelphia in 1793. Legaux, a Frenchman, was convinced he could succeed in cultivating *Vitis vinifera* vines, but his attempts failed just as all the others have until recent times.

The repeal of National Prohibition was met in Pennsylvania with state monopoly restrictions which, until they were modified in the 1960s, did not allow the industry to develop. Even today, limited production and marketing regulations curb the full potential of Pennsylvania winegrowing. A 1900 USDA report stated that Pennsylvania had 57 operating commercial wineries. In 1995 there were 40 commercial vintners operating in the Keystone State, about half of them producing less than 10,000 gallons each vintage.

Located southwest of Westfield, New York, and just over the state line on the shore of Lake Erie is the town of North East, Pennsylvania—the gateway to Great Lakes winegrowing. The history of this area is tied to that of the Lake Erie-Chatauqua region and, as it does there, the Concord vine, for Welch's, still predominates in this Pennsylvania locale.

Founded in 1964 by Doug Moorhead, son of the late chairman of the Welch Grape Juice Coooperative, Presque Isle Wine Cellars has made its mark as one of the premier vintners in Pennsylvania. Even more important, Moorhead has become a major grape and winemaking equipment supplier to other smaller vintners in the eastern United States.

Eric Miller, son of Benmarl Wine Company owner Mark Miller, founded his own Chaddsford winegrowing estate in 1985, aptly named after the nearby hamlet of Chadds Ford, Pennsylvania. Whereas Miller the elder planted hardy French-American cultivars in the Hudson Valley region of upstate New York, Miller the younger has devoted production to Old World *Vitis vinifera* varieties with remarkable success. The Chaddsford reputation is becoming one of the best in the state.

The southeastern tier of Pennsylvania, between Harrisburg and Philadelphia, is simultaneously the state's oldest and newest viticultural region. As mentioned earlier, colonial Pennsylvania has a rich history in the early development of vineyards and vintners. After a cenury of political and social oppression, several modern-day winegrowers are taking up the challenge once again.

In Stewartstown, near York, Richard Naylor commenced operations at Naylor Wine Cellars in 1978. Naylor has earned a fine reputation for fine red wines made from estate-grown Cabernet Sauvignon and Chambourcin grapes.

❖ NEW ENGLAND

King Charles II ordered vines to be planted in colonial Rhode Island, which resulted in yet another failed attempt to grow the *Vitis vinifera*. John Mason offered to trade the British monarch all of what is now New Hampshire in return for 300 tons of French wine, but Charles II rejected that proposal.

Ephraim Bull was a mid-1800s vine breeder of Concord, Massachusetts. His venerable "Concord" vine was the offspring of very hardy native *Vitis labrusca* parentage and remains today the quintessential grape juice and jelly grape and the most widely planted native American vine in the United States.

In 1995 there were eleven commercial vintners operating in Massachusetts, ten in Connecticut, four in Rhode Island, three in Vermont, two in Maine, and one in New Hampshire.

The Westport Rivers Vineyard and Winery stands out as one of the largest and most progressive in Massachusetts, despite having been founded only in 1989. The Russell family have devoted their 50 acres of vineyard to Chardonnay, Johannisberg Riesling, and Pinot Noir vines. The first vintages have been very impressive, achieving a quality thought to have been virtually impossible only a decade ago. The winery tasting facility features works of art created by local Fall River and New Bedford artisans. Westport Rivers has been heralded by *The Boston Globe* as "The toast of the Bay State."

FIGURE 5.28 Concord. *(Photo by author.)*

Sherman P. Haight, Jr., founded Haight Vineyard in 1978, a dream he had built throughout his career as a textile executive in Georgia and distinguished military service as a senior officer in Korea. On the Connecticut family homestead, which dates back to Revolutionary times, Haight built an impressive vineyard and winery estate that is now one of the winegrowing jewels of New England.

Sakonnet Vineyards, founded in 1975, is the epitome of boutique winemaking in eastern America. Owned by the Samson family, Sakonnet cellars are housed in a modern structure and outfitted with the finest of equipment, tankage, and barrels, from which come some of the most highly respected wines made in the east.

In a climate far too harsh for fine wine viticulture, Kathe and Robert Bartlett designed their 1983 Gouldsboro, Maine, winery for the production of exceptionally high quality fruit wines. Their Bartlett wines from apples and blueberries are popular in local markets and frequent winners of gold medals and accolades from the press.

✠ NEW JERSEY

Wine grapes have been grown in New Jersey for more than a century. The Renault Winery, located in Egg Harbor City, northwest of Atlantic City, has been in operation since 1868. It made its mark for good sparkling wines prior to the turn of the century and survived National Prohibition by producing Renault Tonic, a widely distributed over-the-counter wine "medicine."

Interest in restoring the wine industry in the Garden State continues to build. In 1995 there were 17 commercial vintners operating in New Jersey.

Despite heavy urbanization of the area, Renault still cultivates vineyards and produces estate wines. A rarely found vine cultivated at Renault is the Noah, a historical native variety that is grown nowhere else in such volume. A large collection of antique wineglasses are beautifully displayed in a gallery near the entrance of the old stone winery, through which thousands of visitors on their way to or from nearby Atlantic City are welcomed each year.

Founded in 1993 near Ringoes, New Jersey, Unionville Vineyards is already one of the state's most award-winning vintners. Owners Patricia Galloway and Kris Nielsen are world-renowned industrial engineers with the means to build and constantly improve every phase of winegrowing on their impressive estate. The wine in each bottle of Unionville is made, as would be expected, with precision craftsmanship and quality, winning the attention of consumers and critics alike.

❖ THE GREAT LAKES ❖

The Great Lakes, from Lake Ontario in the east, to Lake Superior in the west, provide a climatic buffer zone along their coastlines, offering protection to vines in the region, just as Lake Erie does for western New York State vines. Cold northwestern air blowing across the lakes is warmed by the stable temperatures of deep lake water. Thus, growing seasons are increased because of a reduced threat of late spring and early fall frosts. The southern tier of Michigan and northern tiers of Indiana and Ohio are famous for constituting a heavy "snow belt," serving to insulate dormant vines from harsh midwinter windchill.

The expanse of the Great Lakes winegrowing region, however, which for the purpose of this text includes Ohio, Michigan, Indiana, Illinois, Wisconsin, and Minnesota, reaches across far more land mass than just the lake coastlines. Although the region's history has been rocky owing to recurrent biological, economic, and political disorders, Great Lakes winegrowing has endured. With

FIGURE 5.29   Great Lakes wine-growing regions.

commitments continuing in vinicultural research, the resulting cool-climate production technology and advanced marketing concepts give promise for dynamic growth to continue.

⬧ OHIO

The Ohio River Valley, the first area in the Great Lakes Region to be settled, was also the first to have a significant commercial wine industry. Nicholas Longworth, an ambitious young lawyer and one of the largest landowners in the country during his time, had an avid interest in wine. He began planting vineyards in Cincinnati in the 1820s. After an initial search for the "right" vine varieties, he settled on the Catawba grape, which he had received from John Adlum from Georgetown, D.C., and quickly made a fortune by producing and marketing sparkling Catawba wine. By the 1840s, Longworth had accumulated more than 1,000 acres of vineyard, and numerous other growers in the area were supplying him with even more grapes. But the empire fell almost as quickly as it had risen. By the time of Longworth's death in 1863, most of the 3,000 acres of vineyards along the Ohio River were dead from infection by *oidium,* or powdery mildew, for which there was no means of control at that time.

In the 1830s vineyards began to appear on the Lake Erie shoreline and on the little Bass Islands in Lake Erie north of Sandusky. E.M. Erskine, in an 1859 British consul report to his government, observed:

> *The banks of the River Ohio are studded with vineyards, between 1,500 and 2,000 acres being planted in the immediate vicinity of Cincinnati, with every prospect of a vast increase.*

This is a particularly curious statement in view of the fact that Longworth and his growers were being wiped out by the oidium mildew at the time. Erskine went on:

In Kentucky, Indiana, Tennessee, Arkansas, and generally, in at least 22 out of the 32 states now constituting the Union, vineyards of more or less promise and extent have been planted.

This statement is more accurate. Of the hundreds of wineries, large and small, that existed at the turn of the century in Ohio, only a few survived Prohibition and its aftermath. A special U.S. Department of Agriculture study in 1900 revealed that New York and Ohio combined had more than 22,500 acres of vineyards.

During Civil War times the Golden Eagle Winery was opened on Middle Bass Island. By 1875 it had become the largest single winery in the United States, producing upwards of 500,000 gallons per year, yet it was only one of many wineries in the Lake Erie shoreline and Bass Islands vicinity. Commercial winegrowing had grown to become a very important part of the northern Ohio agricultural scene in the late 1800s.

Today the Ohio wine industry advances under the leadership of the Ohio Wine Producers Association, supplemented with research from Ohio State University. New plantings of classic Old World vines are at an all-time high, and wine quality from some vintners has reached world-class proportions. In 1994 there were 47 commercial wine producers in Ohio.

Meier's Wine Cellars in the Cincinnati area is a fascinating combination of old and new, north and south, in the Ohio wine industry. Founder John Meier was an 1800s contemporary of Nicholas Longworth. Meier survived the oidium plague by buying grapes from the Bass Islands. During National Prohibition, the Meier's winery became a grape juice plant and was acquired by Henry Sonneman.

Sonneman quickly popularized his Unfermented Catawba Grape Juice, more of which found its way into home wine fermenters than was consumed "unfermented." Following the repeal of National Prohibition he bought the Isle St. George vineyards on North Bass Island in Lake Erie and set about promoting Isle St. George wines. These found a ready market, and dessert wines such as Meier's No. 44 Cream Sherry, along with many other products, were added to the line. Meier's Wine Cellars became the largest winery in the Great Lakes region and one of the largest in the entire United States.

In 1976 distillery executive Robert Gottesman bought Meier's and began to enlarge the company even further. He acquired the historical Golden Eagle Winery on Middle Bass Island which had, in the interim, become the fabled Lonz Winery. Gottesman also acquired the Mantey Vineyards and Mon Ami

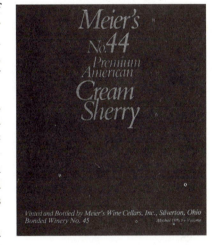

FIGURE 5.30   Lonz Winery on Middle Bass Island in Lake Erie. *(Photo by author.)*

Champagne Company near Sandusky and other Ohio properties. He hired expert winemaker Ted Moulton, winner of many production awards. Many native *Vitis labrusca* vines were replaced with plantings of *Vitis vinifera*. Meier's continues today as the largest and one of the most progressive vintners in the Great Lakes Region.

Northwest of Cincinnati, in Morrow, Ohio, is Valley Vineyards, owned by the Schucter family. Kenneth Schucter, a Detroit automobile manufacturing executive tired of the corporate life, started planting French-American hybrid vines on a truck farm his family owned. In 1970 Valley Vineyards winery was opened and remains today as one of Ohio's most innovative vintners. The Schucter family are master marketers too, and Valley Vineyards is the site of frequent wine festivals and other interesting activities.

The Chalet Debonne Vineyards winery was founded in 1971, when Tony P. Debevc, a pomology student, graduated from Ohio State University. Tony persuaded his father, Tony J. Debevc, to plant about 10 acres of French-American hybrid grapes on the family farm near Madison, Ohio. Together they built a winery and tasting room in the style of a Swiss chalet and commenced their labor of love. They succeeded on their own very well, but with the hiring of gifted winemaker Anthony Carlucci, the quality of Chalet Debonne wines became world-class. Carlucci convinced the Debevcs that *Vitis vinifera* would be a superb supplement to their product line. Indeed, his Chalet Debonne Johannisberg Riesling won the Best White Wine of Show at the San Francisco Fair Wine Competition in 1994.

⬧ MICHIGAN

The winegrowing history of Michigan is modest as compared with that of Ohio or Indiana. Although there were a few wineries in Michigan prior to National Prohibition, they were small, located mostly on the east side of the state, and were unable to survive the long "dry" experiment.

Most of Michigan's grapes are grown in the southwestern corner, in Berrien County, along the beautiful Lake Michigan shore. This industry emerged circa 1900 as a result of a growing demand for grape juice across the conservative Midwest, supplied by acre upon acre of Concord vineyards. With repeal, the market underwent a change as consumers turned their preference to wine, and sweet, fruity Concord fit the bill—for a couple of decades. Michigan adopted a protectionist excise tax measure whereby wines made outside Michigan were taxed at 54 cents per gallon, while Michigan-grown wines were taxed at a rate of only 4 cents a gallon. The Michigan wine industry survived with the help of this discriminatory tax for several decades, but eventually most of the larger wineries, principally in and around the villages of Paw Paw and Lawton, collapsed from an inability to turn production away from Concord and toward wine grapes. In the last decade or so this situation has changed for the better.

Michigan State University has an exemplary record in both creating and applying technologies in close support of the remarkable transformation of Michigan wine. Since the early 1970s, Professor Gordon S. "Stan" Howell, of the MSU Department of Horticulture, has provided capable leadership for this development. It is largely due to Howell's research and development that Michigan can now successfully grow Old World vines, once thought impossible to cultivate in the Great Lakes Region.

The Michigan wine industry has evolved to resemble that of New York State, with small high-grade estate wineries replacing giant producers of low-grade plonk. Adding to this excitement is the establishment of several new wine-

DEBEVC Vineyards 1987

GRAND RIVER VALLEY
JOHANNISBERG RIESLING
GRAPES GROWN BY DEBEVC VINEYARDS
ALCOHOL 10% BY VOLUME
PRODUCED & BOTTLED BY CHALET DEBONNE VINEYARDS, INC.
MADISON, OHIO 44057

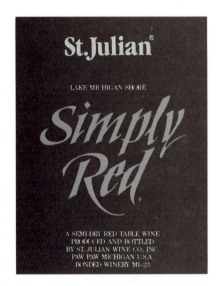

FIGURE 5.31 Tabor Hill Winery in southwestern Michigan. *(Courtesy of Tabor Hill Winery.)*

growing appellations. The Leelanau Peninsula, located in the northwest section of the state, seems an unlikely place for fine wine vines to thrive, but with Lake Michigan on the west and Grand Traverse Bay on the east, vines enjoy protection through the tempering of Great Lakes water. Small boutique vintners have founded wineries on the peninsula and now make award-winning wines from both *Vitis vinifera* and French-American hybrid grapes. In 1995 there were 21 commercial wine producers in Michigan.

The attractive St. Julian Winery is a popular tourist stop, off Interstate 94 in Paw Paw, Michigan. Owned by the Braganini family, St. Julian is a well-preserved pre-Prohibition facility that produces a wide range of table, sparkling, dessert, and fruit wines. Under the expertise of winemaker Charles Catherman, St. Julian wines win impressive awards in national competitions.

As mentioned earlier, much of the renaissance in Michigan winegrowing has taken place in northern Michigan. There is no greater evidence of this than at Château Grand Traverse, situated just north of Michigan's cherry-growing capital, Traverse City. Founded in 1975 by Edward O'Keefe, a descendant of the famous O'Keefe beer-brewing giant in Canada, Château Grand Traverse has been a leader in the planting and development of Chardonnay and Johannisberg Riesling vineyards for fine wine production.

Born of wealth accumulated in the lumber business, the Welsch family founded Fenn Valley Vineyards near Fennville, Michigan, in 1973. This vintner's innovation in processing technology has resulted in table wines of exceptional quality.

◈ INDIANA

The beginnings of commercial winegrowing in Indiana occurred during the late 1700s, when Jean Jacques Dufour emigrated from Vevey, Switzerland. Dufour first settled in Kentucky but later moved across the Ohio River to southeastern Indiana. Dufour's first vines were planted during the very early 1800s near his namesake riverside village of Vevay, just north of Madison, in what is now Switzerland County. Following his success, others planted more vines, and with their successes, even more plantings were made. It became a monumental winegrowing region, often referred to as "The Little Rhineland," with terraces ascending from the Ohio River banks.

Thomas Jefferson and Henry Clay, who had also expressed great interest in the Alexander grape of Pennsylvania, became interested in Jean Dufour's Indiana wine, corresponded with him, and provided encouragement for Dufour to write *The American Vine Dresser's Guide*, first published in 1826. The Little Rhineland became quite large, with what was thought by some to be thousands of acres of vineyards; Indiana was becoming one of the top 10 wine-producing states in the Union.

The grand project was short-lived, as the Alexander was susceptible to mold diseases that thrived in the hot, humid summers along the Ohio River. Other vine varieties, it remains unknown which, were planted to replace the Alexander, most failing because of the *Phylloxera* root louse. Catawbas were planted to supply Nicholas Longworth's wine empire in nearby Cincinnati, but these fell to the same oidium mold that wiped out the Ohio vineyards. National Prohibition all but eradicated winegrowing in the state, except for home winemakers.

Indiana passed a small winery bill in 1971, largely as the result of the efforts of one of those home winegrowers. It was William Oliver, a law professor from Indiana University, who put together the proposal that would open the door for commercial Indiana wine once again. His expertise in law was matched by an ability to make good wine. The Oliver Wine Company was founded in 1972 and has now grown into a monumental success, directed by Bill Oliver Jr. The Oliver winery, with a Stonehenge-like entry and inviting lakeside picnic area, is one of the most popular tourist attractions in southern Indiana. More important, the quality of its wine, particularly those made from Gewürztraminer and Merlot grapes, has made Oliver a leader in the Midwest.

A retired World War II Navy carrier pilot, Ben Sparks, and his wife, Lee, founded the quaint Possum Trot Winery near the summer resort town of Nashville, Indiana, south of Indianapolis. The Sparkses also created the Indiana Winegrower's Guild in the early 1970s. From this evolved an annual conference, The Indiana Grape/Wine Symposium, which has become a midwestern mecca for aspiring winegrowers.

The Huber homestead has been in the family for more than 100 years. With its own bakery, cheese-making facility, fruit farm, petting zoo, antique center, restaurant, and other features, the Huber Orchard Winery is another of the Hoosier wineries attracting thousands of tourists every year. Displaying an impressive array of medals, ribbons, and other awards won for quality, the Huber label is synonymous with superb Seyval Blanc, Chambourcin, and berry wines.

In the late 1980s yet another giant step for the Indiana wine industry was taken by Jim Butler, owner of the Butler Winery in Bloomington. Butler gathered an impressive amount of economic and historical data to support a proposal for a small portion of the excise tax collected on all retail wine sales in Indiana to be devoted to grape and wine research at Purdue University. His was a landmark success, as this mechanism generated enough revenue to support a wine marketing effort as well. In 1995 there were 17 commercial vintners in Indiana, with 5 more on the drawing board.

Founded in 1986 by Dr. Donald Shumrick, a medical professor at the University of Cincinnati, Château Pomije was named with his wife's maiden name. The estate winery and vineyards are situated in Guilford, Indiana, near Milan, of *Hoosiers* movie fame. Château Pomije vineyards are the largest in Indiana, including Chardonnay, Johannisberg Riesling, Pinot Noir, and Cabernet Sauvignon—all of which are made into wines of impressive quality and sold at equally impressive prices in the winery restaurant.

Even closer to Milan is the aptly named Villa Milan winery, which makes wines from native Concord and Catawba vines. To the south, in historical Switzerland County, where Jean Dufour planted vines nearly two centuries ago, an Indiana winegrowing renaissance is taking place. Central to this rebirth are the newly opened Lanthier and Thomas Family wineries, both popular attractions in the riverboat city of Madison. Nearby, in Vevay, two more vintners are in the process of building.

ILLINOIS

In 1995, there were nine commercial vintners operating in Illinois. The oldest winery in the state is Baxter's Vineyards on its western border in the town of Nauvoo. Founded in 1857 by the Icarians, a French utopian society that had settled in Nauvoo, the winery continues today under the direction of the Logan family, who produce a range of *Vitis labrusca* wines.

An hour's drive or so south of Chicago, in the little town of Monee, is the Thompson Winery and surrounding vineyards. The vineyards were originally planted in 1963 by Bern Ramey, an Ohio sparkling wine aficionado, who set out to prove that fine wines could also be grown in Illinois. He succeeded in this effort but lost his vineyards to a deadly weed-killer spray that had apparently been windblown from a nearby property. Bitter litigation followed, and eventually John Thompson acquired the winery in 1970. Thompson restored the vineyards and resumed wine production.

In Roselle, Illiniois, Lynn and Fred Koehler commenced making wine at their small Lynfred Winery in 1977. Most Lynfred wines are made from grapes grown in California and other states. The Koehler talent has won some coveted awards in both national and international wine competitions.

WISCONSIN

Count Agoston Haraszthy, of Sonoma County and Buena Vista wine fame, first settled in Wisconsin during the 1840s, but cold weather discouraged his attempts to grow classic Old World wines there. In the ensuing 150 years there has been considerable progress in adapting new cool-climate hybrid vine cultivars, as well as some selections of *Vitis vinifera* vines, to the rigors of Wisconsin winters. In 1995 there were 10 commercial vintners operating in this state.

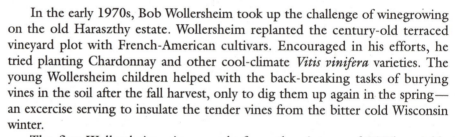

FIGURE 5.32   The Wollersheim
Winery in Wisconsin—the first
Haraszthy winery. *(Courtesy of
Ocooch Mountain News.)*

In the early 1970s, Bob Wollersheim took up the challenge of winegrowing
on the old Haraszthy estate. Wollersheim replanted the century-old terraced
vineyard plot with French-American cultivars. Encouraged in his efforts, he
tried planting Chardonnay and other cool-climate *Vitis vinifera* varieties. The
young Wollersheim children helped with the back-breaking tasks of burying
vines in the soil after the fall harvest, only to dig them up again in the spring—
an excercise serving to insulate the tender vines from the bitter cold Wisconsin
winter.

The first Wollersheim wines, made from the vintage of 1975, quickly
became a standard for perennial award winners. Visitors to the winery can see
the original wine cave Agoston Haraszthy carved in the hillside on the estate
above the Wisconsin River and sample some of the finest wines grown in the
entire Great Lakes region.

✠ MINNESOTA

The demand for the fruit of the vine in Minnesota, and in Wisconsin as well,
reflects the grand Norse taste for brandy. Although no wine spirits are grown
there, these states consume more brandy than the other 48 states combined.

If winegrowing in Wisconsin may be called difficult, in Minnesota it must
be called heroic. Nevertheless, there are three commercial vintners in Minnesota
who have answered this monumental challenge—and succeeded.

The Bailly family decided on a vineyard site south of Minneapolis on the
Mississippi River. Their first vines were planted in 1973; most, however, were
killed during the devastating winter of 1976. The Baillys planted again in 1977
and commenced the Wollersheim practice of burying all their vines in late
autumn for protection from killing freezes.

Virtually all of the Bailly production is from French-American hybrid cultivar vines. Some native vines are grown; this estate is one of the very few to cultivate native *Vitis riparia* vines. Wines from these grapes are crisply acidic.

❖ THE ATLANTIC SEABOARD ❖

The Atlantic Seaboard Region has a long and distinguished history of viticultural struggle. The determination of the seaboard people to produce fine wines has been more than equalled by the magnitude of problems they faced in doing so.

The Maryland and Virginia colonists often built their community inn or tavern near their church. Between services the worshipers would gather around the tavern's log fire, enjoying food, drink, and good fellowship. Vineyards were mostly private plantings and the wines homemade. A visitor to Colonial Williamsburg can easily see that wine was an essential part of life in early America.

George Washington planted vines at Mount Vernon, but apparently little came of them, because there is no record of his producing any wine there.

Thomas Jefferson, unquestionably the most determined of all prospective winegrowers, brought thousands of vine plant materials from Europe, along with European vineyard experts to direct his new vineyards. After 30 years of experimentation and disappointment, he was finally forced to admit that efforts should perhaps be concentrated on native varieties such as the Alexander.

In 1835, D.N. Norton, of Richmond, introduced a vine that produced grapes of an intense red color, the "Norton," touted as the red counterpart to the Catawba vine for white wines in Virginia and neighboring states. The Norton lacked the strong foxy flavor inherent in most native vine varieties. A Norton "Claret" produced by the Monticello Wine Company at Charlottesville won a gold medal at a Vienna wine competition in 1873 and a silver medal at a Paris exposition in 1878.

The Civil War had the expected effect on the wine industry south of the Mason-Dixon line. Inability to fight vine diseases, economic struggle, and the emerging politics for National Prohibition caused the commercial wine industry in the Atlantic Seaboard region to falter during the late 1800s.

Following repeal in 1933, the next chapter in the history of wine centered on Philip Wagner, a Maryland journalist with a taste for fine wine. With California grapes once again in demand for commercial winemaking, Wagner was unable to obtain them for his home winemaking hobby. He tried many other American grapes and found them all unsatisfying. Unwilling to give up, Wagner imported some of the French-American hybrid cultivars developed in France decades earlier as an alternative to resist the *Phylloxera* root louse blight and the cold winters. He propagated those that made the best wine and encouraged both amateur and commercial winegrowers throughout North America to give them a try. In 1945, Wagner and his wife, Jocelyn, founded the Boordy Vineyards winery and began to market their wines along with their vines. It was the Wagner influence that marked the begining a revolution that would awaken the eastern wine industry and give promise of a major step forward in quality and consumer appeal.

⬢ VIRGINIA

Disappointment with the native American vines, and with the unfamiliar wines they made, no doubt prompted the plantings of European *Vitis vinifera* varieties in the Colonies during the 1600s. The London Company of Virginia may have made the first attempt at growing Old World grapes in the New World. Lord Delaware brought French viticulturists and vines to establish Virginia vineyards in the 1620s. The vines died, however, and colonists blamed the failure on the French vignerons' mishandling of the project.

In 1995 there were 47 commercial vintners in Virginia. Most of these exist as a result of Wagner's pioneering work with the French-American hybrids, along with Dr. Frank's trail-blazing efforts with *Vitis vinifera*. As might be expected, Wagner and Frank had very different views, but in this case the rivalry was monumental, often extending to public ridicule of each other. The Virginia wine industry is tempered today with science and technology provided by Dr. Bruce Zoecklein at Virginia Tech.

The climate of Virginia varies more from east to west than from north to south because of a coastal plain elevating into the foothills of the Appalachian mountain chain. Today it is possible to graft Old World vines to rootstocks resistant to the *Phylloxera* that nearly bankrupted Jefferson in his attempts two centuries ago. Newly developed dusting and spray materials ward off molds and other diseases in the vineyards. Virginia currently ranks among the most progressive winegrowing states in the east.

One of the first three estate wineries to open in Virginia during 1976, Meredyth Vineyards is situated south of Middleburg in the foothills of the Bull Run mountains 50 miles west of Washington, D.C. Meredyth was founded by the Archie Smith family. Their pioneering efforts showed the way for twentieth-century applied technology. Hedging their bets, they planted both French-American hybrids and Old World vines. By the early 1980s gold medals and blue ribbons from national competitions covered the walls of the Meredyth tasting room. It has grown to become one of the largest wine estates in Virginia.

Also near Middleburg, a few miles west of Meredyth, is Piedmont Vineyards. This estate was owned by the late Mrs. Thomas Furness, who was the first to plant classic Old World vines in Virginia since Jefferson at Monticello. Planted in 1973 and cultivating primarily Chardonnay and Sémillon, hers was the first successful commercial vineyard of *Vitis vinifera* in the state.

The Barboursville Winery, owned by Zonin S.P.A., an Italian wine marketing firm, is located near Charlottesville, Virginia. A farm exceeding 800 acres was purchased in 1976, on which experimental *Vitis vinifera* vineyards were planted. Today the early Barboursville experiments have given rise to Chardonnay, Cabernet Sauvignon, and other Old World style varietal wines that are truly world-class competitors.

In eastern Virginia, situated between the Rappahannock and Potomac Rivers, is the Ingleside Plantation Winery. This grand old southern mansion, listed in the National Register of Historic Places, is owned by the Flemer family. They compare the site to the Entre-Deux-Mers region of Bordeaux. Initially the Ingleside farm was a nursery, producing young vines for other growers. The Flemers became interested in wine and produced 2,800 gallons in 1980. Just three years later Ingleside was crushing more than 20,000 gallons. Ingleside's winemaker, Jacques Recht, with considerable winegrowing experience in his native France, crafts an array of delicious award-winning table wines from both French-American hybid vines and *Vitis vinifera* varieties.

❖ MARYLAND

An era in Maryland wine history ended in 1980 when Philip and Jocelyn Wagner decided to retire and sell their Boordy Vineyards winery in Riderwood, Maryland. It had become a mecca for many hopeful vintners who came to get Wagner's advice. Far more important than his wines and his vintner apprenticeships were his public tastings and the thousands of consumers he won for quality eastern wines. The Deford family bought Boordy Vineyards and subsequently moved the facility to nearby Hydes, Maryland.

Northwest of Boordy Vineyards, in the little town of Silver Run, University of Maryland professor G. Hamilton Mowbray founded the Montbray Wine Cellars in 1966. In 1969, Montbray introduced the first commercial Chardonnay and Johannisberg varietal wines grown in Maryland. In 1974 he made history again by producing the first American "ice wine" when an October freeze caught his Johannisberg Riesling yet unharvested. In 1976, Mowbray added Cabernet Sauvignon to the list of Montbray wines gaining increased attention in the Baltimore-Washington vicinity.

The Byrd family opened Byrd Vineyards winery near Frederick, Maryland, in 1976. Their 1980 Cabernet Sauvignon won a gold medal at the American Wine Competition—the only eastern wine from this variety so honored. Catoctin Vineyards was a partnership firm founded by Bob Lyon, former winemaker at Byrd Vineyards, and a number of Maryland winegowers. Their first crush of Catoctin Chardonnay and Cabernet Sauvignon in 1983 heralded Catoctin's becoming one of the best names in fine eastern winegrowing. The Catoctin list of accolades, awards, and medals is truly outstanding.

❖ THE SOUTHEAST ❖

As the Alexander, Concord, Catawba, and Norton became champion grape producers in the north, so the Muscadine variety "Scuppernong" became the pride of the south. This name was derived from the Indian word for an aromatic tree they called *Ascuponung*, which also appears on early North Carolina maps as the name of a river. By 1800 the name had evolved to Scuppernong, and census-taker James Blount, a decade later, reported that 1,368 gallons of wine were made in the town of Scuppernong.

◈ NORTH CAROLINA

North Carolina's first commercial winery was founded by Sidney Weller in 1835. He later sold the business to Dr. Francis Garrett and his brother, who were successful with both grape juice and wine production. But it was Francis Garrett's son, Paul Garrett, who achieved the greatest success with wine in the South. Young Garrett opened his own winery in 1900. Garrett & Company quickly became a wine empire, with 17 facilities in six states generating millions of dollars in revenue. His most famous and best-selling wines were those sold under the Virginia Dare label.

In 1995 there were five commercial vintners operating in North Carolina, along with eleven in Tennessee, ten in South Carolina, seven in Georgia, six in Florida, and three in Mississippi.

The magnificent Vanderbilt château is the center of a huge landmark estate situated in western North Carolina near Asheville. William A. Vanderbilt Cecil, grandson heir, decided in the early 1970s to try his hand at Old-World-style winegrowing. Because Asheville was highland country, it was appropriate to first select cool-climate vines such as Chardonnay and Johannisberg Riesling. Philippe Jourdan, a winemaker from France, was hired to oversee all wine operations, including the refurbishing of the old Biltmore dairy and creamery buildings into a winery that today rivals any such facilities anywhere.

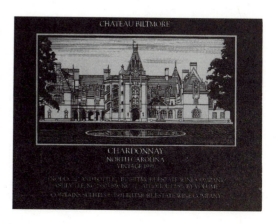

Technology, a good share provided by Professor Dan Carroll at North Carolina State University, has served to add Sauvignon Blanc and Cabernet Sauvignon to the Château Biltmore vineyards. The project has been a success, fully in the Vanderbilt style.

In modern times, there has been renewed interest in Muscadine grapes in North Carolina, as evidenced by the award-winning wines from Duplin Wine Cellar at Rose Hill (See Figure 5.33, color insert). In response to a sagging market for their grapes, a number of growers pooled their resources under the leadership of David Fussell and opened the Duplin winery in 1975. Their first crush totaled about 3,500 gallons of Scuppernong, Carlos, and Noble — all Muscadine varieties. By 1983 production had tripled in volume, and the product line has since expanded to include sparkling wines and brandy.

◈ TENNESSEE

Wine production in Tennessee was hampered by a long-standing controversy between wine wholesalers and vintners. As would be expected, the large, well-established wholesalers had political clout, and the result is very restrictive winery law. On the brighter side, Tennessee has been blessed with a large number of wine enthusiasts who formed the progressive Tennessee Viticultural and Oenological Society (TVOS), which has blazed the trail for continuing research and lobbying efforts.

One of the most picturesque wineries in northern Tennessee is Beachaven, located on the northern edge of Clarksville about 35 miles northwest of Nashville. It was founded by the late Judge William O. Beach and his son-in-law, Edward Cooke, who were champion amateur winemakers prior to entering the commercial ranks. The facility is a charming Nordic-styled building that attracts many visitors to taste the delicious wines made from *Vitis vinifera, Vitis labrusca,* and French-American hybrid vines.

Another of Tennessee's Nordic-style wineries is Highland Manor, owned and operated by the Martin family, also well known in the mid-south as master crafters of elegant cherry furniture. At this winery, situated a lofty 1,700 feet in elevation near Rugby, Tennessee, visitors can enjoy fine table wines along with a magnificent view of the Cumberland Plateau.

The largest winery in Tennessee is the Smoky Mountain Winery in the beautiful resort city of Gatlinburg, high in the mountains southeast of Knoxville. The facility is well known for producing award-winning fruit and berry wines.

◈ SOUTH CAROLINA

The Montevino vineyard, once owned by Dr. Joseph Togno of Abbeville, was a good example of 1860s winegrowing in South Carolina, as was the Benson and Merrier Winery at Aiken. In 1989, Robert Scott founded Montmorenci Vineyards, also in Aiken, and has since earned one of the highest reputations for quality in the Deep South. The best of Montmorenci is a superb light red table wine made from Chambourcin, reminiscent of fine Beaujolais.

◈ GEORGIA

In 1730 an enthusiastic grower from Portugal, Abraham de Lyon, planted a large-scale *Vitis vinifera* vineyard in Savannah, Georgia. Despite encouragement throughout the community, his project failed. A historian of the times reported that Lyon's vineyard "which was to supply all the plantations . . . resulted in only a few gallons, and was then abandoned."

FIGURE 5.34 Château Elan Winery. *(Courtesy of Château Elan.)*

Georgia, a top wine producer since the mid-1700s, recorded nearly a million gallons of production annually by the 1880s. At the onset of National Prohibition it had become the sixth largest wine production state in the United States. Not every Georgian was pleased with the repeal of Prohibition, and there are still whispers of fundamentalist support for the "Dry Movement" in Georgia.

Until relatively recently the only winery in Georgia was Monarch in Atlanta, established in the mid-1930s to alleviate the Georgia peach surplus.

One of the most remarkable new vintners in the Deep South was launched in the early 1980s near Braselton, Georgia, by pharmaceutical magnate Donald Panoz. This magnificent château is state-of-the-art at every turn. Located just 50 miles or so northeast of Atlanta, this estate epitomizes the good life. Winemaker Brad Hansen has won medals for both his Muscadine and Old World wine types.

⬧ FLORIDA

With the exception of the native Muscadine, Florida has not succeeded in growing grapes for commercial purposes until very recently. Selections of *Vitis labrusca* vines were planted in the late 1800s and a huge planting of Texas hybrids was made in the 1920s. All eventually succumbed to disease and pests. Today wines are made in Florida from citrus fruits, Muscadine grapes, and disease-resistant hybrid vines developed by University of Florida research.

Dr. Terrell Bounds, a California physician, has been the driving force in establishing the impressive Chautauqua winery estate near DeFuniak Springs in northern Florida. Chautauqua innovation has made great strides in advancing winemaking methods, which has resulted in capturing the enticing, rich essence of Muscadine flavors and eliminated the traditional oxidized character of these wine types.

1994
BLANC DU BOIS
PREMIUM FLORIDA WINE
ALCOHOL 11% BY VOLUME

Visitors come to the attractive Lakeridge Winery in Clermont, located amid the popular central Florida theme parks, to taste and buy the delicious wines made by Jeanne Burgess. The Lakeridge product line includes wines made from hybrids born from research at the University of Florida. The best of these is a vine called "Blanc du Bois," bearing delicious white grapes with flavors best described as somewhere between Sauvignon Blanc and Gewürztraminer. Lakeridge Muscadine wines are the equal of Chatauqua's; both vintners now proudly display medals won at national competitions.

❖ MISSISSIPPI

J.M. Taylor, an 1870s winegrower, in Rienzi, was the first vintner in Mississippi. By the turn of the century, the Magnolia State could boast of 31 commercial wineries in operation. If there are whispers of the Dry Movement in Georgia, support for the movement in Mississippi is obvious. The Magnolia State is commonly referred to in the Deep South as the "buckle of the Bible belt." It was the last state to vote for repeal, not until 1966, and dry counties remain.

During the 1970s and 1980s, Mississippi State University, under the encouragement and direction of Vice President Louis Wise, made a monumental effort to bring commercial winegrowing back to the position it enjoyed in the late 1800s. It was a project with little support other than the Wise influence, and, after his death in 1988, the project was discontinued.

During the latter 1970s Dr. Scott Galbreath, a successful Natchez veterinarian, converted a pre-Prohibition beer warehouse into a quaint winery. Production is entirely from *Vitis rotundifolia* Muscadine varieties.

❖ THE SOUTHWEST ❖

Thomas Volney ("T. V.") Munson generated much of the latter 1800s viticultural interest in the Southwest, primarily with his experimental vineyards in Denison, Texas. T. V. Munson's name is still revered by grape enthusiasts in memory of his intensive work in combating the European *Phylloxera* blight, his breeding of grapevines, and the essential text he wrote entitled *Foundations of American Grape Culture*. It was T. V. Munson who said, "There is no more delightful and healthful employment than vine culture."

Though few of Munson's hybrid cultivars are grown commercially in modern times, his name has been immortalized by the species *Vitis munsoniana*, a name given to a native grape lineage with which he worked most of his life.

❖ TEXAS

The Dry Movement continues in some areas of Texas, yet unlike Georgia and Mississippi, Texas has a very large cosmopolitan population that enjoys wine. On the other hand, Tarrant County, centered by Fort Worth, remains legally dry. Given such hurdles, there was little interest in developing a commercial wine industry in Texas directly after repeal of Prohibition.

However, Texas is doubtlessly also the most provincial state in the Union. Texans are famous for believing that everything in Texas is either the biggest, the best, or both. This may have been the tenor that changed the outlook for winegrowing in Texas during the early 1970s.

In 1974, the University of Texas, in search of a profitable industry to utilize its vast acreage in west Texas, began experimenting with wine grape culture.

Knowing that the oil wells that swelled the university's endowment fund would one day diminish, the institution's Board of Regents hoped to find alternative uses for the land that would provide a continuing income. Experimental plots of *Vitis vinifera* vines were planted in several locations, and by 1980 the university was sufficiently encouraged to proceed with commercial plantings. The Board of Regents approved the development of 320 acres of vineyards and began searching for a commercial company interested in developing the industry. The firm of Gill-Richter-Cordier, a consortium combining French vineyard and winemaking expertise with U.S. marketing and management skills, won the University of Texas contract and commenced operations with the 1984 vintage.

The decade of experimentation and development by the University of Texas generated widespread publicity in the media for this renaissance of viniculture. Interest grew across Texas, indeed, across all the southwest, the nation, and the world, as evidenced by the French involvement previously indicated. Sufficiently convinced, another dozen or so independent vintner projects commenced operations throughout Texas during the 1980s.

The huge land mass of Texas and its vast range of mesoclimate extremes make it difficult to generalize about suitable environs for viticulture within the state. The greatest successes have been achieved in those districts that combine high altitude, dry climate, and comparatively cool temperatures during the growing and ripening seasons. The plains of north Texas and the hill country of south Texas have shown the greatest promise for fine *Vitis vinifera* winegrowing to date. In some locales sufficient irrigation water can be a problem, along with unusually severe winters and spring hailstorms.

Texas is overcoming its commercial winegrowing hurdles, and with continuing research and development by Professor George Ray MacEachern at Texas A & M University, the future for Texas seems very bright. Texas joins Indiana, Michigan, New York, and Virginia as one of the most progressive winegrowing states east of the Rocky Mountains. In 1994 there were 31 Texas vintners in operation and nearly 3,000 acres of vineyards in cultivation.

The oldest of the new breed of Texas vintners, located in the panhandle near Lubbock, is called Llano Estacado (Spanish for "staked plains"). The firm began with a group of Texas Tech University professors who experimented with their own amateur wines. Several of these men were chemists and agriculturists interested in developing a high plains wine industry. In 1976, Llano Estacado was founded for commercial operations, and a winemaker from the Napa Valley was hired. The winery began cautiously with French-American hybrids, but the rapidly advancing technology encouraged management to move steadily toward *Vitis vinifera* production. Quality at Llano Estacado has won it a plethora of prestigious awards in national wine competitions, and, as a result, growth in production has been remarkable.

FIGURE 5.36 Reception and tasting center at Cap Rock Winery in Lubbock, Texas. *(Courtesy of Cap Rock Winery.)*

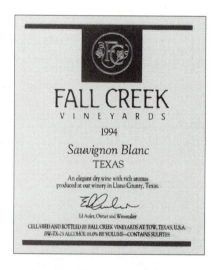

The showplace of Texas winegrowing is the Cap Rock Winery, offering a spectacular hospitality facility and a view of state-of-the-art wine production. Cap Rock is a resurrection of the Teysha winery, which failed, but with new ownership and the expert winemaking of Kim McPherson, its magnificent cellars exemplify the dynamic growth of commercial winemaking across the Lone Star State in recent years. Cabernet Sauvignon and Merlot are the wines of note bearing the Cap Rock label—every bit the equal of wine from the same vines grown anywhere else in America.

Susan and Ed Auler, cattle ranchers in the magnificent Hill Country district west of Austin, not far from the old Chisholm Trail, became interested in commercial winegrowing while visiting France in the early 1970s. After considerable study and consultation, they founded Fall Creek Vineyards in 1975, now a very upscale estate winery beautifully situated on the shores of Lake Buchanan near Tow, Texas. Dedicated to the cultivation of *Vitis vinifera* varieties, the Aulers best express their talent for fine wine in their vintages of Sauvignon Blanc and Cabernet Sauvignon. The Fall Creek Cabernet Sauvignon 1989 was selected for the Texas Hall of State dinner during the 1991 visit of Queen Elizabeth II.

Founded by Merrill and Paul Bonarrigo in 1977, the Messina Hof estate vineyard and winery is located in Bryan, Texas, in the Brazos Valley only a few miles from Texas A & M University. Their family roots are traced to Messina, Sicily, where 200 years ago the Bonarrigos were winegrowers. Transplanted from New York to Texas, Paul Bonarrigo is a sixth-generation vintner who has an impressive display of wine quality awards and medals in the nineteenth-century manor home that serves as the Messina Hof Guest Center. Messina Hof wines are grown from Old World *Vitis vinifera* vines, among the very best of which are vintages of Cabernet Sauvignon.

❖ ARKANSAS

Much of the increase in the reputation of Arkansas winegrowing must be credited to Professor Justin Morris in the Department of Food Science at the University of Arkansas in Fayetteville. Dr. Morris is one of the most prolific contributors to enology research literature and is frequently called upon nationwide as a consultant and mentor to both academic and commercial winegrowing concerns. In 1995 there were five commercial vintners operating in the state of Arkansas.

On top of St. Mary's Mountain, near the town of Altus, Arkansas, is the site of Wiederkehr Wine Cellars. Johann Wiederkehr, having emigrated from Switzerland, dug his cellar and made his first wine there in 1880. The Wiederkehr family has ever since continued to build the Wiederkehr estate into one of the premier winegrowing firms in Arkansas—and one of the first in the entire Southwest Region to commercially cultivate *Vitis vinifera* vines successfully.

Over St. Mary's Mountain, on the way to Altus, is the Post Familie Winery, founded by Jacob Post in 1880—the same year in which cousin Johann Wiederkehr founded his. The winegrowing philosophy of the Post family has been applied to cultivating native *Vitis labrusca* and *Vitis rotundifolia* vines, although the most recent generation of Posts have commenced to cultivate some *Vitis vinifera* vines as well.

❖ NEW MEXICO

Grapevines were first introduced to New Mexico by Franciscan monks and have been commercially cultivated there for several hundred years, flourishing especially well in the Rio Grande and Pecos River valleys. After repeal of National Prohibition many of the state's small wineries reopened, but the industry declined until it was virtually defunct by the early 1960s.

The 1960s wine boom across the United States caught on in the "Land of Enchantment," and now commmercial winegrowing is beginning to set deep roots once more. Much of the revived industry is located in the southeast corner of the state, where considerable European capital is being invested. Local winegrowers are expanding acreage on smaller scales along the Rio Grande from Las Cruces to north of Santa Fe. Plantings in the southern portion of this valley have been devoted to *Vitis vinifera* varieties. The higher elevations, from Albuquerque north past Santa Fe, are primarily planted to French-American hybrid vines. In 1995 there were 18 commercial vintners operating across the State of New Mexico.

❖ COLORADO

Constituting one of six Colorado wineries founded since 1978, Colorado Cellars winery and vineyards are situated at the base of the Rocky Mountains in the Colorado River valley. Technology in the advancement of viticulture has been essential in developing commercial winegrowing in such mesoclimates, which would have been marginal, or even impossible, just a decade or two ago. Still, this winery fully exemplifies the "struggling vine theory," that richer, heavier wines can be produced from smaller berries yielded by vines under stress for survival.

❖ THE PLAINS STATES ❖

According to the U.S. Department of Agriculture, Iowa, Missouri and Kansas combined included 11,000 acres of vineyard in 1900, truly a significant portion of American winegrowing at that point in time. In 1995 there were 28 commercial vintners operating in Missouri, along with 10 in Iowa and 3 in Kansas.

⬧ MISSOURI

The Teutonic influence in the history of winegrowing in Missouri was pivotal. Although the first wine was made in the state by French Jesuits who established a seminary near St. Louis in 1823, the cultivation of the vine was largely undertaken by German immigrants. Viticulture flowed west with the settlers, down the Ohio River to the Mississippi and then up the Missouri River valley. Jacob Fugger planted the first vines in the town of Hermann, Missouri, in 1843.

The area southwest of St. Louis near St. James, Missouri, known as Big Prairie, is part of the Ozark Plateau. Most of the grapes in Missouri are grown here, primarily native *Vitis labrusca* varieties. The Hofherr family decided to build their St. James Winery here in 1970 because of the proximity of vineyards to supply their needs, but have since added considerable vine acreage of their own. John Hofherr, trained in California, is one of the young winemakers who is returning national prominence to Missouri winegrowing.

Established in 1847 by emigrants from the German Rhineland, Stone Hill in Hermann, Missouri, is one of the oldest U.S. wineries, and the second largest in 1900. Aptly named, Stone Hill is a charming old stone building fronting caves that were used for growing mushrooms during National Prohibition. Today the Held family owns and operates Stone Hill in grand fashion. In 1994 their wines were among the most consistent medal-winners in America. Stone Hill is one of the very finest vintners of enticing white wine from the vaunted Vignoles vine and delicious dark, dense red wine from the historical Norton vine.

Also located in Hermann is the Hermannhof Winery; its cellars were constructed in 1852. Like Stone Hill, this is a restoration of a defunct winery. The new owner, James Dierberg, added a *wein garten* and a smokehouse in the German style and planted French-American hybrid vines. Located downtown near the Missouri riverbank, Hermannhof is ideally situated for the Mayfest held in Hermann each year on the third weekend in May. Hermannhof stunned the wine world in 1993 when its Vignoles won Best of Show for white wines at the New World International Wine Competition.

⬧ IOWA

The Amana Colonies consist of seven villages southwest of Cedar Rapids that were communally owned by a religious sect called the "Community of True Inspiration." The founding members arrived there in 1854 and purchased about 25,000 acres of prairie land for their settlement. Known as the Amana Society, the colony survived in its communal form until the Great Depression of the 1930s, when it incorporated and began paying its members wages for their work. Amana Refrigeration is the best known of the original Amana industries. Today winemaking survives there as a cottage industry, catering mostly to tourists and visitors. The majority of the wines made in the locale are from fruits and berries.

6
THE WINES OF FRANCE

I n 1993, France shipped 17.5 million gallons of wine to America—worth nearly half of the $1 billion the United States spent on foreign wine imports that year. Although Italy exports more wine gallonage to the United States than does France, the cost and unit value of imported French wines are far greater.

The French mainland and Corsica total approximately 213,000 square miles, an area about 80 percent the size of Texas. Yet within this relatively small area the French cultivate more than three times the total vineyard acreage of the United States.

About 12 percent of the 50 million people who live in France earn their living in some way connected with wine. Three out of every 100 French persons are winegrowers. The average per capita consumption of wine in France is nearly 20 gallons, or tenfold the per capita consumption in the United States.

When all aspects of the wine art are considered, there can be no question that France is foremost among nations. Although Italy produces more gallons of wine, Spain has more acres of vineyards, and the United States has arguably more advanced enotechnology, France has a wine heritage and diversity unmatched by any other country.

In 1875, France produced nearly 2 billion gallons of wine—a level never again attained. Nowadays France produces about 700 million to 1.4 billion gallons annually. This wide disparity reflects the effects of weather on vine yields from vintage to vintage.

The single most important word in French winegrowing is *terroir* (the soil). Whether it is the chalky subsoil in Champagne, the deep gravel of Graves in Bordeaux, the unbelievably stony ground of the Rhone, or the mineral-rich earth of Burgundy, *terroir* is everything to the winegrowers in France. To an outsider this reverence can be rather curious, as these soils, for any other agronomic crop, would be nothing short of *terrible*.

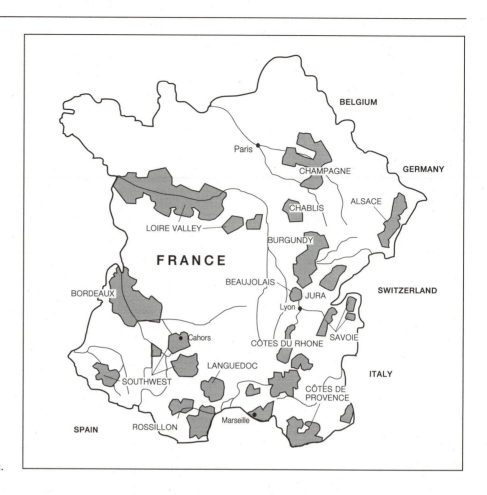

FIGURE 6.1 Wine regions of France.

Irrigation is not permitted in French vineyards, and extremes of drought and rainfall are rather frequent. Spring and autumn frosts often inflict great losses of fruit. Moderate weather is the key, resulting in grapes with a good sugar-acid ratio and rich flavor. Hot, dry summers yield light crops with high sugar content, resulting in strong (high alcohol) wines with lower acidity. Cool, wet summers generally produce grapes that never quite ripen, yielding wines of lower strength and tart acidity. Consequently, winegrowers and wine merchants endeavor to offset the considerable yearly differences through variable pricing in order to survive economically.

There are, of course, exceptions to this practice, particularly in the case of noble growths that maintain such high standards that only the finer vintages are marketed under the esteemed labels of the estate. Poorer vintages are often sold in bulk to *négociant* (negotiant) firms that blend, process, and bottle finished wines under their own labels. Although such labels may display the region of origin and the vintage year the grapes were grown, the individual vineyard or estate wine identity is lost, the wine thus becoming "generic" in character.

Prior to the nineteenth century there were few laws regulating the wines of France. Guidelines as to the quality of each estate were primarily hearsay reputation and each individual's determination of previous vintages, plus, of course, the price levels that the market would bear. The shortage of wine following the *Phylloxera* root louse epidemic in the latter half of the nineteenth century led to considerable fraud and abuse of the consumer. The French government legislated against this deception in 1905 with regulations that repressed "the deceits and attempted deceits of nature, quality, species, origin, and denomination of wine."

Following World War I the demand for wine greatly increased, and again dishonest merchants marketed large quantities of poor-grade wines at high prices. By 1919 exacting definitions for French appellations of origin had been determined. Nevertheless, further loopholes were discovered in the vinicultural regulations.

A lasting decree was enacted on July 30, 1935, which provided designations for wines from a controlled geographical origin. This act, although not perfect, has been lauded by winegrowers and consumers the world over and has been the basis of similar legislation in other countries. Consumers desiring authentic wines from specific French geographic locales should learn to look for label statements that disclose those sources.

◈ CLASSIFICATION

Much of the wine imported to America from France is of a different quality than that which the French consume on a daily basis. The French are typically frugal people, and economic pressures make it necesary to export much of their best production. The origin of French wines is classified into four broad quality, or nobility, echelons.

VINS DE CONSOMMATION COURANTE

As its name suggests, Vins de Consommation Courante is the category of wines for current consumption, the famous French *vin ordinaire*. No origins are specified, or required, for these wines, which are sold and drunk about as widely and with as little discrimination as soft drinks in America. Some markets sell such wines by the liter, dispensed in a manner closely akin to that of gasoline pumps at a filling station.

VINS DE PAYS

Established in 1973 by the French government, the Vins de Pays category translates as "wines of the area" or, more loosely as "country wines." Wines in this category are usually rather ordinary, and the designation may be applied to wines of an entire region or to wines of a small *commune* (township). For the most part, the Vins de Pays designation allows people to enjoy inexpensive carafe or jug-type wines made from locally grown grapes.

VINS DÉLIMITÉS DE QUALITÉ SUPÉRIEURE (VDQS)

The Vins Délimités de Qualité Supérieure classification is translated as "wines designated as being of superior quality," but not from a finite geographical origin. The VDQS category was established in 1945 to help popularize many previously unknown vineyard locales. These wines are also controlled by French winegrowing regulations, but not to the degree of AOC growths. Most VDQS wines are consumed in France, with less than 5 percent of French wines exported to the U.S. being labeled as belonging to this category.

APPELLATION D'ORIGINE CONTRÔLÉE (AOC)

The Appellation d'Origine Contrôlée (AOC) classification translates as "wines of controlled place names." This is the most specific and important statement of origin to be found on French wine labels. In total, only about 15 percent of the entire French wine production qualifies for an AOC label.

The AOC is regulated and enforced by the Institut National des Appellations d'Origine (INAO), which is a privately administered organization, but empowered by the French government to "service de la repression des fraudes."

FIGURE 6.2 Components of a French wine label. *(Adapted from Food and Wines from France.)*

Accordingly, AOC wines must be labeled with a statement identifying the place where the grapes were grown. These controlled geographic origins, or appellations, have constant boundaries, specified grape variety requirements, viticultural limits, and consistent winemaking rules.

Figure 6.2 shows the following key elements of a French wine label:

1. A statement that the wine is a product of France.
2. The region in which the wine was produced, for example, Burgundy, Bordeaux, Champagne.
3. The appellation for which the wine qualifies, accompanied by AOC or VDQS, except in the case of Champagne, for which the label need only read "Champagne."
4. The name and address of the shipper, except in the case of Champagne, where, usually, the Champagne vintner is also the shipper.
5. The name and address of the importer.
6. The alcoholic percentage by volume.
7. The net contents of the bottle.
8. Vintage—year the grapes were grown.
9. Brand name, estate name, or château name.
10. "Estate bottled" or "Château bottled"—for wine made and bottled at the same domaine estate or château where the grapes were grown.

The varieties of vines permitted to be cultivated in specific appellations are closely monitored, as is the sugar content in their grapes. In some regions, such as Burgundy and Champagne, AOC regulations prescribe exact guidelines for vine spacings and trellising. In other areas, such as Bordeaux, such cultivation techniques are less important.

Winemaking regulations are precisely stipulated too. For example, even though the black grape, Pinot Noir, is grown in both the Burgundy and Champagne regions, it can be commercially made into red table wine only in Burgundy. In Champagne it must be a white sparkling wine.

Each AOC has its own maximum-yield limitation, called the "Basic Yield," or *Rendement de Base*. Generally, the greater the prestige of the AOC, the lower the limit set on Basic Yield. For each vintage, local commissions can authorize crops to exceed Basic Yield, the amount dependent on the growing conditions during that year. The yield permitted over and above the Basic Yield in any given vintage is called the Annual Yield. Above the Annual Yield there is a crop maximum known as the Ceiling Yield, or *Plafond Limité de Classement*. Production that exceeds Annual Yield, but is less than Ceiling Yield, may qualify for an AOC label if it passes a taste test conducted by local authorities.

The French classification system is a common source of confusion to both expert and neophyte. Not only are there new terms to learn, but often a particular term has a slightly different meaning from one region to the next. The best approach is to master a clear understanding of how the system is employed in one region and then move on to the next.

Learning a few French words can help to grasp the sense of wine classification in France. Consider the following terms and translations:

barrique	wooden barrel or small cask
blanc de blanc	white juice pressed from white grapes
blanc de noir	white juice pressed from black grapes
cave	underground wine cellar
cépage	vine variety
clos	vineyard surrounded by a wall
côte	slope or hillside
château	mansion or grand vineyard estate
commune	township of a few square miles or less
cru	vineyard or growth
domaine	vineyard estate
élèveur	*négociants* who blend, process, and bottle
grand	great or finest
haut	higher than or superior to
millesime	vintage year
monopole	sole owner of a specific vineyard
mousseau	foaming or effervescence
négociants	wine dealers and shippers
nouveau	new, unaged wine
premier	first or primary
sec	dry, without sugar
vendange	grape harvest, vintage season
vignoble	vineyard

The old adage *Respectez les crus,* or "Respect the vineyards," may offer encouragement to memorize the names of some major *crus* in each region. It isn't necessary to commit the entire apparatus to memory, but there is a need to understand the system. A good solid knowledge will provide confidence that each new label can be positively identified—and the wine behind it fully appreciated.

❖ BURGUNDY ❖

The most important wine region in eastern France is Burgundy, or Bourgogne, as it is known by Burgundians. Winegrowing in Burgundy preceded the Roman occupation there by several centuries. The Roman Pliny the Elder gave credit to Helvetius, a Swiss, for bringing the vine to Burgundy. There are those who maintain that the northern Italian Tuscans were the first to make wine in Burgundy. A case can also be made for the Phoenicians, who brought viticulture to the mouth of the Rhone River at Marseilles at about 600 B.C. Whether they managed to navigate vines and wines some 200 miles northward to Burgundy is questionable.

It was the Romans, however, who taught the Burgundii peasants, originally Nordics and Teutons, how to make wines from cultivated vines. As the Roman Empire began to fall, the church became increasingly dominant over Burgundian vineyards. Monks of various religious orders planted and cultivated many landholdings bestowed upon the monasteries, some given in the late eighth and early ninth centuries by the great monarch Charlemagne.

Both the Benedictine and Cistercian orders grew wine in Burgundy, and the monks created many of the now famous vineyards of the Côte d'Or—the "Slope of Gold." Wine was, in fact, nearly as valuable as gold (a circumstance that may have been the source of the financial term "liquid assets"). As a result, the church became wealthy.

The monks' epicenter of winemaking was the great Abbey at Cluny, a grand structure located near Mâcon. In its day Cluny maintained a huge vineyard expanse and produced the finest wines in the region. Saint Bernard offered harsh criticism for the great wealth amassed at Cluny, once the greatest religious structure in all of France. Today, however, the locale is known as the Mâconnais, and its wine production is generally regarded as good but a step below the grand wines of the golden slope to the north.

Many Benedictine monks moved out of luxurious Cluny in order to establish more serene abbeys. One group, formed in the latter part of the eleventh century, called themselves Cistercians, after the bulrushes, or *cisteaux*, that grew in the swampy area where they settled near the medieval city of Beaune. Their motto was "By the Cross and the Plow."

Although their religious ideals may have been realized, the only agricultural crop in which the Cistercians found success was grapes, perhaps from vines that were descendants of the native Allobrogian vine. These produced grapes in small clusters shaped like pine cones *(pinot)* packed with tiny black *(noir)* berries. Although the Pinot Noir vine yielded superb wine, it was a shy producer.

The most celebrated Cistercian monks were those of the Clos de Vougeot, the twelfth-century abbey that grew to comprise 125 acres of vineyards, which many connoisseurs contend still produce some of the very finest red Burgundy. A thirteenth-century nunnery vineyard of equal stature is the Clos de Tart, neighboring Vougeot to the north.

The church planted new varieties of vines, doubtlessly some failing to fully ripen their grapes in the short Burgundian growing season and others unable to withstand the harsh winters. A variety that did flourish was discovered in the *commune* of Gamay. The Gamay vine produced much heavier crops than the vaunted Pinot, and Gamay wine was much darker in color and had a bold fruit flavor. Favor for Gamay grew quickly among winegrowers. The dukes of Burgundy, however, rejected the exotic nature of Gamay and remained steadfast in their insistence that the more delicate and sophisticated wine from the modest Pinot held virtues that would continue the true nobility of red Burgundy wine.

Philip the Bold banished Gamay from the golden slopes in 1395, but it found great acceptance to the south, in Beaujolais, where it has since reemerged as classic Burgundy in an entirely different mode. Louis XI, who ruled France from 1461 to 1483, prohibited the use of lesser grapes in winemaking throughout all the winegrowing regions of the nation.

Burgundian vintners operating during the Middle Ages experienced difficulty in trading with the provinces and countries to the north. Heavy loads of

FIGURE 6.3 *Barriques* of wine aging in Burgundy caves. *(Courtesy of Mommessin.)*

wine were hard to transport overland, and highwaymen were a common peril. Nevertheless, the fine quality of Burgundy wines was enhanced by the splendor and *gentillesse* with which the dukes of Burgundy presented them. All of this impressed the Parisians, in particular, who were willing to pay the high cost of shipment. As trade increased, the city of Beaune became the business center for the burgeoning business of Burgundy wine. With the advent of the Renaissance new and higher standards for Burgundy wines began to emerge.

Following the French Revolution, the large church properties were divided into small plots and sold to the laity. Any one *vigneron* could diversify his holdings by owning a portion of any number of AOC properties—a good hedge against the unpredictable ravages of hail, which could shred one vineyard or another indiscriminately. Today, because of this division, most of the important Burgundy vineyards have multiple ownership. The Clos de Vougeot, for example, is divided into more than 60 separately owned parcels.

Tiny parcels of vineyard, each having its own story, place, and personality, are part of the charisma of modern-day Burgundy. Only a few Burgundy estates remain that total more than 50 acres, and even these are collections of precious small vineyard plots here and there around the region.

Up until the eighteenth century most Burgundy wines were drunk from the *barrique* (barrel). Bottling was a convenience for marketing, rather than used for aging.

Burgundy is comparatively light in color but typically rich in a bramble-coffee bouquet, supple texture, firm acidity, and lingering flavor. It has been aptly called "the iron fist in a velvet glove."

Burgundy is the wine of scarcity. Most highly ranked vineyards produce only a few thousand bottles each year, with price levels providing a good indication of the extent to which demand outdistances supply.

❖ THE REGION

Burgundians are fond of proverbs, and there is one particular favorite of the people who grow wine in the Côte d'Or: "If our slopes were not the richest, they'd be the poorest." The passion of an eloquent Burgundian expounding upon a distinctively separate vineyard *terroir* can be contagious. There is, of course, a profound effect on Burgundy quality rendered by the struggle this soil

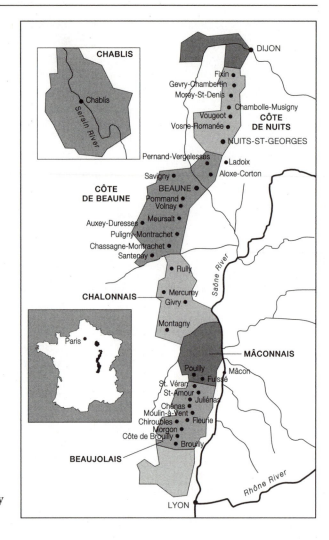

FIGURE 6.4 Burgundy winegrowing region.

imposes on its vines, eager to bear a few tiny berries bursting with color and flavor. Burgundy is a gift of nature; fine wines were grown there long before the advent of twentieth-century technology.

Most of Burgundy is situated in a narrow 90-mile strip of land between the cities of Dijon and Lyon. The entire region cultivates approximately 100,000 acres of vineyard, amounting to 4 percent or so of total French winegrowing. To the northwest is the disconnected district of Chablis, which, although technically part of the Burgundy region, has its own unique character.

The Burgundian landscape is serene and picturesque, but not dramatic, except perhaps for the wind-eroded cliffs to the west of Mâcon city. This is a region of marvelous agrarians, thousands of farmers making a decent living growing precious grapes on soil probably unsuitable for any other commercial agriculture. It is a region of several dozen small villages and a few modest cities. Burgundians are friendly, eager to please visitors who show respect for their craft and gentle to those who try their language.

Burgundy is often referred to as only the prestigious Côte d'Or, to the casual exclusion of the other four districts in the region. Although Côte d'Or wines are the most celebrated of Burgundies, all wines grown in the area have a legal right to the name *Burgundy,* and will be so considered in this text.

Thus, Burgundy consists of five districts:

Chablis—often referred to as the "Yonne," or the "Auxerrois"; centered on the village of Chablis.

Côte d'Or—the magnificent "Slope of Gold"; its capital city is Beaune.

This district is divided into two subdistricts:

Côte de Nuits, the northern portion

Côte de Beaune, the southern portion

Chalonnais—centered on the city of Chalon.

Mâconnais—centered on the city of Mâcon.

Beaujolais—the largest district in Burgundy.

In each township *(commune)* surrounding a village in Burgundy, the vineyards are divided into small parcels known as *climats*. Perhaps the best way to visualize this is to consider a model vineyard, AOC Petite Canard, composed of 30 rows of vines. Pierre may own the first 9 rows, Marie may own the next 10 rows, and Marcel the remaining 11 rows. A tourist driving down the road could easily assume the 30 rows to be a single entity, whereas the vineyard actually comprises three individually owned *climats*. Pierre, Marie, and Marcel are each permitted to sell their grapes, or their wine made from those grapes, under the name "Petite Canard."

VILLAGE *(COMMUNE)*.

Burgundy labels displaying only the AOC village name certify that the wine in those bottles was grown entirely within that *commune's* limits; for example:

Vosne-Romanée

Aloxe-Corton

Most village wines are made from grapes grown in the flatland vineyards in the *commune*.

PREMIER CRU

One step up from AOC Village Wine is AOC *Premier Cru*, or "First Growth." The name of the Premier Cru may appear after the *commune* name on the label, as in the following examples:

Vosne-Romanée Malconsorts

Aloxe-Corton Moutottes

Premier Cru vineyards are generally situated on choice sites on the upper or lower reaches of the slopes.

GRAND CRU

The highest-ranking Burgundy vineyard is the coveted *Grand Cru*, or "Great Growth." Typically, the labels on these wine bottles will display only the vineyard name as the appellation; for example:

Romanée-Conti

Corton

Grand Cru vineyards are always found in the very choicest sites in every Burgundy *commune*, as a rule about midway between the very top and the very bottom of a given slope or hillside.

Wines from Grand Cru and Premier Cru vineyards may be declassified to Village status. This is rather unusual, typically occurring when a vintage of particularly poor quality is experienced. Village wines cannot, of course, be elevated to either Grand Cru or Premier Cru. All vineyards are permanently and rigidly classified with their AOC rankings; they do not change from year to year.

ESTATE BOTTLING

Two phrases frequently found on Burgundy labels or corks are *Mise en Bouteilles au Domaine* and *Mise en Bouteilles à la Propriété*. Both are translated as "Bottled at the Estate," and are roughly equivalent to *estate bottled,* the term used in America. In Burgundy most wine estates are known as *domaines,* and in Bordeaux they are usually called *châteaux.*

The phrase *Mise en Bouteilles dans Nos Caves* translates as "Bottled in Our Cellars." Unless the bottler is also the owner of the *climat,* such words offer little assurance of any special quality.

NÉGOCIANTS

Because many of the Burgundy vineyards are divided into individual *climats,* it can often be difficult for the consumer to know which particular label to choose within a given AOC.

A way around this problem is to become familiar with the better *négociants,* or shippers, whose names appear somewhat as "brand names" on Burgundy labels. *Négociants* buy grapes and/or wine from many of the private growers, then blend, process, bottle, and market the resulting wines under their own labels. The better *négociants* have fine reputations to protect and are, therefore, very careful about ensuring that each of their Grand Cru, Premier Cru, and Village wines are sterling examples of their AOC pedigrees.

Among the better Burgundy shippers exporting to America are Bichot, Boisset, Bouchard Père et Fils, Joseph Drouhin, Faiveley, Louis Jadot, Laboure-Roi, Louis Latour, Mommessin, Moillard, Moreau, and Antonin Rodet—this is not an exhaustive list.

✤ THE CHABLIS DISTRICT

Chablis is sometimes referred to as "Lower Burgundy" because of its relatively low elevation. On a map, however, Chablis is unmistakably in the upper portion of the Burgundy region toward Paris.

The history of Chablis reaches back to the twelfth century. Pontigny, a Cistercian monastery, was founded there in 1114. Four years later the monastery acquired adjacent vineyards from the Benedictines of St. Martin at Tours. The Pontigny monks were undoubtedly the first to plant the great Chardonnay vine in Chablis. Thomas à Becket was exiled to Pontigny in 1164. During the mid-1100s a glorious church was built there, which in modern times serves as a seminary and remains the oldest surviving Cistercian church in all of France.

The Chablis district lies in the Department (county) of Yonne, which is the countryside centered by the charming medieval city of Auxerre. The village of Chablis is situated, a dozen miles or so east of Auxerre, on the banks of an aptly named small river, Le Serein (the serene), which empties into the Yonne River to the north. Many wine people refer to the district as Chablis or the Yonne, interchangeably. The Yonne River empties into the Seine, which runs through Paris. This river system has been important in providing water transportation for centuries.

There are about 4,000 acres of vineyard in the Yonne, which are divided among hundreds of growers. Less than 10 percent of Yonne wine production is AOC, all of which is from the Chablis village locale. One subdistrict, Sauvignon-de-St.-Bris, is designated as VDQS. Other lesser subdistricts in the Yonne are Auxerre and Tonnerre.

The soil of the district is very calcareous, consisting of clay mixed with limestone. The climate is rather harsh; winters are cold and dry, and summers are

FIGURE 6.5 Grand Cru Chablis vineyards across the Serein River. *(Photo by author.)*

hot and humid. Spring frosts can damage or destroy the fruiting buds on the vines, which wary growers protect with various heating devices. Hailstorms are a common threat in both spring and summer and are impossible to guard against.

Chablis makes up about half of all the Auxerrois vineyards and produces only dry white wines exclusively from the Chardonnay variety. Barrel aging in this region has given way to the use of glistening stainless steel. Wines from superior vintage years are of a very pale golden straw color. Contemporary Chablis expresses a clean green apple bouquet that carries over to the palate, finishing with crisp acidity and a distinct flinty-stony aftertaste.

To the north of Chablis village, across the river Serein, are the 86 acres that make up the eight AOC Grand Cru vineyards in the district. There are 30 AOC Premier Cru Chablis vineyards, totaling about 500 acres.

CHABLIS GRAND CRU	CHABLIS PREMIER CRU	
Blanchots	Beauroy	Monté de Tonnerre
Bougros	Beugnons	Montmains
Les Clos	Butteaux	Monts de Milieu
Grenouilles	Chapelot	Morein
Moutonne	Châtains	Pied d'Aloup
Preuses	Côte de Fontenay	Roncières
Valmur	Côte de Lechet	Séché
Vaudésir	Côte des Près Girots	Troesmes
	Epinottes	Vaillons
	Forêts	Vaucoupin
	Fourchaume	Vau de Vey
	Fourneaux	Vaugirard
	L'Homme Mort	Vaulorent
	Lys	Vaupulent
	Mélinots	Vosgros

Of the remaining AOC vineyards in Chablis are those that may be labeled in the Village Wine classification as AOC Chablis, along with some marginal plots that are permitted an AOC Petit Chablis appellation.

The firm of J. Moreau & Fils has the distinction of being both the oldest and the largest *négociant* in the Chablis district. Founded in 1814, the estate has grown to include large holdings of both Grand Cru and Premier Cru vineyards, most noteworthy being a major share of the coveted Grand Cru "Les Clos." In stark contrast to the antiquity of this estate, observed by visitors to the Moreau cellars, are the stainless steel tanks, high-tech processing, and automated equipment producing the finest of modern Chablis.

Laroche is a highly regarded vintner-*négociant*, exemplifying the Chablis tradition. The estate comprises the original family vineyards, which include an important share of the Grand Cru "Blanchots," and the Domaine La Jouchère, which includes major holdings of the Premier Cru "Vaillons," among others. Wines made from the Domaine La Jouchère may also be found under the Bacheroy-Josselin label. A tour of the old Laroche caves recalls medieval times when monks once crafted Chablis in oak barrels, but modern Laroche Chablis is precisely that—modern—with clean, crisp acidity and a rich fruit character.

The villages of Auxerre and Tonnerre produce considerable red *vin de pays* from the Pinot Noir variety, but this wine doesn't compare with the famous Pinot *crus* of Burgundy.

❖ THE CÔTE D'OR DISTRICT

As the Cistercian monks learned 1,000 years ago, the red soil of the Côte d'Or is so poor that the only sensible crop is grapes. Chardonnay and Pinot Noir survive on these slopes to produce wines of unequalled richness of texture and complexity of flavor.

The Côte d'Or is located about 160 miles southeast of Paris. The district commences at the lower edge of the French mustard capital of Dijon. At one time there was an AOC Dijon classification, but it is long since defunct. Côte d'Or vineyards run southward continuously for about 37 miles, ending near the village of Santenay.

There are about 9,000 acres of vineyard on the golden slopes, cultivated by hundreds of growers who produce three to six million gallons of precious wine from most every vintage. Perhaps once or twice in each decade, severe weather befalls the slopes and wine will be acutely scarce. About half of the vineyards in the Côte d'Or are AOC ranked, and red wine production dominates the regional output.

Perhaps the best way to first study the Côte d'Or is with a map. In this district, people often say that their *communes* are the "pearls of the Burgundian necklace." The long, narrow string of villages, each making truly exquisite wine, does fit the metaphor quite accurately.

CÔTE DE NUITS

The upper half of the Côte d'Or, called the Côte de Nuits, is a subdistrict with slopes gently facing east to the Saône River. The soil here is of an oolitic calcareous (chalky) composition, mixed with varying concentrations of iron and marl. The southeastern exposure gets the early morning sun, which has the dual advantage of quickly burning off the dew, which can harbor disease microorganisms, and maximizing the daily sunlight needed for optimal vine growth.

Generally, the land between the upper and lower levels of these slopes is the most desirable and is classified as AOC Grand Cru. The topsoil of this sector has layered fragments of crumbled rock rising from the subsoil, adding potassium and phosphorous to the chalk, iron, and marl. Pinot Noir grapes harvested from these vineyards have an intense amber-scarlet color and bramble-coffee-earthy flavors unequaled anywhere else.

MARSANNY

The northernmost village in the Côte de Nuits in Marsannay, where the great Pinot is grown mostly for rosé table wines. These are usually very good, but fall short of the superb reds grown to the south.

FIXIN AND BROCHON

The great vineyards commence in Fixin and Brochon, both situated just below Marsannay. The best wines of Fixin and Brochon are from their nine Premier Cru vineyards; these *communes* have no Grand Cru. Some of the better vintages can be compared to other good growths in the Côte de Nuits. Fixin and Brochon receive less attention from the wine press and are, therefore, sometimes overlooked by American wine enthusiasts.

FIXIN AND BROCHON PREMIER CRU

Arvelets	Perrière
Cheusots	Queue de Hareng
Clos du Chapitre	En Suchot
Hervelets	Le Village
Meix-Bas	

GEVREY

In A.D. 630 the Burgundian Duke Algamaire bequeathed vineyards at Gevrey to the Benedictine monks at the Abbey of Bèze. The Gevrey vineyards became known as the Clos de Bèze. Next to the Clos was a small piece of land owned by a peasant named Bertin. He became so impressed with the quality of the monks' wine that he planted his small property with vines and began to employ the monks' methods of winegrowing. Bertin's vineyard became known as *Champ* (field) *Bertin,* eventually combined to become "Chambertin." Some historians contend that Chambertin was the favorite wine of Napoleon Bonaparte.

Gevrey, like many townships in Burgundy, has added the name of its most famous vineyard, Chambertin, to its own; thus, the 1,000-acre *commune* of Gevrey-Chambertin. There are eight Grand Cru vineyards in Gevrey-Chambertin. At the top of the list is Chambertin itself and the equally prestigious Chambertin-Clos-de-Bèze. The other six Grand Cru vineyards have all added "Chambertin" to their own particular names.

GEVREY-CHAMBERTIN GRAND CRU	GEVREY-CHAMBERTIN PREMIER CRU	
Chambertin	Bel Air	Ergots
Chambertin-Clos-de-Bèze	La Boissière	Estournelles
Chapelle-Chambertin	Cazetiers	Fontenay
Charmes-Chambertin	Champeaux	Gémeaux
Griotte-Chambertin	Champitonnois	Goulots
Laticières-Chambertin	Champonnets	Issarts
Mazis-Chambertin	Clos du Chapitre	Lavaut
Ruchottes-Chambertin	Cherbaudes	Perrière
	Closeau	Poissenot
	Combe-aux-Moines	Clos Prieur
	Combottes	La Romanée
	Corbeaux	Clos St.-Jacques
	Craipillot	Véroilles

The Boisset success can be attributed to a clever assessment of changing consumer tastes and preferences and, more important, the ability to reach those consumers with good quality wines at attractive prices. The Boisset family owns and operates an enviable list of classified Côte d'Or vineyards, but even more impressive is their new wine production center. This combination of prime vineyard appellation and high-quality, low-cost winemaking has resulted in Boisset labels achieving vast distribution.

MOREY-ST.-DENIS

The next "pearl" to the south is the *commune* of Morey-St.-Denis. Within its total acreage of some 250 acres or so, there are five Grand Cru vineyards totaling about 80 of these acres.

MOREY-ST.-DENIS GRAND CRU	MOREY-ST.-DENIS PREMIER CRU	
Bonnes Mares	Clos Baulet	Genevrières
Clos des Lambrays	Blanchards	Gruenchers
Clos de la Roche	Brulées	Millandes
Clos St.-Denis	Clos Bussière	Monts Luisants
Clos de Tart	Chaffots	Clos des Ormes
	Charmes	Riotte
	Charrières	Côte Rôtie
	Chénevery	Ruchots
	Aux Cheseaux	Sorbés
	Façonnières	Clos Sorbés

The Convent of Le Tart was founded by Cistercian nuns, sometimes called "Bernardines," in this village in 1125. The sisters cultivated vineyards to demonstrate that they were true Cistercians, and their wines were thought to be as good as any in the entire Côte d'Or prior to the French Revolution. The old nunnery vineyard, long since called the Clos de Tart, is one of the Grand Cru growths in Morey-St.-Denis.

CHAMBOLLE-MUSIGNY

As the Grand Cru Chambertin name was added to Gevrey, so the Grand Cru vineyard of Les Musigny was added to the village name of Chambolle, creating the township of Chambolle-Musigny.

CHAMBOLLE-MUSIGNY GRAND CRU	CHAMBOLLE-MUSIGNY PREMIER CRU	
Bonnes Mares	Amoureuses	Fousselottes
Musigny	Baudes	Fuées
	Beaux-Bruns	Grosseilles
	Borniques	Gruenchers
	Charmes	Hauts-Doix
	Châtelots	Lavrottes
	Combottes	Noirots
	Aux Combottes	Plantes
	Cras	Sentiers
	Derrière-la-Grange	

Note that the AOC Grand Cru Bonnes Mares is shared by the *communes* of Morey-St.-Denis and Chambolle-Musigny. It is common that vineyards cross township lines. Note, too, that many vineyard names, such as "Charmes," are taken in several different townships.

It is in Chambolle-Musigny that the only AOC Grand Cru white wines in the Côte de Nuits are grown. Regulation permits AOC Musigny red to have up to 15 percent of the white Chardonnay in its composition. Rarely is Musigny le Blanc bottled separately.

VOUGEOT

Route National 74 connects all the pearls of the Côte de Nuits. The next village south on this road is Vougeot. It is here, along the narrow river Vouge, that the Cistercian monks developed their legendary Clos de Vougeot. The abbey remains in pristine condition today, nearly 900 years later, as a gathering center for the Chevaliers du Tastevin (Soldiers of the Tasting Cup), a large international brotherhood of Burgundy wine enthusiasts.

Today there are only about 125 acres of AOC Grand Cru vineyard in the Clos de Vougeot. The balance are planted with fine red Pinot except for five acres of Chardonnay, which does not qualify as Grand Cru and is aptly labeled "Clos de Vougeot Blanc." The red wines from the Clos de Vougeot vary considerably nowadays, because there are so many individual *climats* from which different owners make their own wines.

VOUGEOT GRAND CRU	VOUGEOT PREMIER CRU
Clos de Vougeot	Clos de la Perrière
	Petits-Vougeots
	Vigne Blanche

Even when the Clos de Vougeot was a single large Cistercian estate, there were different grades of wines identified by the monks who worked in the monastery cellars. The *Cuvée des Papes* (Blend of the Popes) came from the higher elevations of the vineyard slopes, and the *Cuvée des Rois* (Blend of the Kings) was taken from the central slopes. A third wine, grown from the lower flatland vineyards, was the *Cuvée des Moines* (Blend of the Monks).

FIGURE 6.6 Clos de Vougeot abbey and vineyards. (*Courtesy of* Food and Wines from France.)

VOSNE-ROMANÉE

Still farther south on R.N. 74 are the fine vineyards of Flagey-Echézeaux, which total about 178 acres. Today these are generally included in the neighboring *commune* of Vosne-Romanée, bringing the township total to 548 very precious acres. It is said that Vosne-Romanée is the "center pearl of the Burgundian necklace." This is Burgundian *terroir* at its worst and, in classic paradox, at its very best.

Within Vosne-Romanée reigns what is lauded the epitome of red Burgundy —La Romanée-Conti. To Burgundy lovers this 4.5 acres of vineyard has no peer. As would be anticipated, wines from this tiny vineyard are very expensive, often surpassing $300 per bottle for younger vintages and much more for older ones.

La Romanée-Conti is blessed with distinguished neighbors as well, among which are the AOC Grand Cru vineyards La Tache, Richebourg, and Romanée-St.-Vivant. All of these priceless vineyards, including those in Flagey-Echézeaux, were once owned by the Duchess of Burgundy, who bequeathed them to the Benedictine Abbey of St.-Vivant in 1232.

VOSNE-ROMANÉE GRAND CRU	VOSNE-ROMANÉE PREMIER CRU	
Echézeaux	Beaux-Monts	Malconsorts
Grands Échézeaux	Brûlées	Petits-Monts
Richebourg	Chaumes	Clos des Reas
La Romanée	Gaudichots	Reignots
Romanée-Conti	Grande Rue	
Romanée-St.-Vivant		
La Tache		

Legend has it that the wines from Romanée St.-Vivant were given to King Louis XIV for an illness he was suffering. Following his recovery, Le Roi Soleil (the Sun King), as he was often called, remarked that "an illness which helps one discover such a remedy is indeed a present from heaven."

In 1720 La Romanée became the property of the Cronembourg family. Despite the efforts of Madame de Pompadour to acquire it, the 4.5-acre jewel was sold in 1760 to the Prince de Conti, who added his name to make it Romanée-Conti. Like the vineyards of the Clos de Vougeot, those of the Abbey of St.-Vivant became public property after the French Revolution. After all the buildings were destroyed so that the monks would not try to return, the vineyards were auctioned off.

FIGURE 6.7   Romanée-Conti vineyard. *(Photo by author.)*

Curiously, the vines of Romanée-Conti escaped the *Phylloxera* disease until 1945, when older vines were uprooted in favor of grafted stock.

NUITS-ST.-GEORGES

The largest village in the Côte de Nuits is Nuits-St.-Georges, from which the entire *côte* (slope) gets its name. With no Grand Cru vineyards, Nuits-St.-Georges is known for wines that are darker, denser, and coarser in structure than the lighter, refined Pinots grown to the north. Technology has, however, been able to make great strides in advancing the winemaking art in Nuits-St.-Georges, producing some of the best bargains from Burgundy in the marketplace. A visit to the facilities of Jean-Claude Boisset and Labouré-Roi can illustrate how science has been carefully adapted to make fine Burgundy even better.

NUITS-ST.-GEORGES PREMIER CRU

Aux Argillats	Perrière
Les Argillats	Perrière-Noblet
Boudots	Porets
Bousselots	Poulettes
Cailles	Procès
Chaboeufs	Pruliers
Chaignots	Richemone
Chaîne-Carteau	Roncière
Champs-Perdrix	Rousselots
Cras	Rue-de-Chaux
Crots	St.-Georges
Damodes	Thorey
Didiers	Vallerots
Hauts-Pruliers	Vaucrains
Murgers	Vignes Rondes

Wine production among the *négociants* operating in Nuits-St.-Georges relies on modern technology. A drive through the eastern side of the town reveals new construction in which state-of-the-art tankage and machines are bringing the world a new breed of Burgundy with clean, new oak barrel complexity, and greater expression of fruit flavors.

PREMEAUX

The southernmost vineyards in the Côte de Nuits are those of the *commune* Premeaux, a small village generally considered to be a part of the Nuits-St.-Georges township. The greatest distinction of Premeaux is that it marks the border between the Côte de Nuits and the Côte de Beaune. The wines of Premeaux are similar in style to Nuits-St.-Georges and are, in fact, entitled to use AOC Nuits-St.-Georges on their labels.

PREMEAUX PREMIER CRU

Cerdrix	Clos des Corvées
Clos-Arlots	Clos des Forêts
Clos de Grandes Vignes	Clos St.-Marc
Clos de la Maréchale	Corvées-Paget
Clos des Argillières	

The high acclaim given many vineyards in the central portion of the Côte de Nuits is not generally awarded to most of the vineyards situated at the northern and southern extremes of the slope. Among the villages and *communes* affected by this discrimination are Comblanchien and Pressey, both situated near Premeaux, and, as mentioned previously, Fixin and Brochon, bordering Chambertin.

Red wines from wines grown in any of these four townships may be labeled "Côte de Nuits-Villages." This designation lends a bit of prestige and recognition to wines of generally good quality that would probably otherwise go unnoticed in the market. It also provides good values for red Burgundy enthusiasts. White wines from these villages may be blended together as "Bourgogne Blanc."

CÔTE DE BEAUNE

The southern half of the Côte d'Or is called "the Côte de Beaune," a namesake of the magnificent medieval city of Beaune that remains the wine center for the entire Burgundy region.

The Côte de Beaune makes both red and white table wines but, in sharp contrast to the Côte de Nuits, is more famous for its Grand Cru whites. Indeed, the Chardonnay vines in the great vineyards of Corton and Montrachet yield wines of a deep golden hue, bold fig-olive-boxwood flavors, and a long stony-vanilla aftertaste.

The best slopes of the Côte de Beaune face southeasterly and are composed of soils similar to those of the Côte de Nuits, but with a bit more clay and iron. More important, however, is their much higher level of limestone, which expert viticulturists insist is essential in growing the Chardonnay to yield such classic white Burgundy.

LADOIX-SERRIGNY

Ladoix-Serrigny is the first *commune* to greet a traveler entering the Côte de Beaune from the north. Many consider it an annex to the neighboring *commune* of Aloxe-Corton. Although it is regarded as a bit lower in overall quality in the Corton locale, it has, nevertheless, an impressive array of Grand Cru and Premier Cru vineyards.

LADOIX-SERRIGNY GRAND CRU	LADOIX-SERRIGNY PREMIER CRU
Carrières	Basses Mourettes
Grandes Lolières	Bois Roussot
Basses Mourettes (W)	Le Clou d'Orge
Hautes Mourettes (W)	La Corvée
Moutottes (W)	Hautes Mourettes
Le Rognet et Corton (W)	Joyeuses
La Toppe-au-Vert	Micaude
Vergennes	

The Grand Cru white wines of Ladoix-Serrigny are entitled to AOC Corton-Charlemagne. The reds are similarly permitted the AOC Corton designation.

ALOXE-CORTON

Close to the *commune* of Aloxe-Corton are the remains of a twelfth-century church constructed by the monks of Saulieu. Land for this structure was given by the Emperor Charlemagne in 775, along with most of his personal Corton vineyards behind the nearby village.

FIGURE 6.8 The Corton "Dome."
(Courtesy of Albert Bichot.)

Charlemagne hoped, no doubt, that the Saulieu monks would provide him with the finest wine from the Montagne de Corton vineyards. Today this mountain is called the "Corton Dome," as it is decidedly shaped more like a dome than a mountain. The eastern half of the Corton hillside is devoted to Pinot Noir vines, and the southern and western portions are planted to Chardonnay. Both are AOC Corton Grand Cru, the Pinot Noir vineyards being the only red AOC Grand Cru in the entire Côte de Beaune.

The crown of Corton today is Louis Latour, a family owned and operated estate surrounding the magnificent Château de Grancey. There is little new technology to be found here, and none is needed, as the reputation of this estate for the best wines grown on the Corton Dome is known around the world. A visit to the Latour vineyards and caves, where Charlemagne once ruled, is an experience that every wine lover will cherish forever.

Legend has it that the first white wine vineyards of the Corton Dome were ordered to be planted by Charlemagne personally so that he could drink white wine in public and avoid staining his beard with red wine from the Pinot.

Burgundies from Bichot and its estates are more apt to be found on shelves in the United States than almost any other. Founded in the 1830s, the Bichot family estate has grown ever since and is now actually a wine empire. Most of the firm's wines are made by the classic *négociant* method of buying, blending, and finishing—the process of *élevage*. Wines from each of the estates are bottled under their individual labels. Among these are the regal Clos Frantin of the Côte de Nuits and the Long-Depaquit of Chablis. Among other estate labels are Bouchot-Ludot, Charles Drapier, and Remy Gauthier. All are housed in the original Beaune cellars, which have the combined romance of old caves and craftsmanship of modern equipment.

ALOXE-CORTON GRAND CRU		ALOXE-CORTON PREMIER CRU
Bressandes	Meix	Chaillots
Corton-Charlemagne	Meix-Lallemand	Coutière
Chaumes	Pauland	Fournières
Combes	Perrières	Guérets
Corton	Pougets	Maréchaudes
Fiètres	Renardes	Meix
Grèves	Clos du Roi	Pauland
Languettes	La Vigne au Saint	La Toppe-au-Vert
Maréchaudes	Voirosses	Valozières
		Vercots

Corton was the favorite wine of Voltaire, which is rather ironic in that he was a sworn enemy of the monastic system. Voltaire is reported to have poured lesser wines for his guests while drinking Corton himself. His taste was prophetic, as Aloxe-Corton is the only *commune* to have far more Grand Cru than Premier Cru growths.

Pernand-Vergelesses is another annex to the Aloxe-Corton *commune*. Wines from this small *commune* that are not bottled as Aloxe-Corton may be appropriately labeled as Pernand-Vergelesses; as such, they are generally sold for much lower prices and are often very good bargains.

PERNAND-VERGELESSES GRAND CRU	PERNAND-VERGELESSES PREMIER CRU
Corton-Charlemagne	Basses-Vergelesses
Corton	Caradeux
	Creux de la Net
	Fichots
	Île de Vergelesses

Savigny-les-Beaune, yet another of the small Corton Dome villages, borders Pernand-Vergelesses to the west. Although it has no Grand Cru appellations, its 22 Premier Crus have a sterling reputation as appellations for truly fine red Pinot at comparatively attractive prices.

SAVIGNY-LES-BEAUNE PREMIER CRU

Basses-Vergelesses	Lavières
Bataillère	Marconnets
Charnières	Narbantons
Clous	Petits-Godeaus
Dominode	Petits-Liards
Fourneaux	Peuillets
Grands-Liards	Redrescuts
Gravains	Rouverettes
Guettes	Serpentières
Haut-Jarrons	Talmettes
Haut-Marconnets	Vergelesses

Defining the exact geography for each vineyard across the Corton Dome can be an exasperating task. As can be seen in the preceding listings, some vineyard names are found in both Grand Cru and Premier Cru appellations, and across township borders. In most such cases, vineyard names far predate the AOC classification system and even some of the townships themselves.

BEAUNE

South of the Corton Dome is the city of Beaune, surrounded by well-preserved bastions much as they were during medieval times. Beaune has several interesting sightseeing stops—most notably the fifteenth-century Hotel-Dieu, now the famous Hospices de Beaune. Nicholas Rolin, chancellor to the duke of Burgundy in the mid-fifteenth century, constructed the hospital for the needy and gave it vineyards from which wines, sold at an annual auction, funded its operation. The Hospices de Beaune is now a museum, but the auction is still held in late November every year. Prices achieved there have become a barometer of both wine quality and the wine economy for each vintage of Burgundy.

FIGURE 6.9   The Hospice de Beaune. *(Photo by author.)*

The best visit for a wine enthusiast in Beaune includes a tour of the dark caves of Bouchard Père & Fils, beneath the bastions still standing guard around part of the old city. In cellars having walls more than 20 feet thick, bottles of great Burgundy vintages remain as monuments to some of the richest wine history in the world. This winery was founded in the 1730s. The first Bouchards were cloth merchants who made regular sales trips to Paris with books of sample swatches. Small wine deliveries were taken along to help defray travel expenses. The wine business grew to exceed dry goods sales, and the pages of the sample book became order lists for the next shipments of wines. Today the Bouchard estate comprises more than 175 acres of Grand Cru and Premier Cru vineyards, by far the greatest single holding in Burgundy.

There are 34 AOC Premier Cru appellations among the 2,500 acres of Pinot Noir and Chardonnay vineyards cultivated in the large winegrowing *commune* of Beaune.

FIGURE 6.10   Old bottles of Burgundy. *(Courtesy of Bouchard Père et Fils.)*

BEAUNE PREMIER CRU

Aigrots	Marconnets
Avaux	Mignotte
Bas des Teurons	Montée Rouge
Blanches Fleurs	Montrevenots
Boucherottes	Clos des Mouches
Bressandes	Clos de la Mousse
Cent Vignes	En l'Orme
Champs Pimonts	Perrières
Chouacheux	Pertuisots
Coucherias	Reversées
Cras	Clos du Roi
Écu	Seurey
Epenottes	Sizies
Fèves	Theurons
En Genét	Tiélandry
Grèves	Toussaints
Sur-les-Grèves	Vignes Franches

It is the AOC classification of Beaune that often generates uncertainty among wine neophytes trying to make sense of the system. Beaune is, of course, a township in the much larger Côtes de Beaune subdistrict.

In the early 1880s, Louis Jadot was a grape grower whose destiny was to become one of the great Burgundy wine *négociants*. The original Jadot caves are in the medieval Jacobin convent in central Beaune, but the wines that keep the Louis Jadot name among the finest of all Burgundies are made in a modern facility on the outer edge of the city. Jadot estate vineyards are a veritable Who's Who of Côte de Beaune Grand Cru; among these are Corton-Charlemagne, Pougets, and Chevalier-Montrachet. Although these wines are, of course, very expensive, the Jadot *négociant* end of the business has expanded to offer some affordable wines grown in other parts of Burgundy.

The Côte d'Or is replete with some tiny Premier Cru and Grand Cru vineyards, some of just several acres or even less. Burgundian vintners often combine the wines in a given subdistrict that have the same classification, such as Beaune Premier Cru.

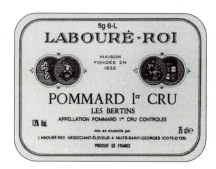

Founded by Joseph Drouhin in the 1880s, the Drouhin family estate now comprises vineyards at the very pinnacle of classic Burgundy classification: Les Clos, Chambertin, Musigny, Clos Vougeot, Grands-Echézeaux, Bonnes Mares, Corton-Charlemagne, Bâtard-Montrachet, and many others. The Drouhin cellars include some of the earliest Roman caves and Burgundian dukes' cellars existing under the streets of Beaune. Much more recently, the Drouhins were the first Burgundians to recognize and invest in the promise of Oregon for growing Pinot Noir in the United States. The combined history, pedigree, and vision of this vintner are brought into focus with truly superb winemaking skill and facilities. The consistency of highest quality achieved by Drouhin is perhaps unmatched in all of Burgundy.

POMMARD

South of Beaune, on the banks of the river Avant Dheune, are the vineyards of Pommard, its entire 820 acres divided into small plots devoted to exceptional red wines from the regal Pinot Noir. The Dutch scholar Erasmus is thought to have been particularly fond of Pommard.

POMMARD PREMIER CRU

Argillières	Épenots
Arvelets	Fremiers
Bertins	Jarollères
Clos Blanc	Clos Micot
Boucherottes	Petits-Épenots
Chanière	Pézerolles
Chanlins-Bas	Platière
Chapponières	Poutures
Charmots	Refène
Combes-Dessus	Rugiens
Clos de la Commaraine	Saussiles
Croix-Noires	Clos du Verger
Derrière St.-Jean	

The brothers Cottin have converted the old Labouré-Roi *négociant* house into one of the most intricate fine wine production and marketing firms in all of France. With access to an increasing amount of grapes from prestige Grand Cru and Premier Cru Côte d'Or vineyards, they have constructed new facilities that exemplify the modern approach to Burgundy winegrowing at affordable prices.

FIGURE 6.11   Volnay vineyards.
(Photo by author.)

VOLNAY

A short walk south from Pommard is the comparatively smaller township of Volnay, with only 375 acres of small plots cultivated to the red Pinot.

VOLNAY PREMIER CRU

Angles	Fremiets
Aussy	Lurets
Barre	Mitans
Bousse d'Or	Ormeau
Brouillards	Petures
Caillerets	Petures-dessus
Caillerets-dessus	Pointes d'Angles
Carelle sous la Chapelle	Pousse d'Or
Carelle-dessous	Robardelle
Champans	Ronceret
Chanlin	Santenots
Clos des Chenes	Taille Pieds
Chevrets	En Verseuil
Clos des Ducs	Volnay
Durets	

In this area some of the growers still make their own wine, which is marketed in bulk to the *négociants*. Here the wine cellar, called a *chai*, is usually a small building that is at least partially buried in order to maintain stable temperatures inside. It is common to find the *maître de chai* (cellar master) wielding the famous *tastevin*. This device is a small shallow cup in which strategically placed "dimples" are indented to facilitate the reflection of light through the wine when it is being evaluated. It is usually made of silver, measuring about three to four inches in diameter and perhaps an inch deep, and is generally carried about by a leather neck strap or fine silver chain. In some of the more modern *chais*, however, the wine masters have taken to using the more common *verre* (glass) to better examine the color and clarity of their wines.

FIGURE 6.12   Silver tastevin.
(Courtesy of Mississippi State University; photo by Marko Nicovich.)

MONTHÉLIE

Nearly all of the wine grown in the small village of Monthélie is red and has the general reputation of being a bit lighter and less distinctive than the more well-known Burgundies.

MONTHÉLIE PREMIER CRU

Cas Rougeot	Lavelle
Champs-Fulliot	Meix-Bataille
Duresses	Riottes
Gaillard	Taupine
Gauthey	Gignes Rondes

The wines of Monthélie have never been able to garner much attention in the world marketplace and are, therefore, usually good values when one is fortunate enough to find them in America.

AUXEY-DURESSES

Even more obscure than Monthélie is Auxey-Duresses, a small *commune* that is another of the lessser known, but good quality red wine appellations.

AUXEY-DURESSES PREMIER CRU

Bas des Duresses	Grand Champs
Bretterins	Reugne
Duresses	Clos du Val
Ecusseaux	

MEURSAULT

The most diverse *commune* in the Côte d'Or is Meursault, which produces a comparatively large number of both red and white wines. It is centered by the town of Meursault, but the village of Blagny is also part of the *commune*.

As early as the twelfth century the Cistercian monks of Citeaux Abbey owned vineyards in Meursault, principally the magnificent manor vineyard of Perrières, now a Premier Cru. The Huguenots destroyed the manor in the sixteenth century, and the property was seized by the government after the French Revolution. Despite this tumultuous history, the large wine cellars have survived. Cardinal de Bernis, adored by Madame de Pompadour, is believed to have traditionally celebrated Mass during the mid-1700s with Meursault wine so that he would not grimace when confronting his Lord.

Sarah Jane English, in her charming book *Vin vignettes,* tells of the name of Meursault being derived from the Latin *muris saltus,* or "mouse leap"—a colloquial term, meaning "short cut," used by Roman foot soldiers. When they referred to a shorter pathway, that could not be used by carts or chariots, they would take a *muris saltus.*

There is ample evidence in and around Meursault that Thomas Jefferson, as U.S. ambassador to France, traveled a number of times to these vineyards to sample and buy for his private stock.

MEURSAULT PREMIER CRU

Bouchères	Perrières-dessus
Caillerets	Petures
Charmes-dessous	Pièce-sous-le-Bois
Charmes-dessus	Plures (R)

Cras	Porusot
Genevrières-dessous	Santenots-Blancs (R)
Genevrières-dessus	Santenots-dessous (R)
Goutte d'Or	Santenots du Milieu (R)
Jenelotte	Sous de Dos d'Âne
Perrières-dessous	

Note in the preceding list that the AOC Premier Cru rank is permitted only for the red (R) wines grown in four of these vineyards, but not for the whites. The rest are permitted the AOC Premier Cru appellation for both red and white wines.

Although the caves of the Jacques Prieur *négociant* firm are located in the village of Meursault, and its wines from that township superb, attention must focus on the diversity and quality of wines grown in the Jacques Prieur collection of classic vineyard plots in Chambertin, Clos de Bèze, Musigny, Clos de Vougeot, Montrachet, and Chevalier-Montrachet—all of Grand Cru rank. The ratings and scores awarded to Jacques Prieur wines are typically very high and match the price tags one should expect for exquisite Burgundy.

PULIGNY-MONTRACHET

What Vosne-Romanée is to Pinot Noir and the Côte de Nuits, Puligny-Montrachet is to Chardonnay and the Côte de Beaune. Many wine experts contend that the five Grand Cru vineyards that cross the townships of Puligny-Montrachet and Chassagne-Montrachet yield the very finest wines grown from Chardonnay anywhere.

Sarah Jane English also tells of the name Montrachet evolving from the Latin *mons rachicensis,* meaning "bald hill," or from *mons racemus,* "grape hill." In any case, the Montrachet vineyards are comparatively young by Burgundian standards; few existed prior to the seventeenth century.

PULIGNY-MONTRACHET GRAND CRU	PULIGNY-MONTRACHET PREMIER CRU	
Le Montrachet	Caillerets	Garenne
Chevalier-Montrachet	Chalumeaux	Homeau de Blagny
Bâtard-Montrachet	Champs-Canet	Pucelles
Bienvenue-Bâtard-Montrachet	Clavoillons	Refferts
	Combettes	Sous le Puits
	Folatières	

FIGURE 6.13 Chevalier-Montrachet vineyard in springtime. *(Photo by author.)*

The sources of the names of the Grand Cru appellations recall a number of legends and tales when the topic is brought up among well-informed Burgundians. One of the most colorful accounts begins in the grand medieval castle at Montrachet, where an elder nobleman seduced one of the young maidens and fathered a son. The nobleman already had a fully grown son—a soldier off to war. The duke of Burgundy was very displeased with the elder Montrachet's indiscretion and decreed that his two sons be distinguished as the *Chevalier-Montrachet*, or "Soldier Montrachet," and the *Bâtard-Montrachet*, or "Bastard Montrachet." The brave young warrior was killed in battle shortly afterward, and Père Montrachet passed away. As time went by, the castle was destroyed and the grand vineyards were parceled into plots bearing the legendary names.

With a history continuing since the 1740s, Domaine Leflaive has built a reputation for some of the finest white wines in Burgundy, arguably the very best in the *commune* of Puligny-Montrachet. The Leflaive domaine includes parcels in the Grand Cru vineyards of Bâtard-Montrachet and Chevalier-Montrachet, along with the Premier Cru Clavoillon, Combettes, and Pucelles.

CHASSAGNE-MONTRACHET

Two of the Grand Cru Montrachet vineyards transcend the boundary between the townships of Puligny-Montrachet and Chassagne-Montrachet. The majesty of these vineyards has come to overshadow the significance of the *communes* in which they are located. In the case of Chassagne-Montrachet, the presence of red wine vineyards among such highly pedigreed whites has veiled what is one of the very best winegrowing locales in the region.

CHASSAGNE-MONTRACHET GRAND CRU	CHASSAGNE-MONTRACHET PREMIER CRU	
Le Montrachet	Boudriotte	Grandes Ruchottes
Bâtard-Montrachet	Brussoles	Maltroie
Criots-Bâtard-Montrachet	Caillerets (W)	Abbaye de Morgeot
	En Cailleret (R)	Morgeot
	Champs Gain	Romanée
	Chenevottes	St.-Jean
	Macherelles	Vergers

AOC Chassagne-Montrachet "Caillerets" is permitted for white wines only, and AOC Chassagne-Montrachet "En Cailleret" is permitted only for reds. All the remaining vineyards are Premier Cru ranked for both white and red.

SANTENAY

The southernmost of the Côte de Beaune *communes* is Santenay, another of the obscure Burgundy appellations that have yet to be fully discovered in the marketplace. Santenay produces both red and white wines of a lighter, more delicate expression than its famous neighbors to the north.

SANTENAY PREMIER CRU	
Beauregard	Maladière
Beaurepaire	Passe Temps
Comme	Clos des Tavannes
Gravières	

At the extreme southern tip of the Côte de Beaune are several small villages that produce rather delicate red and common white wines. Red wines from these villages and other *communes* in the subdistrict (except for Aloxe-Corton, Beaune, Volnay, and Pommard) may be blended together for AOC Côtes de Beaune-Villages in sequel to AOC Côtes de Nuits-Villages, discussed earlier. In much the same manner, this designation gives a measure of prestige and recognition to the labels of these typically good red wines. White wines from these same villages may be blended for "Bourgogne Blanc."

◈ CHALONNAIS

Directly south of the Côte d'Or is the Chalonnais, which takes its name from Chalon-sur-Saône, an industrial city situated a few miles to the east of the vineyards. The Chalonnais is about 20 miles long, composed mostly of vineyards cultivated on the slopes of the Charollais hills which, for the most part, have the east and southeasterly exposures desired for the early morning sun.

Although the lower plains have more clay than mineral components, soils at the upper levels have varying mixtures of limestone, iron, and silica. The usual order holds: the best wines come from the middle- to higher-elevation slopes. Pinot Noir is grown for red wines in the Chalonnais, and both Chardonnay and Aligoté are cultivated for whites. Although there are no Grand Cru wines in the district, there are 25 AOC Premier Cru.

The district is not continuous, but rather a collection of four small subdistricts that are, from north to south, known as Rully, Mercurey, Givry, and Montagny.

RULLY

Rully vineyards produce both red and white wines in about equal amounts and are known as a source for some very good wines priced considerably below those in the Côte d'Or.

RULLY PREMIER CRU	
La Bressande	Meix-Caillet
Champ-Clou	Moulesne
Chapitre	Les Pierres
Cloux	Pillot
Ecloseaux	Preau
La Fosse	Rabourcey
Gresigny	Raclot
Maix	La Renarde
Margoteys	Sous Mont-Palais
Marissou	Vauvry

Moillard is a huge *négociant* house, often called the "banker of Burgundy" in reference to its large inventory of bulk wines from most every notable village in the region. The firm is owned and operated by the Thomas family, which has descended from the founding Moillard family. The estate includes some very prestigious Côte d'Or vineyards, mostly in the Côte de Nuits, but the stock and trade of the Moillard name is its position, from which it can market so many different wines in bottle, and in bulk to other *négociants*. The ardent wine shopper can find some truly outstanding values from Rully.

MERCUREY

Mercurey has been building an impressive reputation among wine enthusiasts, to the extent that some are calling it by its own individual name—"La Region de Mercurey." Most of this new popularity stems from the dramatically improved quality of its red wines, which account for more than 80 percent of the total Mercurey production. Some of these approach the finesse of the Côte d'Or reds; Mercurey is typically a little shy in bouquet and a bit more firm in acidity.

MERCUREY PREMIER CRU

Clos-des-Fourneaux	Clos-du-Roi
Clos-Marcilly	Clos-Voyens
Clos-des-Montaigus	

The wines of Givry are mostly lowland red wines, which can be pleasant but do not approach the quality of Mercurey. Montagny is a relatively new white wine locale that has a budding reputation and deserves attention. Neither Givry nor Montagny has any Premier Cru vineyards.

One of the most important grower-*négociant* firms in the Chalonnais is Antonin Rodet. The estate, directed from the magnificent Château de Chamirey, includes most of the Premier Cru Clos-du-Roi vineyard in Mercurey. Its reputation is for good quality wines at attractive prices.

Although all of the AOC Premier Cru vineyards in the Chalonnais should be afforded every consideration for their rank, it must be remembered that these are wines made in a manner far removed from that employed in Chablis or the Côte d'Or. Fine Chalonnais is made crisp and fresh to capture the youth of every vintage, attributes that cannot, however, compare with the maturity, or the price, of the great pearls of the Burgundian necklace.

◈ MÂCONNAIS

The slopes of the Mâconnais commence a few miles below Montagny in the Chalonnais, continuing virtually uninterrupted for 35 miles south. The Mâconnais embraces the historical Roman city of Tournus and the remains of the huge Abbey of Cluny, the grand center of winegrowing in the entire region before the dukes of Burgundy brought Beaune to prominence. The capital city of the Mâconnais today is, of course, the district's namesake, Mâcon.

The Mommessin château in the city of Mâcon remains symbolic of one of the oldest winegrowing families in the Mâconnais. Mommessin is a *négociant* for good quality wines throughout Burgundy; its claim to fame is ownership of the Grand Cru Clos de Tart, the old nunnery vineyard estate in Morey St.-Denis, in the upper Côte d'Or.

Terroir in the region presents a contrasting profile, ranging from granite cliffs to steep rocky ridges and limestone slopes descending to clay flatlands. Excavations at the base of these cliffs have revealed thousands of prehistoric animal bones. Archaeologists contend that early dwellers chased wild animals over the ledge as a manner of hunting.

The Mâconnais yields a considerable amount of good white wines, particularly from the foothill slopes, but most of the valley reds are of average quality.

The classification system for Mâconnais seems a bit more complicated than it really needs to be. All AOC white wines in the district must be made exclusively from the Chardonnay variety. These can be labeled as *Mâcon* or *Mâcon*

FIGURE 6.14 Mâconnais landscape. *(Photo by author.)*

Blanc, and, curiously, the designation *Pinot Chardonnay Mâcon* is also permitted. With sufficient natural sugar to reach a strength of at least 10 percent alcohol, the term *Mâcon Supérieur* may be used. The best of these often add the name of their village to the label, as exemplified by the popular *Mâcon-Viré-Village.* White wines blended from more than one village in the district may be called *Mâcon-Villages.*

Some of the district townships cross into Beaujolais, which is home to the bountiful Gamay variety. Reds made from Gamay and Pinot Noir may be labeled as *Mâcon* or *Mâcon Rouge,* provided they reach a natural strength of at least 10 percent alcohol by volume. With a minimum of 11 percent alcohol, the reds may be labeled as *Mâcon Supérieur.*

In the lower part of the Mâconnais, on the ridges below the wind-eroded granite cliffs, are the storybook villages of Chaintré, Fuissé, Solutré, and Vergisson, each a part of the white wine AOC Pouilly-Fuisse. Although its fame, price, and distinctive apple-lemon character might well justify Pouilly Fuissé's often being referred to as a Premier Cru, it is not of this rank. In similar fashion, Pouilly-Loche, Pouilly-Vinzelles, and Saint-Véran are also AOC designations permitted for wines grown in other villages belonging to the same locale.

◆ BEAUJOLAIS

The Beaujolais district reaches some 45 miles from its northern juncture with the Mâconnais to the southern extremes approaching the outskirts of Lyon. Comprising nearly 40,000 acres, it is by far the largest district in Burgundy. During the Middle Ages the Beaujolais was not included as part of the Duchy of Burgundy. Some argue even today, on both sides of the border, that Beaujolais should be given its own regional status totally separate from Burgundy. In any event, there can be little question that the massive popularity of Beaujolais wines has built an enviable demand in the world marketplace.

Although the topography of the Beaujolais continues the granite hills and heavy soils of upper Burgundy, its wines are very different. Beaujolais is made from the Gamay vine, which yields heavy crops as compared with the more prestigious Pinot Noir. In many parts of the Beaujolais the Gamay is grown without aid of a trellis and takes a berry bush shape, called a *gobelet.*

The vast majority of Beaujolais production is red table wines. At the northern extremes of the district are several *communes* transcending the Mâconnais-Beaujolais border, where whites are grown from Chardonnay vines and legally designated as *Beaujolais Blanc.*

Beaujolais is named for the ancient Château Beaujeau, which no longer exists. During the ninth century a small portion of Beaujolais was made into red wine for drinking when just several weeks old *(nouveau)*. In a rather Bacchanalian-like rite that has become a famous tradition, Beaujolais winegrowers herald the arrival of every new vintage—Beaujolais Nouveau.

American and French wine drinkers alike have taken to the Beaujolais Nouveau. This wine is made by a process called *macération carbonique.* Whole clusters of Gamay grapes are deposited in special fermenting tanks, which are then closed. The weight of the grapes on top crushes those on the bottom, releasing juice, which begins to ferment. Carbon dioxide generated by fermentation macerates color and flavor components in the skins of the whole clusters above. When the maceration and fermentation process nears completion, the tanks are opened and the must is pressed. The result is a fresh, rich, densely purple wine with an overtly cherrylike flavor—Beaujolais Nouveau! Each year the hoopla grows as the first cases reach the market in late autumn. Some vintners enter competitions to see who can make the wine and get it to market first, sometimes shipping the first cases by air freight in order to win the race.

The great majority of Beaujolais wines, however, are vinified in the traditional manner for red wine—open fermentation "on the skins." These are generally regarded as modestly priced quaffing wines, often labeled as simply Beaujolais, Beaujolais Supérieur, or Beaujolais-Villages.

Any red wine properly grown within the Beaujolais district can be labeled "AOC Beaujolais." To become AOC Beaujolais Supérieur, the grapes must have had sufficient natural sugar to yield at least 1 percent more alcohol than AOC Beaujolais.

There are 39 villages in the district from which wine production may be labeled "Beaujolais-Villages." Historically, wines from these villages have been a bit darker and more flavorful than ordinary Beaujolais. As a rule, Beaujolais-Villages are blends crafted from wines grown in several villages. However, the AOC Beaujolais-Villages designation provides for single-village wines, examples of which are Beaujolais-Beaujeu and Beaujolais-Vaux.

BEAUJOLAIS CRU

The finest wines of Beaujolais are grown in 10 villages that are distinguished by AOC *cru* status. Sometimes the word *cru* is bandied about rather loosely in discussions of Beaujolais, and the designation ends up being referred to as "Grand Cru" or "Premier Cru," but these are inaccurate. Most vintages of Beaujolais Cru express the darkest pigmentation and richest texture grown in the district.

BEAUJOLAIS CRU	
Brouilly	Julienas
Chenas	Morgon
Chiroubles	Moulin-à-Vent
Côtes de Brouilly	Regnie
Fleurie	St.-Amour

The 10 Beaujolais Cru villages are included in the 39 Beaujolais-Villages mentioned previously. Consequently, Beaujolais Cru wines not quite meeting the standards of the best *négociants,* such as Duboeuf, Ferraud, Sarrau, and Vernaux, are often reclassified downward to become constituents for Beaujolais-Villages blends.

Morgon and Moulin-à-Vent wines are typically the most intense in color, flavor, and body, generally taking several years of bottle aging to reach maturity

FIGURE 6.15 Moulin-à-Vent village and vineyards. *(Courtesy of* Food and Wines from France.*)*

and a few more dollars to purchase. Chiroubles, Fleurie, and St.-Amour are generally more delicate and softer in texture, perhaps ready to drink after just a year or two of aging in bottle.

The standard for highest-quality Cru Beaujolais is set by Georges Duboeuf; his wines are easily identified on the shelf by colorful "flower" labels. Every November this "King of Beaujolais" brings the first case of Beaujolais Nouveau to New York City down Park Avenue in a horse-drawn carriage. It is this type of creative marketing that has made Beaujolais wines so popular in the world marketplace. Georges Duboeuf Moulin-à-Vent Cru Beaujolais is considered by many wine experts as the epitome of the district.

⊠ SPARKLING BURGUNDY

New York State Sparkling Burgundy became a popular festive item following the repeal of Prohibition. This was, of course, not really Burgundy at all but, instead, a rather sweet and fruity bubbly made from Concord grapes that was pleasant enough. However, as interest in wine grew after World War II, the term *Sparkling Burgundy* fell to disrepute across America. This is unfortunate, as there are some bona fide sparkling Burgundy wines that are well worth the search—and at prices much less than the cost of Champagne.

A measure of prestige has been regained for sparkling Burgundies through the efforts of the Syndicat des Producteurs de Vins Mousseux Méthode Champenoise de Bourgogne, which guarantees that all sparkling wines produced in the Burgundy region are made by the same bottle-fermentation process employed in Champagne (explained later in this chapter).

Sparkling Burgundies may be either white or red, and at least 30 percent of either wine must result from noble vines such as Chardonnay and Pinot Noir. Thus, the 70 percent balance may be, and usually is, made from lesser grapes, which nevertheless may attain good quality in the hands of talented Burgundian wine masters.

❖ BORDEAUX ❖

The seaport city of Bordeaux is built along the Garonne River, some 60 miles southwest from the Atlantic coast. Pre-Roman Bordeaux was known as Burdigala and subsequently became the capital city of Gascony, the setting for many tales of the age of chivalry. Today it is the fifth-largest city in France, and wine is, by far, its most famous export.

Downstream from Bordeaux the Garonne merges with the Dordogne River to form the Gironde River, which empties into the Atlantic Ocean. The greatest of the renowned Bordeaux château wine estates are found along these three rivers.

As mentioned in Chapter 2, the *Pax Romana* was brought to Bordeaux by Crassus in 56 B.C. Vineyards were already flourishing there. Some historians believe a Spanish vine called *Biturigia,* thought to be an ancestor of the now renowned Cabernet varieties, was among those cultivated in pre-Christian Bordeaux. Under Roman influence, winegrowing in the Gascony region prospered for the next four centuries.

One of the most renowned figures on the early Bordeaux wine scene was Ausonius, a Bordeaux-born son of a Roman senator. Ausonius had a brilliant career as a lawyer and politician, poet, and wine connoisseur—all of which made him a favorite of the Roman court during the early fourth century A.D. He spent his retirement days at a villa near the site of what has become the city of St.-Émilion in Bordeaux. The estate stands today as Château Ausone, one of the most prestigious and highly ranked vineyards in the region.

The 1152 marriage of Eleanor of Aquitaine to Henri Plantagenet united her dowry, which included all of the Bordeaux wine region, with much of the Loire Valley in northern France. Although Plantagenet was born French, he became King Henry II of England in 1154, and thus his great vineyard *domaines* came under the rule of the British crown. The first taste of Bordeaux wine exported to England sparked an enormous demand, which could be supplied only by an armada of ships. And that is precisely what the wine trade created for England—an armada of ships that gave Henry II and his successsors mastery of the seas for more than 300 years.

The term *claret,* often used by the British in reference to red Bordeaux wines, dates back to the Middle Ages. It was common practice to blend red and white wines together then (now forbidden), and all such lighter wines were known as *clairet,* from which *claret* evolved as a name for all Bordeaux reds.

Louis XIV is credited with fostering an appreciation for Bordeaux wines throughout France. The Sun King called the wines of Bordeaux the "nectar of the gods." Many less august persons are still inclined to agree with him.

FIGURE 6.16 Ancient Bordeaux city of St.-Émilion. *(Photo by author.)*

Members of the nobility in disfavor were sometimes banished to Bordeaux—a curious punishment. This was the fate of the duc de Richelieu in the mid-eighteenth century. The story goes that Richelieu's friends played a trick on him by switching labels on bottles of Burgundy and Bordeaux. Richelieu proclaimed the wine labeled Burgundy superior, but when his friends revealed it was actually Bordeaux, he immediately adopted it as his new favorite. Richelieu's new support gave Bordeaux wine a big boost in popularity. As a result, Madame de Pompadour, mistress of Louis XV, began serving Bordeaux at her famous private dinner parties.

In 1723 a glass factory was founded in Bordeaux and "château bottling" was begun. By 1797 the entire vintage of the prestigious Château Lafite was bottled in glass. The practice of château bottling fine Bordeaux estate wines arose in response to demands from merchants who wanted some guarantee that the wines they sold were not being blended with lesser growths. It was not until the late 1800s, however, that château bottling became a common practice throughout the entire Bordeaux region.

Thomas Jefferson loved many different types of wines, not the least of which were the fine wines of Bordeaux. Among the châteaux he particularly favored were Château Latour, Château Margaux, Château Haut-Brion, and Château d'Yquem. This was truly a magnificent selection, as these were four of the five estates that would attain the epitomal "First Growth" status in 1855, nearly 30 years after Jefferson's death.

With Jefferson's enthusiasm exemplifying the rapid growth in popularity of Bordeaux wines during the late eighteenth and early nineteenth centuries, it became clear that some château estates consistently produced better wines than others, and some were indeed superior, one vintage after another.

Consistently superior wines sold for consistently higher prices, but those were trends and track records, not criteria that distinguished one from another. The great Paris Exposition of 1855 provided the occasion for the first official classification of Bordeaux wines. From several thousands of Bordeaux estates, 87 of the designated Grand Cru estates were selected for more definite classification. (These are discussed further in subsequent sections of this chapter.)

Consequently, the entire classification became thus:

Grand Cru châteaux ranked First Growth–Fifth Growth

Grand Cru châteaux unranked

Cru Bourgeois châteaux

Artisan Growths, or Petits Châteaux

Village or *Commune* wines (Margaux, Pauillac, etc.)

District wines (Medoc, Graves, etc.)

Bordeaux regional wines

    Bordeaux

    Bordeaux Clairet (rosé)

    Bordeaux Mousseux (sparkling)

    Bordeaux Superieur (superior in natural alcohol strength)

Bordeaux regional wines can be made from grapes grown anywhere in the Bordeaux Region.

Although many European wine regions were devastated by the oidium mildew and the *Phylloxera* root louse blights during the late nineteenth century, as well as two world wars in the twentieth century, Bordeaux was comparatively fortunate and escaped large-scale destruction.

FIGURE 6.17 Old wine bottles in Château Lafite-Rothschild cellars. *(Courtesy of Domaines Baron de Rothschild.)*

CHATEAU
LACHESNAYE
1980

CRU BOURGEOIS

MIS EN BOUTEILLE AU CHATEAU

APPELLATION HAUT-MÉDOC CONTROLÉE

HAUT-MÉDOC

ALEXIS LICHINE & Cⁱᵉ

GFA des Domaines BOUTEILLER
Propriétaire à CUSSAC-FORT-MÉDOC (33)

RED TABLE WINE - PRODUCT OF FRANCE
CONTENTS 750 ml - ALCOHOL 11% TO 14% BY VOLUME

IMPORTED BY SHAW ROSS INTERNATIONAL IMPORTERS INC.- MIAMI, FLORIDA

England continues to thirst for "claret," as it has since King Henry II and Eleanor introduced Bordeaux wine to the British during the mid-1100s. Thomas Jefferson may be given credit for the popularity of Bordeaux, certainly the reds, in America. England and the United States continue to be major export markets for Bordeaux, as do Japan and Belgium.

Bordeaux remains the quintessential wine for collectors. The great château wines are stylized with hard tannins for the long period of aging, easily several decades for most, as the vintages generally appreciate quite handsomely along the way. Few gifts say as much about the giver, and the recipient, as a bottle of perfectly cellared old Bordeaux.

❖ THE REGION

Bordeaux, with ships at portside, its hurried, cosmopolitan flair, and a concentration of all manner and forms of humanity, is reminiscent of the flavor of San Francisco. Fine food and grand wine provide an ambience that pervades the Bordeaux region, much as California wine and cuisine have earned their own identity in the United States. Bordeaux even has a smaller version of the Golden Gate Bridge, which spans the Gironde from "Centre Ville" to the north toward

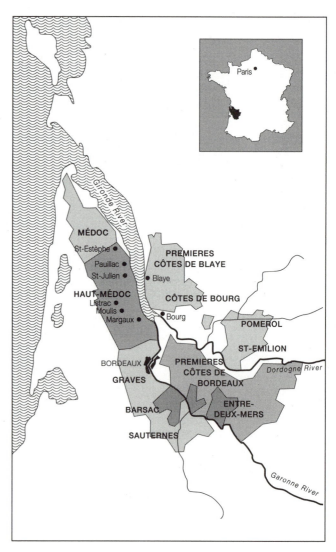

FIGURE 6.18 Bordeaux winegrowing region. (*Courtesy of* Food and Wines from France.)

FIGURE 6.19   Harvest at a Bordeaux
château estate.   *(Courtesy of Château
Dauzac.)*

Libourne. The most important similarity is, of course, that both cities have great
vineyards flourishing around their periphery.

Bordeaux has approximately 250,000 acres of vines that yield 100 million
gallons of wine in an average vintage. It is the largest fine wine viticultural
region in France—and in the world. Of this production about 60 percent is
white, but most of the highly classified vineyards are red, with a few exceptions.
While Burgundy has an agrarian character, with small *climats* divided among different owners, Bordeaux is typified by an aristocracy of individual owners operating large wine estates, or châteaux.

Visitors to the region can expect gentle rolling landscapes rising up from
the rivers. The vista of Bordeaux is seemingly endless vineyards, with one magnificent château mansion after another. A drive through the Médoc defies one's
ability to comprehend the magnitude of wealth that created this wonderland of
agriculture in its finest form. The character of the region is aristocratic—quiet
and rather distant to casual visitors. Although there are some open public tastings to be found in Bordeaux châteaux, it is a good idea to arrange visits and
reservations well ahead of time.

Most people envision a Bordeaux château as a regal mansion surrounded by
a large estate of manicured vineyards, and this is generally the case. However,
Vins à Appellation d'Origine Contrôlée (AOC) regulations decree the term
château to mean a vineyard. There need not be any house on a château estate at
all, and, in fact there are a number of châteaux that do include a house.

AOC law prohibits use of the word *château* on a Bordeaux wine label unless
there is a bona fide vineyard existing on the property. The following legal conditions also apply to such labeling:

- The château must be entitled to the appropriate AOC designation.
- The château name must be authentic, constant, and in conformity with
  local requirements.
- Winemaking from the grapes grown on the estate must take place on the
  estate.

None of these regulations, unfortunately, truly guarantees that any château
wine will be great or even good. As one considers row upon row of Bordeaux
bottles from which to choose in a fine wine shop, it is, in the final analysis, soil
virtue *(terroir)* that ultimately determines value.

As discussed earlier, the 1855 classification rigidly ranked 87 châteaux, leaving several thousand others without any specific order of hierarchy. This exclu-

sion eventually resulted in a lack of identity in the marketplace and brought financial hardship to owners of the lesser growths. In 1920 the first of a numbber of supplemental classification systems were adopted which, aside from bringing considerable complexity to the modern-day Bordeaux pecking order, are dynamic and allow for consistently better wine estates to achieve higher grades.

Of the 87 estates decreed in the 1855 classification, there are 62 that are generally considered a step up from the rest. Five of these 62 were awarded the highly coveted First Growth designation. There were 15 Second Growths selected, 14 Thirds, 10 Fourths, and 18 Fifth Growths. The remaining 25 are discussed in a subsequent section devoted to the Sauternes district.

Except for the 1973 upgrading of Château Mouton-Rothschild from Second Growth to First, the Grand Cru ranking has remained rigid. As would be expected, changes in ownership and operational philosophies over the ensuing years have had a profound effect on the quality of wines today. There are a number of instances in which most experts would agree that some Fourth and Fifth Growths are superior to several Thirds and Seconds. The important thing to remember, however, is that all five echelons are Grand Cru and even Fifth Growths are among the 62 highest-ranked châteaux among several thousand in Bordeaux.

There are a number of small marketing organizations that operate in Bordeaux, generally along the docks, or *quays,* as they have since the Renaissance days of the sailing fleets. Although they are often called *négociants,* as in Burgundy, they differ chiefly in that many Bordeaux wines are aged and bottled at the châteaux; in Burgundy the grapes or young wines are sold to a *négociant* for further processing, or *élevage.* Some châteaux market independently, and still others contract with large shippers and foreign importers. Kobrand, Heublein, and Schieffelin are among the most well known importers of Bordeaux wines to America, but the giant Château & Estate Wine Company (a division of Seagram) is by far the largest importer of high-profile château wines to the United States.

Most young red Bordeaux wines are nearly undrinkable. They are usually densely purple in color, astringent from unmellowed tannins, and awkward on the palate. But when patiently matured in French oak puncheons and aged in bottles, Bordeaux reds can be richly rewarding. The best are heavy bodied, dark garnet-ruby in color, and heavily structured with delicious orchestrations of black currant (cassis), bell pepper, vanilla-oak, and creosote flavors. Along with the Côte de Nuits of Burgundy, the Médoc yields some of the very finest and most expensive red wines on the face of the earth.

There are 27 *communes* in the Haut-Médoc, of which 7, Margaux, St.-Julien, Pauillac, St.-Estèphe, Listrac, Moulis, and Haut-Médoc, may display their name on labels. Along with the great internationally known chateâux of the Médoc are many lesser châteaux (from which often the best values can be found) and several large cooperatives. A few whites are grown, but these are limited to only regional AOC Bordeaux classification.

❖ MÉDOC

The Médoc, particularly the higher portion, the Haut-Médoc, is the single most important subdistrict of the entire Bordeaux region. About 7 miles wide and 35 miles long, it is situated between the small city of Blanquefort, just north of Bordeaux city, and Pointe de Grave, extending northwestward along the left bank of the Gironde estuary.

The lower Bas-Médoc, which comprises some 40 percent of the Médoc district in area, is the northwest portion consisting of light, moist soil which produces good, but lesser, red wines as compared with those of the higher ground.

The Haut-Médoc soil is typically quartz-gravel-iron oxide topsoil on clay subsoil. The gravel stones, called *cailloux,* retain heat from the daytime sun and thus aid in ripening the grapes. The *cailloux* also allow drainage from excess rainfall.

To find one's way around the Médoc, it is essential to know of its four principal villages, or *communes.* Southernmost is Margaux, then St.-Julien, Pauillac, and St.-Estèphe. Each of these villages have classic château estates known worldwide by accomplished appreciators of fine Bordeaux wines.

MARGAUX

Château Margaux, in the *commune* of Margaux, was originally known as Château Lamothe and belonged to the crown of England. After passing through the hands of several owners, Margaux became the property of Count Fumel, lord of Haut-Brion, who planted the first vineyards on the estate in the mid-1700s. After the French revolution the state sold Château Margaux to the marquis de la Colonilla, who demolished the old building and built the magnificent Grecian château that is the now famous Margaux landmark. Today it is owned by the Mentzelopoulos family, who have completely renovated vineyards, *chais* (cellars), and the mansion.

Château Margaux is the only *Grand Cru Classé 1855,* First-Growth, in the *commune* of Margaux. Its vineyards are spread over approximately 150 acres of the total 625-acre estate. Some 90 percent of the vines are Cabernet Sauvignon. One section of the estate is planted with Sauvignon Blanc vines, which are classified simply as AOC Bordeaux. These vineyards yield a sumptuous dry white wine, not unlike fine Graves Blanc but labeled as *Pavillon Blanc de Château Margaux.* It is the superb red wine, however, which has made this estate famous.

The origins for Second-Growth Château Lascombes in the *commune* of Margaux date back to feudal times when it was part of a much larger property owned by the dukes of Duras. A separate identity emerged in the eighteenth century when this magnificent parcel of 225 acres was acquired by Chevalier Antoine de Lascombes. Whether he gave his name to this grand estate or took his name from it may never be known for certain. During the post–World War II years Château Lascombes was owned by renowned wine writer Alexis Lichine, who was then married to screen actress Arlene Dahl. Lichine recently passed away, and the property has since been purchased by the Bass-Charington beverage firm in England.

FIGURE 6.20 Château Margaux. *(Photo by author.)*

ST.-JULIEN

Although no *Grand Cru Classé 1855,* First Growth, estates were classified in the St.-Julien *commune,* there are several Second-Growth estates that produce equally superb wine today. Given price comparison, they are bargains.

The original Léoville estate, created in 1638, was among the earliest of the now famous Bordeaux wine châteaux. In 1722, Thomas Barton arrived from Ireland and became a wine merchant, his family successors acquiring a small portion of Léoville in 1821. Subsequently, the vineyards of Château Léoville-Barton were selected as Second Growth at the 1855 Paris Exposition and remain one of the highest-ranked vineyards in the St.-Julien *commune.* This grand estate is still owned and managed by the Barton family.

Many people view Château Beychevelle as the greatest architectural expression of all the classic Bordeaux estates, some likening it to the majesty of Versailles. Its origins are traced back to the early 1400s. A long reputation for fine wine earned Beychevelle a Fourth-Growth Grand Cru rank in the 1855 classification. The Château Beychevelle label, with its logo of an old ship with lowered sails, has stirred many curious notions. Among the most romantic is the legend that ships moving up and down the Gironde estuary running along the shores of the estate would dip their sails in respect for the grand quality of the wine grown there. More likely, perhaps, is that during the 1500s Beychevelle was owned by the duc d'Epernon, first sea lord of France, and passing ships would "lower sails" *(baisse voiles,* from which the Beychevelle name may have originated) in a salute to the admiral's rank.

PAUILLAC

Pauillac is the richest of all the towns in Bordeaux. It is geographically in the center of the greater Haut Médoc and the only *commune* to embrace three First-Growth Grand Cru estates designated in the 1855 classification.

First-Growth Grand Cru Château Latour is comparatively small, only about 100 acres in all. The owners of this ancient Pauillac estate sided with the English Plantagenets during the Hundred Years' War and lost their castle in the destruction that accompanied the final battle when the English general, John Talbot, was killed and the Aquitaine returned to French rule. Only the tower remains, from whence the name *Latour* was taken. The tower is a very familiar logo, prominent on the labels of Château Latour.

FIGURE 6.21 Pauillac and its vineyards along the Gironde estuary. *(Courtesy of Château Lynch-Bages.)*

FIGURE 6.22 Château Pichon-Longueville-Baron. *(Courtesy of Jean-Michel Cazes.)*

The property was purchased in 1670 by a Monsieur de Chavanaz, councillor to Louis XIV, and seven years later was passed on to the Clauzel family. Through marriage, it became the property of the de Ségur family and continued so for more than two centuries. In 1842 a corporate Societé Civile de Château Latour was established to manage the estate. The Latour vineyards are planted with about two-thirds Cabernet Sauvignon and the rest with mostly Malbec and Cabernet Franc. Total production from an average vintage is about 20,000 gallons. Château Latour is a red wine of intense ruby color, dense body, and robust acidity. It often takes two decades or more to approach maturity.

Baron de Longueville's only daughter was married to Bernard de Pichon in 1646, the title shifting to Pichon after the passing of de Longueville. Succeeding generations married into the families of other wealthy landowners, creating a massive winegrowing estate by the time Joseph de Pichon-Longueville was born in 1755.

Baron Joseph lived to be 95 years of age, having sired two sons and three daughters. Anticipating a family dispute over how the château would be divided after his death, he shrewdly willed a split beforehand. One of his sons had died, so the château and 40 percent of the vineyards went to his other son, Baron Raôul. Ever since, this portion has been known more simply as "Château Pichon—the Baron."

The remaining 60 percent of the property went to the baron's daughters, administered by the eldest, Marie-Laure de Pichon-Longueville, a widow. Near her land were the famous Latour vineyards, owned by the comte de Beaumont, reputed to be Marie-Laure's lover. Latour did not have a château building upon it at that time, and to construct an obvious convenience, the dashing count gave her a parcel of Latour sufficient to build her own château, which was added to her holdings of Château Pichon-Longueville. There could not, of course, be two identical château names—and Marie-Laure would not relinquish her birthright. Consequently, she named her estate "Château Pichon-Longueville, Comtesse de Lalande," known more simply as "Château Pichon—the Countess."

Both châteaux are exemplary of truly superb red wine from the Pauillac *commune*. Château Pichon—the Baron, Grand Cru, Second-Growth, is now owned by the large AXA insurance group, which has completely refurbished the

FIGURE 6.23 The late John Grisanti with his $31,000 bottle of Château Lafite-Rothschild 1822—a record price in 1980. *(Courtesy of John Grisanti.)*

château to its original magnificence, along with building a completely new winemaking facility that, at this writing, may be the most modern in the entire world.

The Domaine de Bages has a history reaching back to the 1500s. John Lynch, a young Catholic exiled from his native Ireland in 1691, bought the estate in 1749. It has ever since been known as Château Lynch-Bages.

The estate was purchased in the 1930s by the Cazes family, who have transformed these vineyards into one of the very finest Grand Cru estates in the prestigious Pauillac district. Under the leadership of Jean-Michel Cazes, thought by many to be the "king" of Bordeaux, Château Lynch-Bages is a Fifth-Growth estate, which experts insist makes wine at least as good as the Seconds and perhaps the Firsts. Thus, this estate is a good example of why the great 1855 classification is much more an honored relic than a true measure of modern quality.

Perhaps the single most famous wine producer in the world is Grand Cru First-Growth Château Lafite-Rothschild, beautifully situated on the top of a hill (*Lafite* is translated as "hilltop") in the *commune* of Pauillac. It was christened the "Prince of Vineyards" during the Middles Ages by a magistrate who felt even then that this was a superior growth.

King Louis XV preferred Lafite, and, in keeping with the desires of the court, Madame de Pompadour also began serving the delicious red wines from Château Lafite. Prior to the French Revolution, Lafite was owned by Nicholas Pierre de Pichard, then high court president of the Parlement de Bordeaux. In 1867, Lafite was purchased by Baron James de Rothschild. It then became Château Lafite-Rothschild and has remained ever since in the Rothschild family, now directed by Baron Eric de Rothschild.

Château Lafite-Rothschild comprises about 312 acres, of which a little more than half are planted with vineyards. About 60 percent of the vines are Cabernet Sauvignon, the rest mostly Merlot and Cabernet Franc. Production each vintage averages about 45,000 gallons. Lafite is moderately dark and heavy bodied, as compared with wines of other First Growth estates in Pauillac. Given a decade or so to achieve its typical character, the young wine has an enticing complexity of cassis-cedar-tobacco flavors mellowed in finest French oak *barriques* to a silky-soft texture.

Since 1797 a few cases from each vintage have been placed in a cellar vault under the mansion. The cache now numbers several thousand bottles, an overwhelming sight when one considers that many of these bottles command prices in excess of $25,000 each, and others more than $100,000! Some, particularly the very oldest, are priceless. This was a treasure openly coveted by Nazi air

FIGURE 6.24 Château Lafite-Rothschild. *(Courtesy of Domaines Baron de Rothschild; photo by Michel Guillard.)*

FIGURE 6.25 Modern chai-in-the-round cellars at Château Lafite-Rothschild. *(Courtesy of Château Lafite-Rothschild.)*

marshal Hermann Goering during the German occupation of France in World War II. Ironically, the wine cellar remained in the hands of the Jewish Rothschilds.

FIGURE 6.26 Château Mouton-Rothschild. *(Photo by author.)*

The current world-record price for a bottle of wine is $156,450. It was paid at a Christie's London auction in 1986 by Christopher Forbes, son of the late Malcom Forbes Sr. of *Forbes* magazine fame, for a Château Lafite-Rothschild 1787 thought to have once belonged to Thomas Jefferson.

Mouton is also located in the *commune* of Pauillac and, as noted earlier, was originally classified as a Second-Growth in the 1855 Classification. Because of owner Baron Philippe de Rothschild's monumental diligence in improving wine quality, and an even greater tenacity in persuading government, the wines of his estate gradually became accepted on a par with those of the First-Growths. In 1973 the elevation from Second to First became official.

The duke of Gloucester in England owned the estate in 1430 and, after passing through several other proprietors, Château Mouton became the property of the duc d'Epernon in 1587 and remained in his family until 1741, when it was acquired by Baron Brane. Baron Nathaniel de Rothschild purchased Mouton in 1853 and added his name to form the now familiar Château Mouton-Rothschild. Like cousin Lafite, Mouton has remained a Rothschild property ever since, now under the direction of Baroness Philippine de Rothschild.

Mouton vineyards total about 150 acres and are planted almost exclusively to Cabernet Sauvignon vines. The wine has a powerful green pepper and cigar box aroma, with rich cherry-plum flavors that linger for several minutes after each taste. Texas wine wholesaler Tony LaBarba, at auction, paid $38,000 for a single bottle of 1870 Château Mouton-Rothschild.

ST.-ESTÈPHE

Whereas the wines of Margaux are often referred to as silky smooth and faster to mature, young St.-Estèphe wines are generally coarse, tannic, and age at a slower pace. Much of this can be attributed to the *terroir* and the climate, of course, and an additional case can be made for the winemaking techniques employed in St.-Estèphe being a bit more traditional than the modern equipment and updated technology employed in the other *communes* in the Medoc.

Château Calon-Ségur epitomizes the rich history found in the St.-Estèphe district. The Romans called the locale "Calones," as many small boats, also called *calones,* sailed in and out of the canals in the *commune*. For centuries afterward the district was known as St.-Estèphe de Calon. The grand château mansion that now centers the estate was built during the late 1400s, and with the marriage of the owner's widow to the marquis de Segur, the title "Château Calon-Ségur" was established. It was not a marriage for money or power, as the marquis was already very wealthy. Indeed, at the time he already owned both Châteaux Lafite and Latour. He often stated, however, that his "heart belonged to Calon," and thus he placed the heart logo on the label, which remains today. Château Calon-Segur was sold in 1894 to the Capbern-Gasqueton family, which continues ownership and operation of this magnificent Grand Cru St.-Estèphe Third Growth.

MÉDOC GRAND CRU—SECOND GROWTHS

Château Brane-Cantenac (Margaux)

Château Durfort-Vivens (Margaux)

Château Lascombes (Margaux)

Château Rausan-Ségla (Margaux)

Château Rauzan-Gassies (Margaux)

Château Ducru-Beaucaillou (St.-Julien)

Château Gruaud-Larose (St.-Julien)

Château Léoville-Barton (St.-Julien)

Château Léoville-Las-Cases (St.-Julien)

Château Léoville-Poyferré (St.-Julien)

Château Pichon-Longueville Baron (Pauillac)

Château Pichon-Longueville Lalande (Pauillac)

Château Cos d'Estournel (St.-Estèphe)

Château Montrose (St.-Estèphe)

MÉDOC GRAND CRU—THIRD GROWTHS

Château Boyd-Cantenac (Margaux)

Château Cantenac-Brown (Margaux)

Château Desmirail (Margaux)

Château Ferrière (Margaux)

Château Giscours (Margaux)

Château d'Issan (Margaux)

Château Kirwan (Margaux)

Château Malescot-St.-Exupéry (Margaux)

Château Marquis d'Alesme-Becker (Margaux)

Château Palmer (Margaux)

Château Lagrange (St.-Julien)

Château Langoa-Barton (St.-Julien)

Château Calon-Ségur (St.-Estèphe)

Château La Lagune (Haut-Médoc)

MÉDOC GRAND CRU—FOURTH GROWTHS

Château Marquis-de-Terme (Margaux)

Château Pouget (Margaux)

Château Prieuré-Lichine (Margaux)

Château Beychevelle (St.-Julien)

Château Branaire-Ducru (St.-Julien)

Château St.-Pierre (St.-Julien)

Château Talbot (St.-Julien)

Château Duhart-Milon Rothschild (Pauillac)

Château Lafon-Rochet (St.-Estèphe)

Château La Tour-Carnet (Haut-Médoc)

MÉDOC GRAND CRU—FIFTH GROWTHS

Château Dauzac (Margaux)

Château du Tertre (Margaux)

Château Batailley (Pauillac)

Château Clerc-Milon (Pauillac)

Château Croizet-Bages (Pauillac)

Château Grand-Puy-Ducasse (Pauillac)

Château Grand-Puy-Lacoste (Pauillac)

Château Haut-Bages-Libéral (Pauillac)

Château Haut-Batailley (Pauillac)

Château Lynch-Bages (Pauillac)

Château Lynch-Moussas (Pauillac)

Château Mouton-Baronne-Philippe (Pauillac)

Château Pédesclaux (Pauillac)

Château Pontet-Canet (Pauillac)

Château Cos Labory (St.-Estèphe)

Château Belgrave (Haut-Médoc)

Château de Camensac (Haut-Médoc)

Château Cantemarle (Haut-Médoc)

✣ GRAVES

Graves is French for "gravel," in this case a gravel plain, often of nearly snow-white stones, on which this district's best vineyards are cultivated. It is about 38 miles long, borders the Médoc to the south, embraces the city of Bordeaux, and extends southeastward just past the village of Langon.

This famous gravel topsoil has a subsoil of chalk, clay, and ironstone, all of which are thought to infuse Graves wine with an earthy taste, termed the *goût de terroir*. Wines from the vineyards bordering the Medoc are mostly red and are the finest of the district. All of the classified growths of the Graves are situated in the northern portion of the district, centered by the villages of Pessac and Léognan, the names of which may be added to labels of wines grown in those *communes*. At the center of the Graves are the best white wine vineyards. Traveling south, one finds a greater output of Graves and Graves Supérieur, white wines that become noticeably sweet as the district approaches the Sauternes border.

In general, the red wines of Graves are as good as those of equal classification in the Médoc, perhaps somewhat less full bodied but often more silky-smooth in texture. The major difference between the two districts is the large amount of white wine grown in Graves along with the reds. Graves Blanc, from Sauvignon Blanc and Sémillon vines, has built a well-deserved high reputation for dry whites with delicious blossom-melon flavors balanced with crisp acidity.

Château Haut-Brion is the only 1855-classified First Growth in the Graves district. It belonged to the lord d'Aubrion during the Middle Ages and in 1529 was given over to Jean de Pontac as part of the dowry of Jeanne de Bellon, daughter of the mayor of Libourne. In 1801, Charles de Talleyrand-Perigord, minister of foreign affairs for France, acquired Château Haut-Brion and sold it three years later to a Parisian banker. In 1935, Château Haut-Brion was bought by the American banker Clarence Dillon, father of the former American ambassador to France, C. Douglas Dillon.

Haut-Brion produces about 25,000 gallons of wine annually from about 105 acres of undulating vineyards. Experts say that the wines of this château are as tasty as the three Médoc First Growths, but with more finesse.

Decades—indeed, nearly a century—passed before the other châteaux in Graves were classified in 1953, when the district decreed its own lists, and the adoption was fully ratified by the AOC in 1959. Two châteaux were recognized as Grand Cru for white wines only, six exclusively for red, and seven for both red and white.

Classification resulted in the following order:

1855 GRAND CRU—FIRST GROWTH

Château Haut-Brion (R)

1953

Château Bouscaut

Château Carbonnieux

Château Couhins (W)

Domaine de Chevalier

Château de Fieuzal (R)

Château Haut Bailly (R)

Château La Mission Haut-Brion (R)

Château La Tour Haut-Brion (R)

Château Latour Martillac

Château Laville Haut-Brion (W)

Château Malartic Lagravière

Château Olivier

Château Pape Clément (R)

Château Smith Haut-Lafitte (R)

It was Georges Smith, in 1720, who founded Haut-Lafitte amid the Graves. In 1990 the estate was acquired by sporting goods magnate Daniel Cathiard, a former French ski champion who, in partnership with his advertising executive wife, Florence, have resurrected this magnificent château to its 1800s prime and dedicate themselves to maintaining the eloquent character of the exemplary Bordeaux wine.

⬖ SAUTERNES

In comparison to the Médoc and Graves, Sauternes is demure. Somewhat triangular in shape, the Sauternes district measures about seven miles on each side and is nearly surrounded by the Graves. The township of Sauternes is situated in the extreme south of the district. Four other *communes* in the district are entitled to AOC Sauternes labels: Barsac, Bommes, Fargues, and Preignac. Its very unusual wine makes Sauternes a fascinating place to visit, but it is rather ordinary as a typically friendly French agricultural locale.

There is a unique combination of mesoclimate and *terroir* in Sauternes. Both the morning mist and the midday autumn sun are more intense here than in the surrounding Graves district. The best topsoils lie on rolling upland gravel with a subsoil of clay and sandstone, containing somewhat more limestone in the Barsac *commune*. Only white wines are grown in the district, and nearly all of these are from the Sauvignon Blanc and Sémillon varieties.

The grapes are harvested radically overripened, left on the vines until they become infected with the famous "noble" grape mold called *pourriture noble* by the French and *Botrytis cinerea* by microbiologists (see Figure 6.27, color insert). This mold permeates the skins of the fruit and allows water to evaporate from the interior pulp of each grape berry. If the cool morning mist continues during the harvest season, the *Botrytis*-infected grapes commence to look a bit like rotten raisins but yield an exceedingly luscious sweet nectar reminiscent of fig, peach, and raisin flavors. Sugar percentage may increase to half again or more than is produced in normally ripened wine grapes. If the rains come during this critical period, another mold generally develops, the dread greenish-blue *Penicillium,* which ruins the grape crop and the entire vintage.

To qualify as AOC Sauternes, the resulting wine must reach at least a 13 percent alcohol strength and retain a high level of sweetness from the remaining unfermented sugars. Specific sweetness levels, which vary from one vintage year to another, are usually from 3 to 7 degrees "extract" — an analytical term roughly equivalent to percentage of sweetness by weight. If these requirements are not met, the wine may be marketed only as AOC Bordeaux. Indeed, some wines are made dry intentionally, such as "Ygrec" at Château d'Yquem and the more well known "R" at Château Rieussec.

The French insist that the sweet honey taste of Sauternes makes for an excellent appetizer wine. For other wine enthusiasts, the rich flavor and heft of the golden Sauternes makes it a good dessert wine. Some connoisseurs rate the fine vintages of Sauternes as the finest sweet white wines in existence, which

FIGURE 6.28 Château d'Yquem. *(Photo by Jacques Vargues.)*

generally have prices to match. There are others who argue that the late-harvest wines from Germany are equal or even superior.

There is only one First Growth in the Sauternes district, and it is also the only white wine First Growth in all of Bordeaux—the fabled Château d'Yquem. It is named for Michel Eyquem Seigneur de Montaigne, an extravagant patron of the arts who was an owner of the estate during the Middle Ages. Montaigne, who had himself awakened each day by gentle tunes from the flute, offered these profound thoughts concerning the good life:

> *Drinking wine at two meals a day, in moderation—surely the good Lord did not intend us to be restricted to so little. The Ancients spent all their days and nights drinking.*

In 1782, when Ambassador Thomas Jefferson first arrived in Bordeaux, having walked most of the several hundred miles from Paris, he entered in his journal that the best white wine of France was the Sauternes of "Monsieur d'Yquem." That wine was not, however, the same lavishly sweet product resulting from the noble mold that we know in modern times but, rather, a drier table wine made by traditional methods.

Passed through a number of owners via sales and marriage dowries, Château d'Yquem eventually became the property of the comte de Lur-Saluces just three years after Jefferson's visit. The Lur-Saluces family continues ownership and operation of the 370-acre estate.

The 1855 Classification resulted in an interesting twist for the wines of Sauternes. Château d'Yquem was recognized as a Grand Cru "Exceptional Growth," as compared with the First Growths in the Médoc and Graves. This designation can be a source of confusion, as the next two levels below Yquem comprise 11 First Growths and 14 Second Growths, accounting for the remaining 25 Grand Cru estates in the total of 87 that were classified. There are those who contend that this implies that Yquem stands alone as the single greatest wine estate in all of Bordeaux. Another understanding is that the term *First Growth* in the Médoc and Graves designates a higher echelon of excellence than in Sauternes. In whatever manner one may choose to compare the hierarchy of the estates in these three districts, it must be remembered that the entire classsification in Sauternes is for sweet white wines, which have no standard for comparison in either the Médoc or Graves.

For historical purists the situation can be even further confusing, in that many of the estates classified in 1855 have been divided or in some other manner altered from the original. Nevertheless, the current classification of Sauternes is as follows:

EXCEPTIONAL GROWTH

Château d'Yquem

FIRST GROWTH

Château Climens

Château Coutet

Château Guiraud

Château Clos Haut-Peyraguey

Château La Tour-Blanche

Château Lafaurie-Peyraguey

Château Rabaud Promis

Château Rayne-Vigneau

Château Rieussec

Château Sigalas-Rabaud

Château Suduiraut

SECOND GROWTH

Château d'Arche

Château d'Arche Lafaurie

Château Broustet

Château Caillou

Château Doisy-Daëne

Château Doisy-Dubroca

Château Doisy-Védrines

Château Filhot

Château Lamothe

Château de Malle

Château Myrat

Château Nairac

Château Romer

Château Suau

❖ ENTRE-DEUX-MERS

The name of the Entre-Deux-Mers translates as "between two seas" or, less literally but more accurately, "between two rivers"—the Garonne to the southwest and the Dordogne to the north. At the extreme northwestern tip of the district these rivers meet, forming the Gironde estuary, which continues flowing northwesterly along the Medoc and on out into the Atlantic. This is the great shipping lane that has built Bordeaux into the largest seaport in France.

In east-west length the Entre-Deux-Mers measures a full 40 miles and in width about 20 miles—the largest wine district in Bordeaux. It is not fully covered with vines as are the more famous districts in Bordeaux. Between the vineyards are orchards, row crops, fields of grain, and other agricultural endeavors competing for the land. However, there are few places in the region that are more inviting and beautiful to visit.

The wines of the district are equally attractive. Only dry white wines, made principally from Sauvignon Blanc and Sémillon, are permitted AOC Entre-Deux-Mers labeling. Reds grown in this district may be labeled only AOC Bordeaux or, with higher alcoholic strength, AOC Bordeaux Supérieur. These are grown principally from Cabernet Sauvignon and Merlot vines. The best of these whites and reds represent some of the finest values in all of Bordeaux. It is interesting to compare good no-name Entre-Deux-Mers wines against high-brow châteaux offerings at several times the price.

◈ ST.-ÉMILION

Some 20 miles or so northeast from Graves and Sauternes, across both the rivers Garonne and Dordogne and the entire breadth of the Entre-Deux-Mers, is the medieval village of St.-Émilion. The finest estates are situated on slopes, or *côtes,* of limestone hills that border the old town and plateau vineyards. The *côtes* are found along the southeastern perimeter of the town, sometimes rather steep, all combined totaling an area some two miles wide and five miles long. Another sector of St.-Émilion, a rolling tract of land northwest of town on a lowland plateau, is called *graves.* Despite being named for gravel soil, it is composed mostly of clay and should not be confused with the spectacular deep gravel soils in the Graves district discussed earlier. Least noble of the grand St.-Émilion vineyards are found in the *sables,* or sandy soils, southwest of the village down near the Dordogne riverbank.

St.-Émilion may be the most interesting town, certainly the most tourist-oriented, in all of the Bordeaux outlying vineyard districts. Named for an eighth-century monk who chose to remain inside the monastery cellars for most of his life, St.-Émilion remains a fine example of a medieval city, some of its gates and battlements remaining as they were 1,000 years ago. The old stone steps in the nooks and crannies were carved hundreds of years ago. Today they are lined with shops, offering every imaginable artifact having to do with wine, along with romantic outdoor restaurants. The grand influence of the church in St.-Émilion history is seen everywhere; nearly every proper name is attributed to a saint.

There are 14 *communes* in the St.-Émilion district, as follows:

St.-Émilion

Lussac-St.-Émilion

Montagne St.-Émilion

Parsac-St.-Émilion

Puisseguin-St.-Émilion

Sables-St.-Émilion

St. Georges-St.-Émilion

St.-Christophe des Bardes

St.-Étienne de Lisse

St.-Hippolyte

St.-Laurent des Combes

St.-Pey d'Armens

St.-Sulpice de Faleyrens

Vignonet

FIGURE 6.29   Château Ausone.
(Photo by author.)

It has been only since 1936 that the St.-Émilion appellation has included the last seven of these townships, and these cannot attach the name "St.-Émilion" to their own as can the traditional first seven in the list.

All of the great St.-Émilion wines are red, mostly from the Merlot vine. Cabernet Sauvignon requires a longer growing season, which St.-Émilion, being further inland from the Atlantic, does not have. Superior St.-Émilion, fully aged, expresses a deep tawny-scarlet color, good heft in mouth feel, with significant bramble-fruit and cigar-box complexities in the nose and on the palate.

It is in St.-Émilion that the ancient Roman poet Ausonius built his villa and planted his vineyards—an estate now known as Château Ausone. Many relics of its antiquity may still be seen, among them a chapel in which there are the remains of a mural depicting the Last Judgment.

The Dubois-Challon family owns the property, but it is managed by the Moueix family. The great success of the Moueix family is discussed in the following section on the Pomerol district. The average yearly output of Château Ausone is only about 6,000 gallons.

Château Cheval Blanc, or "White Horse Mansion," is situated in the *graves* plain a short distance to the west of St.-Émilion village. It was originally built as an inn by the Englishman Roger Leyburn in 1269. Travelers on the way to and from the nearby city of Libourne would stop there for food and drink. Neighboring sharecroppers planted the first vines there. Gradually, as they left, the estate was formed from their remaining vineyards. Cheval Blanc has been handed down to succeeding generations of the Fourcaud-Laussac family. Annual production is about 40,000 gallons.

The 1855 classification in Paris did not include any château estates in the St.-Émilion district—a source of rivalry with the Médoc and Graves that has continued ever since. In 1954 the INAO officially classified the St.-Émilion châteaux, devising a dynamic and farsighted system that requires updating every 10 years. Unfortunately, this virtue is outweighed by the overuse of superlatives in elaboration. After combining "Premier" and "Grand Cru" for the top category, the Institut added "Premier Plus" as well.

PREMIER GRAND CRU CLASSÉ
PREMIER PLUS

Château Ausone

Château Cheval blanc

PREMIER GRAND CRU CLASSE

Château Beauséjour Duffau-Lagarrose

Château Beauséjour Societé-Becot

Château Belair

Château Canon

Château Clos Fourtet

Château Figeac

Château La Gaffelière

Château Magdelaine

Château Pavie

Château Trottevieille

There are another 63 château estates that are entitled to use the title "Grand Cru Classé" on their labels. This is truly unfortunate, as some of these are out-and-out misrepresentations of such lofty recognition and the prices that accompany them. Even worse is the last step in the St.-Émilion pecking order—the confusing and infamous Grand Cru designation, which means nothing at all. Perhaps the next update of the system will succeed in a classification order worthy of the historical St.-Émilion name.

❖ POMEROL

Pomerol *terroir,* an extension of the *graves* reaching northwest of St.-Émilion, is characterized by an ironstone subsoil beneath its clay-gravel topsoil. AOC Pomerol is, like St.-Émilion, authorized only for red wines that are grown mostly from Merlot vines, because of its comparatively short growing season. The higher, more fertile, northwestern sector of the district is the Lalande-de-Pomerol. The lower, less fertile, southeastern sector, called the Neac, is where all the great growths of Pomerol are situated.

Although Pomerol may have the least impressive scenery and fewest tourist attractions of any Bordeaux wine district, it has one distinction: it has escaped the overdone classification. It is ironic that the most expensive wine grown in all of Bordeaux is Pétrus—without any château, title, or classification whatsoever.

The best Pomerols are typically described as the most slowly developing reds grown in Bordeaux. But when they mature, they produce one of the most mouth-filling red wines found anywhere. Fine aged Pomerol is dense in ruby-garnet color, massively full-bodied, almost chewy, with an intense bouquet of complexities—black cherry, truffle, cedar, vanilla, and more.

There is no long history or grand tradition at Pétrus. In just two generations of Moueix family ownership it has emerged as the top estate in Bordeaux —if not in wine quality, certainly in price. A bottle of young Pétrus can easily exceed $200 at retail, and older vintages are now appreciating to much more. Reading old Pétrus prices on the wine lists in great restaurants can be great entertainment in itself.

Such success can be traced to great attention in vineyard management, and the epitome of niche marketing. In simple terms, Pétrus has capitalized on its wine's being above classification, unconcerned with its not even being a "château." Those who can afford it have bought into the notion. Pétrus is magnificent wine with great structure and powerful flavors, all embraced in a silky elegance. Each year there are only about 5,000 gallons, or some 25,000 bottles, available to the entire world wine market.

FIGURE 6.30 Pétrus. *(Photo by author.)*

Thus, Pétrus cannot be for everyone. The following are other fine châteaux in Pomerol:

POMEROL
UNCLASSIFIED

Château Beauregard

Château Bourgneuf

Château Certan de May

Château Clinet

Château Clos Rene

Château Conseillante

Château de l'Église

Château L'Evangile

Château Gazin

Château Giraud

Château Haut Ferrand

Château La Croix

Château La Croix de Gay

Château Lafleur

Château Lagrange

Château Latour Pomerol

Château Le Gay

Château Marzelle

Château Moulinet

Château Rouget

Château Trotanoy

Château Vieux Certan

The success of Pétrus has given a coattails ride to the prices of most all of the Neac Pomerols. Some remain affordable for special occasions.

Visitors in Pomerol should not expect rural boulevards of grand mansions as in the Médoc or Graves. Indeed, even Pétrus is a modest *chai* (groud-level wine cellar) that can easily be missed rounding the bend amid its vineyards. To picnic in Pomerol is to be surrounded by truly outstanding agriculture.

⬧ FRONSAC AND CANON-FRONSAC

Fronsac is another district that awaits discovery by the wine world, probably because it is very small, 10 square miles at best, a mile or so west of Pomerol. The wines of Fronsac are very good, but most lack true bargain excitement.

A good share of the vineyards here are planted to the Cabernet Franc vine, which yields red wine expressing an earthy-tobacco character. When aged in fine French oak, these wines can be delicious, but still different from the more traditional Cabernet Sauvignon and Merlot.

Red wine grown anywhere in the district may be labeled as AOC Fronsac. Reds grown on a series of slopes called the Côtes de Canon Fronsac, situated in the northern part of the district, may be aptly labeled as AOC Canon-Fronsac. Fronsac white wines may be labeled only as AOC Bordeaux.

⬧ BOURG AND BLAYE

Many wine enthusiasts have been to Bordeaux many times, yet never tour the enticing wine districts of Bourg and Blaye. That is unfortunate, as both their châteaux estates display all the grandeur of any other district in the region. Uninformed wine enthusiasts are often quick to blame the *terroir* as the problem, but that is not the case at all. Bourg and Blaye are replete with good gravel soils and actually have better exposure to sunshine than the left bank of the Gironde.

History has dealt this portion of Bordeaux a poor hand. During the formative decades of winegrowing in the region, it was much more chic to move directly up the left bank, which is the same side of the river on which Bordeaux city is located. Consequently, it was the Médoc that was the "in" place for the wealthy to spend their summers and little attention was given Bourg and Blaye.

FIGURE 6.31 Château Tayac in Blaye. *(Photo by author.)*

These districts have fine wine discovery potential, but their "poor cousin" reputation denies prices that can finance fine wine production. Consequently, they must compensate by making high volumes of low-grade wine in order to survive, and the reputation continues. However, several key estates are now in the hands of progressive owners, and it will be interesting to see if modern-day concerns for wine quality at reasonable prices will increase consumer interest in Bourg and Blaye. Until then, this region remains uncrowded and as fine a wine frontier as one can hope to find in France. Proud winegrowers are quick to explain that Bourg and Blaye vineyards were among the first to be cultivated in all of Bordeaux.

The Côte de Bourg and Côte de Blaye combined make up one of the larger geographical districts in the Bordeaux region, fully twice the size of St.-Émilion and Pomerol combined. Much like the Entre-Deux-Mers, the two *côtes* are green rolling farmland with vineyards divided by other agriculture.

Straightforward simplicity characterizes the best wines grown on the Côte de Blaye, primarily Cabernet Franc and Merlot reds of good color and body with expressive berry-cherry fruit. Prices are moderate, and some château bottlings are interesting. Some of the best buys are wines blended and bottled by *négociants* and cooperatives.

Bourg is smaller than Blaye but produces more wine. Most experts contend that Bourg wine is generally better, too. Many estates in Bourg have been outfitted for barrel aging and the whole gamut of modern château winegrowing techniques employed in other Bordeaux districts.

❖ BERGERAC

The wines of historical, romantic Bergerac are rather evenly divided between red and white table wines. Traditionally, the best have been sweet white wines made from late-harvest Sémillon in much the same style as Sauternes from nearby Bordeaux.

Château Monbazillac, the crown jewel of Bergerac, is a classic producer of this expensive special wine. Monbazillac, high atop a vineyard-covered hill overlooking the legendary city of Bergerac, is the center for wine enthusiasts in the region. Truly fine values can be found among the red wines from the small district of AOC Pecharmant.

FIGURE 6.32 Château Monbazillac. (*Courtesy of* Food and Wines from France.)

Bergerac is, of course, famous as the home of Cyrano, and this lore is worth a day in the city. Fortunately, neither his dignity nor the wine industry has suffered from his name being hyped on a sea of wine labels. The vinicultural reputation of Bergerac has been in the hands of large cooperatives, which have marketed fair-to-good wines at very attractive prices.

A new classification system for Bergerac is under consideration, but this must rely upon the success of new plantings, principally Merlot, which has by any measure been proven to be the red variety in demand. Look for a number of now obscure estates, such as Château Fongrenier, already making superb Merlot, to emerge from this new development in Bergerac.

With some 27,000 acres of vineyard, and the savvy to transform technology and investment into greater quality, Bergerac wine seems on the brink of wider renown. Identities for Bergerac wines include AOC Saussignac, AOC Bergerac, and AOC Côtes de Bergerac.

❖ CHAMPAGNE ❖

Champagne is one of the most legendary wine regions in all of France—indeed, the entire world. It is located about 100 miles northeast of Paris in the Department of the Marne. Although some Burgundy and Bordeaux selections are priced far higher, Champagne is still considered to be the most luxurious of wines. The reason, of course, is that its bubbles, which number about 50 million per bottle by most estimates, add an extra measure of festivity.

By national decree, a wine labeled as "Champagne" can only be a sparkling wine. Nonsparkling, "still" wine made in the region must be labeled as *Côteau Champenois* or *Côteaux de Champagne*. The region has two capital cities, Reims and Epernay, and as should be expected, they have had a colorful, long-standing rivalry.

Winegrowing in Champagne shares a Roman history with most other major wine regions in France and western Europe. Vines were cultivated in the Reims and Epernay vicinity during the first century. There are many references to Champagne wines in St. Remis's *Testament,* including mention of specific vineyards. In A.D. 496, Remi, then bishop of Reims, laid the crown upon the head of Clovis, the first Christian monarch of France. Every king of France thereafter was crowned in Reims, most in the great cathedral that remains the jewel of the city.

The sparkling Champagne wines of modern times were not known in the Middle Ages. The vineyards surrounding Epernay and Reims then produced red and white table wines similar to those grown in Beaune and Chablis in Burgundy.

In the eleventh century, Pope Urban II praised the nonsparkling red wines from the area of Reims. The great Champagne vineyards of Ay, Cumières, Damery, and Hautvillers were among the favorites listed by the poet Deschamps in 1398. The archaic nonsparkling red Champagne was preferred by Pope Leo X in the early 1500s, at the beginning of the Renaissance, and continued as the preferred wine in Paris until the seventeenth century, when Burgundy first became fashionable.

Dom Pérignon was born in January 1638 at St.-Menehoulde and became a Benedictine monk at the age of 19. He was appointed wine master of the Abbey of Hautvillers, near Epernay, in 1668. Despite the popular belief that Dom Pérignon invented sparkling wine, he may not have. There is evidence indicating that Saumur vintners in the Loire Valley region could have captured bubbles in their wine decades earlier.

FIGURE 6.33 Roman caves used for making Champagne. (*Courtesy of* Food and Wines from France.)

FIGURE 6.34 Dom Pérignon.
(Courtesy of Moët & Chandon.)

FIGURE 6.35 Dom Pérignon's Abbey of Hautvillers above Champagne vineyards near Epernay. *(Courtesy of C.I.V.C.)*

Pérignon did make better wines in Champagne than had been made before his time, and he did, in fact, make sparkling Champagne wines. But his fame should be placed in the proper perspective. Pérignon was an expert blender and the first to use cork stoppers to seal wine bottles.

In both Champagne and Saumur, winemakers found that wines bottled during the cool winter "rest" continued to ferment after the spring warming, because the carbon dioxide gas generated during the resumed fermentation could not escape from bottles securely stoppered with Pérignon's corks. The carbon dioxide gas dissolved in the bottled wine, causing a "sparkling" effect, or effervescent bubbling, when the wine was uncorked and poured.

This process was, like all fermentations, believed to be a mystical reaction, and winemakers had little control over it until, in 1810, Joseph-Louis Gay-Lussac formulated his relationship of sugars in fermentation and created the densimeter. This device, now known as a hydrometer, allowed the precise measurement of sugar in wine before bottling and secondary fermentation. This, in turn, permitted control over the amount of carbon dioxide gas generated, resulting in far fewer explosions of bottles because of excessive fermentation. Pasteur's later discovery of yeasts served to explain the winter "rest"—that cells suspended growth in colder temperatures. The technology of Champagne winemaking today is, of course, far more advanced, but the basic principles remain the same.

Sparkling Champagne arrived in the French court during the last years of Louis XIV's life. His own enjoyment of this new wine doubtlessly suggested to him that it would export at great value. He was monumentally correct. The ensuing trade in Champagne with England and other countries markedly increased the wealth of France. This was, however, a time marred by the death of the king's son in 1711, and his grandson a year later. When the Sun King died, in 1715, the next in line for the throne was grandson Louis XV, who was only five years old and so was entrusted to the care of Philippe, duc d'Orleans, a bon vivant of grand proportions. Louis XV lived in an extravagant life-style, as did his court, which he moved to Versailles. There Champagne captured the hearts of royals, courtiers, nobles, and everyone in France who could afford it.

FIGURE 6.36 Inspection of Champagne in the Pol Roger caves. *(Courtesy of Frederick Wildman.)*

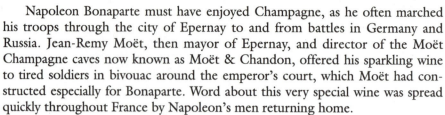

Napoleon Bonaparte must have enjoyed Champagne, as he often marched his troops through the city of Epernay to and from battles in Germany and Russia. Jean-Remy Moët, then mayor of Epernay, and director of the Moët Champagne caves now known as Moët & Chandon, offered his sparkling wine to tired soldiers in bivouac around the emperor's court, which Moët had constructed especially for Bonaparte. Word about this very special wine was spread quickly throughout France by Napoleon's men returning home.

Following Napoleon's defeat, it was the Germans and the Russians who traveled through Champagne. Some Germans remained and started Champagne production of their own; the names Bollinger, Deutz, Geldermann, Heidsieck, Krug, and others, remain today as testimony to their success. Russian soldiers looted many of the caves. This deed eventually backfired, because by the time political order was restored to the Champagne province, Russia had acquired an insatiable thirst for Champagne, for which the Russians have been paying dearly ever since.

Although the genesis of sparkling Champagne must be credited to Dom Pérignon, the commercialization of this glorious wine—a story far more interesting and important—is due to the intuition, ambition, and foresight of three remarkable widows.

Madame Cliquot-Ponsardin was widowed at age 27 during the early 1800s. She took the reins of her newly inherited Champagne house with unprecedented zeal. The *veuve* (widow) Cliquot-Ponsardin pioneered more efficient and profitable methods of producing sparkling wine, in particular by inventing the clarification technique now referred to as the *rémuage* and *dégorgement*. To *veuve* Cliquot we can be thankful for the production methods of Champagne.

In 1858, Madame Louise Pommery was widowed. With the rationale that drier (less sweet) Champagne would be more acceptable among the aristocracy who could afford it, she acquired 150 acres of land at the periphery of Reims city under which were some of the most spectacular Gallo-Roman caves in the region. Her vision was superb, as Champagne became the rage in Paris and throughout Europe. To *veuve* Pommery we can be thankful for the marketing of Champagne.

It was the widow Olry Roederer who developed the notion of "luxury" Champagne. Czar Alexander II of Russia had, years before, demanded a Champagne of peerless quality to be made just for him. The house of Roederer created "Cristal," a small lot of crème-de-la-crème Champagne from only the best vintages bottled in crystal glass—and priced to match. Cristal became the first of what are now many "Grand Marque" Champagnes. To *veuve* Olry Roederer we can attribute the grand image of Champagne.

American soldiers in both World Wars enjoyed Champagne, the slang word *booze* arising, unfortunately, from the village of Bouzy. Winston Churchill was an avid Champagne drinker, naming one of his race horses "Pol Roger" after his favorite Champagne vintner. It is ironic that it has been through war that Champagne has evolved to become synonymous with celebration and festivity.

❖ THE REGION

There are approximately 55,000 acres of vineyards and 16,000 growers in the Champagne region. Production ranges from 3.5 to 11 million gallons, depending on the bounty of each vintage. More than 90 percent is white wine production; much of the rest is sparkling rosé wines, which continue to increase in popularity.

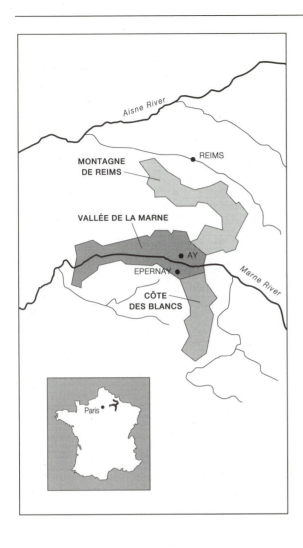

FIGURE 6.37 Champagne winegrowing region. *(Courtesy of* Food and Wines from France.)

Only three varieties of vine, one white and two black, can be cultivated for Champagne wine: Chardonnay, Pinot Noir, and Pinot Meunier. The vines, by regulation, must be planted one meter apart, one meter between the rows, and are trained not to exceed one meter in height.

Champagne winegrowing is regulated by the Comité Interprofessionelle du Vin de Champagne (CIVC). One of the more recent heroes of Champagne is the late Comte Robert-Jean de Vogue of Moët & Chandon who, at the beginning of World War II, resisted the efforts of the Nazis to loot the great caves— an effort that led to his imprisonment in a German concentration camp. After the war, Comte de Vogue founded the CIVC, which enforces vineyard and wine production throughout the region. This association continues to function as a board of directors, which has an equal number of grower and winery representatives. It is funded through a marketing order on each kilogram of grapes and each bottle of wine sold.

The climate of Champagne is characterized by cold winters, but also long summers. Virtually every vineyard has heating and air movement devices, which are used in the vineyards during the spring to ward off the frosts that can damage buds. The CIVC determines when harvest should begin each year and how much fruit may be harvested per acre. The CIVC also prescribes the use of spray materials to control vineyard pests. Spraying is usually effective, but when mold does occur, a *triage,* or culling, of fruit, laboriously, cluster by cluster, may be required.

FIGURE 6.38 Chalk subsoil in the Champagne Region. *(Photo by author.)*

Champagne subsoil is one of the most famous in viticulture. The best vineyards are planted on a base of belemnitic and oolitic chalk, a layer raised by earthquakes that shook the region thousands of years ago. The chalk, or calcium carbonate, rests under a shifting topsoil layer and absorbs heat in the fall, which advances the ripening of the grapes. The topsoil often erodes with heavy rains or melting snows and must be replaced with organic deposits from the nearby hilltops. The chalk subsoil provided the ancient Romans with a material that could be readily quarried to form vast storage caves underground. These caves remain and have long since been used as ideal wine cellars. A cellar master in Champagne is called the *chef de caves*.

However, Champagne's famous chalky subsoil varies in composition and density across the region. Its constituency is the crucial determinant of *commune* quality; this is a figure, precisely determined by the CIVC, ranging from 75 percent to the maximum of 100 percent. Note that it is the entire *commune* that is rated, not just the specific vineyards as in Burgundy. Nevertheless, the Champenoise insist that their 100 percent classification is the equal of a Burgundian Grand Cru classification. Similarly, 90 to 99 percent growths are compared to Premier Cru. One may also hear or read of Champagne Deuxieme Cru (Second Growth) and Troisieme Cru (Third Growth) vineyards, which are not so designated in Burgundy. Except to identify a specific *commune*'s pedigree, these tertiary designations don't mean very much, and they are rarely used on a label.

Champagne production and marketing are dominated by a group of several dozen large wineries, known as "houses," located in the cities of Reims and Epernay. Their caves are found 100 feet or so beneath the streets and buildings. Pommery & Greno has more than 12 miles of caves, some with magnificent wall carvings, under its facility in Reims. Moët & Chandon has more than 20 miles of caves in its remarkable system beneath Epernay. Although there are no powerful *négociants* in Champagne, most of the houses are owned or controlled by large distribution companies and, therefore, each house has its own broad marketing program.

The Champagne vineyard region is divided into four districts:

Montagne de Reims

Vallée de la Marne

Côte des Blancs

Aube

Each district has its own character, producing grapes with individual virtues of color, flavor, body, and acidity. These are the heart and soul of Champagne—the essential focus of blending. These special attributes, in concert with production in compliance with the *méthode champenoise,* the celebrated "method of Champagne" devised by the widow Cliquot, results in the famous bubbling wine that continues to demand dear prices.

❖ MÉTHODE CHAMPENOISE

A ton of Champagne grapes contains about 180 gallons of juice. The CIVC, however, allows only 80 gallons of juice to be extracted—the first reason for the high price of this wine. The *vin de cuvée* is the free-run juice collected from the press before any pressure is applied, accounting for a little more than 60 gallons of the total. The *premiere taille* or "first pressing," accounts for another 15 gallons, and the *deuxieme taille,* the "second pressing," adds the final 5 gallons from each ton.

The juice is kept separate by vintage, by vineyard, and by pressing, each lot fermented into dry white table wine. The young table wines are gently clarified, stabilized, filtered, and aged.

Juice pressed from Chardonnay is referred to as *Blanc de Blancs,* or "white of whites," a designation that is sometimes used on the labels of Champagne made exclusively from Chardonnay grapes. It follows that *Blanc de Noirs* would be "white from blacks." The light pressing of the Pinot Noir and Pinot Meunier grapes extracts very little color from the skins—a faint pink at best, which soon oxidizes to a golden hue. The Blanc de Noirs designation is seldom used on Champagne labels.

Pink, or rosé, Champagne is typically made by adding a small amount of red wine from Pinot Noir to the white cuvée wine. The village of Bouzy is best known as the source of this red wine, made in much the same manner as red wine in Burgundy.

FIGURE 6.39 Pressing grapes in the Champagne Region. *(Courtesy of* Food and Winers from France.*)*

ASSEMBLAGE

Then comes the all-important blending operation, the *assemblage*. New white table wines from various lots are brought to a laboratory where owners, winemakers, *chefs de caves,* and other masters cast judgment on how each assemblage should be made. Most houses carefully guard the secrecy of their fundamental assemblage recipe.

The assemblage for lower-priced nonvintage Champagne is made to perpetuate the "house style," blending wines from various vintages and vineyards in order to maintain consistency from one assemblage to the next.

For higher-priced vintage Champagne, the assemblage must, of course, be limited to table wines from a single vintage year, but is frequently a blend from various vineyards. Typically, vintage Champagne is assembled from wines grown on land with 90 percent chalk grades and higher. Vintages are "declared" when these wines are exceptional in quality, typically just twice or thrice each decade.

For the highest-priced luxury *Grand Marque* (sometimes referred to as *tête de cuvée)* vintage Champagne, the assemblage is taken from the best wines from the best vineyards, some entirely from 100-percent *communes*. Examples of these are as follows:

Pommery & Greno	"Madame Louise"
Moët & Chandon	"Dom Pérignon"
Perrier-Jouet	"Belle Epoque"
Roederer	"Cristal"
Piper-Heidsieck	"Rare"
Veuve Cliquot–Ponsardin	"La Grande Dame"

CUVÉE

Once an assemblage is completed, a *liqueur de tirage,* a carefully calculated amount of sugar, is added. In modern times, this step also includes an addition of free amino nitrogen and B vitamins, which improves conditions for yeast growth. The *cuvée* is then inoculated with cultured yeast and put into bottles specially designed to withstand the high pressure resulting from the secondary fermentation.

SECOND FERMENTATION

The filled bottles are sealed with a temporary "crown" cap and then laid on their sides in rows, stacked row upon row in what is called the *tirage*. A tirage is built on the floors of the caves, which hold a natural year-round temperature of about 55 ° F—perfect for fermentation to take place slowly over several months. Pressure in the bottles may exceed 80 pounds per square inch as this fermentation nears completion.

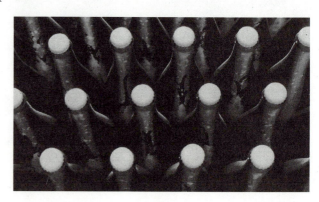

FIGURE 6.40 Yeast sediment in Champagne tirage. (*Photo by author.*)

After the sugars have been fully fermented to alcohol and carbon dioxide gas, the yeast cells commence to die and disintegrate, or *autolyze*. Dead yeast cells break up and precipitate to a sediment, during which yeast protoplasm diffuses a "yeasty" flavor through the wine. The greater the amount of time in tirage, the more this flavor will develop from the yeast sediment—an essential component in fine Champagne. Vintage Champagnes may remain in tirage for years, and Grand Marque Champagnes for decades.

RIDDLING

The dangerous task of shaking down the yeast sediment from the sides of the bottles, collected during tirage, into the bottle neck is called the *rémuage* in France, "riddling" in America. Many Champagne houses now employ machines that riddle boxes filled with bottles pointed downward, or *sur pointe*.

DISGORGING

Once the riddling operation has shaken all yeast sediment down into the bottle neck and onto the crown cap, the *dégorgement* operation proceeds, freezing the bottle neck so as to suspend the sediment in an ice "plug." When the disgorger removes the temporary cap, internal pressure blows out the ice plug like a bullet from a gun, carrying the sediment with it. About 10 percent of the carbon dioxide gas is lost during disgorging.

DOSAGE

Promptly after disgorging, bottles are transferred to machines that permit the addition of a dosage liqueur without further loss of carbon dioxide bubbles. The liqueur replaces the volume lost to the ice bullet, and the sweeter the liqueur, the sweeter the resulting Champagne. Labels on Champagne bottles disclose sweetness levels by the following terms:

Naturel	no sugar added, bone dry
Brut	very little sugar added, dry
Sec	little sugar added, nearly dry
Demi-Sec	sugar added, "half dry"
Doux	sweet

CORKING AND HOODING

Comparatively little carbon dioxide gas is lost during the dosage operation. A special cork is required to withstand the pressure that develops once carbon dioxide gas equilibrium is regained inside the bottle. Corks are squeezed under tons of pressure in the jaws of a specially designed corking machine that exerts tons of force to drive the cork into the mouth of each bottle. A wire hood is then applied over the cork and beneath the lip of bottle mouth so as to prevent the cork from popping out until the wine is ready to be served. Bottles are then inverted back and forth to mix the dosage.

PACKAGING

Bottle dressing is not part of the *méthode champenoise*, but it bears noting that some Champagnes, particularly the luxury Grand Marque editions, are lavishly dressed. Piper-Heidsieck "Rare," for example, has a label designed by Fabergé more than a century ago. Although Roederer "Cristal" is not made in crystal bottles anymore, the package is, nevertheless, nothing short of spectacular.

FIGURE 6.41 The riddler. *(Courtesy of C.I.V.C.; photo by Jean-Pierre Leloir.)*

FIGURE 6.42 The *dégorgement.* *(Courtesy of C.I.V.C.; photo by Jean-Pierre Leloir.)*

⬧ MONTAGNE DE REIMS

As its name suggests, Montagne de Reims is a hilly district around the city of Reims, comprising the best vineyards on the higher slopes along the southern perimeter. Except for those grown in four major *communes*, the Montagne de Reims cultivates black grapes almost exclusively. The nine 100-percent *communes* in this district are planted to black grapes only. The white juice pressed from these grapes make wines that are deeply golden in color, "toasty" in bouquet, with rich briar flavor, heavy body, and crisp acidity.

MONTAGNE DE REIMS
100-PERCENT GRAND CRU COMMUNES

Ambonnay

Beaumont-sur-Vesle

Bouzy

Louvois

Mailly

Puisieux

Sillery

Tauxières-Mutry

Verzenay

A guided tour of the Pommery & Greno caves, founded in the 1830s, with their magnificent carved chalk walls embracing many millions of bottles, is one of the best visits in Champagne. As mentioned earlier, Madame Louise Pommery took control of these vast cellars in 1858. Under her leadership Pommery Champagne and her château, now the regal Boyer les Crayères hotel and three-star restaurant, became the standard of elegance in Reims. She made a fortune, much of which was spent in buying classic French artworks in America so they could be returned to the Louvre museum in Paris. The winery now under corporate management, her memory is forever preserved with the Grand Marque vintage Champagne wine of the house, labeled "Cuvée Madame Louise."

⬧ VALLÉE DE LA MARNE

Again, as the name suggests, the Vallée de la Marne district is a valley through which the Marne River flows. From the renowned *commune* of Ay westward to the city of Château-Thierry are some 50 miles of gentle vineyard slopes on either side of the valley. This is the part of Champagne in which to take an outing. Visitors are greeted with picturesque croplands on the riverbanks, separated by small villages in which there are some fascinating restaurants.

Traditionally, the Marne district of Champagne has been the source of comparatively less expensive Pinot Meunier grapes. Although Pinot Meunier vineyards still flourish, an increasing number of new Pinot Noir plantings replace the Meunier. There are comparatively few Chardonnay vines cultivated in this district.

New wines from the Marne Valley vineyards are typically delicate in character and weight, although the Pinot Meunier offers a pleasing earthy truffle flavor. Marne vineyards offer crucial blending elements used in taming the intense wines grown in the Montagne de Reims situated 10 miles to the north.

Ay

Mareuil-sur-Ay

Champagne Perrier-Jouët appeared in 1811, when the marriage of Pierre-Nicholas-Marie Perrier and Adele Jouët combined their family estates. The prominence of their house did not emerge, however, until later when their son, Charles, acquired a tract of coveted Côte de Blancs vineyards near Epernay. The light, chalky subsoil of this land is the quality standard for prime Champagne grapes, as first demonstrated at the turn of the century when the very best Perrier-Jouët assemblage was introduced in the now famous "Fleur de Champagne" *Belle Epoque* "flower" bottle designed by the art-glass worker, Emile Galle. A tingling, toasty-apple bouquet and rich complexity of flavors distinguish this wine today as one of the very finest Grand Marque Champagnes.

❖ CÔTES DES BLANCS

In the Côte des Blancs (slopes of whites) region, the whites are virtually all Chardonnay, growing on hillsides that reach continuously for 15 miles or so south of Epernay city. The Côtes des Blancs is a great place for a picnic, but less so for sightseeing.

The excellence of this region's delicious wine, however, cannot be denied. Its color, as would be expected in Chardonnay, is very light in both hue and density. The bouquet of young Côtes des Blancs is rather like green apple and celery, with lingering stony-fig flavors, and some *communes* identified by nuances of honey and olive. On the palate it is light, with acidity ranging from moderate to crisp. Obviously, wines from this district add yet another dimension to the broad complexity of Champagne assemblage.

CÔTES DES BLANCS
100-PERCENT GRAND CRU COMMUNES

Cramant

Avize

❖ AUBE

The district of Aube lacks distinction as a finite locale dominated by vineyards. It is a geographic area between the Aube and Seine Rivers, south of the Côtes des Blancs, which has a scattering of quaint villages surrounded by a number of winegrowing *communes*. The poor reputation for the locale is undeserved, unfortunately perpetuated by some wine writers who seem not to have visited there recently. During the past several decades new plantings of Pinot Noir and advanced facilities have served to create Aube wines of good quality and very good value. Although the subsoil lacks the intensity of chalk found in the three major districts of Champagne, this deficit is compensated by a longer mesoclimate that allows the Pinot Noir to mature more fully.

❖ THE LOIRE VALLEY ❖

The Loire, more than 600 miles in length, is the longest river in France. It originates in the central highlands west of Lyons and gathers the tributary rivers of Cher, Indre, Layon, Loir, Sevre, Vienne, and others on its way toward the

Atlantic seaport city of Nantes. Situated along the banks of these rivers are the four important wine districts of the region: the Central Vineyards, the Touraine, Anjou-Saumur, and the Nantais. More than 200,000 individual growers cultivate more than 350,000 acres of vineyard across this vast region.

The Loire Valley vineyards were established by the Romans during the first and second centuries. St. Martin of Tours, the first viticulturist monk, was born circa A.D. 316 in Hungary. He was so popular locally that the people of Tours, France, forced Martin to become their bishop, escorting him with an armed guard to their city. Martin was a successful evangelist who brought Christianity to the pagan country people and built churches in many early French villages. He carried out his episcopal duties faithfully and found time to establish an abbey of hermits at Marmoutier, on the banks of the Loire River. The discovery of the now famous Chenin Blanc grape variety in the Loire Valley is credited to St. Martin, and each year toward the end of January a festival is held in his honor. St. Martin died in 397, a red cloak thought to be his becoming one of the most sacred relics in all of France.

During the Renaissance the many different varieties and styles of red, white, and rosé wines of the Loire began to improve in quality. Hence, producers retreated from exporting their wines to England and the Netherlands in order to supply the thirst of Paris and other internal French markets.

During the reigns of Louis XIII and XIV (1610–1715) the Anjou vineyards became one of the finest wine sources in France. Anjou was praised by Alexandre Dumas as being "le premier vin de France."

Anjou eventually lost its postition of popularity to other growths, among these the vineyards of neighboring Saumur, which may have provided grapes for sparkling wines even before Champagne. In any case, many French wines were developing superb reputations. Perhaps Cardinal Richelieu best described the happy condition of French wine when he said, "If God forbade drinking, would He have made wine so good?"

Although there are more châteaux in Bordeaux, the largest and most spectacular are in the Loire Valley; some of them, indeed, are palaces of the first order. Among these are Chambord, of Da Vinci design and more than 400 rooms, and Madame de'Medici's Chenonceaux, dating from the Renaissance, built over the Cher River, not to mention Louis XV's Versailles and many other landmark estates.

FIGURE 6.43 Château Chambord.
(Photo by author.)

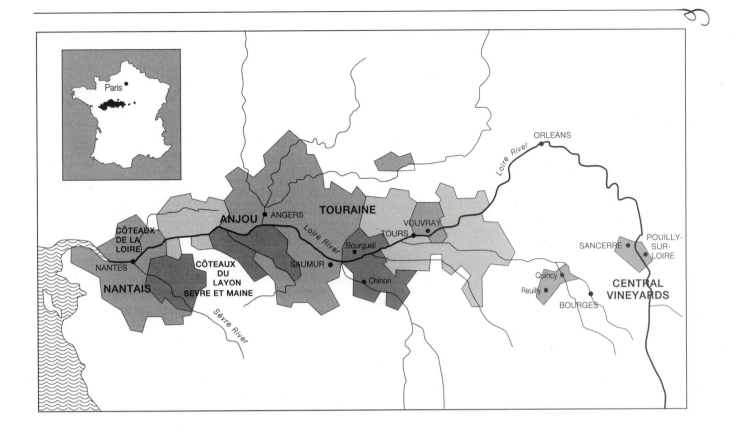

The Loire Valley probably attracts more visitors than any other region in France. Its small vineyard plots, divided by orchards and many other forms of manicured agriculture, are inviting. Indeed, a summer drive along the Loire may present more acres of sunflowers than vineyards. The region is viticulturally diverse, cultivating a greater variety of vines for more types of wines than any other region in the nation. There are no individual vineyard or estate classification systems operating in the Loire, simply AOC designations for locales of special merit. Many of these wines are good, but it is clearly the grand châteaux that bring most people to this beautiful countryside.

It is interesting that the Loire wine trade is conducted a bit in the château style too. Although *négociants* operate throughout the region, most fine wines rely heavily on the estate name for marketing, rather than vineyard classification and the *négociant's* brand name, which in Burgundy mean everything.

FIGURE 6.44 Loire Valley wine-growing region. (*Courtesy of* Food and Wines from France.)

❈ THE CENTRAL VINEYARDS

The Central Vineyards district is sometimes called "the Nivernais." It is also referred to as the Upper Loire, owing to its location upriver about 90 miles to the southeast of the city of Orléans.

This is the smallest district in the region, with only about 5,000 acres of vines. Most of the Central Vineyards area is located on the right bank of the Loire between the villages of Gien to the north and La Charité to the south. White wines are the most highly regarded here, particularly those made from Sauvignon Blanc, sometimes called "Blanc Fumé" by the locals. The term *fumé* arises from the opulent fruity element in the aroma that is found in better examples of the type. Red and rosé wines are made from Gamay and Pinot Noir.

The two most important subdistricts in the Central Vineyards are AOC Sancerre and AOC Pouilly-sur-Loire. The latter is further subdivided to distin-

FIGURE 6.45   Château du Nozet.
(Photo by author.)

guish AOC Blanc-Fumé-de-Pouilly, which is generally considered to have the finest vineyards in the entire district. The best wines from these vineyards may be found under the "Comte Lafond" label produced by Baron Patrick de Ladoucette at the grand Château du Nozet.

Kings Henry IV and Louis XVI thought Sancerre was the best wine they had ever tasted, each stating that if more people drank it, there would be fewer wars.

There are red Sancerres that have bold berry-cherry flavors resembling Beaujolais *nouveau*. Like most of the Loire Valley wines, those from the Central Vineyards should be consumed young, while flavors are fresh and fruity. Good examples of Pouilly-Fumé and Sancerre are under the labels of Henri Bourgeois and Didier Dagueneau.

A few miles west of Pouilly and Sancerre are the AOC vineyards of Ménétou-Salon, Quincy, and Reuilly. Ménétou-Salon and Quincy are planted with Sauvignon Blanc on poor gravel soil, and Reuilly cultivates the white Sauvignon on marly soils.

Downriver are a group of vineyards called the Côteau de Gien, and farther down is the Côteau de l'Orléanais, which surrounds the city of Orléans. Both of these subdistricts produce good-quality whites and reds, mostly for local consumption.

❖ TOURAINE

Touraine is the largest district in the Loire Valley region. It commences at the city of Blois and continues on both sides of the river for abut 75 miles west to the city of Chinon.

This district has a viniculture generally considered more common and ordinary, certainly less distinctive, than those of the other three districts in the Loire Valley Region. Yet some of the most glorious history and the finest of old castles and châteaux are embraced by this enchanting place.

As mentioned earlier, most historians credit St. Martin with planting the first vines, perhaps the Chenin Blanc variety, in the Touraine a few years after founding the Abbey of Marmoutier there in A.D. 372. Legend has it that he left his donkey to graze in the vineyard grass one day, but returned to find that the animal had preferred to eat the supple shoots growing from the vines instead. At the following harvest it was observed that grapes from these vines were fewer in quantity, but of much greater quality. Although this may be a more romantic account of discovering the benefits of pruning, there is considerable evidence that Columella had practiced pruning in Roman vineyards centuries earlier. On the left bank of the Loire, about 20 miles west of Tours, is the lovely village of Candes, where St. Martin is enshrined.

One should not miss taking the time to visit Chinon. As discussed in Chapter 2, Chinon castle was home to Henry II, king of England, husband of Eleanor of Aquitaine from Bordeaux, and father of Richard the Lionhearted. It is thought that Richard died at Chinon after being wounded in battle at Chalus in 1199.

But it was two centuries later that this castle gained even greater historical significance. Having heard a divine calling as a shepherd girl, Joan of Arc came to Chinon in 1429 to offer Charles VII, heir to the French throne, her leadership of his army against the English who then occupied northern France. She was not received with much credulity, but day after day, for weeks, she successfully responded to questions in matters she could not possibly have known about except through holy intervention. Finally, Charles gave her his army and she drove the English out of France. Subsequently, Joan took a place of honor at Charles's coronation in the Cathedral of Reims. She was later captured by Burgundian soldiers and was turned over to their English allies, who burned her at the stake in Rouen.

Soil strata in the better Touraine subdistricts are primarily clay and limestone on a subsoil of tufa chalk, a fascinating porous pumicelike chalk produced by prehistoric volcanic activity. This is a special *terroir*, which retains both heat and moisture well. The cliffs lining both sides of the river have many natural caves, most of which are fashioned into homes and wineries, with facades that seem to melt into the earth behind them.

On the north side of the river, just to the east of Tours, is AOC Vouvray, one of the most notable wine subdistricts in the Touraine. Vouvray whites are made both dry and sweet, still and sparkling, all from the Chenin Blanc variety,

FIGURE 6.46 Touraine vineyards with "cave-homes." *(Photo by author.)*

which the locals call "Pineau de la Loire." On the south side of the river is the Montlouis subdistrict, which produces similar wines.

In the western Touraine are the vineyards of AOC Bourgueil, which produce distinctive red wines, rather bramble-berrylike in flavor, from Cabernet Franc vines. Next to AOC Chinon, the most notable *commune* in this vicinity is AOC St.-Nicholas-de-Bourgueil, for which the subdistrict is named. One of the best reputations for fine Chinon and Bourgueil wines is held by Marc Bredif, where caves contain vintages bottled more than a century ago and wine presses that were used during the 1500s.

Alexandre Dumas spent much of his younger life in Orléans and around the Touraine, which doubtlessly influenced his life-style as a bon vivant. He once remarked that history would remember him for his *Grand Dictionnaire de la Cuisine,* not for *The Three Musketeers.* The Dumas food dictionary is a rare book of 818 pages that includes suggestions for serving wines with such exotic dishes as elephant's feet and kangaroo.

❖ ANJOU-SAUMUR

The white table wines of AOC Anjou are grown from Chardonnay, Chenin Blanc, and Sauvignon Blanc vines, often made just slightly sparkling, or *petillant.* Some are a bit sweet. AOC Anjou reds are grown principally from Cabernet Sauvignon and Cabernet Franc, along with a separate AOC designation called Anjou-Gamay. Undoubtedly the most internationally famous product from this locale is the AOC Rosé d'Anjou wine made to a medium-dry finish. AOC Cabernet d'Anjou-Rosé and AOC Cabernet de Saumur Rosé are grown exclusively from Cabernet vines. All of these wines—whites, pinks, and reds—are relatively inexpensive and best when consumed within a year or two.

This locale might be better named the "Layon District," as the Layon River runs through the heart of the Anjou vineyards, and the principal subdistrict is called the AOC Côteau du Layon. In this same locale are three more subdistricts: AOC Côteau de l'Aubance, AOC Quarts de Chaume, and AOC Bonnezeau. Chenin Blanc is the principal vine variety cultivated here, and the *Botrytis cinerea* noble mold (*pourriture noble)* is allowed to grow on ripened grapes. As may be expected, the resulting wines have a character somewhat similar to those grown in the Sauternes district of Bordeaux.

Both red and white wines from the Saumur, the most important subdistrict in this area, are permitted the AOC-Saumur designation. AOC Saumur-Champigny grows red wines from Cabernet grapes. The best-known Saumurs are sparkling wines made by the bottle-fermented method similar to that employed in Champagne. Locals insist that there were sparkling wines made in Saumur many years before the more famous Champagne wine was invented.

Situated on the north side of the Loire River is the comparatively small subdistrict AOC Anjou Côteau de la Loire, in which delicate dry, or near dry, white wines are made from Chenin Blanc.

Wines from the Anjou-Saumur can be a good starting point for the beginner wishing to enjoy a broad array of French wine types and styles at reasonable prices.

❖ NANTAIS

The Nantais district embraces the final 60 miles of the Loire River as it flows through the city of Nantes toward the Atlantic. Wine grown in the Nantais is labeled "AOC Muscadet." It is white wine made from the grape variety Melon

de Bourgogne, first brought from Burgundy during the 1700s to replant vineyards destroyed by a devastating winter. Confusingly, some vine experts call the vine Melon, others call it Pinot Blanc, and still others refer to the Nantais vine as simply Nantais. In any event, the best of these are dry, tart, and crisp with a light blossomy-citrus bouquet. This character is elusive as Muscadet ages quickly, but when fresh it can be delightful. It is, therefore, not the best choice off the shelves in the United States, but the finest bottles are from such vintners as Domaine Henry Pelle and Robert Michele.

AOC Muscadet de Sevre-et-Maine is considered the best winegrowing subdistrict in the Nantais. This locale embraces the southern perimeter of Nantes city, which is composed of flatlands of clay evolving to more sandy constituency on the slopes. AOC Muscadet des Côteaux de la Loire is a smaller subdistrict situated on chalky slopes along the northern side of the river.

❖ THE RHÔNE VALLEY ❖

The majestic Rhône River valley stretches about 120 miles from the large industrial city of Lyons southward to Avignon, perhaps the most picturesque winegrowing landscape in France. Along the way various winegrowing *communes* are separated by orchards and truck cropping. This region is divided into two subregions, quite simply, the Upper Rhône in the northern sector and the Lower Rhône in the southern. In all, the region cultivates more than 100,000 acres of vineyards.

The Rhône Valley has a rich heritage, primarily because of its being the only navigable waterway between the Mediterranean Sea and central France. Between 800 and 600 B.C. political tyranny and economic chaos in Greece had commenced to crumble the once mighty Hellenic nation. Their country divided by this turmoil, many Greeks left to establish new colonies along the southern coast of Italy, in Sicily, and westward to the mouth of the Rhône. Although the Greeks may have been the first influence in winegrowing along the Rhône, it was the Romans 1,000 years later who widely planted vineyards near the river port settlements of Aix, Orange, Valence, and Vienne, among others, all of which are now cities that center the grand Rhône Valley viniculture.

As Roman power began to diminish during the fourth and fifth centuries A.D., Teutonic barbarians took over many of the colonies and territories Rome had established in western Europe. Rather strange partnerships existed for some time; Romans and Teutons often fought together against the invading Huns. It was the combined forces of the Visigoths from the central Gallic highlands and the Romans that finally defeated Attila, king of the Huns, in 451. Among other Teutonic invaders were the Angles and the Saxons who forced their way into Great Britain, the Burgundians who took eastern Gaul, and the Franks who invaded the Rhône. In A.D. 486 the Frankish king, Clovis, defeated Syagrius, the last Roman governor in Gaul. Under Frank rule, Gaul became France.

In the sixth century, Christian monks took up the tools of grape growing and winemaking. There were hundreds of monasteries in the Rhône region—Cornas, Gigondas, and St.-Péray, among many others—which remain famous today as communal centers of fine winegrowing. The Rhône River carried supplies to the Crusaders in the Middle East and brought back rich cargoes. Among these was a viticultural jewel, the renowned grape variety *Syrah*. This ancient vine, known as the *Shiraz* in Iraq, may have been Noah's vine brought down from Mount Ararat to the Fertile Crescent long before. The grand blackred wine from the Syrah is today the region's finest.

The weather in the Rhône Valley can often be quite harsh. There are four seasons in the north, but the south has Mediterranean mesoclimates, with sum-

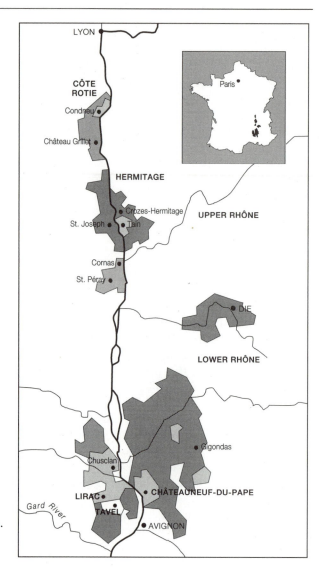

FIGURE 6.47 Rhône Valley winegrowing regions. (*Courtesy of* Food and Wines from France.)

mers separated by mild winters. The entire region is chilled with a relentless cold glacier wind, the Mistral, which sweeps down from the Alps more than 200 days a year, sometimes at near-hurricane velocity. The mistral can, and often does, bring serious damage to the Rhône Valley vineyards.

Most Rhône wines are marketed in similar fashion to those of Burgundy, albeit with far less distinction in the classification system. The Rhône is, for the most part, a region in which many small vineyard owners depend heavily on *négociant* distribution in the world marketplace.

❖ UPPER RHÔNE

The northernmost area of the Rhône, designated AOC Côte Rotie, is linked to the west bank of the river just south of Lyons city. Syrah vines are cultivated for reds, and Viognier for whites. Côte Rotie reds are the area's best, with a dark ruby color, heavy texture, and bold berry-plum-earthy-resin flavors. This district is subdivided into two subdistricts, the Côte Brunette and the Côte Blonde. Legend has it that these are names given by a medieval winegrower who had two daughters, one a brunette and other a blonde. If one looks closely at the soils in the two locales, it is evident that one is dark with iron oxide and the other pale with limestone.

To the south of Côte Rotie, still on the west bank, are the neighboring vineyards of AOC Condrieu, planted exclusively to the Viognier, which yields white wines with an expressive spicy-pear bouquet and a rather stony-citrusy flavor. Condrieu is generally affordable and a good choice for those on a budget wanting a taste of Rhône white.

Further south is AOC St.-Joseph, where the Rhône begins to widen out. The west bank vineyards are devoted to the Syrah, although the white Viognier is also cultivated here and sometimes blended with the dense, heavy red Syrah to create a lighter, fruitier style of red wine, generally consumed with comparatively little aging.

Still farther south is AOC Cornas, which cultivates the Syrah on some of the steepest slopes to be found in the entire region. As one would expect, production is small, but the wine is exceptionally heavy and its flavor intense.

The last of the west bank vineyard districts in the Upper Rhône is St.-Péray, where full-bodied white wines are grown from the varieties Marsanne and Roussane, expressing rich olive-resin bouquet and bold vinous-vanilla flavors. There is also significant production of white sparkling wine in this locale, which may be labeled as AOC St.-Péray Mousseux.

On the east side, opposite the town of Tournon, is the village of Tain-l'Hermitage. Situated around the village and up in the nooks and crannies of the hillsides are the famous Syrah vineyards of AOC Hermitage. When young, hermitage is like Cornas, very dense, peppery and tannic, and usually undrinkable for at least several years—more than a decade for some vintages. When this wine is mature, however, it is a rare treat. Marsanne and Roussane vines yield white Hermitage with their own distinction, dry white wines that are exceptionally full-bodied, high in alcohol strength, and long on the palate with leathery-nutty flavors.

Bordering the Hermitage to the south is AOC Crozes-Hermitage, which unfortunately pales in the shadow of its famous neighbor. Some experts contend that both the red and white wine from Crozes-Hermitage, made from the same varieties as cultivated in the Hermitage, are a touch or two lighter and less concentrated. They are also less expensive and, therefore, make good values.

The Upper Rhône ends at the northern limits of the city of Valence.

FIGURE 6.48 Jaboulet Vineyards in the Rhône Valley. *(Courtesy of Frederick Wildman.)*

◈ LOWER RHÔNE

The Upper and Lower Rhône Valley are divided by about 50 miles in which very little commercial viniculture is found. The first districts of importance in the Lower Rhône are the Côtes du Vivarais and the Côteaux de l'Ardeche, which embrace more than 20 winegrowing villages nestled in the hills across the river west of Montelimar. None of these is AOC designated, but 11 are classified VDQS for white, rosé, and red wines made from 13 authorized vine varieties.

A few miles farther south of Montelimar, and back on the east side of the river is AOC Côteaux du Tricastin (elevated relatively recently from VDQS), where 12 villages cultivate Carignane, Grenache, and several other red wine varieties. Tricastin wines are berry-cherry in bouquet, a bold fruit aroma that carries over to the palate. They are generally quite reasonable in price and are a good choice for neophytes as an introduction to Rhône reds.

Southeast of Tricastin are 17 villages scattered among the hills that, when their wines are made in compliance with strict rules governing alcohol strength and flavor, are entitled to be classified as AOC Côtes du Rhône-Villages. One of these villages, Gigondas, was awarded its own AOC in 1971 for rosé and red wines produced mostly from the Grenache variety. Some of the Côtes du Rhône villages in this locale are also permitted to make AOC Vins Doux Naturels, a fruity, sweet fortified dessert wine made from Muscat de Frontignan grapes.

The Côtes du Rhône villages, scattered throughout the countryside northeast of Orange, are the best places in the entire region for a day of touring. Quiet back roads wind through vineyards cultivated on the Dentelles de Montmirail hillsides at the base of Mont Ventoux. Many centuries of the relentless Mistral wind have formed natural rock sculptures at the tops of the hills, and more recent winds are evidenced by trees with trunks permanently bent to the south.

Across the river, to the west of Orange, is the district of AOC Lirac, which is well known locally for perhaps the best bargains in red wines to be found in the entire Rhône Valley. This locale, along with AOC Tavel, is world famous for its superb dry rosé wines.

CHÂTEAUNEUF-DU-PAPE

The Côtes du Rhône region ends at the junction of the Durance and Rhône Rivers, south of the city of Avignon. Clement V, previously bishop of Bordeaux, was elected pope here in 1305, the first of seven popes to reside in Avignon. He was also the first occupant of the Châteauneuf-du-Pape, the "new home of the

FIGURE 6.49 Ruins of the Châteauneuf-du-Pape. *(Photo by author)*

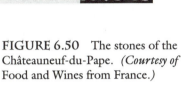

FIGURE 6.50 The stones of the Châteauneuf-du-Pape. (*Courtesy of* Food and Wines from France.)

pope," which was a large castle situated on a bend of the Rhône about seven miles north of Avignon. Today only a small portion of the original castle remains, but it is well worth a visit to experience the dominance of the site over its surroundings in every direction. Vineyards in this district long preceded the popes, and some historians say the first vines cultivated here preceded even the Romans.

Today the wine of AOC Châteauneuf-du-Pape is unquestionably the jewel of the Rhône, continuing to command the same high regard it has enjoyed for the many centuries vines have been cultured there. Along with its rich history, however, this district has some of the most remarkable vineyard soil, or lack of it, to be found anywhere. Seeing virtually nothing but smooth stones, mostly three to five inches in diameter or length, causes visitors to stop by the roadsides and look in utter amazement at this rather moonlike landscape. There is, of course, soil beneath, in which vine roots take up water and nourishment, but the stones hold heat absorbed from the sun during the day to help ripen fruit, which would otherwise remain green from the Mistral chill.

There are more than a dozen vine varieties permitted for AOC Châteauneuf-du-Pape. The most widely cultivated are Grenache and Syrah, with Cinsault, Mourvèdre, Roussanne, and others, including some whites, making up the rest. With this broad selection, one would expect Châteauneuf-du-Pape to have an equally broad variance from one estate to another. There are differences, but the more traditional vintners seem to achieve a remarkable similarity in their wines. These have dark ruby color, heavy consistency, and powerful truffle-plum flavors, all of which need years of aging to tame the bristling young tannins.

❖ ALSACE ❖

The Alsace is situated in northeastern France, but it is much more German in character than French. Fossils of vine leaves and grape seeds provide evidence that grapes were cultivated in the Alsace long before the Romans arrived in the region during the second century. This region is a narrow 65-mile strip of slopes along the Vosges foothills just west of the Rhine, between the old Roman cities of Strasbourg and Mulhouse. The hill barriers, fine vineyard land, fertile valley soils, and the Rhine waterway made the Alsace a valuable outpost. Indeed, the name *Strasbourg* translates as "road castle," implying its strategic position.

Teutonic Frankish tribes drove the Celts and Romans out of the Alsace during the fifth century and proceeded to establish small villages with, as would be

FIGURE 6.51 Alsatian vineyards and village. *(Courtesy of* Food and Wines from France.*)*

expected, Teutonic names. Dambach Kayserberg, Wintzenheim, Guebwiller, and others remain today, their names sounding unexpectedly different from those of other villages in France.

The Alsatian Franks were not winegrowers, but they were gardeners on a grand scale, these gardens remaining a great pride of twentieth-century Alsatians. During the reign of Emperor Charlemagne, the Treaty of Verdun, drafted in A.D. 870, allocated the German king, Louis, all of the Alsace Province, renamed *Alemannia,* so that winegrowing could and would be expanded. It was at this time that the Germanic character of winegrowing was rooted in the Alsace, and it has remained ever since.

The Alsace has one of the most war-ridden histories in France. Following Charlemagne's rule, control of the region was disputed by the French and Germans for more than eight centuries. The Thirty Years' War ended with the Treaty of Westphalia in 1648, which ceded Alsace to France. When the Franco-Prussian War ended in 1871, the Alsace went back to Germany. The armistice of World War I returned the region to France, Hitler took it back for Germany in 1940, and the end of World War II once again returned the Alsace to France.

Since the French Revolution, when all of France was changed from provincial to departmental structure, the Alsace has been divided into the Departments of Haut-Rhin and Bas-Rhin, the "high" and "low" Rhine districts, respectively. The small storybook villages continue as the centers of Alsatian winegrowing. This is one of the most picturesque and charming wine regions in all of Europe.

The Alsace cultivates approximately 30,000 acres of vineyards, the Haut-Rhin embracing both the largest portion of this acreage and the best quality. More than 90 percent of Haut-Rhin production is AOC Alsace white wine. The Bas-Rhin also produces 90 percent white wine, but only a little more than half of this is classified as high as AOC Alsace.

The hillside soils of the region are varied, with combinations of gneiss, gravel, granite, marl, and limestone found in different locales. In the Haut-Rhin, the better vineyards are planted on calcareous slopes with southern and southeastern exposures. In both districts the lower valley plains yield more ordinary wines.

The Alsace is located more than 500 miles inland from the Atlantic and is, therefore, not significantly affected by the tempering effects of ocean currents. The Vosges mountains to the west offer some protection from inclement weather approaching from that direction, but Alsatian summers are hotter and winters colder than in any other major French winegrowing region.

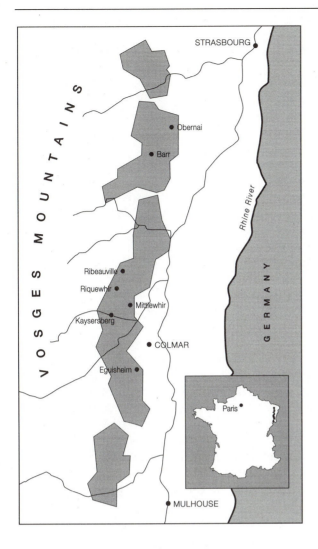

FIGURE 6.52 Alsace wine-growing region. (*Courtesy of* Food and Wines from France.)

Most of the fines Alsatian wines are estate bottled; some of the most highly regarded of these are produced by Dopff & Irion, Hugel, Meyer, Trimbach, and Zind-Humbrecht. Cooperatives generally market less distinctive, but good-quality, wines at lower prices. The most distinguishing factor of Alsatian wine labels is their use of vine variety names for labeling in conjunction with geographical origins. An increasing number of sparkling wines are made, which are labeled as AOC Alsace Crémant.

There are seven noble vines that make up virtually all viticulture in the region. The most famous is the Johannisberg Riesling, a variety native to Germany but cultivated in the Alsace for wine of a more dry and delicate style. The jewel of the Alsace is Gewürztraminer. It was once simply called *Traminer*, but a genetic mutation was discovered that was thought to produce superior white wines of *Gewürz*, or spicy, character. The Gewürz-Traminer was heavily propagated and is now the most widely planted variety in the region. Gewürztraminer is the world standard for wines having a rich, spicy-apricot flavor.

Other Alsatian varieties of note are Muscat Ottonel, Pinot Blanc, Pinot Gris (sometimes called Tokay d'Alsace), Sylvaner, and Pinot Noir. Many of these, or similar, vine varieties are also cultivated in Germany, but the significant difference is that in Alsace most of the wines are finished dry, with little remaining unfermented sweetness.

Both Alsace and Vin d'Alsace are permitted AOC designations. When a vine variety name is combined with either of these on a label, then all the wine

must be made from that varietal. Alsatian AOC wines must have a minimum alcohol strength of 8.5 percent, and grapes must be harvested within the regulations set forth by the Comité Regional d'Experts. Wines from the Alsace are usually bottled in a tall, slender, green Germanlike bottle, known as the *flute d'Alsace*.

A provision is made for ordinary Alsatian wines that are made from other than the seven AOC-permitted vine varieties mentioned earlier. These may be blended with wines made from noble grapes, as long as they are labeled with the archaic AOC designation "Alsace Edelzwicker." Such labels may not display the names of any noble grapes.

Alsatian vintners sometimes add the names of their *communes* to labels, and the addition of specific vineyard names is equally common. Labels that indicate variety name, village name, and vineyard name, along with the shipper's brand, are likely to indicate the best wines.

Alsatian Grand Cru wines were first permitted in 1983 for 48 vineyards of historically superior-quality wine production. An AOC Alsace Grand Cru further requires a minimum of 10 percent alcohol for wines from Johannisberg Riesling and Muscat. Eleven percent is the minimum for both Gewürztraminer and Pinot Gris.

There are two classifications of sweet late-harvest wines in the Alsace. The *Vendange Tardive* (VT), although made from grapes harvested well overripened, is not finished in the semidry style as the German *Spätlese* and *Auslese* cousins are. Alsatian Vendange Tardive is generally dry and must reach at least 12.9 percent alcohol for Johannisberg Riesling, and 14.3 for Gewürztraminer and Pinot Gris. It is rare to find a *Selection des Grains Nobles* (SGN), or "Selection of Noble Overripened Grapes," as alcohol level minima are increased to 15.1 and 16.4, respectively, yet these wines must still retain enough residual sugar to create sufficient sweetness for the type. As would be expected, the big bouquet and rich flavors of fine Selection des Grains Nobles are bold and exotic, as are their prices.

❖ THE MIDI ❖

The Midi is the oldest and largest winegrowing region in France. It is situated along the Mediterranean coast between the Spanish border and the Rhône Valley. This is the locale, centered on the city of Narbonne, in which the Romans first settled nearly 2,000 years ago.

Although rich in history, wines from the Midi have been ordinary, at best, and have suffered the reputation of being perhaps the worst-quality wine grown in France. In recent years, however, following huge investments in new vineyard plantings and modernized winemaking facilities, wines from the Midi have gained considerable attention in the world marketplace.

Traditional white wines of the region are made from Aramon, Clairette, and Mauzac, all standard vin ordinaire. Muscat de Frontignan and several other Muscat varieties make very fruity wines, which are often preferred by beginners. Rather thin and lackluster reds made from the bountiful Alicante Bouchet and Carignane bear the major brunt of criticism in regard to Midi wines. The modern makeover of the Midi has included replacing some of these varieties with Chardonnay, Sauvignon Blanc, Sémillon, Cabernet Sauvignon, Merlot, Mourvèdre, Syrah, and other noble vines. Consequently, geographical consistency will be a problem until this transition is complete. Until then consumers have little alternative but to look for brand names that are emerging as superior products. Prices, on the other hand, are very attractive, which allows for ample experimentation.

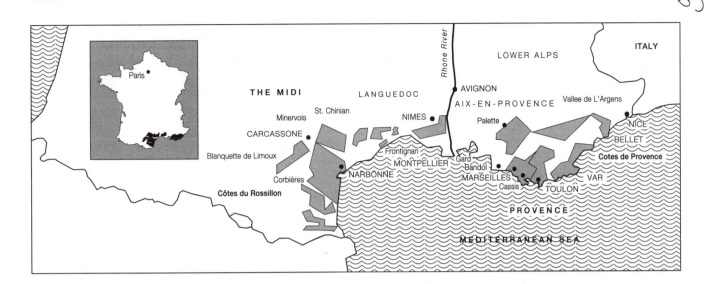

FIGURE 6.53 The Midi and Provence winegrowing region.

❖ LANGUEDOC

The Languedoc is by far the largest district in the Midi. It extends 30 miles around the land perimeter of Narbonne and twice that distance to the northeast. The best wines in the district are grown on the slopes designated as AOC Fitou, AOC Corbières (also Corbières Superieur) and AOC Minervois—all of which offer fresh, berrylike reds made by the same carbonic maceration process as employed in Beaujolais for its famous Nouveau.

Languedoc also includes Carcassone, an impressive medieval city still enclosed by high stone walls and bastions, where a recent version of *Robin Hood* was filmed. Nearby are the vineyards of Limoux, where good AOC Blanquette de Limoux sparkling wines are grown. This is truly magnificent countryside, easily accessible and well worth spending an extra day there to taste the local wines, along with enjoying dinner and lodging inside the old city.

A few miles north of Carcassone are the hillside vineyards of AOC Faugères and AOC St.-Chinian, both of which produce interesting fruity red wines. In the extreme northeastern part of the district, near Montpellier, is AOC Clairette de Bellegarde vineyards, producing whites, and AOC Costières du Gard producing reds. Connecting the southwestern and northeastern extremes of the Languedoc is the huge Côteaux du Languedoc, which produces the same general types of whites, pinks, and reds as the AOC growths, but for less money.

FIGURE 6.54 Machine harvesting grapes in the Midi. *(Courtesy of Food and Wines from France.)*

FIGURE 6.55 Vineyards in Roussillon. *(Courtesy of* Food and Wines from France.*)*

❖ ROUSSILLON

About 40 miles south of Narbonne are the AOC Côtes du Roussillon, AOC Côtes du Roussillon-Villages, and AOC Colliore. The vineyards surrounding these small towns and villages produce perhaps the very best red wines in all of the Midi. Many of these are comparatively small vineyards, cultivated in the slate-laden Pyrenees foothills. Careful selection can result in very good wine values for the money.

Les Vignerons du Val d'Orbieu was founded in 1967 by a small group of foresighted vintners who planted vineyards along the banks of the Orbieu River, which runs through the Corbières district of the Languedoc. It has grown to become one of the largest producers of wine in France, with vineyards stretching all along the Mediterranean coast from the Pyrenees Mountains to the Rhône River.

The Roussillon district is also famous in France for rather Port-like dessert wines called *vins doux naturels* (wines of natural sweetness). These are made by the addition of grape brandy at some point during fermentation, which serves to arrest any further yeast activity and preserve the remaining natural grape sugar. AOC Banyuls, AOC Maury, and AOC Rivesaltes are the principal growths, producing white, rosé, red, and tawny Madeira-style dessert wines.

❖ PROVENCE ❖

The geographical region of Provence begins where the Rhône Valley winegrowing region ends, at Avignon, the "cité des Papes." Provençal winegrowing, however, commences considerably farther south, the first district of note being AOC Côteaux des Baux-en-Provence, situated around the southeastern periphery of Les Baux. This is poor, rocky soil, which gives full meaning to the "struggling vine theory," as Grenache and Syrah vines yield lighter, fruitier wines here as compared with the heavy red Rhônes to the north.

The city of Aix-en-Provence typifies what many feel southern France is all about—good food, fine wine, and great people. It is easy for one to be captured by the ambiance of this enchanting countryside. AOC Côteaux d'Aix-en-Provence and AOC Palette are arguably the best vineyards in the region, yielding mostly hearty dry reds grown from Cinsault and Mourvèdre made in the Lower Rhône style. AOC Bandol vineyards are situated in the extreme south, near the Mediterranean coast, offering similar reds but at higher prices. AOC Cassis brings to mind black currants and red wine, but in fact cultivates Marsanne vines for whites expressing rather guava- and figlike flavors.

The largest winegrowing district in Provence, by far, is AOC Côtes-de-Provence, which embraces much of the Mediterranean inland slopes between Marseilles and Nice. This is a locale brimming with history. Seven centuries before the birth of Christ, Greek expeditions landed in southern Gaul and colonized the port of Massilla, the city now known as Marseilles. Following the conquest of Asia Minor by the Persian king, Cyrus, in 546 B.C., more Greeks carried their culture westward and founded the port colonies of Monoikos (Monaco) and Kikai (Nice). Several centuries later, the Romans arrived and occupied the "Province," for which its name remains.

Much of the Côtes-de-Provence wine production is consumed along the glitzy nearby Côte d'Azur. A large portion of its vineyards are devoted to the rather ordinary Carignane variety. Such plantings, along with some untidy vineyards, stoke the fires of an ongoing controversy about the Côtes-de-Provence red and rosé wines lacking finesse, being underaged and overpriced, and whether the district deserves the AOC status received in 1977.

❖ OTHER REGIONS ❖

❖ THE SOUTHWEST: CAHORS, GAILLAC, MADIRAN, JURA, AND SAVOIE

The Cahors district, located on the Lot River in the southwest of France, is best known for good red table wines made principally from Auxerrois, Merlot, Syrah, and Tannat vine varieties. This is a locale in which winegrowing is shared with other agriculture such as tobacco fields and fruit orchards. The best wines of the Cahors seem to exude a distinct note of plum and green-cigar-like character. Château de Cayrou and Château Pech de Jammes are two of the better estates in Cahors, and the local cooperative offers very good wine values.

Some historians believe that Gaillac may have existed as a winegrowing area before Bordeaux and, like the Rhône Valley, even before Roman occupation. In modern times the most notable Gaillac wines are whites produced from a rather broad array of varieties, including Mauzac, Muscat, Sauvignon Blanc, and Sémillon. Despite this selection of vine varieties being typically among the most bold in the generation of exotic fruit flavors, the Gaillacs are quite neutral. Gamay is cultivated for "*nouveau*-type" reds in the full-blown Beaujolais style, and some good sparkling wines are also made in Gaillac. The best for the money are offered by the cooperatives, which dominate production in the district.

Wines from the Madiran may be the best red table wines grown in the southwest region of France. With about equal portions of grapes from the varieties Cabernet Sauvignon, Cabernet Franc, and Tannat, Madiran red has an enticing character all its own, with firm tannins to allow long-term aging. The Madiran white, Pacherenc du Vic Bilh, is a blend of Courbu, Sauvignon Blanc, Sémillon, and other locally known varieties. Although equally complex, the white is no match for the quality of the red. This is a fascinating locale to visit, with at least a dozen fine estate vintners to be found, as well as the ever-present cooperatives that maintain the business of production on a steady course.

Vineyards of the Jura are situated south of the town of Pau on the lower slopes of the Pyrenees in a picturesque setting. The two principal vine varieties

FIGURE 6.56 Vineyards and village in the Jura. *(Courtesy of* Food and Wines from France.*)*

cultivated in this district are Gros Manseng and Petit Manseng—Gros for heavy yield and Petit for exceptionally aromatic and bold-flavored white table wines. The situation of the slopes allows them to gather intense daytime sun and heat, although they reach near freezing cold at night. During the vintage harvest season this near-ideal combination results in the grapes achieving exceptionally high sugar levels. Vineyards are manually harvested selectively, the first picking going for dry *moelleux* types. Later pickings, often infected with the noble mold, *Botrytis cinerea,* may surpass 30 percent sugar by weight in some vintage seasons. These grapes are relegated to *passerillage* and are partially fermented to a rather Sauternes-like sweet wine, justifiably the pride of Jurançon winegrowers.

To many people the thought of Jura and Savoie first brings skiing to mind. These are in a region located due east of Burgundy, situated on the eastern border between France and Switzerland. There are few trips through the French countryside that offer more beautiful views than the overlooks from the highway going up into the mountains from Burgundy enroute to Geneva. Here, vineyards are a bit scattered, sharing slopes and plateaus with cattle, row crops, and other agriculture.

The main wines of the Jura are those of AOC Côtes du Jura, AOC Arbois, and AOC Château-Chalon, the last being a township rather than an estate. Best are the light reds from Pinot Noir and other local varieties. Some are tasty, the most notable being from Arbois, birthplace of Louis Pasteur, but none of the reds in the district can be compared in any manner to Burgundy. One of the local Jura whites is Vin Jaune, translated as "yellow wine," which is more Spanish than French in character. This is coarse wine that is allowed to go through a secondary fermentation by *flor* yeasts, which impart a Sherrylike nutty flavor. Another white is the sweet Vin de Paille, made from grapes hung on racks to dry like raisins.

The Savoie is the most mountainous winegrowing locale in France and one of the most breathtaking vinicultural landscapes in all of Europe. It is located on the Upper Rhône River between Lyons and Geneva. Most Savoie wine production is light white table wines made from Chardonnay, the best of which are grown at Bugey and Crépy. The thin, fruity reds from Pinot Noir are pleasant, but the dense reds made from Mondeuse and Jacquère vines are serious fare. Some of these could rank among more noble growths if they were given a chance in the marketplace. Sparkling wines from the town of Seyssel in this area are building a good reputation.

❖ CORSICA

The sunny island of Corsica, located north of Sardinia and due west of Italy, is heavily influenced by Italian culture. Corsica's most famous historical figure is, of course, Napoleon Bonaparte. The island is replete with beautiful mountain vineyards, which yield ordinary, but dry and strong, wines, made principally from the white Malvoisie, Trebbiano, and Vermentino vines, along with the reds Nielluccio and Sciaccarello.

7
THE WINES OF ITALY

Depending on the bounty of each vintage, Italy generally produces 1.4 to 1.6 billion gallons of wine every year—with some vintages yielding more production than in France. In 1993 the 25 million gallons of wines shipped from Italy accounted for more than 38 percent of all wines imported into the United States that year.

The Italian mainland totals about 116,000 square miles, an area just slightly larger than the state of Arizona. Within this comparatively small geographical region, the Italians produce about four times the total volume of wine produced in the entire United States each year. There are approximately four million acres of land devoted to winegrowing in Italy. Three-quarters of the Italian wine produced is also consumed there, with per capita wine consumption at nearly 20 gallons annually.

The Italian "boot" peninsula reaches from the 37th to the 47th parallels north latitude, stretching from the Alps to within easy reach of Africa. Much of the terrain is austere and mountainous, the Alps and the Dolomites forming the northern extremes and the Apennines dividing almost the entire length of the country.

In the northern provinces bordering France, Switzerland, Austria, and Slovenia, the winters are cold and summers hot, although the climate is somewhat tempered by the Alpine barrier to cold winds from the north.

South of the Po River Italian mesoclimates take on a more temperate character, with warmer winters and cooler summmers. As one would expect, wines grown in these milder climes generally exhibit less strength and character than the distinctive classics cultivated in the upper Italian vineyards.

In southern Italy the climate is typically Mediterranean, with warm winters and sultry, humid summers, resulting in many wines that have high alcohol strength but are shy in overall character.

FIGURE 7.1 The wine regions of Italy.

FIGURE 7.2 Vineyards in northern
Italy. *(Courtesy of Italian Wine
Promotion Center; photo by Flavio
Faganello.)*

FIGURE 7.3
Etruscan amphorae,
first century B.C.
*(Courtesy of Lowie
Museum of
Anthropology,
University of
California,
Berkeley.)*

Italy's diversity of climates is matched by differing categories of soil types from one region to another. The result is a range of distinctive wine types, with variation even within individual regions. The comprehensive scope of Italian winegrowing is expanded further by the seemingly endless number of vine varieties cultivated across the nation. Some varieties, such as Nebbiolo, Barbera, Dolcetto, and Freisa, are limited to cooler mesoclimates. Others, including Trebbiano, Sangiovese, Malvasia, Moscato, and Verdicchio, are cultivated in warmer environs.

There are few places in Italy where vineyards do not constitute the major share of the agriculture. The vine is cultivated virtually everywhere—on the coastal plains, the plateaus, and the lower mountainsides. About 30 percent of the national work force in Italy is employed either full- or part-time in vineyards, most of which are owned by farmers in parcels that average less than three acres each.

There are nearly 200 different types of Italian wine recognized officially by controlled classification. Even so, less than 10 percent of the annual wine production is conducted under those regulatory parameters. It is, however, from this small portion that most of the wines reaching American retailers and restaurants are grown.

The largest export markets for Italy's wines are Germany, Switzerland, the United States, the United Kingdom, and France. The major share of exports to France and Germany are bulk lots of low-cost wines used in blending according to European Economic Community (EEC) rules.

Greeks arriving in Italy called it Enotria, or "the land of wine." There are records of Italian winegrowing that predate Rome by 1,000 years, but the culture and style of early Italian wines progressed in parallel with the Roman Empire—and regressed in much the same manner. As discussed in Chapter 2, Rome spread the art and science of winegrowing throughout what is now western Europe.

The many writings of Cato the Elder, Columella, and Pliny the Elder, among others that have survived history, portray an Italian winegrowing art that was remarkably advanced even before the advent of Christianity. There is considerable evidence to suggest that the Roman vineyards of 2,000 years ago were quite similar to some of those found in rural Italy yet today.

University of Maryland archaeologists have excavated an ancient vineyard from beneath the volcanic debris at Pompeii, the legendary Roman city destroyed by the eruption of Mount Vesuvius in A.D. 79. That dig revealed that these vines were planted about four feet apart and trained on chestnut, poplar, and willow trellis stakes, with several hollows dug in the soil at the base of each vine to collect rainwater. Such cultivation practices are still employed in many Italian vineyards. The citizens of ancient Pompeii enjoyed outdoor restaurants and wine retail shops. A typical wine merchant would provide tables and seats for customers, displaying wines on shelves where cups and glasses were also stored. The wine "bartender" would pour and serve wines from a countertop that generally faced a busy street.

Benedict of Nursia, the founder of Benedictine monasticism, played an extremely important role in the history of Western civilization. Born circa A.D. 480, St. Benedict studied in Rome and, sensing a call to the monastic life, spent several years in seclusion near the ruins of one of Nero's palaces. Neighboring monks invited him to be their abbot, but Benedict's discipline was more severe than they had anticipated, and it was decided to assassinate him with poisoned wine. Witnesses attested that when Benedict raised the cup of his doom and made the sign of the cross, the cup shattered, saving his life.

St. Benedict established another monastery at Monte Cassino, in central Italy, with a dozen or so monks of a more obedient nature. His rule emphasized agricultural work, particularly in the farming of grain, olive oil, and wine. Benedict remained committed to his ethics of moderation in the consumption of both wine and food.

The lofty reputation of Benedict's monks won for them a measure of peace from the violence and pillaging that swept Europe after the fall of Rome. Vineyards could again be tended without harassment, and lay workers in search of sanctuary soon joined the vigneron work forces in the monastery. This protective, productive life-style was soon emulated in monasteries across Europe.

FIGURE 7.4 Fifth-century fresco from the Castello Buon Consiglio. *(Courtesy of Italian Wine Promotion Center; photo by Flavio Faganello.)*

Benedictine monasteries remain monuments to the widespread development of commercial European winegrowing.

Yet, although the monks had inherited the vineyard lands of Europe, they also found themselves amid continued invasion from the barbarians to the north and east. Following the death of St. Benedict, circa 543, the Italian abbeys were sacked by Byzantines (Turks) from the east who held these outposts for only a short time before they themselves were overcome by Germanic Lombards from the north.

The Benedictine monastery of Monte Cassino was reconstructed in 717, and once more the winegrowing arts were practiced in the vineyards of St. Benedict. The Black Monks, a suborder of Benedictines, relaxed certain aspects of the strict code originally laid down by St. Benedict. Wine from some of these vineyards became so highly regarded that it was offered as a prize to winners of the Olympic games.

Winegrowing declined along with the fall of the Roman Empire. Indeed, vines and wines virtually ceased to exist in Italy for several centuries. The sparse records that remain indicate that is was not until the ninth century that Italians resumed the culture of the grape. But Italian red wines in the Middle Ages lacked the color, tannins, and strength that the classical Roman wines needed to endure decades of maturation.

It was during this period that Greek-speaking refugees from the Byzantine conquest of Greece built the magnificent cathedral of Greco di Gerace, largest of all in Calabria, located in the toe of the Italian boot. These refugees grew the fabled *Greco di Gerace* white wine on soils so poor that often two vines struggled to yield just one bottle.

Greco di Tufo, also white and one of the lightest of Italian wines, has origins similar to those of the heavier, stronger Greco di Gerace. Both wines have their roots in the church. Greco di Tufo was grown at the Benedictine hermitage of St. William, built high on Monte Vergine in Campania near Naples during the eleventh century.

In 1282 a Florentine wine merchants' guild was formed, perhaps the first such regulatory body for marketing wines. It was unquestionably the ancestor of the modern-day consorzi, which operate in much the same capacity of behalf of Italian wines today.

A white wine called *Trubidiane,* which resembled the *Trebulan* of Caesar's time and the *Trebbiano* of modern times, was exported to London in 1373. English literature mentions the wines of Florence and *Lacryma Christi,* as well as *Leattic,* known today as *Aleatico.*

Most of the wine produced in Italy during the Middle Ages was also consumed there, although some was exported to England. There is, however, little evidence to indicate that Italian wine exports were encouraged with any enthusiasm or effort in this era.

Despite some eloquent phrases quoted from Michelangelo and Galileo in praise of wine, there is little evidence that the Italian wine art benefited as much from the Renaissance as the other art forms. Yet there are a few elaborate sixteenth- and seventeenth-century Italian wineglasses in museums, indicating the De'Medici influence on wine.

It was not until the mid-1700s that Italian winegrowing began to attract agricultural scholars. Even then, another century passed before any improvement in wine products became noticeable. Cyrus Redding, a British wine enthusiast, wrote of his experiences during an 1850 trek through Italian wine country: "Italian wines have stood still and remain without improvement."

Perhaps it was the lack of regimentation which then—and still today, to a large degree—separated the Italian winegrowing industry from the French. In assembling material to write a treatise on Italian wines, one could easily identify

FIGURE 7.5 St. Giovanni Church, home of the Shroud of Turin. *(Photo by author.)*

several hundred grape varieties cultivated for commercial winemaking across Italy. Some wine varieties have been given different names in different regions, and there is a seemingly endless number of blends, some named by custom more than geographical origin. Thus, one can understand why Redding may have felt that the Italian wine industry was rather chaotic.

Whether the Italians approached this problem as a matter of housecleaning, or they observed the classified French wines gaining profitable footholds in export markets, or for another reason, in the early 1930s the *consorzio* system was introduced in Italy.

❖ CLASSIFICATION

An Italian governmental decree authorized the creation of local wine associations called *consorzi,* or consortiums, each with its own constitution designed to regulate wine production and marketing in its particular region or locale. The *consorzi* created geographic limits and production standards and authorized district names of origin that had real meaning. The *consorzi* also enforced national regulations and promoted Italian wine exports. This was the first national effort to formulate definitions and standards.

The *consorzio* system had several early problems, including the differences in the individual constitutions from region to region and renegade vintners who refused to acknowledge their authority. Yet, despite these and other difficulties, establishment of the *consorzi* was the first step toward organizing the then vast and chaotic vineyard system of the nation.

In 1963, the Italian government issued the Italian Wine Law, which fixed the basis for wine industry control according to the principles endorsed by the EEC. This comprehensive statute, modeled on the French Appellation Controlée (AOC) regulations, specifically defines areas of production, designates the grape varieties that may be grown in the various regions, and regulates wine quality. The Italian wine decree is known as the DOC statute, the Denominazione di Origine Controllata, which translates as "controlled appellation of origin."

The original law has since been elaborated to have four different wine grades, as explained in the following paragraphs.

VINO DA TAVOLA

Wines of the lowest grade were designated Denominazione di Origine Semplice. Wines in this category originated within specified areas, but production methods were not defined. This grade was subsequently replaced by the EEC grade of "table wine," or Vino da Tavola, which remains today.

INDICAZIONI GEOGRAFICHE TIPICHE (IGT)

The Indicazioni Geografiche Tipiche (IGT) classification was established in 1995 for wines having a specific character resulting from typical soil type and climate, as well as for approved vine varieties within a specific geographical locale. In short, the IGT classification is much like the French Vins de Pays with some of the VDQS limitations.

DENOMINAZIONE DI ORIGINE CONTROLLATA (DOC)

The next higher grade, and the most well known, is Denominazione di Origine Controllata (DOC). To qualify for this category, Italian wines must conform to production rules laid down by the *consorzio* for each particular region or locale of origin. The regulations for DOC wines also govern bottling, alcohol levels, and aging requirements. A DOC wine carries the initials "DOC" on a red label affixed to the bottle, often as a seal over the capsule.

Depending on the region involved and the assigned category, Italian wines may be geographically designated with the name of a large region, such as *Chianti;* or a district, such as *Asti;* or a village, such as *Montalcino.* Wines may also be named for the sole or primary grape variety used in their production, but if they are DOC designated, they must also carry the name of the place where the grapes were grown, such as *Nebbiolo d'Alba,* indicating that Nebbiolo is the grape and Alba is the place.

A national 28-member committee of industry and government officials considers applications from vintners for DOC recommendation. On the committee's advice, the applications are processed by the Ministries of Agriculture, Commerce, and Industry. Given recommendation, DOC status is conferred by presidential appointment. For a table wine to receive a DOC seal, at least 20 percent of the vineyards in the region must meet the standards and receive endorsement. For dessert and sparkling wines, 30 percent is required. If the vintner is a *consorzio* member, a paper seal authenticating this association is placed over the closure or capsule of the bottle.

Yet large portions of each region remained unclassified, and it soon became rather obvious that the wine world would demand a guarantee for each endorsement.

DENOMINAZIONE DI ORIGINE CONTROLLATA E GARANTITA (DOCG)

The sought-after guarantee arrived with the highest category in Italian wine classification, the DOCG (Denominazione di Origine Controllata e Garantita), which ensures that the appellation of origin is controlled and guaranteed by both the *consorzio* and the national government. This designation is reserved for wines of only the highest distinction.

There are, at this writing, only 13 DOCG winegrowing districts in all of Italy, as follows:

WINE DISTRICT	REGION
Asti Spumante	Piedmont
Barolo	Piedmont
Barbaresco	Piedmont
Gattinara	Piedmont
Albana di Romagna	Emilia-Romagna
Brunello di Montalcino	Tuscany
Carmignano	Tuscany
Chianti	Tuscany
Vernaccia di San Gimignano	Tuscany
Vin Nobile di Montepulciano	Tuscany
Sagrantino di Montefalco	Umbria
Torgiano Rosso Riserva	Umbria
Taurasi	Campania

The term *Classico* on a label signifies that the wine was grown from an inner, and superior, portion of a larger region. For example, *Chianti Classico* indicates the choice inner district of the Chianti region. When the DOC seal is approved, other terms of identification may also appear on an Italian wine label, such as the following:

abboccato	slightly sweet
amabile	moderately sweet
annata	year
azienda agricola	winegrowing estate
bianco	white
botte	barrel or small cask
bottiglia	bottle
casa vinicola	negotiant
classico	classic center of a DOC zone
consorzio	consortium of wine authorities
dolce	sweet
etichetta	label
fattoria	vineyard estate
frizzante	slightly effervescent
imbottigliato	bottled by or at
liquoroso	wine with brandy added
nello stabilimento	on the producer's property
passito	wines made from late-harvest grapes
produttore	producer
recioto	wine made from dried grapes
rosato	rosé or blush
rosso	red
secco	dry
spumante	sparkling
tenuta	estate
vendemmia	vintage
vigna, vigneto	vineyard
vitigno	vine variety
zona d'origine	zone, or district, of origin

Descriptive terms for wine, each *consorzio* prescribing its own variations in levels of meaning, interpretation, and regulation, are also allowed, such as the following:

riserva	reserved for longer aging in barrel and/or bottle as determined by each *consorzio* regulation
vecchio	old or aged
superiore	higher in alcohol strength

Italy has 20 carefully defined winegrowing regions, each producing wines of distinctive types and styles. Although the northern Italian provinces of the Piedmont, Veneto, and Tuscany are generally regarded as the leaders in quality Italian wine, the import price leaders in the American marketplace are wines coming primarily from the central and southern reaches of Italy.

FIGURE 7.6   Vineyard landscape in the Piedmont. *(Photo by author.)*

◈ PIEDMONT

Piedmont means foot of the mountains, and the region is aptly named, as it is located at the foot of the Alps in the far northwestern corner of Italy. Some wine experts consider this region Italy's best. With its classic whites, reds, sparklers, and being the birthplace of vermouth, it is certainly the most diverse of the fine wine provinces. Visitors will also enjoy truly superb candy, crafted in old wine towns and villages, as well as the world's finest hazelnuts and white truffles.

As most of the automobile production of Italy takes place in Torino, it is thus a very industrial capital city of the Piedmont. It also features historical treasures, such as the famous Shroud of Turin, thought by some to have been wrapped around Christ after his crucifixion.

Popular with tourists are small restaurants in the central city square of Torino, where barks, herbs, and spices were first used to flavor Italian sweet vermouth years ago. It is said that the secret recipe of Cinzano is made from no less than 92 such ingredients.

Commercial winegrowing in the Piedmont is documented well before the beginning of the sixteenth century. As Cyrus Redding implied, its history was not a glorious one, nor very progressive. Of particular note, however, was one Giuseppe Garibaldi, whose sage advice to winegrowers, based on his knowledge of French science, made him a national hero. Garibaldi had been a militant revolutionary throughout his life. He was twice captured and condemned to death, first by the Austrians and then by the French, each time escaping to another country. In 1854 he again returned to his beloved Italy and effected an alliance of compromise with Victor Emmanuel II, a liberal nobleman aspiring to be king of Italy. Garibaldi, long since a seasoned veteran, led Emmanuel's forces victoriously through battles in Sicily, Naples, and Gaeta.

In 1861, Victor Emmanuel II was proclaimed king and Italy was unified, except for Rome, which was proclaimed a papal possession. Garibaldi went to war several more times and was eventually elected a member of the Italian Parliament in 1874. The later years of his life, until he died in 1882, were devoted to vineyard experiments that were to become everlasting examples of science and order in Piemontese vineyards.

The city of Asti, just several miles from Victor Emmanuel's palace, is the production center for the very fruity Spumante sparkling white wines well

known throughout the U.S. marketplace. Much of this light, very fruity wine is produced by the *charmat* (tank-fermented) process from several varieties of Muscat *(Moscato)* vines.

About 20 miles south of Asti is Alba, a small town famous for mighty red table wines grown from Nebbiolo vines cultivated in the Barolo and Barbaresco districts. Arneis, an archaic white wine vine variety, is being resurrected to prominence there by the Ceretto winegrowing family.

During the harvest season grape pickers awake to a light fog *(nebbia)* over the vineyards. This cool mist serves to chill the vines and preserve the precious sugars that would otherwise be lost to higher-temperature respiration. The name of the Nebbiolo vine thus translates as "the fog," and the clusters of grapes on these vines do indeed have a gray-purple, foggy appearance. Nebbiolo's wine is dark ruby red with flavors of plums, licorice, and a bit of pine resin.

Classic *Barolo* has traditionally been a coarse, dense red wine made from the great Nebbiolo vine, generally undrinkable until aging for a decade or longer, or even for several decades. Better vineyard management, less extraction of astringent phenols during fermentation, and large investments in oak barrels, among other factors, have resulted in Barolo's becoming a serious contender among the grand red estate wines of the world. Barolo can be released for sale after three years of aging, *Barolo Riserva* must be four years old, and *Barolo Riserva Speciale* requires five years of aging before it can be sold.

Barbaresco, grown in a neighboring area, is softer than Barolo and usually has less body and slightly less color intensity. It was its gentility that, until recently, often made Barbaresco the choice for drinking among younger vintage Piedmont reds. Barbaresco can be marketed after two years of aging, Riserva after three, and Riserva Speciale after four. Both Barolo and Barbaresco must be made exclusively from Nebbiolo, and both are DOCG classified.

Gattinara and *Ghemme* are wines made from Nebbiolo vines blended with wines from other varieties grown in the region. These are generally considered somewhat inferior to Barolo and Barbaresco, but still a better bet for the money than the simple varietal Nebbiolo wines.

Although the Nebbiolo vine enjoys the highest regard in the Piedmont, the Barbera is more widely planted throughout the region because of its greater productivity. Barbera wines are dry, fruity red table wines, typically rather

FIGURE 7.8 Oak aging casks and barrels in the Ceretto cellars. *(Photo by author.)*

intensely pigmented with ruby red hues, and quite acidic. This variety, too, has benefited well from new technology in production and vinification. *Barbera d'Asti* is one of the most well known wines made from the variety. It is also made into a few rather sweet wines, as well as some *frizzante* (slightly effervescent) offerings.

Grignolino, Freisa, and Dolcetto are other vine varieties that yield notable red wines grown in the Piedmont region. Grignolino typically produces light, reddish-orange dry red wine that varies in flavor and finish from vintner to vintner. Well-made Freisa has a light berry character which, if captured by a talented winemaker, can result in a pleasant, fruity, rather Lower-Rhone-like, light red wine. Dolcetto is darker than the other two in color and is usually a bit heavier, often slightly tannic and astringent, needing a bit more aging. Three good examples of these wine types are *Grignolino d'Asti, Freisa di Cheri,* and *Dolcetto d'Alba.*

East of Alba, and just north of Genoa, is the town of Gavi, where the Cortese vine produces a dry, typically stony-citrus-honey-flavored white wine called Gavi di Gavi, which gained widespread attention throughout the wine world during the 1980s—much of which was generated by astronomical prices.

Despite *Gavi di Gavi* being comparatively new to the world market, it is nevertheless centuries old in the small locale where this complex white wine is produced. Tenuta Rusca was established on the twelfth-century Santa Seraffa estate, where the Rusca family now produces some of the most sumptuous Gavi grown in the region, more fresh and expressive than most, with a rich buttery-olive bouquet and lingering vanilla-fig flavors.

Gaja is one of the premier brand names for top quality Piedmont wines—with prices to match. The family firm was founded in 1859, and today Angelo Gaja is the quintessential "new breed" Italian vintner, adapting advanced winemaking methods and thus revolutionizing standards for traditional Gavi di Gavi and Barbaresco. As if the Italians didn't already have a profusion of vine varieties available for cultivation, they are now adding new plantings of Chardonnay and Cabernet Sauvignon. Angelo Gaja is one of the leaders of this development, and his wines are on a par with the best grown anywhere.

Bruno and Marcello Ceretto are the land barons of the Piedmont, overseeing more than 60 acres of top vineyard properties, such as the Bricco Rocche in Barolo and Bricco Asili in Barbaresco. The Ceretto label assures dark, heavy, traditional Nebbiolo reds with the fullest and richest of textures.

Carlo Gancia studied winemaking in the Champagne region of France in the late 1840s and subsequently returned to his native Piedmont to commence building his own wine estate. Gancia set about making sparkling wines from rich fruit-flavored Muscat grapes, so sweet that bottle fermentation pressures reached higher levels than the bottles could withstand. In 1865 he devised a method by which he could bottle partially fermented wine so that residual sugar was precisely calculated and bottles were not broken, thus producing the first of Italy's now famous "spumante" sparkling wines. The Charmat bulk-tank method is often used today to make Gancia Asti Spumante.

It was in 1863 that the initial production of a dark amber, richly flavored "Italian style" aperitif was shipped from the cellars of Martini, Rossi & Sola in the Piedmont. That firm is now famous as Martini & Rossi, the world's premier vintner of sweet vermouth. The company name is equally accepted as one of the leading producers of Asti sparkling wine.

Since 1981, the Pio Cesare winery has steadfastly held to the tradition of making Barolo and Barbaresco in the dense, high-extract style, some vintages taking decades of aging to reach maturity. After years of experimentation, careful application of new winemaking methods is bringing Pio Cesare reds to market with the same heavy character, but with drinkability achieved with far less cellaring. In stark contrast, Pio Cesare Gavi is fermented in stainless steel to preserve a rich fruit character, bottled fresh, and marketed promptly.

PIEDMONT DOC AND DOCG GROWTHS

Asti Spumante (DOCG)
Barolo (DOCG)
Barbaresco (DOCG)
Gattinara (DOCG)

Barbera d'Alba
Barbera d'Asti
Barbera del Monferrato
Boca
Brachetto d'Acqui
Bramaterra
Carema
Colli Tortonesi
Cortese dell'Alto Monferrato
Dolcetto d'Acqui
Dolcetto d'Alba
Dolcetto d'Asti
Dolcetto delle Langhe Monregalesi
Dolcetto di Diano d'Alba
Dolcetto di Dogliani
Dolcetto d'Ovada
Erbaluce di Caluso, or Caluso
Fara

Freisa d'Asti

Freisa di Chieri

Gabiano

Gavi, or Cortese di Gavi

Ghemme

Grignolino del Monferrato Casalese

Lessona

Loazzolo

Malvasia di Casorzo d'Asti

Malvasia di Castelnuovo Don Bosco

Nebbiolo d'Alba

Roero

Rubino di Cantavenna

Ruche di Castagnole Monferrato

Sizzano

⊠ VALLE D'AOSTA

Located north of the Piedmont, in the extreme northwestern corner of Italy, the Valle d'Aosta is the smallest Italian viticultural region, perhaps more famous for ski resorts than for winegrowing. Visible in the distance, to the north, is the spectacular Matterhorn peak in neighboring Switzerland.

The snow-capped Alps rise majestically, dwarfing the hillside vineyards along the Aosta Valley. The comparatively small yield of richly concentrated Nebbiolo grapes is made into a wine called *Donnaz,* a rather coarse red that is the hallmark of the region. Petit Rouge grapes are cultivated at higher elevations to make *Enfer d'Arvier,* a rather acidic, but pleasantly berrylike, dry red wine. There is a single regionwide DOC, aptly called the Valle d'Aosta.

⊠ LIGURIA

To the south of the Piedmont, along the Italian Riviera playground of the wealthy, is the Ligurian winegrowing region. Although it may not be the most important wine-producing locale in Italy, Liguria is surely one of the country's most picturesque.

At its center is the historical port of Genoa, and in the southeastern portion of La Spezia, growers have carved vineyards into the cliffs, many of which can be reached only by boat. Between the cliffs and the sea a delicate dry white wine called *Cinqueterre* is grown, its name referring to the five villages located there. Cinqueterre is made from blends of wines grown from Albarolo, Bosco, and Vermentio vines.

Dolceacqua, sometimes called *Rossese di Dolceacqua,* is a heavy, fruity red wine, which, despite the romance of Cinqueterre, is usually a better value.

LIGURIA DOC GROWTHS

Cinqueterre

Colli di Luni

Riviera Ligure di Ponente

Rossese di Dolceacqua, or Dolceacqua

FIGURE 7.9 The village of Arona on Lake Maggiore. *(Photo by author.)*

◈ LOMBARDY

The Lombardy region, located northeast of the Piedmont, is among the largest and busiest provinces in Italy, as its capital city, Milan, is one of the most important cultural and commercial centers in Europe.

In the northern portion of Lombardy the Adda River flows through the Valtellina Basin, where vineyards of Nebbiolo yield the most noted red wines grown in the region. Most of the wines of the Valtellina are named after subdistricts, breathtakingly beautiful vineyard landscapes rising into the Alpine foothills to altitudes exceeding 2,500 feet above sea level. The subdistricts of highest regard are Grumello, Inferno, and Sassella. *Sfursat* is a very heavy-bodied red wine made in the Valtellina from partially dried Nebbiolo grapes.

At the far western extreme of Lombardy is magnificent Lake Maggiore, which, although not a center for fine winegrowing, is a place where visitors can easily find Italian wine, food, and scenery combined into an unequalled synergy of the good life.

Situated in the southern heart of Lombardy are the Oltrepo Pavese vineyards, which produce wines with such catchy names as *Sangue di Giuda,* or "Judas blood." Barbera vines are cultivated here to make sturdy red *Buttafuoco,* which is often blended with wines from other red varieties to make the coarse and hearty *Bonarda.*

A rather dark rosé, called *Chiaretto del Garda,* or "Claret of Garda," is made from Gropello vines grown on the southwestern shores of Lake Garda, another grand vacation mecca, which borders the region of Veneto.

LOMBARDY DOC GROWTHS

Botticino

Capriano del Colle

Cellatica

Colli Morenici Mantovani del Garda

Franciacorta

Lambrusco Mantovano

Lugana

Oltrepo Pavese

Riviera del Garda Bresciano, or Garda Bresciano

San Colombano al Lambro

San Martino della Battaglia

Valcalepio

Valtellina

❖ VENETO

With an output of about 250 million gallons per vintage, the Veneto is consistently among the top five Italian regions in volume of wine produced each vintage. Situated between the Piave and Po Rivers and the Lake Garda resorts, it produces some of the most well recognized, and most reasonably priced, wines to be found in American wine shops and restaurants. Along the Swiss border, this region is mountainous, flattening out as it drops southeastward to its capital city of Venice and the Adriatic Sea. In the Euganean hills of the Province of Padua are vineyards that are more than 1,000 years old. Seventeen *communes* there produce white and red wines called *Colli Euganei.*

Bardolino is quickly recognized by American wine enthusiasts. This light, dry red table wine is grown primarily from Corvina and Molinara vines, but some vintners blend these with wines grown from Rondinella and other grape varieties. Minimum alcohol allowed by *consorzio* regulation is 11.5 percent by volume. Bardolino is grown across a group of 16 *communes* in the Province of Verona on the southeastern shores of Lake Garda. Six of these *communes* form the inner *Bardolino Classico* district. The wine may be labeled *Bardolino Superiore* if aged in the vintner's cellars for at least one entire calendar year before being released for sale.

Although the world hears much about Venice—and rightly so, as its canals and gondolas and romantic charisma are truly unique— it is the much smaller city of Verona that is the true wine capital of the Veneto. Verona is the city of Dante and his *Inferno,* of Shakespeare's *Romeo and Juliet,* and of many other literary milestones. It is also a mecca of truly superb small restaurants, serving first-rate Italian cuisine matched with wine from their local vineyards.

The crown jewel of fine Veneto is *Valpolicella,* silky-smooth red wine grown from vineyards cultivated upon the hillsides facing the Adige River to the east of Bardolino. Valpolicella is blended from essentially the same varieties as Bardolino and identified across 19 *communes,* 5 of which have been awarded the coveted *Valpolicella Classico* designation. Wines grown exclusively in the Valpantena Valley may also add the Valpantena name to their labels, as in "Valpolicella Valpantena." *Recioto della Valpolicella* is made from grape berries that ripen only on the outside of the cluster—the choice berries that receive the greatest exposure to the sun. Such production is more highly controlled than that of the standard Valpolicella. Minimum alcohol strength required for Valpolicella is 12 percent, and, if aged for at least one year in the vintner's cellars before being released, it may be labeled *Valpolicella Superiore.*

The classic *Amarone* is made from grapes harvested from Corvina, Molinara, and Rondinella vines cultivated in Valpolicella Classico *communes.* Harvested grape clusters are placed on bamboo or straw lattice trays to dehydrate for several months. Each day the clusters are turned to prevent rotting and to promote an even greater

FIGURE 7.10 Juliet's balcony in the ancient Veneto city of Verona. *(Photo by Philip DiBelardino.)*

evaporation of natural grape water content in order to concentrate sugars and flavors. The shriveled grapes are crushed and fermentation progesses slowly, resulting in a high-alcohol and bitter red wine, which is then barrel aged for several years to achieve the rich, full-bodied, matured elegance of expensive Amarone.

A fragrant white table wine is made in the Veneto from the Prosecco vine cultivated on the hillsides around the village of Conegliano north of Venice. As in the Piedmont, the Veneto has added new plantings of Cabernet Sauvignon and Merlot to its stable of vine varieties. Vintners generally add a local name to the grape varietals on their labels, such as *Cabernet di Pramaggiore* or *Merlot di Montello.*

Located about 12 miles east of Verona is the small town of Soave, which gives its name (or vice versa) to the light white wine grown there known to most everyone in the wine world. Made from the grape varieties Trebbiano and Garganego, Soave has a crisp green apple, citrusy character at its best. Otherwise, it is rather neutral and common. *Recioto di Soave,* like Recioto della Valpolicella, is made from the outer berries of each cluster of grapes. The district *consorzio* regulates special geographical designations and natural alcohol requirements for *Soave Classico* and *Soave Superiore* in much the same manner as for Bardolino and Valpolicella.

The Anselmi brand has become one of the standards of quality in the Veneto. Once a large producer of ordinary wines, the Anselmi family have downsized their operations to concentrate on truly superb Bardolino, Soave, and Valpolicella wines. Production is directed in a winery that demonstrates the epitome of sanitary methods.

Three generations of Bolla family winemakers have followed innkeeper Abele Bolla's founding of the now famous wine estate. Bolla's great pride was in offering guests the very finest wines available, and he visited many other wineries to discover new wine types and better winemaking methods. Having three strong sons at his side, Bolla expanded his vision to embrace his own wine production and developed a passionate insistence on top quality. The Bolla name today is synonymous with fine Soave and Valpolicella.

The Masi winery in Verona began in the 1400s with the Boscaini family, who still operate the estate. The Boscainis are among the oldest continuous vintners in Italy. Despite this classic history, Masi is one of the most modern innovators of winemaking technology in the Veneto. The firm is best known for its superb Valpolicella and has set the standard for Amarone.

The founding of Santa Margherita is quite recent by Italian standards. The Marzotto family, famous as producers of fine textiles in Venice, commenced wine operations in the mid-1950s. The Santa Margherita label has been perhaps

the single greatest influence in bringing varietal wines from the Pinot Grigio (Pinot Gris) vine to world attention and appreciation.

VENETO DOC GROWTHS

Bardolino
Bianco di Custoza
Breganze
Colli Berici
Colli di Conegliano
Colli Euganei
Gambellara
Lessini Durello
Lison-Pramaggiore
Montello e Colli Asolani
Piave, or Vini del Piave
Prosecco di Conegliano-Valdobbiadene
Soave
Valpolicella

✥ TRENTINO-ALTO ADIGE

The Trentino-Alto Adige is the most northern of the Italian wine regions, better known to some as the Italian Tyrol. As the Alsace is a bit of Germany in France, the Trentino-Alto Adige is a bit of Alpine Switzerland in Italy.

Viticulture in the region dates back to the formation of the Roman Empire. Then, as now, parts of the Adige Valley, from below Trentino to Bolzano and Merano, were literally covered with vineyards. The Alps provide a barrier for the Adige vineyards, protecting them from cold wind blowing down from the Scandinavian peninsula and northern Europe.

FIGURE 7.11 Trentino vineyard terraces. *(Courtesy of Italian Wine Promotion Center; photo by Flavio Faganello.)*

The wines of this region are also Teutonic in character; the vine variety Gewürztraminer is native to the Alto Adige locale. As described in Chapter 6, the *Traminer* vine produced wine of a *Gewürz*, or "spicy", character when grown in the Alsace, and thus the compound name, Gewürz-Traminer. The village of Terlano is the center of one of the most notable areas of white wine production, principally from *Pinot Bianco* (Pinot Blanc), Traminer, and Johannnisberg Riesling vines.

Red wines from the upper part of the region, approaching Bolzano, are a bit astringent but usually well balanced for tartness. Lake Caldaro is one of several highly regarded red wine locales, as is Santa Maddalena.

The lower valley, the Trentino, cultivates vineyards of the Teroldego variety, which yields heavy red table wines labeled with the same name. The native Moscato, along with newer plantings of Cabernet Sauvignon, Pinot Noir, and Johannisberg Riesling, are also grown in the Trentino vicinity. *Casteller* is a rather heavy blush wine grown in the lower valley.

TRENTINO-ALTO ADIGE DOC GROWTHS

Alto Adige

Caldaro, or Lago di Caldaro

Casteller

Sorni

Teroldego Rotaliano

Trentino

Trento

Valdadige

✪ FRIULI-VENEZIA GIULIA

In the comparatively small region of Friuli-Venezia Giulia, situated along the Adriatic seacoast in northeastern Italy, wine has been grown for so long that it is not certain when it originated, certainly long before the birth of Christ. This is perhaps the single finest white wine region in Italy.

Collio, a small locale situated west of the town of Gorizia, produces mostly white table wines and some sparkling whites, which are marketed as *Collio Goriziano.*

The principal vine varieties cultivated here are Ribolla, Malvasia, and Tocai. These and other varietals, such as Pinot Bianco (blanc), and Pinot Nero (noir), and Traminer, are also permitted the Collio Goriziano label, provided the wine so designated has been made exclusively from the variety named on that label.

With fifth-generation family management, Felluga wines continue a tradition that has grown to embrace several estates exceeding 300 acres of fine wine vineyards. Felluga Pinot Grigio is one of the best produced in the region.

FRIULI-VENEZIA GIULIA DOC GROWTHS

Aquileia, or Aquileia del Friuli

Carso

Collio Goriziano, or Collio

Colli Orientali del Friuli

Grave del Friuli

Isonzo, or Isonzo del Friuli

Latisana, or Latisana del Friuli

✦ EMILIA-ROMAGNA

Bordering the south of both Lombardy and the Veneto, the Emilia-Romagna Region produces more than 250 million gallons of wine annually—the second-largest volume of wine production among the regions in Italy.

This historical region centers on the famous city of Parma, world renowned for some of the greatest cheese (Parmesan) and ham (prosciutto) in the world. Thirty miles to the southeast is Modena, whose historical wine and food production is highly contrasted by ultramodern Ferrari sports car production.

Relatively little of the wine produced in the Emilia-Romagna ever leaves there. One remarkable exception is *Lambrusco,* a rather sweet, or *amabile,* purple-red wine, something of a "sweet nouveau," with a bouquet that some say is reminiscent of violets. Lambrusco caught on across the United States as the "in" wine during the 1970s, replaced by wine "coolers" as the fad wine of the early 1980s. Some Lambrusco *amabile* is still exported to America, but far less than during the 1970s. The great share of Lambrusco has reverted to the drier style preferred by Italians. It is grown in four locales centered by the city of Modena.

The native Albana vine is cultivated, a few miles to the southeast of Bologna city, to produce large clusters of white grapes. *Albana di Romagna* is one of the newer DOCG growths, the best of which are sweet white wines grown in vineyards in the Apennine foothills. Other wines, Sangiovese reds and Trebbiano whites, are also grown and shipped from the Emilia-Romagna. Principal among these are *Trebbiano di Romagna,* which is grown east of Bologna, and *Sangiovese di Romagna* from vineyards situated in the southern perimeter of the region along the Tuscan border.

EMILIA-ROMAGNA DOCG AND DOC GROWTHS

    Albana di Romagna (DOCG)

    Bianco di Scandiano
    Bosco Eliceo
    Cagnina di Romagna
    Colli Bolognesi-Monte San Pietro
    Colli di Parma
    Colli Piacentini
    Lambrusco Grasparossa di Castelvetro
    Lambrusco Reggiano
    Lambrusco Salamino di Santa Croce
    Lambrusco di Sorbara
    Montuni del Reno
    Pagadebit di Romagna
    Sangiovese di Romagna
    Trebbiano di Romagna

✦ TUSCANY

Tuscany, situated south of the Emilia-Romagna, cultivates some very famous and noble vineyard growths, as well as some that are ordinary. About 125 million gallons of wine are produced in a typical vintage across the entire region of Tuscany. Although not the largest producer, Tuscany is unquestionably the most historical and considered by most wine authorities to be the single most important winegrowing region in Italy. Many are also of the opinion that Tuscany is the most characteristically "Italian" of Italy's wine regions. Introducing this topic of conversation in Italy, outside Tuscany, instantly brings controversy and argument.

The Etruscans cultivated vineyards in Tuscany during the ninth century B.C., and the Romans who followed them advanced the art and craft of wine-growing. During and after the fall of the Roman Empire, the Christians advanced grape growing and winemaking even further. In the Middle Ages, Tuscany was a frequent battleground. Its vineyards were often laid waste, only to be planted again and again. Florence, "Firenze" in Italian, is the magnificent capital city of the region; here the Renaissance first flowered under the influence of the de'Medici family. Following her marriage to Henry II, Catherine de'Medici carried haute cuisine to France, teaching the French and all of Europe how to use a fork at the table.

Tuscany was the birthplace of Amerigo Vespucci, Leonardo da Vinci, Machiavelli, and Giovanni da Verazano. Florence was where Michelangelo worked, as did Galileo and many other noted geniuses in the arts and sciences. Artists from around the world still study in Florence. Yet wine, along with olive oil, remains the most important agricultural production in the region.

Perhaps the best known of all Italian wines is Chianti, a dry everyday red wine grown primarily from Sangiovese vines. In recent years the Tuscans have had difficulties in agreeing on precise boundaries for the Chianti and Chianti Classico districts. Grape crops are governed for Chianti Classico, and wines made from these grapes must have an alcohol content of at least 11.5 percent by volume.

Some of the Chianti wines are made by a traditional system called the *governo* process, in which up to 10 percent of the grapes are left to dry while the rest ferment. After fermentation the dehydrated grapes are added to the new wine, and fermentation resumes. Some of the sweetness and all of the raisinlike flavor

FIGURE 7.12 The harvest in Chianti Classico. (*Courtesy of Frederick Wildman.*)

FIGURE 7.13 Bottling at the Mellini cellars in Chianti. *(Courtesy of Frederick Wildman.)*

remains in the finished wine, resulting in complexities of clove, anise, and cherry flavors. Chianti is typically light to medium in body and has a pleasant tannic astringency on the palate. If a Chianti wine has a minimum of 12 percent alcohol and is allowed to age for two years or more, vintners may add the term *vecchio* (aged) on their labels. Chianti Classico may also be labeled *vecchio* under the same conditions, except the natural alcohol content must be at least 12.5 percent. After three years of aging, both Chianti and Chianti Classico may be entitled to the distinction of *riserva*.

Surrounding the central Chianti Classico region are six individual districts that may use the term "Chianti" in labeling, as long as it is followed with the name of the particular district in which the grapes were grown:

Chianti Colli Arentini

Chianti Colli Fiorentini

Chianti Colli Pisane

Chianti Colli Senesi

Chianti Montalbano

Chianti Rufina

White Chianti wines are unknown, but some white wines are grown from Malvasia and Trebbiano vines cultivated in other areas of Tuscany.

Since the 1200s the *Vin Nobile di Montepulciano* has been grown as a wine for religious celebrations by the local aristocracy. By the 1300s it was already being exported and is reputed to have been a favorite of Pope Paul II. Deep red in color, it is made principally from the Prugnolo Gentile vine, which some believe to be a superior clonal selection of Sangiovese. Wine grown in the Vin Nobile di Montepulciano district must achieve at least 11 percent alcohol and receive two years of aging in cask. It may be designated *riserva* after three years aging, or *riserva speciale* after four, and can age well in the bottle for decades.

Perhaps the most noble red wine grown in all of Italy is *Brunello di Montalcino*. The Brunello vine, a cousin of the Prugnolo Gentile mentioned earlier, is another of the superior clones selected from the vaunted Sangiovese vine genealogy. South of the historical city of Siena is the village of Montalcino, which centers this comparatively small vineyard township in which the Brunello is grown. The young wines are very dark and dense and must be aged for a minimum of six years to become *riserva*. They are often aged in bottle for decades

FIGURE 7.14   Village of Montalcino in Tuscany. *(Photo by author.)*

more. Some vintages of *Brunello di Montalcino Riserva* are among the most expensive table wines sold anywhere.

There are few vintners in the world that can match the grand contributions of the Marchese Piero Antinori. At the magnificent Renaissance palace of Antinori, in the Antinori Plaza of Florence, Antinori wines are tasted by thousands of visitors every year. This grand influence of Antinori history and vision is perhaps best symbolized by *Tignanello,* an expensive and exceedingly complex dry red blended from traditional Sangiovese and newly planted Cabernet Sauvignon vines. The bouquet includes nuances of cinnamon, cloves, anise, brambles, and cherry, all structured in dense color and full tannins matured in new oak barrels. However, Chianti Classico and other traditional Tuscan and Umbrian wines are made with equal attention to advancing the state of the art.

Another of the very impressive estates in Tuscany is Castello Banfi, a magnificent eleventh-century flagship fortress in the village of Sant' Angelo Scalo, some 30 miles or so south of the city of Siena. Amid seemingly endless vineyards, this old castle is truly symbolic of the huge Banfi global wine marketing company. Castello Banfi, complete with an extensive wine museum, is one of the most popular tourist attractions in the region. Under the direction of the Mariani family, Banfi won the prestigious Gran Vinitaly Award in 1994 for producing wines of consistently high quality. Castello Banfi Brunello di Montalcino, an exceptionally rich and heavy red wine, exemplifies this grand tradition.

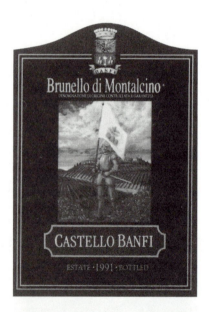

It was in the early 1840s that Clemente Santi founded the Santi winery near the small town of Montalcino. The estate was inherited by grandson Ferruccio Biondi-Santi, who was the first to market the now classic *Brunello di Montalcino,* the very dark, heavy red wine made from the Brunello clone of the Sangiovese vine first isolated in the Greppo vineyard on the Biondi-Santi estate. The winery has remained small, with a capacity to produce only several thousand cases from each vintage—the most expensive wines grown in all of Italy.

The Ricasoli family settled on a rocky *brolio* (hill) near Siena, 40 miles south of Florence, in the early 1140s. This site is where the original Brolio Castle was built and where many ensuing medieval battles were waged. Some of the castle ruins remain for visitors to see. In the early 1800s a young Baron Bettino Ricasoli commenced to experiment and apply what was then a very young but deliberate science to the identification of superior vineyards, improved viticultural technique, and advanced winemaking methods for his Tuscan red wines.

The result was what is thought by many wine historians to be the first great Chiantis, and the roots for creating the Chianti Classico designation.

The Frescobaldis, a banking family of enormous wealth in the historical Italian winemaking tradition, first made wine in 1308. The Frescobaldi castle displays a number of Renaissance artworks, several by Michaelangelo, who traded some of his paintings for fine Frescobaldi wines. In modern times, brothers Vittorio and Ferdinando are twenty-ninth-generation directors of the family wine empire, best known for its grand Chianti and the regal *Castelgiocondo Brunello di Montalcino.* The Frescobaldi reputation has recently been earned by fine new editions of Chardonnay and Cabernet Sauvignon.

Founded by cousins Ilario and Leopoldo Ruffino in 1877, the Ruffino wine estate was sold to the Folonari family in 1913. Today it is directed by members of both families. With several thousand acres of vineyards in Tuscany, the Ruffino name is synonymous with affordable Chianti and Chianti Classico around the world.

TUSCANY DOCG AND DOC GROWTHS

Brunello di Montalcino (DOCG)

Chianti (DOCG)

Carmignano (DOCG)

Vernaccia di San Gimignano (DOCG)

Vin Nobile di Montepulciano (DOCG)

Bianco dell'Empolese

Bianco della Valdinievole

Bianco di Pitigliano

Bianco Pisano di San Torpe

Bianco Vergine Valdichiana

Bolgheri

Candia dei Colli Apuani

Colli dell'Etruria Centrale

Colli di Luni

Colline Lucchesi

Elba

Montecarlo

Montescudaio

Morellino di Scansano

Moscadello di Montalcino

Parrina

Pomino

Rosso di Montalcino

Rosso di Montepulciano

Val d'Arbia

Val di Cornia

Vernaccia di San Gimignano

✜ MARCHES

Located east of Tuscany on the Adriatic coast, the Marches is another of Italy's ancient winegrowing districts. White wines made from Verdicchio vines are the principal production of the region. In that these are generally rather astringent, quite strong in alcohol, and have a light fruitiness which does not do well with extended aging, Marches whites are best when drunk young.

The Verdicchio grape is also made into a crisp, dry white wine, sold in a distinctive amphora-shaped bottle, grown in the coastal vineyards near the Adriatic Sea. Verdicchios from Castelli di Jesi and Matelica, both farther inland, are also highly regarded.

MARCHES DOC GROWTHS

Bianchello di Metauro

Bianco dei Colli Maceratesi

Falerio dei Colli Ascolani

Lacryma di Morro d'Alba

Rosso Conero

Rosso Piceno

Sangiovese dei Colli Pesaresi

Verdicchio dei Castelli di Jesi

Verdicchio di Matelica

Vernaccia di Serrapetrona

✜ UMBRIA

Umbria, the heartland region of Italy, has many vineyards planted on the Apennine mountain slopes facing westward into the valley of the Tiber River. In ancient times boats carried large volumes of wine from this region to Rome.

Downriver, just north of Lake Bolsena, is Orvieto, the ancient Etruscan town that makes the well-known wines of the same name. The vines cultivated here are the Trebbiano, as well as the Malvasia Greco and Verdello varieties. *Orvieto* must contain at least 12 percent alcohol; it may be either dry or sweet and is sometimes *frizzante*. In Roman times Orvieto was a holy shrine, and misuse of its vineyards was severely punished.

The traditional pride of Orvieto has been the *abboccato*, a semisweet white wine, but in recent years the dry *secco* has become popular too. During some vintages the noble mold, the *Botrytis cinerea,* here called the *muffa nobile,*

grows in the humid river valley, bringing more richness to the wines made in this locale.

In the higher portion of the Tiber valley is Torgiano, a small district that embraces Assisi, famous as the home of St. Francis. Today the area produces white and red *Torgiano* wines from Trebbiano, Canaiolo, and Sangiovese vines.

The third Umbrian wine of note is *Colli del Trasimeno*. This is grown in the district that is located along the border with Tuscany and produces red wines from Gamay, Ciliegiolo, and Sangiovese grapes, often bearing a similarity to Tuscan reds. White wines are also made in Colli del Trasimeno, chiefly from Trebbiano, Malvasia, and Grechetto vines.

Although the history of his winery dates only to the early 1960s, founder Giorgio Lungarotti has made up for this lack of tradition with exceptional innovation. It was Dr. Lungarotti's *Torre di Giano,* made from Trebbiano, that was the first Umbrian DOC designated wine—DOC Torgiano. Similarly, it was *Rubesco Riserva* from the Lungarotti Monticchio vineyard that was the first Umbrian DOC red. Plantings of Chardonnay, Gewürztraminer, and Cabernet Sauvignon bring promise for even more firsts from the Lungarotti cellars.

UMBRIA DOCG AND DOC GROWTHS

Sagrantino di Montefalco (DOCG)

Torgiano Rosso Riserva (DOCG)

Colli Altotiberini

Colli del Trasimeno

Colli Martani

Colli Perugini

Montefalco

Orvieto

Torgiano

◈ LATIUM

The Latium region embraces the city of Rome and the lower Tiber River basin, an area steeped in history and legend. Situated in the upper portion, near Lake Bolsena, is the village of Montefiascone, from which the fabled sweet white wine called *EST! EST!! EST!!!* originated. Although there are a number of different yarns explaining how this name came to be, the most widely recognized version has to do with the German bishop Fugger of the diocese of Fulda in Franconia during the twelfth century. While traveling through Italy, Bishop Fugger quite naturally wanted to make his trip as enjoyable as possible. It was fashionable at the time for VIP travelers to send scouts ahead to seek out good inns with superior food and wines. They marked a chosen inn by writing the word *est* on the door, apparently an abbreviation for *vinum bonum est,* or "the wine is good." The wine in the village of Montefiascone must have been truly superb, because the door of the inn there was marked with "EST! EST!! EST!!!" The bishop obviously agreed wholeheartedly, as he abandoned his journey and dwelled in Montefiascone for the rest of his life. The bishop's wine was a sweet dessert wine made from Moscato grapes. Today's EST! EST!! EST!!! is made both dry and sweet from Trebbiano blended with Malvasia. Although they are good, the EST! EST!! EST!!! wines of today do not appeal so as to capture clergy from their designed missions.

The volcanic Alban hills that rise south of Rome, known as *castelli,* have produced wines since the first Greek settlers arrived there 3,000 years ago. In

modern times the vineyards, planted amid quaint scenery and ancient castles, yield *Frascati,* the most well-known wines of the Castelli Romani. Most typically, Frascati is made slightly sweet, or *abboccato,* in style, but it is also made sweet and sparkling—all from Trebbiano and Malvasia vines. *Marino, Colli Albani,* and *Colli Lanuvini* are other white table wines grown in the locale. Latium reds are grown from Cesanese and Sangiovese vines, but they are not widely known outside the region.

LATIUM DOC GROWTHS

Aleatico di Gradoli

Aprilia

Bianco Capena

Cerveteri

Cesanase del Piglio

Cesanase di Affile

Cesanase di Olevano Romano

Colli Albani

Colli Lanuvini

Cori

Est! Est!! Est!!! di Montefiascone

Frascati

Genezzano

Marino

Montecompatri-Colonna

Velletri

Vignanello

Zagarolo

⊠ ABRUZZI

With a grand Roman history all its own, Abruzzi is nevertheless one of the newer commercial wine regions in Italy, having been largely developed just since World War II. Most of the vines in the region are cultivated on the narrow plain along the eastern coast of the country.

This region is located east of Latium and produces a red wine called *Montepulciano d'Abruzzo,* which should not be confused with the Vin Nobile di Montepulciano of Tuscany, although they are similar in dense color and complexity of flavor. The Montepulciano d'Abruzzo is typically a bit lighter in body and less tannic than Vin Nobile di Montepulciano. The most important wine of the district is *Trebbiano d'Abruzzo,* a white that overcomes a shy acidity with delicate apple-pear-melon flavors. Montepulciano d'Abruzzo and Trebbiano d'Abruzzo are the only DOC growths in the Abruzzi region.

⊠ MOLISE

The comparatively small region of Molise was actually the southern part of Abruzzi until it was separated in the early 1960s. In that much of Molise wine-growing comprises small, fragmented estates, many but an acre or two, it is difficult to discern the rationale for the division.

Perhaps the answer lies in the significant history of Molise, some accounts supporting the idea that cave-dwelling human beings may have lived in this

FIGURE 7.15 Mastroberardino cellars in Avellino, Campania. *(Courtesy of Heublein, Inc.)*

locale more than 100,000 years ago. If this is the case, Molise may be where man first made wine.

In simplest terms, the wines of Molise are still archaic, perhaps not harking back to caveman basics, but nevertheless lagging well behind most Italian wines, which have been improved and upgraded with advancing technology in both the vineyards and the cellars. The *Montepulciano* clone of Sangiovese is the most widely planted red wine vine, as the Trebbiano is for whites. There are two DOC zones, Biferno and Pentro.

▨ CAMPANIA

The magnificent Campania, surrounding the city of Naples on the west coast of Italy, is another winegrowing region rich in history and lore. It includes the renowned vineyards of *Lacryma Christi*, which are grown on the famous volcanic slopes of Mount Vesuvius. Several legends have arisen to explain the origin of this great religious name. The most accepted version is that Lucifer, manifested as the devil and cast out of paradise, stole a portion of the heavenly soil and hurled it iniquitously into the Gulf of Naples, to this day called "the bit of paradise dropped by the devil." When Christ visited the area, he looked at how the devil's work could lure people into sin and was moved to tears. Where his tears fell upon the Campanian slopes, vines of sacred origin sprang forth and produced the white wine of the Lacryma Christi, the "tears of Christ."

One white wine of merit mentioned earlier in this chapter is the Greco di Tufo, or "the Greek wine grown on boiled stone." Soils of the Tufo are similar to those of the Touraine in France, and so are the white "smoky" wines that these two separate districts produce.

Fiano di Avellino, a white, and *Taurasi,* a red, are also popular wines grown in the montainous vineyards of Campania. *Solopaca* is medium-bodied red wine produced in the northeastern sector of the region. The island of Ischia, not far from Naples, produces both whites and reds of good everyday quality.

Mastroberardino is one of the most highly regarded vintners in southern Italy, with family roots going back to the early 1700s. Its traditional Lacryma Christi white is light and crisp, with raisin-apple flavors; its red expresses bold cherry-raspberry flavors.

CAMPANIA DOC GROWTHS
Taurasi (DOCG)

Aglianico del Taburno, or Taburno

Asprinio di Aversa

Capri

Castel San Lorenzo

Cilento

Falerno del Massico

Fiano di Avellino

Greco di Tufo

Guardia Sanframondi, or Guardilio

Ischia

Lacryma Christi del Vesuvio

Sant'Agata de' Goti

Solopaca

⊞ APULIA

The Apulia region, the "heel" of the Italian boot, is the largest wine producing region in Italy. Winegrowing in Apulia is done on a gigantic scale, typically producing more than 350 million gallons each vintage. Only six countries produce more wine than this single region.

The wines grown in Apulia are mostly common and strong in alcohol, resulting from large clusters of sweet grapes matured under long, hot growing seasons. Many Apulian wines are exported to other European countries for use as blending wines in the production of European Economic Community (EEC) table wines.

Inexpensive Apulian wines became so popular in France during the early 1970s that many French winegrowers, especially in the Languedoc, became concerned about the heavy volume of Italian imports diluting prices and market demand. In 1976 the first of several riots erupted on the docks of Marseilles as wines from Apulia were unloaded. To date the situation has not been fully resolved, and a rivalry between the large ordinary wine regions of Italy and France continues.

Aleatico di Puglia is a heavy-bodied red dessert wine made medium sweet, or *dolce naturale,* from Aleatico and Primitivo grapes. Sweet, or *liquoroso,* Aleatico di Puglia is made from grapes dried on racks to concentrate sugar and flavors.

Inland, between Bari and Foggia, good white, rosé, and red table wines can be found at the Castel del Monte, the rosé considered by most to be the best in Apulia and one of the best pink wines grown in all of Italy.

APULIA DOC GROWTHS
Aleatico di Puglia

Alezio

Brindisi

Cacc'e Mmitte di Lucera

Castel del Monte

Copertino

Gioia del Colle

Gravina
Leverano
Lizzano
Locorotondo
Martina, or Martina Franca
Matino
Moscato di Trani
Nardo
Orta Nova
Ostuni
Primitivo di Manduria
Rosso Barletta
Rosso Canosa
Rosso di Cerignola
Salice Salentino
San Severo
Squinzano

❖ BASILICATA

The soils of the Basilicata are doubtlessly the worst in all of Italy, which makes one wonder why the Greeks chose to settle in this region some 3,000 years ago. Winegrowing is the only agriculture attempted on the slopes of the dormant volcano, Mount Vulture, in this area. The vine cultivated in, or on, Basilicata is the highly revered Aglianico. As may be expected, the best wine in the region is *Aglianico del Vulture,* a dark red, typically tannic, table wine. With three years of aging, Aglianico may be labeled *vecchio,* and with five years age it can be sold as *riserva.* White table wines made from Malvasia and Moscato grapes are also popular in local consumption. Aglianico del Vulture is the only DOC growth in the Basilicata.

❖ CALABRIA

The rugged and austere terrain of Calabria is breathtakingly beautiful, the region being perhaps more famous for its scenery and for being the "toe" of the Italian boot than for any of its wines. One possible exception is the *Greco di Gerace,* a dark golden dessert wine famous since Roman times, which some say has a bouquet reminiscent of orange blossoms. What little is offered for export brings high prices.

The table wines grown in the Ciro and Melissa districts along the central Ionian coast on the east side date back to Grecian times. The best Ciros are reds from Gaglioppo vines and are mostly consumed in the region. Donnici, Pollino, and Savuto are central and western districts in which good reds are made from Gaglioppo, Greco Nero, and Sangiovese grapes. Whites, generally of lesser repute than the reds, are made from Trebbiano and Greco Bianco.

CALABRIA DOC GROWTHS
    Ciro
    Donnici
    Greco di Bianco

Lamezia

Melissa

Pollino

Sant'Anna di Isola Capo Rissuto

Savuto

❖ SICILY

The island of Sicily has more acreage of vineyards than any other winegrowing region in Italy and is second to Apulia in the volume of wine produced—more than 250 million gallons from most vintages. Sicily also ships considerable amounts of wine in bottle and bulk to other regions and countries.

Sicilian wines have been famous for centuries; evidence of winegrowing on the island goes back to early Greek times. In the city of Syracuse, originally a Greek colony, archaeologists have found many ancient coins with the head of Bacchus embossed on one side and a cluster of grapes on the other. Despite this grand history and great production, the best Sicilian winegrowers have never competed aggressively in the world's wine markets. Consequently, many of the truly fine wines from this region remain relatively unknown outside its borders.

Perhaps the very best of Sicily's wines is *Marsala*, a dessert wine first made there by Englishman John Woodhouse in the 1770s. Marsala production begins with blends of table wines made from Catarrato, Grillo, and Inzolia grapes (see Figure 7.16, color insert).

Woodhouse brought with him the knowledge of how the famous Sherry wines were made in southern Spain. *Vino cotto*, or "cooked wine," which is really just grape juice boiled down into a sweet concentrate, is added to the blends along with brandy to create the strong, sweet Marsala. The cooking and aging oxidize color pigments and caramelize the sugars in the wine, a process called *maderization*, named after the method used to make Madeira wine. After four months of aging, Marsala can be called *fine* and may be either dry and light in color, or sweet and dark. *Marsala superiore* must be aged in casks for at least two years. If no *vino cotto* is added and if the wine is aged in a *solera*, the resulting wine may be called *Vergine*, a drier and lighter Marsala. The *solera* blending and aging system is fully described in the section on Spanish Sherry in Chapter 9. *Marsala Speciale* wines are also made with the addition of fruit, nut, and/or other flavors.

Another Sicilian dessert wine is made from late-harvested Zibibbo grapes, resulting in a strong amber-colored product known as *Moscato Passito di Pantelleria*.

The white wines of Etna, produced mostly from Carricante grapes grown in the province of Catania, are also well regarded. When grown in the *commune* of Milo, and fermented from at least 80 percent Carricante grapes to at least 12 percent alcohol strength, the wines may be labeled "Etna Superiore."

Most experts agree that the finest wines grown on the island of Sicily are from the cellars of Corvo Duca Di Salaparuta under the familiar Corvo label seen in fine wine shops around the United States. With a tradition reaching back to its founding in 1824 by the duke of Salaparuta, Corvo is made in a new winery constructed as one of the most technologically advanced in Europe. *Corvo Bianca di Valguarnera* is its flagship white; *Corvo D'Agala* and *Duca Enrico* are the best reds.

SICILY DOC GROWTHS

Bianco Alcamo, or Alcamo

Cerasuolo di Vittoria

Contessa Entellina
Etna
Faro
Malvasia delle Lipari
Marsala
Moscato di Noto
Moscato di Pantelleria
Moscato di Siracusa

SARDINIA

Nearly the equal of Sicily in size, Sardinia lags far behind its island sister in both the quality and quantity of wine produced. This inequality is mainly due to the lack of advancement in applied winegrowing technology and in developing markets.

One white wine made from Nuragus vines and a red from Cannonau are considered to be the best table wines grown on the island. Perhaps the most typical of Sardinian wines is the dessert wine *Vernaccia di Oristano,* which is very similar to Marsala.

SARDINIA DOC GROWTHS

Arborea
Campidano di Terralba, or Terralba
Cannonau di Sardegna
Carignano del Sulcis
Giro di Cagliari
Malvasia di Bosa
Malvasia di Cagliari
Mandrolisai
Monica di Cagliari
Monica di Sardegna
Moscato di Cagliari
Moscato di Sardegna
Moscato di Sorso-Sennori
Nasco di Cagliari
Nuragus di Cagliari
Vermentino di Gallura
Vermentino di Sardegna
Vernaccia di Oristano

8

THE WINES OF GERMANY, AUSTRIA, AND SWITZERLAND

GERMANY

There are 136,000 square miles of land, lakes, rivers, and mountains in Germany. The country, politically reunited East and West, forms a land mass comparable in size to the State of Montana. In a typical vintage, German vintners produce more than 250 million gallons of wine, a bit more than half the U.S. output.

Germans are not the greatest wine consumers in the European community, owing, in part at least, to their thirst for beer. By most accounts, the annual per capita wine consumption is about seven gallons. The most important export markets for German wine are Russia, the United Kingdom, and the United States.

German wine production spans a comparatively narrow range of unique wines, mostly whites, created through a struggle against the elements of nature. The wine land of Germany is primarily situated in the southwestern portion of the nation, directly atop the 50th parallel of north latitude. Although the northern location and steep slopes of the best vineyards present growers all the hazards expected in cool-climate viticulture, there is some compensation in planting vineyards along the rivers, where flowing water helps to stabilize day/night temperatures. In addition, mist and fog rise from the water surface during the ripening season, offering some protection from early frosts.

FIGURE 8.1 Winter in a German vineyard. *(Courtesy of German Wine Information Bureau.)*

The vineyards of Germany lie at the very northern limits of the zone where grapes may be commercially grown for fine wines. Further north, the summers are too short to provide enough heat summation for the adequate ripening of grapes. With marginal weather conditions the rule rather than the exception, the German winegrowing situation is precarious even within the most choice locales. Once the vine buds open in springtime, there is the threat of frost killing the emerging new shoots that are essential to producing the grape crop. Some winegrowers continue the tradition of solemn prayer to St. Sophia, or "Cold Sophie," the patron "Ice Saint," who is called upon to protect the vineyards from frost damage.

As in most fine wine regions, the best soils are paradoxically the worst, forcing the vines to struggle to produce sparse crops of tiny berries bursting with flavor. The "struggling vine" theory is perhaps better exemplified in Germany than in any other country. Soils here are often nothing more than flakes of shale, which can be washed down the mountainsides during violent rainstorms.

There are two major rewards for conquering such handicaps. The first of these is the production of some of the most delicious white wines in the world, and the second is doing it amid some of the most breathtakingly beautiful countryside anywhere.

Although many nations have planted German wine vines, no other country has yet succeeded in matching the many complex nuances of flavor in Germany's whites. Their characteristics range from fresh apple-citrus aromas and thin consistency in wines grown in the lowland vineyards, to bold honey-apricot flavors and rich textures from the cliffside vines.

When all the hurdles imposed by Mother Nature are surmounted, the German wine industry faces further problems in pursuit of a place in the global market. While world wine consumption is gradually moving to dry red wines, Germany is well established in making sweeter whites. With every other major winemaking nation building on wine classification by geographical origin, Germany classifies its wines based on the natural sweetness attained by its grapes. As the more progressive winegrowing nations find new ways to define wine origins, Germany makes more blends with meaningless names that dilute the identity of each component wine. The situation cries out for reform.

The river of major importance to winemaking in Germany is the Rhine, teeming with both commercial and pleasure craft during the months of milder weather. The Rhine passes by the winegrowing regions of Baden, Rheinpfalz, Rheinhessen, Hessische Bergstrasse, Rheingau, and Mittelrhein, before flowing northward through the Netherlands and emptying into the English Channel.

Württemberg winegrowing is served by the Neckar River, and the Franken region by the Main; both rivers are major tributaries of the Rhine. The rest of Germany's wine regions are named for additional tributaries of the Rhine: the Nahe, the Ahr, and the Mosel-Saar-Ruwer, which is, in itself, yet another system of rivers.

Nearly 90 percent of all German wines are white and come from four major vine varieties, some of which are restricted to certain vineyard locales and others of which may be cultivated in any region. With this comparatively narrow choice of suitable vines, there is an equally limited number of wine types and styles.

Without question, the great *Johannisberg Riesling,* often called "White Riesling" or just "Riesling" in California, is the most noble vine cultivated in Germany. It accounts for about 20 percent of all vineyard plantings in the nation and responds to severe deficiencies of soil fertility and rainfall with profoundly rich, russet-speckled golden clusters of grapes. It is this vine that garners most of the world's accolades for elegant German white wines. On the other hand, the Johannisberg Riesling requires a bit more heat summation to ripen its fruit than most other German vines and, in some years, falls short of total maturity.

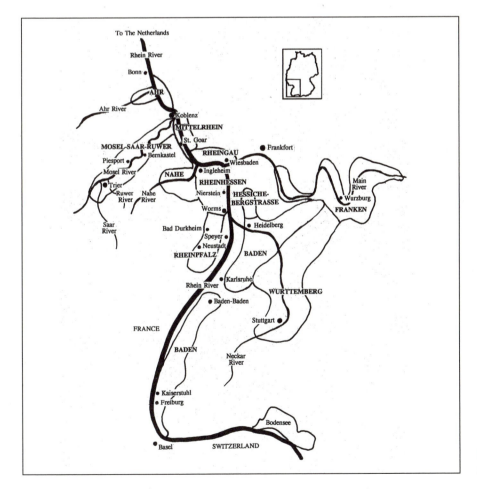

FIGURE 8.2 German winegrowing regions.

At one time *Silvaner* was the most widely cultivated vine in Germany, but today it accounts for less than 10 percent of the total vineyard acreage nationally. Although it ripens considerably earlier than Johannisberg Riesling and produces consistently larger crops, the wine quality of Silvaner has never been rated as high.

In 1882, Professor Müller of Thurgau, Switzerland, succeeded in crossing Riesling and Silvaner in order to achieve an offspring vine that would yield fruit with Johannisberg Riesling-like richness and flavor, but with Silvaner-like hardiness in the vineyard. The result was the now-famous *Müller-Thurgau* cultivar, which has since become the most widely cultivated vine in Germany, accounting for more than 25 percent of the total German vineyard acreage.

Another major vine variety grown in Germany is red, the *Spätburgunder*, equivalent to Burgundy's Pinot Noir. Other principal grape varieties cultivated in Germany are *Gewürztraminer, Rulander*, known as Pinot Gris in France, *Koerner*, and *Scheurebe*.

By the time the first German settlements were established by Roman soldiers during the second century, wine had long since become a staple in the diet of Rome. Each soldier was allotted, and required to drink, one liter of wine each day. Consequently, great quantities of wine were needed to fill this requirement. Fresh wine from local Rhineland vines was much preferred to that which was shipped from the smoky *fumaria* cellars back in Italy.

As the Roman Empire expanded in search of land for grain agriculture, there was no encouragement to plant vines in Germany. Yet the steep hillsides along the Rhine, Mosel, and other great rivers in Germany could, of course, never serve as grainfields. So it was on these precipitous slopes that the Teutonic natives were first called upon to establish the great vineyards in Germany.

The influence of the Roman occupation lives on in the winemaking terms still used in Germany today: *flasche* (bottle), from the Latin *flasca*; *keller* (cellar), from *cellarium*; *winzer* (vintner), from *vinitor*, and many others.

From the early 400s to the middle 700s A.D., Huns, Vandals, and Visigoths laid siege to the German provinces time and time again. As the Roman Empire and its once-mighty legions were destroyed, so were vineyards, wine cellars, and their journals and records. Gone was an essential historical link to the earliest winegrowing in Germany.

The German rival to Monte Cassino in Italy was the great Abbey of Fulda, founded by St. Boniface in 744. The planting of the Fulda vineyards was directed personally by St. Boniface, a missionary and viticulturist who had planted a number of vineyards near Mainz. Fulda, however, won a special place for itself in German wine lore, because it was there that the now famous *kabinett* wine classification originated. Many of the abbots at Fulda were wine connoisseurs, each having a special cellar in which the finest wines were stored and dispensed from a secret "cabinet."

The Benedictine Abbey of St. Maximin at Trier established vineyards at Detzen, Leiwen, and Longuich. The best wine at St. Maximin was *Abtsberg*, grown at the top of the hill and drunk only by the abbot. Farther down the hill grew *Herrenberg* wines, the wine reserved for the choir monks. *Bruderbar* came from still farther down the hill and was consumed by novice clerics. The very lowest vineyards produced *Biertelsberg*, a wine that was allocated to the laity.

In the early ninth century, Charlemagne became the driving force for expanding the cultivation of vineyards across Germany. He is credited with planting the original "Schloss Johannisberg" vineyards in what is now the Rheingau region just west of Wiesbaden. Charlemagne brought artisan monks from other parts of Europe to teach Germans the ways of commercial viniculture. He issued regulations for grape growing, and it was during his era that the earliest records were kept for the great Rhineland vineyards.

FIGURE 8.3 German "Romer" wineglass, late 1600s. *(Courtesy of the Corning Museum of Glass.)*

FIGURE 8.4 Schloss Rheinstein on the Rhine. *(Courtesy of German Wine Information Bureau.)*

The famous modern-day vineyards found in Geisenheim and Rudesheim on the north bank of the Rhine River owe their existence largely to Charlemagne's influence in promoting the use of wine in households at that time. The great emperor gave land to the monasteries and nunneries in Germany, much as he had given land to the church in other countries.

Between the many wars that took place across the vast Holy Roman Empire, Charlemagne's successors maintained his tradition of benevolence for several centuries. During the Middle Ages the church became the largest single owner of vineyards in Germany. As a result, the church emerged as a very wealthy entity, as well as a powerful spiritual force.

During the eleventh century a medieval archbishop bequeathed to the Benedictine monks of St. Alban's Priory the Mons Episcopi, or "Bishop's Hill," overlooking the Rhine River near the village of Winkel. It was renamed Johannisberg, or "St. John's Hill," and eventually became Schloss Johannisberg, today the most famous vintner in all of Germany.

The splendid work of the church in Germany continued during the twelfth century at the large vineyard of Steinberg, located near Schloss Johannisberg in the Rheingau region. Here the Cistercian monks created the Kloster Eberbach, the most magnificent abbey and vineyard in the nation. Eberbach was the "Clos de Vougeot" of the Rhineland. The monks devoted themselves to attaining the highest possible wine quality, although they achieved quantity too. The Kloster Eberbach abbey warehouse in Cologne grew to hold more than 100,000 gallons and had its own flotilla of barges to carry wines in trade to the British Isles and other markets in Europe.

FIGURE 8.5 Ruins of the medieval nunnery abbey Stuben on the Mosel. *(Photo by author.)*

Another monumental abbey, the Mühlen Brunnen, or "Mill Well," was constructed near Speyer, 100 miles or so up the Rhine, by the knight Walter von Lomersheim. It is thought that St. Bernard inspired the project when he visited to preach for the second Crusade. This great monastery prospered magnificently, eventually acquiring more than 100 vineyard parcels on both sides of the river.

Some experts believe that it was also St. Bernard who brought the classic red Burgundian Pinot Noir vine from Burgundy and introduced it to the Kloster Eberbach. It was renamed Blauburgunder, and later Spätburgunder, but in any event, its wine from the abbey vineyards fell far short of the great Burgundy reds. The Pinot was taken downriver to Assmannshausen, a few miles past Schloss Johannisberg, where it yielded better quality but was still not a wine to compare with Burgundy.

The medieval wine markets played a very important role in the economic development of the many towns and villages in which they operated, primarily because of the revenue generated by different types of vine and wine taxes. During the time of the Renaissance there was a trend toward developing higher-quality wines, which led to many new plantings of the Johannisberg Riesling vine. Unfortunately, the Thirty Years' War, fought on Rhenish soil, brought massive destruction once again to vineyards and cellars, as it did to all aspects of life in the Rhineland.

In 1716, Schloss Johannisberg and all the monastic vineyards of the Rheingau came under the control of the prince-abbot of Fulda. The dual title had evolved from the merger of two formerly separate offices, primate of imperial abbots and hereditary chancellor of the empire. By 1752 the office had been elevated even further to the level of prince-bishop, and successive monarchs ruled the tiny principality with regal splendor. One of the many duties of the prince-bishop was to announce the starting date for the vintage season. A notoriously absent-minded prince-bishop forgot the proclamation in 1775, and the fruit on the vines commenced to shrivel and mold because of overripening.

Frantic with worry, the monks of Johannisberg dispatched a courier to Fulda to secure permission to begin the harvest. The horseman was detained, either by a highwayman or by an attractive young lady—the tellers of the story divide nearly equally at this point. In any event, by the time the youth returned, the Schloss's grapes had already rotted with *Edelfäule*, or "noble rot," the very same *pourriture noble* that is essential to Sauternes in Bordeaux. Nevertheless, the monks gathered the moldy fruit and made wine with it. The result, to their astonishment, was a magnificent sweet golden wine. The process was developed and became traditional. Today such wines are revered as the famous *Beerenauslese* and *Trockenbeerenauslese* wines described in detail later in this chapter.

Until the mid-seventeenth century the English called all German wines *Rhenish*, whether or not they were actually from the Rhine. Perhaps the finest of all the Rhenish wines then were from Bacharach. Pope Pius II was convinced that Bacharach was Germany's best. As more and more wines were shipped down the Rhine to England during the early to mid-1600s, the term *Rhenish* was replaced in England by *Hock*, derived from the shipping-dock village of Hochheim on the river Main, which flows into the Rhine.

In 1830, German officials mandated that the names of all vineyards, along with the vineyard owners' names, be recorded in a land register used as a tax

FIGURE 8.6 Statue of courier at Schloss Johannisberg. *(Photo by author.)*

roll. The resister also contained such information as the vineyard soil type, grape variety planted, and wine quality, as well as the nearest village. Although it was not originally designed as such, this eventually became a system for classifying the vineyards in Germany. As would be expected, the first result of keeping the register was to encourage greater demand for the better quality wines. This brought about a desperate situation for the owners of the poorer vineyards, who were sometimes forced to sell all the wine a person could carry for just a few pennies. In despair, many of the lower-class growers sold their vineyards for a pittance and emigrated to Australia and the Americas.

The church-owned German vineyard estates ended with Napoleon's invasion from France. The monastic vineyards were parceled out to private owners, much as they had been in Burgundy. Most of the secular estates became the property of provincial governments.

Like the rest of Europe, Germany was infected with the *Phylloxera* root louse, first reported in the Rheinpfalz region in 1874. Noble and common vineyards alike were completely obliterated. Yet, in the long run, not all of the effects of this pest were negative. The clearing of older, lower-class vineyard sites provided an opportunity for upgrading vineyards by replanting with American rootstocks, highly resistant to the *Phylloxera,* and top grafting with scion wood from Johannisberg Riesling and other classic varieties greatly improved German wine quality.

Private wine collections came into vogue among the aristocracy. During the late 1800s the death of Sir Walter Trevelyan occasioned the probate of his London estate, which included an extensive wine cellar. Among the prized bottles found were some very old bottles of Hock, the oldest being from the superb vintage of 1540! Some of these bottles were opened in 1961, the wine being then 421 years old, and declared sound enough to taste. Aside from some browning caused by oxidation, the wine was agreeably pleasant, according to those fortunate few who had the opportunity to taste it.

◆ CLASSIFICATION

Control and regulation, of one sort or another, of German winegrowing dates back even before the days of Charlemagne. But most of the modern-day German wine regulations have arisen as a result of technological advances in quality control and increased sophistication in identifying grape and wine characteristics.

The winegrowing lands of Germany are classified into 13 *Gebiete* (regions). Each is further divided into *Bereiche* (districts).

The labels of the better German wines may carry the name of the township (usually with an "-er" added to the end of the village name) and the vineyard name. For example, "Bernkasteler Doktor" indicates that the wine comes from the classic Doktor vineyard situated in the township of Bernkastel.

A wine labeled with a village and vineyard name is likely to be superior to a wine with only a *Bereich* (district) name. For example, "Niersteiner Brudersberg" is generally better quality wine than that labeled simply "Bereich Nierstein." The more finite the geography, usually, the better the grade of product.

The following are terms that further divide German winegrowing geography.

Gemeinden	winegrowing village
Grosslagen	Groups of vineyard parcels having similar geographical characteristics
Einzellagen	specific vineyard parcels
Lagen	individual vineyard

German wine regulations, however, do not parallel those in France or Italy, which recognize specific geography or history as the primary element in the classification system. Instead, the wines of Germany are classified by the amount of sugar in the grapes each vintage and by assurances of authenticity in production processes. Wine labeling artwork often includes a black eagle logo, over which the letters "VDP" (Verband Deutscher Prädikats) proudly indicate the union of science with industry.

This devotion to technical devices results in some of the world's highest quality wines, but ignores a heritage every bit as old and rich as that of any other country in Europe. As a consequence, German wines do not attract nearly as much consumer interest in the world marketplace as those from France or Italy. Whereas wines from Charlemagne's Corton vineyard in Burgundy are given the epitomal "Grand Cru" classification and sell for $100 per bottle, the wines from Charlemagne's Ingelheim vineyard along the Rhine have no ranking and go relatively unnoticed at $10 per bottle.

To compensate, the Germans have traditionally made sweeter wines in order to supply that segment of market demand. More recently the trend has been toward producing dry table wines, which can be truly delicious. Nevertheless, the great value of the history and geography of German wines continues to be muted in their classification system.

Grapes commercially grown for German wine must contain strictly stipulated degrees of sugar at harvest in order to legally carry labels designating specific type and quality. Poor weather often leaves grapes unripe or deficient in the required sugar content. This condition can be rectified by *chaptalization,* the addition of sugar to the fermenting juice. Although adding sugar would seem to challenge the justification for natural grape sugars as the basis for a classification system, it is authorized nevertheless. Each region is strictly regulated as to the maximum amount of sugar that may be added, if any, each year. Most of the superior classified growths are not allowed any chaptalization at all, in any vintage.

German winegrowers report grape harvest data to government inspectors who inspect vineyards and cellars, as well as wines in inventory. These inspectors use the results of their analyses, performed at designated testing stations, to authenticate specific requirements regarding grades of quality. Under the most recent update of German wine law, there are three major categories of wine quality, as described in the following praragraphs.

TAFELWEIN

Tafelwein is the lowest grade of wine produced commercially in Germany. It never carries a vineyard name on the label and is generally consumed as the everyday wine of Germany. *Deutscher Tafelwein* must be made entirely of German-grown wine, whereas wine designated simply as *Tafelwein* may be a blend of German and wines from another EEC member country, usually Italy. Wine labeled only as *Wein* may be grown and vinified outside the EEC.

DEUTSCHER LANDWEIN

Deutscher Landwein, a relatively new official German wine category, distinguishes between ordinary Tafelwein, which can be grown anywhere, and wines of a little better quality from broad geographical or "land" demarcations. It is roughly the equivalent of the French Vins de Pays category. Deutscher Landwein labels may carry the name of the region in which the wine was grown; this wine may be chaptalized.

QUALITÄTSWEIN

Qualitätswein is divided into two subcategories: Qualitätswein bestimmte Anbaugebiete (QbA) is quality wine from designated regions, typically indicated by only the simple statement of "Qualitätswein" on the label. Qualitätswein mit Prädikat (QmP) is the top quality wine and is labeled with very important "predicate" qualifications.

All Qualitätswein must be analyzed by German governmental officials at regional analysis laboratories. Following testing, and with final approval, a *Prüfungsnummer,* or national certificate number, is issued to each wine. This number consists of as many as 11 digits, for example, 43417141594. The last two digits indicate the application year (94). The preceding three digits (415) denote the serial number given to the vintner's application. The next previous three digits (171) reveal the vintner's own code identity. The next two prior digits (34) disclose the vintner's village code, and the first digit (4) identifies the particular inspection station that performed the evaluation.

Qualitätswein bestimmte Anbaugebiete (QbA)
The QbA wines must originate from one of the 13 Qualitätswein regions in Germany and must be made from government-approved grape varieties. A rather nebulous regulation requires grapes for QbA wines to achieve sufficient ripeness each vintage to result in wine that has the typical style of bouquet and flavor traditional to that region, although chaptalization is also permitted.

It is in the QbA category that the largest quantity of German Qualitätswein is made and marketed. In everyday jargon, QbA wines are often referred to simply as *qualitätswein.*

Qualitätswein mit Prädikat (QmP)
QmP wines may not be chaptalized and must exhibit special attributes and distinction. As one would expect, the QmP classification is awarded to the very finest wines of Germany. Consequently, the system is dynamic, reflecting the effects of the growing season—literally changing with the weather—as compared with the constancy of geographical classification in France and Italy.

Each QmP wine must display one of six special distinctions on the label. The individual attributes primarily reflect the natural sugar content and ripeness of the grapes at harvest. Designations in the following list are ranked according to an ascending order of quality:

Kabinett. Wines made from grapes harvested at peak ripeness. They must measure at least 17.8 degrees Brix, an expression of sugar content as total dissolved solids by weight. Finished *Kabinett* wines usually contain little, if any, residual sweetness. The name is derived from special wines once reserved in "cabinets" by St. Boniface at the Fulda Abbey in the Rheingau region.

Spätlese. "Late-harvest" wines made from grapes picked at least seven days after peak ripeness and after having reached at least 20.4 degrees Brix. The idea is to ensure optimal flavor development, and the finished wine may have some slight sweetness. The name is derived from a courier who arrived late one vintage with the absent-minded prince-bishop's decree to commence the harvest.

Auslese. "Select harvest" wines made from grape clusters specially selected for superior quality. The natural Brix level must be at least 21.6 degrees, and these wines are often finished with light-to-moderate residual sweetness.

Beerenauslese. "Selected harvest berries." These are wines made from auslese grapes that have reached at least 28.0 degrees Brix. Individual berries infected with *Edelfäule,* or "noble mold," are laboriously hand selected. The finished wines are always sweet—and expensive.

Trockenbeerenauslese. "Dry selected harvest berries." These wines are made from Beerenauslese grapes that have attained at least 36.0 degrees Brix. The individual berries infected with *Edelfäule* must have achieved a raisinlike dry state. These wines are rare, very sweet, and very expensive.

Eiswein. "Ice wine." Eiswein can be made from any form of late-harvest or select-harvest grapes as long as they are harvested while naturally frozen and the juice pressed out prior to thawing. The finished wines are very concentrated in bouquet, flavor, and sweetness. They are rare and very expensive.

German-grown wines that are varietal labeled, that is, having labels that indicate the variety of grape from which the wine was made, must have at least 85 percent of that specific variety as the source of the particular wine.

QUALITÄTSWEIN GARANTIERTEN URSPRUNGSLAGE (QbU)

The newest addition to the German system of wine labeling is the category *Qualitätswein garantierten Ursprungslage,* or QbU. Such names are quickly given an acronym for ease in writing and speaking. This term has caused some confusion, generating the notion that it may be yet another higher, greater, category of sweetness or goodness. It is not. The QbU label statement simply guarantees, in rather Italian-like fashion, that 100 percent of the grapes came from the locale indicated on the label. For example, a "QmP Auslese" can now be a "QmP Auslese QbU."

Typically, German wines are bottled in the tall, slender *Schlegelflaschen,* still often referred to as "Hock" bottles. Amber-colored Hock bottles are generally used for wines grown in the Rhine River regions, green for wines from the Mosel-Saar-Ruwer, and sometimes blue from the Nahe. The short flagon, or *Bocksbeutel,* is commonly used for wines grown in the Franken region and, occasionally, for Baden wines. Legend has it that the short stubby *bocksbeutel* shape evolved from a design made by monks, who could more easily hide *bocksbeutels* under their habits while laboring in the vineyards and cellars.

FIGURE 8.7 Harvesting *eiswein* grapes in the Rheinhessen. *(Courtesy of Die Weinwirtschaft; photo by Claudia Chauvin.)*

LIEBFRAUMILCH

The name of *Liebfraumilch* wine was originally *Liebfrauminch* (*minch* is an archaic German word for "monk"; thus Liebfrauminch was wine belonging to the monks of the Liebfrauenkirche, or the "church of the loving wife" (i.e., St. Mary, mother of Jesus Christ). As the language evolved, the *n* in *minch* became an *l*, and hence, *Liebfraumilch*. Some contend that this word originated as *Liebfraumilch* and is thus translated as "milk from the loving mother," but this is not the case.

The Liebfrauenkirche vineyards surround the Worms church, now known as the Liebfrauenstift, and yield about 4,000 gallons of wine annually—far less than the millions of gallons of Liebfraumilch marketed each year around the world. Consequently, any Qualitätswein grown in the Rhineland today may be labeled "Liebfraumilch" as long as the label displays no other name to indicate a more specific origin. If the wine qualifies, Liebfraumilch may also display the special designations *Kabinett* or *Spätlese*. The grapes for Liebfraumilch must attain at least 14.8 degrees Brix natural sugar, and the names of the grape varieties used in making it may not be displayed on the label.

MAY WINE

In an old German custom called the "mixing of cups," a *Bowle* (cup) is used to mix convivial drinks. One of these is May Wine. The *Bowle* is used to blend ordinary light white wine and strawberries along with *Waldmeister,* the fragrant woodruff herb found growing wild in German forests. The mixture is then sweetened with sugar. The strawberries may be replaced with peaches or pineapple, or some portion of these and/or other fruits may be mixed together. Some May Wines are bottled, using woodruff and fruit essences, but genuine May Wine is made and consumed fresh from the *Bowle* during the late springtime.

MOSELBLÜMCHEN

Moselblümchen, translated as "little blooms from the Mosel," is generally a very inexpensive wine produced anywhere in the Mosel region of Germany. It is considered only as *Tafelwein.*

STROHWEIN

Strohwein, translated as "straw wine," is a wine made from late-harvest grapes allowed to dry on straw mats into a raisinlike form. The finished wines are, as would be expected, very sweet.

OTHER DESIGNATIONS

Some shippers of German wines choose to add still other special designations to labels for export, often expressed in English owing to the substantial trade with English-speaking nations.

Produced and Bottled by indicates only that the bottler actually produced at least 75 percent of the wine; the balance may have been purchased from another vintner.

Made and Bottled by reveals that the bottler had to have produced at least 10 percent of the wine.

Bottled at the Winery stipulates that the wine was bottled at the same location where it was produced and/or blended.

Gutsabfüllung, roughly equivalent to "Estate Bottled," indicates that the bottler made the wine from grapes grown on the vintner's estate.

Erzeugerabfüllung—bottled by the producer.

Abfüller—bottler.

Winzergenossenschaft—winery.

To the beginning appreciator of German wines, vineyard names can be rather imposing in both pronunciation and meaning. The late Frank Schoonmaker, in his book *The Wines of Germany,* made a good suggestion for overcoming this obstacle. He pointed out that if the neophyte would memorize just a few German words and their English translation, it would be much easier to make sense of many vineyard titles. The following list is a start:

Bad	bath
Berg	hill
Burg	castle
Dom	cathedral
Garten	garden
Herren	men, or lords
Hof	court, or manor house
Kloster	convent, or monastery
Schloss	castle
Stück	tract of land

Furthermore, German vineyard names are quite colorful. They range from "the dove" (*Taubenberg*) to "the dragon" (*Drachenstein*), and from "heaven" (*Graacher Himmelreich*) to "hell" (*Johannisberger Hölle*).

With a little time and effort devoted to building up these terms, one can soon become adept at unraveling the meanings of even the most seemingly complicated German vineyard names and wine labels. A knowledge of the following terms is helpful:

Anbaugebiete	quality wine regions
Halbtrocken	semidry
Sekt	sparkling wine
Trocken	dry
Weinlese	vintage

There are 11 contiguous German winegrowing regions located in the far southwestern corner of the nation, bordered by France and Switzerland.

✠ BADEN

Baden is the southernmost *Anbaugebiet* (wine region) in Germany. Commencing with the Bodensee at its extreme southeast end, the district proceeds along the north bank of the Rhine westward to the city of Basel, in Switzerland, where the river turns northward. The Baden extends north for about 250 miles ending at the Franken region border. Seven *Bereiche* (districts) and 17 *Grosslagen* (subdistricts) constitute the Baden region.

With more than 35,000 acres of vineyards under cultivation, Baden ranks third in quantity of wine produced in the nation, and its wines are the most varied. Its soils include a range of consistencies: clay, gravel, limestone, loess, shell-lime, and volcanic stone.

Approximately 38 percent of the vines planted here are the Müller-Thurgau hybrid cultivar. Another 13 percent are Rulander, but only 7 percent or so are devoted to Johannisberg Riesling. Red wines from Spätburgunder account for approximately 20 percent of Baden wine production. Most vineyards in the region have been replanted during the past several decades in a massive project, undertaken with the latest viticultural technology.

Bereich Bodensee, isolated from the main portion of the Baden, encompasses fewer than 1,000 acres of vineyards. The specialty of the district is a rosé wine made from Spätburgunder, called *Weissherbst*.

The major share of the Baden vineyards is situated along the east bank of the Rhine River, between Basel and Heidelberg, the heart of the region lying between the cities of Freiburg and Karlsruhe. Kaiserstuhl-Tuniberg, situated around an extinct volcano, is the largest *Bereich* in the locale. The volcanic ash soil has a pronounced effect on the wine grown there, imparting a distinctively smoky element to the bouquet and a rather metallic component to the flavor. Other important *Bereiche* in the Baden heartland are Markgräflerland, Breisgau, and Ortenau.

Farther north, bordering the romantic city of Heidelberg, is Bereich Badische Bergstrasse/Kraichgau, producing heavy-bodied white wines replete with rich, flowery fragrance and firm acidity.

Situated at the far northern reaches of the Baden Anbaugebiet is Bereich Badisches Frankenland, which, as its name suggests, borders the Franken region. The wines grown in this district are often similar to those of Franken, even to the extent that some are bottled in the squat *Bocksbeutel* bottle.

❖ WÜRTTEMBERG

The Württemberg Anbaugebiet is located east of Baden on both banks of the Neckar River, which flows into the Rhine at the city of Mannheim. The capital city of the region is Stuttgart, one of the most dynamic industrial centers of the nation—the "Detroit" of Germany.

As in Baden, much of the wine produced in Württemberg is also consumed there; comparatively little is exported. The finest wines of the region, as may be expected, are grown from the classic Johannisberg Riesling. The *Trollinger* vine is cultivated widely through Württemberg and yields distinctive red and rosé table wines. The "Black Riesling," or *Schwarzriesling,* is another important red wine variety cultivated in Württemberg. Schwarzriesling is the very same variety as the Pinot Meunier, which is widely grown in Champagne. Spätburgunder and *Portugieser* are also cultivated in significant acreages.

There are three *Bereiche* in Württemberg, commencing with Remstal-Stuttgart at the south, proceeding northward downriver to Württembergisch Unterland, and finally, Kocher-Jagst-Tauber. The majority of winegrowing in Württemberg is done by large cooperative vintners.

❖ HESSISCHE BERGSTRASSE

With about 1,000 acres of vines, the Hessische Bergstrasse is the smallest *Anbaugebiet* in Germany. The region, bordering the north side of Baden, is nearly surrounded by rivers: the Neckar, the Main, and the Rhine.

Johannisberg Riesling is the predominant vine planted in the southern Bereich Starkenburg. Müller-Thurgau is cultivated in the northern Bereich Umstandt. Within these two *Bereiche* the tiny Hessische Bergstrasse region is made up of three *Grosslagen*—all of which typically produce wines that are full-bodied, moderately fragrant, yet often low in acidity. As in Württemberg, most of the wine grown in Hessische Bergstrasse is accounted for by cooperatives, and most of this production is also consumed there.

❖ FRANKEN

The Franken, or Franconia, located about 40 miles east of Frankfurt, in the northwest corner of Bavaria where the Main River joins the Rhine, is a very colorful winegrowing region with a unique character.

Much of the stony-earthy flavor found in Franken wines is thought to be due to a climate that often brings heavy rainfall, early autumn frosts, and bitter cold winters. Consequently, the early-ripening Müller-Thurgau has found great acceptance in the Franken and now accounts for about half of all vines cultivated in the region. Silvaner represents another 23 percent of all plantings, and Johannisberg Riesling a scant 2 percent or so.

Another token of Franken's individuality is the traditional *Bocksbeutel*, the short, rounded flagon in which Franken wines are bottled.

The westernmost of Franken's three *Bereiche* is Steigerwald. This is a comparatively small district that cultivates its vines on predominantly clay soil, which some experts say imparts a rather honeylike element to the complexity of the district's wines.

There are nine *Grosslagen* in Bereich Mandreieck, with vineyards cultivated on predominantly limestone soils, yielding, in general, the best wines grown in the region. At the center of Bereich Mandreieck is the old Gothic city of Würzburg, the capital of Franken.

Another rather unique aspect of the Franken is its charity hospitals funded by winegrowing profits. One of the most interesting of these is the old

FIGURE 8.8 Casks in the Burgerspital cellars at Würzburg. *(Courtesy of German Wine Information Bureau.)*

Burgerspital, a geriatric hospice that is supported by the wine made from the most famous vineyard in this district, the Stein. It is from the Stein that the term *Steinwein* is derived, used by some wine enthusiasts in reference to all Franken wines.

To the far west is Bereich Mainviereck, where sandstone and loam soils yield wines which, in the better vintages, can be powerfully rich and fruity.

❖ RHEINPFALZ

The Rheinpfalz produces more wine annually than any other *Anbaugebiet* in Germany, even though its acreage (54,000 acres of vineyards) ranks second to the 58,000 acres in neighboring Rheinhessen. Some 50 miles or so of the Rhine River serve as the eastern border of the Rheinpfalz, and France borders the region on its western side.

The term *pfalz* is rooted in the Roman *palatium,* for "palace," which is also thought to be the origin of the English name for the region known as the Palatinate. During the Middle Ages the Rheinpfalz was known as the "wine cellar of the Holy Roman Empire." Whatever building an emperor chose for his headquarters during a visit to the region became a palace, or *palast* in German. This term eventually evolved to become *pfalz,* hence the "Rheinpfalz."

About 25 percent of the vineyards in the region are planted to Müller-Thurgau vines, with 14 percent devoted to Johannisberg Riesling. Silvaner, Koerner, Morio-Muskat, Portugieser, and Scheurebe make up most of the remaining Rheinpfalz viticulture.

Despite its comparatively large size, the Rheinpfalz has only two *Bereiche.* The Deutsche Weinstrasse, or "German Wine Route," which predates even the Roman occupation, remains a very picturesque vineyard landscape, with the Haardt mountains creating a rugged profile through the Rheinpfalz.

Today, Bereich Mittelhaardt-Deutsche Weinstrasse is the heart of the great Rheinpfalz vineyards, particularly in the countryside between the cities of Neustadt and Kallstadt. This is where much of the Johannisberg Riesling vineyards yield wines that are typically delicate and unassertive, with a finesse that exemplifies superior German white table wine.

In striking contrast, the village of Forst centers a small portion of this district that has black basalt soil, existing nowhere else in German vineyards. This

locale is known for wines of heavy body, coarse flavors, and firm acidity, best exemplified by the famous vineyards of the Jesuitengarten, or "Jesuits' Garden." Well known in the U.S. marketplace are Deidesheimer wines, and with good reason, as the township of Deidesheim is one of the largest producers of *Qualitätswein* in the entire Rheinpfalz.

The southern half of the Rheinpfalz is known as the Bereich Sudliche Weinstrasse. Winegrowing in this historical district has made great strides in modernization, owing to new plantings and updated winemaking techniques. Much of this progress has resulted from government support and the emergence of cooperative vintners. Once known primarily for ordinary wines, the Sudliche Weinstrasse is now achieving accolades for its fine varietal wine production.

✣ RHEINHESSEN

As mentioned in the preceding section, the Rheinhessen has the largest acreage of vineyards in Germany. This region is Germany's second largest producer of wine. Bordered by the Rhine River both to the east and to the north, the Rheinhessen is limited by the Nahe River to the west. It is a region of rolling hills and fertile valleys in which there is a wide array of soil types and microclimates. The vine varieties cultivated here are similar to those in the Rheinpfalz.

The great history of the Rheinhessen centers on the town of Ingleheim, where Emperor Charlemagne built a palace overloooking the Rhine. He noticed that the snow melted first across the river, in what is now the Rheingau region, and reasoned that this might be a better site for vineyards.

There are three *Bereiche* in the Rheinhessen. The southernmost of these is Bereich Wonnegau, a name derived from the German *Wonne*, meaning "bliss." At the ancient city of Worms are the historical vineyards of the Liebfrauenkirche, birthplace of the now corrupt Liebfraumilch wine discussed earlier. Chalk, loam, marl, sandstone, slate, and other soil types, readily identified just short distances from each other in this locale, bring a similar complexity to the characer of wines grown here.

Most experts agree that the best Rheinhessen wines are grown in Bereich Nierstein. Without question, Niersteiners are the most easily found Rheinhessens throughout the U.S. marketplace. This district, characterized by red slate soils, extends from Gunterblum north to the ancient city of Mainz.

FIGURE 8.10 Liebfrauenkirche at Worms. *(Courtesy of German Wine Information Bureau.)*

The history of Mainz wine dates to 38 B.C., when Roman soldiers established a camp next to a Celtic community there and were rationed wines from Italy. Some 25 years later, Emperor Augustus's stepson, Drusus, launched his campaign against the Teutons from that headquarters. Mainz eventually became the seat of the Roman commander in chief of Upper Germania, and the site of extensive vineyard plantings.

The hillsides rising from the riverbanks of the Mainz area are fashioned into terraces, on which grapes may ripen to yield rich wines expressing an opulent floral bouquet. One noteworthy village here is Oppenheim, known for its softer wines from gentler slopes.

The wines of Bereich Bingen have, not surprisingly, many qualities in common with the wines grown in the neighboring Nahe region to the immediate west across the Nahe River. The Bingen slopes impart richer texture and more flavor than typical of the wines of other *Bereiche* in the Rheinhessen Anbaugebiet. The best wines in Bereich Bingen are grown in the townships of Scharlachberg and Charlemagne's Ingleheim.

◈ NAHE

Most of the vineyards of the Nahe are carved into steep slopes that form the banks of the Nahe River. The topography has a captivating austerity: cliffs, terraces, and small sleepy villages, centered by the city of Bad Kreuznach.

It is in the Nahe district, at the old Burg Layen castle, that Dr. Ingo Diel operates one of Germany's more eccentric wineries. A tour of his cellars is a bit like a visit to a modern art exhibit, with commissioned Dali-like avant-garde paintings on his tanks. Diel produces some excellent QmP wines in the 200-year tradition of his Schlossgut Diel estate, and he also makes some wines that defy classification according to the German system. Having planted several French vine varieties officially banned for Nahe *Qualitätswein,* Diel makes some rather Burgundy-like whites and reds. These, legally relegated to simple *Tafelwein,* are marketed with a fanfare for great quality, at prices marked higher than many highly-ranked QmPs. His wines are in great demand by eclectic German restaurants.

The Nahe has only two *Bereiche.* To the south is Bereich Schlossböckelheim, which surrounds a village of the same name. The slate soils of this district produce wines that express an enchanting floral-honey bouquet and fresh green apple flavor. The most famous vineyard of the Schlossböckelheim is the Kupfergrube, which relates to a local copper mine.

Bereich Kreuznach is the industrial city of Bad Kreuznach. As its name suggests, there is a "bath," or spa, in Bad Kreuznach. The best vineyards of Bereich Kreuznach yield truly fine wines, leading some to argue that the Nahe, in this choice geography, serves as the transition between the great wines of the Mosel-Saar-Ruwer and the revered Rheingau.

⬥ RHEINGAU

Although only about 3 percent of total German vineyard acreage falls within the boundaries of the Rheingau, it is nevertheless one of the most important wine-growing centers in the nation. Steeped in a history of wine excellence, the Rheingau continues to produce some of the world's most aristocratic wines.

All Rheingau vineyards lie on southern exposures along the Rhine River and are thus protected from the direct north winds by the Taunus hills behind them. There are about 7,000 acres of vines cultivated across the region, of which approximately three-quarters are planted with the classic Johannisberg Riesling, and most of the rest with Müller-Thurgau and Silvaner. The most well known Spätburgunder reds of Germany are also grown in the Rheingau.

The Rhine provides a temperature buffer, which protects somewhat against frost and increases the humidity level during the ripening season in autumn, which is necessary for the proper development of the *Edelfäule* mold.

There are 28 wine villages in the Rheingau, most of whose names are quickly recognized by connoisseurs of German wines. The region has only one *Bereich*, Johannisberg. It has 10 *Grosslagen* and more than 100 *Einzellagen* (named vineyards).

In 1984 several major winegrowers in the Rheingau decided to form the Charta Association. The mission of this group is to preserve the great history and tradition of Rheingau wines, but at the same time to advance their quality. Its trademark (three Roman columns connected by arches), found on bottle capsules, has evolved to become identified mostly with *Kabinett* and *Spätlese* wines as a special designator for dryness, as opposed to the residual sweet finish to which consumers are, or were, accustomed. The Charta objective was to gain the attention of enophiles devoted to the dry white wines of Bordeaux, Burgundy, and other major winegrowing regions and to offer these at a lower price. Charta has had some success, but, ironically, suffers because wines of the region have had difficulties in passing the standards.

At the eastern extreme of the Rheingau Anbaugebiet, near Winkel, the soils are of a loess and quartzite consistency. Along the riverbank here lies the small village of Erbach and its neighboring town of Hattenheim. Between these communities is the legendary vineyard of Marcobrunn, named after the Marcobrunnen, or "boundary fountain." For decades a dispute raged over whether the long-lived wines from that vineyard were officially "Erbachers" or "Hattenheimers." In 1971, German authorities pronounced the growth an Erbach, leaving Hattenheim to console itself with being home to the classic Steinberg vineyards first planted by Cistercian monks in the twelfth century. These vineyards retain their Hattenheim origin and yield white wines considered by some experts to be among the finest grown in all of Germany. Two miles to the north is the great abbey of Kloster Eberbach, approaching 900 years in age, still intact and a proud monument to the glorious heritage of the region.

One of the most highly revered wine estates in Germany is Schloss Vollrads, near the village of Winkel. This estate has been in the Matuschka-Greiffenclaus family since the beginning of the 1100s—a continuity of 30 generations! Schloss Vollrads wines are usually a bit lighter and more delicately elegant than those of the rich golden color and honey-apricot flavor typically associated with Rheingaus.

At the center of the region is another of the glorious German wine estates, the legendary Schloss Johannisberg. Vines extend from the front of the old palace down toward the Rhine River, a truly superb site yielding vintages of luscious whites that are often the most expensive wines produced in the nation. Schloss Johannisberg identifies different *Prädikats* of its wine through label statements, of course, but also by using capsules of different colors to seal and

FIGURE 8.11 Schloss Vollrads tower. *(Courtesy of German Wine Information Bureau.)*

dress the top of the bottle over the corks. Since the Napoleonic auction, the estate has been owned by the von Metternich family. German law provides exceptions to both Schloss Vollrads and Schloss Johannisberg, permitting their labels to carry only the name of their estate; the name of a vineyard site is not needed.

Also located in the Rheingau is the little village of Geisenheim, home of the Institut fur Kellerwirtschaft, the world-famous German school of enology and viticulture.

Farther west is the village of Rüdesheim, where vineyards are terraced into steep slate and schistous slopes known as the "Rüdesheimer Berg." As would be expected, this very poor soil yields tiny berries, making wines of rich color, body, and flavors, the very best of which are four *Einzellagen: Bischofsberg, Berg Roseneck, Berg Rottland,* and *Berg Schlossberg.*

In the extreme western reaches of the Rheingau the land is composed of slate rock on steep slopes, where the village of Assmanshausen centers a small area of red wine production from Spätburgunder vines. This wine has traditionally been given a residually sweet finish in order to meet QmP regulations, but there are an increasing number of dry *Assmanshausens* that are forgoing these rules in order to make more Burgundy-like dry reds.

MOSEL-SAAR-RUWER

There are records of Roman vines being cultivated on the banks of the Mosel River since the time of Christ. The Mosel runs about half its entire length in France before becoming the border between Germany and Luxembourg. It then turns northward and finally flows as a tributary into the Rhine at the city of Koblenz. It winds in such a serpentine course that it takes about 150 miles to progress less than one third that distance as the crow flies.

With about 30,000 acres of vineyards, the Mosel-Saar-Ruwer (M-S-R) is the fourth largest winegrowing region in Germany. Its history rivals that of the Rheingau, as does its wine quality. The M-S-R produces virtually all white wine principally from Johannisberg Riesling, along with a lesser portion from Müller-Thurgau.

The southwesternmost *Bereich* of the Mosel Anbaugebiet is the Obermosel, or Upper Mosel. It is here that the Saar and Ruwer river tributaties merge with

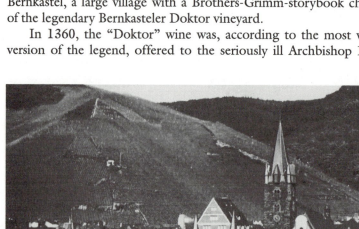

FIGURE 8.12 Mosel-Saar-Ruwer vineyards. *(Courtesy of German Wine Information Bureau.)*

Deinhard

BOTTLED BY
DEINHARD & CO.

KOBLENZ-GERMANY
AN RHEIN & MOSEL.

Mosel · Saar · Ruwer

Piesporter Goldtröpfchen

Riesling Kabinett

Qualitätswein mit Prädikat

A. P. Nr. 190700305684

750 ml   PRODUCT OF GERMANY WHITE WINE   ALCOHOL 9 % BY VOL.

the Mosel. In Trier, the capital city of this district, one can see the ruins of the ancient Roman sector, an impressive monument to a winegrowing heritage reaching back nearly 2,000 years.

Nearby, in the Bereich Saar-Ruwer, is found the rather uncommon vine variety *Elbling*, which is thought to be native to the locale and, therefore, to predate the Romans. The Elbling lacks finesse and, in a combination of sandstone and slate soils, yields wines that are tasty but often harshly acidic. When these wines are extremely harsh, the locals make what they call, with tongue-in-cheek, *Dreimannerwein*, or "three-man wine"—it takes two men to force a third to drink it!

Downriver is Piesport, home of the famous *Piesporter Goldtröpfchen* wine, the "little drops of gold." At this point in its course the Mosel River makes numerous sharp bends, and the very steep hillsides and cliffside vineyards, planted mainly with Johannisberg Riesling on both sides, make an unforgettable sight.

The Bereich Bernkastel has a truly magnificent countryside and wines to match. Indeed, some of the finest and most expensive wines grown in Germany are *Bernkastelers*. The capital of the district is generally recognized to be Bernkastel, a large village with a Brothers-Grimm-storybook charm and home of the legendary Bernkasteler Doktor vineyard.

In 1360, the "Doktor" wine was, according to the most widely accepted version of the legend, offered to the seriously ill Archbishop Boemund II of

FIGURE 8.13 City of Bernkastel at the foot of the Doktor vineyard. *(Photo by author.)*

Trier by Herr Ritter von Hunolstein, a local winegrower. Von Hunolstein was a personal friend of the archbishop and, feeling desperate to help in some way, prepared a bottle of the best wine from his Bernkastel vineyards and managed to get it into the hands of the ailing prelate. The archbishop eagerly drank the wine, doubtlessly assuming that drinking it could give pleasure while it eased his pain. After consuming several glasses, Boemund fell asleep. When he awakened the next day, he proclaimed full recovery from his illness, rejoicing, "This splendid doctor cured me!"

Since then the vineyard has received countless accolades regarding its healing powers. Eventually the property became part of the estate of Dr. H. Thanish, who is often mistakenly thought to have been the original "Bernkasteler Doktor." The Doktor is a vineyard, not a physician, and the scant 12 acres of Doktorberg vineyard today yield wines of grand blossomy bouquet and complex fruit flavors but can produce only enough to satisfy a fraction of its great world demand.

Other important vineyard towns in the Bereich Bernkastel are Brauneberg, Erden, Graach, Ürzig, Wehlen, and Zeltingen. The "Heaven's vineyard of Graach," or Graacher Himmelreich, produces very fragrant wines with a delicate consistency. The Ürziger Wurzgarten, or "spice garden of Ürzig," is well-known for wines with a delicious spicy-apricot flavor.

Farther on downriver is the town of Wehlen, famous for its "sundial vineyard," the Wehlener Sonnenuhr, named after a sundial carved in one of its riverside cliffs. The wines of Wehlen are green apple and a bit citrusy in flavor, long-lived, and the equal of most any other fine Mosel wine.

The steepest vineyards of the entire Mosel-Saar-Ruwer are found at Erden, the most remarkable being the Treppchen, or "little stairway." Erdener wines typically express a fresh fruit bouquet and complex earthy flavor on the palate. Braunebergers and Zeltingeners are rich and full-bodied, with distinctive Riesling bouquet and flavor.

Still farther down the river is Bereich Zell/Mosel, where increased plantings demonstrate the growing popularity of the Müller-Thurgau vine. The riverbanks are not as steep here, and soils gradually become a little more fertile as the river nears its confluence with the Rhine at the city of Koblenz. The central town of Zell is the home of the renowned Kellar Schwarze Katze, or "Black Cat Cellar."

Legend has it that many years ago a very superstitious keeper of the Electoral Castle Inn in Zell, having worked all his life with little to show for it, turned to growing grapes as a last resort. During the spring of his vineyard's first crop year,

FIGURE 8.14 Wehlener Sonnenuhr vineyard on the Mosel. *(Photo by author.)*

on a cold and rainy day, a black cat happened through the vines, saw the man, hissed and spat at him, and backed away. The man fell into despair, but his depression slowly lifted as his grapes ripened to perfection and the wine they yielded was superb. In gratitude, the man promptly named his new enterprise after the black cat. It is said that, to this day, no dogs are allowed in the old inn at Zell.

MITTELRHEIN

The Mittelrhein begins where the Rheingau ends. This region proceeds northwesterly some 60 miles downriver to the city of Bonn. It is in the Mittelrhein that the very steepest cliffside vineyards in Germany are cultivated, many of which offer the utmost challenge to anyone desiring to grow wine.

A visit to the vineyards of the Mittelrhein is not for the fainthearted; however, the legendary castles and ancient ruins perched upon rocky peaks, along with natural scenery of the region, are unmatched anywhere for spectacular sightseeing. Not to be missed is the classic monastery of St. Goarshausen, which overlooks some of the finest vineyards in the Mittelrhein.

Nearly three-quarters of the vines tended in the Mittelrhein are Johannisberg Riesling; much of the rest are Müller-Thurgau. The wines from these vines are almost always tart and, when excessively so in poorer vintages, are generally marketed in bulk for the production of sparkling wines, which in Germany are called *Sekt.*

AHR

Before the reunification of Germany, the Ahr was the northernmost of Germany's wine *Anbaugebiete,* the only region where more red wine is grown than white. Of all the winegrowing regions, only the Hessische Bergstrasse is smaller than the Ahr. The vineyards of this region line steep hillsides along both banks of the Ahr River for about 15 miles until it joins the Rhine at Bonn.

Approximately 32 percent of the vines cultivated in the Ahr region are Spätburgunder, and another 28 percent are *Portugieser.* The resulting red wines are light and fruity; most are consumed locally.

SAALE/UNSTRUT

Since political reunification, the Saale/Unstrut has become the northernmost of Germany's winegrowing regions. It has a long tradition of light wines, few of which ever achieve more than a *Kabinett* or *Spätlese* level of natural grape sugar.

The Saale/Unstrut gets its name from the Saale and Unstrut river valleys, just west of Leipzig, in which Müller-Thurgau, Silvaner, and Weissburgunder vines are cultivated, along with some vineyards on the hillsides near Freiburg. Virtually all of the wines grown in the region are also consumed there.

SACHSEN

Most of the Sachsen vineyards are situated on slopes along the Elbe River, about 30 miles from Pillnitz, past Dresden, Radebeul, and Meissen. Sachsen wines are grown from Müller-Thurgau, Weissburgunder, and Gewürztraminer, along with some Spätburgunder grown for *Elbtal Sekt,* a red sparkling wine that is very popular with the locals and some of the many tourists who visit the cultural and historical centers in Dresden and Meissen each summer.

❖ AUSTRIA ❖

As in most other western European countries, winegrowing in Austria and Switzerland was rooted by Roman colonizers and advanced through the Middle Ages by the church. Thus, the Austrians and the Swiss, having been isolated both politically and geographically, offer wines from vine varieties that have survived from ancient times. Enhanced by modern winemaking techniques, these wines offer a very interesting departure from the norm across Europe.

Although Austria is not one of the largest producers of wine in the world, the nine gallons average per capita wine consumption by Austrians ranks them among the world's leading imbibers.

The winegrowing regions of Austria are all located in the eastern part of the nation, distributed in a 150-mile sector replete with rivers, the Danube serving as the main artery in the north.

The climate of the principal Austrian vineyard districts is drier and warmer than that of most vineyard locales in Germany, primarily because the Alps east of Austria create a barrier to cold westerly winds and rain-filled clouds. As a result, grapes grown in the dry Continental Basin often reach the overripe state necessary to produce the prized late-harvest Beerenauslese and Trockenbeerenauslese wines of obvious German influence.

Grape seeds have been found in Austria which are estimated to be more than 2,500 years old, indicating that vines were harvested then and possibly made into wine. When Germanic tribes overran the Roman Empire, winegrowing, for all intents and purposes, ceased to exist. Charlemagne, through his decrees for the planting of vines, began the resurrection of the winemaking arts in Austria as he had in France and Germany.

Among the most active forces in the reestablishment of Austrian winegrowing were the monasteries. One of the finest of these is in Heiligenkreuz, built by St. Leopold in 1141, near Mayerling in the Voslau region. It remains one of the most splendid examples of Cistercian monastic architecture in the country, and its flourishing vineyards today bring to mind the many vintages of flowery white wines enjoyed in the nearby Vienna woods.

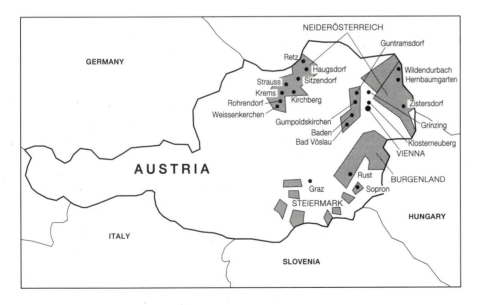

FIGURE 8.15 Austrian winegrowing regions.

FIGURE 8.16
Heurigen vintner in
Vienna. *(Courtesy
of University of
California at Davis;
photo by Philip
Hiaring.)*

✪ CLASSIFICATION

During the early 1100s, Viennese winegrowers maintained a powerful association that rigidly restricted wine imports allowed into their region. These restrictions no doubt constituted at least one reason why Austrian wine quality generally suffered during the next few centuries. In 1582, Johannes Rasch wrote an impressive book about the need for upgrading Austrian viticulture. This work unquestionably influenced the Austrian imperial court to ratify a wine quality classification system.

It is in Austria that one finds *Heurigen,* literally translated as "young wine," which refers to the fresh young wines available at low prices in the many Vienna wine pubs following the vintage season. The first *Heurigen* became available in 1780 when Empress Maria Theresa proclaimed that each winegrower was allowed to sell wine made from his or her own vines without having to pay taxes. As new wines became marketable in November, the vintner would display a crown or wreath of straw or fir above the entrance door of the establishment, advertising to passersby that the *Heurigen* was ready. With the new vintage, the vintner would welcome new friends and renew ties with old ones. By the following November, when a new *Heurigen* was ready, the previous *Heurigen* became *alte wein,* or "old wine."

During the early 1970s, Austria embarked upon an ambitious program of reform for its wine industry. Previously, the nation had only a rather loose set of national wine regulations that did little to define origins or set production controls. When neighboring Germany adopted its new wine law in 1971, the Austrian government took steps to enact a very similar set of regulations—the major categories of which are as follows:

Tafelwein. Natural grape sugar must have reached a minimum of 13 degrees Brix. In Austria sugar content is measured by KMW degrees (short for *Klosterneuberger Mostwaage),* a scale that is virtually identical to the more familiar Brix measurement used in the United States. Chaptalization is permitted.

Qualitätswein. Natural grape sugar must have reached a minimum of 15 degrees Brix, and alcohol level must be at least 9.5 percent by volume. Chaptalization is permitted.

Kabinett Wein. Natural grape sugar must have reached a minimum of 17 degrees Brix.

Besonderer Reife. Kabinett Wein that has higher natural grape-sugar levels and exhibits the organoleptic characteristics typical of overripe grapes.

Spätlese. Natural grape sugar must have reached a minimum of 19 degrees Brix.

Auslese. Natural grape sugar must have reached a minimum of 21 degrees Brix.

Beerenauslese. Natural grape sugar must have reached a minimum of 25 degrees Brix.

Ausbruch. Natural grape sugar must have reached a minimum of 27 degrees Brix.

Trockenbeerenauslese. Natural grape sugar must have reached a minimum of 30 degrees Brix.

Eiswein. Natural grape sugar must have reached a minimum of 22 degrees Brix, and the grapes must have been naturally frozen.

All Austrian-grown wines, except for the *Tafelwein* grade, must display the geographical origin of the grapes on the labels.

The addition of sugar is permitted under much the same circumstances as prescribed in Germany. Should natural grape sugar fall below the minimum for a particular vintage, then the wine may be chaptalized, provided that the sugar addition brings the resulting juice up to only a 13 degrees Brix maximum. A maximum addition of 5 Brix is permitted under any conditions.

One of the chief differences between Austrian and German quality levels is the higher sugar requirement in Austria, a result of the warmer and drier climate, as discussed earlier. Another difference has to do with government testing. No *Prüfungsnummer* is awarded in Austria. Instead, wines that successfully pass the evaluation of government cellar inspectors may be awarded the *Weingütesiegel,* or "Wine Seal." This circular seal is red, white, and gold and should not be confused with the triangular Austrian trademark, the *Österreichermarke,* which is placed on some wines that have not earned the quality wine seal of approval.

Austrian wine-labeling laws allow a bottle label to carry the name of a region, a district, a village, and the predominant grape variety, which, in some cases, makes for confusion. Adding further complexity is that both vintner and grape variety names are permitted in combination with origins. However, when a geographic claim is made for a white wine, it must have originated entirely from that designated locale. Austrian red wines are allowed to be blended with up to 15 percent of wines from outside the designated origin on a label.

❖ NIEDERÖSTERREICH

The Niederösterreich region, located in the northeastern corner of Austria, is the largest winegrowing center in the country. Niederösterreich, often referred to as "Lower Austria," because of the lower elevation of this land, which borders both banks of the Danube as it flows through the central part of the beautiful countryside.

Vineyards in the Niederösterreich embrace the romantic old city of Vienna both to the north and to the south. Soils in this lowland region are varied, including chalk, gravel, sandy loess, and schist.

The wines of the Niederösterreich are typically white, light, and dry, but because of the relatively higher Brix levels attained, some are also strong in alcohol content. The vaunted *Grüner Veltliner* vine variety is very heavily planted in the region.

The Niederösterreich comprises 9 districts, as follows:

Baden	Traismaur
Falkenstein	Vöslau
Krems	Wachau
Langenlois	Wildendurnbach
Retz	

FIGURE 8.17 Austrian wine cellar. *(Courtesy of University of California at Davis; photo by Philip Hiaring.)*

Perhaps the best-known wine of Austria is the legendary *Gumpoldskirchner,* grown in the Baden district from *Rotgipfler* vines. These rich, golden, fruity wines are the product of grapes grown on the slopes below the exquisite resort town of Gumpoldskirchen.

Forty miles to the west of Vienna is the town of Krems, its lovely display of vineyard slopes directly facing the Danube. To the northeast of Krems is the Langenlois district, with several miles of the Kamp River valley connecting the two districts. Despite the great presence of the Grüner Veltliner vine being cultivated throughout the region, it is the Johannisberg Riesling wines that are the best quality.

To the southwest of Krems is the famed Wachau district. One could almost mistake the Danube for the Rhine as it flows past the storybook villages of Weissenkirchen and Dürnstein. The white wines grown here are definitively Austrian Grüner Veltliner, the norm being light-bodied, shy flavors, and a bit tart. It was in Dürnstein that Richard the Lion-Hearted was imprisoned and held for ransom during the twelfth century. Although arguments on the subject persist, it is generally conceded that the Wachau is among Austria's finest quality winegrowing districts.

❖ VIENNA

Vienna is Austria's smallest viticultural region, embraced both north and south by the Niederösterreich. The Vienna vineyard locale is really more of a large district than a region. The importance of Vienna winegrowing, however, lies not in its size, but in the social activity and tourist traffic it engenders, principally in the many *Heurigen* offered during and after the vintage season. The most noteworthy Vienna vineyard districts are Grinzing, Nüssdorf, and Sievering.

❖ BURGENLAND

About 25 miles southeast of Vienna is the Burgenland, where some of Austria's most impressive wines are grown. In the center of region is the large lake Neusiedler See, which tempers the climate of the area and provides essential humidity to nurture the *Edelfäule* noble mold needed for making sweet late-harvest wines. It is common for as much as half of the Burgenland's white wine production to reach the upper Brix sugar levels. A few of the finer estates may produce, in some years, a preponderance of Beerenauslesen and Trockenbeerenauslesen.

The most widely cultivated vine varieties in the Burgenland region are Müller-Thurgau, Neuburger, and Weissburgunder. Gewürztraminer, Muskat-Ottonel, Johannisberg Riesling, and Welschriesling vines are planted to a lesser extent.

There are two subdistricts in the Burgenland, Neusiedler See and Rust. Neusiedler See whites are generally superior Austrian growths, but this district is probably best known locally for some of its red wine production from *Blaufränkischer* (Pinot Noir) and *Blauer Portugieser* (Merlot).

Rust is where *Ruster Ausbruch* originates, a Trockenbeerenauslese that often achieves the high quality of German wines of the same type. Rust is the best known of the Burgenland subdistricts, primarily due to an "antifreeze scandal" that became worldwide news during the summer of 1985. A number of wines from Rust were found to contain diethylene glycol, commonly used as a refrigerant, apparently added in an attempt to increase sweetness levels without employing chaptalization, which could be detected. Ingestion of this chemical in sufficient quantities can cause serious brain and kidney damage. As might be expected, this scandal has had a devastating impact on the entire Austrian wine industry.

◈ STEIERMARK

The Steiermark region, composed of five comparatively small districts, stretches from the southwest to the southeast of Graz, and on both sides of the Mur River. The terrain is stark, with many vineyards established upon the poor rocky soils of the Alpine foothills. Much of the abundant rainfall here either quickly runs down the steep slopes or arrives during the dormant season, consequently adding little to the constant moisture levels in the vineyards.

Southern Styria and Klöch-Oststeiermark are the two principal districts in the Steiermark Region. The city of Leibnitz is the capital of Southern Styria. This locale is conducive to white wine production from Sauvignon Blanc (which locals call "Muskat-Silvaner"), Johannisberg Riesling, Weisser Burgunder (Chardonnay), and Welschriesling. Klöch-Oststeiermark has volcanic soils, which seem to impart a smoky character to the white wines grown primarily from Gewürztraminer and Ruländer vines.

❖ SWITZERLAND ❖

As in Austria, Swiss wine production does not equal that of most other European countries, although average per capita wine consumption of 13 gallons annually ranks it fifth among nations in the world.

Switzerland is a nation of three cultures, each of which maintains its own language. In the eastern portion of the country, centered by Zurich, is the German region. In the western sector, around Geneva, is the French region, and in the south is the Italian sector. The country is politically divided into 29 autonomous states called *cantons,* each with its own customs, regulations, traditions, and life-styles. Similar distinctions and contrasts can be found in the vineyard topography from one region to another.

Down the spectacular mountains of Switzerland flow the beginnings of three of Europe's most important rivers, the Rhine, the Rhone, and the Po. The Rhine flows northward through the German region, through Holland, and into the English Channel. The Rhone flows westward through the Valais district and then south, down the Rhone valley into France, toward the Mediterranean Sea. The Po flows southward through the Italian sector and on into Italy, finally emptying into the Mediterranean Sea.

The vines in these mountain districts are planted at higher elevations than in most other vineyards in Europe; the very highest is at Visperterminen, some 3,700 feet above sea level.

Virtually all of the average 23 million gallons of wine produced in Switzerland annually is white and dry. In recent years, however, much more attention has been given to the planting of red wine vines. Nevertheless, it is the white *Chasselas* variety that is most widely planted, along with Müller-Thurgau, often called *Riesling-Silvaner* locally. *Amigne* and *Competer,* other white wine vines, are also cultivated in Swiss vineyards. Principal reds are *Blauburgunder*

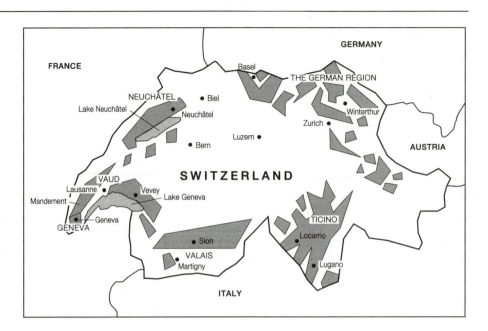

FIGURE 8.18 Winegrowing regions of Switzerland.

and *Klevener,* both of which are the same as Pinot Noir. Gamay and Merlot are also planted.

In Switzerland, as in all other western European winegrowing nations, the ancient Romans and the church had the greatest influence on the origins of wine production, particularly in the Vaud and Neuchâtel Cantons. The oldest monastery in Switzerland is the Abbey of St. Maurice, located near Monthey. The monks of St. Maurice owned many vineyards near the eastern shores of Lake Geneva. Monks are also credited with introducing the vine into the area centered now by the city of Lausanne on the northern shore of the lake. The Clos des Abbayes and the Clos des Moines are the best known of these vineyards that remain, and both continue to produce superior wines from Chasselas vines.

Switzerland served as a battleground for Germanic tribes and Romans for centuries during and following the days of the Roman Empire. In the ninth century, Switzerland became part of the German Empire. Later in the same century, in 888, the French Burgundians invaded the Rhone Valley to the southeast of Lake Geneva in the region now known as the Valais. The ensuing Burgundian occupation contributed a great deal to the art and craft of viniculture in that area, and a Burgundy character remains unmistakable in the wines grown here even in modern times. Wealthy Swiss often make weekend jaunts west, across the Jura mountains to Beaune, to buy selections of Grand Cru and Premier Cru Burgundies to stock their personal cellars.

The white varieties Pinot Gris and Traminer (the *Gewürz* prefix came centuries later in the Alsace) are still grown in the Valais region, although they are known locally as *Malvoisie* and *Païen,* respectively. The Burgundian king Rodolphe gave the vineyards at Bevais, north of the Valais, near Neuchâtel, to the grand Abbey of Cluny, near Mâcon in Burgundy, during the latter part of the tenth century.

Switzerland remained under foreign dominance until 1291, when the first three cantons of Schwyz, Unterwalden, and Uri were established so as to resist the Hapsburgs. During the next two centuries another 10 cantons entered the Swiss confederation. These 13 cantons remained self-governing and, despite their differences and quarrels, were still sufficiently unified to build one of the best armies in all of Europe, defeating Charles the Bold of Burgundy repeatedly in the latter portion of the fifteenth century. By 1648, the Swiss had achieved total political independence from the Holy Roman Empire, guaranteed by the Treaty of Westphalia.

Despite its fiercely guarded independence, Switzerland continued to be influenced by neighboring nations. The loose federation of Swiss cantons then gave way to the Helvetic Republic in 1798. This alignment was short-lived, and the Swiss, inspired by America's success in federating a United States, resumed the earlier form of government, in which the cantons were unified. In 1848 the new federal constitution was drawn and adopted. No set of political instruments, however, could unify the essentially tripartite nature of Swiss culture and history. And Swiss winegrowing, like Swiss society, continued to reflect its distinctive French, German, and Italian extractions. There is no true "Swiss" style.

Interpreting Swiss wine labels today can be difficult, because the information on the labels varies according to the canton in which the wine was grown. As in France and Italy, each region has its own traditions and regulations. In general, wines are named for the places in which they were grown, for the vine variety cultivated to grow them, or by the name of the wine type. As may typify the Swiss penchant for frugality, economy, and profit, their wine bottles contain 700 milliliters instead of the normal 750 milliliters found in most other major winegrowing nations.

The following terms, which may be found on Swiss wine labels, should be noted:

Avec Sucre Residuel—a label term that means that the wine has some residual sweetness

Légèrement Doux—a term meaning the same as *Avec Sucre Residuel*

Premier Cru—wine grown on the vintner's vineyard estate, virtually the same as "estate-bottled"

Oeil de Perdrix—a label term used for rosé wines made from Pinot Noir grapes

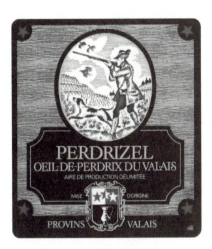

From the point of view of the American consumer, the most essential information printed on most labels is the vintner's name, a statement that has virtue in nearly every vinicultural area in the world.

❖ THE VALAIS

The Valais is the largest winegrowing region in Switzerland, cultivating more than 10,000 acres of vineyards and producing nearly 10 million gallons of wine each year. The Valais is a long, wide valley situated on both sides of the Rhone River, flowing westerly through the French sector in the southwesternmost reaches of the country. The climate here is one of the warmest and driest in

FIGURE 8.19 Vineyards in the Valais. *(Photo by author.)*

Switzerland, requiring many of the mountain vineyards to be irrigated by the thaws of the upper glaciers. The most noteworthy winegrowing townships in the region are Ardon, Chamason, Conthey, Leytrol and Vétroz, all centered by the capital city of Sion.

The most famous wine of the Valais is the light, refreshing white *Fendant*, named for the principal vine variety cultivated in the region. The Swiss cultivate the Silvaner vine here too, and perversely call the resulting wine "Johannisberg." This is generally a wine with firm acidity and light, fruity bouquet. The true Johannisberg Riesling vine is also grown in the area. Other whites of the region are grown from Malvoisie and Amigne which, along with several other varieties, are also made into sweet dessert wine types. *Ermitage* is a rather neutral dry white wine made from Marsanne vines.

The Valais red of note is *Dôle*, a wine blended from light reds crafted from Gamay and Pinot Noir. It has neither the deep red color nor the coffeelike bouquet of French Côte d'Or wines grown in Burgundy, a little more than 100 miles to the west. Dôle is light, berryish, and simple, and the Swiss readily admit that this wine is their everyday quaff. Nevertheless, it is a guarded commodity, as the Swiss government requires each Dôle blend be submitted for testing before it can be legally labeled as such.

❖ THE VAUD

The greater portion of Vaud vineyards are situated in a crescent along the entire north shore of Lake Geneva. The region also includes some vineyards on both sides of that portion of the Rhone River between the Valais and the lake. Most experts agree that the Vaud is the premier quality winegrowing region of Switzerland.

The Vaud, generally considered to be a French region, has three subdistricts: the Chablais, the Lavaux, and La Côte.

The Chablais is the Rhone River sector centered by the town of Aigle. Chasselas grapes grown in this locale yield light white wines of good quality, but not usually equal to the wines grown in the neighboring Lavaux district.

FIGURE 8.20
Vineyards in the Vaud.
(Courtesy of Office Des Vins Vaudois; photo by Max F. Chiffelle.)

The lakeside villages along the eastern shores of lake Geneva are travelogue picturesque, with acre upon acre of beautifully terraced vineyards ascending the Lavaux mountainsides. The epitome of Swiss winegrowing is found here on the famed Dézaley slope situated above the villages of Rivaz and Treytorrens in the Lavaux. Shy crops of the Chasselas grapes are fully ripened to make full-bodied white table wines, typically expressing a fragrant melon-fig bouquet and flinty-peach flavors.

Other notable winegrowing towns in the Lavaux district are Chardonne, Cully, Epesses, St.-Saphorin, and the very famous Vevey, where the annual Fête des Vignerons has been held every year since 1651, when it was initiated by the monks of the Abbey of St. Urban. A namesake of Vevey is Vevay in Switzerland County, Indiana, where Swiss immigrant winegrowers, under the leadership of Jean Dufour, established one of the single largest winegrowing regions in America during the mid-1800s.

The district of La Côte extends westerly from the city of Lausanne to the borders of the Geneva region. The wines from this locale are generally less flavorful and less distinctive than those from the Lavaux, but good quality vineyards can be found in the vicinity of Fechy, Luins, Perroy, and Vinzel townships.

Chasselas is grown for more than three-quarters of the wine produced in the Vaud. Gamay is the other principal vine, cultivated here for wine called *Salvagnin*, which may be blended with a small percentage of Pinot Noir, creating a product similar to the Dôle grown in the Valais, which also must pass Swiss government testing for authenticity before it is permitted to be labeled as Salvagnin.

❖ GENEVA

The Geneva region surrounds the western tip of Lake Geneva and is one of the smaller winegrowing regions in Switzerland. Chasselas, the preferred vine in the locale, yields dry white wines called *Perlan*, which closely resemble the wines made in the neighboring La Côte, but are often finished with a "spritz" of residual effervescence. In recent years new plantings of the Gamay grape variety have significantly increased production of red wines in the region.

Geneva is much less mountainous than most of Switzerland's wine regions, a factor that has permitted mechanization in the vineyards and thus reduced costs, as reflected in lower wine prices.

The Mandement, located north of the Rhone River as it flows out of Lake Geneva, is the largest of three Geneva winegrowing districts. A deed dated in the year 912 gave the Mandement vineyard to the Old Priory of Satigny, now the center village of the district. South of the city of Geneva are the districts of Arve-et-Rhone and Arve-et-Lac, situated, as their names suggest, near the river and the lake.

❖ NEUCHÂTEL

The region of Neuchâtel is the very smallest vinicultural area in Switzerland. Its vineyards commence at the periphery of the Vaud, stretching northeastward along the northern shores of lake Neuchâtel to the city of Biel. The French-style wines grown in the locale are considered to rival the better growths in the Vaud. Without question, the wines of Neuchâtel, along with its cheeses, are well known around the world.

Virtually all of the white wines produced in the Neuchâtel region are made from Chasselas, which constitute 75 percent of the total regional output. It is common for these wines to be bottled very young, still containing some of the effervescence from primary fermentation. "To make the star" is a local term denoting a slight sparkle in the wine. The other 25 percent of Neuchâtel wine production is devoted to red and rosé wines vinified from Pinot Noir vines. The most notable rosé is the legendary *Oeil-de-Perdrix* ("eye of the partridge"), which is also grown in the Valais. The best red is known as *Cortaillod,* named for the village where it is grown.

◈ THE GERMAN REGION

The many small vineyard locales across the Rhine valley, which embraces the entire northern portion of Switzerland, is known as the German Region. The Swiss Rhine flows northward through the Grisons Canton, bordering Liechtenstein, and continues north to the Bodensee, then westward to the historical city of Basel, after which it becomes the German Rhine.

Vineyards in this part of the country, often referred to as "Eastern Switzerland," are scattered among 300 villages and towns within nine cantons. The most noteworthy of these communities are Hallau, Wädenswil (where a large vinicultural research center is located), Winterthur, and the world-renowned Zürich.

Chasselas, called *Gutedel* here, still reigns as the predominant white grape variety. Local winegrowers and merchants refer to the Müller-Thurgau as *Riesling-Silvaner,* a combining of the names of the parent vines of this hybrid. It was Professor Müller who developed this cross at the Thurgau experiment station in this region. Pinot Gris and Completer vines are also cultivated here, but to a much lesser extent than the Chasselas. The major red vine planted in the German Region is the *Blauburgunder.*

◈ TICINO

The Italian winegrowing sector of Switzerland, Ticino, is best known for its good quality Merlot, commonly labeled "Merlot di Ticino." If this wine passes a government test for superior bouquet, flavor, and body, it may be labeled "VITI." In the Italian tradition, the best of the VITI may be labeled "Riserva" after further aging.

The Italian region is situated in the Alpine foothills surrounding Lake Lucarno and Lake Lugano in the Ticino Canton. The area is somewhat subtropical in climate, with palm trees and other vegetation one would normally expect to find far to the south.

In addition to the Merlot, small vineyard plots of Gamay and Pinot Noir, among other vine varieties, can be found in Ticino. Blends of these are made into *Nostrano,* an ordinary wine that is consumed locally.

9
THE WINES OF SPAIN AND PORTUGAL

SPAIN

Spain is the third largest wine producer in the world, some of its vintages yielding more than one billion gallons. It ranks first among nations, however, in the acreage of vineyards cultivated. With more acres and fewer gallons in comparison with top-producers France and Italy, it is obvious that Spanish vineyards have lower yields.

Switzerland is the only European country with more mountainous terrain than Spain. Five rivers flow from the majestic peaks rising in the center of the country. Each provides essential moisture to parched plateaus and lowlands, permitting the many different vineyard regions of Spain to exist.

The oceanic coastal climate in northwestern Spain is similar to that of neighboring Portugal to the south. Ocean-borne clouds from the southwest touch the cool mountains and produce rain, often rather torrential. Across the mountains to the east and south, the levels of rainfall taper off dramatically until, particularly in some of the plateau regions of Spain, there is only scant precipitation.

Long before the Iberian peninsula was divided into the countries of Spain and Portugal, the Phoenicians and Carthaginians brought the knowledge of winemaking to the eastern coast of this western Mediterranean land. The Greeks followed, bringing even greater art and craft to the cultivating of vines and making wines.

Hannibal used Spain as a base for the conquest of Rome in the third century B.C. During the Second Punic War, he crossed the Pyrenees and the Alps to attack Italy but was cut off from Spain by Roman forces. This marked the first occupation of Hispania by the Romans, but it was several hundred years more before the Iberian provinces were totally secured for the Roman Empire.

The Romans spread winegrowing to the northern provinces of Spain during the first two centuries after the birth of Christ. The eastern coastal vineyards in Tarragona, Andalusia, and Alicante were heavily developed during these early times. In the fifth century the Iberian peninsula was pillaged by Germanic invaders, and although winegrowing suffered, it survived.

The Moors occupied southern Spain from the early eighth century through the Middle Ages. Despite the Islamic prohibition on alcohol, there is much evidence to suggest that the Moors enjoyed Hispanic wines to the fullest. In the eleventh century the poet Al-Motamid wrote:

I certainly intend
Complaining to my friend
About this glass, alack,
Garmented all in black.

I set therein to shine
The sunlight of the wine;
The sun is sinking thence
To darkness most intense.

That the translation rhymes raises the question of accuracy, but the poet's agreeability to wine seems evident.

During the Middle Ages wine was one of Spain's most important products, but it was not until the tenth century that the Spanish wine export trade began to flourish. This commerce continued until the twelfth century, when economic conditions pushed Spain outside the mainstream of European trade. Consequently, more and more Spanish-grown wines were consumed domestically.

Alfonso X led his forces into Jerez, near Cádiz on the Mediterranean coast across from Gibraltar, in 1262. His victory confined the Moors, along with their proclaimed prohibition against wine, to reservations in Granada and several other locales along the Mediterranean coast. During the next 150 years or so the Christians gradually gained control of Spain, although Moorish and Jewish influences lingered in both language and politics.

With the 1469 marriage of Isabella I, queen of Castile, and Ferdinand II, king of Aragon, Spain made great advances in uniting as a powerful nation. Laws were recodified, the judicial system was reorganized, and an absolute monarchy emerged, which centralized governmental power. Isabella and Ferdinand were dynamic as well as decisive. They succeeded in driving the Moors out of Granada in 1492 and, of course, in that same year sponsored Christopher Columbus on his voyage of discovery to the New World.

The development of this new Spain included a rejuvenation of the vineyards, especially on the Cádiz and Granada frontiers. Spain's Catholic monarchs had many political and economic differences with other European nations, particularly England, and this discordance served to soften trade even though some of the exported Spanish wines had gained superb reputations abroad. A raid by Sir Francis Drake on Cádiz in 1587 resulted in the seizure of more than 350,000 gallons of Sherry wine, but the booty only created increased demand back in England.

Because it did not spoil, Sherry was an international favorite. This was due to the fortification of its alcohol content with brandy. Despite the Moors having been prohibitionist, they are curiously given credit for discovering wine distillation into high-alcohol brandy spirits. This grand Sherry "sack" wine from Spain was the preferred beverage of Shakespeare and is mentioned in many of his works. In *Henry IV*, Falstaff explains,

> *If I had a thousand sons, the first human principle I would teach them should be,*
> *—forswear thin potations and to addict themselves to sack.*

and

> *A good Sherris-sack hath a two-fold operation in it. It ascends me into the brain; dries me there all the foolish and dull and crudy vapours which environ it, makes it apprehensive, quick, forgetive, full of nimble, fiery, and delectable shapes; which delivered o'er to the voice—the tongue,—which is the birth, becomes excellent wit.*

Some of Shakespeare's contemporaries insisted that Sherry was a foreign wine, made and consumed by foreigners. This referred to the fact that British merchants had heavily influenced Sherry's method of vinification with Moorish brandy at least as far back as 1340. Following the recapture of the winegrowing lands near Cádiz from the Moors in 1492, the British merchants gradually developed the market for Sherry back in England. Sherry was known as *sacar*, meaning "export" in Spanish, which eventually became Anglicized into *sack*. According to the many references to sack during the Renaissance, it was probably much sweeter than the "dry sack" we know in modern times.

King Edward III made the initial ties with Portugal for England after Bordeaux was lost in the Hundred Years' War. A treaty was signed that gave

FIGURE 9.2   Sherry casks reserved for kings and queens. *(Courtesy of Sherry Institute of Spain.)*

Portuguese ships fishing rights off the English coast. Portuguese sailors traded their casks and skins full of tart dry wine called *vinho verde,* or "wine made from green grapes," for English goods. This was far different from the claret the British had beome accustomed to, and they turned to dry red *Port* (not the famous sweet Port dessert wines that were developed later), but this was also disappointing.

Spanish wines lost international popularity again during the early 1700s, resulting, to a large extent, from the Methuen Treaty in 1703, which favored Portuguese wine imports into England. But the demand for Sherry expanded once more during the latter part of the eighteenth century and the beginning of the nineteenth. During this era many of the present-day large Sherry houses in Jerez were founded.

Spanish table wines, for the most part, had been a dead issue since the Moorish occupation, and they remained so until the *Phylloxera* root louse invaded the vineyards of Europe in the 1860s and 1870s. The demand that could not be supplied by the customary French and German growths opened the door to the Spanish winegrowers. But the new markets were not handled properly, and disorganization created confusion and discord. Eventually, the *Phylloxera* invaded Spain too, and by the end of the nineteenth century the Spanish wine industry was in shambles.

The twentieth-century resurrection of Spanish winegrowing has been nothing short of magnificent. Resurging from the late 1800s, Spain now has approximately 4.5 million acres of vineyard under cultivation. From this great expanse of viticulture, about 750 million gallons of wine are produced annually.

✛ CLASSIFICATION

In the 1920s the post of *consejo regulador* (wine governor) was established for each region to administer wine production and wine marketing activities. Appointments for the position are made by the Spanish minister of agriculture. Inspections stations are maintained in some regions for the analysis and inspection of wines assigned for export. There are also inspectors who make checks in the vineyards and bodegas to ensure that regional regulations are met. The principal types of Spanish table wines are as follows:

blanco	white wines, both dry and sweet
clarete	light reds with a fruity bouquet
rosado	rosé wines, usually light and dry
tinto	dark reds, full-bodied and strong in alcohol

The entrance of Spanish wines into the international marketplace has had a profound influence upon the winegrowers of Spain. Quite apart from additional sales, there has been a significant improvement in the quality of wines from Spain, and their reputation, alongside classic wines from France and Italy, has advanced. It was in 1970 that the Ministerio de Agricultura promulgated the Statute of Vines, Wines, and Spirits. Subsequently, the Instituto Nacional de Denominaciónes de Origen (INDO) was established. INDO enforces regulations that empower 40-odd regional *consejos* to conduct a system very similar to the Italian system of *consorzi* and DOC classification.

VINO DE MESA

The Vino de Mesa category is similar to the ordinary wine classifications found in other European countries. Labels for wines of this type may not state a vintage, and virtually all Spanish *vino de mesa* is consumed within Spain.

The Spanish are the prizewinners when it comes to the variations they have managed to differentiate formally into separate categories. All wine grown in Spain that is "quality wine," or not *vino de mesa,* is designated as *Vino de Calidad Producido en Region Demarcada* (VCPRD).

VINO COMARCAL

There are 30 geographical areas in Spain where VCPRD *vino comarcal* wines are grown. Their labels may indicate both the vintage and the region in which the grapes were grown. With little increase in production cost, this new designation has given incentives for winegrowers to improve quality in order to pursue markets traditionally enjoyed by wines of higher qualifications.

VINO DE LA TIERRA

The VCPRD *vino de la tierra* classification is the ultimate interim appellation category. Although wines from within the borders of these locales must comply with the traditional identity set by the INDO, quality is not considered high enough to warrant Denominación de Origen status.

DENOMINACIÓN DE ORIGEN (DO)

The *Denominación de Origen* (DO) echelon of distinction is similar to the AOC in France and the DOC in Italy. Consistently high wine quality, vintage after vintage, and a well-known geographical identity are the basic elements necessary for each of the 40-odd Denominación de Origen locales authorized by INDO. Every DO is administered by its own *consejo,* who works with INDO to regulate production and marketing.

DENOMINACIÓN DE ORIGEN CALIFICADA (DOC)

In Spain, the *Denominación de Origen Calificada* (DOC), like the DOCG in Italy, is the ultimate classification for wine. It is reserved for the very highest expression of tradition, uniqueness, quality, and prestige. To date, only the *Rioja* has attained DOC rank in Spain.

Aging statements on Spanish table wine labels are controlled in the DO and DOC classifications as follows:

crianza	minimum aging of 1 year—1 year must be in cask
reserva	minimum aging of 3 years—1 year must be in cask
gran reserva	minimum aging of 5 years—2 years must be in cask

The table wines of northern Spain, perhaps best exemplified by those from the Rioja region, are considered by many to have the most character and highest quality of all Spanish wines. The central regions of the country grow most of the common *vino de mesa* (table wine). The south is famous for regal dessert wines, with Sherry and Malaga enjoying classic status.

◈ RIOJA

Located less than 75 miles south of the French border, the Rioja is the northernmost winegrowing region in Spain. Its name derives from the Rio Oja (the Oja River), a tributary that joins the Ebro at the town of Haro.

When the *Phylloxera* invaded Bordeaux, many of the winegrowers there crossed over into Spain, particularly to the Rioja, bringing with them their French vinicultural expertise and high hopes of filling the world demand for

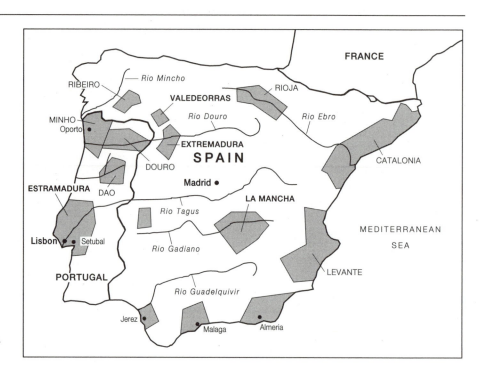

FIGURE 9.3 Wine regions in Spain and Portugal.

wine with Spanish supply. The French heritage lingers, and in modern times the wines of Rioja are made in a manner that readily recalls French style.

In the opinion of many wine enthusiasts, Rioja wine could be much better if it were not aged so long in the *barricas* (equivalent to the traditional 225-liter oak *barriques* in France), which impart a distinct vanillalike character and tawny-brown color when overdone. However, technology is catching up quickly in the Rioja, and critics are awarding increasingly higher grades.

Both white and red table wines are grown in the Rioja. The reds are made principally from *Tempranillo* and *Garnacho* vines, the latter of which is the same variety as the Grenache widely cultivated in the Rhone Valley region in France. White Rioja wines are grown from the classic *Malvasia* and the *Viura*, also known as the *Macabeo* in the Catalonia region.

Most Rioja wines are made in *bodegas* (wine cellars) which are very large as compared with the many small *caves* in Burgundy, or *Weinkellerei* in Germany. Indeed, some vintners in the Rioja region rival the largest Bordeaux estates in

FIGURE 9.4 Vineyards in the Rioja.
(Photo by author.)

size, but there are few Spanish villas that can match the splendor of the French châteaux.

The western districts of the Rioja, the Alta and Alavesa, have a moderate climate without excessive rainfall or summer heat. The environment changes drastically, however, as one proceeds down into the Rioja Baja, where the meso-climate becomes nearly arid and very warm. As would be expected, the wines grown at the Alta (higher) and Alavesa vineyards are more acidic and full-bodied, and the Baja (lower) wines are strong and bland. It is common to find wines blended together from all three districts of the region. Such blending ensures consistency of production, without the annual variation that is customary in districts comprising most other European viticultural regions.

In recent years the red wines from Rioja have become increasingly popular across the United States, particularly in the larger metropolitan market outlets. Much of the overaging is being tamed by the better vintners, and as popularity and publicity increase, so do the prices. What were once great bargains are now sometimes found to be competitive with other fine reds from around the world.

The AGE S.A., bodegas that produce the well-known "Siglo" brand are among the largest in the Rioja. They are part of a company that was founded in the city of Fuenmayor by the merging of Bodegas Las Veras and Bodegas Romeral during the late 1960s. The *reserva* and *gran reserva* are both made in the newer style of the region—more fruit and less oak. Siglo bottles are distinctively wrapped in a burlap-type material.

Founded in 1860, Vinos de los Herederos Marques de Riscal is the oldest operating bodega in the Rioja. It produces the epitome of the traditional Rioja —good red wine, but oak-aged to a fault by most Western standards. Nevertheless, its years of history, awards won, worldwide distribution, and comparatively high pricing, firmly illustrates that this wine is in great demand.

❈ NAVARRA

The Navarra, which borders the Rioja to the north and east, has historically been pegged as a producer of ordinary rosé table wines.

In the tenth century, during the time of Charlemagne, this region centered the kingdom of Navarre, a vast domain extending south into the Rioja, north into Bordeaux, and west to the Atlantic Ocean. It may have been during this time that the *Vitis biturgia*, perhaps an ancestor vine to the now famous Cabernet varieties, ascended from northern Spain into southern France.

FIGURE 9.5 Navarra vineyard. *(Photo by author.)*

Navarra is perhaps better known to Americans for its capital city of Pamplona, where locals conduct the annual running of the bulls through the streets. This world-famous event has generated increasing tourism for the region, whereby attention has been drawn to its red wines, which are similar in nearly every way to those of the Rioja Baja. The best Navarra wines are *Reserva* and *Gran Reserva* reds grown near the medieval town of Puente de la Reina.

The Vinicola Navarra estate was founded by a French firm, which commenced operations in 1864. Most of its production continues a heritage of good everyday red wines with modest fruit flavor and high acid, often balanced with a touch of residual sweetness. The *Las Campañas Cabernet Sauvignon* varietal is receiving good reviews by the wine media.

❖ CATALONIA

The Catalonian winegrowing region is located about 100 miles east of the Rioja and is centered by the cities of Barcelona, Sitges, and Tarragona.

To the north of Barcelona are the vineyards of the Alella district. Alella table wines are grown from the same four major vine varieties that are widely cultivated in the Rioja.

Embracing the port city of Sitges is the sandy lower sector of the Penedès district, historically known for its sweet, light amber dessert wine called *Malvasia de Sitges*.

In the higher limestone soils of the Penedès uplands are traditional vineyards planted to Macabeo and Parellada vines, which make good everyday white table wines. There are, however, a number of winegrowers planting Chardonnay, Cabernet Sauvignon, and other classic French vines in the Penedès with superb results.

The Torres family have become world-famous vintners of delicious table wines from Catalonia. Since the 1870s beginning of their winegrowing estate, founded amid a picturesque medieval landscape just west of Barcelona, they have become pioneers in the planting of the world's most celebrated vine varieties. The resulting grapes have made fascinating wines, thought by many experts to be the very finest grown in Spain. The highly respected *Torres Gran Coronas mas la Plana Estate* is a blend of Cabernet Sauvignon and Cabernet Franc, increasingly compared favorably to Grand Cru Bordeaux.

Sparkling wines produced in Spain are called *Cava,* made in the Penedès both by the French Champagne method and by the *charmat* (tank) process. The best are those made from white grapes selected cluster by cluster for superior quality, much as in the *triage* selection process employed in Champagne. Cava is finished in the following sweetness levels:

bruto	bone dry
seco	dry
semiseco	semidry
semidulce	semisweet
dulce	sweet

The Raventos family was the first to make wine in the magnificent Catalan countryside, near the town of San Sadurni de Noya, during the 1500s. But their worldwide fame today is for their sparkling Cava made by the Champagne bottle-fermentation method. The Raventos caves are immense, each more than one-half mile long, built side by side in parallel, each series atop another, several levels deep into the earth. The Codorniu brand Cava made in these caverns is of both world-class quality and world-class quantity, by one of the largest sparkling wine vintners in the world.

The Tarragona district in Catalonia has endured a reputation for producing very strong red dessert wines of poor quality, known as "Red Biddy" in England. In recent years Tarragona has improved its name somewhat with the production of quality aperitif wines. This expansive vineyard locale is perhaps best known, however, for its *sangria,* a light red wine mixed with citrus fruit slices, sparkling soda, and a dash of brandy. Sangria was the rage across the entire United States during the late 1960s and early 1970s.

Within the Tarragona district is a subdistrict called the Priorato, perhaps somewhat equivalent to Italy's "Classico" designation. The Priorato gets its name from the priory of a Carthusian monastery, Scala Dei, now only ruins on the volcanic slopes of the Sierra de Montsant. Dry red wines grown from the *Cariñena* and *Garnacho Negro* vines are often vinified to more than 16 percent natural alcohol content. *Mistela,* a brandy and grape juice blend, is also made in Tarragona. Although some mistela is consumed straight, some of it is also used for blending to make aperitif and dessert wines.

In recent years some of the larger, better-known vintners of Catalonia have found great success in American markets. Among these firms are Torres, Jean Leon, and Raimat for table wines, along with Codorniu and Freixenet for Cava.

✠ CARIÑENA

Located between the Rioja and Catalonia, the Cariñena is one of Spain's smaller wine regions, even when the neighboring Aragon district is included.

Very strong red and white table wines are grown in the Cariñena from the *Garnacho Negro, Garnacho Blanco,* and the region's namesake vine, the *Cariñena,* which is the same as the Carignan so widely grown in California's Central Valley region. The Aragon reds resemble some of the lighter reds grown in the Rioja.

✠ LA MANCHA

Situated about 150 miles south of the Rioja, La Mancha is renowned as the homeland of the regal Don Quixote. The region is a high plateau on which about one third of all the table wine grown in Spain is produced.

The soils of La Mancha are of a poor chalky base with an arid topsoil. The best district in the region is the Valdepeñas, or "Valley of Stones." Red wines grown in the Valdepeñas from *Cencibel* and *Garnacho Negro* vines have a good reputation, as do the whites made from *Airen, Cirial,* and *Pardillo.*

Most of the La Mancha wines are dry, bland, and thin. Those seen in the American market will seem even drier and thinner as compared with other table wines. But this blandness is partially compensated by low prices.

✠ LEVANTE

East of La Mancha is the Levante, another of the huge Spanish vinicultural regions, bordered by more than 100 miles of Mediterranean coastline along the southeastern reaches of Spain. The best of the Levante wines are grown in the districts of Utiel-Requena and Valencia, the latter named for its capital port city. Almost all of the dry red, white, and rosé table wines in this locale are strong in alcohol, which is typical of wines grown in fertile soils of warmer climates.

1993
Vega
SERENA
Red Wine
LA MANCHA
DENOMINACION DE ORIGEN

PRODUCT OF SPAIN
Bottled by Rodriguez & Berger, S.A. Cinco Casas. ESPAÑA
SOLE U.S. AGENTS: SHAW-ROSS INTL. IMPORTERS, MIAMI, FL
750 ml   R.E.Nº 2060 CR   ALCOHOL 11.5% BY VOLUME

✣ GALICIA

The region of Galicia is best known as the burial site of St. James in the Cathedral of Santiago. James was the son of Salome, famous as the dancer of the seven veils. James and his brother, John, were apostles of Jesus Christ. John provided a written account of Christ's life, as included in the New Testament of the Bible. James preached the ways of Christ while walking from place to place across Spain; upon returning to Judea, he was executed under order of King Herod. James' remains were secretly taken back to Spain and interred in a Galician tomb, over which the magnificent Cathedral of Santiago was built.

Today there are many walking pilgrimages retracing the steps of St. James through Galicia. Along the way visitors can find both red and white table wines grown in the region. The best are red, doubtlessly successors to similar wines used in the celebration of Mass by St. James. Galician reds, when aged six years or more, qualify for a *reserva* label designation.

The most well-known Galician wine is, however, a white that is called "green wine," similar to the famous *vinho verde* of Portugal, discussed later in this chapter. Green wines are made from unripened white or red grapes and, as would be expected, are aggressively acidic on the palate. Wines of this type are often described as "eager" wines, perhaps because of the eagerness of the vintners to gather their grapes before rain can ruin the crop.

The Galician province of Orense is located along the northern border of Portugal and is made up of three districts: the Ribeiro, Valdeorras, and the Valle de Monterrey. The largest of these locales is the Ribeiro, where red table wines of good balance are grown from *Garnacho Negro, Caino,* and *Brancellao* vines. Whites are made from *Treixadura* and *Albarino*. Valdeorras vineyards are planted on gently sloping hills, which rise to elevations surpassing 2,500 feet. The varieties *Garnacho Negro, Alicante,* and *Mencia* yield good red wines, and *Godello Blanco* good whites. The vineyards and wines of the Valle de Monterrey are similar to those of Valdeorras.

✣ EXTREMADURA AND LÉON

The Douro River flows through the rural reaches of the provinces of Badajoz and Caceres, which together make up the Extremadura. The clay, granite, and slate soils yield good wines in some locales of this region, but few are exported. The best red table wines are grown from *Almendralejo, Garnacho Negro,* and *Morsica* grapes. *Cayetana* is the most prominent white wine vine, along with *Lairen, Moscatel, Macabeo, Palomino,* and *Pedro Ximenez.*

The Provinces of Léon and Zamora produce a large amount of ordinary wines called *corrientes,* although some superior growths are noted from the vicinity of La Bañeza and Toro.

✣ MONTILLA AND MORILES

The Montilla and Moriles region is located about 75 miles from Valdepeñas and some 20 miles or so to the southeast of Cordoba. Soils in the region vary but are predominantly calcareous. The principal vine variety cultivated here is the *Pedro Ximenez,* which is vinified into a very strong wine similar to Sherry and Madeira. Although *Montilla* is not fortified with brandy, it reaches an alcohol content well above that of most natural table wine fermentations.

The light, medium, and dark amber wines of Montilla were once even more popular than those from the Sherry region to the south. The name of the famous *Amontillado* wines of Sherry is translated as "like the wine of Montilla," an indication of how highly esteemed these wines are. The bodegas of Montilla recall ancient Roman times, as they still use huge earthenware amphorae, called *tinajas,* to ferment and store wines. These containers are often more than seven feet in height and contain more than 700 gallons.

✠ MALAGA

Malaga, another of the Spanish winegrowing regions rich in history, retains many signs of Roman occupation. The capital of this region is the coastal city of Malaga, situated amid the famous Costa del Sol vacationland.

The mild climate here yields large clusters of grapes produced from Pedro Ximenez and Moscatel vines, the latter dried into raisins before being pressed for very sweet dark brown juice, which is then fermented. Like the wines of Montilla, the wines of Malaga were well known long before the Sherries of neighboring Jerez de la Frontera.

Lagrima, considered by many to be the best type of Malaga, is made entirely from Moscatel raisins. Vines cultivated on the hillsides make wines that are drier and lighter than Lagrima. *Virgin* is the driest of the Malaga wines.

✠ HUELVA

Malaga is located at the eastern end of Spanish Andalusia, world-famous equine country, Huelva is at the western end, and the Jerez region is nestled in between.

The climate, soils, and vine varieties cultivated in the Huelva are quite similar to those of neighboring Jerez de la Frontera. However, experts agree that the Huelva wines lack the delicate character of grand *fino* Sherry.

✠ JEREZ DE LA FRONTERA

The Greek historian Theopompos referred to the ancient capital of the Spanish Sherry region in the fourth century B.C.: "Xera, city situated in the proximity of the Columns of Hercules."

Xera, on Spain's south coast near Gibraltar, was already an old city at the time of Theopompos. The Phoenicians had founded a settlement called Shera at the same location in the eleventh century B.C.

The Roman agriculturist Columella lived in the ancient fortress city of Cadiz, located on the Mediterranean coast about five miles south of Xera, then called Ceritium. Columella wrote that Ceritium was an important winegrowing center in his time.

Conquering Moors renamed Xera again, this time changing it to Xerez, which they pronounced as "Sheris." The medieval wine produced by the Iberians during the Moorish occupation was simple and sweet, made so by boiling down freshly pressed juice into syrup, which was added to wines after fermentation.

The history of Sherry wine commenced with the invasion of Xerez in the mid-thirteenth century by Alfonso X, who encouraged the expansion of winegrowing across his new "frontier"; hence the name Jerez de la Frontera.

The citizenry of Jerez de la Frontera were instrumental in preparing Christopher Columbus for his voyages to the New World. In 1493 they contributed more than 1,200 bushels of wheat to the provisions for his second journey to the west.

FIGURE 9.6 Cork tree in southern Spain. *(Photo by author.)*

It was in the large monastery called "Of the Defense of the Blessed Virgin Mary" that many faithful believe the first Sherry wine was fortified with brandy, circa 1475. Some historians credit the Moors for inventing the brandy distillation process during their occupation of Xerez, although others suggest that if this were the case, then Spanish brandy would have been exported long before Sherry.

Southern Spain is also heavily planted with cork oak trees, employed in making a large share of the cork stoppers used to seal wine bottles. The outer bark can be harvested only once every six to ten years.

The climate of the Sherry region is, except for very warm summers, rather mild. Prevailing southwesterly winds bring only a bit more than 20 inches of rainfall during most years, most of which falls in late autumn. This precious rain is diverted by shallow ditches dug along the rows and absorbed by the chalky soil. Given that mechanical irrigation is not permitted, keeping these ditches functional is an essential mission for successful Sherry viticulture.

The soil of the Albariza district has approximately 40 percent chalk content, less than half the chalk found in the finest Champagne vineyards but ideal for Sherry vines. Other principal districts in the region that have this essential soil are Añina, Balbaina, Carrascal, and Macharnudo.

The semiarid climate of the Jerez de la Frontera vineyards makes labor arduous, although tractors and other equipment have alleviated much of the hardship during the past several decades. Each year the chalky soils dry into a crust, which must be broken. As in the French Beaujolais region, some vineyards are managed without benefit of trellising, but this practice is changing because better fruit quality and great economic efficiencies have been attained through the use of modern training systems.

A characteristic malady of the grapes harvested from the Jerez de la Frontera vineyards is a deficiency in acid strength. Wines made from low-acid grapes are more subject to microbiological degradation and are generally more difficult to stabilize than balanced wines. This problem is overcome in the Sherry region with a process called "plastering," in which gypsum (*yeso* in Spanish) is dusted on the grapes. Natural tartaric acid ions in the fruit react with the gypsum, resulting in calcium tartrate, potassium sulfate, and tartaric acid. The salt crystals precipitate as part of the eventual wine lees, but the acidity remains, increasing total acidity content to desired levels.

Nowadays the golden ripe Palomino grapes of the Jerez de la Frontera are harvested and taken immediately to wineries for crushing and pressing. Pedro

FIGURE 9.7 Heavy Sherry grapes supported by props. *(Photo by author.)*

FIGURE 9.8 Bending staves in a Sherry butt with heat from fire. (*Courtesy of Sherry Institute of Spain.*)

Ximenez and Moscatel grapes continue to be dried in more traditional styles on woven grass mats before being shipped to the Sherry bodegas. The fruit from each vineyard locale is kept separate so that vintners can judge the components from each growth in blending a final wine that will remain consistent from year to year.

In the traditional process, tumultuous primary fermentation takes place in just several days, as the Jerez bodegas are warm during the autumn and yeast cells multiply quickly. The new wines, having reached about 12 percent alcohol, are allowed to rest for three months or so in the Sherry *butts* (oaken casks of about 132 gallons capacity), filled to only about three-fourths capacity. The air space, or *ullage*, provides an oxygen source for the growth of *flor* yeasts, or wine "flowers." These very special microbes grow on the surface of the wine in a white rather meringue-like form and serve to oxidize ethyl alcohol and acetic acid into acetaldehyde, which has the famous nutlike flavor inherent to fine Sherry wines.

It is at this point that Sherry vintners decide upon Sherry qualities:

Fino—A thick layer of *flor* is developed, imparting a very distinctive, but delicate, nutlike flavor; color is slightly amber.

Manzanilla—Similar to *fino*, but a bit more tart.

Amontillado—Often described as "medium" Sherry; more fully developed in flavor and color.

Palo Cortado—Similar to *amontillado*, but with a bit more complexity and flavor intensity.

Oloroso—Often described as "cream" Sherry; the most fully developed in flavor, color, and body.

To the novice it may seem that from *fino* to *oloroso* is a progression in quality. On the contrary, *finos* are the most highly regarded of all Sherries. Overdeveloped *olorosos* are called *raya* and can be blended or culled for distilling material.

FIGURE 9.9 A *Capataz* sampling Sherry from a cask with a *venencia*. (*Courtesy of Sherry Institute of Spain.*)

In another part of each bodega, juice from raisinized Pedro Ximenez and Moscatel grapes is made into a very sweet mistela by the addition of brandy. A more delicate *dulce mistela* is sometimes made from *Palomino*. A "color" wine can also be made by concentrating the juice from these grapes even further and blending the resulting tawny-brown syrup with fresh juice prior to fermentation.

The new wines, along with mistelas, brandies, and color wines are assembled by the wine masters into blends that are designed as dry *finos*, along with *amontillados*, which are a bit darker and sweeter, as well as *olorosos*, which are typically the darkest and sweetest of all Sherries.

Until a few decades ago, much was left to chance as to whether the resulting wines would achieve the high *fino* level, or become an *amontillado*, or an *oloroso*, or culled as a *raya*.

As in most of the world's classic wine regions, modern methods have found acceptance in making Sherry too. The pressing of crushed, but not destemmed, grapes is now performed with large modern presses rather than the traditional barefoot treading in the shallow wooden vats (*lagares*) of just a few decades ago.

Today most of the large Sherry houses employ much more advanced technology in order to reduce the number of lesser-grade wines. After the initial rest of the new vintage (*añada*), the new wines are reclassified every few months. The wine from each separate vineyard is also regularly evaluated.

Once all the new wines are categorized, they are blended by type and introduced to a *solera* in the bodega. A solera is a fractional blending system in which

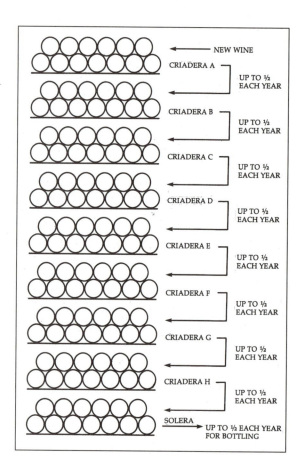

FIGURE 9.10 A solera blending system.

FIGURE 9.11 José Domecq, the famous "nose," examines new Sherry from the solera in his bodegas. (*Courtesy of National Geographic Society; photo by David Alan Harvey.*)

criaderas, or rows of stacked Sherry butts are maintained full of wine from previous years. Once each year a prescribed amount of wine, up to 50 percent of the total volume, may be taken from each of the butts in the bottom or lower *criadera* for bottling. The void left in this final *criadera* is replaced with wine taken in the same manner from each butt in the next to last *criadera,* which, in turn, is refilled with wine from the next *criadera,* and so forth, through perhaps as many as 15 *criaderas* in the entire solera. The new vintage replaces the void left in the first *criadera.*

This process brings a superb consistency to the Sherries from each solera and, because such wines depend on long periods of aging, the solera also continuously effects a progressively older cumulative age for the entire volume of wines in the system.

Finos are typically marketed as fresher, younger Sherries, and thus fewer *criaderas* are generally employed in a *fino* solera than for the *amontillado* or *oloroso* grades. Because the storage butts in the *criaderas* are wooden and therefore porous, water, having such small molecules, can slowly evaporate from Sherry wines during long periods of aging. The much larger alcohol molecules are retained inside the butts, in time causing the alcohol percentage to increase slightly.

One special type of Sherry is grown and matured in Manzanilla, located near the port of Sanlucar de Barrmeda. This is the region of the chalky Albariza soils adjoining the Mediterranean Sea a dozen miles or so northwest of Jerez de la Frontera. Classic *Manzanilla* has a distinctly seaside element in its bouquet and a hint of saltiness on the palate.

One of the greatest of the British-Spanish alliances formed for commercial production of Sherry occurred in 1855, when London wine broker Robert Byass joined with Jerez vintner Don Antonio Gonzalez. Their distinctive *Tio Pepe fino* demonstrates their unique expertise with the solera and is the largest selling Sherry of all.

John Harvey became master of an English wine-importing company in Bristol during the early 1820s, the firm having been founded some 20 years earlier. The Harvey family leadership resulted in great success with marketing sweet dessert wines. During the 1960s Harvey's Bristol Cream was one of the American "boom" wines. Its name translated *oloroso* into "sweet," and clever marketing made it the "in" cocktail and dessert wine of the times. With the passing of that fad, Harvey's sold out to a large brewing corporation that also bought the McKenzie Sherry bodegas and vineyards in Spain. The combination has renewed the Harvey's reputation as a vintner of fine Sherry.

It was in 1790 that George Sandeman, with a small loan from his father, founded the equally small House of Sandeman in London. It became one of the world's largest and most respected shippers of fine Sherry and Port wines. The Sandeman "Character Oloroso" is, as the name suggests, rich in the nutty-caramel bouquet character that the golden-amber *oloroso* type promises.

Other respected names in Sherry are Duff Gordon, Emilio Lustau, and Williams and Humbert.

❖ PORTUGAL ❖

Winegrowing in Portugal began with the Phoenicians, even though Portugal as a nation did not exist at the time. Following the Phoenicians were the Greeks, who added their expertise; then the Romans, with even more advanced technology in treating vines and wines. In the southern reaches of the Iberian peninsula, Roman *dolia,* very large amphorae, have been found, which closely resemble the *tinajas* still employed in the area. Strabo (circa 63 B.C.–A.D. 21), a Greek geographer, told of how vineyards were being planted along the western coast of what is now Portugal and Spain.

The Moors brought suffering to Portugal as they had to Spain. Following the Christian conquest that drove them out, much of the remaining primary vineyard land in Portugal was divided into large estates. Curiously, interest in winegrowing seems to have disappeared for several centuries thereafter.

The first date of importance in the more recent history of Portuguese winegrowing is 1093, the year in which King Alfonso VI of Castile arranged the marriage of his illegitimate daughter, Teresa, to Count Henry of Burgundy. The dowry included large Portuguese estates, and Count Henry brought many vines with him to his new land. The native Portuguese immediately adopted the new vines and renamed them *Tinta Francisca,* or *Tinta da Franca* and *Francesca,* all of which translate as "French Red." The wines that resulted were much heavier and richer than those that had previously been produced on these estates.

Count Henry's domain, stretching across much of northern Portugal, became known as the Terra Portugalensis, and Henry extended the borders even farther through taking the spoils left after his successes in settling civil wars. Henry's son, Alfonso, inherited these lands, promoted himself to duke, then prince, and finally to king of the Terra Portugalensis. However, his cousin, Alfonso VII, successor to King Alfonso VI of Castile, did not take kindly to these titles and declared war on the ascender in 1130. An ensuing peace brought little satisfaction and eventually, King Alfonso VI, with the Treaty of Zamora, acknowledged the royal status of his cousin and granted him the title "King of Portugal." The Pope did not concur, however, and would recognize only a dukedom for the renegade king.

Throughout the next two generations of monarchs, the Portuguese wine industry became well established and trade with England resumed. During this time the Portuguese borders were expanded through conquests by the Crusaders, Templar Monks, and the Knights Hospitalers.

British king Edward III negotiated a treaty that served to exchange Portuguese wine for fishing rights off the coast of England. These wines, called "Port," were dry reds of poor quality as compared with the fine reds from Bordeaux that had been shipped to Britain for two centuries. It was a situation that caused considerable unrest among English wine imbibers.

Another wine, *Osey,* a white probably from the Oporto area, was also exported to England, but the British seemed to accept this rich golden product, which was most likely sweetened with honey. A poem of the time comments:

> *Portyngalers....*
> *Whose merchandise cometh much into England.*
> *Their land hath oil, wine, osey, wax and grain.*

Lisbon, a large port city and trade center during the fifteenth century, may have introduced the West to spices, tea, and other culinary treasures from the East. Portuguese sailors of the day were renowned for their adventuresome spirit and fearless disposition.

Among these was one João Gançalves, also known as "Zarco the Blue-Eyed." Zarco boldly sailed into the forbidding Atlantic and discovered the rocky isle of Madeira, located about 400 miles from the west African coast. In colonizing the island, Zarco set fire to the forests, fires that were reported to have lasted almost seven years. The ashes may have given fertility to the sparse volcanic soil, as the Madeira vineyards flourished, but wood for building the casks needed for wine storage was lost to the great fire. Visiting the island in 1455,

Alvise da Mosta, a Venetian, praised Madeira wines, especially those made from the *Malvasia* vine, which produced large clusters of grapes. This reputation spread quickly, and by the end of the fifteenth century, the popular Cretian Malmsey wines exported to England were in stiff competition with the new Madeira.

Following the defeat of King Sebastian in 1580, Philip II of Spain marched into Portugal and brought an end to the wine trade with England. Sixty years later the Portuguese kingdom was restored and trade resumed once again, although the poor quality of the red wine once again created a strained relationship. Another poem reveals the discontent with the dry Port wine:

Mark how it smells. Methinks, a real pain
Is by its colour thrown upon my brain.
I've tasted it—'tis spiritlesss and flat
And it has as many different tastes,
As can be found in compound pastes…

Although Portuguese dry red wine found little acceptance in England, there was still an interest in the sweet grapes grown in Portugal. During the late 1600s a number of British wine merchants went to Portugal with the idea of trying their own hand in making wines that they could successfully market back in the British Isles. They literally invented the Port wine we know today. In short, they added brandy to the partially fermented wine. The brandy arrested further yeast growth, which left the remaining unfermented sugar as sweetness in the finished wine.

This practice, however, was quickly challenged, as purists insisted that such wines were not natural—a complaint that continues within some circles even in modern times. The British wineries, or "wine lodges," still operate near Oporto in Portugal, bearing the now famous names of the original inventors and shippers: Croft, Dow, Gould-Campbell, Graham, McKenzie, Offley, Sandeman, Warre, and others.

Oliver Cromwell is credited by historians with introducing the new sweet Port dessert wine to England. It soon became the favorite wine of the nation, just as Madeira became the preferred wine in the British colonies.

It was in Oporto that the first cylindrical bottles were employed for wine aging, at about 1770. Prior to this time, bottles were typically rather short flasks. Most could not be laid down, and thus their corks would not stay wet. Instead, they were stored upright, and when corks dried out, air entered the bottles, allowing for bacterial spoilage and/or oxidation.

Tiny Portugal ranks well below the leading nations in wine production, but is first in the density of vineyards as compared with total land area and may also lead the world in per-capita wine consumption, at just over 20 gallons a year. The Portuguese produce about 350 million gallons of wine per year from some 900,000 acres of exquisitely beautiful vineyard locales.

The winegrowing regions of Portugal rise steeply from the narrow sandy plains of the Atlantic coast, where there are very warm mesoclimates, to the cooler mountainsides that dominate most of the countryside. In many areas the mountains must be terraced to accommodate the vineyards. Hardy laborers dedicate their lives to winegrowing in Portugal, tending their precious vineyards almost as one would care for a garden, with most of the work performed by hand. Much of the soil, especially in the northern portion of Portugal, is granitic rock and must be broken up manually. The magnificent terraces and walled vineyards of the Douro make for some of the most picturesque landscapes in the world.

FIGURE 9.12 English wine bottle, circa 1800. *(Courtesy of Corning Museum of Glass.)*

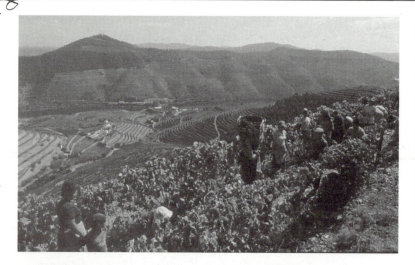

FIGURE 9.13   Terraces of vineyards in the Douro Region of Portugal. *(Courtesy of James Symington.)*

❖ CLASSIFICATION

Responsibility for regulation of Portuguese wines is held by the Junta Nacional do Vinho (JNV), which is headquartered in Lisbon. Port wine is excepted from this jurisdiction, as it is controlled by its own institute in Oporto. The JNV coordinates the work of local, regional, and national authorities in somewhat the same manner as the federal DOC cooperates with the regional *consorzi* in Italy. Vinifying practices, standards of production quality, and marketing regulations are functions of the JNV. Most of the enforement operations authorized by the JNV are delegated to regional authorities.

VINHO DE MESA

The ordinary white, rosé, and red wines of Portugal are called *vinho de mesa* and are loosely comparable to the ordinary wines grown in neighboring Spain and other countries. Much of the popular Portuguese table wine imported into the United States originates from blends of these wines.

Wine from the Quinta do Carmo estate exemplifies the increase of inexpensive wines made under *vinho de mesa* labels. This estate, now part of the Rothschild wine empire, which includes Château Lafite-Rothschild in Bordeaux, has received great praise from wine consumers and the wine press.

VINHO REGIONAL (VR)

Wines grown in various districts are permitted to be blended into *vinho regional* (VR) wines, labels for which may express both vine variety and vintage year. This classification has given Portuguese vintners located outside the more prestigious winegrowing locales an opportunity to establish an identity from which to pursue new markets.

VINHO DE QUALIDADE PRODUZIDO EM REGIÃO DETERMINADA (VQPRD)

VQPRD *(Vinho de Qualidade Produzido em Região Determinada)* is another relatively new level of wine quality and authenticity regulated by the JNV. Perhaps because the name of this category is cumbersome, and obviously patterned after the VDQS designation in France, wines in the category are now also known as *Indicação de Proveniência Regulamentada* (IPR). A major feature of IPR appellations is their potential, with consistent quality and consumer appeal, to advance into DOC status.

DENOMINAÇÃO DE ORIGEM CONTROLADA (DOC)

The *Denominação de Origem Controlada* (DOC) level of quality and authenticity was decreed by the JNV in 1990. DOC-classified wines undergo laboratory testing to ensure that they meet the particular specifications set by the JNV for each particular region and district. Bottled wines from Portuguese demarcation areas have a printed seal, varying from region to region, taped across the bottle neck and cork before being capsuled.

✖ MINHO

The Minho, located in the northwestern corner of Portugal, is the region of the *vinhos verdes* (green wines), sometimes called "eager wines," as they are produced from grapes that have not fully ripened in the vineyards. More than 75 percent of *vinho verde* is made from unripened red grapes. The common winemaking procedure does not include removing the stems, which, along with green fruit high in malic acid, usually results in *vinho verde* being both astringent and acidic and a bit like "leathery" green apples in flavor. This wine, in fact, is a favorite of only a very small portion of wine lovers outside the region.

Minho vines are often cultivated to heights of about eight feet above the vineyard floor in an overhead system that provides shade for other crops beneath the trellises. The black *Vinhao* variety is the most heavily planted, and *Azal Tinto, Borracal,* and *Espadeiro* are also popular. White vine varieties are *Alvarinho, Azal Branco,* and *Dourado.*

There are approximately 90,000 winegrowers in the Minho region, who together produce more than 60 million gallons each year. The districts included in the region are Amarante, Basto, Braga, Lima, Monçao, and Peñafiel.

✖ DÃO, BAIRRADA, AND TRÀS-OS-MONTES

The Dão, a region of granite soils, is high plateau land divided by steep canyons and bordered by mountains. It is situated in the north-central section of Portugal about 40 miles south of the Minho. The region takes its name from the Dão River, which cuts through it in a southwesterly direction and flows as a tributary into the Mondego River.

FIGURE 9.14 Villa Mateus, museum center of Mateus rosé wine. *(Photo by author.)*

From very early times, the wines grown in this region have been good, but still ordinary. In the twelfth century the Dão citizenry voted to prohibit sale of any wines made outside the region as long as stocks of the native Dão wines remained unsold in inventory. Since the establishment of the regional authority in 1908, the Federação dos Vinicultores do Dão, wine quality has improved along with labeling standards.

There are abut 50,000 acres of vineyards in the neighboring Bairrado and Tràs-os-Montes, or "Across the Mountains," some cultivated at elevations of more than 5,000 feet. In contrast to the Minho, the vineyards of the Dão are maintained in a low-trellis system. Mostly bland red wines are made from the varieties *Tourigo, Preto Mortagua,* and *Tinta Pinheira,* this last thought to be a descendant of the Pinot Noir brought centuries earlier by Count Henry of Burgundy. Whites are made from *Doura Branca* and *Arinto,* the latter considerd to be a descendant of the German Johannisberg Riesling.

At the center of these three regions is the ancient Roman crossroads town of Viseau, which doubtlessly had a profound influence on the earliest winegrowing development in this part of Portugal. The largest of Portugal's vintners is Sogrape, Vinhos de Portugal SARL, producer of the widely distributed Mateus Rosé wines made primarily from the vine varieties *Alvarelhao, Bastardo, Mourisco,* and *Touriga.*

All the districts in this region grow *vinhos maduros* (mature wines) from ripened grapes. One of the landmark townships is Pinhel, noted for its rosé table wines.

❖ CARCAVELOS

The tiny region of Carcavelos is composed of vineyards cultivated on the alluvial soils bordering the Tagus River estuary. A red dessert wine grown from the *Galego Dourado* vine is made to varying sweetness levels. Rather rare as exports nowadays, the drier wines of Carcavelos are treasured in the Scandinavian countries, where they are enjoyed as aperitifs.

❖ ESTREMADURA

The region of Estremadura, located north of Lisbon, is usually divided into two main districts: the "Plain" and the "Ocean." Most of the wine production in the Estremadura is *vinho de mesa.*

The wines from the flatland plains, centered by the Tagus River, are reds from the *Cartaxo* vine and both reds and whites from *Almeirim, Bucelas,* and *Torres Vedras* vines.

The vines cultivated in the Ocean district are some of the oldest in the world. The sand is so deep and hot in this locale that the *Phylloxera* root louse could not wreak its damage here during its late nineteenth century rampage through Europe. Consequently, these vines survived the scourge. To prevent grape clusters from being burned on the hot vineyard floor, vines must be propped up to keep them off the blistering sand during the summer and early fall.

◈ SETÚBAL

South of Lisbon in the upper portion of the Setúbal are vines which, like those in the Ocean district of the Estremadura, have survived the *Phylloxera.* These vineyards are bordered by the Atlantic Ocean on one side and the limestone Arrábida hills on the other.

White grapes from the *Moscatel do Setúbal* vine and reds from *Moscatel Roxo* are vinified into a golden dessert wine aptly named *Setúbal Moscatel,* thought by many wine experts to be the finest muscatel in the world, and by others to be the best overall dessert wine of all.

The Setúbal peninsula is also the location of the giant vintner, J. M. Da Fonseca, Internacional-Vinhos, Lda. This company is more easily recognized as the producer of the Lancers brand of rosé, the first of the popular Portuguese rosé wines marketed in America.

◈ MADEIRA

The isle of Madeira is 30 miles long and scarcely 16 miles wide, and only about one-third of the land surface is suitable for viticulture. The entire island is a dormant volcano dotted with high cliffs and caves. Most of the arable land must be created by breaking up the lava by hand.

The vines cultivated on Madeira include the *Malvasia,* which the Renaissance British often referred to as "Malmsey," a variety originally brought to Madeira from Crete. *Bastardo* was often mentioned by poets of the eighteenth and nineteenth centuries. Perhaps the most important variety on the isle is the *Sercial* vine, thought to be a relative of the Johannisberg Riesling.

Perhaps the reason Madeira was so popular in colonial America was that King Charles II excluded Madeira wines from a regulation that required wines to be shipped in a British ship out of a British harbor. Produce from other English possessions and territories was prohibited from direct export. Christopher Columbus lived in Madeira for a time and, in bringing his wines to the New World, he perhaps blazed the trail for the eventual shipping of Madeira by wealthy ship owners in Boston, Charleston, New York, and Philadelphia.

In modern times, Madeira is made in classic dessert wine style. Grapes are still crushed by bare feet in *lagares,* shallow open-top vats. The resulting must is carried in goatskins to the winery lodges, most of which are located in the capital city of Funchal. Following fermentation, the wine is aged for six months or so in heated cellars called *estufa,* where temperatures of about 110° to 115° F "bake" the wine. For sweeter Malmsey and Bual Madeiras, the *estufado* baking process is performed after brandy is added to fortify the wine. The drier Sercial and Verdelho Madeiras are baked in *estufa* before the fortification brandy is blended in.

Legend has it that some casks consigned to a colonial American wine buyer were once accidentally topped-up from a barrel of rainwater. The Madeira shippers discovered this mistake only after shipment and expected a wrathful response. However, the lighter Madeira wines were received even more warmly than the traditional vintages, and reorders were placed for larger shipments. This legend continues, with "Rainwater" Madeira still commercially produced.

There remain a few bottles of *Madere de Napoleon*, which was produced in 1772. This wine was offered to Napoleon in 1815 on his way to exile at St. Helena, but he was too ill to take any.

In contemporary times Malvasia, or Malmsey, is obtained from the pressing of the ripest of the grapes harvested in the hottest region of the island. Sercial is produced from vines on the peaks and cliffs, some suspended in truly precarious positions. Sercial Madeira is not usually drunk until it is at least eight years old, and it may be aged for decades longer before consumption.

◆ DOURO (PORT)

Aside from the use of more modernized equipment, the making of the sweet Port dessert wine designed by British merchants in Oporto several centuries ago has not markedly changed.

Port is a fortified wine made from red grapes that are crushed and fermented so as to use about half of the natural grape sugar in making alcohol. Brandy is added to inhibit any further fermentation by the yeasts and to raise the alcohol content to about 20 percent by volume. Because Port contains unfermented grape sugars it is, by definition, sweet. The British, who have long dominated Port production and trade, consider it the supreme after-dinner drink.

FIGURE 9.15 Back-laden baskets of Port grapes carried down a Douro vineyard terrace. *(Courtesy of James Symington.)*

FIGURE 9.16   Barefoot trodders
in a Port *lagare*. *(Courtesy of James
Symington.)*

Both soil and weather conditions for vineyards in the upper Douro River
region are extreme. The climate includes temperatures of biting cold in winter
and more than 100° F during most summers. Rainfall often measures more than
50 inches per year. The rocky shale soils on the mountainsides and cliffs are
composed of a compressed clay, which commonly protrudes from a dense granite overlayment. The labor required to plant just a small vineyard on a terrace
supported by a high wall is monumental. The land is often so unmanageable
that dynamite is needed to blast holes for planting vines. Few other plants, and
no other crops, can be grown economically in this locale. Its soil has few nutrients or other redeeming qualities, yet the Douro remains one of the most beautiful vineyard regions on earth.

The finest growths are situated near Pinhão, located in the center of the
Douro region approximately 60 miles east up the Douro River from the great
English wine lodges in the cities of Oporto and Vila Nova de Gaia.

More than 30 grape varieties are grown for Port in the Douro. Among the
best are *Alvarelhão, Mourisco, Tinta Cao, Tinta Francisca, Souzão,* and
Touriga. At one time barefoot trodders crushed the grapes in *lagares,* but now
most of the lodges have taken to using modern machinery in the vinification
processes. The vintage commences in September with the gathering of grapes,
still done by hand, and the fruit is carried from the cliffside terraces on the
backs of workers.

As the fermenting process converts sugar to alcohol, wine masters monitor
progress until just the right amount of sweetness remains in the fermenting
must. Then brandy, at a strength of 155 degrees proof (about 77.5 percent
alcohol), is added to arrest the fermentation. Each vintner individually sets his
own precise sweetness standards.

Of the 30 million gallons or more of wine made annually in the Douro,
only about one third is *approveitado* (government approved) for Port. This designation is determined by a points system that is governed by the Instituto do
Vinho do Porto. Points are derived by a complex equation, which considers
productivity, altitude, geographical position, vineyard maintenance, age of vines,
soil composition, climate, and other factors to determine the classes of Port
vineyards.

Class A vineyards must achieve more than 1,200 points and are permitted
to use no more than 600 liters of wine for making Port from each 1,000 vines.
A Class B vineyard totals between 1,001 and 1,200 points and can use not more

FIGURE 9.17 A *barco* in harbor at Oporto. *(Courtesy of James Symington.)*

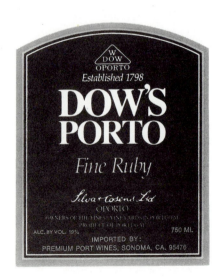

than 570 liters per 1,000 vines. This scale ends with Class F vineyards, which tally less than 400 points and are allowed to use no wine for Port production.

Once a new wine is judged suitable to be processed into Port, it is taken from its *quinta* (estate lodge) and shipped to one of the Port lodges in Vila Nova de Gaia. Single-sailed boats called *barcos rabelos* hauled the pipes (81-gallon barrels) down the Douro River across the rapids until more recent times, when hydroelectric dams made the trek impossible. Nowadays semi tractor-tanker units and rail cars haul most of the new Port downriver.

Founded in the late 1790s as Silva & Cosens, Ltd., the Dow's brand, now respected as one of the very fines names in Port, originated from the name of an Englishman who joined the firm later. The principal vineyards for Dow's Ports are cultivated on the exquisite Quinta do Bomfim estate situated near the Duoro capital city of Pinhão.

Most Ports are blends of various wines and vintages, each lodge blending to maintain its own consistent style. The new wine is stored in *toneis,* large wooden casks, which contain approximately 3,000 gallons each.

When these wines undergo long periods of aging in wooden casks, they are known as "Wood Ports." There are four distinct types of Wood Ports, as follows:

Ruby Port—aged for abut four years in pipes before bottling

Old Ruby Port—matured for seven years prior to bottling

Tawny Port—aged for more than eight years in pipes

White Port—made from white grapes and aged for about four years in pipes before bottling

When the Port producers and shippers think that a given year has been truly exceptional for the production of fine Port, they "declare" a vintage; this occurs only abut twice each decade.

Of all Ports, *Vintage Port* is deepest ruby in color and fullest in flavor. Ports of this type are aged in pipes for just two years or so before bottling, but they are given the benefit of long periods of aging in the bottle before being shipped. Despite the claims of some authorities, Vintage Ports will not live forever, and certainly not as long as Madeira. Vintage Ports are more expensive than Wood Ports, but in the opinion of most connoisseurs, they are well worth the price. Few wines receive the accolades bestowed on well-aged Vintage Port.

Founded circa 1670, Warre's was the first of the Port lodges to operate under British influence in making fortified sweet red wines. It remains in very high repute and at very high prices. Warre's is typically bold in fruit aroma, with firm acidity and lengthy aftertaste.

Another of the old Port lodges, W. & J. Graham & Co., has become one of the most prestigious names in fine vintage Port wines. Malvedos is the premier estate for Graham's grapes and is where the Symington family owners often spend a summer weekend retreat. Graham's Vintage Ports are heavily structured, with a very dark ruby color and complex berry-plum and cedarlike flavors, all in perfect sweet-tart balance.

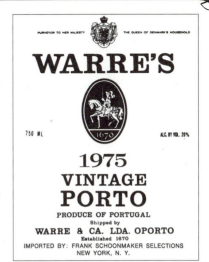

LATE-BOTTLED VINTAGE PORT

Late-Bottled Vintage Ports, sometimes labeled simply "LBV Port," are aged in wood about twice as long as Vintage Ports. LBV Ports generally have a lesser degree of color and flavor, are often filtered (which enhances appearance at the expense of some flavor), and cost less than Vintage Ports. They are a good value when produced by one of the better lodges.

CRUSTED PORT

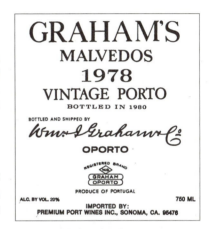

Crusted Ports are made in much the same manner as Vintage Ports, except that they are blended from at least two different vintages and are aged for much longer periods of time in bottle. During this aging, the sediment that develops hardens on the sides of the bottle into the familiar crust.

EXPORTS FROM THE REGION

A Port lodge may not ship more than one third of its inventory in any single year. Apart from the Instituto do Vinho do Porto, which exercises control over

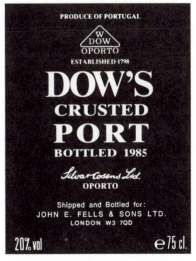

FIGURE 9.18 LBV Port casks in the Dow's cellars. (*Courtesy of James Symington.*)

Port production, there is also a winegrower's union, the Casa do Douro, that was formed in 1933. This cooperative regulates trade and manufactures the brandy used in arresting fermentations and fortifying total alcohol content.

Their position dwarfed by the immense international popularity of Port, the table wines made in the Douro are often forgotten. Unclassified red table wines enjoy the best reputation. The famous Mateus rosé found in wine shops across America is blended, processed, and shipped from Oporto, across the river from the Port city of Vila Nova de Gaia.

The great Port names found in the U.S. marketplace are Burmeister, Cockburn, Croft, DaSilva, Dow, Ferreira, Fonseca, Gould-Campbell, Graham, Sandeman, Taylor, and Warre.

10

THE WINES OF AUSTRALIA, NEW ZEALAND, AND CANADA

Although they rank relatively high on the wine consumption scale, each of the British Commonwealth nations still lags well behind the major winegrowing nations in the quantity of wine produced. Canadians drink nearly three gallons of wine per year on average, the English a fraction more than that, and the Australians and New Zealanders are now approaching five gallons annually—more than twice the rate of American consumption.

Nevertheless, the modest production growth in Australia, New Zealand, and Canada has been accompanied by a truly remarkable ability to make world-class quality wines, in some cases in climates and soils that are far less than ideal.

Each of these Commonwealth nations shows the unmistakable influence of European winegrowing traditions and practices. In the Barossa Valley of Australia, a rich German heritage is still evident. The German language is still widely spoken there, and the wines grown throughout the southern states of Australia display a pronounced Teutonic character.

Vines cultivated in New Zealand are also of German origin, along with the typical New World immigration of vines from France, Italy, Portugal, and Spain.

A comparatively small portion of Canada's wines are grown in the Province of Quebec, but the French influence is so deeply rooted there that it spills over into the other Canadian winegrowing regions, save perhaps British Columbia, where there is a decided Italian flavor. Canada's rather rigorous climate restricts most of the wine industry to southern sectors of the country, particularly where Ontario and New York State, in close proximity, share cool-climate technologies.

❖ AUSTRALIA ❖

Australians, like the Germans, drink a lot of beer. To the uninformed it may be surprising that Australia also ranks among the world's most progressive wine producers. Wine production here has increased more than sixfold during the past three decades. Most of this output is consumed by Australians, but wine exports, now shipped to more than 70 nations, have grown to become a trade factor of national economic significance. Although America has 15 times the population of Australia, U.S. wine production is just 4 times larger. There can be no question that winegrowing has become an essential industry in modern-day Australia and is advancing to levels of commercial significance approaching that in Europe.

Most of the notable winegrowing regions of Australia are situated in the southeastern coastal countryside, a bit closer to the equator than those of Europe. Such a location provides Australian vines with abundant sunshine, normally sufficient to fully ripen grapes in most of the regions virtually every year. These same locales are generally also rather dry, and a large share of the vineyards located in the states of South Australia, New South Wales, and Victoria require irrigation. Heavier productivity is generally achieved from the irrigated vineyards, resulting in wines of comparatively lighter bouquet and flavor, but of higher alcohol strength, than the products of the cooler, higher-elevation, non-irrigated districts in the same regions.

The lower levels are usually alluvial flatlands with sandy loams, somewhat lighter in consistency in South Australia and Victoria than in New South Wales. The soils at higher elevations are mixtures of limestone, sandstone, ironstone, and heavier sand in varying blends of brownish-red and gray earth. Although Australia's vineyards may not display the diversity of some other major winegrowing nations, there is quite enough variety to offer an interesting breadth of character and style.

FIGURE 10.1 Australian wine-growing regions.

Captain Arthur Phillip brought the first vines to Australia in 1788. Phillip had ordered the stocks from Rio de Janeiro on his way from England to New South Wales, where he had been directed by the Crown to establish a penal farm. By 1791, Phillip, then governor of the colony, had an experimental vineyard that had grown to about three acres. Phillip became ill and returned to England shortly thereafter, but his work with vines had shown such promise that two French prisoners were released from the penal farm to manage the vinicultural experiments. This enterprise, however, proved unsuccessful, as the two Frenchmen, atypically, knew little about winegrowing.

The next figure on the early Australian wine scene was explorer Gregory Blaxland, who established a vineyard in 1816 on his Brush Farm on the banks of the Parramatta River near Sydney. Six years later Blaxland won the Silver Medal for his red wine entry in a London competition administered by what is now the Royal Society of Arts. When his red won the Gold in 1827, wine authorities in England began to look favorably on Australia's potential for commercial wine production.

Many Australians, however, consider John MacArthur to be the true father of their wine industry. MacArthur, the first importer of Merino sheep to Australia, was exiled from Australia from 1809 to 1817, the result of a bitter argument with the infamous Captain Bligh of the Bounty, then governor of New South Wales. In exile, MacArthur toured some of the better winegrowing regions of France in order to gather vine stocks and information about their cultivation. After his return to Australia, he established his first vineyard plot at Camden in 1820 but later moved to the alluvial banks of the Nepean River near Penrith, where the first Australian commercial winery was constructed. By 1827, MacArthur's production had grown to exceed 20,000 gallons per year.

There are still others in Australia who consider James Busby to be the patriarch of their wine industry. Busby came to the new colony from Scotland in 1824 and was appointed headmaster of an orphanage. One of his topics of study was viticulture, which he taught with special enthusiasm since he was authorized to supplement his meager salary with one third of the income from the school vineyards. Busby took wine samples with him on a journey back to England in 1830. Those wines were so highly regarded that he was commissioned, at the government's expense, to tour Spain and France for the purpose of selecting the finest vine stocks for propagation in the Hunter Valley district of New South Wales. Starting with these original plant materials, the Hunter Valley has grown and flourished. Its success is a monument to Busby's dedication to wine quality.

In 1837, Colonel William Light became the first Britisher to explore the vast Barossa Valley of South Australia. A later explorer in that locale, Johann Menge, made a prophecy of remarkable accuracy:

> I am certain that we shall see the place flourish, and vineyards and orchards and immense fields of corn throughout. It will furnish huge quantities of wine; it will yield timber for our towns, and superior stone and marble abounds for buildings.

It was in 1842 that non-British immigrants were first permitted to settle in Australia, thus paving the way for the employment of trained vineyard and winery workers from the European continent. Subsequently, many German winegrowers came to the new colony and, as mentioned previously, the German influence has since become an integral part of the rich Australian wine heritage.

Johann Gramp planted vineyards in the Barossa Valley, at Jacob's Creek, in 1847. Soon afterward the legendary Joseph Seppelt came to the valley from Germany with a dream of growing tobacco. When he saw how very well the vine adapted to the beautiful Barossa, his interests quickly changed to winegrowing, and thus the internationally famous House of Seppelt was born.

FIGURE 10.2 Celebration of the vintage by the Barons of Barossa, an Australian fraternity established by German immigrants. *(Courtesy of Australian Information Service; photo by Douglas McNaughton.)*

Gold fever gripped Australia at about the same time and with the same exuberance that gripped the American West. Just as in the 1849 gold rush in the United States, prospectors flocked to Victoria in 1850, frantically searching for the precious metal. In similar fashion, most of those ventures also failed, leaving many native European entrepreneurs with little opportunity for earning a living other than by winegrowing. Two of the most important villages to emerge from the gold rush days were Great Western and Rutherglen, which have since become classic viticultural districts in Australia.

Samuel Sidney wrote of the 1852 viniculture scene in his *Three Colonies of Australia:*

> *Men who have been previously slaves to spirit-drinking, on going to work at a vineyard, have sobered down to two bottles of Australia wine daily, to the infinite benefit of their health and finances.*

It was Edward Henty and William Ryrie who pioneered winegrowing in Victoria, near Melbourne. By the mid-1860s their wines had won so many awards in European competitions that some wine experts talked of Victoria's becoming a world-class vineyard region. The British generally preferred heavier and sweeter wines, however, and Victorian wines made by French and Swiss immigrants were usually light and dry. This trend, along with the invasion of the *Phylloxera* blight, dashed the hopes for Victorian wine greatness in the latter portion of the nineteenth century.

During this time it was also found that much of the vineyard lands of South Australia needed to be irrigated for optimal production. Two Canadian brothers, Ben and George Chaffey, had established irrigation systems in California and in 1887 were invited to Australia to engineer similar projects. They set up a watering system in South Australia at Renmark, and a second in Victoria at Mildura. News of the Chaffey irrigation process spread throughout the upper Murray River in South Australia, fostering the establishment of vineyard plots and wineries, which have since become huge operations. Later, the advancing technology of irrigation to Griffith in New South Wales and other now-important Australian winegrowing districts.

The Parliament of South Australia enforced a strict vine stock import quarantine so as to avoid the ravages of *Phylloxera,* but it could not avert an economic wine blight similar to the overproduction glut that plagued the United States during the 1870s and 1880s.

Commerce in wines between Australia and England was greatly curtailed following the outbreak of World War I. The Armistice brought renewed activity in the wine export trade, but some of the social tensions between the British and German cultures remained. Many German family names remain today in every region of Australia winegrowing, although the character of the land and the climate are far different from any in Germany.

The Australian Great Depression preceded that in America by several years, but U.S. winegrowers had the added hardship of facing National Prohibition at the same time. Australian and American winegrowing history diverged even more widely during World War II. In the United States many of the manufacturing resources for wine were diverted to the victory effort. Production and exports of wine were reduced in Australia too, but domestic per capita consumption more than doubled from 1939 to 1945. Wines, sold by the carafe and by the glass, were quaffed without any particular regard for vineyard region or producer.

In the late 1940s the profile of wine marketing changed dramatically in Australia, with more and more wine being sold in bottles labeled with pertinent source information. As a result, even greater interest in wines from their own country was generated among Australian wine consumers. As interest grew, the wines themselves improved greatly because of advances in winemaking technology and art.

✛ CLASSIFICATION

A move toward more definitive classification of Australian winegrowing geography and the establishment of label guarantees was initiated in 1990 by the adoption of the Label Integrity Program (LIP). Bottles expressing vintage, vine variety, and specific origin on their labels must contain a minimum of 85 percent of wine in compliance with each of those identities. Inspections and audits are made to ensure compliance.

PRODUCT OF AUSTRALIA

The broadest appellation permitted is "Product of Australia"; the labels of wines in this category, without further definition, may not express either a grape variety name or vintage. This is similar to the rather generic "American" appellation enforced by the ATF in the United States. Many of the Australian "Champagne" and "Port" wines are classified as Product of Australia, as these types are traditionally nonvarietal and nonvintage anyway.

AUSTRALIA

A second classification, "Australia," should not be confused with the appellation "Product of Australia." Within the category, Australian vintners are permitted varietal/vintage labeling, but the national identity is virtually meaningless. It does, however, encourage the blending of wines across the nation, which serves to balance supply and demand from region to region.

SOUTH-EASTERN AUSTRALIA

The most successful segment of the new Australian classification system is the regional appellation of "South-Eastern Australia." This includes the states of South Australia, New South Wales, and Victoria, transcending the poor image of broad identity, yet providing in volume vintage-dated wines of good quality and reasonable price for the export market. It is the South-Eastern Australia appellation that has become very popular in wine stores across the United States.

STATE OF ORIGIN

The "State of Origin" appellation is much the same as in America. California, Washington State, Oregon, and other states earn their reputations in much the same way as South Australia, New South Wales, Victoria, and the other three winegrowing states do in Australia.

REGIONS AND DISTRICTS

Traditional appellations remain in Australia as regions, exemplified by Barossa, Clare Valley, and Coonawarra in the state of South Australia. Some of these, however, are further identified by specific districts, such as the Barossa Valley in Barossa.

▣ SOUTH AUSTRALIA

ADELAIDE AND SOUTHERN VALES

The city of Adelaide was founded in 1836, a busy seaport nestled on the eastern shore of Gulf St. Vincent where many of the German settlers arrived during the middle of the nineteenth century. Most of the vineyards that once graced the hills and plains embracing the old city, with the production of some excellent dessert wines, have long since given way to an expanding modern metropolis.

The Southern Vales district in the South Australian region commences at the southern suburbs of Adelaide, extending south along the Gulf of St. Vincent coast through the cities of Reynella and McLaren Vale to Willunga. The Southern Vales is particularly well suited for volume winegrowing, as it has a consistently temperate climate and light soils composed of sand, sandy-loam, and limestone.

One of the most famous names in the Southern Vales is Reynell. Walter Reynell and Sons Wines, Ltd., has a colorful heritage going back to the very beginnings of Australian winegrowing with the 1838 plantings of Richard Hamilton and John Reynell, for whom the city of Reynell is named.

CLARE VALLEY

Clare Valley is the northernmost district in South Australia, yet it is moderately cool, owing to its being situated on a series of upland plateaus ranging from 1,300 to more than 1,600 feet in elevation. Clay subsoils with sandy loam topsoils are typical along the 20-mile stretch of Clare Valley vineyards.

The city of Clare, established at the northern end of its valley, was settled in the 1840s by John Horrock, from England, who discovered copper and silver in the region. It soon became a mining boom town. Winegrowing commenced there in the 1850s when a monastery was founded, soon, of course, accompanied by vineyards. Commercial vineyards following in the early 1900s were relegated to making Port and brandy products. With consumer demand forcing a tack away from higher alcohols in the 1960s, major moves were made toward planting Shiraz, Cabernet Sauvignon, and other superior Old World *Vitis vinifera* vine selections.

Penfolds produces wines from organically grown grapes in the Clare Valley. Founded in the early 1890s as the Stanley Wine Company, this firm was taken over by the American H. J. Heinz Company, of catsup fame, in 1971. It has since become the Leasingham Domaine, the largest wine-producing firm in the Clare Valley.

BAROSSA

The great Barossa is perhaps the best-known winegrowing region in all of Australia, certainly the most notable in the region of South Australia. Situated approximately 35 miles northeast of metropolitan Adelaide, at its widest point the Barossa spans seven miles. From the towns of Kalimna and Bilyara at the north, to Williamstown at the south, the valley measures 20 miles in length. The principal communities in the district are Angaston, Nuriootpa, and Tanunda.

As may be expected, the temperatures of the Barossa Range hills are generally cooler than those of the valley floor. Soils range from light sandy loams to the richer loams on clay subsoils, the latter known as "red-brown earth," on which some of the finest wines in the region are grown. The commercial appeal of the Barossa is its overall combination of very warm weather, agreeable soils, and sufficient irrigation. These combine to produce consistently heavy crops of good grapes.

The South Australian Department of Agriculture operates one of the finest research facilities for viticulture in the nation just two miles east of Nuriootpa. Considerable acreage is devoted to working out solutions to the area's viticultural problems and to the advancement of the state of the wine art.

The most important institution in Australia for the research and teaching of viticulture and enology is Roseworthy Agricultural and Oenological College. This school, located near the city of Adelaide, also operates a large plot of research vineyards and a pilot winery where students have an opportunity to study wine marketing along with wine production.

One of the most historical vintners in the Barossa region is Kaiser Stuhl, (Seat of the Emperor). The firm is better known by locals as the Barossa Cooperative Winery, Ltd. From a rather difficult start and virtual failure during the Great Depression years, it has risen and prospered since World War II. The

FIGURE 10.3 Kalimna vineyard in the Barossa Valley. *(Courtesy of Rubin/Hunter Communications, Santa Rosa, California.)*

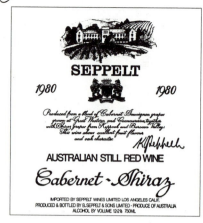

FIGURE 10.4 1879 Port barrels at
Seppelt. *(Courtesy of B. Seppelt & Sons, Ltd.)*

firm adopted the name Kaiser Stuhl from a nearby hilltop named after the
Kaiserstuhl hilltop vineyards in the Baden region of Germany.

One of the most famous vintners in the Barossa is B. Seppelt & Sons, Ltd.
Joseph Ernst Seppelt emigrated from Silesia in 1849, accompanied by his family
and other families associated with his tobacco and spirits business in
Wustewaltersdorf. Since its first plantings, the House of Seppelt has grown to
become one of the largest wine producers in the nation.

Of particular note is the locally famous 1879 Port made at the firm's large
winery facility at Seppeltsfield. That vintage year marked the first reserve held
from the finest Port wine made at Seppelt, a tradition that continues each year.
Bottles of the 1879 and other early vintages are now very rare, often selling for
several thousands of dollars each. In modern times Seppelt has adjusted its
product portfolio to reflect the increasing demand for varietal table wines in
Australia. Most of the varietals are produced in the firm's impressive Château
Tanunda winery complex.

Without question, the wine of highest regard throughout Australia is
Penfolds Grange Hermitage. The late Max Schubert, nationally acclaimed winemaker at Penfolds, toured the great Bordeaux château wine country in 1950
and was inspired to produce a wine of dense color and body, beyond anything
yet achieved from Australian grapes, perhaps even beyond Bordeaux itself.

FIGURE 10.5 Crushing Shiraz
grapes at Penfold's Magill Estate.
*(Courtesy of Rubin/Hunter
Communications, Santa Rosa,
California.)*

It was an idea that attracted a great deal of attention, and the Penfolds marketing people advanced the notion to Herculean proportions. Grapes were selected from the most struggling of vines in the coolest vineyards on the poorest soils—tiny berries packed full of color and flavor. The result was, and remains, a monument to fine winemaking—and an equally monumental price.

One of the comparatively newer names in the Barossa is that of Wolfgang Blass. The first of his Wolf Blass wines were released in 1966. Just one year later the first of what has become a plethora of awards and medals for excellence was won. Demand continues to build for the wines of this progressive vintner.

Established in 1863 by the Hill-Smith family, their Yalumba brand is one the oldest and most prestigious in the Barossa. The Yalumba vineyards are located in the Eden Valley district, situated a dozen miles or so southeast of Barossa Valley. Eden has higher ground, a cooler climate, and is arguably the source of Australia's finest Chardonnay and late-harvest Rieslings.

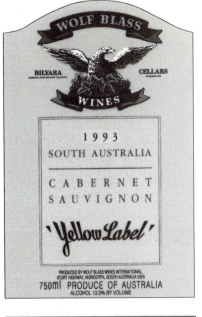

COONAWARRA

Situated to the extreme southeast of South Australia, along the border of Victoria, is the small wine district of Coonawarra, meaning "wild honeysuckle" in the language of the Australian Aborigines. Located near the cold ocean waters to the southwest, Coonawarra is the coolest vineyard district in the state of South Australia.

When full ripening is achievable, the wines of Coonawarra can be some of the finest grown in the nation. Whereas the more northerly and warmer regions yield fruit of rather uniform quality each vintage, Coonawarra is subject to widely varying conditions. Frosts are always a hazard during both budding and harvest. The harvest season here, in April, is usually more than a month later than in the Barossa, sometimes extending into a season of rainy weather, which can ruin maturing fruit. As one might expect, the cold-hardy German "Rhine Riesling" vine is widely cultivated in the limestone soils typical of this area.

Some 40 miles northward from Coonawarra, and offering a distinct contrast, are the comparatively new winegrowing Padthaway and Keppoch districts, both rather desertlike terrains of red and gray sandy loam soils. Seppelt and Thomas Hardy & Sons planted the first vines there, mostly Chardonnay and other cool-to-moderate climate varieties. Lindemans, founded in 1870, the third largest wine producer in Australia and a well-known brand of Chardonnay heavily distributed across the United States, has substantial vineyard holdings in Padthaway.

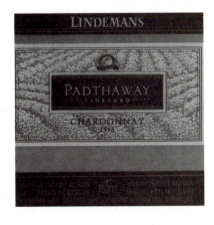

FIGURE 10.6 Wynn's Coonawarra Estate Winery. *(Courtesy of Rubin/Hunter Communications, Santa Rosa, California.)*

Despite Coonawarra's reputation being built on Chardonnay and other cool-climate whites, Wynns has earned respect by growing rich, full-bodied Shiraz and Cabernet Sauvignon wines since its founding in 1918.

RIVERLAND

Settled by the Canadian-born Chaffey brothers mentioned earlier, who emigrated from California winegrowing in the late 1880s, the Riverland was, despite its name, a desert wasteland situated a hundred miles to the northeast of Adelaide.

The Murray River, flooded every year by melting snows flowing down from the mountains in the Great Dividing Range far to the east, was tamed by the Chaffeys through the clever engineering of channels, locks, and dams. As a result, the desert was awakened with irrigation. Today large crops of Riverland grapes make good blending wines in several cooperative wineries. Much of this production finds its way into wines bearing the new "South-Eastern Australia" label appellation.

◈ NEW SOUTH WALES

The State of New South Wales, to the east from South Australia, is fringed by the southeastern coastline of Australia and is centered by the magnificent city of Sydney.

HUNTER VALLEY

About 135 miles north of Sydney, near the coastal city of Newcastle, is the renowned Hunter Valley, the New South Wales viticultural district that is well known internationally for wines of exceptionally high quality. The general regard of Australians for the Hunter Valley may be compared to the American devotion for the Napa Valley of California. Both have colorful histories and certain similarities of background. Busby was the founding hero of the Hunter Valley, playing a role rather like that of George Yount, the father of the Napa. Both regions struggled with a lack of respect and recognition until recent years. Yet, despite their renown, each contributes proportionately only a minor share of their respective national wine output.

The Hunter Valley may be divided into two main vineyard locales. The older, more traditional vineyard sites are located in the parishes of Pokolbin and Rothbury. In the upper reaches of the valley are many of the newer vineyards, established in the district since the end of World War II.

The soils of the Hunter Valley range from alluvial river flatlands to podzolic loams, sandstone, and shales. Temperatures are warm, and rainfall is erratic from year to year. Frost and hail are frequent hazards, as is mildew. Each year can be distinctly different. There are very good, even great, growing years, as well as miserable vintages that yield only common fruit.

Hunter Valley vintners continue to cultivate the traditional varieties of Sémillon, Cabernet Sauvignon, and Shiraz, but the most recent plantings there have included Chardonnay, Gewürztraminer, and Merlot, among others.

Founded in 1969, Rosemount Estate has become one of the large wine-growing firms in Australia. With a reputation built on powerful Gewürztraminer and Rhine Riesling wines, Rosemount has more recently directed its efforts toward other fine white table wines. Its Roxburgh vineyard, planted on soils heavy with limestone, yields a particularly rich Chardonnay, even by Australian standards, and its *Rosemount Fumé Blanc* is no less intense. Both wines are perennial winners in the better international wine competitions.

Established in 1828 by George Wyndham, the Wyndham Estate is one of Australia's oldest vintners and is now part of a consortium of estates in the Hunter Valley. Its "Bin" series, which includes *Bin 222 Chardonnay* and *Bin 444 Cabernet Sauvignon,* is typified by the strong, full-bodied, rich-flavored character resulting from the warm weather and fertile soils in this district.

HASTINGS VALLEY

Some 200 miles along the coastline north of Sydney is the remarkable Hastings Valley. Despite having some of Australia's hottest weather and highest rainfall, this district produces wines that are amazingly good.

Emigrating from his native France, John Cassegrain pioneered winegrowing in the Hastings Valley during the early 1980s. The bounty of heat and rain in this locale demand exceptional expertise in management of its vineyards. The *Cassegrain Chambourcin,* a French hybrid vine able to withstand these elements, produces a tasty spicy-fruity red wine reminiscent of Gamay.

MUDGEE

Approximately 140 miles west of the Hunter Valley is the Mudgee district, which exhibits nearly the same growing conditions as the Hunter Valley. Some of the most important vintners in Mudgee are Augustine, Botolbar, Craigmoor, Huntingdon, Miramar, Montrose, and the Mudgee Winery.

RIVERINA

Located about 350 miles west of Sydney is the largest winegrowing district in the New South Wales region, the Riverina, also known as Murrumbidgee, centered principally by the towns of Griffith and Yenda.

Comparatively heavy crops of grapes devoted principally to making dessert wines are the traditional production of the Murrumbidgee Irrigation Area, or MIA, as it is better known to the local wine trade. This region is undergoing a dynamic transformation, however, with new planting of the finer Old World grape varieties producing higher-quality table wines through the use of the latest vinicultural technologies. It is in connection with this transformation that the difficult-to-market name of Murrumbidgee was changed to Riverina. The larger vintner operations in Riverina are McWilliams, Penfolds, and Seppelt's.

COROWA

More than 100 miles south of Riverina, the Corowa district has been established on the north bank of the Murray River, which marks the border between New South Wales and Victoria. This locale is best known for dessert wine production, particularly by the large Lindeman's firm.

✛ VICTORIA

The Victoria Region is bordered by South Australia to the west, by New South Wales to the north, and by the Bass Strait to the south. It is situated at the extreme southeastern tip of Australia, and its hub is the port city of Melbourne.

The northeastern portion of Victoria is centered by Rutherglen, which was an 1850s gold rush boomtown. The prosperity of the vicinity diminished with the decline of gold strikes. European prospectors-turned-winegrowers fostered renewed economic growth in the several decades that followed the gold rush, but the scourge of *Phylloxera* brought desperation and poverty to the area once more.

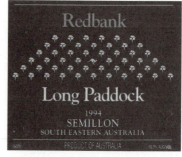

The town of Great Western is situated in the eastern foothills of the Grampian Mountains and near the town of Ararat, about 135 miles west of Melbourne. With poor soils and little rainfall, it recalls Old World environs. Given the abundance of fertile soils in Australia, this is an unlikely place to find commercial winegrowing. Such adverse conditions bring stress to the vines, of course, which respond by producing small crops of truly superb fruit. Some vintages of sparkling wines made from Pinot Noir and Chardonnay grown in this locale challenge the finer growths in the Champagne region of France. One of these is the "Yellowglen" brand produced by the firm of Home & Landragin, located between Melbourne and Great Western.

Redbank is a small boutique-style vintner, founded on the rolling foothills of the Pyrenees in 1973 by the Robb family. This locale which, along with the Grampians, is part of the Great Dividing Range of mountains, has the same adverse growing conditions that yield smaller crops of top-grade wine grapes.

The Victorian northwest shares a history with the Riverland district, described earlier. The region was a desert with no viticultural use until it was developed through irrigation settlements on the Murray River. The project was expanded for the repatriation employment of returning World War II veterans. This is a district of lowlands, most less than 400 feet above sea level, surrounding the town of Mildura. A good share of the viticultural output of the area is seedless table grapes, although quantities of Sémillon and Shiraz are also cultivated for volume wine production.

Mildara Wines, Ltd., has been in business at Merbein, just north of Mildura, since 1891 and is nationally famous for its production of fine Sherry-type wines from the traditional Spanish Sherry vine varieties, Palomino and Pedro Ximenez.

YARRA VALLEY

One may need to do a bit of searching to locate the tiny Yarra Valley district, pushed up against the Great Dividing Range peaks along the northeast outskirts of Melbourne. Yet although it is dwarfed by some of the larger commercial vineyard districts of Victoria, the Yarra has an outstanding reputation for its truly fine table wines. Chardonnay, Gewürztraminer, Johannisberg Riesling, Cabernet Sauvignon, Merlot, and Pinot Noir are the important vine varieties cultivated here. Soils are generally rich and well-drained, ranging from red sands to grey podzolic loams. The district has typically cool temperatures, as compared with most other Australian winegrowing districts, allowing for near perfect ripening conditions during the vintage season.

Many of the wines grown in the Yarra district exhibit a Swiss character, owing principally to the families de Castella and de Pury, who immigrated to this beautifully landscaped valley during the late 1840s.

Dr. Bailey Carrodus was the first to plant Cabernet Sauvignon and Shiraz vines in the Yarra Valley during the 1960s, although his wine labels do not express these varietal names. Nevertheless, the small production of only several thousand cases each vintage find great demand in nearby Melbourne.

GEELONG

About 50 miles west of Melbourne, across Port Phillip Bay, is the city of Geelong, for which the historical Geelong vineyard district is named. This was a site settled by the Swiss, by the Breguet and Pettavell families who planted their namesake "Neuchatel" vineyard there in the early 1840s. The area also became attractive to German immigrants, but shortly thereafter the Geelong was invaded by the *Phylloxera* root louse. Consequently, the popularity of the region as a premium table wine supplier fell off rather abruptly during the 1870s.

Today the Geelong is undergoing a rebirth of winegrowing. The finest European red and white wine varieties are being planted, some on sites that require irrigation, but all in a generally cool climate. The leader of this renaissance in the Geelong is the Sefton family, whose vines planted on the hillsides near the Moorabool River during the mid-1960s now yield high-quality wine grapes produced in their Idyll winery.

GOULBURN VALLEY

Located about 80 miles north of the great international port city of Melbourne is the Goulburn Valley Region. Rich, sandy loam and gray alluvial soils, coupled with extended warm growing seasons, typically yield bountiful crops of very sweet grapes, which make thin wines high in alcohol strength.

The Goulburn Valley is the site of the remarkable Château Tahbilk, which has a rich history dating back to 1845. Several families have owned the estate through the years, a line of French winery managers having brought a distinctly continental flair to the winery. Château Tahbilk has thus evolved into a true French-style château estate within an enchanting Australian landscape.

Founded in the late 1960s on the banks of the Goulburn River, Mitchelton was built with an imposing architecture. It is identified by an elaborate tower, from which visitors gain a magnificent view of the estate. Fine-quality wines and a superb restaurant make Mitchelton a popular tourist stop. Michelton's specialty is *Marsanne,* a vine from the Rhone Valley that yields white wine particularly rich in a guava-fig bouquet and toasty-vanilla flavor.

◈ WESTERN AUSTRALIA

There are comparatively few wines from Western Australia found in the U.S. marketplace. Nevertheless, the region's winegrowing history is the very oldest in the nation. Thomas Waters planted the first vines in this locale at his Olive Farm in the Swan Valley shortly after Western Australia became a state in 1829. (South Australia and Victoria did not gain statehood until several years later.)

SWAN VALLEY

The Swan Valley district is located about 25 miles northeast of the coastal city of Perth. Clay subsoils support very fertile sandy topsoils which, coupled with extended dry and sunny growing seasons, consistently produce heavy yields of very sweet grapes that make strong wines with comparatively shy bouquet and flavor.

Founded in 1859, Houghton is the most famous vintner in Swan Valley and, until recently, the only winegrower in the district. Historically, Houghton's reputation was for rather ordinary white wines blended from Chenin Blanc, Verdelho (from Madeira), and Sémillon, among others. Now, under Thomas Hardy & Sons' ownership, Houghton has become transformed into a fine wine vintner of Shiraz and Cabernet Sauvignon reds.

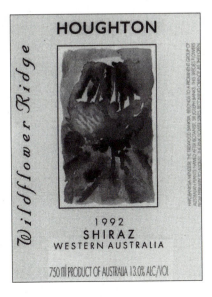

MOUNT BARKER-FRANKLAND RIVER

The district of Mount Barker-Frankland River is located about 200 miles to the southeast of Perth. It is much less developed than Swan Valley, but its cooler climate and less fertile soils are attracting new vintner interest.

MARGARET RIVER

The Margaret River district is situated near the breezy coast at the extreme southwestern tip of Australia. Although red wines from Margaret River continue to gain attention, cool-climate whites have built its reputation for fine quality.

Founded in the early 1970s, Leeuwin Vineyards is generally considered one of the best vintners in Western Australia. The Leeuwin Chardonnay is exceptionally heavy bodied and full flavored.

Winegrowing at Evans and Tate extends into both Swan Valley and Margaret River, as the John Evans and John Tate families operate vineyards in both districts. Their "Two Vineyards" Chardonnay expresses the balance of acidity, body, and flavor complexity expected from grapes grown in such diverse environs.

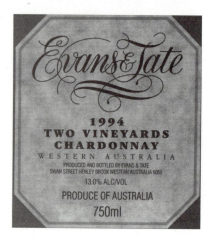

❖ QUEENSLAND

Comparatively little wine is grown in Queensland. The forbiddingly hot climate continues to discourage many vintners from risking investment here. One notable exception is the Bassett family, who have had success at their winery situated more than 300 miles west of Brisbane. Samuel Bassett planted the first Rhine Riesling and Muscat vines in Queensland in 1863, and his son carried on the legacy until 1973, when the firm was acquired by the Wall family.

❖ TASMANIA

The island of Tasmania is situated 100 miles or so south of the Australian continent. Bartholomew Broughton first made wine here in 1827. In the 1830s William Lawrence cultivated vineyards near the city of Launceston. In modern times commercial winegrowing must contend with very cool temperatures, although several entrepreneurs have braved the investment risks.

❖ NEW ZEALAND ❖

North Island and South Island, the two major islands that make up New Zealand, total a bit more than 103,000 square miles, just slightly less than the State of Colorado. Despite its comparatively small size, New Zealand has a long north-south profile that spans latitudes comparable to the finest temperate winegrowing zones in Europe. With its wide variances in soils and mesoclimates, this small country offers some of the most ideal viticultural conditions in the world.

The Reverend Samuel Marsden's vineyards of the 1800s were the first to be planted in New Zealand. James Busby, of note in Australian winegrowing in the 1830s, was also an important figure in the early development of New Zealand viticulture. But, other than some isolated vineyard plots, there was no viable commercial wine industry in the nation prior to the twentieth century.

During the early 1900s, immigrant "gum diggers" from eastern Europe and Lebanon zealously planted *Phylloxera*-resistant native American *Vitis labrusca* and French-American hybrid vines. Much of the resulting production was vinified into dessert wines that were of poor general quality and not very well

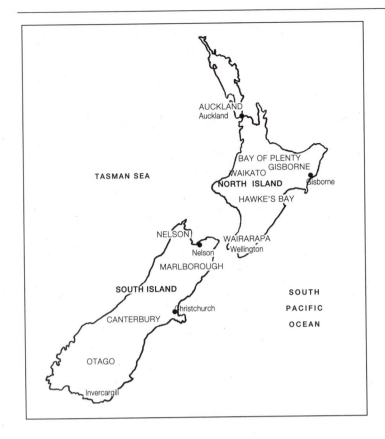

FIGURE 10.7
New Zealand
wine regions.

received in the New Zealand marketplace. The situation was made even worse by a highly restrictive New Zealand marketplace. Wine was prohibited from being sold for consumption in most public places. An ensuing wine glut caused many vineyards to be uprooted.

Consultants hired from Europe urged viticultural research so as to match Old World *Vitis vinifera* vine selections with the diversity of New Zealand's environs. The most appropriate sites were planted, and the wines from these vineyards held great promise. Although enthusiasm again resulted in the planting of too many vines, this time the New Zealand wine industry dealt with overproduction by applying supply-side economics, primarily through developing both domestic and export markets. Ever since, New Zealand winegrowing has been advancing with world-class quality.

❖ CERTIFIED ORIGIN

At this writing a system of "Certified Origin" is under design in New Zealand. The basic system of such regulation is to guarantee that at least 85 percent of the wine in each bottle complies with the geographical source, vintage, and vine variety displayed on the label.

❖ NORTH ISLAND

AUCKLAND

The Auckland region of North Island is the northernmost, the warmest, and the most humid of New Zealand's winegrowing locales. It includes the Kumeu/Huapai district, situated to the northwest of Auckland city, and the

FIGURE 10.8 Drawing a sample, with a "wine thief," from French oak barrels at the Nobilo cellars in Auckland. *(Courtesy of New Zealand Wine and Food Annual; photo by Julie Dalzell.)*

Henderson district to the immediate west. A relatively new viticultural area south of Auckland promises to be a significant contributor to New Zealand's growing wine industry.

New estate vintners are joining the older, established firms in the production of truly fine table wines. Sauvignon Blanc and Sémillon head the list of white wine varieties cultivated, and Cabernet Sauvignon and Pinot Noir are the most widely planted reds.

Joseph Babich left his native Yugoslavian wine lands in 1910 to join three older brothers farming in northern New Zealand. Although crops prospered, young Babich was drawn to winegrowing in the fertile Henderson Valley at the base of the majestic Waitakere mountain range. His estate grew slowly, but with more and more classic European vines planted, his production of world-class wines have become a national pride. Vintages of Babich Chardonnay express an enticing vegetable-citrus bouquet with rich olive-oak flavors.

The Kumeu River vineyard estate, nestled in the picturesque landscape of New Zealand's North Island, continues centuries of noble vintner traditions unique to the Brajkovich family. Their ancestral Yugoslavian coat of arms, displaying three clusters of grapes, dates back to 1420. Of special note are the vintages of Kumeu River Merlot/Cabernet Sauvignon blend, which exemplify the famous Brajkovich art and style. It is a dry red wine expressing an enchantingly complex bouquet of black cherries, tobacco leaf, and cedar, with rich flavors of plums and vanilla-oak.

BAY OF PLENTY

Despite the fact the Bay of Plenty has agreeable natural growing conditions for fine wine grapes, it has never emerged as a popular winegrowing region. As table wines replaced dessert wines across most of New Zealand's larger vineyard regions, the Bay of Plenty failed to attract the special expertise necessary to plant and maintain Old World vines. With land prices driven up by the continuing growth of suburbia, interest in renewing commercial winegrowing ventures in this region has been slow in coming. A notable exception is the Morton Estate Winery, which celebrated its premier vintage of Chardonnay in 1983 and is generating considerable attention with its superb Chardonnay, Sémillon, and Cabernet Sauvignon.

THE WAIKATO

About 50 miles south of Auckland, and perhaps twice that distance west of the Bay of Plenty, is the Waikato wine region, centered by the city of Hamilton. The New Zealand Ministry of Agriculture and Fisheries operates a viticultural research station near Te Kauwhata under the direction of Dr. Richard Smart, who is called upon for consultation on cool-climate viticulture around the world.

GISBORNE AND HAWKE'S BAY

The region of Gisborne and Hawke's Bay, surrounding the city of Napier, is located along the southeastern coast of North Island. The historical wineries and widespread fruit and vegetable production in this locale attract a great deal of tourist traaffic. There is a stark contrast between the subtropical climate and heavy clay soils of the Auckland region and the more temperate, well-drained loam soils of Gisborne and Hawke's Bay.

About two thirds of all the wine grapes grown in New Zealand are cultivated in the Gisborne and Hawke's Bay region. An upsurge of the *Phylloxera* root louse during the 1980s has given cause to replant many of the vineyards to Chardonnay and other cooler-climate vine varieties.

WAIRARAPA

Situated on the southern tip of North Island, around the northern outskirts of Wellington, is the Wairarapa region. Mountains on three sides of the Wairarapa protect it from cold winds, but deny rainfall to the extent that irrigation is required. Chardonnay and Pinot Noir grown from the region's best foothill gravel sites can be outstanding wines.

❖ SOUTH ISLAND

MARLBOROUGH AND NELSON

The uppermost winegrowing region of South Island includes the districts of Marlborough and Nelson. Marlborough is located west of the city of Blenheim, and many of its vineyards are devoted to Johannisberg Riesling, Müller-Thurgau, and other cool-climate varieties. Dry growing and ripening seasons

FIGURE 10.9 Machine harvesting grapes in Montana's Marlborough vineyard. *(Courtesy of New Zealand Wine and Food Annual; photo by Julie Dalzell.)*

necessitate irrigation for most vineyards. Some of the vintners having earned fine reputations for wine quality in this locale are Cloudy Bay, Grove Mill, Montana, Stoneleigh (Corbans), and Wairau River.

Nelson is another relatively new viticultural outgrowth in New Zealand, located near the southwestern shores of Ruby Bay. Its climate, soils, and varieties of vines cultivated are similar to those of Marlborough.

CANTERBURY

The vineyards of Canterbury, located just north of the city of Christchurch, are the southernmost commercial plantings in New Zealand. As would be expected, this is also one of the coolest mesoclimates in the nation. The varieties Johannisberg Riesling, Gewürztraminer, and Müller-Thurgau are widely planted in this very new winegrowing region.

OTAGO

Perhaps the most unlikely place to find a rapidly growing winegrowing industry is in central Otago, traditionally a haven for winter sports enthusiasts. Nevertheless, the rocky lakeshores in the Otago retain sufficient temperature and growing conditions to ripen cool, hardy varieties such as Gewürztraminer and Johannisberg Riesling.

❖ CANADA ❖

Canada includes a bit more than 3.6 million square miles of land, just a fraction more than the combined area of the 50 states of its neighbor to the south. Canada's coast-to-coast topography is very similar to that of the United States. Most of the commercial winegrowing activity is in the provinces of Ontario, British Columbia, and Quebec.

Despite the rigors of short growing seasons and cold winters, Canadian wine production has rapidly increased during the past decade or so, during which per-capita consumption has more than doubled to exceed the two-gallon annual level of consumption in America. The close parallel between Canada and the United States is further evident, in that both nations were brought up on beer and whiskey but continue to move toward a preference for wine. Both have survived National Prohibition and have experienced periods when dessert wines and pop wines were consumed at higher levels than table wines.

The Vineland described by Leif Erikson at about the year 1,000 is thought by some geographers and historians to actually have been the southeastern coast of Canada, not northeastern America.

In any event, the first fully documented explorer of Canada was John Cabot, who, in the commissioned service of British King Henry VII, anchored off the North American coast in 1497. During the next century voyages were made to Canada by three other nations in search of a new western passage to Asia. The first expedition was made by Portugal and headed by navigator Gaspar Corte-Real. The next was by Giovannia da Verrazano of Italy. Later, a series of explorations were made by the Frenchman Jacques Cartier.

Between 1595 and 1605, French interest in the new western land grew rapidly. Although some called the territory "New France," a more popular name was *Canada,* an Indian word misconstrued as meaning "country," which actually meant "town." Fur trading attracted French settlers into the St. Lawrence River region during the earliest years of the seventeenth century, the region that is today the French-speaking Province of Quebec. These French colonists were probably the first winegrowers in Canadian history.

FIGURE 10.10 Pruning grapes in Ontario. *(Courtesy of Wine East magazine; photo by Hudson Cattell.)*

The Roman Catholic Church was an early influence in the development of commercial Canadian winegrowing, as it was in the United States and most European countries. In 1615, Franciscan missionaries arrived in Quebec; there they cultivated native *Vitis labrusca* vines for both sacramental and secular needs.

Canada's fledgling wine industry may have developed more fully had it not been for the Thirty Years' War, during which the British seized Acadia and Quebec. The Acadians were banished from Canada, and some settled in southern Louisiana, where the "Cajuns" still speak French but grow very little wine in the forbiddingly hot, humid bayous of the American Deep South.

The next 50 years were a period of political unrest in Canada. Nevertheless, emigrants from Europe continued to settle there. One of these was a German, Johann Schiller, who founded Canada's premier winery just south of Toronto in 1811.

Following National Prohibition and the Great Depression of the 1930s, Canada instituted provincial control of wine distribution. In some provinces the government assumed monopoly control of all wine bought and sold at wholesale within provincial borders, a system similar to that still operating in Pennsylvania and a few other states. This served to discourage smaller vintners from entering the industry, as provincial listings were difficult to obtain unless comparatively large quantities of each wine lot offered were available. At the same time, provincial control allowed the established firms to grow in oligopolistic fashion until the late 1960s, when cottage vintners were given an opportunity to retail their wines to tourists and visitors. The provincial wine marketing control authorities also changed several other regulations so as to give the smaller vintner firms a chance to succeed.

Many cottage wineries emerged during the late 1960s and through the 1970s and 1980s, but the wine boom of Canada has included continued growth of the large wineries as well, most of which now have production facilities in each of the more important wine-consuming provinces.

❖ VINTNERS' QUALITY ALLIANCE

The newly established Vintners' Quality Alliance (VQA) sets limits to winegrowing geography and provides guidelines for quality in the provinces of Ontario and British Columbia. Vintners desiring to display the VQA seal of

FIGURE 10.11 Henry of Pelham Estates Winery in St. Catherines, Ontario. *(Courtesy of Wine East magazine; photo by Hudson Cattell.)*

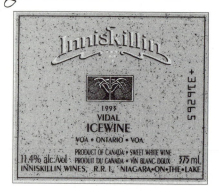

FIGURE 10.12 Ontario vineyards. *(Courtesy of Vintners' Quality Alliance.)*

compliance must submit their wines to a panel of judges who evaluate the wines in blind tastings, from which superior wines are selected.

All VQA wines must be made from *Vitis vinifera* grapes, excpt for ice wine, which can be made from the French hybrid cultivar *Vidal Blanc*.

❖ ONTARIO

The largest winegrowing province in Canada is Ontario, with most of its vineyards cultivated along the southwestern shores of Lake Ontario and the northern coast of Lake Erie. Some of the newest vintners have established wineries in the district of the Niagara Peninsula, which separates Niagara Falls from the city of Hamilton.

Deep, well-drained fertile soils in the Niagara Peninsula are protected from cold north and west winds by an escarpment that surrounds the locale except on the Lake Ontario side. The tempering effects of the cold lake waters help to deter the occurrence of false springtime, when extended periods of warm March and April weather can cause bud break, resulting in the damage or destruction of fruiting shoots when winter temperatures resume. Sudden springs frosts are also a recurring problem. Summers are consistently warm, with adequate rainfall, and autumns usually have sufficient heat summation to ripen most varieties of wine grapes cultivated here.

The VQA has established three viticultural districts in Ontario: Lake Erie North Shore, Niagara Peninsula, and Pelée Island. Wines displaying these appellations on their labels must be made exclusively from *Vitis vinifera* vines grown within the boundaries of these districts.

The first vineyard plantings in the Niagara frontier were devoted to native *Vitis labrusca* vines, but now more than half of the commercial vineyards in the locale are planted to Old World varieties and French-American hybrids. A significant share of vineyard acreage is also dedicated to hybrid cultivars developed by Vineland Station, the highly respected vinicultural research facility operated in the Niagara Peninsula by the Ontario Provincial Government.

Andres Wines, Ltd., one of the largest wine firms in Canada, has facilities in Ontario and several other provinces. With more than nine million gallons of capacity, this vintner is comparable in scale to the larger corporate firms in California. Founded in British Columbia by Andrew Peller in 1961, the winery expanded quickly. Headquarters for the firm were moved to Ontario after Peller acquired the Beau Chatel winery in Winona.

T. G. Bright and Co., Ltd., was established in 1910 when the Bright family acquired F. A. Shirriff's interest in a Niagara Falls winery they had started together in 1890. The firm can actually be traced back even further, to 1874, when Bright and Shirriff first made commerical wine in Toronto. Bright's continues as another of the large Canadian wineries.

Château des Charmes commenced winery operations in 1978 and has built its production of Chardonnay, Johannisberg Riesling, and Gamay, among other varietals, into a table and sparkling wine facility comprising more than 250,000 gallons.

The London Winery, Ltd., was founded in 1925 in the Ontario provincial city of the same name. This three-million-gallon winery operates a chain of retail wine shops and offers a full range of grape, fruit, and honey wines.

◈ BRITISH COLUMBIA

In stark contrast to the thundering Niagara and fertile flatlands of southern Ontario, British Columbia is characterized by a serene, austere terrain with stunning mountains, valleys, and lakes. One of these valley districts, the Okanagan, located about 250 miles east of Vancouver, is the heart of winegrowing in this breathtaking countryside.

The Okanagan Valley is referred to as "Napa North" by some Canadians, but the Okanagan, with a north-south length exceeding 100 miles, is several times larger than California's Napa Valley. The mesoclimates of this area have distinct differences too. Spring frosts following bud break are more frequent in Napa, whereas frosts occurring during the September and early October ripening season are more apt to occur in the Okanagan. Very harsh winter temperatures, sometimes below 0° F, are a perennial threat to vines culti-vated in Okanagan, as is the lack of rainfall, often measuring less than 10 inches for an entire year. Conse-quently, the Okanagan and Napa valleys really have little in common aside from their winegrowing splendor.

Despite the natural viticultural limitations of this region, the light loam soils of the Okanagan can yield some truly fine table wines from Old World and hybrid vines.

Perhaps the most well-known vintner in British Columbia is Calona Wines, Ltd., which commenced initial operations during the early Depression years in the city of Kelowna, the urban center of the Okanagan Valley. An Italian immigrant grocer, Pasquale Capozzi, and W. A. C.

Bennett, owner of a neighboring hardware store, started the original company, Domestic Wines and By-Products, Ltd., to manufacture wines and associated products so as to assist impoverished local fruit growers. Under very difficult circumstances, Capozzi and Bennett sold several thousand shares at $1 apiece and marshalled the great dedication of their employees to develop one of the largest and most successful wine production firms in the nation. The winery has grown to more than five million gallons of capacity and is now owned by the beverage giant Heublein.

In 1982, the Gray Monk Cellars, Ltd., Estate Winery was established by the Heiss family, who make only table wines in their comparatively small 60,000-gallon winery. Most of the Gray Monk production uses grapes grown in their own Okanagan Valley estate vineyards.

FIGURE 10.13 Okanagan vineyards. *(Courtesy of Heublein, Inc.)*

The Sumac Ridge Estate Winery of Summerland, British Columbia, was founded in 1980 by Harry McWatters and Lloyd Schmidt. The 200,000-gallon Sumac Ridge winery makes table and sparkling wines principally from Chardonnay, Pinot Blanc, and Gewürztraminer.

❖ QUEBEC

One of the best examples of perseverance—enduring the rigors of harsh climate to make good wine—is found in the province of Quebec. From just several steadfast vintners operating in the early 1980s, the Quebec wine industry grew to number more than 20 commercial winemakers in the early 1990s.

The Andres operation and Les Vins La Salle, both in Ste. Hyacinthe, are two of the larger wine producers in Quebec. The oldest operating winery in the province, founded in 1965, and with more than two million gallons of capacity, also the largest, is Vin Geloso, located in Laval.

❖ NOVA SCOTIA

If Quebec is a fine example of determination amid challenging mesoclimates, Nova Scotia is nothing short of spectacular. Five small wineries, Gaspereau, Grand Masters, Grand Pre, Jost, and Ste. Famille, have continued operations since the 1980s. Some of the Russian cold-climate vine varieties from the *Vitis amurensis* species are being cultivated in Nova Scotia, along with native vines and the hardier selections of French-American hybrid cultivars.

11

THE WINES OF SOUTH AMERICA AND MEXICO

The Spanish Jesuits who followed Columbus west from Spain were the first to plant vines in the New World. In South America, Spanish monks established vineyards at their missions during the mid-1500s, following the invasions of Pizarro and the Conquistadores. Vines were planted in Peru in 1563. Chile was the next to grow wine, modeling its industry on that in France. Commercial winegrowing was undertaken by Italian immigrants in Argentina more than two centuries later. Brazilian viniculture emerged in the early twentieth century under Portuguese influence. Uruguay was settled by people who emigrated from all four of these European nations. All of these enterprises have been very successful; today there is more wine produced and consumed in South America than in North America.

Traditionally, few wines have been imported into the United States from South America. This is due in part to the unstable economic and political situations that have plagued these nations, and in part to a history of rather poor quality wines. In the last several decades, however, there has been dramatic change. The larger urban markets in North America offer truly spectacular values in lower-priced, higher-grade South American wines, particularly from Chile and increasingly from Argentina.

�֍ ARGENTINA

With about 380 million gallons of wine produced in 1995, Argentina ranks fifth among the world's winegrowing nations. It is also ranked fifth in per-capita wine consumption; at an average of about 13 gallons annually, it is in the same league as Old World nations such as Italy, France, and Portugal. The Argentines make more commercial wines than all other South American countries combined.

FIGURE 11.1 Winegrowing nations and regions in South America.

Two thirds of the wine grown in Argentina is red table wine. Most of the rest is white table wine, although some dessert and sparkling wines are made in significant quantities as well. Industry regulations are promulgated and enforced by the military through the Instituto Nacional Viniviticola. Inspectors monitor all phases of winegrowing, from planting and cultivation to production, transportation, and marketing. Yet despite this policing, there is little real regulation or standardization. Label information is not generally instructive, and brand names are usually the most reliable indicators of authenticity and/or quality and value.

The extreme western limits of Argentina are guarded by the Andes, the great chain of mountains that form the South American continental divide and a natural border between Argentina and Chile to the west. To the east are the Argentine plains, gradually sloping from about 2,000 feet in elevation to just above sea level. It is on the western plateau of these plains, centered by the Province of Mendoza, where most of the wines in this nation are grown.

FIGURE 11.2 A young Argentine vineyard east of the Andes. *(Courtesy of Finca Flichman.)*

FIGURE 11.3 Finca Flichman estate vineyards and winery in the upper plateau sector of the Mendoza. *(Courtesy of Finca Flichman.)*

There are more than 2,000 vintners and *fincas* (vineyard and winery estates) in Argentina making wines from the traditional Italian vine varieties, Barbera, Nebbiolo, and Sangiovese. Other principal vines cultivated are *Criolla, Sémillon, Malbec,* and *Tempranillo,* all of which produce good, but rather ordinary, table wines that are quaffed daily as diet staples throughout the nation.

The national governing authority for Argentina winegrowing has failed in its mission to control wine quality. Now that world markets are accepting exports from Australia, New Zealand, rival neighbor Chile, and other New World countries, there is renewed interest in moving towards regulation, which should eventually allow Argentine exports to compete.

Accelerating this movement is an industry consortium formed by more than a dozen major Argentine vintners, the Asociacion Vitinivinicola Argentina (AVA). It operates mostly as an information and promotional agency for exports, although there is a move afoot for the AVA to resolve better production methods.

Among most of the larger Argentine wineries, and many of the smaller firms, there is an increasing movement toward cultivation of the classic European Old World vines. Sacrificing quantity for quality, new Argentine vineyards of Chardonnay, Gewürztraminer, Johannisberg Riesling, Sauvignon Blanc, Cabernet Sauvignon, Merlot, and Pinot Noir mirror the wine renaissance that continues across the United States.

Some wineries in Argentina have been updated with state-of-the-art production facilities and are directed by professional personnel who command international respect. These operations are producing increasing quantities of very good table wines for the export trade. Athough they are still some distance in quality from the better export wines coming out of Chile, the gap is narrowing.

MENDOZA

The Mendoza plain was first irrigated by Italian immigrants from the Piedmont, who employed Swiss technology to channel melted snow from the Andes to the vineyards. As in many other large winegrowing regions, the *Phylloxera* root louse has become a major threat. In some Argentine vineyards irrigation water is allowed to flood the vines, serving to drown many of the pests and washing others downstream. Some viniculturists criticize this practice as crude and harmful to the vines, but the results cannot be disputed. Both grape quality and quantity continue to increase.

RIO NEGRO AND LA RIOJA

The very best wines of Argentina are generally considered to be those grown in the cooler Rio Negro and Neuquén Regions to the south of Mendoza. At 39.2 degrees south latitude, the Rio Negro valley is the southernmost winegrowing region in the world.

To the north of Mendoza is the warm climate vineyard region of La Rioja, along the eastern banks of the Rio Jague, namesake of the grand winegrowing region along the Rio Oja in northern Spain. Vines were first planted in the city of Todos los Santos de la Nueva Rioja in 1591, where Spanish immigrants employed native Indians to work in the vineyards.

Other important regions are the Norte and Occidente, both of which are located in the northwestern part of the county on the eastern Andean plains. The Cordoba region is situated in the central part of Argentina, and Entre Rios and Litoral are regions in the eastern sector.

The Barrancas vineyards of Mendoza, established in 1873, became the founding cornerstone of the Flichman wine estate, now one of the leading vintners in Argentina. Having won awards of excellence in global competitions, vintages of Flichman Cabernet Sauvignon are a national pride. These are typically modest in color intensity and body, but express pleasant ripe plum and minty-cedar flavors with soft vanilla tannins.

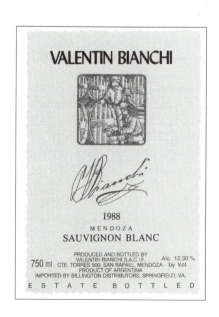

Valentin Bianchi was a pioneer Mendoza vintner, emigrating from Italy in 1910 and founding the vineyards that now bear his name in 1928. The Bianchi estate includes four *fincas*—Asti, Doña Elsa, Las Paredes, and Cuadro—totaling more than 2,000 acres of vineyards under cultivation. An Italian-style tradition of white wine quality is exemplified in the blossomy bouquet, grassy-vanilla flavors, and crisp acidity found in vintages of Bianchi Sauvignon Blanc.

Arriving in 1880, Pascual Toso settled in the rich Mendoza flatlands along the magnificent Andean plateau. Toso was reared in the Piemonte of northern Italy, one of Italy's premier winegrowing regions, and was well versed in the production of fine wines before emigrating to Argentina. By 1890 he had succeeding in establishing the vineyards and winery needed to make the first of what have become some of Argentina's best Cabernet Sauvignon, with rich cedar bouquet and full cassis-vanilla flavors balanced on soft acidity and mellow tannins.

Trapiche is one of the largest vintners in the world. Founded in 1883, the Trapiche estate now embraces more than 5,000 acres of vines and retains both vineyard and winery expert consultants to help the company continue to bring quality in line with quantity. These efforts are paying dividends, as the "Fond De Cave" line of premium Chardonnay and Cabernet Sauvignon varietals are exemplary of wines that are gaining increased attention and respect in the world markets.

Nicolas Catena, another of the great Italian winegrower immigrants, planted his first Mendoza vineyard in 1902. He selected a gravel plain that was irrigated by melting snow from the peaks of the Andes. Three generations of the Catena family have since cultivated classic French vines in these ideal environs and have built a lofty reputation for superb winemaking. Bodegas Esmeralda Sauvignon Blanc typically has rich blossom-melon flavors, with a delicate acidity and creamy texture.

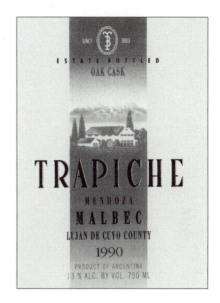

The grand cellars of Navarro-Correas, founded in 1798, are now among the most prominent in all of Argentina. The pride of Navarro-Correas is its "Coleccion Privada" Cabernet Sauvignon, which, in the fashion set by Château Mouton Rothschild, is identified by the artwork selected for its label decor with each successive vintage. Patient aging in both barrel and bottle results in a Cabernet Sauvignon that is rather soft and delicate, with a light tobacco-leaf bouquet and sumptuous wood-plum flavors.

FIGURE 11.4   Vintage season in the vast Mendoza. *(Courtesy of Trapiche.)*

CARRASCAL
CABERNET - MERLOT - MALBEC
1985
RED WINE   VIN ROUGE
BODEGA Y CAVAS DE WEINERT S.A.
SAN MARTIN 5923 - LUJAN DE CUYO - MENDOZA
PRODUCT OF ARGENTINA   PRODUIT D' ARGENTINE
12.5 alc./vol.   MENDOZA   750 ml
SOLE AGENTS FOR CANADA
JOHN HANNA & SONS, LTD.
TORONTO - ONTARIO

In constrast to the modern technology now implemented by many of the larger and more well established vintners in Argentina, the Weinert family built their enviable name by bringing together Old World art and New World craft. The Weinert estate produces some very interesting proprietary white wines, such as the "Carrascal" Sémillon-Sauvignon Blanc, a Graves-style blend recalling the grassy-melon flavors found in superb white Bordeaux.

◆ BRAZIL

There was virtually no commercial wine grown in Brazil prior to 1900. Most Brazilians relied on wines imported from Europe and other South American countries—a practice that continues for those who can afford such wines.

Although still a long way from world ranking in either production or consumption of wine, Brazil has achieved remarkable growth in both since the turn of the twentieth century.

Most of Brazil's vineyards are located in the state of Rio Grande do Sol at the extreme southern tip of the country, on the northeastern border of Uruguay. The rest are located in the regions of Minas Gerais, Rio de Janeiro, Santa Catarina, and São Paulo. Considerable research has been directed toward cultivating vines in the warmer and more humid regions of northern Brazil near the equator. By forcing vine dormancy through restriction of irrigation water, some growers have reported raising two grape crops per year.

The principal Brazilian white wines are now made from Malvasia, Johannisberg Riesling, and Trebbiano, and reds grown from Barbera, Cabernet Sauvignon, and Merlot vines. At one time the native American Isabella vine was widely cultivated here.

The most noteworthy vintners in Brazil are Vinicola Riograndense, Profivin, Viamao, and Dreher. American and European firms have made significant investments in the growing wine industry of Brazil.

◆ CHILE

Chile is a country of extremes. At 2,650 miles in length and an average of only 110 miles wide, it is comparable to the State of Tennessee stretched from the Atlantic to the Pacific. Within this narrow geography Chile ascends from Pacific sea level to the tops of the Andean peaks. This country has a very warm climate in the tropical north and frigid cold toward the Antarctic south. The entire nation sits atop a division of dynamic continental plates, which causes frequent tremors and devastating earthquakes.

With all of its new vineyard plantings, Chile now produces about 100 million gallons of wine each year. Chileans consume an average of eight gallons each year, four times the average consumption by Americans.

Although Argentina indisputably makes the largest quantity of wine in South America, most wine experts award Chile the honor of being the highest-quality producer. Without question, viniculture in Chile is most reminiscent of that in Europe.

Spain discovered Chile in 1536, and the first winemaker there was Francisco de Aguirre, on his land grant in Copiapo. It was in 1548 that Carabantes, a Spanish priest, brought the first vines to this part of the New World. These early stocks were of the Pais variety, quite similar to the traditional Criolla of Argentina and the Mission vine of California. The classic varieties from France, Germany, and Spain were not introduced into Chile until 1851, when Silvestre Ochagavia, a progressive

FIGURE 11.5
Entrance to Vina
Concha y Toro
bodegas.
*(Courtesy of Vina
Concha y Toro.)*

winemaker of Spanish descent, planted the first Chardonnay, Johannisberg Riesling, Cabernet Sauvignon and *Cot* (Malbec) vines, among others.

These vines adapted well and continue to flourish, as Chile is the only major winegrowing nation to have totally escaped the ravages of the *Phylloxera* root louse. The giant Andes peaks to the east, the desert to the north, and the cold polar Humboldt current from the west are thought to provide natural barriers against the pest. Yet similar description could be made of the environs of northern California, where *Phylloxera* continues to wreak havoc upon winegrowers. Whatever the answer is, Chilean vines continue to be grown on their own roots with no apparent need for grafting to resistant rootstocks. There is, however, another root insect in Chile, the *Margarodes vitium,* which is equally deadly to grapevines, but does not seem to spread as quickly as the *Phylloxera*.

By 1875 the commercial wine industry in Chile had grown to a production level exceeding 13 million gallons annually, and to triple that in the next decade or so. Since then various crises have prompted statutes, control laws, and reforms, leaving the country with a wine history equally as rocky and diverse as that in the United States. In 1979, however, a total restructuring was implemented that permitted Chilean winegrowers an open opportunity to enter the mainstream of New World production. There has been New World marketing, too, as Chilean wine exports have become popular fare on the shelves of the United States, the United Kingdom, and other large markets.

The magnificent snow-capped Andes mountains, with some peaks reaching four miles high, dominate the topography of Chile and form a natural border between Chilean vineyards and the Argentine Mendoza to the east. There is comparatively little rainfall in Chile. There are few rain clouds arriving from the Pacific for the high Andean peaks to block in order to produce rainfall. But there is plenty of irrigation water flowing from melted snows into mountain streams down the western Andean slopes.

Most Chilean vines are cultivated on plateaus of clay, limestone, and gravel soils. Like the United States, Australia, and New Zealand, Chile has nearly ideal enivrons of natural land and weather for viticulture.

FIGURE 11.6 Chilean vineyard west of the Andes. *(Courtesy of Cousiño-Macul.)*

A severe problem that plagues vintners in both Chile and Argentina is damage causesd by earthquakes and tremors. One of many archaic methods of dealing with the shifting earth can be found in the cellars of Concha y Toro, where mortar for *casillero* bricks is made by mixing egg whites, sand, and horsehair. Such bricks seem to have been very resilient, as the Roman-style arches there have survived numerous earthquakes. New wineries, constructed from complex architectural and engineering designs, are able to absorb massive shocks and movement.

Technological advances are enabling Chileans to realize the superb potential of their growing table wines, particularly from the classic vines of Chardonnay, Sauvignon Blanc, Cabernet Sauvignon, and Merlot.

The Ministry of Agriculture controls the use of appellations of origin in Chile's four winemaking regions. The volume of wine output is also controlled by the Chilean government. Surplus wine, amounts made above these limits, is distilled into brandy or industrial alcohol. White table wines for export must reach an alcohol strength of at least 12 percent, and reds a minimum of 11.5 percent. Export wines labeled as "Courant" must be at least one year old. "Special" wines must be aged at least two years and "Reserve wine" at least four years; "Gran Vino" Chilean table wines are six years old or older.

ACONCAGUA

The Aconcagua, a region of magnificent landscape, is named for the highest peak in the Western Hemisphere, Mount Aconcagua, exceeding 22,800 feet in elevation. Aconcagua winegrowing is spread across most of this exceptionally narrow part of Chile.

At the base of the Andes foothills is the Panquehue district of this region, centered by the city of San Felipe. This is dry, desertlike irrigated vineyard land made productive by the Maximiano family, who own and operate the grand Vina Errazuriz estate.

One of the most exciting developments in Chilean winegrowing is the development of the Casablanca district near the port city of Valparaiso. Cool Pacific breezes and poor soils are giving a rather California Carneros-like promise to Chardonnay, Pinot Noir, and other cooler-climate varieties, making wines of truly superb quality.

MAIPO

The Maipo Region has long enjoyed Chile's highest reputation for fine wines. The capital of the region, the large international city of Santiago, has grown to such proportions that some vineyards are actually part of the city.

FIGURE 11.7 Vintage season in the Maipo. *(Courtesy of Vina Conchay Toro S.A.)*

There is perhaps no other winegrowing region in the world that has such diverse climate and soil conditions within such a comparatively small area. The soil and weather conditions, referred to as "Mediterranean" by Maipo vintners, range from semiarid desert in the north to more humid and fertile environs in the south. The Andean slopes are cool-climate rocky massifs, descending to a warm plateau of alluvial soils, then cooler again as they become sandy in texture along the Pacific coast. Vineyards are found in all combinations of these conditions, and, consequently, it is difficult to bring any single *terroir* character to the Maipo.

The following are the nine principal winegrowing districts of the Maipo region:

> Buin
> Coelemu
> Isla de Maipo
> Llano de Maipo
> Pirque
> Santiago
> Santa Ana
> Talagante
> Yumbel

Although the Viña Santa Rita vineyards and winery estate were founded by Don Domingo Fernandez in 1880, the site was first employed for winegrowing a century earlier. General Bernardo O'Higgins, the father of Chilean independence, hid 120 soldiers in the wine cellars at Santa Rita during an 1814 battle retreat. This historical event is maked by an entire line of fine wines from Santa Rita bearing the "120" label. This large estate, having been divided over the years, has since 1980, when Don Ricardo Claro Valdes bought the winery, undergone reassembly. This restoration includes a magnificent hacienda manor house and chapel and many new acres of vineyards.

FIGURE 11.8   Cousino-Macul bodegas.   *(Courtesy of Cousiño-Macul.)*

Although Carmen is one of the older Chilean wine estates, it failed to advance along with the twentieth-century renaissance of the entire Chilean wine industry, having changed ownership several times. Claro Valdes, owner of the huge Santa Rita estate described earlier, purchased Carmen in 1988. With prime quality grapes from the cool ocean climate of the district of Casablanca, this estate promises to become a grower of truly luxury boutique wines.

Grandson of a member of the first Chilean governmental junta, Don Melchor de Concha y Toro was one of the pioneers in the development of commercial winegrowing in Chile. In 1883 he founded the Viña Concha y Toro, an estate which, along with a large tract of prime vineyard land inherited by his wife in 1892, grew rapidly. The winery became a corporation in the early 1920s, and foresighted management has directed Sociedad Viña Concha y Toro in becoming the nation's largest vintner, now maintaining more than 5,000 acres of vineyards. Vintages of "Don Melchor" Cabernet Sauvignon are its best, which, with deep ruby color, full-bodied texture, and blackberry-oak flavors, are priced for everyone across the United States.

With generous soils and moderate climate, the esteemed Maipo central region, pivotal on the capital city of Santiago, may be the single most auspicious environment for producing larger crops of quality wine grapes in the world. The Macul land grant is one of the oldest in Chile, much of which was sold to the Cousiño family in 1856. The Cousiño-Macul Cabernet Sauvignons are rich in color, body, and texture, with a berry-cedar bouquet and velvety vanilla-plum flavors.

Don Luis Pereira Cotapos, educated in France, founded Viña Santa Carolina in 1875, naming it in honor of his wife, Doña Carolina Iniguez. Cotapos employed French expertise in building his grand Maipo river estate— an enologist who brought with him the most adaptable Old World vines and an engineer whose buildings are now national monuments. With a long list of accolades and awards, Santa Carolina has managed to maintain top quality while becoming one of the largest vintners in Chile.

RAPEL

Across the Andean slopes, reaching down to the Pacific Ocean, the Rapel has some of the most productive soils employed in growing grapes in Chile. There is also plenty of water for irrigation, with its five tributaries flowing from the slopes to form the Rapel River. The city of San Fernando is capital to this rich agricultural production and processing land. The best wines from both the Rapel and the Maipo are reds from Cabernet Sauvignon, Merlot, and Malbec.

The following are the principal winegrowing districts in the Rapel region:

Cachapola	Peumo
Colchagua	Rengo
Chimbarongo	San Fernando
Lihueimo	Santa Cruz
Nancaugua	Tinguiririca
Peralillo	

The Bisquertt family, immigrants from the Basque region of northwestern Spain, have developed a large winegrowing estate in the Colchagua district in the heart of the Rapel region. The Viña Bisquertt label is found only on rare vintages of the most exceptional high-quality wines. Most domestic and world markets recognize the Las Garzas label on superb Sauvignon Blanc, Cabernet Sauvignon, and Merlot varietal table wines, made in a rather California-like style with both cutting-edge technology and Old World know-how.

Operated since 1750 by the Eyzaguirre-Echenique family, Los Vascos is one of Chile's oldest wine estates, with an advancing reputation for good quality wines offered at very reasonable prices. In the late 1980s, French wine magnate Baron Eric de Rothschild purchased an interest in Los Vascos and assigned Gilbert Rokvam, *regisseur* winemaker at the famous Château Lafite-Rothschild in Bordeaux, to also guide wine production at this Chilean estate in the Colchagua district of the Rapel region. The resulting red wines have been, as expected, Bordeaux-like in character.

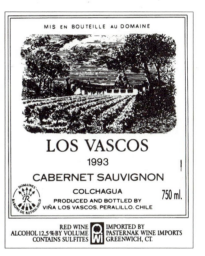

MAULE

Maule is by far the largest of the Chilean winegrowing regions. Its generally warm climate has much the same range of temperatures throughout the seasons as those of the Rapel and Maipo regions. There is more rainfall in Maule, however, and its soils are more volcanic. It is here that the best Chilean white wines are made, principally from Sauvignon Blanc and Chenin Blanc vines.

The following are winegrowing districts in the Maule:

Cauquenes	Parral
Chillan	Quillon
Curico	Sagrada Familia
Linares	San Clemente
Lontué	San Javier
Molina	Talca
Palmilla	Villa Alegre

The Torres family in the Catalonia region of Spain are world-famous winegrowers; their name has been associated with fine wine since the end of the seventeenth century. Miguel Torres, the late patriarch, was an aggressive innovator. With production operations already established in the United States and other countries, in 1979 he purchased about 120 acres of existing vineyards near Curico in the northern Maule region. In the years since, Viña Miguel Torres-Chile has become one of the most respected names of quality table wines in the country.

The name *Caliterra* derives from *cal,* or "calcium-lime," and *terra,* or "earth-soil," recalling the vital importance of *terroir* to winegrowing. The Viña Caliterra winery has an abundance of *cal-terra* in the Maule region on which to grow truly superb Sauvignon Blanc and Cabernet Sauvignon wines. This is one of the newest wine estates, founded in 1989 as a joint venture between Viña Errazuriz of Chile and Franciscan vineyards in California.

⬧ URUGUAY

There are four small provinces in Uruguay that grow wine commercially: Canelones, Colonia, San José, and Soriano. All of these are adjacent to the capital city of Montevideo.

This region is predominantly lowland, with sultry heat and humidity, somewhat comparable to the more southern vineyards locales in Italy. About 50,000 acres of vines are cultivated in Uruguay, and annual wine production is generally about 20 million gallons.

Little of the Uruguayan wine output has earned a quality reputation. The best grapes harvested from traditional French and Italian vine varieties are made into rather ordinary table wines. The most inferior white and red wines are usually distilled into brandy or blended to make "Vino Seco," a fortified wine in the Madeira style. Nearly all of the wine produced in Uruguay is also consumed there.

⬧ PERU

According to the writings of Garcilaso de la Vega, the first vineyard was planted in the tropical paradise of Peru along the Ica River in 1563. The vines were transported there from the Canary Islands by Francisco de Carabantes. Again, as throughout the entire history of the vine through Western civilization, it was the necessity of wine for the church that was a major influence in this elemental agriculture. It is thought by some historians that the very first vines planted in Argentina and Chile came from mother vine stocks in Peru.

Winegrowing in Peru continues along the Ica River, where the summer months between December and March are celebrated by winegrowers with the "new water" rainfall in the Andes. It rarely rains in the Ica Valley; thus, water runoff from the foothills is an essential part of successful grape growing in the region.

The main irrigation artery is "La Achirana," a channel some 50 feet wide and 30 miles long that brings water to the entire upper portion of the valley. Ricardo Palma, in his book *Peruvian Traditions,* relates the legend that La Achirana was dug by 40,000 soldiers in 15 days. Inca Emperor Pachacutec ordered the project in order to pay tribute to an Ica maiden whom he could not seduce.

Because of its close proximity to the equator, one might first think that there is too much sunsine, and therefore too much heat summation, for the cultivation of classic vine varieties. Peru does, in fact, have a sunny climate most of the year. But during the more active times in the annual growth cycle of the vine there are actually fewer daylight hours each day than in more temperate winegrowing regions. Furthermore, the wide range of temperatures between day and night allows for near perfect vine respiration, and thus superior development of natural grape sugar.

About 150 miles southeast of Lima, and just several miles northeast of Ica, is the grand expanse of vineyards that make up the Tacama wine estate. Originally part of a very large Spanish land grant to the Convent of St.

Augustine, this property was first known as Santo Tomás de Villanueva de Tacama. During the Agrarian Reform movement in 1970, this vast holding was divided and became simply "Tacama" under the ownership of the Olaechea family. Production is implemented with modern methods, not unlike those used by some of the medium-sized vintners in California. As would be expected, most of the Tacama wines are made from warm-climate vine varieties, blends of Sauvignon Blanc and Sémillon for whites, and blends of Malbec and Cabernet Sauvignon for reds.

✤ MEXICO

In the 1520s, Cortez gave land grants to settlers in Mexico, with the proviso that they plant 10 vines for every person living on their land. Despite this land giveaway, the colonists who followed were slow to develop viniculture in Mexico.

The greater portion of Mexico is a large elevated plateau bordered by two mountain ranges, the Sierra Madre Oriental to the east and the Sierra Madre Occidental to the west. Both fall off sharply to form narrow coastal plains. The ranges meet at La Junta, where mountain elevations rival all but the very highest Andean peaks in South America.

With five million gallons of production each vintage, Mexico does not rank among the leading wine-producing nations, perhaps primarily because the climate and soils across the country are not generally well suited to winegrowing. Where rainfall is sufficient, temperatures are typically too high to adequately cultivate fine wine vines. Where climate is more temperate, there is usually an insufficiency of water.

There are exceptions to these conditions along the northern border of the country, especially in the San Solano Valley near Ensenada, where the old Santo Tomás de Aquino Mission produces good red table wines on the Pacific side of the Baja California Peninsula. Santo Tomás was founded in the early 1790s by Padre José Loriente, a Dominican monk who recognized that the rich loam soils and abundant sunshine were valuable vinicultural resources. Loriente found that cool ocean breezes tempered the Baja climate and mountain water could provide ample irrigation to supplement the scant rainfall. The vineyards of Santo Tomás expanded for the next three decades until the Mexican government took control of all the missions in 1825. The twentieth-century renaissance of Santo Tomás was realized under the consultation of expert winemaker Dmitri Tchelistcheff, son of the late dean of California winemakers, Andre Tchelistcheff. His recommendation that the mission vineyards be replanted with classic European vine varieties was a major factor in the resurrection of Santo Tomás.

The Guadalupe Valley is also situated in the Baja near Ensenada, and it is here that the Domecq winery operates under the direction of its internationally famous parent facility, Bodegas Pedro Domecq, vintner of premium Sherry wines. Industrias Vinicolas Domecq is best known in Mexico for the production of "Los Reyes" table wines, which enjoy a good reputation.

Perhaps the most important Mexican winery is Casa Madero, located near Monterrey at the base of the Yucatan Peninsula. The second oldest commercial vineyard in the Americas, Casa Madero was founded by Don Lorenzo Garcia, who secured the original land grant from King Philip II of Spain in 1597. Garcia constructed his winery near the ancient Mission of Santa Maria de las Parras, translated as "St. Mary of the Vineyards," named after the profusion of native vines found growing there in the wild. Casa Madero continues its great heritage, but it is the new viticulture of Old World vines and new winemaking technology adapted to make good varietal table wines that have drawn attention to this vintner.

The first commercial vineyard in the Americas, also at Parras, was planted in the early 1600s by Don Francisco de Urdinola. This site is still operated as a producing vineyard by the Marques de Aguayo winery located nearby.

Mexican wines are also grown in Chihuahua and Aguascalientes; production in these regions is led by the firms Delicias and Compania Vinicola de Saltillo, respectively. The Cavas de San Juan in Querataro, at 6,000 feet, has the highest elevation of any winery in Mexico.

12
THE WINES OF SOUTH AFRICA

Modern-day wines from South Africa rank with any in the world. Since South Africa, politically and socially, has experienced more peaceful times recently, the wines from this nation have achieved some renewed measure of success in finding retail shelf space in the larger U.S. wine markets. South Africa remains, however, a significant source of fine wines that much of the world has yet to discover.

It was in 1487 that the Portuguese sailor Bartholomeu Dias named the southern tip of Africa Cabo Tormentoso, or "tormenting cape," inasmuch as it is spendidly docile in calm weather, but in storms it is violent and deadly. Back in Portugal this name brought fear to King Henry who worried that, in hearing it, his sailors might refuse to make voyages around the cape. Consequently, he renamed it Cabo do Boa Esperanca, or the "Cape of Good Hope." Subsequently, Vasco da Gama successfully sailed from Portugal around the cape. He was followed in 1580 by Sir Francis Drake on his historical voyage around the world. Drake wrote in his diary: "This Cape is the most stately thing and the fairest cape we saw in the whole circumference of the earth."

By the 1640s regular passage around the Cape of Good Hope had been established, Cape Town becoming a routine port of call for international trade. In 1647 a Dutch East India Company ship was wrecked off the coast, and its sailors were forced to bivouac in Cape Town. They eventually built several forts there, which signalled the beginning of Dutch influence in South Africa.

The first South African vines were planted by Jan van Riebeeck in the early 1650s, soon after the Cape colony was founded. Van Riebeeck wrote in his diary on February 2, 1659:

Today, praise be to God, wine was made for the first time from Cape grapes, namely from the new must fresh from the vat. The grapes were mostly Muscadel and other white, round grapes, very fragrant and tasty. The Spanish grapes are still quite green, though they hang reasonably thickly on several vines and give promise of a first class crop. These grapes, from three young vines planted two years ago, have yielded about 12 quarts of must, and we shall soon discover how it will be affected by maturing.

Apart from the Muscat vines he indicates, van Riebeeck's plantings were thought to include Chenin Blanc, Sémillon, and Cinsault, all from mother vines in France. He planted more vines on his Boschheuvel farm, but few others in the colony followed up on his success, as row crops and grain were in greater demand and provided a more immediate cash return.

Simon van der Stel became governor of the Cape of Good Hope in 1679 and, being a wine lover, planted many vines on his picturesque Groot Constantia farm. Van der Stel encouraged growers to plant vines throughout the colony and, helped along by the expertise of some French Huguenot immigrants, vineyard plantings increased by more than 500 acres by 1687. In addition to Constantia, vineyards were established in the communities of Franschhoek, Paarl, and, Stel's namesake, Stellenbosch. The vine seemed to thrive immediately in South Africa. Captain William Dampier entered the following passage in his log in 1691:

The country is of later years so well stocked with vineyards that they make an abundance of wine. This wine is like a French High Country white wine.

Although Dutch control grew during the late 1600s and early 1700s, it began to diminish in the late 1700s. Increasingly, Dutch control of South Africa became diluted by France. Fearing the loss of the Cape Town port enroute to India and Asia, the English seized the colony in 1795.

For the next half century, South African winegrowing expanded widely in order to satisfy the thirst of the British. Some of the wines earned the praises of the great French author and gourmet, Alexandre Dumas, and Frederick the Great, king of Prussia. But, for the most part, South African winegrowers concentrated on increasing quantity, rather than improving quality. Nevertheless, success continued until 1861, when Gladstone, who was then Chancellor of the Exchequer in England, abolished the preferential tariff. That event, along with the invasion of the *Phylloxera* root louse blight some 20 years later, all but destroyed the wine industry in South Africa.

Great Britain liberated Cape Town as a free trade zone in 1802, but took occupation again in 1806 and remained in political control there until the early 1900s. In 1910, the Union of South Africa was created as an independent commonwealth under the British Crown. In the late 1890s resistant graftings were employed by South African viticulturists. The replanting of vineyards progressed very quickly, resulting in sufficient wine production to satisfy domestic demand in just several years. But, as in many post-*Phylloxera* replanting projects, growers overplanted, and a glut of production created a market for wine at very low prices. By the start of the twentieth century, the South African wine industry was in desperate need of moderation and regulation.

One answer to this economic problem was to reduce production costs, which was achieved by the formation of cooperatives during the early 1900s. A more effective method of stabilization was introduced in 1918, when Die Kooperatiewe Wijnbouwers Vereniging van Zuid Afrika (KWV), or "The Cooperative Winegrowers Association of South Africa," was founded by several leaders from the cooperatives. Today the KWV is a wine-producing giant governed by 12 directors, all of whom are elected from the rank and file of several thousand member vintners. This directorate maintains supply in balance with demand for South African wines by the administration of production quotas and price floors for all members. In addition, buffer stocks are maintained and bonus payments made in lean vintage years in order to ensure stability across the

FIGURE 12.1 La Concorde—
headquarters of the KWV. *(Courtesy
of Cooperative Winegrowers Association of
South Africa, Ltd.)*

nation's industry. The KWV is the most powerful and effective self-imposed winegrowing regulatory organization in the world.

Under pressure by the free world to abolish apartheid (racial separation), South Africa chose Nelson Mandela to be its first freely elected president. Following the demise of apartheid, a previously thriving wine export trade, some 140,000 gallons per year to the United States alone, receded to comparatively nothing, but is now actively advancing once again.

In 1993 there were 160 independent vintners in South Africa, as compared with 70 cooperatives. However, the co-ops, some of which are truly giant firms, produced more than 95 percent of the 250 million gallons of wine grown in South Africa. Per-capita wine consumption has grown to approach approximately 2.5 gallons per year.

The cooperatives make sense for South African winegrowers. Apart from the obvious advantages of their united strength in buying power and a perpetual outlet for every vintage, the co-ops have the ability to study market dynamics and prepare products to best serve changing consumer demands. Most important, however, because the highest-quality winegrowing regions in South Africa are situated 1,000 miles south of Johannesburg and major foreign outlets are continents and oceans away, the co-ops serve in marketing far beyond the capabilities of most independent vintners.

The climate—especially levels of seasonal rainfall—is the primary factor in determining vineyard locale in South Africa. The lack of rain confines most commercial vineyards to the southwestern reaches of the country, in a narrow section connected to the north and east by the city of Cape Town. Most winegrowing regions are situated among the beautiful mountain ranges and foothills, where rainfall can vary from 30 to more than 300 inches per year. Soils are typically sandstone in the west, granitic in the east, shales in the dry valleys, and sandy loams in the river valleys. The climate is mild overall, with heavier rainfall along the coastal areas and irrigation required across the interior sectors.

It has only been in the last several decades that there has been a movement among South African vintners to plant more of the classic fine wine varieties. More than half of the nation's wine production continues to be reasonably good white wine derived from Chenin Blanc, Johannisberg Riesling, Ugni

Figure 12.2 Stellenbosch vineyards. (Courtesy of Cooperative Winegrowers Association of South Affica, Ltd.)

Blanc, Palomino, and Muscat of Alexandria. Chenin Blanc is called "Steen," and Johannisberg Riesling is referred to in some locales as "Cape" and in others as "Weisser Riesling." Ugni Blanc is "Trousseau Grey Riesling," Palomino is "Fransdruif," and Muscat of Alexandria has become "Hanepoot." Included in this broad white wine portfolio are Pinot Blanc, Sauvignon Blanc, Thompson Seedless, Green Hungarian, and some European-African hybrids.

Much of the red table wine production seems to be patterned after that of the Rhone Valley region in France. The Rhone variety Cinsault, sometimes spelled *Cinsaut* or called "Hermitage" in South Africa, accounts for about one third of the red wine vines cultivated here. The nation's now famous Cinsault-Pinot Noir hybrid, Pinotage, accounts for another large share of the reds. A large portion of Syrah rounds out the Rhone varieties, and there are significant shares of Cabernet Sauvignon and Souzão vines as well.

Prior to the recent table wine renaissance, South African vintners were noted for their fine Sherry and Port-type wines. These were, and remain, generally superb products grown from the same Palomino and Souzão vines and made by the same time-honored methods that are traditional in Spain and Portugal.

❖ CLASSIFICATION

In 1973 the South African government enacted official regulations for wine labeling, including a complex Wine of Origin (WO) system, along with specific requirements for vine variety, vintage year, and other information. With modifications in 1990 and 1993, the fundamental premise of the WO is to prohibit the use of geographical origins existing in other nations. Seals of authenticity are provided to compliant vintners, recalling the DOC and DOCG seals found on bottles of superior Italian wines. WO enforcement is maintained by the nation's Wine and Spirit Board, an official body with membership from both the South African government and the wine industry. Chairmanship of the board is held by the director of the Viticultural and Oenological Research Institute (VORI) at Stellenbosch. The VORI continues to be very active in vinicultural research, contributing much to the worldwide state of the art in winegrowing.

FIGURE 12.3 Winegrowing regions in South Africa.

⬧ COASTAL REGION

Vineyards of the Coastal Region, centered by the capital city of Cape Town, are situated along the periphery of False Bay. As in California and many other premium New World winegrowing locales around the world, some vineyards have fallen to expanding urban development. The Coastal Region is cooled by the Benguela Current, which rides up the Atlantic and Indian Oceans from Antarctica.

Of understandable concern to this winegrowing community is the spread of vine-killing diseases into many of the lower flatland vineyards. Although many of the sites are planted with certified disease-free vines grafted on resistant rootstocks, there is a move toward finding new sites, particularly in the foothills of the mountain ranges that divide one breathtaking valley from another in this magnificent landscape. The advantage is cooler temperatures, of course, but also more rainfall and better soil drainage, resulting in greater fruit quality, but at the expense of lower quantity. For the purposes of building important export markets, such as the United States, this improved quality is essential.

CONSTANTIA

Within the Coastal Region, bordering Cape Town to the south, is the historical Constantia district, one of the coolest and certainly the smallest vineyard ward in South Africa. The 750 acres that make up Constantia are devoted to very high quality wines made principally from Hanepoot (Muscat of Alexandria) vines. One notable exception to this concentration of Muscat vines is found in the Groot Constantia winery estate, founded in the 1670s by pioneer vintner and governor Simon van der Stel. These vineyards are composed of Chenin Blanc, Johannisberg Riesling, Sauvignon Blanc, Cabernet Sauvignon, and Syrah.

DURBANVILLE

The district of Durbanville also has historical roots dating back to van der Stel. It is situated on the north side of Cape Town near the Atlantic coast, where cool breezes temper the hot sun and heavy clay soils retain rainfall. Durbanville touts an ideal mesoclimate for winegrowing. Its celebrity has also served, ironically, to destroy many vineyards, as well-to-do people from nearby Cape Town are increasingly drawn to construct new homes in the balmy Durbanville environs. This locale is probably best known for big red wines grown from Cabernet Sauvignon and Shiraz vines. Bloemendal, Meerandal, and Diemersdal are the best vintners of these. One of the pioneer vintners in this locale is Altydgedacht, also a fine Cabernet producer, but known principally for full-structured white wines grown from Chardonnay, Chenin Blanc, and Gewürztraminer.

OVERBERG

The Overberg district is one of the newer viticultural appellations established by the WO. Although it is not officially included in the Coastal Region, it borders Constantia to the south and is embraced by the southernmost coastline of the region. As a result, this locale has the coolest temperatures of all South African winegrowing districts. Plantings of cool-climate vines such as Chardonnay, Johannisberg Riesling, and Pinot Noir may attain quality approaching that of Constantia and Durbanville.

SWARTLAND

Swartland is one of the largest and most fertile winegrowing districts in the Coastal Region, although most of the land is devoted to growing grain. The Swartland Cooperative dominates the wine scene. Rich soils have consistently provided heavy production, allowing for attractive prices and a strong consumer following. The reputation of this district has been built mainly on good value Cabernet Sauvignon and Cinsault reds. Recently, however, it has included equally fine white wines grown from Sauvignon Blanc vines.

STELLENBOSCH

With more than 38,000 acres of prime quality vineyards, Stellenbosch is unquestionably the most prestigious wine district in all of South Africa. Most of the world's classic vine varieties are cultivated across this grand expanse.

With vineyards that have a recorded history from the time of Dutch colonization, the Kanonkop is a hallmark winegrowing estate in Stellenbosch. *Kanon* in its name relates to a cannon on the estate that was fired when ships approached in nearby Table Bay. That cannon could well be used today in saluting Kanonkop as the vintner that brought the hybrid vine *Pinotage* into acceptance among red wine aficionados.

The Kanonkop name has become synonymous with the very best in red wine. The estate still produces an exceptionally rich and heavy Cabernet Sauvignon each vintage, thought by many South Africans to be their very best.

Four Stellenbosch cooperatives are recognized for producing good quality table wines from grapes grown in the Coastal Region. The Bottelary co-op is best known for its award-winning Gewürztraminer. Chardonnay and Sauvignon Blanc are highly regarded wines from the Eesterivier co-op, and good Cabernet Sauvignon and Shiraz come from both the Helderberg and Welmoed cooperatives.

Bergkelder, an independent vintner, is another of the large Stellenbosch producers marketing good quality wines, under the brands "Fleur du Cap" and "Grünberger," both found in the larger outlets throughout the U.S. wine market.

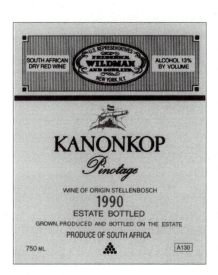

Founded in 1924, the Stellenbosch Farmers' Winery is the largest single vintner in South Africa and ranks among the top 10 largest in the world. This publicly held company comprises several important estates. Along with wines from the Stellenbosch Farmers' Winery itself, the company operates four other wine-producing firms, Zonnebloem, Château Libertas, Sable View, and Tasheimer.

Winner of many awards and accolades for quality, Zonnebloem is one of Stellenbosch Farmers' super-premium vintners. With a history reaching back to the days when this property was an original land grant from Simon van der Stel in 1689, Château Libertas was named in honor of liberty. It remains one of the very few "château" winegrowing estates in South Africa and is corporate headquarters for the Stellenbosch Farmers' winery.

The Sable View brand is founded on lower-priced wines made from classic grapes—Chardonnay, Sauvignon Blanc, and Cabernet Sauvignon—which are cultivated to yield large crops on heavily fertilized and irrigated soils situated in locales of warmer climates. Such wines, referred to as "fighting varietals" in the United States, are often involved in price wars and can be good values, but they usually lack the intensity of color, body, and flavor found in wines grown under more controlled conditions.

PAARL

Only part of the more than 50,000 acres of vines cultivated in the Paarl district are classified within the borders of the Coastal Region. Paarl is the largest single vineyard district in the entire nation. Table wines constitute its principal production, but they have yet to gain the international reputation attained by the district's dessert wines. Paarl "Sherries," made by the same flor yeast method used in Spain, continue to be held in high regard. The best are considered by many wine experts to be fully the equal of Sherry. Granitic soils, a warm climate, and adequate natural rainfall hold great promise for Paarl's becoming one of the world's finest winegrowing locales.

Paarl cooperatives concentrate on making good value red table wines. The Boland cooperative's Cabernet Sauvignon and Pinotage are consistently high in quality, as are those from the Perdeberg and Simonsvlei cooperatives. The Franschoek cooperative makes the best co-op whites in the district, primarily Sauvignon Blanc and Sémillon under the brand name "La Cotte."

It is in the Paarl district, at the Nederburg wine estate, that an annual auction is held during the vintage season each March. This event, in rather Burgundian fashion, now attracts more than 2,000 wine-buying hopefuls from afar, and, with 1994 sales of $600,000 as a standard, the Nederburg auction continues to enhance the reputation of all South African wines.

Founded in 1791, the Nederburg Wine Farm estate vineyards and wine cellars are situated in the heart of the magnificent Paarl Valley. Owned by the

Stellenbosch Farmers' Winery, Nederburg is independently operated as an autonomous facility. With a diversity of deep topsoil types and plenty of natural rainfall, the Nederberg vignerons are provided the luxury of cultivating Chardonnay, Sauvignon Blanc, Pinot Noir, Cabernet Sauvignon, and other classic vines within ideal environs. The result is wines that many experts rank among the very best produced in South Africa. The Nederburg Wine Farm was declared a national historical monument in 1990.

TULBAGH

The Tulbagh district is situated about 30 miles north of Paarl, in the highlands. Most of its 10,000 acres of vineyards are devoted to white table wine production, principally Teutonic cool-climate varieties such as Johannisberg Riesling and Gewürztraminer.

◈ BREEDE RIVER VALLEY REGION

About 20 miles east of the vast Paarl district is the Breede River Valley Region, which also includes the Hex River Valley. This is another of the warmer and dryer regions in South Africa.

WORCESTER

The largest district in the region is Worcester. With five subdistricts, each with distinctly different mesoclimates, this is another locale known primarily for the production of dessert wines and brandy, although truly superb Muscat white table wines are also grown here. Bergsig Furmint and late-harvest Gewürztraminer are notable Worcester whites.

ROBERTSON

Robertson has nine subdistricts, all more or less similar in soil and weather patterns, that are famous for dessert wine and brandy. These, like many other wine-growing areas in South Africa, are changing as recent plantings of classic table wine vines bring increasing attention to this district.

FIGURE 12.4 Vineyards in the Worcester Region of South Africa. *(Courtesy of Cooperative Winegrowers Association of South Africa, Ltd.)*

One of the most modern winery facilities in Robertson is Madeba Vineyards, which, along with considerable Cape Riesling and Muscat acreage, includes new plantings of Chardonnay and Pinot Noir. Mont Blois, owned since 1884 by the Bruwer family from Blois in the Loire Region of France, has built a fine reputation for sweet white wines from Muscat vines. More recently, Mont Blois has been engaged in wine production from Sauvignon Blanc in the Blanc Fumé style of the Loire.

The town of Bonnievale centers winegrowing activity in the easternmost reaches of this district. Late-harvest sweet white wines made from Gewürztraminer and Cape Riesling win prestigious awards repeatedly even though, paradoxically, the reputation for Bonnievale wines has traditionally been built on marginal value for easy prices. Bon Courage cellars, three times South Africa's champion wine estate, has turned to making drier wines. The Rietvallei Estate, well known for fine sweet red Muscat wines, has shifted to planting Chardonnay and Rhine Riesling for dry whites. The De Weshof Estate was the first of the Swellendam pioneers to win a major table wine award, the coveted Vinexpo Award in Bordeaux, in 1987.

There is similar activity among Roberston cooperatives. The Rooiberg cooperative and Nuy, a small co-op with an equally small name, have both won prestigious awards for their whites. The Robertson and Roodezant co-ops both produce superb Cabernet Sauvignon.

SWELLENDAM

Despite the agreeable coastal location of the Swellendam district, the advantages of cool temperature and adequate soils in some mesoclimates have failed to generate much change to quality table wine production. It remains a large producer of inexpensive dessert wines, ordinary table wines, and wines for distilling into brandy.

◈ OLIFANTS RIVER REGION

Starting about 125 miles north of Cape Town, and 10 miles inland from the west coast, the Olifants River Region stretches northward to become a large expanse of vineyards cultivated in very warm and dry environs. This region supplies a good share of the vin ordinaire for South Africa.

PICKETBERG

The Picketberg district borders Paarl to the north. With a hot climate and scant rainfall necessitating widespread irrigation, this area is known for large cooperatives that vinify lower-priced table wines, dessert wines, and brandy.

KLEIN KAROO REGION

Perhaps more famous for its ostrich feathers than for wine, the Klein Karoo region is located northeast of the Breede and Hex Rivers in an east-west stretch of plain that is virtually arid. As would be expected, this region accounts for still more of South African dessert wine, brandy, and ordinary table wine production.

DOUGLAS AND LOWER ORANGE RIVER

The Douglas and Lower Orange River Region reaches even farther north from the Klein Karoo and is the northernmost winegrowing region in South Africa. As such, it is the hottest and dryest, including the southern extremes of the Kalahari Desert. The region is divided by the town of Prieska, the Douglas sector to the northeast and lower Orange River to the west. Winegrowing in both locales is totally dependent on the river for irrigating the parched, sandy soil. Much of the grape production in this region is devoted to Muscat varieties and Thompson Seedless for raisins. As would be expected, Douglas and Orange River wines, principally from Chenin Blanc and French Colombard vines, are light and thin. They have, however, the advantages of both lower price and being 500 miles closer to the large Johannesburg market than the quality wines grown in the Cape Town vicinity.

MOSSEL BAY

Two hundred miles due east of Cape Town is the coastal city of Mossel Bay. At this writing, Mossel Bay has not yet been declared an official region by the WO, but new vineyards in the relatively cool-climate Elgin and Walker Bay locales are giving promise that this may become recognized as an appellation of origin.

GLOSSARY

abboccato. Italian term referring to level of sweetness; semidry.

acerbe. French term referring to wines made from acidic, harsh-tasting grapes.

acetic acid. Colorless, pungent substance commonly known as vinegar.

acetification. The process by which acetic acid is formed; the oxidation of ethanol (alcohol) into acetic acid by bacteria called *acetobacter.*

acid. A compound in wine that, in proper balance, contributes a tart freshness to taste and helps a wine age; sometimes used in reference to the harshness of grapes and wine.

acidity. Term used to indicate tartness or sharpness on the palate; does not relate to astringency or dryness.

aerobic. Term used to describe microorganisms requiring oxygen in order to grow.

aftertaste. Term used to refer to the flavor that remains in the mouth after a wine has been swallowed; an olfactory function of sensory receptors located in the mouth and nose.

age. Length of time a wine has existed, often taken as a sign of quality. However, greater age does not in itself make better wines.

aged. Refers to wine kept in storage (either in bulk or in bottle) under conditions designed to improve its qualities.

aging. The maturation of wine; the oxidation (reaction of one or more wine constituents with oxygen) process in which wines become mellowed.

alcohol. One of the essential components of wine resulting from the fermentation of grape juice or must. When fermentation is complete, the natural alcohol content will have reached about 12 percent by volume. In making dessert and aperitif wines, additional ethyl alcohol (ethanol) is added in the form of grape brandy (usually at about 190 degrees proof or 95 percent pure ethanol), which increases the resulting wine alcohol content to about 20 percent by volume.

Alicante. Winegrowing region located on the southeastern coast of Spain.

Aloxe-Corton. Winegrowing village located in the Côte d'Or district of the Burgundy region of France.

Alsace. Winegrowing region located in northeastern France, composed of the Haut-Rhin and Bas-Rhin. Alsatian wines often show their Teutonic heritage in type, style, and packaging, but usually do not equal the finer German growths.

amabile. Term often used to refer to level of sweetness; sweeter than *abboccato*.

amaro. Term often used to refer to bitterness.

amelioration. Addition of water and/or sugar to juice or wine. In most European countries, when natural sugar levels are insufficient in a given vintage, a vintner is allowed to add sugar to grape juice and must prior to fermentation. California juice and must may not be ameliorated at all; juice and must in other states may be ameliorated in accordance with U.S. Bureau of Alcohol, Tobacco and Firearms regulations.

amontillado. Popular type of Sherry; may be dry but is usually noticeably sweet.

amoroso. Sherry that is darker and sweeter than *amontillado*.

amphorae. Ancient Greek jars, vases, or jugs with oval bodies and narrow necks.

anaerobic. Term used to describe a microorganism able to grow in an environment lacking in oxygen.

Anjou. Winegrowing district in the central Loire Valley region of France.

anthocyanins. Color pigments found in the skins of grapes from which the color of wines originates.

aperitif wine. Wine that contains added essences and flavors of spices, herbs, roots, etc.; for example, vermouths.

appearance. The visual aspect of wine evaluation, concerned with color and clarity.

Appellation d'Origine Contrôlée (AOC). Translated from the French as "authenticity guaranteed"; the highest level of wine quality authorized by the French government as regulated and enforced by the Institut Nationale des Appellations d'Origine (INAO).

apre. French term used to refer to wines that are very harsh.

Arbois. Winegrowing district in the Jura region of eastern France.

aroma. Term used to refer to the fragrance of a juice, must, or wine. Aroma is contributed by the fruit and is one constituent of the total bouquet.

aromatized wines. Generally regarded as the same as *aperitif wines*.

arome spiritueux. French term used to refer to the bouquet of a wine at the time of serving; usually a bouquet that lasts longer than the flavor. See Sève.

Asti. Capital city of the Piedmont region of northern Italy. Asti Spumante is a white sparkling wine that is usually rather sweet and very fruity.

astringency. Term used to refer to the response of the palate to tannin, a response similar to that produced by aspirin.

ATF. Acronym used for U.S. Bureau of Alcohol, Tobacco, and Firearms.

Auslese. Famous German wine made from specially selected clusters of over-ripened grapes that may or may not be infected with *Edelfäule* mold.

Ausone. Ancient St.-Émilion château in the Bordeaux region of France once owned by and named for Ausonius, a Roman consul.

austere. Term used to to describe strong wines. See *heady*.

bacteria. One-celled microscopic plants. The bacteria called *Acetobacter* are responsible for turning wine into vinegar.

balance. Term used in describing the proportions of dryness (or sweetness) and acidity in wine.

Balling. Graduated viscosity scale that indicates the simultaneous influences of alcohol and dissolved solids as read on a Brix hydrometer.

barrique. Wine cask used principally in the Bordeaux region of France, containing approximately 60 U.S. gallons. Similar-sized casks of the same name are found in other regions of France.

Barsac. Winegrowing *commune* located in the Sauternes district of Bordeaux, France.

Baume. Scale measuring dissolved solids (mostly sugar) content in grapes.

Beaujolais. Winegrowing district in the southern portion of the Burgundy region of France.

Beaujolais Nouveau. Newly made, or very young, Beaujolais wines (fermented by the carbonic maceration process), which are meant to be consumed within several months following harvest.

Beaujolais-Villages. Blends of wines grown in various villages in the Beaujolais district of Burgundy; generally considered superior to wines labeled only as "Beaujolais."

Beaune. Capital city of the Burgundy region of France.

Beerenauslese. German wine made from individually selected grape berries of specially selected bunches of overripe grapes infected with *Edelfäule* mold.

bentonite. A montmorillonite clay compound used in winemaking (usually in younger wines) as a clarification agent. Through its great adsorptive capacity, precipitates suspended solids and colloids; may also tend to diminish color intensity of the wine as a side effect.

bereich. German for "area." Used to refer to vineyard origins; for example, "Bereich Bernkastel" (from vineyards located within the legal bounds of the Bernkastel district).

Bernkastel. Central city of Mosel-Saar-Ruwer winegrowing region in Germany.

bianco. Italian for "white."

big. Term generally used to describe wines that exhibit an abundance of positive qualities.

binning. Storage of bottled wines in bins, usually for the purpose of aging.

bite. Term used to refer to an unpleasant taste value that generally results from high acidity.

Blanc de Blancs. French for "white from whites"; denotes a white wine made entirely from white grape varieties.

Blanc de Noirs. French for "white from blacks"; denotes a white wine made entirely from black grape varieties.

bland. Term used to describe wines lacking in acidity and/or overall character.

blended wine. Two or more wines mixed together, generally in an effort to improve overall character through melding individual attributes.

Bocksbeutel. The short, squat flagon-type "ram's-head" bottle generally associated with the Franken winegrowing region of Germany.

bodega. Spanish for "wine cellar," usually constructed above ground. The term also refers to a Spanish "wine house."

body. Term used to describe how wine feels in the mouth. This feeling is caused by dissolved solids. A wine may be "light-bodied," or thin, as opposed to "heavy-bodied," or thick.

bonded. A term used by the U.S. Bureau of Alcohol, Tobacco and Firearms (ATF) in reference to wines on which the federal excise taxes have not yet been paid. A "bonded area" denotes the borders within which wine may be made and stored. A "bond" is a financial document that guarantees payment of excise taxes. Both a "bond" and a "bonded area" must be applied for and approved by the ATF as part of a vintner's operating permit in the United States.

Bordeaux. Large winegrowing region in southwest France. Its center is the port city of the same name. "Claret" is an often-used English term for red Bordeaux wines.

Botrytis. See *pourriture noble* or *Edelfäule*.

bottle. Glass container in any U.S. government-approved size used for wine packaging and marketing.

bottle aging. Designed program of improving wine quality through periods of storage in bottles.

bottle fermentation. Secondary fermentation of wine in bottles to capture carbon dioxide gas in the production of sparkling wines.

bottle sickness. Term used in wine production, usually referring to a temporary change or reduction of bouquet and flavor in wines just bottled, often a result of the addition of preservatives and the rigors of cask-to-bottle cellar treatment.

bottoms. Sediment in wine tanks after fermentation, racking, clarification, etc.; more often called *lees*.

bouquet. Term used to describe the fragrance of a wine. The bouquet consists of the fruit aroma and the volatile constituents that result from the cellaring techniques used to make the wine.

brandy. Distilled wine; the "spirits" of wine.

breathing. Practice of uncorking a wine bottle well in advance of serving to allow the wine to expel head-space gases. The usefulness of letting a wine breathe is questionable.

bright. See *brilliant*.

brilliant. Term used to describe wines that have a flawless clarity.

Brix. Graduated hydrometer scale used to measure dissolved solids in grape juice; not to be confused with *Balling*, which is influenced by alcohol in solution along with dissolved solids.

brut. French for "raw" or "natural" unsweetened wines (usually Champagne); the very driest.

Bual. White wine vine variety cultivated on the isle of Madeira. Also a type of Madeira wine that is generally heavy bodied and sweet.

Bucelas. Vineyard region north of Lisbon in Portugal.

bulk process. Production of sparkling wine in special tanks rather than through the traditional *méthode champenoise* of fermenting sparkling wine in individual bottles. *Charmat* is another name for the bulk process.

bung. Stopper, usually made of wood or glass, used to seal a keg, barrel, or some other bulk wine-storage vessel.

bunghole. Opening at the top of a bulk wine-storage vessel into which the bung is placed as a seal.

Burgundy. Winegrowing region in central France. The finest wines are generally considered to be grown in the Côte d'Or (comprising the subdistricts Côte de Beaune and Côte de Nuits) district. "Burgundy" is also a generic term sometimes used indiscriminately on the labels of U.S.-produced red wines which have no resemblance to true Burgundy.

butt. English term for Spanish cooperage. Each butt contains approximately 126 imperial gallons (about 151 U.S. gallons).

Cabernet. Short for Cabernet Sauvignon, the premier red wine grape of the Bordeaux winegrowing region in France and other New World nations. Also used incorrectly to refer to the hybrid Ruby Cabernet.

Cabernet Franc. Red wine vine variety cultivated in the St.-Émilion district of Bordeaux, France, and, increasingly, in the New World.

Cabernet Sauvignon. See *Cabernet*.

Cabinett-Wein. See *Kabinett*.

candling. Process of judging clarity in a bottle of wine by holding it in front of a filament bulb or lighted candle.

cantina. Italian for "cellar" or "winery."

Cantina Sociale. Cooperative winery of Italian grape growers.

capiteaux. French term meaning "warmly rich in alcohol."

capsule. Seal over a wine bottle used to protect the neck and closure and enhance the packaging.

carbohydrate. Carbon, hydrogen, and oxygen chemically bonded as a compound. Sugar and ethyl alcohol are carbohydrates.

carbonated wines. Wines injected with carbon dioxide gas, rendering them effervescent.

carbon dioxide. The gas produced by fermentation; CO_2.

carbonic maceration. Method by which whole grapes are fermented in a closed container, during which the carbon dioxide gas generated from fermentation permeates the grapes. A process employed for nouveau wines grown in the Beaujolais district of the Burgundy region in France.

carboy. Glass bottle, usually with a capacity of 5 gallons.

Carignan. Red wine vine variety grown widely in southern France and Central California.

casa vinicola. Italian for "winery."

case. Container in which bottled wine is held, usually made of heavy paperboard, wood, or plastic, and normally with a capacity of twelve 750 milliliter bottles (24 half-bottles, 6 magnums).

cask. Wooden container for bulk wine storage and aging, usually made of some species of white oak and containing at least 200 U.S. gallons; generally built with bulging sides. Not to be confused with the smaller butts, hogsheads, pipes, barrels, puncheons, or the larger tuns.

caskiness. Term generally used to refer to wines that may have been aged in casks that were not cleaned or treated properly beforehand. Same as "tanky."

casse. Term used to describe the haze that develops in wines as a result of excessive metal content.

Cassis. Winegrowing seaport village near Marseilles, France; also refers to a black currant aroma often found in wines made from Cabernet Sauvignon grapes.

Catawba. Native American grape variety cultivated principally in New York State and Ohio.

cave. French for "wine cellar."

Cellared and Bottled by. Same as Made and Bottled by.

cellar treatment. The materials and methods used in the various phases of the winemaking process.

cépage. French for "grape cultivar."

cerasuolo. Italian for "light red."

Chablis. Winegrowing district in the Burgundy region of France; produces some of the finest white wines from the Chardonnay variety. Petit Chablis is a lesser grade grown within the district. Chablis is also used as a generic term indiscriminately for some U.S.-produced white wines bearing little or no resemblance to true Chablis.

Chagny. Winegrowing village in the Côte d'Or district of the Burgundy region in France.

Chambolle-Musigny. Winegrowing township in the Côte d'Or district of the Burgundy region in France.

chambrer. The act of bringing a wine, usually red, carefully to cool room temperature.

Champagne. Winegrowing region northeast of Paris, France, important in producing sparkling wine. Champagne is also used as a generic term for U.S.-produced sparkling wines bearing little resemblance to true Champagne.

Champagne Rouge. Refers to red sparkling wines often labeled "Sparkling Burgundy."

chaptalization. Addition of sugar to juice or must in order to increase the resultant alcohol strength from fermentation (note that the term *amelioration* denotes the addition of water and/or sugar).

character. The sum of the qualities that distinguish a wine: color, taste, and bouquet of a particular wine type.

Chardonnay. White wine vine variety grown for all of the great white Burgundies and across much of the New World.

charmat. Bulk or tank method of producing sparkling wines, usually a much faster process (and generally less respected) than the traditional French *méthode champenoise* bottle-fermentation technique.

charnu. French term generally used to refer to wines that have body, but not much alcohol strength.

charpente. French term used to describe wines that have been well made.

Chassagne-Montrachet. Red and white winegrowing district in the Côte d'Or district of the Burgundy region in France.

Chasselas. Common grape used for both eating and winemaking in Europe. The variety is called Gutedel in Germany and the Alsace, and Fendant in Switerland.

château. French for "castle." A wine estate comprising vineyards and a winery in France, usually in Bordeaux.

Châteauneuf-du-Pape. Literally means "new home of the pope." A winegrowing district located in the southern Rhone Valley, near Avignon, France.

Chenas. Winegrowing village in the Beaujolais district of Burgundy, France.

Chianti. Winegrowing district in the Tuscany region of Italy. Chianti Classico wines are from superior, centrally located vineyards.

chiaretto. Italian for "light red."

Chinon. Historical winegrowing town in the Loire Region of France.

Chiroubles. Winegrowing village in the Beaujolais district of Burgundy, France.

claret. Term used by the English for red wines grown in the Bordeaux Region of France, rarely used as a generic term by U.S. vintners.

clarete. Spanish term denoting a red wine that is light in body and color; generally refers to wines from the Rioja.

clarify. To make a wine clear by adding refining agents (such as bentonite) in order to precipitate suspended solids.

classico. Inner zone of an Italian DOC. Generally refers to superior growths.

classified growth. A particular vineyard, domaine, estate, or other geographical locale that is officially recognized by a national government as a controlled appellation of wine origin.

clean. Term used to describe a wine free from the detrimental effects of unsanitary cellar treatment or overprocessing. When the palate experiences the full varietal character and detects no interference from other varieties blended in, the wine is called *clean*.

clear. Describes wine that has been clarified and/or filtered successfully from visible solids, but is not brilliant.

clos. French for "walled vineyard." Generally found in Burgundy.

cloudy. Describes a wine with a rather heavy presence of suspended solids.

cloying. Excessively sweet.

coarse. Harsh and overpowering in taste; may refer to young wines not allowed to mellow through sufficient cellar treatment and aging.

Colares. Winegrowing locale near Lisbon in Portugal.

colloidal suspension. Hazy or cloudy suspensions of semisolid particles in wine; not to be confused with *metal casse*.

Colmar. Capital city of the Alsace winegrowing region in northeastern France.

color. The hue and intensity of pigmentation in wine. Usually refers to recognized values such as "light straw," "ruby," or "tawny," along with "light," "dark," etc.

complex. A term used to describe a wine in which bouquet and/or flavors are composed of many different constituents that may be difficult to separate and classify.

concentrate. Dehydrated grape juice, either red or white, used for sweetening grape juice and wines that are deficient in natural grape sugar.

Concord. American hybrid grape cultivar developed by Ephraim Bull of Concord, Massachusetts. The Concord, very popular as a juice grape, also finds acceptance as a table grape and wine grape, most notably for kosher wines produced in the northeastern United States.

Conegliano. Winegrowing district north of Venice in the Veneto region of Italy.

consorzi. Association of grape growers, vintners, academics, and government officials in Italy who regulate winegrowing within their region; compliance is indicated by affixing a seal on bottle necks.

cooked. Term used to describe a "baked" character or an oxidized bouquet and flavor. Generally used positively in reference to madeirized wines and negatively in regard to wines that have endured excessive heat in shipping and/or storage.

cooperage. Term that traditionally refers to wine containers made from wood. The word derives from *cooper*, a British sailing term for a ship's barrel maker. In modern times *cooperage* refers to any container used for wine, whether of wood, steel, glass, or any other material.

cooperative. Winery owned by more than one grape grower, generally formed to share the cost of winery establishment and operation among members.

cork. Bark from the cork oak tree, grown in large acreages in Mediterranean countries, harvested and processed into stoppers for both still and sparkling wine bottles.

corkscrew. Spiral metal device with a sharp tip used to remove corks from wine bottles.

corkiness. Term used to describe an unpleasant flavor and bouquet in a wine that has been tainted with trichloroanisole (TCA) from a moldy cork.

corps; vin qui à du corps; vin corsé. (body, wine with body, full-bodied wine). French terms used to describe wines that possess substance, pronounced taste, and vinous strength, and that "fill the mouth"; the opposite of a light, dry, cold, or watery wine.

Côte de Beaune. Southern winegrowing subdistrict in the Côte d'Or district in the Burgundy region of France.

Côte d'Or. "Golden Slope" of northern Burgundy, where the finest red wines of the region are grown. In the opinion of some experts, in certain years some of the finest red wines of the world are grown here.

Côte-Rotie. Winegrowing district in the extreme north of the Rhone Valley region of France, famous for the "blond" and "brunette" vineyards.

Côtes du Rhone. See *Rhone River.*

court. French term used to describe wines that are deficient in taste and flavor.

cradle. Device, usually made of wicker in one or another basket weave, in which a wine bottle is placed at an angle for serving.

Cramant. Important winegrowing *commune* in the Champagne region of France, which produces Blanc de Blancs (not to be confused with *Crémant*).

cream of tartar. Colorless crystalline deposit of potassium bitartrate that precipitates from unstable wines during refrigeration. See *tartaric acid.*

Crémant. Sparkling wine that has a reduced level of effervescence.

cru. French for a specified vineyard "growth," classified for a specific echelon of quality, such as a Premier Cru Classé or a Grand Cru Classé.

cru; crudité. French terms meaning "rawness." Applied to wines that are too young and, thus, retain a disagreeable greenness. See *vert.*

crust. Sediment of unstable solids from wine that have collected and solidified on the surface of the bottle; common in red wines. Most often associated with very old wines, especially Ports.

crystalline deposits. Crystal deposits composed primarily of tasteless potassium bitartrate that accumulate either at the bottom of the bottle or at the bottom of the cork. They are often the result of white wine's exposure to low temperature. See *tartaric acid.*

cuvée. Literally means "tub full" or "vat full"; in the winemaking sense, refers to the quantity of production from a vineyard. The term *cuvée* is often synonumous with "cru." The most common use of the term is in identifying blends of base wines fermented a second time for sparkling wines.

Dão. Winegrowing region in Portugal.

decant. Operation of delicately transferring wine from a bottle to a decanter so as to separate any sediment that may have formed in the bottle during aging.

dégorgement. French for "disgorge." The technique of removing the frozen plug of sediment from a bottle of sparkling wine after *rémuage* (riddling), but prior to the addition of dosage.

degrees Balling. Divisions for dissolved solids on the Balling hydrometer scale when used as a measurement of viscosity in solutions containing ethanol (ethyl alcohol), such as wine.

degrees Brix. Divisions for dissolved solids on the Brix hydrometer scale when used as a measurement of viscosity in solutions that do not contain ethyl alcohol, such as grape juice or must.

Delaware. Native American grape variety discovered growing wild in Delaware County, Ohio, during the early 1900s. The fruit is light red in color, but yields white wines.

delicate or **delicatesse.** French term meaning "delicate." Refers to a wine that has very little acidity and color. Though the wine may have one or more coarse constituents, it has been blended to mask that imbalance. Often used synonymously with *elegant.*

delicate. Term used to describe wines with subtle bouquet and flavor values.

demijohn. Small glass container for wine; usually wicker-covered. A common misnomer for *carboy* (5-gallon jug).

demi-sec. French for "nearly dry" or semidry." Most often used in the description of sparkling wines.

Denominazione di Origine Controllata. Instituted by the Italian government in 1963 as the official regulatory system for wine quality and origin control. Usually referred to by the acronym "DOC." It specifies the regulations and requirements for each wine name or title prescribed by the Italian Ministry of Agriculture.

dessert wine. In the United States, a wine that has received an addition of brandy, or has been "fortified," usually resulting in a sweet Port-type or Sherry-type wine. The term may also refer to any sweet wine that is served with dessert courses.

developed. Degree of wine maturity; a measurement of aging.

dinner wine. See *table wine.*

disgorging. English form of the French sparkling wine term *dégorgement,* meaning to expel the frozen plug of sediment in the neck of a sparkling wine bottle with the carbon dioxide gas pressure that has developed during secondary fermentation.

distinctive. Term for a wine with finesse and the qualities that distinguish its special character from that of lesser wines.

dolce. Italian for "sweet."

domaine. French for "vineyard estate" or "wine estate"; most commonly used in Burgundy.

Dom Perignon. Famous wine-master monk at the Abbey of Hautvillers in the Champagne region of France who is given credit for inventing sparkling wines during the seventeenth century. In modern times, "Dom Perignon" is a brand name for a very fine Champagne produced by Moët & Chandon in Epernay, France.

dosage. Addition of a rather high-alcohol, very sweet syrup to sparkling wines directly after *dégorgement* to balance acidity. The dosage usually contains a preservative to prevent a third fermentation.

Douro. Winegrowing region of Portugal where Port wine is made. It is named for the Douro River that flows through the valley to the city of Oporto.

doux. French for "sweet"; most often used in the description of sparkling wines.

dry. Absence of fermentable sugar; opposite of sweet.

dull. See *flat.*

dur or **dureté.** French term meaning "hard." Used for coarse wines that affect the palate in a disagreeable manner.

earthy. Sensory term relating to the smell of soil as a constituent in the bouquet and/or flavor of a wine.

Edelfäule. Fungus *Botrytis cinerea,* or "noble mold," that permeates the skins of grape berries, allowing moisture to evaporate and concentrating sugar and flavors that remain. *Edelfäule* is the German term for *Botrytis* and is associated with Beerenauslese and Trockenbeerenauslese wines. See also *pourriture noble.*

Égrappage. French for the "destemming" of grapes.

elegant. See *delicate.*

enology. Art, science, and study of making wine; same as *oenology.*

Entre-Deux-Mers. Winegrowing district located between the Dordogne and Garonne Rivers in the Bordeaux region of France.

Epernay. Wine city in the Champagne region of France.

erzeuger abfüllung. German for "estate bottled."

épluchage. Removal of poor-quality berries from bunches of grapes; see *triage.*

essential oils. Organic oils generated in grapes, which are distinctive in aroma and taste; the organoleptic profile of a particular grape.

Est! Est!! Est!!! Legendary wine grown in the Montefiascone district of the Latium region of Italy.

estate bottled. Labeling statement that generally signifies that the same authority who vinified the wine also grew the grapes that made the wine. Because this term is often misused, it may not always be the indication of a superior wine for which it is intended.

esters. Volatile (evaporative) organic compounds that make up the bouquet or the "nose" of a wine. Some esters are contributed by grapes, and others arise due to specific vinification procedures, such as aging in oak barrels.

ethyl alcohol. See *alcohol.*

event, goût d'. French for "flat" or seemingly lifeless. A condition that may arise when wines are overaged or have been stored in containers not properly sealed.

extract. Term for total dissolved solids in wine, including sugar, color pigments, glycerols, etc.

extra dry. "Bone" dry or totally lacking in residual sugar; the absolute opposite of *sweet.* Sometimes used incorrectly in labeling sparkling wines that are really slightly sweet, but not as dry as Brut or Sec.

faible. French for "weak." Generally associated with wines that exhibit thin body and little alcoholic strength, but may also be used for wines having little flavor—a characteristic preferred by some.

false wines. Wines made from sources other than grapes.

fattoria. Italian for "wine producer."

ferme or fermeté. French for "firm." A term used to describe strong and vigorous wines exhibiting heavy body. May also refer to young green wines. Generally a fault in finished wines, but may be a positive attribute in blending wines meant to add greater character.

fermentation. Generally signifies the transformation of sugar to alcohol (ethanol), carbon dioxide, and energy through the action of yeasts, although bacterial fermentations also occur in wines.

fermentation lock. Device on fermenting vessels that allows fermentation CO_2 to escape from the fermenter, but prohibits air and other outside elements from entering.

fermenters. Containers, generally constructed of stainless steel or oak, in which the process of wine fermentation takes place.

filtering. Passing a wine through filter media for removal of suspended solids.

finish. Term that refers to the last impression of the wine before, during, and after swallowing; includes the aftertaste as well.

fino. Lightest and driest of the Spanish Sherries.

firm. Term usually referring to wines that exhibit an aftertaste of tannin.

fixed acidity. Organic acids in wines that are nonvolatile, such as tartaric acid, malic, and lactic acids.

flat. Term for a wine devoid of interesting qualities; lacking finesse or polish. Also, sparkling wine that has lost its effervescence.

flavored wines. Wines that have values of taste and aroma added to the natural fermented grape juice used to make the wine, such as vermouth and some pop wines.

flavorous. Term used to describe full or extra-full flavor values.

flavors. Term used to describe distinct tastes as experienced by the palate.

Fleurie. Wine village in the Beaujolais district of Burgundy in France.

flinty. Term used to describe the stony or rocky flavors found in some white wines.

flor. Spanish for "flower." Generally refers to the surface-growing yeasts that synthesize acetaldehyde, the compound that contributes the nutty flavor common to Sherry-type wines.

flowers of wine. Development of a white film on the surface of wine that denotes the growth of *Acetobacter*. The acetification process is the development of vinegar.

flowery. Term used to describe the aroma and bouquet of wine that smells like flowers in blossom; an example is the white wine made properly from the vine variety Johannisberg Riesling.

fort. French for "strong." Wines that exhibit a superior alcoholic strength and, perhaps, a very pronounced flavor.

fortified wine. Wine that has been increased in alcohol content by the addition of brandy; good examples are Sherry and Port.

fortify. The act of adding brandy to wine to increase the alcohol content.

foxiness. Aroma and flavor generally attributed to grapes from the *Vitis labrusca* species, among others.

franc de goût. French for "natural taste," referring to wines that have no flavor other than that of the grape itself. Does not include wines of natural earthy or herbal flavors.

Franken. Winegrowing region in Germany.

Franken Riesling. See *Silvaner.*

free run. Juice or wine that flows freely from the press without the exertion of pressure.

Freisa. Red wine, sometimes *frizzante,* produced in the Piedmont region of Italy.

fresh. Term used to describe a lively bouquet and flavor.

frizzante. Italian for "petillant" or "slightly sparkling"; fizzy.

Fronsac. Winegrowing district in the Bordeaux region of France.

Frontignan. Winegrowing district in the Midi region of southern France. May also refer to the grape variety Muscat de Frontignan.

fruit wines. Wines made from fruits or fruit concentrates other than grapes. Not to be confused with fruit-flavored wines, which are base wines to which fruit flavor essences are added.

fruity. Term applied to wines having high values of bouquet and flavor captured from the grape (or whatever fruit from which it was made). Often used in evaluating wines made from *Vitis labrusca* and *Vitis rotundifolia*.

full. Term for wines that are heavy bodied, strong in values of bouquet and flavor, or both.

full-bodied. Term used to describe wine that feels thick, rich, and heavy in the mouth, such as Port, as opposed to thin and light, such as Chablis.

fumé. See *Sauvignon Blanc*.

fumé-aux. French for "heady." A term for wines with such high alcohol strength that they evaporate excessively, perhaps irritating the membranes of the nose.

Gamay. Red wine vine variety grown primarily in the Beaujolais district of the Burgundy region of France.

Geisenheim. Winegrowing town in the Rheingau region of Germany. Also the location of the Geisenheim Institute, a center for teaching and research in enology and viticulture.

genéreux. French for "generous." A term used to describe wines that offer abundant bouquet and flavor; wines that tend to warm and soothe the palate.

generic. Labeling term that describes wines from or characteristic of a particular geographical region or political boundary, such as Burgundy or Champagne in France. This can be contrasted with varietal labeling, which takes the name of the principal grape variety used in making the wine, such as Pinot Noir, which is the most important red grape variety grown in Burgundy. Some countries, such as the United States, are permitted to use some of the more common generic terms originating in Europe, such as "California Burgundy" or "New York State Champagne."

Gevrey-Chambertin. Winegrowing village in the Côte d'Or district of the Burgundy region in France.

Gewürztraminer. White wine vine variety grown principally in the Alsace region of France, but native to northern Italy.

grain. Term denoting a distinct, but not excessive, roughness or harshness, especially apparent in many young wines. Not necessarily a negative attribute.

Grand Cru. French for "great growth." Used primarily to classify vineyards in France, the term has a different significance from one wine region to another.

Graves. Winegrowing district in the Bordeaux region of France.

Gray Riesling. White wine vine variety in California, especially in the Livermore Valley. Some claim it is identical with the Chauche Gris grape of the Arbois district in the Jura region of France.

green. Term used to describe undeveloped wines; also wines that display a grassy or herbaceous bouquet and flavor, exemplified by Vinho Verde grown in Portugal.

Green Hungarian. White wine vine variety grown widely in California.

Grenache. Red and rosé vine variety grown widely in the Rhone Valley region of France and in California.

Grignolino. Red wine vine variety grown in northern Italy.

grossier. French term used to express coarseness.

Gumpoldskirchner. Delicate white wine grown in Austria.

Gutedel. See *Chasselas*.

Hallgarten. Winegrowing village in the Rheingau region of Germany.

Hammondsport. Winegrowing center of the Finger Lakes region of upstate New York.

hard. Term used to describe wines that affect the palate as coarse and/or harsh. The opposite of delicate and soft.

Hattenheim. Winegrowing village in the Rheingau region of Germany.

haut. French for "high," but more often taken, in wine terminology, to mean "higher than" or "farther away from" or "better than," such as in "Haut-Medoc," the superior section of the Medoc district of Bordeaux.

Hautvillers. Winegrowing abbey in the Champagne region of France. Dom Perignon, a monk, is credited with inventing Champagne in this abbey.

heady. Term usually referring to wines with excessive alcohol content. Roughly equivalent to "strong" wines. Also used loosely as a term for sparkling wines that show a persistent foam on their surfaces.

heavy. Refers to heady or strong wines that are not necessarily equally strong in bouquet and flavor. Also used in describing the viscosity of wines, especially sweet dessert wines.

Hermitage. Winegrowing district in the northern Rhone region of France.

Heurige. Young wine traditionally quaffed in Austrian pubs right after the vintage season.

Hippocras. Ancient medicinal elixir made by blending wine, spices, and honey or sugar.

Hochheim. Winegrowing village in the Rheingau region of Germany. The origin of the term "Hock."

Hock. English term for German wines in general. Thought to have originated from Hochheim, once a port city from which many German wines were shipped to the British Isles.

Hogshead. Small wine cask, usually found in Bordeaux, containing approximately 225 liters, or about 59.5 U.S. gallons.

Hospices de Beaune. Old hospital located in the city of Beaune, capital of the Burgundy region of France. The hospital has become famous for an annual auction sale of wines from vineyards it has acquired over the years through charitable donation.

hybrid. Result of a crossbreeding of two different varieties of vines. New cultivars may exhibit, in varying proportions, the properties contributed by each parent.

hydrometer. Floating instrument used to measure the density, specific gravity, or viscosity of liquids, such as grape juice or wine.

ice bucket. Device used to chill wines prior to serving. Should be large enough to hold at least a 3-liter bottle along with cracked ice.

Jerez. See *Sherry*.

Jeroboam. Large wine bottle that usually has a capacity of three liters, or four times the capacity of a common, standard wine bottle. Four-liter jeroboams are also available.

Johannisberg. Winegrowing town in the Rheingau region of Germany; often used to refer to "Schloss Johannisberg," which is located nearby.

Johannisberg Riesling. See *Riesling*.

Julienas. Wine village in the Beaujolais district of the Burgundy region in France.

Jura. Winegrowing region in eastern France near the Swiss border.

Jurançon. Winegrowing region in southern France near the Spanish border.

Kabinett. German wine made without the addition of sugar, generally considered the driest and lowest grade of Qualitätswein mit Pradikat.

keg. Very small wooden container used to store wine, usually less than 30 U.S. gallons in capacity.

kellar. German for "cellar"; often short for "wine cellar."

kelter. German for "press." Often short for "grape press" or "wine press."

Knipperle. White wine vine variety cultivated in the Alsace region of France.

kosher wine. Jewish sacramental wine made under rabbinical law and supervision.

kreuznach. Winegrowing district in the Nahe region of Germany.

Labrusca. Short for *Vitis labrusca,* the native grape species indigenous to the northeastern part of the United States and the southernmost reaches of Canada.

Lacryma Christi. Legendary white wine grown upon the slopes Mount Vesuvius in the Campania region of Italy.

lactic acid. Important acid constituent of grapes and wine that accounts for a cheeselike flavor. Lactic acid is fermented from malic acid during a malolactic fermentation.

lage. German for "locale." Generally used to describe a specific vineyard site.

lagrima. Type of Malaga wine made from overripe grapes grown in Spain.

La Mancha. Winegrowing region in central Spain.

late harvest. Wines made from grapes purposely left on the vines past peak ripeness. A practice heavily employed in many of the winegrowing regions of Germany.

lees. Sediment that precipitates from young wines during and after fermentation, which is composed primarily of grape pulp, yeasts, color pigments, acid salts, etc. In clarification procedures, "fining lees" denotes the precipitation of fining agents.

leger. French for "light." Wines that are *leger* have little body and/or color, sometimes because of a higher-than-normal alcohol content.

legs. Term used to describe the condensation of alcohol and other volatile compounds, including glycerol, on the inner surface of a wineglass above the surface of the wine. As this is largely influenced by temperature, the "legs" give no meaningful indication of any particular positive or negative attribute of a wine.

Leognan. Winegrowing *commune* in the Graves district of the Bordeaux region in France.

Liebfrauenstift. Legendary vineyard that surrounds the Liebfrauenkirche (the "loving wife's church," referring to Mary, the virgin mother of Jesus Christ) in the city of Worms, at the southern extremity of the Rheinhessen region of Germany; the birthplace of Liebfraumilch.

Liebfraumilch. Multiregional wine grown in the Rhineland of Germany. First produced by monks centuries ago from the Liebfrauenstift vineyard.

light. Term used to describe a low value of viscosity or body; the "mouth feel" of wines, usually dry white wines; may also be properly used to describe a wine lacking in values of bouquet or flavor.

liquoreux. Term used to describe wines that are sweet and soft and taste as though they had been treated with a liqueur.

liquoroso. Italian for "strong"; generally used for fortified wines.

Livermore Valley. Winegrowing district in the Central Coast region of California just east of San Francisco.

Loire Valley. Winegrowing region in the west-central portion of France.

Lombardy. Winegrowing region of northern Italy.

long. Term used to describe wines that have flavors that linger in the mouth; abundant aftertaste. May also refer to wines that are consistent over a number of vintages.

mâche. French for "mash"; a term used to describe a very heavy-bodied wine, somewhat thick or pasty.

Mâcon. Winegrowing capital city of the Mâconnais district in the Burgundy region of France.

Made and Bottled by. Labeling statement on U.S.-produced wines that indicates the wine was blended and bottled, but not necessarily fermented, processed, and aged, by the bottler.

Madeira. Winegrowing island belonging to Portugal; famous for Malmsey and Sercial wines.

madeirization. The oxidation of ethyl alcohol and acetic acid into aldehydes, considered a benefit in the making of Madeira or Sherry but a detriment in white table wines.

magnum. Wine bottle with usually twice the capacity of a normal 750-milliliter bottle.

Malaga. Winegrowing region in southern Spain; produces wines somewhat similar to Sherry.

Malbec. Vine variety grown for red wines in the Bordeaux region of France; also popular in Argentina.

malic acid. Acid constituent of grapes and wine that accounts for an apple-like flavor. It is malic acid that is fermented into lactic acid during a malo-lactic fermentation.

malo-lactic fermentation. The transformation of malic acid to lactic acid, carbon dioxide gas, and energy by the action of bacteria.

Malmsey. Legendary wine made from Malvasia grapes grown on the Portuguese island of Madeira.

Malvasia. White wine vine variety cultivated on the Portuguese island of Madeira for the making of Malmsey wines; also widely planted in other southern European locales. Known as Malvoisie in France.

Manzanilla. Very dry, pale wine produced near the Sherry region of Spain; it is not, however, a Sherry.

Margaux. Winegrowing subdistrict of the Medoc district in the Bordeaux region of France.

marque. French for "mark"; usually used to designate a trademark, such as *marque déposée.*

Marsala. Sweet dessert wine made in a similar manner to Sherry.

Martillac. Winegrowing *commune* in the Graves district of the Bordeaux region in France.

Mascara. Important vineyard region of Algeria in North Africa.

mature. Term used to describe a wine that has been properly cellared and aged so as to have reached full development of all sensory qualities.

maturity. Level at which a wine has become ready to drink. Also, full ripeness, a state in which grapes have developed on the vine for the use intended by the wine master.

May Wine. Wines made in Germany in which the very aromatic leaves of the woodruff (an herb called "Waldmeister" in Germany) have been infused. Most often served cold in a bowl with strawberries or some other fruit floating in it.

mead. Wine made from honey; traditional in England.

Médoc. Winegrowing district of the Bordeaux region in France. Important subdistricts in the more prestigious Haut-Médoc include Margaux, Pauillac, St.-Julien and St. Estèphe.

mellow. General term usually referring to a wine that is not biting or harsh. May also loosely refer to lower levels of sweetness.

Mendocino. Winegrowing district in the North Coast region of California.

Mercurey. Winegrowing subdistrict in the Chalonnais district of the Burgundy region in France.

Methuselah. Very large wine bottle, most often used in the Champagne region of France; generally eight times the size of a normal 750 milliliter wine bottle.

Meursault. Winegrowing subdistrict in the Côte de Beaune section of the Côte d'Or district of the Burgundy region in France.

mildew. Fungal disease of vines that can destroy both green tissue and fruit. Two noteworthy types are commonly known as downy mildew (occurs when there is an excess of rainfall) and powdery mildew (occurs when there is a deficiency of rainfall).

millesime. French for "vintage"; used in identifying the year in which the grapes that made a specific wine were grown.

Mis en Bouteilles au Château. French for "bottled at the winery estate"; used as an indication of authenticity of origin and quality.

Mis en Bouteilles au Domaine. French for "bottled at the vineyard estate"; used as an indication of guaranteed origin and quality.

mistela. Concentrated grape juice, or grape syrup, made by boiling down, which is used for sweetening some wines produced in Portugal and Spain.

moelle. French for "marrow"; a term referring to oily wines, a bit sweet and heavy, but not as a result of sugar or of being sweet. See *Liquoreux*.

moelleux. French for "mellow."

moldy. Term referring to "off" values of bouquet and flavor, usually applied to wines that have been made from grapes stored or aged in cooperage that has harbored mold.

montant. French for "rising"; a term used to describe wines that are pleasantly heady and spirituous.

Montefiascone. See Est! Est!! Est!!!

Monthélie. Winegrowing *commune* in the Côte de Beaune section of the Côte d'Or district of the Burgundy region of France.

mordant. French for "biting"; a term used primarily to describe overpowering wines or blending wines that dominate the other constituents in a given blend.

Morey-St.-Denis. Winegrowing *commune* in the Côte d'Or district of the Burgundy region of France.

Morgon. Winegrowing subdistrict in the Beaujolais district of the Burgundy region in France.

Moscatel. Dessert wines made from Muscat grapes in Portugal.

Moscato. Italian for "Muscat." The term may refer to any specific variety of Muscat grape cultivated in Italy; also refers to many different wines produced from Muscat grapes in that country.

Mosel. Winegrowing region along both banks of the Mosel River in Germany.

Moselblümchen. Name given to blends of wines grown in the Mosel region of Germany. Primarily fanciful, it carries no significance regarding specific origin or vinification controls.

mou. A French term used to describe wines that lack body and acid balance.

Moulin-à-Vent. Winegrowing subdistrict in the Beaujolais district of the Burgundy region of France.

mousseux. French for "foaming." A term used to describe sparkling wines produced by the French *méthode champenoise* process, but not in the Champagne region, such as the sparkling Loire wine Vouvray Mousseux. Sparkling wines not produced in the Champagne region may not be labeled "Champagne" in France. The Italian equivalent is "mussante."

mulled wine. Sweetened and spiced wine served hot, sometimes with a bit of lemon juice.

Muscadelle. White grape variety cultivated in the Bordeaux region of France.

Muscadine. Common name for *Vitis rotundifolia* grape species indigenous to the southeastern United States.

Muscadet. Winegrowing district in the western portion of the Loire Valley of France.

Muscat. Family of very aromatic grape varieties that spans several species. Muscats may be white, red, or black, but the most famous Muscat wines are white, such as Muscat de Frontignan.

Muscatel. Dessert wine grown from Muscat grapes. In the United States, the term generally refers to inexpensive fortified California wine, but it does not necessarily have this negative connotation in European countries.

must. Crushed grapes that have been destemmed.

musty. Term often used interchangeably with *moldy* or *mousey;* the distinction may be that musty wines can result from aging in decayed or waterlogged cooperage.

mutage. Process of adding brandy to fermenting juice or must to arrest fermentation and retain some of the natural grape sugar.

natural fermentation. Fermentation taking place with natural indigenous yeasts, rather than cultured yeast cells.

natural wines. Wines resulting from natural fermentation; wines produced without the addition of sugar. Also wines that have not been fortified with added brandy.

naturel. French for "natural"; generally refers to wines made without added sugar.

naturwein. German term used to denote wines that have been fermented with only their natural grape sugar.

Nebbiolo. Red wine vine variety grown widely in northern Italy.

négociant. French for "negotiant," or "shipper." The term refers to wine buyers in France who "negotiate" annually for the purchase of each vintage of wine produced by certain vintners. *Négociants* age the wines and bottle them under their labels and then ship them to markets through their distribution networks.

nero. Italian for "very dark red."

nerveux. French for "vigorous'; a term for wines of strength and spirit, or with high alcohol content and flavor, perhaps coupled with high tannin content.

Nahe. Winegrowing region along the banks of the Nahe River in Germany.

Napa. Capital city of the important Napa Valley winegrowing district in the North Coast region of California.

Niagara. White wine vine cultivar grown in the northeastern portion of the United States and the southeastern portion of Canada.

Niagara Peninsula. Southernmost portion of Ontario, Canada, situated between Lake Erie and Lake Ontario; one of the largest winegrowing regions of Canada.

Nierstein. Winegrowing town in the Rheinhessen region of Germany.

noble rot. See *Edelfäule* or *pourriture noble.*

nose. Term relating to the sensory reaction to a wine's odor; often used as a term for the bouquet of a wine or the aroma of grapes, grape juice, and grape must.

nouveau. Term for new or unaged wine that generally has a pronounced fruity bouquet and flavor. Perhaps best exemplified by the annual production of Beaujolais nouveau.

Nuits, Côte de. Northern portion of the famous Côte d'Or district in the Burgundy region of France.

Nuits-St.-Georges. Winegrowing town in the Côte d'Or district in the Burgundy region of France.

nutty. Descriptive term for a wine with a rather nutlike bouquet and/or flavor, usually derived fron a process of madeirization, such as in the making of Madeira, Marsala, or Sherry.

odor. Term that most wine judges use to describe a fault in a wine's aroma and bouquet.

Oeil de Perdrix. French for "eye of the partridge"; rather pinkish gray tint observed in the color of some wines, most often whites made from black grapes, such as Blanc de Noir sparkling wines.

oenology. British spelling of *enology.*

oidium. Same as *mildew.*

oily. Term used to describe noticeable levels of grape stem and/or seed oil found in a wine; generally an indication of poor winemaking.

Oloroso. Darkest and sweetest of the Sherries.

Oporto. Important Port wine trade center in northern Portugal.

organoleptic. Term referring to the impression a wine makes on the sensory organs of sight, smell, and taste.

oxidation. A reaction of wine constituents with oxygen, resulting, for example, in a browning of color and the formation of acetaldehyde from ethyl alcohol. Wine aging is a form of controlled oxidation.

Palatinate. Archaic name for the Rheinpfalz winegrowing region in Germany.

Palomino. White wine vine variety cultivated for Sherry wine production in Spain; may also be found in limited acreages in California.

Passe-Tout-Grains. Blends of Pinot Noir and Gamay wines grown in the Burgundy region of France.

pasteurization. Process of inhibiting harmful microorganisms by the application of heat; in wine, at temperatures ranging from 140° to about 180° F; in *flash pasteurization* the desired temperature is held for only a short time, perhaps less than 30 seconds, and the wine is then cooled to storage temperature. Both are generally considered detrimental to wine quality.

pâteux. French for "pasty." See *mâche*.

Pauillac. Winegrowing *commune* in the Medoc district of the Bordeaux region of France.

petillant. French for "slightly sparkling"; *crémant* is another French term used to describe this quality in wines.

pH. Scale used to measure acidity from strongest acidity (pH 1) to neutrality (pH 7) to the strongest alkalinity (pH 14).

Phylloxera. Root louse (some airborne, leaf-galling types also exist), more precisely known as *Phylloxera vastatrix*. A parasite that attacks grapevines. The great *Phylloxera* epidemic of the mid-1800s killed most European vineyards, which were restored by grafting the vines onto U.S. rootstocks.

Pierce's disease. Bacterial malady that is mortal to grapevines; especially prevalent in warmer, more humid winegrowing climates.

Piesport. Winegrowing town in the Mosel region of Germany.

Pinard. French slang term for ordinary red wine.

Pineau de la Loire. Same white wine vine variety as Chenin Blanc. Of importance in the Loire Valley region of France; traditionally popular variety in California, but decreasingly so.

Pinot Noir. Red wine vine variety; the source of the classic red wines of the Côte d'Or district in the Burgundy region of France. Pinot Noir is being grown with increasing success in the cooler-climate locales in California. In recent times other states, principally Oregon, have achieved superior results from the variety.

pipe. Wine container equal to two hogsheads, or about 81 U.S. gallons.

piquant. French term for sharpness, or high level of acidity in a wine.

piquette. Secondary wine of very low quality made by the addition of water to grape pomace. Generally, a wine made for consumption by winery workers at certain establishments in France.

plat. French for "dull"; a term for wines that have little body, flavor, or spirituousness.

pomace. The pressed seeds, skins, and pulp that remain in a press after the juice or wine has been extracted.

Pomerol. Winegrowing district in the Bordeaux region of France.

Pommard. Winegrowing *commune* in the Côte d'Or district of the Burgundy region in France.

pop wine. Usually refers to wines of rather low alcohol content that have been infused with fruit flavors.

porosity. Size limitation of foreign particles or suspended solids that may pass through a media used in wine filtration.

Port. Sweet dessert wine produced in the Douro region of Portugal; also used as a generic term for similar wines produced elsewhere.

Pouilly-Fuisse. Winegrowing locale embracing two neighboring villages, Pouilly and Fuisse, in the Mâconnais district of the Burgundy region of France.

Pouilly-Fumé. Superior wine type made of Sauvignon Blanc grapes grown near the village of Pouilly-sur-Loire of the Loire Valley region of France.

pourriture noble. French for "noble rot"; *Botrytis cinerea* fungus that permeates the skins of grape berries, allowing moisture to evaporate and concentrating sugar and flavors. *Pourriture noble* is associated with the classic Sauternes wines grown in the Bordeaux region of France. See *Edelfäule*.

pousse. Strong, fresh fruity bouquet and taste, found particularly in wines that have fermented too long in contact with the skins of the grapes.

ppm. Abbreviation for "parts per million." An expression of the number or units of a given substance, such as sulfur dioxide (a wine preservative and antioxidant) found in a total of one million; roughly equivalent to "milligrams per liter."

precoce. French for "precocious"; a term for wines that mature quickly.

Premier Cru. French for "First Growth." In the Burgundy region of France this term refers to a great number of the finest vineyards, but is secondary to Grand Cru.

press wine. Wine that is extracted from a fermented must after the free run has been collected, generally considered inferior to the free run.

pricked. Term used to describe the odor of ethyl acetate (like paint thinner) in wines (not acetic acid or vinegar).

Produced and Bottled by. Labeling statement on U.S.-produced wines that indicates at least 75 percent (51 percent for wines made from *Vitis labrusca* grapes) of the wine has been actually produced from grapes processed by the producer.

proof. Measure of alcoholic strength, usually used for distilled spirits, seldom for wine. One degree of proof is approximately equal to one half of one percent of alcohol by volume.

proprietaire. French for "proprietor," owner.

Puligny-Montrachet. Winegrowing *commune* in the Côte d'Or district of the Burgundy region in France.

puncheon. British wine-container measure equal to 56 imperial gallons, or 70 U.S. gallons.

punt. Indentation in the bottom of a wine bottle, originally intended to provide added strength to the container.

qualitätswein. German for "quality wine," and short for *Qualitätswein bestimmte Anbaugebiete* (QbA). Signifies that the wine has been grown and produced in one of 13 specific German wine districts as identified on the label.

Qualitätswein mit Prädikat. German for "quality wine with special properties" (QmP). A step above QbA because no sugar is allowed to be added in the production processes. The *Prädikat* categories, in ascending order, are Kabinett, Spätlese, Auslese, Beerenauslese, Trockenbeerenauslese, and Eiswein.

quinta. Vineyard estates in the Douro Port wine region of Portugal.

racking. Decanting, or transferring wines from one vessel to another in order to separate out the lees.

rancio. Term used to describe the bouquet of some sweet oxidized wines; has no connection to the term *rancid*.

Raya. Lower grade of Sherry, which is usually distilled into brandy or sold for modest prices.

récolte. French for "vintage season" or "harvest."

red table wine. Wines, usually made by the process of including the skins during fermentation in order to leach out red color pigments (although some are made by heating the must prior to pressing and fermentation), which are predominantly dry.

regional. Wines originating from a general area including specific villages, vineyards, or other geographical locales.

rehoboam. Large wine bottle, generally found in Champagne; the equivalent of about six normal-sized 750 milliliter bottles.

Reims. Winegrowing city in the Champagne region of France.

rémuage. See *riddling*.

reserva. Spanish for "reserve"; wines selected for special aging and/or usage.

residual sugar. Generally refers to the amount of sweetness left in a finished wine; wines that are not fermented dry have residual sugar.

Retsina. Greek wine that has been infused with pine resin to produce a rather turpentine-like bouquet.

Rheingau. Winegrowing region in the Rhineland of Germany.

Rheinhessen. Winegrowing region in the Rhineland of Germany.

Rhine Wine. Wine grown from vineyards in the Rhineland of Germany; also loosely applied to any white wine made in the German style or from grapes indigenous to Germany.

Rhone River. Winegrowing region located on both sides of the Rhône River in southern France.

riddling. The French *rémuage*. The process of working the sediment in bottle-fermented sparkling wine into the neck of the bottle, usually performed on a rack or table that holds the bottles inverted. Riddling of each bottle is performed one or more times daily by raising bottles slightly and, with a quarter turn, firmly reinserting the bottle back to its resting place so as to jar the sediment loose from the sides of the bottle. After several weeks of thrice-daily riddling, all the sediment has been made to spiral downward into the bottle neck.

Riesling. Principal grape variety cultivated for the finest of German wines; also properly referred to as Johannisberg Riesling or, in the New World, as White Riesling; not to be confused with Gray Riesling or Missouri Riesling, which are not true Riesling grapes. The Emerald Riesling is a California-developed hybrid from Johannisberg Riesling parentage.

Rioja. Winegrowing region in northern Spain.

ripe. Term generally used to describe wines that have reached their full term of aging or have achieved a proper state of bouquet and flavor development.

riserva. Italian for "reserved" wines required to be aged for specific longer periods of time; similar to the Spanish Reserva.

rich. Term used to describe wines that have bold bouquet and flavors, along with heavy body and broad complexity.

rosato. Italian for "rosé."

rosé. Generic name for pink table wines made in the same manner as red wines but with less skin contact time during fermentation. Can be dry, near-dry, or rather sweet. Examples are Anjou and Tavel.

rotten eggs. Term used to describe wines that have degenerated because of the formation of hydrogen sulfide (H_2S).

round. Term referring to a wine with a good balance of all characteristics; a wine that has been blended harmoniously.

Ruby Cabernet. California-developed hybrid cultivar from Cabernet Sauvignon parentage.

Sack. Usually refers to a dry, or somewhat dry, Sherry. This was a favorite wine of Shakespeare. The name *Sack* is thought to be a Spanish derivation of the French *sec*, meaning "dry."

St.-Émilion. Winegrowing district in the Bordeaux region of France.

St.-Estèphe. Winegrowing subdistrict in the Medoc district of the Bordeaux region in France.

St.-Julien. Winegrowing subdistrict in the Medoc district of the Bordeaux region of France.

St.-Peray. Winegrowing *commune* in the Rhone Valley region of France.

salamanazar. Largest commercially available wine bottle; the equivalent of 12 normal-sized 750 milliliter bottles. Generally found only in the Champagne region of France.

Sancerre. Winegrowing locale near Pouilly in the Loire Valley region of France.

Sangiovese. Red wine vine variety cultivated widely in the Tuscany region of Italy.

San Joaquin. Winegrowing region in California; also known as the Central Valley region.

Santa Clara. Winegrowing district in the Central Coast region south of San Francisco, California.

Santa Cruz. Winegrowing district in the Central Coast region south of San Francisco, California.

Santenay. Winegrowing *commune* in the Côte d'Or district of the Burgundy region of France.

Sardinia. Winegrowing island region of Italy.

Sauvignon Blanc. White wine vine variety cultivated widely in the Graves and Sauternes districts of Bordeaux, as well as in the Pouilly-Fumé district of the Loire Valley in France. The bold fruity *fumé*-style of wines of Pouilly are the inspiration for the *fumé blanc* style of sauvignon blanc first made by Robert Mondavi and now widely made in the United States.

sec. French for "dry," or without sweetness. Also used to describe sparkling wines that may have some residual sweetness, but are not as sweet as *doux*. Truly dry sparkling wines are generally referred to as *brut* or *naturel*.

secco. Italian for "dry"; however, the term is often used to describe wines that are not totally dry.

sèche. French term used to describe flat wines that have become bitter.

sediment. The precipitated solids formed as a result of fermentation, clarification, or some other cellar process, referred to in the trade as lees. Solid precipitate in wine bottles, however, is properly termed "sediment."

sekt. German for "sparkling wine," made either by the traditional French bottle-fermented method or by the bulk process.

Sémillon. White wine vine variety grown in the Sauternes district of the Bordeaux region of France. Cultivated in limited acreages in California and other areas of the United States.

Sercial. White wine vine variety cultivated on the Portuguese island of Madeira.

Sevé. The perfuming of the palate that lingers after the wine has been swallowed.

Sherry. English name for the fortified wine of the Jerez district of southern Spain; Sherry is characterized by a nutlike bouquet and flavor. More loosely used as the generic name for any wine that has a high aldehyde content deliberately generated in order to make a Sherry-style wine.

Sicily. Winegrowing island region of Italy.

Silvaner. White wine vine variety cultivated in most winegrowing regions in Germany; also grown in Italy and the Alsace region of France. There are only very limited plantings of Silvaner in the United States; may be spelled "Sylvaner" in some locales.

soft. Term usually referring to white or rosé table wines that are low in both acidity and astringency; much the same as *smooth*.

solera. The Spanish fractional blending system used to age Sherry wines. Wines are blended in tiers of casks, each successive tier containing blends of older wines. After a set period, wines are partially drawn from younger tiers and blended into the older tiers. The last *solera* contains the wines that are drawn off for bottling.

Sonoma County. Winegrowing district in the North Coast region of California.

sour. Wine that has turned to vinegar; term often used incorrectly to describe the acidity or astringency of a wine.

soutirage. French for "racking." See *racking*.

soyeux. French for "silky"; a term used to describe wines with no roughness or harshness that produce a very agreeable sensation on the palate.

Sparkling Burgundy. Originally a U.S. term for sparkling red wine, it has caught on in France, and some "Sparkling Burgundy" wines are now produced in the Burgundy region of France.

sparkling wine. Wine, usually white or rosé, in which carbon dioxide gas is captured during secondary fermentation in a closed container. The traditional French method of bottle-fermentation is called *méthode champenoise*. The bulk, or tank, method is called the *charmat* process. The most famous sparkling wine is Champagne.

Spätburgunder. German term for the Pinot Noir vine variety.

spätlese. German for "late picked"; refers to grapes left on the vine for several days or weeks to optimize ripeness, perhaps causing a slight dehydration of the grape berries, which results in higher sugar concentration.

specific gravity. Ratio of the weight of a given volume of liquid to an equal volume of water.

spicy. Term for bouquet and flavor reminiscent of spice, such as cinnamon and nutmeg. The best example is wine properly made from Gewürztraminer.

spritzig. German term for "slight effervescence"; used to describe very young wines that have not fully fermented and produce a prickling sensation upon the palate. Such wines are quaffed during the autumn wine festivals in Germany.

spumante. Sparkling wines made in Italy; the same as "mussante" wines. Produced either by the traditional French bottle-fermented method or the *charmat* (bulk) process.

stalky. Term used to describe wines that have become rather astringent and vegetative in character owing to excessive contact with grape stalks (stems).

stemmy. See *stalky*.

sulfur dioxide. A compound of sulfur and oxygen (SO_2) used in winemaking.

superiore. Italian DOC term relating to a wine of superior grade, usually a result of further aging, either in bottle or in cask.

supple. See *round*.

sweetness. Taste sensation directly opposite to sour; in wine, sweetness results from added or residual sugar content. Wines with sweetness levels that are barely detectable may be properly termed "near-dry"; wines described as "sweet," such as Port and Sauternes, have a noticeably sweet taste.

Syrah. Red wine vine variety cultivated in the Rhone Valley region of France; increasingly planted in the vineyards of California and other U.S. regions. Not to be confused with Petite Sirah, which is a different variety. Spelled "Shiraz" in its native Iran, Australia, New Zealand, and other New World countries.

table wine. In the United States, any wine having less than 14 percent alcohol content, but generally refers to any wine consumed at the table with food.

tafelwein. Wine without any specific quality classification in Germany, but if labeled "Deutsche Tafelwein," it must be German in origin.

tannic. Term generally used for wines that are astringent or stemmy (grape stems contain phenolic compounds that have astringent gustatory values).

tannic acid. Astringent acid with a leathery taste, normally added to increase the life span of a wine by slowing the aging process.

tannins. Special phenolic compounds found in grape stems, seeds, and skins, which contribute to astringency, particularly in young red wines. Tannins are also introduced into wines from the wood of oak aging vessels and may lengthen the life of wines by slowing oxidation reactions.

tart. Term used to describe wines that are high in fixed or total acidity.

tartaric acid. Natural acid of grapes. Tartaric acid is unstable in wine at cold temperatures and will precipitate as the acid salt potassium bitartrate (cream of tartar).

taste. Sensory reaction on the palate that detects olfactory and gustatory characteristics of wine.

tastevin. Small tasting cup; the best are made of silver; used for tasting wines, principally in Burgundy.

Tavel. Winegrowing district in the lower Rhone Valley region of France.

tawny. Amber hue taken on by red wines that have been exposed to high temperature and/or long terms of aging; Tawny Port is a good example.

Teinturier. Very heavily pigmented black grapes generally used for blending to enhance color intensity.

tenuta. Italian for "estate"; usually denotes a wine and/or vineyard estate.

tinto. Portuguese or Spanish for "red."

tirage. Laying of bottles on their sides in tiers for secondary fermentation in the production of sparkling wines.

Tokaji Aszu. Dessert wine produced in Hungary.

tonneau. Traditional Bordeaux wine cask, measuring 900 liters or about 238 U.S. gallons.

topping up. Refilling of casks in order to replace the wine that has been lost in the space known as ullage. See *ullage*.

total acidity. Aggregate of all acids measured in a given wine; the sum of fixed and volatile acids.

Touraine. Winegrowing district in the Loire Valley region of France.

tourne. French for "turned"; a term used to describe wines that have turned into vinegar or decomposed in some other way.

Traminer. See *Gewürztraminer*.

Trentino. Winegrowing region in northern Italy.

triage. Removal of defective clusters and/or berries from the harvest, typically on a moving-belt inspection line.

Trier. Ancient Roman winegrowing settlement, now the capital city of the upper Mosel region of Germany.

Trockenbeerenauslese. German for "dry berry special selection"; the separation of those berries on each bunch of grapes that have been raisinized by the noble mold, *Botrytis cinerea*. The juice is highly concentrated in sugar content and may have a rather caramel-like flavor. Slowly fermented with a very sweet finish, Trockenbeerenauslese is one of the most expensive dessert wines in the world.

Tuscany. Winegrowing region in central Italy.

Ugni Blanc. Same vine variety as the Trebbiano of Italy.

ullage. Air space in a bottle or wooden aging vessel generated by seepage, evaporation, and assimilation of the wine into the pores. In barrels and casks, the ullage should be refilled at least weekly in order to keep the wine from exposure to oxygen. See *topping up*.

Umbria. Winegrowing region in central Italy.

Valdepeñas. Winegrowing district in the La Mancha region of Spain.

varietal wine. Wine labeled for the variety of grape from which it was predominantly or entirely made. Examples are California "Cabernet Sauvignon" and New York State "Seyval Blanc."

variety. Individual natural strain within a group of closely related plants. Though each variety has its own unique characteristics, it is still recognizable as a member of its species.

vat. Wine container constructed to rest in a vertical position, as opposed to a cask, which rests in a horizontal position.

velouté. French for "velvety"; a term used to describe wines with no harshness or bitterness that are, nonetheless, dry, full-bodied, and well balanced.

Veltliner. White wine vine variety cultivated principally in Austria and Switzerland. Sometimes referred to Gruner Veltliner.

velvet. Term used to describe the softness and delicacy of wines of perfect balance that have reached peak maturity.

vendange. French for "grape harvest"; refers to the harvesting of the grapes and the making of new wines.

vendemmia. Italian for "grape harvest"; the same as *vendange*.

veneto. Winegrowing region located in northern Italy.

veraison. French viticultural term used to describe the point in the growing season when grapes start to ripen, become soft, and change color.

vermouth. Wine that contains aromatic essences derived from barks, herbs, roots, spices, etc. Dry vermouth, generally known as the French type, is white. Sweet vermouth, often referred to as the Italian type, is normally very dark because of the addition of caramel color.

vert. French for "green"; a term for young wines with high acidity levels.

vigne. French for "vine."

vignoble. French for "vineyard."

Vila Nova de Gaia. Port wine center located opposite the city of Oporto on the Douro River in Portugal.

vin. French for "wine."

viña. Spanish for "vineyard."

vin de paille. French term for wine made from grapes dried on straw *(paille)* mats in order to enrich sugar and flavor content.

vin de pays. French for "wine of the area"; such wine is usually consumed in the locale where it is grown and is rarely found outside this area.

vineux. French for "vinous"; a term used to characterize wines according to the soil and climate in which they were grown, rather than according to their fruit flavor attributes.

vin gris. French term used to describe wines having only a faint hue of pinkish color. See *oeil de perdrix*.

vinho verde. Wine made from unripened "green" grapes grown in the Minho region of Portugal.

viniculture. The art, science, and study of grape growing and winemaking as related disciplines.

vinifera. Short for *Vitis vinifera*, the most widely cultivated species of wine grape vine grown on earth. Also known as the Old World vine, generally considered to be the finest wine grape species. The cultivars *Chardonnay, Pinot Noir, Cabernet Sauvignon,* and *Johannisberg Riesling* are classic examples of *vinifera*.

vinification. Process of making grapes into wine.

vino. Italian and Spanish for "wine."

vino cotto. Concentration of grape juice by heating or boiling down. The "cooking" evaporates the water from the natural juice and enriches sugar and flavor content.

vino passito. Italian term for wine made from grapes dried in raisinlike fashion to enrich their sugar and flavor content prior to fermentation.

vinosity. Term that refers to vinous (soil and/or vegetative flavors) as opposed to fruity (grape ester flavors) bouquet and taste.

vin rosé. See *rosé*.

vin santo. See *vino passito*.

vin sec. French for "dry wine."

vintage. Year in which a crop of grapes were grown and harvested; the wine from a crop of grapes from a particular year. A *vintage year* is often construed as a good or great growing season that has resulted in a distinguished wine.

vintner. Wine producer; usually refers to the ownership and/or management of a winemaking facility.

viscidity. Lack of tannic acid, which permits a wine to age prematurely.

viscosity. Resistance of a gas or liquid to flow; a measure of adhesion and cohesion.

Vitis. Taxonomic name of the grapevine species, of which there are more than 50 known so far. The most important wine species is the Old World *Vitis vinifera*. See *vinifera*.

volatile acidity. Organic acids in wines that are evaporative or distillable. Chief of these is acetic acid.

Volnay. Winegrowing *commune* located in the Côte d'Or district of the Burgundy region of France.

Vosne-Romanée. Winegrowing *commune* in the Côte d'Or district of the Burgundy region of France.

Vougeot. Winegrowing *commune* located in the Côte d'Or district of the Burgundy region of France.

wein. German for "wine."

weingut. German for "wine estate" or "vineyard and winery estate."

weinkellerei. German for "wine cellar."

wine. Product resulting from the fermentation of grape juice or grape must. The five main categories of wine are Table Wine, Sparkling Wine, Dessert Wine, Aperitif Wine, and Pop Wine.

winegrowing. Art and science of growing grapes and making wine commercially.

winery. Building, cave, room, vault, etc., in which grapes are made into wine.

winzer. German for "vintner" or "winegrower."

winzergenossenschaft. German for "winegrowers cooperative association."

winzerverein. German for "winegrowers cooperative."

woody. Term that refers to wines that have a bouquet and flavor characteristic of wet wood, usually as a result of overaging.

Xeres. Archaic spelling of Spain's Jerez, or Sherry.

yeasts. One-celled plants, about one micron in diameter, that secrete enzymes that convert sugar(s) into ethyl alcohol, carbon dioxide gas, and energy.

yeasty. Term used in a negative sense when describing the characteristic bouquet and flavor of yeast in wines, usually caused by extended contact with the lees; used in a positive sense for Champagne or other bottle-fermented sparkling wines in which a good dissolution of yeast has occurred in *tirage* aging. *Sur-lies,* or "on the lees," aging of some white wines, such as Chardonnay, can create more complexity in bouquet and flavor.

Zinfandel. Red wine vine variety grown primarily in California.

Zwicker. Random blend of white wines grown in the Alsace region of France, primarily for local consumption.

zymase. Enzymes produced by wine yeasts that are essential for fermentation. See *yeasts*.

BIBLIOGRAPHY

Adams, Leon D. *The Wines of America,* 3d ed. New York: McGraw-Hill, 1985.

Adlum, John. *A Memoir on the Cultivation of the Vine in America and the Best Mode of Making Wine.* Washington, D.C.: Duff Green, 1828.

Allen, H. Warner. *The Wines of Portugal.* New York: McGraw-Hill, 1963.

———. *A History of Wine.* London: Faber and Faber, 1961.

Amerine, M.A., and E.B. Roessler. *Wines: Their Sensory Evaluation,* rev. ed. San Francisco: Freeman, 1983.

Amerine, M.A., et al. *Technology of Wine Making,* 4th ed. Westport, Conn.: AVI, 1980.

Anderson, Burton. *The Wine Atlas of Italy.* London: Mitchell Beazley, 1990.

———. *Vino.* Boston: Atlantic Monthly Press, Little-Brown, 1980.

Australian Wine Board. *Wine Australia.* Adelaide: The Australian Wine Board, 1979.

Baldy, Marian W. "How the Nose Knows." *American Wine Society Journal* (Rochester, N.Y.), Spring 1995.

Baxevanis, John. *The Wines of Champagne, Burgundy, Eastern and Southern France.* Totowa, N.J.: Rowman and Littlefield, 1987.

Berger, Dan, and Richard Hinkle. *An Inside Look at Napa Valley.* Wilmington, Del.: Atomium Books, 1991.

———. *An Inside Look at Sonoma County.* Wilmington, Del.: Atomium Books, 1991.

Berry, Charles Walter. *Viniana.* London: Constable, 1934.

Bespaloff, Alexis. "Gemütlichkeit by the Glass." *Food and Wine,* November 1980.

Botwin, Michael. "The Regional Wines of Switzerland." *American Wine Society Journal,* Winter 1974.

Brenner, Gary. *The Naked Grape.* Indianapolis, Ind.: Bobbs-Merrill, 1975.

Broadbent, J.M. *Wine Tasting.* London: Wine and Spirit Publications, 1970.

Bullard, Robyn. "South African Wines on Their Way." *Wine Spectator* (New York), April 1992.

Burroughs, David, and Norman Bezzant. *Wine Regions of the World.* London: Heinemann, 1979.

Butler, Frank Hedges. *Wine and the Wine Lands of the World.* New York: Brentano's, 1926.

Butler, Joel. *The Wines and Wineries of Australia.* Burlingame, Calif.: Australian Wine Importers Association, n.d.

Buzzi, Fernando Vidal. *Mendoza.* Mendoza, Argentina: Alguero Ltd., 1994.

Cattell, Hudson, and Lee Stauffer Miller. *Wine East of the Rockies.* Lancaster, Pa.: L & H Photojournalism, 1982.

———. *The Wines of the East: Native American Grapes.* Lancaster, Pa.: L & H Photojournalism, 1980.

———. *The Wines of the East, The Vinifera.* Lancaster, Pa.: L & H Photojournalism, 1979.

———. *The Wines of the East, The Hybrids.* Lancaster, Pa.: L & H Photojournalism, 1978.

Chilean Traditional Wine Exporter Committee. *ProChile.* Santiago: Larrain and Asociados Editores, 1983.

Chilean Export Promotion Office. *Chilean Wines: A Tradition.* Santiago: August 1983.

Chroman, Nathan. *The Treasury of American Wines.* New York: Rutledge-Crown, 1973.

Church, Ruth Ellen. *Entertaining with Wine.* Chicago: Rand-McNally, 1976.

———. *Wines of the Midwest.* New York: MacMillan, 1964.

Churchill, Creighton. *The Great Wine Rivers.* New York: MacMillan, 1971.

———. *The World of Wines.* New York: MacMillan, 1964.

Clarke, Oz. *Wine Atlas,* New York: Little Brown, 1995.

———. *The Wine Book.* New York: Portland House, 1987.

Cooper, Rosalind. *The Wine Book.* Tuscon, Ariz.: HP Books, 1981.

Domaine Chandon. *A User's Guide to Sparkling Wine.* Yountville, Calif.: Domaine Chandon, 1984.

Dorozynski, Alexander, and Bibiane Bell. *The Wine Book.* New York: Golden Press, 1969.

Edita Lausanne. *The Great Book of Wine.* Lausanne, Switzerland: Edita Lausanne, 1970.

Ellison, Curtis, M.D. *Does Moderate Alcohol Consumption Prolong Life?* New York: American Council on Science and Health, Inc., 1993.

Emerson, Edward. *Beverages, Past and Present.* New York: Knickerbocker Press, 1980.

Evans, Len. *Complete Book of Australian Wine*. Sydney: Hamlyn, 1978.

English, Sara Jane. *Vin Vignettes,* Austin, Texas: Eakin Press, 1984.

Fadiman, Clifton, and Sam Aaron. *The Joys of Wine*. New York: Abrams, 1975.

Farrer, Marshall. "Argentina Poised as the New Chile." *Wine Business Monthly* (Sonoma, Calif.), July 1995.

Fisher, M.F.K. *Wine in California*. Berkeley: University of California Press, 1962.

Fluchere, Henri. *Wines*. New York: Golden Press, 1974.

Ford, Gene. *The French Paradox and Drinking for Health*. San Francisco: Wine Appreciation Guild, 1993.

Frankel, E.N., et al. "Inhibition of Oxidation of Human Low-Density Lipoproteins by Phenolic Substances in Red Wine." *Lancet* 341 (1993): 454–457.

Fridjhon, Michael. *The Penguin Book of South African Wine*. London: Viking Penguin, 1992.

Fuller, Andrew S. *Grape Culturist*. New York: Orange Judd, 1867

German Wine Institute. *German Wines*. Main, Germany, n.d.

Giordano, Frank. *Texas Wines and Wineries*. Austin: Texas Monthly Press, 1984.

Gohdes, Clarence. *Scuppernong*. Durham, N.C.: Duke University Press, 1982.

Gold, Alec, ed. *Wines and Spirits of the World*. Chicago: Follett, 1973.

The Great Wines of Argentina. Buenos Aires: Asociacion Vitivinicola Argentina, n.d.

Grossman, Harold J. *Grossman's Guide to Wines and Spirits and Beers,* 4th ed. New York: Scribner's, 1964.

Hallgarten, S.F. *Vineyards, Estates and Wines of Germany*. Dallas: Publivin, 1974.

Halliday, James. *Wines and Wineries of Australia*. St Lucia: University of Queensland Press, 1982.

———. *Wines and Wineries of Victoria*. St. Lucia: University of Queensland Press, 1982.

———. *Wines and Wineries of South Australia*. St. Lucia: University of Queensland Press, 1981.

Hasler, G.F. *Wine Service in the Restaurant*. London: Wine & Spirit Publications, 1973.

Hayes, C.J.H., et al. *History of Western Civilization*. New York: Macmillan, 1962.

Hiaring, Philip. "The Editor Finds the Latch-String Out in Austria's Wineland." *Wines and Vines,* January 1980.

———. "A Visit to the Argentine Wine Industry." *Wines and Vines,* June 1975.

Hinkle, Richard Paul. "The Merit in Meritage." *The Quarterly Review of Wines* (Winchester, Mass.), Autumn 1993.

Hosmon, Bob. "Wines from Portugal." *The Wine News* (Miami), October/November 1994.

Husmann, George. *The Native Grape*. New York: Woodward, 1868.

Iocca, Pasquale. *Wines of Portugal*. New York: Portuguese Trade Commission, n.d.

———. *Porto*. New York: Portuguese Trade Commission, n.d.

Jacobs, Julius L. "The Greeks' Word was 'Oinos.'" *Wines and Vines,* December 1974.

Jobson's Wine Handbook 1993, New York: Jobson Publishing, 1993.

Johnson, Hugh. *Vintage: The Story of Wine,* New York: Simon and Schuster, 1989.

———. *Modern Encyclopedia of Wine,* New York: Simon and Schuster, 1983.

———. *The World Atlas of Wine,* 2d ed. New York: Simon and Schuster, 1978.

Kaufman, William I. *Encyclopedia of American Wine*. San Francisco: The Wine Appreciation Guild, 1984.

———. *The Traveler's Guide to the Vineyards of North America*. New York: Penguin Books, 1980.

Keehn, Karen. *Structure of Wine and Its Interaction with Food*. Hopland, Calif.: McDowell Vineyards, 1986.

Kressman, Edouard. *The Wonder of Wine*. New York: Hastings House, 1968.

Lallemand Editeur. *Champagne Wine of France*. Paris: Lallemand Editeur, 1968.

Lamb, Richard B., and Ernest G. Mittelberger. *In Celebration of Wine and Life*. San Francisco: The Wine Appreciation Guild, 1980.

Lawrence, R. de Treville, Sr. *Jefferson and Wine*. The Plains, Va.: Vinifera Wine Growers Association, 1976.

Layton, T.A. *Wines of Italy*. London: Harper Trade Journals, 1961.

Lesko, Leonard H. *King Tut's Wine Cellar*. Berkeley, Calif.: Scribe Publications, 1977.

Lichine, Alexis. *Guide to the Wines and Vineyards of France,* rev. ed. New York: Knopf, 1982.

Loubere, Leo A. *The Red and the White*. Albany: State University of New York Press, 1978.

Lucia, Salvatore P., M.D. *Wine and Your Well-Being*. San Francisco: Popular Library, 1971.

Mayson, Richard, ed. *Portuguese Wines*. London: Portuguese Trade and Tourism Office, n.d.

Meredith, T. *Northwest Wine,* 2d ed. Kirkland, Wash.: Nexus Press, 1983.

Milam, James R., and Katherine Ketcham. *Under the Influence*. Seattle: Madrona, 1981.

Moore, Bernard. *Wines of North America*. Secaucus, N.J.: Winchmore Publishing, 1983.

Morris, Robert. *The Genie in the Bottle*. New York: A & W Publishers, 1981.

Morse, Joseph Laffan, ed. *Universal Standard Encyclopedia*. New York: Unicorn, 1954.

Muir, Augustus. *How to Choose and Enjoy Wine*. New York: Bonanza, 1972.

"New Zealand's Wine Industry Is Growing." *Wines and Vines,* December 1979.

"The 1993 Wine Market." *Wines and Vines* (San Rafael, Calif.) 75 (7), 1994.

Palmer, R.R., and J. Colton. *A History of the Modern World,* 2d ed. New York: Knopf, 1963.

Paronetto, Lamberto. *Chianti*. London: Wine and Spirit Publications, 1970.

Pellegrini, Angelo M. *Wine and the Good Life*. New York: Knopf, 1965.

Radford, John. "Decanter's Guide to the Wines of Spain." *Decanter* (London), December 1994.

Ray, Cyril. *Lafite*. New York: McGraw-Hill, 1966.

Read, Jan. *Guide to the Wines of Spain and Portugal*. New York: Monarch, 1977.

Robertson, George. *Port*. London: Faber and Faber, 1978.

Roux, M.P. *Vineyards and Châteaux of Bordeaux*. Dallas: Publivin, 1972.

Roux, M.P., et al. *Vineyards and Domains of Burgundy*. Dallas: Publivin, 1973.

Sandeman Sons & Company. *Port and Sherry*. London: Sandeman Sons & Company, 1955.

Schoenfeld, Bruce. "Spain's Proudest Wine." *Saveur* (New York) January/February, 1995.

Schoenman, Theodore. *The Father of California Wine, Agoston Haraszthy*. Santa Barbara, Calif.: Capra, 1979.

Schoonmaker, Frank. *Encyclopedia of Wine*, 5th ed. New York: Hastings House, 1973.

Seely, James. *Great Bordeaux Wines*. London: Secker & Warburg, 1986.

Seward, Desmond. *Monks and Wines*. New York: Crown, 1979.

Simon, Andre. *Wines of the World*, 2d ed. New York: McGraw-Hill, 1981.

———. *A Dictionary of Wines, Spirits and Liqueurs*. New York: Citadel, 1963.

———. *The Blood of the Grape*. London: Duckworth, 1920.

Smets, Paul. *Kloster Eberbach*. Mainz: Rheingold-Verlan, 1964.

Steiman, Harvey, and Thomas Matthews. "Wine Pioneers Poised to Capture America's Fancy." *Wine Spectator* (New York), February 1992.

Stern, Margaret. "A Skeletal History of South Africa." New York: Margaret Stern Communications, n.d.

———. "Chateau Libertas." New York: Margaret Stern Communications, n.d.

———. "Nederburg Wines." New York: Margaret Stern Communications, n.d.

———. "South Africa's Wine Lands Today." New York: Margaret Stern Communications, n.d.

———. "Stellenbosch Farmers' Winery." New York: Margaret Stern Communications, n.d.

———. "Visiting South Africa: A World in One Country." New York: Margaret Stern Communications, n.d.

———. "Zonnebloem." New York: Margaret Stern Communications, n.d.

Stone, Dee. "The Cape Winelands." *The Friends of Wine*, May/June 1983.

Stone, Frank. *Aids and Resources*. Salt Lake City, Utah: Society of Wine Educators, 1983.

Suckling, James. "A Taste of South Africa." *Wine Spectator* (New York), September 1995.

Sutcliffe, Serena. *Champagne*. New York: Simon & Schuster, 1988.

Tacama. Lima: Negociacion Industrial Vitivinicola Tacama S.A.

Thompson, Bob, and Hugh Johnson. *The California Wine Book*. New York: Morrow, 1976.

"The Top 100." *Wine Spectator* (New York), December 1995.

"The Top 100." *Wine Spectator* (New York), December 1994.

"The Top 100." *Wine Spectator* (New York), December 1993.

"The Top 100." *Wine Spectator* (New York), December 1992.

"The Top 100." *Wine Spectator* (New York), December 1991.

University of California at San Francisco, the Society of Medical Friends of Wine, and the Wine Institute. *Wine, Health, & Society*. Symposium proceedings. Oakland, Calif.: GRT Book Printing, 1981.

Ureta, Fernando, and Philippo Pszczolkowski. *Chile*. Santiago: Editorial Kactus, n.d.

Valaer, Peter. *Wines of the World*. New York: Abelard, 1950.

Veronelli. *The Wines of Italy*. Rome: Canesi Editore, n.d.

Vine, Richard P. *Commercial Winemaking*. Westport, Conn.: AVI, 1981.

Vineyard and Winery Management Desktop Guide, Watkins Glen, N.Y.: Vineyard and Winery Management, 1995.

Wagner, Philip M. *American Wines and Wine-Making*, 5th ed. New York: Knopf, 1972.

———. *A Wine-Grower's Guide*, 2d ed. New York: Knopf, 1972.

Warner, Charles K. *The Winegrowers of France and the Government Since 1875*. New York: Columbia University Press, 1960.

Wasserman, Sheldon. *The Wines of the Côtes du Rhone*. New York: Stein and Day, 1977.

Waugh, Alec. *In Praise of Wine*. New York: Sloane, 1959.

Waugh, Harry. *The Changing Face of Wine*. London: Wine and Spirit Publications, 1970.

———. *Pick of the Bunch*. London: Wine and Spirit Publications, 1970.

Wine Institute. "Compounds Found in Wine May Reduce Health Risks." *Wine Issues Monitor* (San Francisco), April/May 1992.

———. "Current Research Status on the Association Between Alcohol, Hypertension and Stroke." *Wine Institute Research News Bulletin* (San Francisco), March 1995.

———. "Decade-Long Study of 12,000 People Finds Both Male and Female Moderate Drinkers at Lowest Risk." *Health and Social Issues Newsline* (San Francisco), May 1994.

———. "The Facts in Perspective." *Wine Issues Briefing Series*. (San Francisco), 1990.

———. "Moderate Consumption Shown to Curb Other Ills." *Wine Issues Monitor* (San Francisco), December/January 1994/95.

———. "Moderate Drinkers May Cope Better with Stress." *Wine Issues Monitor* (San Francisco), May/June 1993.

———. "New Evidence Strengthens French Paradox Wine Hypothesis." *Wine Institute News Bulletin* (San Francisco), 1995.

———. "New Harvard University Study Finds That Moderate Alcohol Consumption Reduces the Risk Of Overall Mortality in Women." *Wine Institute Newsflash* (San Francisco), May 1995.

———. "New Medical Review Finds Insufficient Evidence for Breast Cancer, Alcohol Connection." *Health and Social Issues Newsline* (San Francisco), October 1993.

———. "New Studies Link Moderate Drinking with Longer Life." *Wine Issues Monitor* (San Francisco), Fall 1995.

———. "New Studies Look at Women, Moderate Alcohol Consumption, and Increased Estrogen Levels. *Health and Social Issues Newsline.* (San Francisco), May 1993.

———. "New Study Finds Moderate Drinking with Meals May Be Most Beneficial." *Health and Social Issues Newsline* (San Francisco), May 1994.

———. "New Study Finds That Moderate Wine Consumption Was Not Related to Increased Risk of Breast Cancer." *Wine Institute Newsflash* (San Francisco), June 1995.

———. "Older Moderate Drinkers Are Healthier Studies Find." *Wine Issues Monitor* (San Francisco), September/October 1993.

———. "Profile of the Wine Drinker: Perceptions and Attitudes." *Issue in Focus* (Wine Institute, San Francisco), November 1991.

———. "Rutgers University Monograph Criticizes Alcohol Research Bias." *Research News Bulletin* (San Francisco), 1: 4, 1992.

———. "A Scientific Examination of Wine, the Heart and the Mediterranean Diet." *Issue in Focus* (San Francisco), February 1992.

———. *A Scientific Look at Wine.* San Francisco: Wine Institute, 1990.

———. "A Scientific Perspective on Alcohol's Effect on Body Weight." *Health and Social Issues Newsline* (San Francisco), September 1992.

———. "Scientist Presents Balanced News on Wine and Health." *Wine Issues Monitor* (San Francisco), December/January 1992/93.

———. "*60 Minutes* Coverage of the Benefits of Moderate Wine Consumption.*"* San Francisco: 1991.

———. "US Government Plans to Study the Health Effects of Moderate Alcohol Consumption." *Wine Institute Newsflash* (San Francisco), March 1995.

———. *Wine & America.* San Francisco: Wine Institute, 1993.

———. *Wine and Medical Practice,* 10th ed. San Francisco: Wine Institute, 1981.

———. "Wine Antioxidants May Be Stronger Than Vitamin E." *Wine Issues Monitor* (San Francisco), July/August 1993.

Wine Institute of New Zealand. *New Zealand Wine Annual.* Auckland: Burnham House, 1983.

———. *New Zealand Wine & Food Annual.* Auckland: Burnham House, 1984.

Young, Alan. *Making Sense of Wine.* Richmond, Australia: Greenhouse, n.d.

Younger, W. *Gods, Men and Wine.* Cleveland, Ohio: World, 1966.

Yoxall. *The Wines of Burgundy,* 2d ed. New York: Stein and Day, 1978.

INDEX

Climate, and grape variety, 4
Cliquot-Ponsardin, Madame, 278
Clones, grapevine, 4
Clos de Vougeot, 65, 228, 237
Clos Pegase, 175
Cluny (France), 228, 250
Coastal region (South Africa), 433–436
Coca-Cola, 175, 201
Cognac, 7
Cold Duck, 89
Colorado Cellars winery and vineyards, 221
Colorado wines, 221
Color of wine:
  enhancement of, 16
  and grape, 15
  judging, 97–98
Columbard (grape variety), 7
Columbia Valley, 193–194
Columbia Winery, 194
Columella, 54, 55, 73, 377
Commune, 231
Competitions, wine, 111–113
Composition of wine, 13–16. *See also* Microbiology of wine
  and color, 15–16
  and flavor, 16
  grapes vs. wine (table), 13
  minerals and metals, 14–15
  nitrogenous compounds, 16
  organic acids, 14
  phenolics, 15
  phenols, 15
  polyphenols, 15
Concannon, James, 186–187
Concannon Vineyards, 186–187
Concha y Toro, 424
Concord (grape variety), 10, 15, 79, 204
Condrieu, 293
Constantia district (South Africa), 433
Consumption of wine, in United States, 40–42, 165
Cooke, Edward, 216
Cooking, wine for, 140–142
Cooling, 22
Cooperatives, wine, 35
Coppola, Francis Ford, 83, 173
Cordorniu brand, 374–375
Corks, 29–30
  Champagne, 283
  uncorking, 148–149
Cork tree, 378
Cornas, 293

Cornell University, 199
Corowa (Australia), 403
Corporate vintners, 33–35
Corsica, 302
Cortaillod, 366
Cortese (grape variety), 6, 313
Corton, 240–242
Corvino (grape variety), 9
Corvo winery, 332
Côteaux d'Aix-en-Provence, 300–301
Côteaux du Tricastin, 294
Côte de Beaune, 240–249
  Aloxe-Corton, 240–242
  Auxey-Duresses, 246
  Beaune, 242–244
  Chassagne-Montrachet, 248
  Ladoix-Serrigny, 240
  Meursault, 246–247
  Monthélie, 246
  Pommard, 244
  Puligny-Montrachet, 247–248
  Santenay, 248
  Volnay, 245
Côte de Nuits, 234–240
  Chambolle-Musigny, 236–237
  Fixin and Brochon, 235
  Gevrey, 235–236
  Marsanny, 235
  Morey-St.-Denis, 236
  Nuits-St.-Georges, 239
  Premeaux, 239–240
  Vosne-Romanée, 238–239
  Vougeot, 237
Côte d'Or district, 234. *See also* Côte de Beaune; Côte de Nuits
Côtes des Blancs district, 285
Côtes du Rhône Villages, 294
Cousiño-Macul, 424
Cream of tartar, 24
Cro-Magnons, 43
Cromwell, Oliver, 383
Cronin, Duane, 188
Cronin Vineyards, 188
Crozes-Hermitage, 293
Crusades, 64–65
Crusted Ports, 391
Cuvée, 282

Damianos, Herodotus, 203
Dart, Alva, 85
Debevc, Tony J., 208
Debevc, Tony P., 208
Decanting, 149–150

Deford family, 214
Degree days, 169
Degrees Brix, 22
Dehydration, wine and, 122
Delaware, Lord, 213
Delaware (grape variety), 10
Delirium tremens, 122
Demi-sec, 31
Denominação de Origem Controlada (DOC), 385
Denominación de Origen Calificada (DOC), 371
Denominación de Origen (DO), 371
Denominazione di Origine Controllata (DOC), 308–309
Denominazione di Origine Controllata e Garantita (DOCG), 309
Dessert, wine selection for, 137–138
Dessert wines, 31
Deutscher Landwein, 342
Diabetes, wine and, 120–121
Diel, Ingo, 351
Dierberg, James, 222
Diglucosides, 15
Dillon, Clarence, 266
Dinner wines, *see* Tables wines
Dionysus, 44, 50, 51, 53
Disgorging, 283
DOC (Denominação de Origem Controlada), 385
DOC (Denominación de Origen Calificada), 371
DOC (Denominazione di Origine Controllata), 308–309
DOCG (Denominazione di Origine Controllata e Garantita), 309
DO (Denominación de Origen), 371
Dolceacqua, 315
Dolcetto (grape variety), 313
Dôle, 364
Domaine———, *see under specific name, e.g.:* Drouhin, Domaine
Domecq, José, 380
Donnaz, 315
Dosage, 283
Double bottles, 29
Douglas and Lower Orange River region (South Africa), 438
Douro region (Portugal), 388–392
Doux, 31
Drake, Sir Francis, 369, 429
Drouhin, Domaine, 196